1 CORINTHIANS

Smyth & Helwys Bible Commentary: 1 Corinthians

Publication Staff

President & CEO
Cecil P. Staton

Publisher & Executive Vice President
Lex Horton

Vice President, Production
Keith Gammons

Book Editor
Leslie Andres

Graphic Designers
Amy Davis
Dave Jones

Assistant Editors
Rachel Stancil
Kelley F. Land

Smyth & Helwys Publishing, Inc.
6316 Peake Road
Macon, Georgia 31210-3960
1-800-747-3016

Printed in the United States of America.

The paper used in this publication meets the minimum requirements of American National Standard for Information Sciences—Permanence of Paper for Printed Library Materials. ANSI Z39.48–1984 (alk. paper)

Library of Congress Cataloging-in-Publication Data

Nash, Robert Scott, 1953–

First Corinthians / by Robert Scott Nash. p. cm.
(The Smyth & Helwys Bible Commentary; v. 25a)
Includes bibliographical references (p.) and index.
ISBN 978-1-57312-082-1 (hardback : alk. paper)
1. Bible. N.T. Corinthians, 1st—Commentaries.
I. Title. II. Title: 1 Corinthians.
BS2675.53.N37 2009 227'.207—dc22 2009031228

SMYTH & HELWYS BIBLE COMMENTARY

1 CORINTHIANS

ROBERT SCOTT NASH

SMYTH & HELWYS
PUBLISHING INCORPORATED MACON GEORGIA

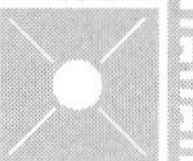

ADVANCE PRAISE

Writing with remarkable clarity, Scott Nash gives us a significant new commentary on Paul's carefully crafted "first" letter to the Corinthians. Nash's work is deceptively sophisticated—it's easy and interesting to read while being loaded with literary, historical, archaeological, and theological information that gives fresh insights into Paul's letter. All readers of this commentary—students, clergy, scholars—will profit from careful study of this work.

—Marion L. Soards
Louisville Presbyterian Theological Seminary

Whereas some commentaries do little more than offer inchoate historical and literary notes on a biblical text, Nash helps the reader to see Paul dealing with questions of identity, relationship, belief, and practice. This book has something for every modern interpreter of 1 Corinthians and I commend it to all.

Two words that describe this excellent commentary are care and creativity. Nash carefully analyzes historical, literary, archaeological, and social dimensions of the text and background of 1 Corinthians as well as Roman Corinth itself. Remarkably, he also creatively engages in a theological dialogue with Paul, his readers, and his interpreters throughout the centuries. Nash's commentary is, at the same time, historically and archaeologically incisive, theologically stimulating, and pastorally sensitive.

—Nijay Gupta
Ashland Theological Seminary

This refreshing new commentary brings thorough, current, and straightforward discussion of the Pauline letter that is probably the most significant for church and pastoral concerns. It is rich in references to social, historical, and Patristic sources, and well informed on current scholarship. Nash examines all the important angles and interpretive theories, makes theologically balanced interpretations of his own, and honestly admits when we just do not know what Paul meant. The pastoral discussions are illuminating and helpful. This is a commentary that will find ready use in many kinds of pastoral contexts.

—Carolyn Osiek
Fischer Professor of New Testament (retired)
Brite Divinity School

Scott Nash's commentary on 1 Corinthians skillfully brings us into genuine conversation with both Paul the author and the first readers of his letter and with the generations of commentators on the text since the first century. Equipped with extensive archaeological experience in Corinth and a clear eye for both physical and theological detail, Nash deftly opens the Corinthian landscape to our view and invites our nuanced reading. The result is a rich, multi-layered, and highly accessible resource for anyone who wishes seriously to grapple with the letter, its context, its history of interpretation, and its continuing influence on the understanding and practice of Christianity in modernity. The volume admirably reflects the series' commitment to provide exegetical and historical depth while bringing contemporary applications to light through a remarkable array of sensitively chosen examples from art, literature, cultural, religious, and intellectual history, the Revised Common Lectionary, and, not least, from the news headlines of our own times.

—Alexandra Brown
Jessie Ball duPont Professor of Religion
Washington and Lee University

CONTENTS

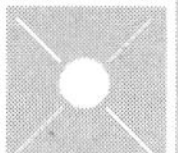

DEDICATION

For Dawn

who

"bears all things, believes all things, hopes all things, endures all things."

ABBREVIATIONS USED IN THIS COMMENTARY

Books of the Old Testament, Apocrypha, and New Testament are generally abbreviated in the Sidebars, parenthetical references, and notes according to the following system.

The Old Testament

Genesis	Gen
Exodus	Exod
Leviticus	Lev
Numbers	Num
Deuteronomy	Deut
Joshua	Josh
Judges	Judg
Ruth	Ruth
1–2 Samuel	1–2 Sam
1–2 Kings	1–2 Kgs
1–2 Chronicles	1–2 Chr
Ezra	Ezra
Nehemiah	Neh
Esther	Esth
Job	Job
Psalm (Psalms)	Ps (Pss)
Proverbs	Prov
Ecclesiastes	Eccl
or Qoheleth	Qoh
Song of Solomon	Song
or Song of Songs	Song
or Canticles	Cant
Isaiah	Isa
Jeremiah	Jer
Lamentations	Lam
Ezekiel	Ezek
Daniel	Dan
Hosea	Hos
Joel	Joel
Amos	Amos
Obadiah	Obad
Jonah	Jonah
Micah	Mic

Nahum	Nah
Habakkuk	Hab
Zephaniah	Zeph
Haggai	Hag
Zechariah	Zech
Malachi	Mal

The Apocrypha

1–2 Esdras	1–2 Esdr
Tobit	Tob
Judith	Jdt
Additions to Esther	Add Esth
Wisdom of Solomon	Wis
Ecclesiasticus or the Wisdom of Jesus Son of Sirach	Sir
Baruch	Bar
Epistle (or Letter) of Jeremiah	Ep Jer
Prayer of Azariah and the Song of the Three	Pr Azar
Daniel and Susanna	Sus
Daniel, Bel, and the Dragon	Bel
Prayer of Manasseh	Pr Man
1–4 Maccabees	1–4 Macc

The New Testament

Matthew	Matt
Mark	Mark
Luke	Luke
John	John
Acts	Acts
Romans	Rom
1–2 Corinthians	1–2 Cor
Galatians	Gal
Ephesians	Eph
Philippians	Phil
Colossians	Col
1–2 Thessalonians	1–2 Thess
1–2 Timothy	1–2 Tim
Titus	Titus
Philemon	Phlm
Hebrews	Heb
James	Jas
1–2 Peter	1–2 Pet
1–2–3 John	1–2–3 John
Jude	Jude
Revelation	Rev

Other commonly used abbreviations include:

AD	*Anno Domini* ("in the year of the Lord") (also commonly referred to as CE = the Common Era)
BC	Before Christ (also commonly referred to as BCE = Before the Common Era)
C.	century
c.	*circa* (around "that time")
cf.	*confer* (compare)
ch.	chapter
chs.	chapters
d.	died
ed.	edition or edited by or editor
eds.	editors
e.g.	*exempli gratia* (for example)
et al.	*et alii* (and others)
f./ff.	and the following one(s)
gen. ed.	general editor
ibid.	*ibidem* (in the same place)
i.e.	*id est* (that is)
LCL	Loeb Classical Library
lit.	literally
n.d.	no date
rev. and exp. ed.	revised and expanded edition
sg.	singular
trans.	translated by or translator(s)
vol(s).	volume(s)
v.	verse
vv.	verses

Selected additional written works cited by abbreviations include the following. A complete listing of abbreviations can be referenced in *The SBL Handbook of Style* (Peabody MA: Hendrickson, 1999):

AB	Anchor Bible
ABD	*Anchor Bible Dictionary*
ACCS	Ancient Christian Commentary on Scripture
AJA	*American Journal of Archaeology*
ANF	*Ante-Nicene Fathers*
ANRW	*Aufstieg und Niedergang der römischen Welt: Geschichte und Kultur Roms im Spiegel der neuren Forschung*
ANTC	Abingdon New Testament Commentaries
BA	*Biblical Archaeologist*

BAG	*Greek-English Lexicon of the New Testament and Other Early Christian Literature*
BAR	*Biblical Archaeology Review*
BECNT	Baker Exegetical Commentaries on the New Testament
BETL	Bibliotheca ephemeridum theologicarum lovaniensium
CBQ	*Catholic Biblical Quarterly*
FCCGRW	First-Century Christians in the Greco-Roman World
FF	Foundations and Facets
GBS	Guides to Biblical Scholarship
GNS	Good News Studies
HDR	Harvard Dissertations in Religion
HNTC	Harper's New Testament Commentaries
HTR	*Harvard Theological Review*
HUCA	*Hebrew Union College Annual*
IBC	Interpretation: A Bible Commentary for Teaching and Preaching
ICC	International Critical Commentary
IDB	*Interpreters Dictionary of the Bible*
JBL	*Journal of Biblical Literature*
JRA	*Journal of Roman Archaeology*
JRASup	Journal of Roman Archaeology Supplementary Series
JSJ	*Journal for the Study of Judaism in the Persian, Hellenistic, and Roman Periods*
JSNT	*Journal for the Study of the New Testament*
JSOT	*Journal for the Study of the Old Testament*
KJV	King James Version
LEC	Library of Early Christianity
LSJ	*A Greek-English Lexicon*
LXX	Septuagint = Greek Translation of Hebrew Bible
MDB	*Mercer Dictionary of the Bible*
MM	*The Vocabulary of the Greek Testament*
MT	Masoretic Text
NASB	New American Standard Bible
NEB	New English Bible
NICNT	New International Commentary on the New Testament
NIGCT	New International Greek Testament Commentary
NIV	New International Version
NovT	*Novum Testamentum*
NRSV	New Revised Standard Version
NTS	*New Testament Studies*
OGIS	*Orientis graeci inscriptiones selectae*
OTL	Old Testament Library
PRSt	*Perspectives in Religious Studies*

RB	*Revue biblique*
RevExp	*Review and Expositor*
RSV	Revised Standard Version
SBLDS	Society of Biblical Literature Dissertation Series
SBLMS	Society of Biblical Literature Monograph Series
SBLSP	*Society of Biblical Literature Seminar Papers*
SNTNMS	Society for the Study of the New Testament Monograph Series
SP	Sacra pagina
TCGNT	*A Textual Commentary on the Greek New Testament*
TDNT	*Theological Dictionary of the New Testament*
TEV	Today's English Version
TynBul	*Tyndale Bulletin*
VC	*Vigilae christianae*
WBC	Word Biblical Commentary
ZNW	*Zeitschrift für die neutestamentiche Wissenschaft und die Kunds der älteren Kirche*

AUTHOR'S PREFACE

My fascination (some might say obsession) with 1 Corinthians began with a graduate seminar on this intriguing letter of Paul conducted by the late Frank Stagg at The Southern Baptist Theological Seminary in 1980. Years later, when Smyth & Helwys Publishing was launched and we began entertaining the prospect of an innovative commentary series, my immediate inclination was to write the volume on 1 Corinthians. That inclination became fixed after participating in a NEH Summer Seminar on "Archaeology and Ancient History" conducted in Greece by Timothy E. Gregory, professor of history at Ohio State University and director of the OSU Excavations at Isthmia. That summer of 1991 marked the beginning of a long and rewarding association with Tim Gregory and the American School of Classical Studies in Athens, Greece. Tim's willingness to permit a New Testament scholar to join the team of the OSU Excavations opened the door to my education in the general aims and procedures of field archaeology and to the particular riches of the archaeological data accumulated at Isthmia and Corinth. I am eternally grateful to Tim for his leadership, collegiality, and friendship. I have learned much from him, as well as from Richard DeMaris, another New Testament scholar who participated in the seminar and who has produced several significant studies bearing on the interpretation of 1 Corinthians. I am also indebted to other members of the OSU team, including especially Richard Rothaus, Jayni Reinhard, and the late Jeanne Marty. I also express debt and gratitude to Charles K. Williams II, former director of the Corinth Excavations; to Nancy Bookidis, also of the Corinth Excavations; and to Elizabeth Gebhard, director of the University of Chicago Excavations at Isthmia. These members of the American School have all labored long and hard to mine and explain the archaeological remains of Ancient Corinth and Isthmia. With deep respect for their scholarship, I have tried to incorporate many of their insights into this commentary while trying to avoid the common mistake made by New Testament scholars of forcing the archaeological evidence to answer questions the evidence itself does not address.

One New Testament scholar who has effectively and judiciously drawn from the deep well of archaeology for insight into the world of the New Testament and early Christianity is obviously Helmut

Koester of Harvard University. I am indebted to him for his many kindnesses during the spring of 2001 when he allowed me to participate in his seminar on "Archaeology and the World of the New Testament" while I was a Visiting Scholar at the Harvard Divinity School. My semester of sabbatical leave at Harvard was also enriched by the scholarship and collegiality of Professor François Bovon, who kindly welcomed me to his graduate seminar on 1 Corinthians. To Mercer University, I express my gratitude for granting the sabbatical leave to study with these outstanding scholars at Harvard in 2001 and for another sabbatical leave to conduct additional research at the American School of Classical Studies in Athens, Greece, and to write the bulk of this commentary during Spring 2008. I also appreciate Mercer's support of my summer study-abroad programs through which I have been privileged to introduce scores of students to the archaeology and culture of Greece.

As the reader will quickly see, this commentary owes much to the efforts of many scholars, including those who have produced their own commentaries on 1 Corinthians. I sincerely appreciate their laudable work, even though I must confess that at times I have resented the thoroughness with which they have examined almost every possible detail of the letter and its interpretation. This is especially true of David Garland, a former professor and colleague of mine at Southern Seminary (now at Truett Seminary), who has written what I consider to be the best exegetical commentary on 1 Corinthians in English. While these scholars have left few exegetical stones unturned, I hope that the reader will find at least a few fresh ideas about 1 Corinthians in this commentary, especially in the restrained use of archaeology and in the suggestions for teaching and proclaiming the text of Paul's letter.

In addition to undergirding my research and writing through sabbatical leaves and financial support, Mercer University has provided an encouraging environment. Richard Wilson, chair of the Roberts Department of Christianity and a longtime friend (who has also written a commentary on 1 Corinthians), has facilitated securing financial support and has fostered a communal spirit within the department that enables me and all my departmental colleagues to benefit mutually from our common and individual interests. Nancy Stubbs, our department's essential administrative assistant, has characteristically done far more than her job description requires in helping to make this commentary a reality. Mercer students have also contributed to the book's completion both by responding to some of the ideas I have presented in classes and by their persistent inquiries about when I would finish. I am especially grateful to Emma Hughes, a member of the 2007 study-abroad program in Greece, for allowing me to include her excellent drawing of the Gallio inscription at Delphi.

In another life when I was a book editor for both Smyth & Helwys and Mercer University Press, I learned from my editorial mentor Edd Rowell, senior editor at MUP, how crucial (and usually unacknowledged) the editorial staff is in bringing a book to fruition. Smyth & Helwys has a superb editor in Leslie Andres, and I would be remiss if I failed to applaud her good work not only for my commentary but also for the entire Smyth & Helwys Commentary series. The format of this commentary series, while richly rewarding to the reader, is daunting to the writer and to the pre-press staff that creates the finished product. Dave Jones, the lead graphic designer, and Amy Davis, the graphic designer responsible for the initial art formatting and for procuring art rights, have once again transformed an author's medley into a book that is aesthetically pleasing and, I hope, accessible for the reader.

Finally, I express my gratitude for all the encouragement for this project through the years that came from students, colleagues, church members, neighbors, and friends. The greatest encouragement and support has come from my family, especially my wife, Dawn, who embodies 1 Corinthians 13:7 so well and who has promised to throw a party when the book is published.

Robert Scott Nash
27 July 2009

SERIES PREFACE

The *Smyth & Helwys Bible Commentary* is a visually stimulating and user-friendly series that is as close to multimedia in print as possible. Written by accomplished scholars with all students of Scripture in mind, the primary goal of the *Smyth & Helwys Bible Commentary* is to make available serious, credible biblical scholarship in an accessible and less intimidating format.

Far too many Bible commentaries fall short of bridging the gap between the insights of biblical scholars and the needs of students of God's written word. In an unprecedented way, the *Smyth & Helwys Bible Commentary* brings insightful commentary to bear on the lives of contemporary Christians. Using a multimedia format, the volumes employ a stunning array of art, photographs, maps, and drawings to illustrate the truths of the Bible for a visual generation of believers.

The *Smyth & Helwys Bible Commentary* is built upon the idea that meaningful Bible study can occur when the insights of contemporary biblical scholars blend with sensitivity to the needs of lifelong students of Scripture. Some persons within local faith communities, however, struggle with potentially informative biblical scholarship for several reasons. Oftentimes, such scholarship is cast in technical language easily grasped by other scholars, but not by the general reader. For example, lengthy, technical discussions on every detail of a particular scriptural text can hinder the quest for a clear grasp of the whole. Also, the format for presenting scholarly insights has often been confusing to the general reader, rendering the work less than helpful. Unfortunately, responses to the hurdles of reading extensive commentaries have led some publishers to produce works for a general readership that merely skim the surface of the rich resources of biblical scholarship. This commentary series incorporates works of fine art in an accurate and scholarly manner, yet the format remains "user-friendly." An important facet is the presentation and explanation of images of art, which interpret the biblical material or illustrate how the biblical material has been understood and interpreted in the past. A visual generation of believers deserves a commentary series that contains not only the all-important textual commentary on Scripture, but images, photographs, maps, works of fine art, and drawings that bring the text to life.

The *Smyth & Helwys Bible Commentary* makes serious, credible biblical scholarship more accessible to a wider audience. Writers and editors alike present information in ways that encourage readers to gain a better understanding of the Bible. The editorial board has worked to develop a format that is useful and usable, informative and pleasing to the eye. Our writers are reputable scholars who participate in the community of faith and sense a calling to communicate the results of their scholarship to their faith community.

The *Smyth & Helwys Bible Commentary* addresses Christians and the larger church. While both respect for and sensitivity to the needs and contributions of other faith communities are reflected in the work of the series authors, the authors speak primarily to Christians. Thus the reader can note a confessional tone throughout the volumes. No particular "confession of faith" guides the authors, and diverse perspectives are observed in the various volumes. Each writer, though, brings to the biblical text the best scholarly tools available and expresses the results of their studies in commentary and visuals that assist readers seeking a word from the Lord for the church.

To accomplish this goal, writers in this series have drawn from numerous streams in the rich tradition of biblical interpretation. The basic focus is the biblical text itself, and considerable attention is given to the wording and structure of texts. Each particular text, however, is also considered in the light of the entire canon of Christian Scriptures. Beyond this, attention is given to the cultural context of the biblical writings. Information from archaeology, ancient history, geography, comparative literature, history of religions, politics, sociology, and even economics is used to illuminate the culture of the people who produced the Bible. In addition, the writers have drawn from the history of interpretation, not only as it is found in traditional commentary on the Bible but also in literature, theater, church history, and the visual arts. Finally, the *Commentary* on Scripture is joined with *Connections* to the world of the contemporary church. Here again, the writers draw on scholarship in many fields as well as relevant issues in the popular culture.

This wealth of information might easily overwhelm a reader if not presented in a "user-friendly" format. Thus the heavier discussions of detail and the treatments of other helpful topics are presented in special-interest boxes, or Sidebars, clearly connected to the passages under discussion so as not to interrupt the flow of the basic interpretation. The result is a commentary on Scripture that focuses on the theological significance of a text while also offering the reader a rich array of additional information related to the text and its interpretation.

An accompanying CD-ROM offers powerful searching and research tools. The commentary text, Sidebars, and visuals are all reproduced on a CD that is fully indexed and searchable. Pairing a text version with a digital resource is a distinctive feature of the *Smyth & Helwys Bible Commentary.*

Combining credible biblical scholarship, user-friendly study features, and sensitivity to the needs of a visually oriented generation of believers creates a unique and unprecedented type of commentary series. With insight from many of today's finest biblical scholars and a stunning visual format, it is our hope that the *Smyth & Helwys Bible Commentary* will be a welcome addition to the personal libraries of all students of Scripture.

The Editors

HOW TO USE THIS COMMENTARY

The *Smyth & Helwys Bible Commentary* is written by accomplished biblical scholars with a wide array of readers in mind. Whether engaged in the study of Scripture in a church setting or in a college or seminary classroom, all students of the Bible will find a number of useful features throughout the commentary that are helpful for interpreting the Bible.

Basic Design of the Volumes

Each volume features an Introduction to a particular book of the Bible, providing a brief guide to information that is necessary for reading and interpreting the text: the historical setting, literary design, and theological significance. Each Introduction also includes a comprehensive outline of the particular book under study.

Each chapter of the commentary investigates the text according to logical divisions in a particular book of the Bible. Sometimes these divisions follow the traditional chapter segmentation, while at other times the textual units consist of sections of chapters or portions of more than one chapter. The divisions reflect the literary structure of a book and offer a guide for selecting passages that are useful in preaching and teaching.

An accompanying CD-ROM offers powerful searching and research tools. The commentary text, Sidebars, and visuals are all reproduced on a CD that is fully indexed and searchable. Pairing a text version with a digital resource also allows unprecedented flexibility and freedom for the reader. Carry the text version to locations you most enjoy doing research while knowing that the CD offers a portable alternative for travel from the office, church, classroom, and your home.

Commentary and Connections

As each chapter explores a textual unit, the discussion centers around two basic sections: *Commentary* and *Connections*. The analysis of a passage, including the details of its language, the history reflected in the text, and the literary forms found in the text, are the main focus of the *Commentary* section. The primary concern of the *Commentary* section is to explore the theological issues presented by the Scripture passage. *Connections* presents potential applications of the insights provided in the *Commentary* section. The *Connections* portion of each chapter considers what issues are relevant for teaching and suggests useful methods and resources. *Connections* also identifies themes suitable for sermon planning and suggests helpful approaches for preaching on the Scripture text.

Sidebars

The *Smyth & Helwys Bible Commentary* provides a unique hyperlink format that quickly guides the reader to additional insights. Since other more technical or supplementary information is vital for understanding a text and its implications, the volumes feature distinctive Sidebars, or special-interest boxes, that provide a wealth of information on such matters as:

- Historical information (such as chronological charts, lists of kings or rulers, maps, descriptions of monetary systems, descriptions of special groups, descriptions of archaeological sites or geographical settings).

- Graphic outlines of literary structure (including such items as poetry, chiasm, repetition, epistolary form).

- Definition or brief discussions of technical or theological terms and issues.

- Insightful quotations that are not integrated into the running text but are relevant to the passage under discussion.

- Notes on the history of interpretation (Augustine on the Good Samaritan, Luther on James, Stendahl on Romans, etc.).

- Line drawings, photographs, and other illustrations relevant for understanding the historical context or interpretive significance of the text.

- Presentation and discussion of works of fine art that have interpreted a Scripture passage.

Each Sidebar is printed in color and is referenced at the appropriate place in the *Commentary* or *Connections* section with a color-coded title that directs the reader to the relevant Sidebar. In addition, helpful icons appear in the Sidebars, which provide the reader with visual cues to the type of material that is explained in each Sidebar. Throughout the commentary, these four distinct hyperlinks provide useful links in an easily recognizable design.

AΩ

Alpha & Omega Language

This icon identifies the information as a language-based tool that offers further exploration of the Scripture selection. This could include syntactical information, word studies, popular or additional uses of the word(s) in question, additional contexts in which the term appears, and the history of the term's translation. All non-English terms are transliterated into the appropriate English characters.

Culture/Context

This icon introduces further comment on contextual or cultural details that shed light on the Scripture selection. Describing the place and time to which a Scripture passage refers is often vital to the task of biblical interpretation. Sidebar items introduced with this icon could include geographical, historical, political, social, topographical, or economic information. Here, the reader may find an excerpt of an ancient text or inscription that sheds light on the text. Or one may find a description of some element of ancient religion such as Baalism in Canaan or the Hero cult in the Mystery Religions of the Greco-Roman world.

Interpretation

Sidebars that appear under this icon serve a general interpretive function in terms of both historical and contemporary renderings. Under this heading, the reader might find a selection from classic or contemporary literature that illuminates the Scripture text or a significant quotation from a famous sermon that addresses the passage. Insights are drawn from various sources, including literature, worship, theater, church history, and sociology.

Additional Resources Study

Here, the reader finds a convenient list of useful resources for further investigation of the selected Scripture text, including books, journals, websites, special collections, organizations, and societies. Specialized discussions of works not often associated with biblical studies may also appear here.

Additional Features

Each volume also includes a basic Bibliography on the biblical book under study. Other bibliographies on selected issues are often included that point the reader to other helpful resources.

Notes at the end of each chapter provide full documentation of sources used and contain additional discussions of related matters.

Abbreviations used in each volume are explained in a list of abbreviations found after the Table of Contents.

Readers of the *Smyth & Helwys Bible Commentary* can regularly visit the Internet support site for news, information, updates, and enhancements to the series at **www.helwys.com/commentary**.

Several thorough indexes enable the reader to locate information quickly. These indexes include:

- An *Index of Sidebars* groups content from the special-interest boxes by category (maps, fine art, photographs, drawings, etc.).

- An *Index of Scriptures* lists citations to particular biblical texts.

- An *Index of Topics* lists alphabetically the major subjects, names, topics, and locations referenced or discussed in the volume.

- An *Index of Modern Authors* organizes contemporary authors whose works are cited in the volume.

INTRODUCTION

Perhaps more than any other "book" in the New Testament, 1 Corinthians offers readers a window to the life of the early church. Through this window we catch a glimpse of a community of faith struggling with questions of identity, relationship, belief, and practice. Other New Testament writings, notably 2 Corinthians and Acts, enhance the view of life within that community of faith. Second Corinthians grants us some sense of how affairs proceeded after 1 Corinthians, and Acts shows how Paul's experience with the Corinthians was remembered, or at least depicted, by one later writer. Furthermore, information from beyond the pages of the New Testament, most notably that provided by extensive archaeological work at Corinth, grants us a fuller picture than we have of most early church communities regarding the environment in which matters of identity, relationship, belief, and practice were shaped.

Yet our vision through the window of 1 Corinthians is not without significant limitations. The author of 1 Corinthians, the apostle Paul, has framed the shape of the window. For the most part, we can see only what Paul has shown us. His window does not provide access to every part of the Corinthian faith community, only to the parts he wished to expose and only in the ways he wished to expose them. We cannot know beyond any doubt that his presentation of the situation was an accurate reflection of that situation, nor can we be certain that we even correctly understand what Paul presented. Filling in the gaps in the partial picture we have of the Corinthian community

Archaeology in Corinth

The Lechaion Road leading to the Forum. (Credit: Scott Nash)

Since 1896, the American School of Classical Studies at Athens, under the supervision of the Greek Archaeological Service of the Ministry of Culture, has conducted ongoing surveys and excavations in Corinth and the surrounding area. In addition, the Greek Archaeological Service has also excavated a few sites itself. While this work has involved the study of the entire history of Corinth from antiquity to the present, the majority of the archaeological remains, especially buildings, have come from the Roman period.

and its struggles involves integrating information from other sources with the selective information provided by Paul. Often those other sources of information do not address our questions directly, and integrating the information they give requires creativity and imagination. Always, in doing this, we run the risk of misreading what Paul wrote and of misapplying the additional pieces of information. Without taking that risk, however, we would find it hard to make sense of much contained within 1 Corinthians. [John Chrysostom's Description of Corinth]

John Chrysostom's Description of Corinth

Early commentators on 1 Corinthians recognized the importance of knowing something about the setting of the letter in order to appreciate its message. John Chrysostom (AD 347–407), who preached forty-one homilies on 1 Corinthians, attempted an imaginative reconstruction of Corinth as it was in Paul's day.

> Today Corinth is the most prominent city in Greece, and in ancient times the citizens took pride in the city's many advantages, above all, in its abundant wealth. This is why one of the pagan authors [Homer, *Iliad* 2.570] called the place "rich." The city is located on the isthmus of the Peloponnesus in a setting well-suited for trade. It was full of rhetoricians and philosophers. One of the so-called Seven Sages is from this city [Periander]. I say these things not to show off or to display the breadth of my education—for what is the significance of knowing these things?—but because they help us understand the subject matter of the letter.

Chrysostom, *Homilies on the Epistles of Paul, Proem*, from *1 Corinthians: Interpreted by Early Christian Commentators*, trans. and ed. Judith L. Kovacs (The Church's Bible, ed. Robert L. Wilken; Grand Rapids: Eerdmans Publishing, 2005) 9.

Even when we have arrived at a satisfying sense of what Paul wrote to the Corinthian community, though, we still face the challenge of "hearing" the message of 1 Corinthians. Can this window that sheds particular light on the life of one early faith community become a medium for "hearing" the word of God for communities of faith today? As a part of the canon of Christian Scriptures, 1 Corinthians holds a position of authority for Christians who believe it can still "speak" to them in matters of identity, relationship, belief, and practice. This commentary proceeds in the conviction our "hearing" is enhanced by our "seeing." The better we can *see* through this window into the life of that early faith community, the better we can hear the message of this part of Scripture. To that end, we will try to obtain as clear a picture as possible of that community to which 1 Corinthians serves as a window, and we will look carefully at the shape and texture of the window itself. In trying to avoid the dangers of filling in too many gaps with too much unsupportable imagination, we will exercise restraint in our reconstruction and err (as inevitably all reconstructions do) on the side of caution.

The Context of 1 Corinthians

Corinth: A Tale of Two Cities

To try to understand the struggles of the faith community to whom Paul addressed the letter we call 1 Corinthians, we need to know something about the environment in which those struggles occurred. Thus, we turn to examine relevant features of the life of that community in ancient Corinth. In doing so, we need to be careful that we examine the right Corinth.

Map of Greece

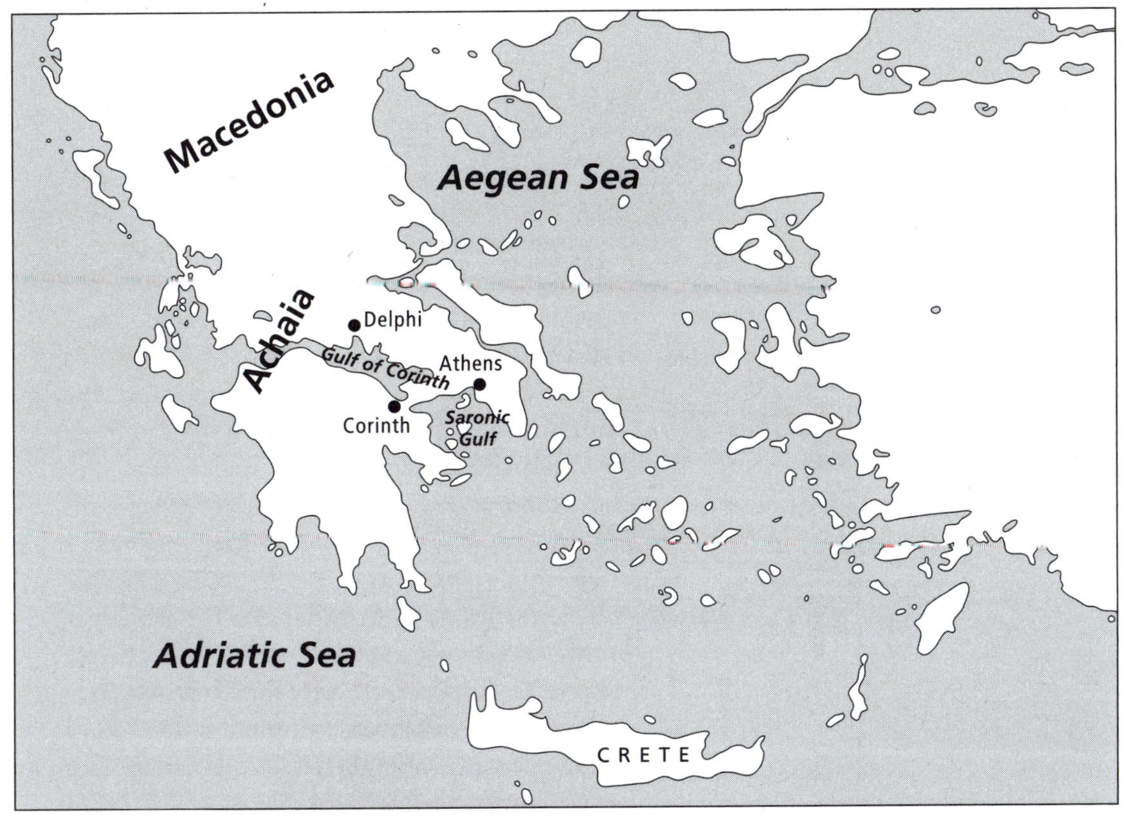

Greek Corinth. Unfortunately, in the history of the interpretation of 1 Corinthians, interpreters have often failed to distinguish between the ancient Greek city-state of Corinth and the Roman colony of Corinth known to Paul. Information about the Greek city found in some ancient writings and archaeological reports has been read as if it applied to Corinth in Paul's time. For example, clay votives of human genitalia found in excavations of the temple of Asklepios have been interpreted as evidence of venereal disease (supposedly indicative of sexual license) rather than as indications of reproductive problems.[1] Similar votives of various body parts have been seen as the "trigger experience" for Paul's use of the body metaphor in 1 Corinthians 12.[2] The relevance of such artifacts proves deficient, however, in light of the fact that the anatomical votives in question had lain buried (and unobservable) for several hundred years by Paul's time.[3]

The most notorious example of not distinguishing between the two cities is the common depiction of Roman Corinth as an especially immoral place on the basis of certain statements by writers in the Classical period and the misreading of certain references by writers closer in time to Paul. Derogatory comments about the promiscuity of Corinthian women and the prominence of prostitution in the city, however, stemmed largely from anti-Corinthian sentiment expressed by Athenian writers of the Classical period who were angered by Corinth's conflict with Athens in the so-called "First" Peloponnesian War (461–446 BC) and Corinth's perceived instigation of the "Second" Peloponnesian War (431–404 BC) that led to Athens's fall to Sparta.[4] The more general perception in ancient Greece regarding prostitution in Corinth saw it as an indication of the city's enviable opulence, not its moral degradation.[5] Undoubtedly, as a wealthy city with two busy ports, Corinth had numerous prostitutes, some of whom were quite famous, as the ancient evidence reports. Indeed, the temple of Aphrodite possessed a large number of prostitutes and other servants dedicated to the goddess, but the evidence is lacking that such prostitutes engaged in "sacred" sexual activity on behalf of an Aphrodisian fertility cult.[6] Furthermore, the scope and nature of prostitution in Greek Corinth is irrelevant for Roman Corinth. Strabo's later reference to one thousand prostitutes dedicated to Aphrodite in Corinth has been erroneously applied to the Roman city that Strabo (and Paul) visited and used as an explanation for problems of immorality within the church; his statement, accurate or not about Greek Corinth, actually points out the absence of such activity in Roman Corinth.[7] [Strabo]

Strabo

Strabo was born in Pontus (in northern Asia Minor) around 63 BC. His educational pursuits often took him to Rome, and on at least one of those trips (29 BC) he passed through Roman Corinth. His description of the city included the statement below about the temple of Aphrodite on the Acrocorinth during the Greek period. His words have often been misconstrued as an indication that sexual immorality was rampant in Roman Corinth. Actually, his description of Corinth clearly indicates that no such center of sexually promiscuous cultic activity existed during the Roman period—if it ever had!

"And the temple of Aphrodite was so rich that it owned more than a thousand temple-slaves, prostitutes, whom both men and women had dedicated to the goddess."

Strabo, *Geography* (trans. H. L. Jones; 8 vols.; LCL; Cambridge: Harvard University Press, 1927) 8:6.20c.

Whatever the state of affairs may have been in the ancient Greek city-state of Corinth, the life of that city came to a tragic end in 146 BC at the hands of the Roman army. Roman military involvement in Greece first came in a series of wars with Macedonia beginning in 214 BC, during which the Greek city-states, including Corinth, were "liberated" by the Romans from Macedonian control in 196.[8] While officially recognizing the freedom of Greece, the Romans moved to strengthen their control of its affairs by weakening the ties of city-states in such alliances as the Achaean league, of which Corinth had often been a prominent member. Open defiance of Roman interference led to the defeat of Achaean forces in 146 BC on the isthmus of Corinth and the punitive sacking of Corinth by the Roman consul Lucius Mummius.[9] According to ancient reports from the second century

AD, the Romans killed the male citizens, sold the women and children into slavery, and hauled off the treasures of Corinth to Rome. [The Fall of Corinth]

Prior to its destruction by the Romans, Corinth had been strategically important to Macedonian control of Greece because of its location at the narrow juncture (the isthmus of Corinth) of northern Greece and the Peloponnesian peninsula and because of the extensive fortifications atop the 575-meter-high mountain (Acrocorinth) incorporated within the city's walls. Corinth's location also made possible its commercial success since, in addition to its control of most land transport between northern and southern Greece, it possessed two excellent harbors. The harbor at Lechaion lay on the southern edge of the Gulf of Corinth, about two kilometers north of the city center, and was joined to the city by long walls. This harbor supplied access to numerous points to the west. On the northeastern edge of the Peloponnesian peninsula, about nine kilometers east of Corinth, lay the harbor town of Cenchreae, Corinth's chief port for sea travel in the Aegean and beyond. Furthermore, Corinth was able to exploit the narrow width of the isthmus (less than six kilometers at the narrowest point) by constructing a stone pavement (the *diolkos*) connecting the Gulf of Corinth on the western side to the Saronic Gulf on the east, over which goods and smaller ships were hauled for a charge. While the *diolkos* sometimes provided timely transport of military vessels (the purpose for which it may originally have been built in the sixth

The Fall of Corinth

The 2d-century writer Pausanias visited Corinth sometime around AD 165. In his description of the Roman city as he found it, he included information about the sack of the ancient Greek city by the Roman general Mummius.

> Mummius held back for the time being from entering Corinth even though the gates were open, suspecting there might be an ambush inside the walls, but two days after the battle he took possession in force and burnt Corinth. Most of the people who were left there were murdered by the Romans, and Mummius auctioned the women and children. He auctioned the slaves as well, those of them I mean who were set free and fought beside the Achaeans, and were not killed at once in the fighting. He collected the most marvelous of sacred dedications and works of art, and gave the less important things to Attalos's general Philopoimen: and in my time at Pergamon they still had the spoils of Corinth.

Pausanias, *Guide to Greece 1: Central Greece* (trans. Peter Levi; New York: Penguin Books, 1971) 267.

Acrocorinth

(Credit: Scott Nash)

The *Diolkos*
The stone passageway by which goods and small ships were transported between the Saronic (east) and Corinthian (west) gulfs.

(Credit: Scott Nash)

century BC), its primary benefit was commercial.[10]

Roman Corinth. Corinth's strategic potential for commerce, and not its military prospects, apparently led to its rebirth as a Roman colony. Thus, unlike other Roman colonies that were designed to establish a strong Roman presence through the settlement of veteran soldiers, *Colonia Laus Julia Corinthiensis* was largely populated by former slaves sent there as freedperson-agents to conduct trade on behalf of aristocrats in Rome who

Map of the Corinthia

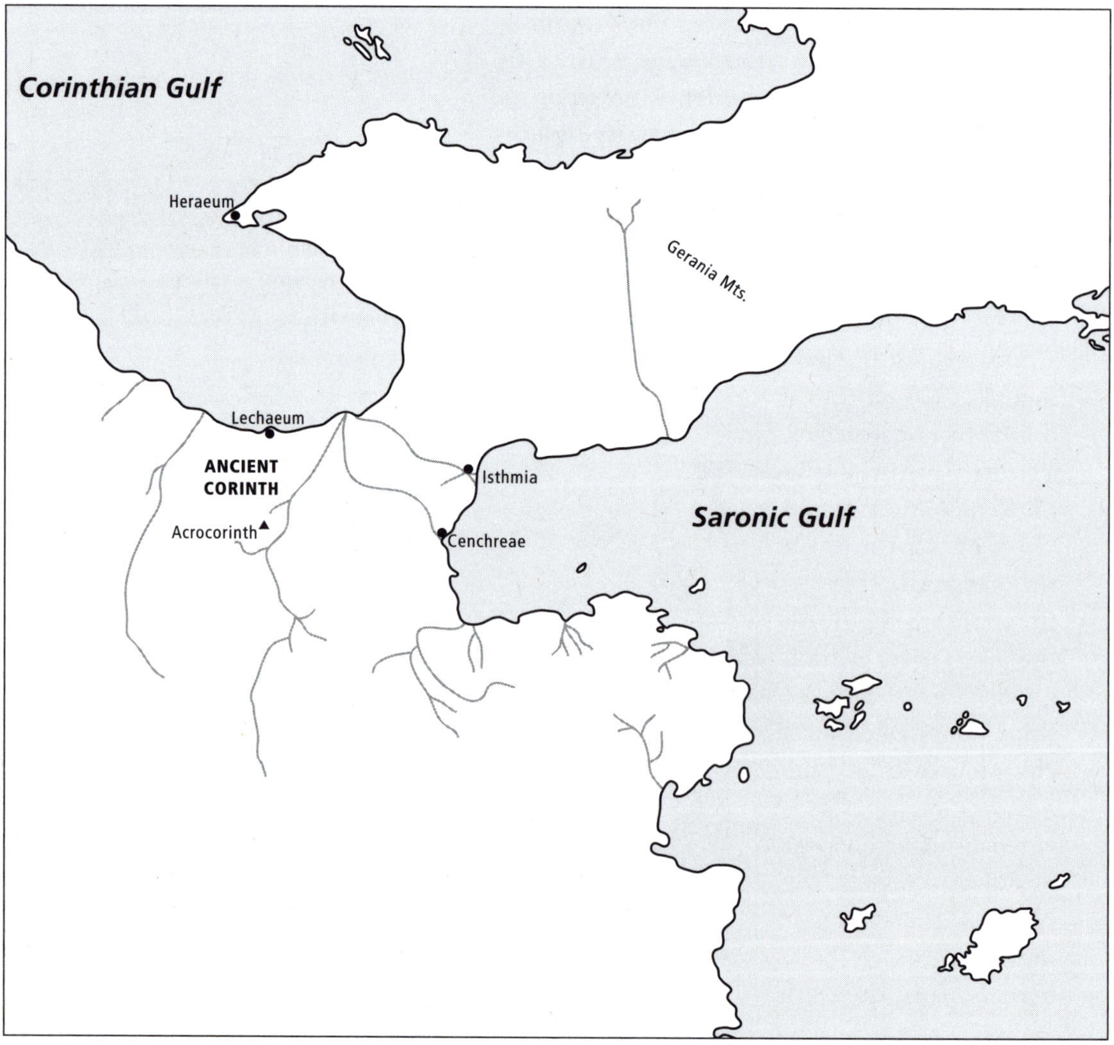

Corinthian Gulf
Heraeum
Gerania Mts.
Lechaeum
ANCIENT CORINTH
Acrocorinth
Isthmia
Cenchreae
Saronic Gulf

were prevented by law from operating such business themselves.[11] The founding of the colony was planned by Julius Caesar shortly before his death in 44 BC and officially enacted by Augustus some years later. Preparations for the design of the urban area and the configuration of surrounding rural territory probably began even earlier.[12] From the beginning of the colonizing process, Corinth was planned as a suitable symbol of Roman triumph and a profitable center for Roman business.

As a colony, the new city of Corinth was intended to be something of a "little Rome" in Greece. The Roman grid system dictated the orientation of streets and buildings, with certain exceptions. The destruction of the old city a century earlier had not been as thorough as some ancient writers would lead us to believe, though Corinth had ceased to exist as a "city." Several major buildings had been left relatively intact, and these were allowed to affect the orientation of the new Roman forum, which served as the central business and administrative district.[13] The basic east-west orientation of the central area was determined by an unusually large building to the south (the South Stoa), which was probably built

Plan of Roman Corinth

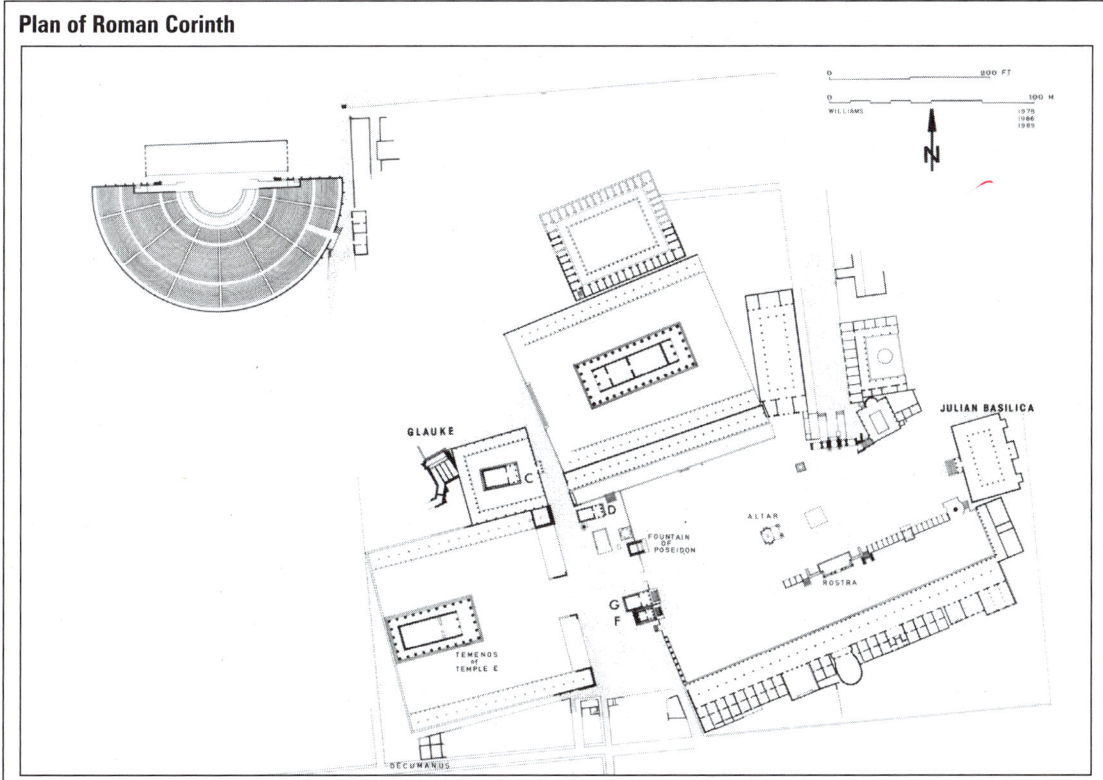

Charles K. Williams II, "General plan of Roman Forum, early 1st-C. AD," in *The Corinthia in the Roman Period* (ed. Timothy E. Gregory; JRASup 8: Ann Arbor MI: Journal of Roman Archaeology, 1993) 32. Courtesy of the Trustees of the American School of Classical Studies at Athens, Greece.

by Philip II of Macedon to house visiting delegates of the Corinthian League.[14] On the north side of the forum, along the western edge, was a prominent ridge atop which stood a large temple (probably to Apollo) that had been built in the Archaic period (sixth century). Along the eastern edge of the north side, at a lower level, stood the venerable Peirene fountain facing north. Between the South Stoa on the south and the archaic temple and Peirene on the north, running east-west, was a long, level area previously occupied by a series of racecourses. The surviving structures from Greek Corinth were restored and incorporated into the architectural design of the new colony.

Despite the influences of these earlier Greek structures, however, the Romans designed their forum with a distinctively "Roman" character. The South Stoa was converted into various administrative offices and shops. A large two-story stoa was erected in front of the temple ridge that partially blocked the view of the old temple of Apollo, which was itself redesigned in the interior while the exterior was restored to its archaic appearance. The Peirene fountain received an elaborate two-storied façade with a typically Roman arcade that permitted a peek at certain features of the old Greek structure.[15] Between the new stoa and Peirene, at the main entrance to the forum via the road from Lechaion, the colonists erected a Romanesque triple-bayed arch. A large *rostra* (perhaps the *bēma* of Acts 18:18) stood prominently near the center of the forum in front of the South Stoa, and in front of it stood a Roman altar. (See "The *Bēma*" below.) A basilica, seemingly dedicated to the Julian family and probably constructed during the Augustan period, framed the east end of the forum. A row of small temples (Temples D, F, G) built in the Roman podium style and dedicated

Forum

(Credit: Scott Nash)

The forum of Roman Corinth was unusually large (180m by 117m at widest point), containing more than 15,300 square meters of open space. Its length seems to have been determined by the long building on the South (South Stoa), which survived Roman destruction of the city in 146 BC. The view from the east in the photograph shows the remains of the archaic temple of Apollo on the northwest (upper left).

Charles K. Williams II, "Roman Corinth as a Commercial Center," in *The Corinthia in the Roman Period* (ed. Timothy E. Gregory; JRASup 8: Ann Arbor MI: Journal of Roman Archaeology, 1993) 33–35.

to deities important to the Romans framed the west end.[16] Farther to the west, beyond these shrines, on a high terrace fronted by a row of large shops, the Romans built a large, visually prominent temple (Temple E). The earliest edition of this temple, which probably dates to the time of Augustus or Tiberius, was replaced after an earthquake in the AD 70s by an even more imposing Roman-style podium temple. Though the dedication of this temple remains disputed, its prominent location supports linkage to Roman state cult, most likely the imperial cult.[17]

This brief sketch of the attention given to the design of the forum for the new colony suggests that public space was intended to communicate a certain sense of identity. The reuse of old Greek-period buildings enabled the new Corinth to claim connection to its illustrious past. Yet the overwhelming appearance of the city was characteristically Roman. The message carried by this medium of architecture was that of a powerful entity, the Roman Empire, as the magnanimous preserver of the Greek heritage while unmistakably visible as the sovereign power. Abundant artifactual evidence exists from Corinth, significantly for the period of Paul's association with the city, that demonstrates the Roman concern to promote the glory of Rome, especially through the imperial cult.[18] Numerous inscriptions, coins, and sculptures from Corinth testify to the prominence of the Roman state and its emperor in every facet of public life.

Augustus

Archaeological Museum of Ancient Corinth (Credit: Scott Nash)

This statue of Augustus with head covered depicts him in his role as Pontifex maximus (chief priest). It was found along with other statues of the Julian family in the basilica on the eastern end of the forum of Roman Corinth, leading the excavators to name the building the Julian basilica.

The Imperial Cult. Corinth's role in promoting the imperial cult and a spirit of *Romanitas* appears to have been enhanced by several significant developments. One was the rise of Corinth to prominence over other Greek cities. In 27 BC Achaia became a senatorial province, with Corinth as its chief city, if not capital. This status ended in AD 15, but in AD 44 (not long before Paul's first visit), Claudius restored Achaia's

Coin of Hadrian and Achaea

Harold Mattingly, et al., eds. *The Roman Imperial Coinage II: Vespasian to Hadrian*. London: Spink, 1923. RIC 938.

On the obverse (front) this coin depicts the emperor Hadrian (AD 117–38) and reads:

HADRIANVS AVG COS III P P

(AUG = Augustus; COS = consul; III = 3 times; P = pater [father]; P = patriae [of his country]).

The reverse side shows the emperor standing on the left, raising Achaea (Greece) with his hand. The engraving reads RESTITVTOR ACHAEA (Restorer of Greece).

provincial status and initiated significant building projects in Corinth. From this period on, then, Corinth functioned as the capital of the province, though evidence of official action stating such is lacking.[19] Another development was the establishment of a "federal" imperial cult in Corinth, possibly around the time of Paul's first visit or soon thereafter.[20] This brought political and financial benefits to the city in that Corinth received obligatory, and sometimes reluctant, contributions from all the other cities in the province for the annual celebration of the emperor's birth. This celebration was in addition to the regular religious ceremonies and special festivals commemorating Rome's beneficent rule, as embodied especially in the generosity of the emperor.

Of the major festivals, the biennial Isthmian games, which had been one of the four panhellenic festivals observed in pre-Roman Greece, were the most important. Significantly, for Roman purposes of self-promotion, a second festival, the Caesarean games, was added to the Isthmian around 30 BC, shortly after Augustus's victory at Actium.[21] Later, either during the reign of Tiberius or Claudius, a third festival honoring the living emperor (the *Caesarea Sebastea*) was added.[22] The public importance placed on the Isthmian games and related contests is evident in the stature of the *agonothetes*, the person elected to oversee them. Roman Corinth's governmental structure somewhat mimicked that of Rome itself, with the annual election of two top administrators, the *duovirs*. Election to the position of *agonothetes*, however, was always the most prized.[23] The *agonothetes* personally financed the games and, thus, was seen as a great benefactor to the city, worthy of great honor.

Isthmia

Ruins of the sanctuary of Poseidon on the isthmus of Corinth, facing east. (Credit: Scott Nash)

The sanctuary of Poseidon on the isthmus of Corinth was the site of one of the four Panhellenic festivals that featured competitions. The Isthmian games were held in the spring of the second and fourth years of the Panhellenic cycle; the Olympic games were held in the summer of the first year, the Pythian games at Delphi in the summer of the third year, and the Nemean games in the summer of the second and fourth years. In the Roman period and perhaps earlier, the Isthmian contests were held in honor of the dead boy-hero Melikertes-Palaimon.

Elizabeth R. Gebhard, "The Isthmian Games and the Sanctuary of Poseidon in the Early Empire," in *The Corinthia in the Roman Period* (ed. Timothy E. Gregory; JRASup 8: Ann Arbor MI: Journal of Roman Archaeology, 1993) 78–94.

Helmut Koester, "Melikertes at Isthmia: A Roman Mystery Cult," in *Greeks, Romans, and Christians: Essays in Honor of Abraham J. Malherbe* (ed. David L. Balch, Everett Ferguson, and Wayne A. Meeks; Minneapolis: Fortress Press, 1990) 355–66.

Patronage. The importance placed on public benefaction by individuals, as well as on a city's display of benevolence in behalf of the emperor, points to an important component of Roman civic life—patronage. Patrons were persons with the power to get things done.

Agonotheteion Mosaic

The elaborate mosaic floor that decorated the administrative headquarters of the *agonothetes* indicates the importance of the office in Roman Corinth. The mosaic dates from the second half of the 1st century AD, but the Agonotheteion was probably constructed during the time of Augustus or Tiberias when the Romans began to convert the eastern end of the South Stoa into civic offices. The mosaic depicts an athlete (note the palm branch and wreath) hurrying from his recent victory to pay homage to Eutychia (the goddess of Good Fortune).

Oscar Broneer, *The South Stoa and Its Roman Successors* (*Corinth* I.4; Princeton: American School of Classical Studies at Athens, 1954) 108, pl 30. Courtesy of the Trustees of the American School of Classical Studies at Athens, Greece.

Their clients were the persons for whom they got things done, in return for services rendered and for the appropriate displays of homage that, in turn, enhanced the patron's clout. In a sense, the emperor was the patron of the whole empire. Persons close to the emperor carried significant clout throughout the empire. In a provincial city, such as Corinth, such persons typically were elected to the highest offices and in those capacities performed acts of benefaction for the city that secured their high standing. Usually, those persons were from aristocratic families and had considerable personal wealth. In Corinth, however, it appears that the potential for wealth accumulation by successful freedperson agents allowed them to rise in rank and hold some offices normally restricted to aristocrats.[24] The pattern of patron-client worked its way from the top of the social pyramid down to the bottom through a network of dependent relationships.

This unofficial system of social interaction affected not only the public political and economic life of Roman Corinth but also its private associations. These associations, including those organized primarily for religious purposes, sought the support of powerful patrons, on whom the association would bestow honors in exchange.[25] Within the associations, the same kind of pyramidal structure that held in the larger society would be followed. Though Roman officials often viewed such associations from the lower classes with suspicion, the decline of traditional Greek city-based cultic ties in the wake of the rise of the empire-based state cult seems to have contributed to the increase in private religious associations in the first century AD.[26] In a growing, cosmopolitan

Babbius Monument

(Credit: Scott Nash)

Cn. Babbius Philinus was probably a freedperson who achieved financial success in Corinth during the early 1st century AD. Inscriptions on structures he either built or refurbished bear no mention of his father, thus supporting the conjecture that he was a freedperson. He served as a magistrate during the reigns of both Augustus and Tiberius.

The so-called "Babbius Monument" was a small, circular structure of the Corinthian order with ornate carvings including a pine cone at the pinnacle of the conical roof. The fine white marble of the superstructure was imported. A dedicatory inscription appeared both on the epistyle and the podium. It reads, [C]N BABBIVS PHILINVS AED[ILIS] PONTIF[EX] D[E] S[VA] P[ECUNIA] F[ACIENDUM] C[URAVIT] IDEMQVE IIVIR P[ROBAVIT] (Gnaeus Babbius Philinus, aedile and pontifex, had this monument erected at his own expense, and he approved it in his official capacity as duovir).

The monument's distinguished appearance, along with its self-congratulatory inscription, served to honor the success of the benefactor.

John Harvey Kent, *The Inscriptions 1926–1950* (*Corinth* VIII.3; Princeton: American School of Classical Studies at Athens, 1966) 73.

James Wiseman, "Corinth and Rome I: 228 B.C.–A.D. 267," *ANRW* 7/1 (1979): 518.

Jerome Murphy-O'Connor, *St. Paul's Corinth: Texts and Archaeology* (Collegeville MN: Liturgical Press, 1983) 27–28.

colony, such as Corinth, religious associations might find a higher degree of freedom from official scrutiny than would have been the case in more traditionally Greek cities, such as Thessalonike, where devotion to civic cult might be monitored and new groups competing for religious loyalties might be discouraged.[27] Even so, associations perceived as threats to social and political norms might be viewed suspiciously even in Corinth. One such association formed in the middle of the first century AD, the *ekklēsia* founded by Paul, would have existed in an environment in which patronage was accepted as the normal way to organize internal, as well as external, relationships.[28]

Religions. In the competitive milieu that patronage fostered, the association founded by Paul would have also found itself in competition with numerous religious options available to the residents of Corinth. While modern interpreters often assume that the official cults supported by the state were purely political in function, those cults also clearly addressed certain religious needs. Even the imperial cult spoke to the religious significance of the emperor as mediator between the human and the divine and not simply to the political reality of his sovereignty.[29] Certain deities of the traditional Greek and Roman pantheons, which had been essentially merged by the first century, were recognized as important to the well-being of the city. Such was the case with Poseidon-Neptune, whose image appears on more types of Roman Corinthian coins than any other deity.[30] One might expect the sea-god to be important to a city so dependent on sea trade, and so, understandably, Corinth's largest sanctuary was dedicated to him, at which the Isthmian games were originally held and to which they eventually returned. Likewise, Aphrodite, as protector of the city, was one of the deities honored in Greek Corinth whose temple (on the Acrocorinth) seems to have been restored early in the life of the colony. Aphrodite's association with the Roman Venus, the patron deity of the Julian dynasty, also contributed to her importance for Roman Corinth.

Poseidon Coin

Issued when L. Paconius Flaminus and Cn. Publicius Regulus were duoviri in Corinth (AD 50–51), this coin's obverse depicts Melicertes, the boy-hero in whose honor the Isthmian Games were held, lying on two dolphins. The reverse has a naked Poseidon, standing and holding a dolphin and trident, and the letters COR SE.

A. Burnett, et al., eds. *Roman Provincial Coinage I: From the Death of Caesar to the Death of Vitellius (44 BC–AD 69)*. London: British Museum Press, 1992. RPC 1188.

With Aphrodite-Venus, however, we move to a dimension of traditional Greek and Roman religion that extends beyond the public to the personal. Excavations east of the theater in Corinth, in a more residential area, have uncovered numerous artifacts related to Aphrodite that demonstrate her importance for female fertility and other wifely responsibilities within the household.[31] Other deities also were honored for the aid they might give to individuals. The reestablishment of the sanctuary of Asklepios, with its focus on individual healing, seems to have taken place early in the colony's life.[32] Exactly when the sanctuary of Demeter-Ceres and Kore-Persephone was reestablished on the slope of the Acrocorinth is unclear, though coinage and some pottery suggests it was before Paul's time.[33] The terracotta figurines found there, as well as the lead "curse tablets" from beginning in the first century AD and continuing through the fourth, suggest that the cult of this mother-daughter pair had special significance for women.[34] Other cults associated with traditional Greek and

Claudius Coin

The obverse of this coin, issued by Licinus iter and Octavius, duoviri of Corinth in AD 42/3–45/6, portrays a laureate head of the emperor Claudius (AD 41–54) and reads:

[TI CLAVD CAESAR] AVG. P P.

([] = text supplied by numismatists; TI = Tiberius; CLAVD = Claudius; AUG = Augustus; P = pater [father]; P = patriae [of his country]).

The reverse depicts a hexastyle temple on the top of the Acrocorinth (probably to Aphrodite) and includes the names of the duovirs (II VIR) who issued the coin, as well as the place of issue (COR = Corinth).

A. Burnett, et al., eds. Roman Provincial Coinage I: *From the Death of Caesar to the Death of Vitellius (44 BC–AD 69)*. London: British Museum Press, 1992. RPC 1180.

Asklepion

(Credit: Scott Nash)

Roman deities, though not part of the more civic observances, also seem not to have been neglected in the new Corinth. Deities not traditionally associated with either Greece or Rome, however, also found a following in Roman Corinth, especially Egyptian ones. Though most of the evidence comes from the second century AD and beyond, some artifactual remains suggest that Isis, Osiris, and Serapis had devotees as early as the first century AD.[35] These deities were often associated with healing and fertility, as well as with life after death. An eastern mother deity with similar associations, Cybele, had a temple in Corinth at least by the middle of the second century AD, and some evidence exists of her worship in domestic settings earlier.[36] One other religious movement with eastern roots calls for special attention—that of the Jews.

Serapis

Archaeological Museum of Ancient Corinth
(Credit: Scott Nash)

That a Jewish community existed in Corinth in the first century seems certain, given that Paul himself was Jewish and that his main coworkers there were Jewish, but all the archaeological evidence comes from much later. (See the photo of the synagogue inscription in chapter 1.) The book of Acts (ch. 18) depicts Paul, in typical Lukan fashion, preaching in the Jewish synagogue in Corinth and eventually alienating most of the Jewish community. Other bits of historical information suggest a significant Jewish presence in Corinth. In AD 39/40, the Jewish philosopher Philo of Alexandria was chosen to head a delegation to Emperor Gaius Caligula to protest the persecution of Jews that had begun in Alexandria under the prefect Flaccus in AD 38. In his account of the argument he presented to Gaius (*Legat.*), Philo pointed out that the Jews had sent "colonies" to numerous places in the Roman world, including Corinth (*Legat.* 281). Exactly what Philo meant by "colonies" is unclear, but it does suggest his understanding that Jewish communities in the diaspora exercised some degree of self-governance as allowed by Roman law.[37] According to Josephus (*Ant.* 16.162-65), Augustus had decreed certain Jewish rights and exemptions in AD 2/3. These rights had been threatened during the reign of Caligula, especially in Alexandria, but Claudius had restored those rights in a pair of decrees issued early in his rule, according to Josephus (*Ant.* 19.5.3).[38] Claudius experienced his own difficulties with Jews in Rome, closing the synagogues there in AD 41 (temporarily) and expelling the Jews from Rome, perhaps, in AD 49. According to Acts 18:2, Claudius's expulsion had brought Prisca and Aquila to Corinth where they became coworkers with Paul. Other Jews may also have migrated from Rome to Corinth on that occasion. Another infusion of Jews came to Corinth after Paul's time when Vespasian apparently sent 6,000 captured Jewish rebels to work on Nero's Isthmian canal project in AD 67.[39]

Menorot

Archaeological Museum of Ancient Corinth (Credit: Scott Nash)

Three Jewish menorot, along with lulav (palm branch) and etrog (citron) appear on a reused block of limestone from Roman Corinth. The lulav and etron were used in celebrating the Succoth (the festival of tabernacles). Probably dating from the 5th century AD, the architectural remains indicate that a Jewish community continued to exist in Corinth even after the establishment of Christianity as the empire's official religion.

The association founded by Paul was, in many respects, another Jewish community in Corinth. "Christianity" had not yet become identifiable as a religion.[40] Paul was, and remained, a Jew, though the particular form of Judaism he espoused had a central role for the Messiah Jesus. While it appears that most members of the community Paul had organized, at least by the time of 1 Corinthians, were Gentile, his use of the Jewish scriptures and his attention to matters of concern to Jewish sensibilities reinforced the perception that his movement was connected to the religious traditions of the people of Israel. To outsiders in Corinth, his group may have looked similar to other Jewish synagogue communities.

The Church in Corinth

According to the book of Acts (18:1-8) and Paul's own words in 1 Corinthians (3:6, 10; 4:15), Paul established the church in Corinth. [Paul's Arrival in Corinth] In this effort he was aided by a "Christian" Jewish wife-husband pair, Prisca and Aquila, as well as his frequent traveling companions Timothy and Silas (Acts 18:5). Later, other associates of Paul also engaged in ministry of various sorts to the congregation, including Apollos, Titus, and unnamed "brothers." While in Corinth, Paul supported himself by working with his own hands, a labor Acts identifies as "tent-making" (or, more precisely, "leather-working"). His initial stay in Corinth lasted about eighteen months, according to Acts. Acts describes no other visits by Paul to Corinth (Acts 20:3 mentions only a visit to

Paul's Arrival in Corinth

The book of Acts gives this account of Paul's initial visit to Corinth.

After this Paul left Athens and went to Corinth. There he found a Jew named Aquila, a native of Pontus, who had recently come from Italy with his wife Priscilla [Prisca], because Claudius had ordered all Jews to leave Rome. Paul went to see them, and, because he was of the same trade, he stayed with them, and they worked together—by trade they were tentmakers. Every sabbath he would argue in the synagogue and would try to convince Jews and Greeks. (Acts 18:1-4, NRSV)

Greece), but 2 Corinthians 13:1 indicates that Paul had made a second visit and was anticipating a third. The third and final visit probably occurred around AD 55/56 and was the occasion for the writing of Paul's letter to the Romans.

Paul's Arrival. Assuming that the account of Paul's initial visit to Corinth in Acts 18 is essentially sound historically, we have from that account two important bits of chronological information.[41] Acts 18:2 places Prisca and Aquila in Corinth as a result of the expulsion of Jews from Italy by Claudius. The event was probably reported by the Roman biographer Suetonius (Claudius 25) around AD 120 and the Christian minister Orosius (*History* 7:6.15-16) in AD 418, and perhaps by the Roman historian Dio Cassius (*History* 60:6.6) around AD 230. [Edict of Claudius] Suetonius wrote that Claudius expelled the Jews from Rome because of disturbances instigated by "Chrestus," which probably means that arguments over the messiah (Gk. *christos*), perhaps caused by "Christian" missionaries, had turned violent. Suetonius gave no date for the event. Orosius, however, citing an otherwise unknown report by Josephus, dated the event to the ninth year of Claudius's rule (AD 49). The lack of corroborating evidence from Josephus renders Orosius's dating suspect. The event reported by Dio Cassius occurred during Claudius's first year (AD 41). Dio Cassius asserted that Claudius did not expel the Jews but rather prevented synagogues from meeting until peace resumed. His report, however, may actually refer to a different episode, although his otherwise complete accounting of the events of AD 49 does not include anything resembling what Suetonius described. The Acts account indicates that Prisca and Aquila had *recently* come from Italy as a result of Claudius's action. This would mesh better with the later date of AD 49, but the exact year of Claudius's expul-

Edict of Claudius

The dating and analysis of the Claudius's eviction of Jews from Rome largely depends on one's interpretation of information given by three ancient writers.

"He expelled from Rome the Jews constantly making disturbances at the instigation of Chrestus." (Suetonius, *Claudius* 25)

"As for the Jews, who had again increased so greatly by reason of their multitude that it would have been hard without raising a tumult to expel them from the city, he did not drive them out, but ordered them, while continuing their traditional mode of life, not to hold meetings." (Dio Cassius, *History* 60:6.6)

"Josephus refers to the expulsion of Jews by Claudius in his ninth year. But Suetonius touches me more in saying, 'Claudius expelled from Rome the Jews constantly making disturbances at the instigation of Chrestus.' It cannot be determined whether he ordered only the Jews agitating against Christ to be restrained and suppressed, or whether he also wanted to expel Christians as being people of related faith." (Orosius, *History* 7:6.15-16)

Jerome Murphy-O'Connor, *St. Paul's Corinth: Texts and Archaeology* (Collegeville MN: Liturgical Press, 1983) 138–39.

sion, whatever its nature and scope, cannot be confirmed.

More substantial confirmation that Paul arrived in Corinth shortly after AD 49 comes from an inscription found at Delphi, north of Corinth. The inscription may be interpreted to date Gallio's term as proconsul either to AD 50/51 or 51/52. Since Gallio did not complete his year of service, the episode in Acts describing the unsuccessful Jewish attempts to get Gallio to hear their complaints against Paul could have occurred no later than AD 51. Acts indicates that Paul ended his eighteen-month stay in Corinth after this event, so Paul would have arrived in Corinth sometime in late AD 49 or early 50.

The Gallio Inscription

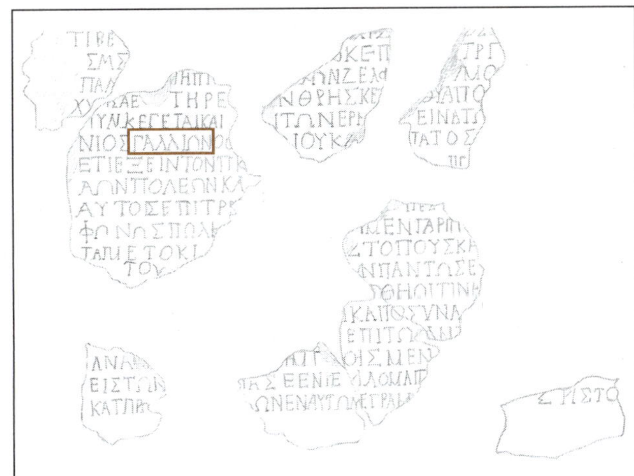

(Credit: Emma Hughes)

An inscription found at the important religious center of Delphi records a letter sent by the emperor Claudius ordering the repopulation of the city. The inscription indicates that Claudius had been informed of the city's destitution of citizens by the proconsul L. Junius Gallio. Because Claudius's letter included information about the year of its publication (12th year of Claudius's tribunician power, acclamation as emperor for the 26th time), one can estimate that Gallio's term of office was likely AD 51–52. (Gallio's name is indicated above.)

Jerome Murphy-O'Connor, *St. Paul's Corinth: Texts and Archaeology* (Collegeville MN: Liturgical Press, 1983) 149–60.

The Corinthian Congregation. More information is available to us about the membership of the Corinthian congregation than of any other church founded by Paul. [Members of the Corinthian Church] Acts describes the early conversion of Crispus the *archisynagōgos* (usually translated "ruler of the synagogue"), and Paul acknowledged having baptized a person by that name (1 Cor 1:14). He also acknowledged having baptized a Corinthian named Gaius and a Corinthian household headed by Stephanas, though Acts is silent about them all. In 1 Corinthians 16:15, Paul possibly indicated that his first converts in Corinth were Stephanas and his household, and in Romans 16:23 (probably to be accepted as part of the letter Paul wrote to Rome while in Corinth), Paul extended greetings from a certain Gaius, whom he described as host for Paul and the whole church. Also named there, evidently as members of the Corinthian congregation, in the extension of greetings to the Romans were Erastus and Quartus. Perhaps also members of the Corinthian congregation were Lucius, Jason, and Sosipater (Rom 16:21), whom Paul identified as "kinsmen," meaning fellow Jews. The only other convert named by Acts (18:7) is Titius Justus,

Members of the Corinthian Church

From 1 Corinthians, 2 Corinthians, Romans, and Acts, we have several names of persons who were either members of the Corinthian congregation or traveling ministers associated with the church.

Corinthian Members	Ministers Associated with Corinth
Achaicus (1 Cor)	Apollos (1 Cor; Acts)
Chloe (1 Cor)	Aquila (1 Cor; Rom; Acts)
Crispus (1 Cor; Acts)	Cephas? (1 Cor)
Erastus (Rom)	Paul (1 Cor; 2 Cor; Rom; Acts)
Fortunatus (1 Cor)	Prisca/Priscilla (1 Cor; Rom; Acts)
Gaius (1 Cor; Rom)	Silas/Silvanus (2 Cor; Acts)
Jason (Rom)	Timothy (1 Cor; 2 Cor; Rom; Acts)
Lucius (Rom)	Titus (2 Cor)
Phoebe—Cenchreae (Rom)	
Quartus (Rom)	
Sosipater (Rom)	
Sosthenes (1 Cor; Acts?)	
Stephanas (1 Cor)	
Tertius (Rom)	
Titius Justus (Acts)	

apparently a Gentile who had participated in the life of the Corinthian synagogue. In his letters, Paul named several other members of the Corinthian congregation: Sosthenes (1 Cor 1:1), Chloe and her "people" (1 Cor 1:11), and Fortunatus and Achaicus (1 Cor 16:17). Tertius, the scribe who wrote himself into the greetings in Romans 16:22, may also have been a Corinthian. To this list of known Corinthians we can add Phoebe (Rom 16:1), a deacon from nearby Cenchreae. In addition, we can identify associates of Paul who, like Prisca and Aquila, spent time in Corinth: Timothy, Silas, Titus, and Apollos.

The question of the relative status of the members of Paul's congregation has received considerable discussion.[42] The once prevailing view that the early Christian movement drew primarily or exclusively from the lowest ranks of Greco-Roman society has been seriously challenged, especially by Edwin Judge, Wayne Meeks, and Gerd Theissen.[43] Their studies, and that of other scholars influenced by them, suggest that the early Christian congregations were made up of a cross-section of persons from various status levels and that some of the leaders were from fairly high up the social scale. In 1 Corinthians 1:26, Paul reminded the Corinthians

Corinthian Ministers

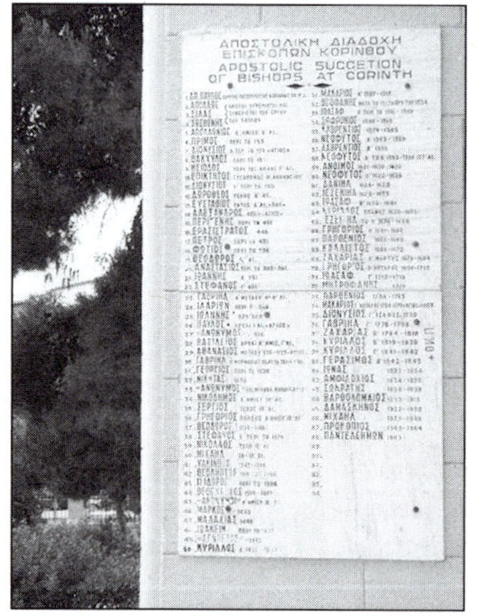

(Credit: Scott Nash)

The church of Sts. Peter and Paul in the modern city of Corinth displays a marble plaque inscribed with the names of those persons the church considers to constitute an "Apostolic Succession of Bishops of Corinth" from the time of Paul until 1965.

that "not many of you were wise according to worldly standards, not many were powerful, not many were of noble birth." While this text clearly places the majority of the Corinthian church in the lower rungs of the status ladder, it suggests that *some* were higher on the ladder. Taking this text as a cue, Theissen and others have accumulated data and arguments to the effect that persons of higher status were part of the cross-section of society reflected in the membership and that the differences in status lay behind many, if not all, of the problems Paul addressed in 1 Corinthians. The idea that the membership of the Corinthian church stretched across the spectrum of social rank (except for the highest ranks) has become something of a "new consensus."[44]

Some problems do exist with this view, however. For one thing, as Steven Friesen has pointed out, social status is difficult to determine since it could be based on a number of factors.[45] A successful freedperson could have considerable wealth, especially in Corinth, and still not be accepted into the elite ranks. In Corinth, freedpersons could be elected to certain high positions, but other positions remained exclusive to those of more aristocratic lineage. Justin Meggitt has argued that only one percent of the population of the Roman Empire could be considered to have been wealthy while the remainder struggled for survival.[46] He rejects the interpretation of supposedly high status indicators by Theissen and Meeks and contends that all the early Christians, like most other people in antiquity, were poor.

While Meggitt distinguishes only between the small minority of the rich and the vast majority of the poor, other scholars have tried to identify a more detailed range of poverty and wealth. Restricting his focus to the matter of economic means, Friesen has constructed a "Poverty Scale" with seven levels. [Friesen's "Poverty Scale"] The top three levels (the rich) comprised only one percent of the population and consisted of imperial, provincial, and municipal elites, none of whom were part of the Christian movement at Paul's time.[47] The lower four levels were those

Friesen's "Poverty Scale"

PS 1 *Imperial Elite*
Imperial dynasty, Roman senatorial families, some retainers, local royalty, some freedpersons

PS 2 *Regional or Provincial Elites*
equestrian families, provincial officials, some retainers, some decurial families, some freedpersons, some retired military officers

PS 3 *Municipal Elites*
most decurial families, wealthy men and women who do not hold office, some freedpersons, some retainers, some veterans, some merchants

PS 4 *Moderate Surplus Resources*
some merchants, some traders, some freedpersons, some artisans (especially those who employ others), military veterans

PS 5 *Near Subsistence Level*
many merchants and traders, regular wage earners, artisans, large shop owners, freedpersons, some farm families

PS 6 *At Subsistence Level*
small farm families, laborers (skilled and unskilled), artisans (especially those employed by others), wage earners, most merchants and traders, small shop-tavern owners

PS 7 *Below Subsistence Level*
some farm families, unattached widows, orphans, beggars, disabled persons, unskilled day laborers, prisoners

Steven J. Friesen, "Prospects for a Demography of the Pauline Mission: Corinth among the Churches," in *Urban Religion in Roman Corinth*, 351–70.

of moderate surplus resources and those who lived near, at, or below the subsistence level. He would place Chloe and Gaius in the "moderate surplus" level and perhaps Erastus, Phoebe, Prisca, and Aquila, although the latter four might belong to the "near subsistence" group.[48] The rest, including Paul, would belong in the "at or below subsistence" groups. A similar assessment is made by Ekkehard Stegemann and Wolfgang Stegemann, who would label the great majority of the early Christians as "relatively rich or relatively poor."[49] On the basis of factors other than economics, however, they would place a few church members in the levels immediately below the elite, that is, among those who were rich but did not belong to any of the social *ordines* (official social rankings) of Roman society.

Wealth may have been "the most important component of social status," as Friesen contends.[50] Still, other factors played a role, though it is difficult to know how those other factors operated in a given context. When Paul noted that not many of the Corinthians had been wise, powerful, or of noble birth (1 Cor 1:26)—perhaps in contrast to the few who were—he did not mention wealth. His sarcastic retort in 1 Corinthians 4:8 that "already you have become rich" probably did not concern wealth either. Questions regarding relative status do seem to have plagued the Corinthian church, but identifying which factors fueled the conflict remains elusive.

Even knowing the status indicators at work in a place such as Corinth (where wealth was clearly a principal factor), applying those indicators to specific persons in the church is difficult. For example, when Paul refers to the church "in the house of Prisca and Aquila" (Rom 16:5; 1 Cor 16:19), one may infer that they owned homes in Ephesus and then in Rome, and therefore probably in Corinth while there. Presumably, Paul stayed in their home in Corinth (Acts 18:3). We cannot know for certain, however, that they actually did *own* their homes or that their homes were large, owned or not.[51] Paul identified Gaius as his host and the host for the "whole church" in Corinth (Rom 16:23). This would suggest he owned a home large enough to accommodate the entire Corinthian congregation, if in fact that is what Paul meant by calling him "host." The term *xenos* usually meant "stranger" or "guest." It could refer to a "host" but usually only in combination with some other word. More frequently it meant "friend," as in a friend who showed hospitality.[52] Thus, Paul acknowledged that Gaius had been hospitable in some sense to him and to the whole church, maybe by providing meeting space in his large home, if he owned such, but maybe his hospitality was of another sort. Even the effect of home ownership on status cannot be determined, however, at least not in regard to the society at large.

Erastus is the person to whom most scholars point as one of those "few" in the Corinthian church who may have been among the "powerful." Paul identified him in Romans 16:23 as the *oikonomos tēs poleōs*, which is often translated as "city treasurer." Assuming that this title refers to a civic position and not a church office or some menial city role (which it may have), many scholars have connected this Erastus to the Erastus named in a famous inscription found at Corinth.[53] The inscription indicates that an Erastus paved a courtyard near the theater at his own expense in return for having been elected to the high office of *aedile*. Thus, Paul's friend Erastus (if the same person) was, presumably, a wealthy and powerful citizen of Corinth. The exact meaning of *oikonomos tēs poleōs*, however, is still uncertain. Furthermore, the connection between the Greek *oikonomos* and the Latin *aedile* is tenuous at best. In addition, questions have arisen about the dating, reading, and interpretation of the inscription itself.[54] The ambiguity surrounding the status of Paul's Erastus and his possible relation to the inscription suggests that Erastus cannot bear the weight of the arguments placed on him in the debate about high-status church members.[55]

Not being able to identify the economic level or status of certain persons, however, does not mean that issues of wealth and status were not important in the Corinthian church. The abuse of the Lord's Supper that Paul condemned in 1 Corinthians 11:17-22 most likely involved members of means acting disrespectfully toward those who had nothing to eat (*tous mē echontas*). Other problems addressed in the letter are also probably rooted in conflicts involving status, as we shall point out in the commentary below. The vast majority of people in Roman Corinth may have been relatively poor,

Erastus Inscription

(Credit: Scott Nash)

In 1929, American excavators in Corinth uncovered in a paved courtyard near the theater a limestone slab sitting *in situ* and engraved with a Latin inscription of seven-inch high letters. Later, two other pieces of the inscription were found, though the remainder has not yet been located. Inlaid with bronze letters, the inscription prominently identified the person responsible for paving the large (62 square feet) courtyard. It reads:

[____________] ERASTVS PRO AEDILIT[at]E
S[ua] P[ecunia] STRAVIT

The missing segment [__________] probably contained the rest of the name (*praenomen*), but what remains is clear: "Erastus in return for the aedileship at his own expense paved (the courtyard)." What is not clear is the connection, if any, the inscription has to the Erastus mentioned by Paul in Rom 16:23. While many NT scholars have concluded that the Erastus of the inscription was the same person as the Corinthian church member named by Paul, that conclusion is highly questionable.

John Harvey Kent, *The Inscriptions 1926–1950* (*Corinth* VIII.3; Princeton: American School of Classical Studies at Athens, 1966) 99.

as Meggitt and Friesen would argue, at least in comparison to the elite minority who do not seem to have been a part of the church there. Beneath the top level of the elite, however, a broad range of economic and status levels existed. Between the very rich and the very poor stood a spectrum of persons of various means and with different standings in society.[56] Especially in a place such as Corinth, where financial possibilities enabled a higher degree of upward social mobility than was typically the case, consciousness regarding status and competition for improving status were intense.

While we may not be able to locate the members of the Corinthian church on a scale of status in relation to Corinthian society, we may accept the probability that they were conscious of such matters and that the same kind of competitions regarding status that existed in the city also existed in the church. Whatever the actual status of the church members in the *outer* society may have been, their participation in the life of the church afforded them a new arena for sorting out issues of status. The competitiveness that held in the larger society probably influenced the church as members engaged in the same kind of jockeying for position that occurred outside. In fact, those excluded from upward movement in the larger society may have found attractive the opportunities for status enhancement offered by membership in this different kind of association.[57] The problem was, as Paul saw it, this association was not different enough from the society at large. Playing the same game of status competition in the church, a game that most of the church members had probably only viewed as envious spectators outside, was in conflict with the nature of the church as Paul envisioned it.

Letters to Corinth

Paul apparently wrote at least four letters to the Corinthian church. Some scholars argue for more.

First Letter	(referred to in 1 Cor 5:9)
Second Letter	(1 Cor)
Third Letter	(referred to in 2 Cor 2:3-4; 7:8-12; possibly contained in 2 Cor 10–13)
Fourth Letter	(probably at least 2 Cor 1–7, though some see 2 Cor 2:14–7:4 as a different letter; may have included 2 Cor 8 and 9, though many scholars see these as two separate letters)

Paul's Relationship with the Church. The tension between Paul's vision for the Corinthian church and the interior life of that church, influenced as it inevitably was by its context, led to a turbulent relationship between apostle and congregation. Charting the course of that relationship depends on how one reads the maps, that is, the letters of Paul to the Corinthians. Most scholars accept that Paul wrote at least four letters to the church in Corinth. [Letters to Corinth] The first, referred to in 1 Corinthians 5:9, is lost. In it Paul had apparently called for some degree of separation between members and "immoral" people. The second, 1 Corinthians, addressed several problems Paul had learned about either through oral reports (some from Chloe's people; 1 Cor 1:11) or from a letter written to Paul by the church apparently asking for his guidance regarding certain matters (1 Cor 7:1). A third letter is indicated by references in 2 Corinthians (2:3-4; 7:8-12). Many scholars think part of this letter actually appears in canonical 2 Corinthians (10:1–13:10).[58] A fourth letter would be the bulk of 2 Corinthians, or at least most of chapters 1–7. Many scholars see 2 Corinthians 8 and 9 as separate letters, too. Some scholars further divide 2 Corinthians, seeing 2:14–7:4 (minus 6:14–7:1) as coming from one letter and 1:1–2:13; 7:5-16; and 13:11-13 as coming from another.[59] How one arranges these different letters in sequence affects how one reads the history of Paul's relationship with the church. To the evidence of these letters, however one divides them and arranges their sequence, one can add the references to visits by Paul and by his associates (such as Timothy and Titus) found in the letters. The picture is one of numerous contacts over a range of years (AD 49–55) and of an "on-again, off-again" relationship.

Apparently, not long after leaving Corinth after his first visit, Paul learned of a problem involving association by some church members with "immoral people." The first, lost letter was Paul's long-distance (and apparently unsuccessful) attempt to correct the problem. Some time later, the church seems to have solicited Paul's guidance regarding other problems by sending him the letter he referred to in 1 Corinthians 7:1. In responding to those matters, Paul also addressed other problems the church had not mentioned in their letter. Paul apparently learned of these issues from Chloe's people and perhaps from other visitors from Corinth (Stephanas, Fortunatus, and Achaicus—mentioned in 1 Cor 16:17—are possible candidates). Paul then seems to have learned that his letter (1 Cor) had not resolved the problems and had, perhaps, created some new ones, especially suspicion of his motives and increased challenges to his status as an apostle. Thus, he sent the "tearful" letter to which he referred in 2 Corinthians 2:3-4 and 7:8-12. Part of that letter may now reside in 2 Corinthians 10–13. From his emissary to Corinth, Titus, Paul learned that his "tearful" letter had prompted reconciliation between the Corinthians and himself. Thus, he penned at least part of 2 Corinthians 1–9 to consolidate this reconciliation. If 2 Corinthians 8–9 were originally a separate letter, then that letter would most likely have been Paul's follow-up to 2 Corinthians 1–7 and would have guided arrangements for the collection he planned to receive on his next visit. If 2 Corinthians 8 and 9 were actually two separate letters, then 2 Corinthians 8 may have been sent prior to 2 Corinthians 1–7 and 2 Corinthians 9 after. The most likely scenario from this reconstruction is that after much painful conflict Paul and the church became reconciled to each other. His last visit to Corinth was probably a peaceful one—peaceful enough for him to compose his letter to the Romans and to make final arrangements for the collection of money received from the Macedonian and Achaian churches for the poor saints in Jerusalem (Rom 15:26).

The Occasion for 1 Corinthians. The situation in Corinth that prompted Paul to write what he did in 1 Corinthians calls for further comment. Obviously, Paul had received a letter from the church in Corinth soliciting his views regarding certain matters. In one sense, then, their letter was the reason Paul wrote 1 Corinthians. Before addressing those concerns, however, Paul took on other issues that he tended to deal with more intensely and with a greater sense of urgency than he tended to do with the matters about which they had written.[60] Those problems, which Paul learned about from oral reports, probably allow a clearer view of the more serious threats to the life of the congregation, at least as Paul read the situation.

From Chloe's people, Paul learned that divisions existed in the church. Paul's reaction to the reported divisions in 1 Corinthians 1–4 has led some scholars to conclude that distinct factions had lined up behind authoritative figures (Paul, Apollo, Cephas, and Christ; 1 Cor 1:12). Earlier commentators took these supposed factions to be representatives of competing theologies.[61] The Cephas party presumably espoused a more Jewish-oriented, torah-abiding position, while the Paul party represented that apostle's more Gentile-oriented, torah-free position. The Apollos party supposedly valued speculative wisdom. The Christ party has received various descriptions including Judaizing Christians, ultraspiritual pneumatics, and Gnostics.[62] Increasingly, however, scholars have agreed with the assessment of Laurence Welborn: "It is a power struggle, not a theological controversy, that motivates the writing of 1 Corinthians 1–4."[63] One may also concur with Donald Ker, however, that "it is hard to imagine that theology was not somehow involved within the conflict."[64]

Identifying the theological positions of Paul's target groups in 1 Corinthians, though, proves difficult. Any reconstruction of those positions must begin with Paul's apparent counter-arguments, which is in itself problematic. Counter-arguments tend to be one-sided and are designed to highlight perceived flaws or weaknesses in an opposing view. Furthermore, Paul did not actually provide much direct information about competing views in the church. Some window into the perspectives Paul refuted may be found in the "slogans" that Paul appeared to quote, presumably from the letter written to him by the Corinthians, but even here we have only Paul's selective presentation of the positions of his opponents. Without confirmed knowledge of their views, we are limited in being able to ascribe any particular theological perspectives to the Corinthians, though scholars have often tried.[65] [The Corinthians' "Theology"]

What does appear to be the case in 1 Corinthians 1–4 (and in some other parts of the letter) is that, whatever theological ideas may have existed among the Corinthians, some members of the *ekklēsia* considered themselves superior in some way to other members.[66] A type of elitism existed that threatened the harmony of the body. Some interpreters understand this elitism to have been primarily "spiritual" in nature and believe that it lay behind not only the divisions in 1 Corinthians 1–4 but also the problems addressed in 1 Corinthians 5 (a stunning case of immorality), 1 Corinthians 12–14 (exalting in certain spiritual gifts), and 1 Corinthians 15 (discounting the bodily resurrection). Increasingly, however, more interpreters have understood this elitism to be "social" in nature and see it lying behind the divisions of 1 Corinthians 1–4 and the problems Paul addressed in several other sections (ch. 6, lawsuits and social permissiveness; chs. 8–10, eating food offered to idols; ch. 11, attire for men and women and divisions at the Lord's Supper; and ch. 16, secular patronage). Probably, the elitism was both social and spiritual (or theological) in nature.[67]

The Corinthians' "Theology"

Scholars have proposed various views regarding the nature of the Corinthians' theology and the sources of the problematic ideas challenged by Paul. These proposals and some representative scholars include:

Christian Judaizers (Baur, Goulder)
Pneumatic Libertines (Lütgert)
Hellenistic Mystery Religions (Heitmüller, Bossett)
Gnosticism (Bultmann, Schmithals)
Hellenistic Wisdom (Horsley, Witherington)
Over-realized Eschatology (Käsemann, Thiselton)
Stoicism (Weiss, Paige)
Cynicism (Downing)
Epicureanism (Tomlin)

David G. Horrell and Edward Adams, "The Scholarly Quest for Paul's Church at Corinth," in *Christianity at Corinth: The Quest for the Pauline Church* (Louisville: Westminster John Knox Press, 2004) 1–43.

One question to be addressed in understanding the occasion for 1 Corinthians is exactly how this elitism related to the divisions. Elitism in itself is divisive, but how did this play out in Corinth? Did the preaching of certain ministers such as Apollos and Cephas in Corinth become an occasion for divisions to occur, and if so, why? Certainly Apollos preached in Corinth, but the evidence that Cephas ever did is totally lacking, despite continuing local tradition to that effect. Obviously, Christ did not preach in Corinth. Since Paul referred primarily to Apollos in his discussion of divisions in 1 Corinthians 1–4, some scholars hold that only two divisions

Church of Sts. Peter and Paul

(Credit: Scott Nash)

The dedication of the church in the modern city of Corinth to the apostles Peter and Paul is based on the doubtful tradition that Peter (Cephas) also ministered in ancient Corinth.

existed, each with loyalties pledged to the two preachers in question. Others hold that no actual factions devoted to these particular leaders existed, but rather "divisiveness" itself over a variety of issues had come to characterize the Corinthian congregation.[68]

The approach Paul took in dealing with divisions in the first major section of the letter suggests that some in the church had begun to question Paul's authority. Nils Dahl proposed that once Paul's authority was challenged, some members of the church advocated looking to Cephas, who was known as the foremost among the apostles, as their authority figure.[69] This would not require that Cephas had actually ever visited Corinth. Others in the church, impressed by Apollos's recent ministry among them, argued that he would be an appropriate authority. Still others, impressed by their own new experience of spiritual gifts, considered themselves sufficiently endowed to decide matters under the direct guidance of Christ. Other interpreters, however, have argued that the actual division focused only on Paul and Apollos and that Paul created the appearance of more factions.[70] Others argue that Paul intentionally cast the problem of division as he did, metaphorically applying it to himself and Apollos, in order to discredit all divisiveness since no such division actually existed between those two ministers.[71]

Paul's argument against divisions will be examined more fully in the commentary on chapters 1–4. Here the issue is the cause of the problem addressed by Paul. From the way Paul addressed the matter, it appears that a significant part of the problem lay in some challenge to Paul's leadership. By the time Paul wrote 2 Corinthians 10–13, someone from outside of Corinth had apparently come to the city and directly questioned Paul's credentials as an apostle (2 Cor 10:12-18; 11:5). That later questioning possibly exacerbated a situation that was already brewing when Paul wrote 1 Corinthians.[72] Numerous suggestions have been offered as to why Paul's position with the church was challenged in the first place. One suggestion has been that Paul actually never had exercised the kind of authority 1 Corinthians was designed to establish.[73] Most scholars, however, accept that Paul's role as founder of the church had granted him an authoritative role that came to be questioned only after he left Corinth. What happened that created a situation in which some members of the church both challenged Paul's authority and adopted an elitist position in regard to other members, leading to an internal culture of divisiveness?

In short, the internal culture of the church had come to reflect the external culture of Roman Corinth. The spirit of competitiveness that reigned in Corinthian society affected those who became a part of the association founded by Paul. The social hierarchy that prevailed in daily life began to assert itself in the relationships within the church. Even if few or none of the members of the church would have been considered of high or moderately high status outside the church, the perceived differences that did exist between members became occasions for conflict as an internal pecking order was established. As will be discussed in the commentary on various parts of 1 Corinthians, this environment of social competition gave rise to many of the problems Paul addressed in the letter.

How this relates to the challenge to Paul's leadership and the rise of "divisions" is informed by a consideration of how visiting preachers such as Paul would have been seen in this environment. "Christian" preachers and teachers were not the only public speakers who gathered groups of followers. Cynic philosophers were one such group of traveling speakers, and several scholars have identified numerous similarities between their activity and Paul's.[74] Paul's self-defense and his argument against divisions, however, suggest that he was deliberately differentiating himself from another group of public speaker-teachers—the sophists. The flowering of the "Second Sophistic" movement came in the second century AD, but Bruce Winter has shown that sophists were already popular in the first century, especially in Corinth, and that Paul cast his own speaking, his ministry, and his message in an antisophistic light.[75] [The Sophist Herodes Atticus] In contrast to modern denunciation of empty speech as *mere sophistry*, successful sophists were esteemed for their intellectual prowess as well as their eloquence. The sophists were extremely popular, drawing large crowds and attracting dedicated disciples (*mathētai*). Just as sophists competed with each other for adulation and disciples, their disciples forcefully expressed their loyalty by espousing their teacher's virtues and criticizing other sophists. Attachment to an eminent sophist could enhance one's own status, so the choice of teacher had social significance.

Paul's defense of his own ministry and his criticism of divisiveness suggest that church members had come to view him as they did sophists. They began to evaluate his speaking using the same criteria applied to sophists. Their expressed preference for other teachers mimicked the bickering and shuffling for position that were part of the competition between sophists and their disciples. The preaching of the reputedly eloquent Apollos (Acts 18:24), which occurred between Paul's departure and the writing of 1 Corinthians, may have served as a catalyst for such competitive comparisons, as Winter has suggested, but evaluation of Paul's speaking performances using sophistic standards was probably inevitable anyway.[76] The letter from the church at Corinth, or at least from some of its members, may have intensified the debate since some might have questioned the solicitation of Paul's views on certain topics about which the church was divided. We cannot know whether the church, or parts of it, also solicited the opinions of other authorities. The fact that Paul seems to have learned of the divisions not from the letter but from Chloe's people may suggest that those who penned the letter did not see competition regarding leaders as a problem. After all, it was the normal way for relating to such leaders in Corinth. Paul, however, did see a problem, and he chose to address the matter at the beginning of his letter. This was necessary both to deal with the issue of divisions and to establish (or reestablish) his authority to speak to the matters about which they had written him.

The occasion for 1 Corinthians, then, was one in which the competitive culture outside the church had

The Sophist Herodes Atticus

Herodes Atticus (c. AD 101–177) was a wealthy Athenian sophist noted for his public benefaction and controversial political career. His friends and students included Marcus Aurelius. His benefactions to Corinth included the refurbishing of the odeion and the Peirene fountain and the gift of a statue group to the temple of Poseidon at Isthmia.

National Archaeological Museum, Athens, Greece. (Credit: Scott Nash)

Constantine P. Cavafy (1863–1933), considered by many to be the greatest modern Greek poet, appeared not to have held the successful sophist Herodes Atticus in high esteem, if his poem below is any indication. It does, however, capture the celebrity of many sophists.

Herod of Attica

Ah, what a glory this is, of Herod of Attica!

Alexander of Seleucia, one of our fine sophists,
arriving at Athens to speak,
finds the city deserted, because Herod
was in the country. And all the young men
had followed him there to hear him.
So Alexander the Sophist
writes Herod a letter,
and begs him to send the Greeks away.
But the shrewd Herod answers at once:
"I too am coming, along with the Greeks." –

How many lads in Alexandria now,
in Antioch, or in Beirut
(tomorrow's orators that hellenism trains),
when they gather at their choice tables
where sometimes the talk is of splendid sophistries,
and sometimes of their exquisite love affairs,
suddenly distracted, they become silent.
They leave the glasses near them untouched,
while they contemplate Herod's good fortune –
what other sophist ever achieved as much? –
Just as he wishes, just as he does
the Greeks (the Greeks!) follow him,
not to judge or to discuss,
not even to choose any more, only to follow.

Trans. Rae Dalven in *The Complete Poems of Cavafy* (New York: Harcourt Brace & Company, 1989) 38.

begun to influence internal affairs. Some within the church approached other members with the same attitude of elitism (whatever it may have been based upon) that prevailed in Corinthian society. That same attitude was extended to the question of leadership, and thus some deemed Paul deficient according to the normal pattern for evaluating sophists. Other problems existed also, some related to the culture of competition and some not. To address the several matters plaguing the church, Paul had first to tackle the competitive perspective that lay behind the challenges to his authority. In doing that, Paul appealed to his "word of the cross" theology, which he believed not only justified his style of ministry but also defined who the Corinthians should be. At the time he wrote the letter, they were behaving essentially as they would have before becoming a part of the *ekklēsia*. Paul wanted to change that, and 1 Corinthians was his first major attempt to do so.

The Corinthian Church after Paul. The church Paul founded in Corinth endured the conflicts reflected in 1 and 2 Corinthians. We learn of other conflicts in the church toward the end of the first century AD from the letter written to Corinth by Clement of Rome (*1 Clement*).[77] In the second century, bishops from Corinth played influential roles in the crystallization of Christian theology and organization.[78] Hagiographic literature includes several accounts of martyrs from Corinth in the third century.[79] The fourth and fifth centuries witnessed the construction of numerous Christian buildings in Corinth, including the ornate basilica on the shore of the Gulf of Corinth near the harbor at Lechaion, the largest Christian basilica yet found in Greece.[80] By then, Christianity had "triumphed" over paganism in the Roman Empire, but the succeeding centuries saw a decline in the financial and political health of Greece. Corinth experienced decline as well, intensified by several destructive earthquakes, yet the church in Corinth continued to exist, as is evidenced by remains of numerous medieval churches and monasteries.[81] In 1858, a devastating earthquake led to the abandonment of the city and the founding of a new Corinth a few kilometers away. Excavation in the old city began in the late nineteenth century, and a village grew up around the site. In the early years of the twenty-first century, the residents of this growing village built a new church dedicated to the Apostle Paul. Paul would have been pleased—perhaps!

Lechaion Basilica

(Credit: Scott Nash)

Church of St. Paul

(Credit: Scott Nash)

The Correspondence Called 1 Corinthians

The above examination of Roman Corinth and the situation that prompted Paul to write 1 Corinthians is intended to aid our understanding of the particular moment in the life of the Corinthian church to which 1 Corinthians was addressed. In a sense, we have been looking *through* the window of 1 Corinthians. Now we must look more closely *at* the window itself.

1 Corinthians as Letter

Though it may seem obvious that 1 Corinthians is a letter, the significance of this bears emphasis. [Ancient Letters] In antiquity, as today, a letter served as a substitute for a personal visit. If Paul had been able, or thought it appropriate, to travel to Corinth to address the church's problems, 1 Corinthians would not have been written. The letter, then, served as a substitute for Paul's presence in Corinth. Carried to Corinth by trusted associates (possibly Stephanas, Fortunatus, and Achaicus; 1 Cor 16:17), the letter would presumably have been read aloud during a meeting of the Corinthian congregation. Knowing that the letter would be *heard* and not *read* by most of the recipients, Paul undoubtedly composed the letter with an oral audience in mind.

In ancient discussions of letters, letters were sometimes described as "one of the two sides of a dialogue."[82] More recently, Calvin Roetzel has referred to Paul's letters as "conversations in context."[83] This particular letter stands within the context of an ongoing conversation between Paul and the Corinthians. Furthermore, the dialogical character of 1 Corinthians is evident in Paul's responses to questions asked of him by the Corinthians in their previous letter to him and by his apparent inclusion of certain slogans from that letter. Still, a dialogue involves give and take as one speaks and then listens, and 1 Corinthians contains more give than take. The "conversation" is largely one-sided. Paul intended that his voice, as heard through the reader, would be

Ancient Letters

Extensive studies of ancient letters relevant for understanding the epistolary nature of 1 Corinthians include the following:

William G. Doty, *Letters in Primitive Christianity* (GBS; Philadelphia: Fortress, 1973).

Hans-Josef Klauck, *Ancient Letters and the New Testament: A Guide to Context and Exegesis* (Waco TX: Baylor University Press, 2006).

Jerome Murphy-O'Connor, *Paul the Letter Writer: His World, His Options, His Skills* (GNS 41; Collegeville MN: The Liturgical Press, 1995).

Stanley K. Stowers, *Letter Writing in Greco-Roman Antiquity* (LEC; Philadelphia: Westminster, 1986).

John L. White, *Light from Ancient Letters* (FF; Philadelphia: Fortress, 1986).

received as authoritative. Thus, even though the letter contains elements of what ancient epistolary theorists called the "friendly style," the bulk of the letter is of another type—the parenetic or exhorting style.[84] The friendly elements stem from the need to cast the exhortation in an atmosphere of positive relationship (e.g., parents-children), but the letter leaves no doubt that Paul expected his friendly advice to be followed. Unlike most letters between friends in antiquity, examples of which are available largely through accidental preservation, Paul would not have considered this letter to be "disposable." The fact that the church did preserve the letter testifies to its eventual reception as an authoritative, even official, apostolic document.

As for the form of the letter, 1 Corinthians follows the pattern of most private Greek letters, except for its uncharacteristic length. [The Pauline Letter Form] Detailed discussion of the parts of the letter will come in the commentary on each section, but here we note the basic design. The letter has an opening consisting of a prescript and a proem.[85] The prescript includes a *superscriptio* (identification of sender), an *adscriptio* (addressees), and a *salutatio* (greeting) in 1:1-3. The proem is rather long and consists of an extended prayer of thanksgiving (1:4-9). The closing is also unusually long and contains an epilogue and a postscript. The epilogue begins at 16:13 and consists of five final exhortations (16:13-14); recommendations regarding Stephanas, Fortunatus, and Achaicus (16:15-18); and various greetings (16:19-20). The postscript (16:21-24) includes Paul's handwritten greeting, a curse on anyone who does not love the Lord, a grace benediction, and an assurance of Paul's love.

The Pauline Letter Form

The letters of Paul typically follow the pattern outlined below, which represents his modification of the standard form found in ancient Greek letters.

The Opening

Sender

Paul usually identified himself as an "apostle"

Recipient

Usually included the word *ekklēsia* = "church"

Greeting

Usually included "Grace to you and peace from God our/the Father and the Lord Jesus Christ."

Thanksgiving/Blessing Prayer

Usually included subtle references to issues discussed in body of letter

The Body

Usually began with standard formulae, such as *parakalō* = "I ask . . ."

Often discussed broader theological principles and then focused on specific issues

Particular topics sometimes addressed in turn with each given a structured argument

Generally concluded with reference to Paul's travel plans

The Close

Always included some of these elements:

(1) Greetings to and from various persons

(2) A prayer for the peace of God

(3) A wish for the grace of the Lord Jesus

(4) Instruction to greet one another with a holy kiss

Sometimes followed by a post script

Hans-Josef Klauck, *Ancient Letters and the New Testament: A Guide to Context and Exegesis* (Waco TX: Baylor University Press, 2006).

Between the distinctive letter opening and closing, we find a rather lengthy letter body. This begins in 1:10 with a typical body-opening request formula: *parakalō* ("I ask . . ."). (See [Parakalō] in ch. 2). The arrangement of the body of the letter is largely dictated by the series of problems Paul addressed. Each section focuses on the issue at hand and employs arguments Paul considered appropriate for that topic. Thus, we do not find the letter moving from a discussion of broad theological issues to a concentration on specific matters, as we typically see in Paul's other letters. Paul began to deal with a specific matter in the opening verse of the letter's body in 1:10.[86] His treatment of theological matters in his argument for unity in 1:10–4:21, however, did establish certain argumentative principles that Paul applied to some of the other problems later in the letter. Thus, there is a degree of coherence in the letter that should prevent seeing it as merely a string of responses to problems. After addressing what he must have considered the most pressing issue, Paul then turned to a serious case of immorality (5:1-13), perhaps lawsuits in secular courts (6:1-11), and immorality of a more general kind (6:12-20). At 7:1, Paul moved to address matters about which the Corinthians had written to him. He clearly indicated this with the phrase *peri de hōn egrapsate* ("Now concerning the matters about which you wrote"). What is not so clear, however, is the range of those matters. The appearance of the phrase *peri de* five more times (7:25; 8:1; 12:1; 16:1, 12) suggests that Paul used it to refer to those matters mentioned in the Corinthians' letter, but this may not necessarily have been the case.[87] [The Phrase *peri de* in 1 Corinthians] The topics addressed from this point include marriage and sexuality (7:1-40), eating foods offered to idols (8:1–11:1), head coverings in worship (11:2-16), disorder in observances of the Lord's Supper (11:17-34), the evaluation of spiritual gifts (12:1-40), questions about bodily resurrection (15:1-57), and the collection for the poor saints in Jerusalem (16:1-4). After dealing with the various matters that prompted the letter, Paul brought the body of the letter to a close in a manner often followed in personal letters: a discussion of travel plans. Paul briefly projected his own travel plans and those of his associates (16:5-12), including a word about the reluctance of Apollos to visit Corinth at that time (16:12).[88]

1 Corinthians as Rhetoric

Paul wrote the letter we call 1 Corinthians to correct certain problems existing in the church at Corinth. In order to correct those problems, Paul had to persuade the Corinthians to accept him as an authoritative leader, to agree with his thinking regarding certain matters, and to conform their behavior accordingly. His letter,

The Phrase *peri de* in 1 Corinthians

ΑΩ Which of the problems addressed from 7:1 on should be included in those matters about which the Corinthians had written to Paul? The phrase *peri de* ("Now concerning . . .") appears six times (7:1, 25; 8:1; 12:1; 16:1, 12). Many interpreters have taken this phrase to mean that Paul was taking up in turn throughout the rest of the letter those issues raised in the Corinthians' letter to him. The six topics introduced in this way are sex between married partners (7:1-24), celibacy (7:23-40), eating food offered to idols (8:1–11:1), spiritual gifts (12:1–14:40), the collection for the poor (16:1-4), and a visit by Apollos (16:12).

Some have argued that other topics in chapters 7–16 not introduced by *peri de* should also be included in this group (head coverings, 11:2-16, and bodily resurrection, 15:1-58). Margaret Mitchell has pointed out, however, on the basis of the use of the phrase in other ancient writings, that *peri de* may simply indicate that Paul was moving from one topic to another, not that he was responding to a particular list of issues raised by the Corinthians. David Hall has observed, on the other hand, that in no other letter did Paul use the phrase so many times and that the impression it gives of Paul's responding to a list posed by the Corinthians remains probable. Paul's reference to plural matters (*hōn*) in 7:1 suggests that he meant more than only what he addressed in chapter 7. There the primary focus is on marriage relationships, with allusions to other issues such as circumcision and slavery being tangential to the main issue. Most likely, at least some of the other matters addressed in chapters 8–16 had been raised by the Corinthians' letter. Furthermore, as J. C. Hurd noted some time ago, Paul's manner of dealing with the matters that he had heard about differed sharply from his manner of treating those items that may have been included in the Corinthians' letter. This latter group (those matters that Paul treated in a calmer tone and with more sensitivity to the Corinthians' struggles) includes the very topics Paul introduced with *peri de*, which supports viewing those matters as ones included in the Corinthians' letter to Paul. Anthony Thiselton, in the most comprehensive commentary on 1 Corinthians in English, has argued that Hurd's criteria for distinguishing between Paul's different responses to his different sources remain useful.

David Hall, *The Unity of the Corinthian Correspondence* (JSNTSup 251; London: T & T Clark Int., 2003) 60.

John Coolidge Hurd Jr., *The Origin of 1 Corinthians* (Macon GA: Mercer University Press, 1983) 61–94.

Margaret M. Mitchell, "Concerning περὶ δὲ in 1 Corinthians," *NovT* 31 (1989): 229–56.

Anthony C. Thiselton, *The First Epistle to the Corinthians: A Commentary on the Greek Text* (NIGTC; Grand Rapids: Eerdmans, 2000) 34–36.

then, was an exercise in rhetoric, if rhetoric is understood more as "the art of persuasion" and less as "empty words of artificial eloquence."[89] While Paul appears at times in 1 Corinthians to have rejected "eloquent speaking" (e.g., 2:1-5), his appeals to the Corinthians repeatedly reveal the use of many ancient rhetorical conventions. Whether Paul consciously adopted such conventions is debated, but their presence is evident. Increasingly, therefore, New Testament scholars have tried to understand the structure and purpose of Paul's argumentation in 1 Corinthians by comparing it to the conventions of ancient rhetoric.[90]

Ancient rhetoric was basically of three types: (1) Judicial or forensic rhetoric concerned attempts to persuade an audience to make a judgment about past events, especially as to the innocence or guilt of someone. (2) Deliberative or advisory rhetoric involved persuading an audience toward some future action, often by showing the advantage of changing course. (3) Epideictic or demonstrative rhetoric sought to persuade an audience to affirm or reaffirm a certain perspective in the present, including a positive view of the orator (writer).[91]

Typically, in antiquity, orators (and writers consciously utilizing rhetorical conventions) began with an *exordium* (Gk. *prooimion*) designed to focus the attention of the audience on the topic at hand and to gain the good will of the listeners/readers. Then one might give a brief account (*narratio*; Gk. *diēgēsis*) of the facts of the case at hand, perhaps including some historical background. This narration, if included, might be preceded or followed by the main point to be argued, the *propositio* (Gk. *prothesis*). Then the heart of the argument would follow, consisting of a series of proofs (*argumentatio*; Gk. *pistis*) supporting the thesis (*confirmatio*) and disputing possible counter-arguments (*refutatio*). Various types of proofs might be presented, including material drawn from stock discussions of certain topics (*topoi*). The conclusion (*peroratio*; Gk. *epilogos*) would summarize the argument and usually appeal to the emotions of the audience for an agreeable decision. [A Rhetorical Scheme]

A Rhetorical Scheme

Forensic rhetoric developed a standard pattern for orations that consisted of four parts. Deliberative and judicial rhetoric often followed the same pattern. The Latin names for those parts are given below, with the equivalent Greek terms in parentheses.

Exordium (*prooimion*)—the opening speech
Narratio (*diēgēsis*)—the statement of the case, including the main thesis
Argumentatio (*pistis*)—the proofs supporting the case
Peroratio (*epilogos*)—the summary and conclusion

In applying this kind of rhetorical criticism to 1 Corinthians, scholars have differed regarding the dominant type of rhetoric in the letter. Some have identified it as judicial,[92] while others have labeled it deliberative.[93] Still, others have focused on its epideictic features,[94] while others have acknowledged a mixture of types.[95] Since Paul's overarching objective appears to have been the correction of perceived problems, then it would appear that whatever epideictic or judicial elements may have been employed in support of this objective, his primary aim was deliberative. His effort to correct problems in the church depended on his gaining a positive hearing for his argument, so one might expect epideictic elements to be prominent in the early part of the letter (esp. in 1:10–4:21).

When it comes to rhetorical analysis of the structure of 1 Corinthians, most studies have focused only on certain parts of the letter. Hermann Probst, however, has undertaken a more extensive study of the letter as a whole.[96] He has identified five sections in 1 Corinthians (1:10–4:21, 5:1–6:20, 8:1–11:1, 12:1–14:40; and 15:1-58), with each containing an *exordium*, *narratio*, *probatio*, and *peroratio*. On this basis, he has argued that each section originally constituted a complete letter. Thus, the major force of his analysis has been to support the idea that 1 Corinthians is a composite of several letters, a view that most scholars now reject.

The analysis of Margaret Mitchell is better informed by the evidence of ancient rhetoric and by her sensitive reading of 1 Corinthians, which she regards as a unified letter.[97] Unlike Probst, who ignored the rhetorical purpose of the thanksgiving prayer in 1:4-9, she has identified this section as the *prooimion* (*exordium*). She has also identified 1:10 as the *prothesis* (*propositio*) that Paul intended to argue in the rest of the letter. In her analysis, 1:11-17 functions as the *diēgēsis* (*narratio*) of the circumstances requiring Paul's argument and 1:18–4:21 as the first of four extensive proofs (*pisteis*) Paul used in support of his proposition. The remaining sections of proofs appear in 5:1–7:40 + 8:1–11:1, 11:2–14:40, and 15:1-57. The *epilogos* (*peroratio*) is brief in her analysis (15:58). A major conclusion to be drawn from her study is that rather than a composite of separate letters or a single letter that treats several topics but has no consistent theme, 1 Corinthians as a whole is a carefully crafted and coherent rhetorical argument. [Mitchell's Rhetorical Scheme for 1 Corinthians]

Mitchell's Rhetorical Scheme for 1 Corinthians

1:4-9	*Prooimion*—the opening speech in the form of a thanksgiving prayer
1:10	*Prothesis*—the thesis statement as a call to unity
1:11-17	*Diēgēsis*—the statement of the facts
1:18–15:57	*Pisteis*—the series of proofs offered in support of the thesis
1:18–4:21	First section of proof
5:11–11:1	Second section of proof
11:2–14:40	Third section of proof
15:1-57	Fourth section of proof
15:58	*Epilogos*—the summation of the argument

Margaret M. Mitchell, *Paul and the Rhetoric of Reconciliation: An Exegetical Investigation of the Language and Composition of 1 Corinthians* (Louisville: Westminster John Knox, 1991).

We will consider the rhetorical analyses of Mitchell and others when we come to the commentary on specific sections, but at this point a few caveats are in order. First, any proposal that imposes a particular form on Paul's argumentation based on ancient rhetorical conventions must be tentative.[98] Discussions of rhetoric in antiquity typically noted that great variety and flexibility were common. Rather than rigidly following the patterns of rhetoric advocated in formal education, Paul more likely used whatever argumentative devices he considered helpful in persuading his readers, some of which may have been drawn from formal rhetoric, though that is not as evident as some scholars argue.[99]

Secondly, the structure of Paul's argument here was determined less by rhetorical conventions of form than by the needs of the situation that made his letter to the Corinthians necessary. This is what several scholars have referred to as the "rhetorical situation."[100] Furthermore, David Aune has observed that early Christian letters were untypically free from many of the literary and rhetorical expectations to which other writers felt cultural pressure to conform.[101] The pressure Paul experienced in framing his arguments in 1 Corinthians came primarily from the situation that existed in Corinth. The information he received both orally and in written correspondence about the problems there, as well as his prior relationship with the church and his hope for the future, dictated much of the shape of his response to that situation, not the supposed requirements of framing his argument according to rhetorical conventions.

Thirdly, the attempt to identify a particular rhetorical scheme in 1 Corinthians confronts the difficulty of applying the conventions of an oral medium (rhetorical speeches) to a written medium (letters). Certainly the letters Paul wrote to churches were read aloud and, in that sense, resembled speeches.[102] But some of the elements in his letters that have been identified as parts of a rhetorical argument may, in fact, have actually been standard features of a particular type of letter.[103]

Cognizant of these caveats, the commentary that follows will make use of rhetorical analysis when it contributes to understanding the flow and focus of Paul's argument without insisting that Paul was following any prescribed rhetorical scheme.

1 Corinthians as Theology

Studies of the historical and social context of 1 Corinthians and epistolary and rhetorical analyses of the letter have provided new avenues of insight for understanding the problems Paul addressed and the manner in which he sought to alter the situation. Somewhat neglected in many such studies, however, has been *theology*. Partly this neglect stems from an aversion to the overly theological readings of earlier interpreters who tended to view Paul's letters as treatises in systematic theology and who often found in them (as one might expect) reflections of their own theological agendas.[104] The diminished attention to theology, however, also reflects the different agendas of modern (and postmodern) interpreters.[105] Theology is often perceived as an attempt to articulate and enforce (through persuasion or other means) claims to truth about God and human existence. As such, theology may be viewed as an instrument of rationality used to acquire or sustain the power of one person or group over others. What is articulated in theological language, then, may be seen as less important than *why* and *how* that language is used. Thus, some studies of Paul's theological language in 1 Corinthians have focused on how he used theology to silence competing voices, while other studies have tended to mute or "de-theologize" Paul's own voice.[106] The former kind of study enables us to consider the contributions of those voices within the early church that reflect an understanding of the gospel different from Paul's. The latter approach helps us see that

Paul's "theology" (and ours) cannot be divorced from social, political, and economic realities. Unfortunately, such studies have often devalued the role theology itself may fill in endeavors to understand the world and human existence.

As a part of the church's canon of Scripture, Paul's own theological voice in 1 Corinthians deserves a hearing. Even so, this proves difficult. Two millennia of interpretation by the church and our own experience have given us numerous filters through which we tend to hear what we want to hear from Paul. We inevitably bring to our reading of 1 Corinthians certain presuppositions about theology that affect how we read. Even when (and if) we recognize these and try to "bracket them out" so as to get to Paul's own theology, we face significant obstacles. Foremost among these is the fact that what we have from Paul are *letters.* In every instance (including Romans, I would argue), we have correspondence addressed to a particular group of people in a particular time and place who were facing particular problems. In the particular instance of 1 Corinthians, we have a letter that appears to focus on behavioral problems rather than theology *per se,* though Paul's response to those problems contains considerable appeal to theological ideas. Paul's letters use theological language, but it is language employed to deal with specific matters, not language designed to educate believers in the "great truths of the Christian faith." [Conzelmann on Theology in 1 Corinthians] Whether Paul had worked out his own core of theological belief or not remains debated, as does the question of what lies at the center of such a core.[107] What we have to work with in trying to hear Paul's voice are bits and pieces of theology brought to bear in a specific context to address specific issues. Because the church in general and countless individual Christians continue to try to hear Paul's own voice, trusting that he still has something important to say for our own theological understanding, we will consider some of the bits and pieces of his theology that appear in 1 Corinthians.

Conzelmann on Theology in 1 Corinthians

First Corinthians has already been criticized [by Walter Bauer] as "that unit among the major Pauline letters which yields the very least for our understanding of the Pauline faith," as being poor in doctrinal content. This criticism misjudges both the character of the epistle and the character of Paul's theology. It understands by theology merely the theoretical development of doctrine. . . . The great attraction of 1 Corinthians, however, lies in the fact that here Paul is practicing applied theology, so to speak. This is not to say that he is doing anything substantially different from what he does in Galatians and Romans, but he does it in a different way. Theology is here translated into an illumination of the existence of the church and of the individual Christian in it.

Hans Conzelmann, *1 Corinthians: A Commentary* (Hermeneia; trans. James W. Leitch; Philadelphia: Fortress Press, 1975) 9.

God as the sovereign and gracious Father. Overall, 1 Corinthians contains little reflection on the nature of God. Since the Corinthians and Paul probably held in common many basic ideas about their "one God" (8:6), Paul felt no need for such reflection.[108] A reminder of the activity of God on their behalf, however, was needed. Throughout 1 Corinthians, Paul worked to move his audience from an anthropocentric focus to a theocentric one. Part of his strategy was to recast their very human behavioral problems as more fundamental matters of *theo*-logy by interjecting God into the picture. More exactly, he reframed the situation to remind them of their place in *God's* picture. He reminded them that their existence as the church of God (1:2, 26-30) and his calling as an apostle of God (1:1) were by God's design and action. Indeed, Paul depicted God as the designer and actor in several dimensions. God created humanity (11:9) and all things (11:12). God assigned the "body" each created thing possesses (15:38) as well as each person's station in life (7:17), including Jesus' (11:3; 15:27). God assigned gifts to members of the church (12:6) and determined the church's structure (12:18, 24, 28). God has given commandments that are to be obeyed (7:19) and will ultimately judge one's compliance (4:5; 5:13). God wills that peace should prevail in the church (7:15; 14:33) and will exclude the unrighteous from the kingdom (6:9-10).

Yet, this God who intends that the divinely established order be followed also acts graciously. God acted in Christ to save those who believe (1:18-21; 6:11). In doing this, God acted in a way that is contrary to the world's standards, accomplishing salvation through the lowly death of Christ (1:20, 25) and imparting salvation to the lowly (1:27-28). This God who acts in unexpected ways is, nevertheless, faithful (1:9; 10:13), revealing God's will to the saved (2:10) and imparting God's spirit to the church (2:11-13). God raised Jesus from the dead (6:14; 15:15) and will raise the saved also (6:14; 15:20-23, 52). This bifocal view of God's sovereign and saving activity is captured in Paul's identification of God as "our Father" (1:3). In this, the sovereign authority of the *paterfamilias*, while posing as the background for his depiction of God, gives way to the emphasis in the foreground on the loving Father who acts graciously on behalf of the children. [*Paterfamilias*] While Paul appealed at times to the image of the disciplining father who judges unrighteous behavior, his dominant approach to correcting behavior was through appeal to the activity of the loving Father who willed and

Paterfamilias

While the father of the family exercised legal and social power over women, children, slaves, and property in all ancient Mediterranean societies, Roman fathers, at least theoretically, wielded unusual authority. Gaius (*Institutes* 1.55) asserted, "There are hardly any other men who have over their children a power such as we have." The father owned all familial property, even that of married sons. Legally, the power of the father (*patria potestas*) included the power of life and death, though by the imperial period significant restrictions to this power in regard to wife and children had been adopted.

Carolyn Osiek and David L. Balch, *Families in the New Testament World: Households and House Churches* (Louisville: Westminster John Knox Press, 1997) 56–57.

worked graciously for the well-being of those called into the new order of God's kingdom.

Christ as the crucified Lord. God's activity, especially God's saving activity on behalf of the church, was typically described by Paul as occurring *in* or *through* Christ.[109] Paul's theocentric focus was often couched in christocentric terms. In fact, the term God (*theos*) appears less frequently (99 times) in 1 Corinthians than terms referring to Christ (129 times). [References to Christ] Particularly interesting are the instances where Paul transformed Old Testament references to God as "Lord" into references to Christ (1:31; 2:16; 3:20; 10:26). Regularly in 1 Corinthians Paul applied to Christ those attributes and activities one might assume belonged to God alone. The letter's opening greeting extends "grace and peace from God our Father *and* our Lord Jesus Christ" (1:3), but "God" is omitted in the closing wish that "the grace of the Lord Jesus be with you" (16:23). The letter opening also refers to calling on (i.e., praying to) "the name of our Lord Jesus Christ" (1:2), while the closing (16:22) includes a prayer to Christ (*marana tha* = "Our Lord, come!"). Paul's apostleship was "by the will of God" (1:1), but the Lord (Christ) directed his itinerary (4:19; 16:7). Paul transformed "The Day of the Lord," which often appears in the Old Testament in reference to God's future judgment, into "the day of our Lord Jesus Christ" (1:8) and cast the Lord (Christ) as the judge on that day (4:4-5; 11:31). These and several other instances of divine activity attached to Christ have led Gordon Fee to observe that "Paul's thinking about God has been expanded to include the reality of Christ as Son and Lord."[110]

References to Christ

In the 129 references to Christ that appear in 1 Corinthians, the term "Lord" is found 63 times, the word "Christ" 44 times, the combination "Jesus Christ" 17 times, and the name "Jesus" 5 times.

Paul's christocentric focus in 1 Corinthians, however, had less to do with espousing a particular Christology than it did in establishing soteriology as the basis for ethics. Thus, the most overtly theological section of the letter appears in Paul's development of his "word of the cross" in his argument against divisional strife in 1:18–2:16. Paul's discussion there makes clear that his christocentric focus was not concerned so much with identifying Christ as a part of the *being* of God as it was with defining Christ, particularly in his death, as the *locus* for God's saving activity. Furthermore, his soteriological interest lay not in explaining *how* Christ's death accomplished salvation but rather in defining what salvation obtained in such a way *means* for the life of the church.

Paul's elucidation of the significance of God's activity in the death of Christ for ethics appears early in the letter in his juxtaposition of worldly wisdom and the word of the cross (1:18–2:5). Paul depicted the problem behind the divisions in the church as stemming from "boasting" (1:29; 3:21; 4:7) and being "puffed up" (4:6). Such behavior might be characteristic of a worldly wisdom that cherishes eloquence (1:17), lofty words (2:1), and clever words of wisdom (2:4), but it is inconsistent with the wisdom of God that utilizes weakness (2:3) and apparent foolishness (1:18, 21) to demonstrate God's power (1:18; 2:4-5). In contrast to the wisdom that empowers through the manipulation of language and, thus, fosters competitiveness, the wisdom that is "Christ crucified" empowers through the recognition and acceptance of God's self-giving love and fosters community. The cross of Christ, then, challenges perceptions of God and humanity that support worldly "power plays" and affirms, instead, solidarity with the self-giving love of God revealed in Christ.[111]

The Spirit as the enabler. The solidarity with God in Christ is effected by the Spirit, which is God's enabling presence with and in the believers. Paul pointed out that confession (12:3) and justification (6:11) come *in* the Spirit. Furthermore, he noted that understanding the thoughts of God comes through the revelation of the Spirit (2:10-12), and communication of that revelation comes through the teaching of the Spirit (2:13). Those who possess the Spirit understand spiritual matters and are able to judge all things (2:14-15). Paul could support his judgment that widows would be better off remaining unmarried by asserting, "I think I have the Spirit of God" (7:40). His claim to have the Spirit of God in 7:40 parallels his assertion in 2:16 that those who possess the Spirit have "the mind of Christ."

The essential equivalence of having the Spirit of God and having the mind of Christ points to the ethical consequence of the Spirit's presence. Paul used two metaphors to illustrate this: temple and body. The Spirit's presence in the church transforms that entity into the holy temple of God (3:16-17). In fact, each person's body is a temple of the Spirit and must not be corrupted by immorality (6:18-20). The Spirit's work within the individual bodies of believers is to build up the *body* of Christ. By the Spirit believers were baptized into the body of Christ (12:13) and from the Spirit received a variety of manifestations of the Spirit's power for the common good of the body (12:4-7). Paul commended the Corinthians for seeking the Spirit's gifts but urged them to pursue the higher gifts of communal edification, especially love (12:31). The members of the body were to seek those manifestations of the Spirit that contribute to the building up of the church (14:12) rather than those that contribute to self-edification (14:4). Thus, the model of God's self-giving love evidenced in the cross of Christ would become operative in the church through the community-oriented working of the Spirit. One can, therefore, understand Fee's contention that in 1 Corinthians the Spirit is "the key to ethical and community life."[112]

The church as an eschatological community. What Paul wrote in 1 Corinthians about such theological ideas as God, Christ, and the Spirit was shaped by his concern for the life of the church. Thus, his theological discussions bear the imprint of ethical interests. Indeed, Paul probably would not have made the distinction between ethics and theology that modern interpreters tend to make.[113] The convergence of theology and ethics is perhaps clearest in his depiction of the church as an eschatological community.

Many scholars have come to see eschatology (from the Gk. *eschaton* = "end") as a major component of Paul's theology, with some holding that it provides the basic structure for the rest of his thought. [Paul's Apocalyptic Eschatology] Furthermore, Paul's eschatological perspective appears to have been largely informed by Jewish apocalyptic thinking, in which a dualistic view of the cosmos and of time prevailed. The cosmic dualism held that the agents of evil (Satan, demons, and worldly powers) were in conflict with agents of good (God, angels, faithful servants). The temporal dualism divided time between this present age in which the agents of evil seem to have the upper hand and the coming age in which the agents of good prevail and establish a new world order. Apocalyptic writings utilized symbolic presentations of this dualism to interpret the struggles of the faithful in the present and, sometimes, to project the events associated with the arrival of the new age of God's kingdom.

Paul's Apocalyptic Eschatology

The importance of apocalyptic eschatology for understanding Paul's theology has been argued in several influential studies, including especially Käsemann, Martyn, and Beker.

Ernst Käsemann, "On the Subject of Primitive Christian Apocalyptic," in *New Testament Questions of Today* (trans. W. J. Montague; Philadelphia: Fortress Press, 1969).

J. Louis Martyn, "Epistemology at the Turn of the Ages: 2 Corinthians 5:16," in *Christian History and Interpretation: Studies Presented to John Knox* (ed. W. R. Farmer, C. F. D. Moule, and R. R. Niebuhr; Cambridge: Cambridge University Press, 1967).

J. Christiaan Beker, *Paul the Apostle: The Triumph of God in Life and Thought* (Philadelphia: Fortress Press, 1980).

While probably influenced by Jewish apocalyptic, Paul's eschatological perspective bore the marks of what he believed God had begun to do in Christ. The death and resurrection of Christ signaled the inauguration of the new age. Yet, unlike in Jewish apocalyptic, the old age with its malevolent rulers has not yet ended (2:6-8). Nevertheless, the present evil age is approaching its demise (7:29-31). The end of this age would come, according to Paul, when Christ returned to defeat the evil powers (15:24-26). At that time, those who had died in Christ and the faithful still alive would be transformed into resurrection existence (15:51-57). The faithful would receive a positive judgment from Christ on that day (1:8) and serve as judges of the world and even of angels (6:2-3).

In the meantime, the church exists in that period between the beginning of the new age and the end of the old. A key text for understanding the implications of this interim existence is 1 Corinthians 10:11 where Paul identified his present generation of believers as "those on whom the *ends of the ages* have come" (NRSV, italics added). [The "Ends" of the Ages] His statement in 10:11 appears in the context of his warning against idolatry (10:6-22). As people already living in the new age, the church cannot follow the habits of the old age. Likewise, in 6:1-8, where Paul possibly condemned members of the church for subjecting their disputes to civil courts, he reminded them that their impending role as judges of the world in the new age certainly qualified them to judge their own disputes in the present. This passage follows the section in 5:1-13 where Paul chastised the church for failing to exercise internal judgment in cleansing the "leaven" of immorality from what should be a new "unleavened" batch of dough (5:7). In 7:1-40, where he addressed matters of marriage, Paul reminded them that the time of this age had been shortened (7:29) and that in light of this world's passing away, they should live as if they no longer had dealings with this world (7:31).

The "Ends" of the Ages

Both *ta telē* ("the ends") and *tōn aiōnōn* ("of the ages") in 1 Cor 10:11 are plural, though many translations obscure this. In a sense, then, Paul understood the ages to overlap. The new age had begun with the crucifixion and resurrection of Christ, but the old age would not end until Christ returned.

The church, then, for Paul, should see itself as an eschatological community living in what remains of the present evil age already endowed with certain aspects of existence in the new age. The vision of life in the new age after the return of Christ should inform and form behavior in the present. Though the church already participates in the life of the new age, the confirmation of individual faithfulness awaits the judgment of Christ (1:8; 3:13-15). Thus, Paul's most glowing depiction of God's final triumph over evil in 15:51-57 ends with an admonition: "Be steadfast, immovable, always excelling in the work of the Lord" (NRSV). The hope provided by Paul's eschatological vision, therefore, could not be divorced from the ethical consequences such a vision impressed (and impresses) upon the church.

NOTES

1. Gordon D. Fee, *The First Epistle to the Corinthians* (NICNT; Grand Rapids: Eerdmans, 1987) 2. Modern society's quest for sexual aids such as Viagra should alert us to similar concerns in antiquity.

2. Jerome Murphy-O'Connor, *St. Paul's Corinth: Texts and Archaeology* (Collegeville MN: Liturgical Press, 1983) 173–74.

3. The misinterpretation of these and other archaeological data has been pointed out by Richard E. Oster Jr., "Use, Misuse and Neglect of Archaeological Evidence in Some Modern Works on 1 Corinthians (1 Cor 7,1-5; 8,10; 11,2-16; 12,14-26)," *ZNW* 83 (1992): 69–73.

4. Many of these statements have been collected and discussed in Jerome Murphy-O'Connor's *St. Paul's Corinth*. For Corinth's involvement in the conflicts with Athens, see Donald Kagan, *The Peloponnesian War* (New York: Viking Penguin, 2003) 25–29, and J. B. Salmon, *Wealthy Corinth: A History of the City to 338 B.C.* (Oxford: University Press, 1984), 257–341.

5. See Salmon, *Wealthy Corinth*, 397–401.

6. In addition to other studies mentioned in a note below, see John R. Lanci, "The Stones Don't Speak and the Texts Tell Lies: Sacred Sex at Corinth," in *Urban Religion in Roman Corinth: Interdisciplinary Approaches* (ed. Daniel N. Showalter and Steven J. Friesen; HTS 53; Cambridge: Harvard University Press, 2005) 205–20. The most cogent argument in support of connecting Aphrodite with sacred prostitution is that of Bonnie MacLachlan, "Sacred Prostitution and Aphrodite," *SR* 21/2 (1992): 145–62, but Lanci has noted her uncritical reliance on Herodotus.

7. For a critical assessment of Strabo's statement, see Hans Conzelmann, "Korinth und die Mädchen der Aphrodite," *NAWG* 8 (1967): 247–61; H. D. Saffrey, "Aphrodite à Corinthe: réflexions sur une idée reçue," *RB* 92 (1985): 359–74; and Murphy-O'Connor, *St. Paul's Corinth*, 57.

8. M. Cary and H. H. Scullard, *A History of Rome: Down to the Reign of Constantine* (3rd ed.; New York: St. Martin's Press, 1975) 150–60.

9. James Wiseman, "Corinth and Rome I: 228 B.C.-A.D. 267," *ANRW* 7/1 (1979): 461–62.

10. James Wiseman, *The Land of the Ancient Corinthians* (SMA 50; Göteborg: Aström Förlag, 1978) 45. See the discussion of the commercial value of the *diolkos* in Salmon, *Wealthy Corinth*, 136–39.

11. Charles K. Williams II, "Roman Corinth as a Commercial Center," in *The Corinthia in the Roman Period* (ed. Timothy E. Gregory; JRASup 8: Ann Arbor MI: Journal of Roman Archaeology, 1993) 31–33.

12. David Gilman Romano, "Urban and Rural Planning in Roman Corinth," in *Urban Religion in Roman Corinth*, 59. See also Romano, "Post-146 B.C. Land Use in Corinth, and Planning of the Roman Colony of 44 BC," in *The Corinthia in the Roman Period*, 9–30.

13. The description of the Corinthian forum given here is largely based on Williams, "Roman Corinth" and Wiseman, "Corinth and Rome I," as well as various reports from excavations conducted by the American School of Classical Studies at Athens.

14. Oscar Broneer, *The South Stoa and Its Roman Successors* (*Corinth* I.4; Princeton: American School of Classical Studies at Athens, 1954) 99.

15. Betsey A. Robinson, "Fountains and the Formation of Cultural Identity at Roman Corinth," in *Urban Religion in Roman Corinth*, 121.

16. Nancy Bookidis, "Religion in Corinth: 146 B.C.E. to 100 C.E.," in *Urban Religion in Roman Corinth*, 153.

17. Charles K. Williams II has published several reports on later excavations of this temple, the most pertinent publication here being his "A Re-evaluation of Temple E and the West End of the Forum in Corinth," in *The Greek Renaissance in the Roman Empire: Papers from the Tenth British Museum Classical Colloquium* (ed. Susan Walker and Averil Cameron; *BICSSup* 55; London: University of London, 1989) 156–62. See the careful discussion of this temple by Nancy Bookidis, "Religion in Corinth," 155–57.

18. Mary E. Hoskins Walbank, "Evidence for the Imperial Cult in Julio-Claudian Corinth," in *Subject and Ruler: The Cult of the Ruling Power in Classical Antiquity* (ed. Alastair Small; JRASup 17; Ann Arbor MI: Journal of Roman Archaeology, 1996) 211–14.

19. Wiseman, "Corinth and Rome," 503. See the argument for the likelihood of Corinth as capital in David Engels, *Roman Corinth: An Alternative Model for the Classical City* (Chicago: University of Chicago Press, 1990) 199 n41.

20. This is argued by Bruce W. Winter, *After Paul Left Corinth: The Influence of Secular Ethics and Social Change* (Grand Rapids MI: Eerdmans, 2001) 271–76. Winter bases much of his case on the evidence presented by Anthony J. S. Spawforth, "Corinth, Argos, and the Imperial Cult: *Pseudo-Julian*, *Letters* 198," *Hesperia* 63/2 (1994): 211–32.

21. The elevation of the status of the Caesarean games by attaching them to the older Isthmian games has been pointed out by James Walters, "Civic Identity in Roman Corinth and Its Impact on Early Christians," in *Urban Religion in Roman Corinth*, 408.

22. John Harvey Kent, *The Inscriptions 1926–1950* (*Corinth* VIII.3; Princeton: American School of Classical Studies at Athens, 1966) 72, dated the games to AD 21/22 on the basis of an inscription. John K. Chow, "Patronage in Roman Corinth," in *Paul and Empire: Religion and Power in Roman Imperial Society* (ed. Richard A. Horsley; Harrisburg PA: Trinity Press, 1997) 108, accepts Kent's reading and dating of the inscription pertinent to this matter, but this has been questioned by Elizabeth R. Gebhard, "The Isthmian Games and the Sanctuary of Poseidon in the Early Empire," in *The Corinthia in the Roman Period*, 87–88. The evidence suggests that, though Corinth regained control of the Isthmian games soon after its refounding, the games were probably not held at the traditional site, the sanctuary of Poseidon on the isthmus, until the reign of Nero. Thus, we should question the imaginative accounts of Paul's visit to Isthmia by Oscar Broneer, "The Apostle Paul and the Isthmian Games," *BA* 25 (1962): 1–31, and "Paul and the Pagan Cults at Isthmia," *HTR* 64 (1971): 169–87.

23. Kent, *The Inscriptions*, 28–30.

24. See Chow, "Patronage in Roman Corinth," 114.

25. Chow, "Patronage in Roman Corinth," 118; also Peter Garnsey and Richard Saller, "Patronage Power Relations," in *Paul and Empire*, 101.

26. James Walters, "Civic Identity in Roman Corinth," 410.

27. The impact of less conflict between the larger community and private, religious associations has been examined in relation to the Corinthian church by John M. G. Barclay, "Thessalonica and Corinth: Social Contrasts in Pauline Christianity," *JSNT* 47 (1992): 49–74, and Craig Steven de Vos, *Church and Community Conflicts: The*

Relationships of the Thessalonian, Corinthian, and Philippian Churches with Their Wider Civic Communities (SBLDS 168; Atlanta: Scholars Press, 1999).

28. Justin J. Meggitt, *Paul, Poverty and Survival* (SNTW; Edinburgh: T & T Clark, 1998) 167–69, has questioned the influence of patronage on the church, but Chow's assessment that "it would be most unrealistic to expect the Christians there [in Corinth] to behave in a completely new way immediately after their conversion" ("Patronage in Roman Corinth," 125) seems reasonable.

29. This point has been clearly made by Simon R. F. Price, *Rituals and Power: The Roman Imperial Cult in Asia Minor* (Cambridge: Cambridge University Press, 1984).

30. Engels, *Roman Corinth*, 96.

31. Charles K. Williams II, "Roman Corinth: The Final Years of Pagan Cult Facilities along East Theater Street," in *Urban Religion in Roman Corinth*, 221–47, esp. 246.

32. Bookidis, "Religion in Corinth," 159.

33. Ibid., 160.

34. Nancy Bookidis and Ronald S. Stroud, *The Sanctuary of Demeter and Kore: Topography and Architecture* (Corinth XVIII.8; Princeton: American School of Classical Studies at Athens, 1997) 434–35. Bookidis and Stroud disagree with Richard E. DeMaris, "Demeter in Roman Corinth: Local Development in a Mediterranean Religion," *Numen* 42 (1995): 105–17, who argued that the emphasis in this cult shifted in the Roman period from fertility to funerary and other worldly concerns.

35. The evidence is presented by Dennis Edwin Smith, "The Egyptian Cults at Corinth," *HTR* 70 (1977): 201–31.

36. Williams, "Roman Corinth: The Final Years of Pagan Cult Facilities," 225.

37. Murphy-O'Connor, *St. Paul's Corinth*, 82, suggests that the Jewish community in Corinth was a *politeuma*, a "corporation of aliens with permanent rights of domicile and empowered to manage its internal affairs through its own officials."

38. Barbara Levick, *Claudius* (New Haven: Yale University Press, 1990) 184.

39. Josephus, *Jewish War* 3.540.

40. Richard Horsley warns against continuation of anachronistic depictions of Paul's movement in his general introduction to *Paul and Empire*, 8.

41. See the extended discussion of this evidence by Murphy-O'Connor, *St. Paul's Corinth*, 137–60.

42. Several articles in *The Journal for the Study of the New Testament* 38/1 (2001): 51–94, were devoted to this subject. See the review of the debate over social status by Bengt Holmberg, "The Methods of Reconstruction in the Scholarly 'Recovery' of Corinthian Christianity," in *Christianity at Corinth: The Quest for the Pauline Church* (ed. Edward Adams and David G. Horrell; Louisville: Westminster John Knox, 2004) 255–71.

43. Edwin A. Judge, *The Social Pattern of Christian Groups in the First Century: Some Prolegomena to the Study of New Testament Ideas of Social Obligation* (London: Tyndale Press, 1960); Wayne A. Meeks, *The First Urban Christians: The Social World of the Apostle Paul* (New Haven: Yale University Press, 1983); Gerd Theissen, *The Social Setting of Pauline Christianity: Essays on Corinth* (Philadelphia: Fortress Press, 1982).

44. Abraham J. Malherbe, *Social Aspects of Early Christianity* (2d ed.; Philadelphia: Fortress Press, 1983) 86–87.

45. Steven J. Friesen, "Prospects for a Demography of the Pauline Mission: Corinth among the Churches,"in *Urban Religion in Roman Corinth*, 351–70.

46. Justin J. Meggitt, *Paul, Poverty and Survival*, 149–51.

47. Friesen, "Prospects," 365.

48. Ibid., 368.

49. Ekkehard W. Stegemann and Wolfgang Stegemann, *The Jesus Movement: A Social History of Its First Century* (Minneapolis, Fortress Press, 1999).

50. Friesen, "Prospects," 362.

51. Meggitt, *Paul, Poverty and Survival*, 120–21.

52. Henry G. Liddell, Robert Scott, and H. Stuart Jones, *Greek-English Lexicon* (9th ed.; Oxford: Clarendon Press, 1968) 1189.

53. The inscription was published by Kent, *The Inscriptions*, 99. See the extended arguments for this identification by Gerd Theissen, *The Social Setting of Pauline Christianity*, 75–83, and Bruce W. Winter, *Seek the Welfare of the City: Christians as Benefactors and Citizens* (FCCGRW; Grand Rapids: Eerdmans, 1994) 179–97. See also the arguments against by Henry J. Cadbury, "Erastus of Corinth," *JBL* 50 (1931): 42–58, and Justin J. Meggitt, "The Social Status of Erastus (Rom 16:23)," in *Christianity at Corinth*, 219–25.

54. Steven J. Friesen, "The Wrong Erastus: Status, Wealth, and Paul's Churches," in *Corinth in Context: Comparative Perspectives on Religion and Society* (ed. Steven J. Friesen and Daniel N. Showalter; Cambridge MA: Harvard University Press, forthcoming).

55. Meggitt, "The Social Status of Erastus," 225, draws the same conclusion.

56. This point is made by Meeks, *The First Urban Christians*, 72–73.

57. This connects with Meeks's discussion of "status inconsistency," 22.

58. David R. Hall, *The Unity of the Corinthian Correspondence* (JSNTSup 251; London: T & T Clark Int., 2003), argues that 1 Cor is the letter mentioned by Paul in 2 Cor. He also holds that 2 Cor should be seen as a unified letter.

59. See the careful discussion of this matter and the new chronology presented by Margaret M. Mitchell, "Paul's Letters to Corinth: The Interpretive Intertwining of Literary and Historical Reconstruction," in *Urban Religion in Roman Corinth*, 307–38.

60. The differences in Paul's responses have been defined by John Coolidge Hurd Jr., *The Origin of I Corinthians* (Macon GA: Mercer University Press, 1983) 65–82. I do not agree with him entirely in his identification of which issues Paul learned about via oral or written reports

61. See the review of this understanding by David G. Horrell and Edward Adams, "The Scholarly Quest for Paul's Church at Corinth," in *Christianity at Corinth*, 13–26.

62. See the discussion of the various identifications along these lines in Anthony C. Thiselton, *The First Epistle to the Corinthians: A Commentary on the Greek Text* (NIGTC; Grand Rapids: Eerdmans, 2000) 123–33.

63. Laurence L. Welborn, "Discord in Corinth: First Corinthians 1–4 and Ancient Politics," as revised in his *Politics and Rhetoric in the Corinthian Epistles* (Macon: Mercer University Press, 1997) 7.

64. Donald P. Ker, "Paul and Apollos—Colleagues or Rivals?" *JSNT* 77 (2000): 83. The likelihood that differences in theology were involved in the divisions is argued well by

David R. Hall, *The Unity of the Corinthian Correspondence* (JSNTSup 251; London: T & T Clark Int., 2003) 14–19.

65. In his extensive commentary, Wolfgang Schrage identified thirteen theories about the theology of the Corinthians. *Die erste Brief an die Korinther* (EKKNT 7/1-4; 4 vols.; Zurich and Braunschweig: Benziger Verlag, and Neukirchen-Vluyn: Neukirchener Verlag, 1991–2001) 1:38–63.

66. The relationship between differences in socioeconomic position and ideological differences is the focus of Dale B. Martin, *The Corinthian Body* (New Haven: Yale University Press, 1995).

67. This is the view now taken by Thiselton in his commentary on 1 Cor (see note 58 above.) Earlier, he had argued that a "realized eschatology" alone prompted the divisions. See his "Realized Eschatology at Corinth," *NTS* 24 (1978): 510–26.

68. Johannes Munck was the first scholar to mount a serious challenge to the once prevailing view that theology divided the church into factions in "The Church without Factions: Studies in I Corinthians 1–4," in *Paul and the Salvation of Mankind* (London: SCM, 1959). See the discussions of the divisions in Corinth by David Hall, *The Unity of the Corinthian Correspondence*, 4–19, and Margaret M. Mitchell, *Paul and the Rhetoric of Reconciliation: An Exegetical Investigation of the Language and Composition of 1 Corinthians* (Louisville: Westminster John Knox, 1991) 65–83.

69. Nils Dahl, *Studies in Paul: Theology for the Early Christian Mission* (Minneapolis: Augsburg Press, 1977) 49ff.

70. This is the position of Donald Ker in the previously cited article "Paul or Apollos," 75–97. Mitchell, *Paul and the Rhetoric of Reconciliation*, 83, also holds that Paul created the slogans of 1 Cor 1:12, but she still sees factions in Corinth claiming allegiance to the named leaders.

71. Hall, *The Unity of the Corinthian Correspondence*, 5–7.

72. I agree with Mitchell, "Paul's Letters to Corinth," 334, that the opposition to Paul reflected in 2 Cor 10–13 should not be attributed to a single event involving visiting preachers. Opposition to Paul was already present when he wrote 1 Cor. Hall, *The Unity of the Corinthian Correspondence*, 1–4, argues that essentially the same situation lay behind both 1 and 2 Cor.

73. Elisabeth Schüssler Fiorenza, "Rhetorical Situation and Historical Reconstruction," in *Christianity at Corinth*, 157.

74. See several articles by Abraham J. Malherbe republished as *Paul and the Popular Philosophers* (Minneapolis: Fortress Press, 1989). See also Ronald F. Hock, *The Social Context of Paul's Ministry: Tentmaking and Apostleship* (Philadelphia: Fortress Press, 1980) and Stanley K. Stowers, "Social Status, Public Speaking and Private Teaching: The Circumstances of Paul's Preaching Activity," *NovT* 26 (1984): 59–82.

75. Bruce W. Winter, *Philo and Paul among the Sophists: Alexandrian and Corinthian Responses to a Julio-Claudian Movement* (2d ed.; Grand Rapids MI: Eerdmans Publishing, 2002).

76. Winter, *After Paul Left Corinth*, 41–43. Hall, *The Unity of the Corinthian Correspondence*, 17, argues that the visit of Apollos is not a sufficient explanation.

77. See the discussion of the situation addressed by *1 Clement* by Barbara Ellen Bowe, *A Church in Crisis* (HDR 23; Minneapolis: Fortress Press, 1988).

78. See the description of the Corinthian church after Paul by Engels, *Roman Corinth*, 116–20.

79. See the discussion of Corinthian martyrs by Vasiliki Limberis, "Ecclesiastical Ambiguities: Corinth in the Fourth and Fifth Centuries," in *Urban Religion in Roman Corinth*, 443–57.

80. See the descriptions of these buildings by Guy D. R. Sanders, "Archaeological Evidence for Early Christianity and the End of Hellenic Religion in Corinth," in *Urban Religion in Roman Corinth*, 419–42, and the discussion of the relationship between Christianity and paganism during this period by Richard M. Rothaus, *Corinth, the First City of Greece: An Urban History of Late Antique Cult and Religion* (Leiden: Brill, 2000).

81. Robert Scranton, *Medieval Architecture in the Central Area of Corinth* (*Corinth* 16; Princeton: American School of Classical Studies at Athens, 1957).

82. Demetrius, *On Style*, 223, credited Artemon, the editor of Aristotle's letters, with this analogy. Demetrius went on to point out differences between a letter and a dialogue. The identity of "Demetrius" and the dating of *On Style* is debated, but most likely it is an anonymous writing from the early first century BC to the late first century AD.

83. Calvin J. Roetzel, *The Letters of Paul: Conversations in Context* (3rd ed.; Louisville: Westminster/John Knox, 1991).

84. Hans-Josef Klauck, *Ancient Letters and the New Testament: A Guide to Context and Exegesis* (Waco TX: Baylor University Press, 2006), 307. See also Stanley K. Stowers, *Letter Writing in Greco-Roman Antiquity* (LEC; Philadelphia: Westminster, 1986) 96.

85. For this description, I am largely using the terminology found in Klauck, *Ancient Letters and the New Testament*, 42.

86. Mitchell, *Paul and the Rhetoric of Reconciliation*, takes 1:10 to be the proposition for the whole letter. So does George A. Kennedy, *New Testament Interpretation through Rhetorical Criticism* (Chapel Hill: University of North Carolina Press, 1984) 24.

87. This common understanding of the function of *peri de* has been challenged by Margaret M. Mitchell, "Concerning περὶ δε in 1 Corinthians," *NovT* 31 (1989): 229–56. It has recently been defended by David Hall, *The Unity of the Corinthian Correspondence*, 60, and Anthony C. Thiselton, *The First Epistle to the Corinthians: A Commentary on the Greek Text* (NIGTC; Grand Rapids: Eerdmans, 2000) 34–36.

88. Some interpreters think the Corinthians had requested a visit by Apollo in the letter they wrote to Paul; *peri de* introduces Paul's words in 16:12. See Archibald Robertson and Alfred Plummer, *First Epistle of St. Paul to the Corinthians* (ICC, 2d ed.; New York: Charles Scribner's Sons, 1914) 392, and, more recently, Winter, *After Paul Left Corinth*, 41.

89. Defining rhetoric either as the "art of persuasion" or "the art of speaking well" is inadequate. Rhetoric incorporated both ends in that it was concerned with effective communication. See George A. Kennedy, *Classical Rhetoric and Its Christian and Secular Tradition from Ancient to Modern Times* (Chapel Hill: University of North Carolina Press, 1980) 4–5.

90. See especially, Mitchell, *Paul and the Rhetoric of Reconciliation*; Ben Witherington III, *Conflict and Community in Corinth: A Socio-Rhetorical Commentary and 1 and 2 Corinthians* (Grand Rapids: Eerdmans, 1995); Stephen M. Pogoloff, *Logos and Sophia: The Rhetorical Situation of 1 Corinthians* (SBLDS 134; Atlanta: Scholars Press, 1992); and several chapters in S. E. Porter and T. H. Olbricht (eds.) *Rhetoric and the*

New Testament: Essays from the 1992 Heidelberg Conference (Sheffield: Sheffield Academic press, 1993).

91. For a description of these three types, see in particular George A. Kennedy, *New Testament Interpretation through Rhetorical Criticism* (Chapel Hill: University of North Carolina Press, 1984) 19ff.

92. Michael Bünker, *Briefformular und rhetorische Disposition im 1, Korintherbrief* (Göttinger theologische Arbeiten 28; Göttingen: Vandenhoeck & Roprecht, 1983).

93. Elisabeth Schüssler Fiorenza, "Rhetorical Situation and Historical Reconstruction in 1 Corinthians," *NTS* 33 (1987): 386–403; Fiorenza's proposal that 1 Corinthians is deliberative is extensively elaborated by Mitchell, *Paul and the Rhetoric of Reconciliation*, whose argument is followed by Witherington, *Conflict and Community in Corinth*.

94. Wilhelm Wuellner, "Greek Rhetoric and Pauline Argumentation," in *Early Christian Literature and the Classical Intellectual Tradition*: in honorem *Robert M. Grant* (ed. W. R. Schoedel and R. L. Wilken; Théologie Historique 54; Paris: Etudes Beauchesne, 1979) 177–88, and Joop F. M. Smit, "Epideictic Rhetoric in Paul's First Letter to the Corinthians 1–4," Bib 84 (2003): 184–201.

95. Kennedy, *New Testament Interpretation through Rhetorical Criticism*, 87; Mitchell, *Paul and the Rhetoric of Reconciliation*, 213–24, who sees 1 Corinthians as predominantly deliberative, identifies epideictic elements in 1:18–4:21.

96. Hermann Probst, *Paulus und der Brief: Die Rhetorik des antiken Briefes als Form der paulinischen Korintherkorrespondenz* (WUNT 2/45; Tübingen : J.C.B. Mohr, 1991).

97. Mitchell, *Paul and the Rhetoric of Reconciliation*. Since Mitchell prefers the Greek terms for rhetorical parts, I use them along with the Latin terms in the description of her analysis.

98. Winter, *Philo and Paul among the Sophists*, 250, holds that imposing rhetorical grids on Paul's arguments fails to appreciate the variety of ways Paul argues his points.

99. Concern about the misapplication of rhetorical analysis to Paul's letters is expressed by Klauck, *Ancient Letters*, 222–27, and Murphy-O'Connor, *Paul the Letter-Writer*, 79–83. See also Stephen M. Pogoloff, *Logos and Sophia: The Rhetorical Situation of 1 Corinthians* (SBLDS 134; Atlanta: Scholars Press, 1992) 87–95.

100. See especially, Fiorenza, "Rhetorical Situation," 393–97, and Pogoloff, *Logos and Sophia*, 91–95.

101. David Aune, *The New Testament in Its Literary Environment* (LEC 8; Philadelphia: Westminster Press, 1987) 203.

102. See Witherington's discussion of the similarities of letters and oral speech, *Conflict and Community in Corinth*, 44–46, and Klauck's warning about overlooking the differences, *Ancient Letters*, 225.

103. Thiselton, *The First Epistle to the Corinthians*, 41–52, discusses the need for a balanced assessment between epistolary and rhetorical analyses.

104. See Jouette M. Bassler, "Paul's Theology: Whence and Whither?" in *Pauline Theology, Vol. II: 1 & 2 Corinthians* (ed. David M. Hay; Minneapolis: Fortress Press, 1993) 8–9. This volume is part of a four-volume collection of papers presented at annual meetings of the Pauline Theology Group of the Society of Biblical Literature from 1986–1996. These papers demonstrate both the difficulties of defining Paul's theology and the continuing interest in the subject.

105. See Thiselton, *The First Epistle to the Corinthians*, 50.

106. An example of trying to hear the competing voices would be Antoinette Clark Wire, *The Corinthian Women Prophets: A Reconstruction through Paul's Rhetoric* (Minneapolis: Fortress Press, 1990), while an example of de-theologizing Paul would be Richard A. Horsley, "1 Corinthians: A Case Study of Paul's Assembly as an Alternative Society," in *Christianity at Corinth*, 227–37.

107. A significant investigation of this issue was made by J. Christiaan Beker, *Paul the Apostle: The Triumph of God in Life and Thought* (Philadelphia: Fortress, 1980). The study group mentioned in note 104 above has continued this discussion.

108. See Gordon D. Fee, "Toward a Theology of 1 Corinthians," in *Pauline Theology, Vol. II: 1 & 2 Corinthians*, 41–42.

109. Fee, "Toward a Theology of 1 Corinthians," 44 n21, stated that the phrase "in/by Christ" occurs 22 times in 1 Corinthians, but I have found only 12 instances.

110. Fee, "Toward a Theology of 1 Corinthians," 43.

111. Alexandra R. Brown, *The Cross and Human Transformation: Paul's Apocalyptic Word in 1 Corinthians* (Minneapolis: Fortress Press, 1995) 157–67, discusses the relationship between Paul's correction of epistemological errors about God and ethical behavior.

112. Fee, "Toward a Theology of 1 Corinthians," 46.

113. See Hall, T*he Unity of the Corinthian Correspondence*, 18–19, and Hans Conzelmann, *1 Corinthians* (Hermeneia; trans. James W. Leitch; Philadelphia: Fortress Press, 1975) 9.

AN OUTLINE OF 1 CORINTHIANS

The Beginning (1:1-9)

I. The Opening (vv. 1-3)
  A. The Senders: Paul and Sosthenes (v. 1)
  B. The Recipients: The Church of God in Corinth (v. 2)
  C. The Greeting (v. 3)
II. The Thanksgiving (vv. 4-9)
  A. The Present Reality of God's Grace-gifts (vv. 4-6)
  B. The Future Realization of Grace's Purpose (vv. 7-9)

The Problems of Divisions (1:10–4:21)

I. Indicting the Corinthians for Divisional Strife (1:10-17)
  A. Identifying the Problem (1:10-12)
  B. Initial Argument against Divisions (1:13-17)
II. Contrasting Worldly Wisdom and the Preaching of the Cross (1:18-2:5)
  A. The Cross as Foolish Wisdom and Power (1:18-25)
  B. God's Choice of the Foolish and Weak (1:26-31)
  C. Proclaiming the Cross as God's Power (2:1-5)
III. Communicating the Wisdom of God (2:6–3:4)
  A. Wisdom Revealed through the Spirit (2:6-13)
  B. Wisdom Incomprehensible to the Unspiritual (2:14-16)
  C. The Corinthians as Unspiritual (3:1-4)
IV. Rightly Perceiving the Servants of the Lord (3:5-17)
  A. Cultivating the Field of God (3:5-9)
  B. Building on the Foundation of Christ (3:10-15)
  C. Caring for the Temple of God (3:16-17)
IV. Appraising with Godly Wisdom (3:18–4:5)
  A. Rightly Discerning One's Self (3:18-23)
  B. Rightly Regarding Christ's Servants (4:1-5)
VI. Applying God's Wisdom to the Church (4:6-21)
  A. An Argument against Boasting (4:6-7)
  B. Apostles as Spectacles and Refuse (4:8-13)
  C. Admonishment from a Father (4:14-21)

Disciplining Immorality (5:1–6:20)

I. Disciplining an Incredible Case of Immorality (5:1-13)

- A. Removing the Guilty Party (5:1-5)
- B. Removing Impurity within the Church (5:6-8)
- C. Clarifying Earlier Instruction (5:9-13)

II. Exercising Judgment within the Church (6:1-11)
- A. Disciplining Fellow Church Members (6:1-8)
- B. Excluding the Unrighteous from God's Kingdom (6:9-11)

III. Keeping Immorality out of Christ's Body (6:12-20)
- A. Misunderstanding Liberty in Christ (6:12-14)
- B. Realizing the Significance of the Body (6:15-20)

Marriage and Sexual Relationships (7:1-40)

I. Counsel Regarding Sexual Relations and Divorce (7:1-24)
- A. Sexual Relations Should Be Maintained in Marriage (7:1-9)
  - 1. Regarding Married Persons (7:1-7)
  - 2. Regarding Unmarried Persons (7:8-9)
- B. Persons Should Remain Married, If Possible (7:10-16)
  - 1. Regarding Marriage with a Believer (7:10-11)
  - 2. Regarding Marriage with an Unbeliever (7:12-16)
- C. One Should Remain in One's State When Called (7:17-24)
  - 1. Regarding Circumcision (7:17-19)
  - 2. Regarding Slavery (7:20-24)

II. Counsel Regarding Marriage for Unmarried Persons (7:25-40)
- A. The Unmarried May Marry, or Not! (7:25-38)
  - 1. A Preference for the Unmarried Life (7:25-28)
  - 2. The Case for the Unmarried Life (7:29-35)
    - a. The Passing of This World (7:29-31)
    - b. Freedom from Anxiety (7:32-35)
  - 3. The Concession for Marriage (7:36-38)
- B. Widows May Marry, or Not! (7:39-40)

Eating Food Offered to Idols (8:1–11:1)

I. The Problem of Eating Food Associated with Idols (8:1-13)
- A. Introduction to the Problem (8:1-6)
- B. The Danger of Hurting a Person of Weak Conscience (8:7-13)

II. The Example of Paul as a Guide to Solving the Problem (9:1-27)
- A. Paul's Relinquishing of His Right as an Apostle (9:1-18)
- B. Paul's Subservience Designed to Win Others (9:19-27)

III. The Theological Danger of Eating Food Offered to Idols (10:1–11:1)
- A. Israel's Example as a Warning to the Corinthians (10:1-13)
- B. The Lord's Supper as Sign of Exclusive Devotion to God (10:14-22)
- C. Eating or Drinking without Offense (10:23–11:1)

Spiritual Gifts (12:1–14:40)

I. The Gifts of the Spirit (12:1–13:13)
  A. The Same Spirit Gives All Gifts (12:1-12)
  B. The Church Is the Body of Christ (12:12-31)
  C. The Way of Love Is the Best Way (13:1-13)
II. The Gifts of Prophecy and Tongues (14:1-40)
  A. Prophecy Edifies More than Tongues (14:1-25)
  B. Order Should Prevail in the Church (14:26-40)

The Resurrection of the Body (15:1-34)

I. An Argument for the Resurrection of the Dead (15:1-34)
  A. The Gospel of First Importance (15:1-11)
    1. Tradition as Witness to the Resurrection (15:1-7)
    2. Paul as Witness to the Resurrection (15:8-11)
  B. The Consequences of Denying the Gospel (15:12-19)
    1. Preaching and Faith Are in Vain (15:12-16)
    2. Sin Remains and the Dead Perish (15:17-19)
  C. The Confirmation of the Resurrection of the Dead (15:20-34)
    1. Resurrection and God's Sovereignty (15:20-28)
    2. Resurrection and Faithful Living (15:29-34)
II. An Explanation of the Resurrection of the Body (15:35-58)
  A. The Glory of the Resurrected Body (15:35-49)
    1. Different Kinds of Bodies (15:35-41)
2. The Body of Spirit (15:42-49)
  B. The Mystery of Transformation (15:50-58)
    1. The Final Victory (15:50-57)
    2. The Present Work of the Lord (15:58)

Final Matters (16:1-24)

I. Preparations for the Collection (16:1-4)
II. Travel Plans for Paul and Associates (16:5-12)
  A. Paul (16:5-8)
  B. Timothy (16:9-11)
  C. Apollos (16:12)
III. Final Instructions for the Corinthians (16:13-18)
  A. Exhortations (16:13-14)
  B. Commendations (16:15-18)
IV. The Closing of the Letter (16:19-24)
  A. Greetings (16:19-20)
  B. Autograph (16:21-24)

STRAINING UPON THE START

1 Corinthians 1:1-9

I see you stand like greyhounds in the slips,
Straining upon the start. The game's afoot:
Follow your spirit . . . .[1]

In 1 Corinthians 1:1-9, "The game's afoot," to borrow a line from Shakespeare's *King Henry V*, and Paul appears to be "straining upon the start." Even as the letter opens, Paul's agenda for writing begins to emerge. This small segment comprises a telling introduction to the first major section of the letter (1:10–4:21) and to the letter as a whole. While these opening verses may not constitute an exact outline of the rest of the letter, they do introduce us to several of the major issues that Paul will discuss in a more substantive way elsewhere.[2] Reread in light of the rest of the letter, these verses subtly suggest elements of the argument that unfolds. [Outline of 1 Corinthians 1:1-9]

Outline of 1 Corinthians 1:1-9

I. The Opening (vv. 1-3)
- A. The Senders: Paul and Sosthenes (v. 1)
- B. The Recipients: The Church of God in Corinth (v. 2)
- C. The Greeting (v. 3)

II. The Thanksgiving (vv. 4-9)
- A. The Present Reality of God's Grace-gifts (vv. 4-6)
- B. The Future Realization of Grace's Purpose (vv. 7-9)

COMMENTARY

The Letter Opening, 1:1-3

First Corinthians has all of the standard components of an ancient Greek letter, including a letter opening containing (1) the identification of the sender, (2) the identification of the recipients, and (3) the greeting. As is true of most of Paul's letters, these opening elements are designed to make important preliminary assertions that support the author's argument in the body of the letter. (See [The Pauline Letter Form] in the Introduction.)

(1) The Identification of the Sender, 1:1

In the opening of the letter, Paul identifies himself as "an apostle of Christ Jesus." Among the letters of the Pauline corpus, only

Rembrandt's Paul

Rembrandt. *The Apostle Paul*. c. 1657. Oil on canvas. The National Gallery of Art, Washington D.C.

Rembrandt has depicted Paul as somber and contemplative, with a hint of strain in his face, taking pen in hand to write one of his letters. Considering the host of problems Paul had to address in 1 Corinthians, one might suspect that Rembrandt had this epistle in mind.

Philippians, Philemon, and the two letters to the Thessalonians make no mention of Paul's identity as an apostle in the letter opening. Of the other nine letters attributed to Paul, all except Titus connect Paul's identity as an apostle with the will and/or calling of God. Here Paul is a "called apostle of Christ Jesus *through* the will of God." The wording of this opening to the letter appears to be carefully chosen to establish Paul's authority to address the matters that prompted him to write.

Probably during or shortly before his first stay in Corinth (c. AD 50–51), Paul had written Galatians, a letter in which Paul's defense of his divinely appointed apostleship undergirded his defense of his apostolic message among the churches in Galatia. In the letter called 2 Corinthians, part of which (chs. 10–13) may have been Paul's third letter to the Corinthian church, Paul had to defend his identity as an authoritative apostle against those in Corinth who had challenged him.[3] (See [Letters to Corinth] in the Introduction.) First Corinthians stands between these two episodes where Paul's right to exercise apostolic authority was challenged. With the trauma of the Galatians incident still fresh for Paul and the initial rumblings of doubt about Paul's authority already present in Corinth—rumblings that would later erupt with the appearance in Corinth of preachers claiming a superior apostolic authority—Paul moves quickly and clearly here in the opening of 1 Corinthians to assert his status as a "God-called apostle." His self-identification here, then, is at least partly rooted in his own tenuous relationship with the Corinthian church.

Launching this letter with the self-designation of being a "called apostle," however, is also connected to the Corinthians' own situation. The Corinthians also have been "called," as Paul repeatedly reminds them (1:2, 9, 24, 26; 7:15, 17, 18, 20, 21, 22, 24). [Call and Calling in 1 Corinthians] Paul asserts later (15:9) that he is not "worthy to be called *as* an apostle," but nonetheless, by the grace of God (15:10), he is a "called apostle." His calling is "*through* the will of God" (1:1), and so is theirs. Paul's identity and their identity have a theocentric basis, not an anthropocentric one. Reorienting the

Call and Calling in 1 Corinthians

ΑΩ First Corinthians abounds in the language of "calling." Paul used both the active (7:15; 7:17) and passive (1:9; 7:18 [twice], 20, 21, 22 [twice], 24; 10:27; 15:9) forms of the Greek verb meaning "to call" (*kaleō*) a total of twelve times. While the verb *kaleō* could be used in the sense of "to call something something," that is "to name it" (as in Matt 1:25, "and he *called* his name Jesus"), Paul seems not to have used the verb this way. Instead, he used *kaleō* to refer to an *act* of "invitation" or "summons." In all but one case (10:27), the invitation or summons comes from God. He preferred to use forms of *legō* (8:5) and *onamazō* (5:11) to refer to what one is called. This conforms to Paul's usage of *kaleō* in all the undisputed letters. Granted, Rom 9:25 and 9:26 appear to use *kaleō* in the sense of "naming," but both instances represent quotations from Hosea. Furthermore, both instances pertain to God's "naming" of a "called" people, so they do not differ in sense from the basic way in which Paul used the term to refer to God's act of summoning someone. 1 Cor 15:9 seems to break the pattern ("I am not worthy *to be called* an apostle"), but the clause would be better rendered "I am not worthy *to be called* as an apostle," thereby keeping with Paul's emphasis on God's *act* of summoning rather than on *what* one is called.

In addition to the verb pair, Paul also used the related adjective *klētos* (1:1; 1:2; 1:24) and the noun *klēsis* (1:26; 7:20) to refer respectively to those who had been "summoned" by God and to the "summons" itself. This also fits the pattern of Paul's usage of these terms in other letters. Paul's use of the *kaleō* family of terms indicates that "being called" lies in the initiative of God and places the one(s) "called" in a state intended by God.

Corinthian mindset from anthropocentric to theocentric is fundamental to Paul's strategy in this letter.

Functioning somewhat as coauthor of the letter, but obviously in a subordinate sense, is Sosthenes, who is simply named and identified as "the brother." Mentioning his name is probably more than a token formality, but the reason for including Sosthenes is unclear.[4] Most likely, Sosthenes was known to the Corinthians, and the inclusion of his name would contribute to the positive reception

The *Bēma*

(Credit: Jim Pitts)

Acts 18:12 states, "And while Gallio was proconsul of Achaia, the Jews together set upon Paul and brought him before the tribunal (*bēma*)." The Acts account goes on to describe how Gallio refused to judge the matter since he determined it concerned Jewish law rather than Roman law, as Paul's accusers had asserted. Then a group, which is not clearly identified (Jews or Romans?) seized the leader of the synagogue (*archisynagōgos*), Sosthenes, and beat him in front of the *bēma*. Since the text seems to indicate that the *bēma* was a place and not the tribunal court, then the reference is most likely to a public rostrum whose location has been identified as the central structure in a row of buildings running east-west that divided Corinth's long forum into lower (northern) and upper (southern) parts (Wiseman, 516). Such a structure would have served as a speaker's platform, allowing the magistrates and other officials to address the audience standing in the lower forum to the north. If so, then the episode in Acts refers not to a formal trial, as tradition often holds, but to the attempt of Paul's critics to gain a hearing with the proconsul while Gallio was making a public appearance in the forum. (See "The Gallio Inscription" in the Introduction.) That later Christians associated the site with Paul is evidenced by the small Byzantine church built upon the base of the *bēma*.

James Wiseman, "Corinth and Rome I: 228 B.C.–A.D. 267," (ANRW 7/1; Berlin: de Gruyter).

Paul intended for this letter. Acts 18:17 mentions a Sosthenes in connection with Paul's brief appearance before the Roman proconsul at the *bēma* (public rostrum) in Corinth's forum. That Sosthenes, identified as "the *archisynagōgos* (ruler or president) of the synagogue," was beaten after Gallio's refusal to give judgment regarding the charges brought against Paul. According to Acts 18:8, another *archisynagōgos* in Corinth, Crispus, had become a believer under Paul's preaching, and in 1 Corinthians 1:14 Paul states that he had baptized a Corinthian named Crispus. Identifying the once-beaten Sosthenes of Acts with the brother Sosthenes of the letter is intriguing (though unprovable), but it still does not explain why he is honored by Paul as coauthor of 1 Corinthians. Paul's inclusion of greetings from Aquila and Prisca near the end of this letter (16:19) indicates that some degree of cordial relationship existed between Jewish and Gentile Christians in Corinth. The substance of the letter, however, does not suggest that Paul needed to shore up support among the Jewish Christians in Corinth by naming one of their own influential members as coauthor. Whether Sosthenes was the same former *synagōgos* mentioned in Acts or not, and even if this Sosthenes was not Jewish, he was someone the Corinthians would have known and was probably prominent.

Synagogue Inscription

Archaeological Museum of Ancient Corinth (Credit: Jim Pitts)

Early in the American excavations in Ancient Corinth (1898), near the propylaeon that was the main entrance into the forum from the road leading from the port of Lechaion to the north, excavators found an inscription in crude Greek letters reading [SYN]AGŌGĒ EBR[AIŌN]. The inscription appears on a broken block of marble entablature of the Ionic order that had apparently been reworked to serve as a door lintel to a synagogue. Benjamin Powell (1903) soon identified the inscription as the one adorning the synagogue in which Paul preached and suggested that the ancient building stood near where the piece was found, a view echoed by many tour guides and some scholars (see Murphy-O'Connor, *St. Paul's Corinth*, 81). Later epigraphical analysis of the style of the inscription by John Harvey Kent (1966) indicated that it dated much later, probably the 4th century. The marble block was not found *in situ*, no other evidence of a synagogue in that location exists, it is highly unlikely that such a structure would have stood so close to the city center, and the broken block had apparently been used for the fill in the foundation of a later construction. Thus, the much-heralded inscription is of no archaeological value in locating a synagogue building that may have stood in Paul's day. It does, however, indicate the continuation of a Jewish presence in Corinth, albeit seemingly not affluent, for centuries after Paul.

Benjamin Powell, "Greek Inscriptions from Corinth," *AJA* 7 (1903): 60–61.

John Harvey Kent, *Corinth 8/3: The Inscriptions 1926–1950* (Princeton: American School of Classical Studies at Athens, 1966) 79.

Richard E. Oster Jr., "Use, Misuse and Neglect of Archaeological Evidence in Some Modern Works on 1 Corinthians (1 Cor 7,1-5; 8, 10; 11,2-16; 12,14-26)" *ZNW* 83 (1992): 55–58.

The fact that Paul identifies him simply as "the brother" undergirds the strategy Paul employs in 1 Corinthians of downplaying one's social status, at least in terms of those standards that typically held in Roman Corinthian society. [Pelagius on Sosthenes] Paul acknowledged certain positions of respect within the church, and "brother" appears to be one of the fictive familial terms he sometimes used for some persons entrusted with special tasks (cf. 1 Cor 16:13; 2 Cor 1:1; 2:13; 8:18, 22; 12:18).[5] Note, however, that Paul never used the term "brother" in reference to himself in his letters; he preferred to label himself as "father" (1 Cor 4:15; 1 Thess 2:11). Nevertheless, the fact that Paul regularly used "brother" to refer to a nonspecific church member and his frequent usage of the plural "brothers" (presumably also including the "sisters") in addressing a church as a whole indicate that his use of the term in regard to Sosthenes (as well as with Apollos in 16:13) aims to undergird his emphasis on the basic equality of all in the family, even those exercising leadership. For Paul, one's true status does not depend on the titles by which one is called by others (anthropocentric); one's true status is determined by God's gracious calling (theocentric).

Pelagius on Sosthenes

"By calling Sosthenes his brother, Paul is both demonstrating his own humility and pointing out that Sosthenes is a fellow worker in the gospel."

Pelagius, *Commentary on the First Epistle to the Corinthians*, in Gerald Bray, ed., *1–2 Corinthians* (vol. 7 of ACCS NT; ed. Thomas C. Oden; Downers Grove IL: InterVarsity Press, 1999) 4.

(2) The Identification of the Recipients, 1:2

Paul addresses his letter to "the assembly (*ekklēsia*; generally translated 'church') of God which is in Corinth." Among the undisputed letters of Paul, five identify the recipients in some sense as "church." [*Ekklēsia*] The other two letters, Romans and Philippians, refer to the recipients simply as "saints." Galatians names the "churches" of Galatia as recipients. First Thessalonians (as well as

Ekklēsia

AΩ The term *ekklēsia* had been used by Greek-speaking people, at least since the Classical period, to refer to the assembly of the *dēmos* (the free citizens) of a *polis* (city-state). While certain obligatory religious rituals apparently accompanied their "assembling," the term basically referred to the citizenry gathered for the purpose of conducting political business. Only rarely was the word used to describe a group gathered for specifically religious purposes. When the Hebrew Scriptures were translated into Greek (primarily the Greek version known as the Septuagint, or LXX), the term *ekklēsia* was used to render the Hebrew term for assembly, *qahal*. The whole of the people of Israel gathered together could be referred to as the *ekklēsia kyriou* ("assembly of the Lord"; Heb. *qahal elohim*; cf. Deut 23:2; 1 Chr 28:8; Neh 13:1; Mic 2:5). The use of the term in the LXX for the assembling of God's people, rather than the general Greek usage of the term to describe a political assembly, provides the context for Paul's use of *ekklēsia* in reference to the "church." The church is a people summoned together by God, and as such the church stands in that long line of those "convened" by God witnessed to in the Old Testament. While the term may be derived etymologically from the prefix ex (out of) and the verb *kaleō* (call), this basic sense is superseded by the derivative meaning of a special group "called together." The early church preferred this term in reference to itself over the term *synagōgē*, which was typically used by Jews for their congregations, although the church could also be referred to as *synagōgē* (cf. Jas 2:2; 5:14). One cannot overlook the probability, however, that in a non-Jewish, Greek-speaking context, such as Corinth, connotations of the more Classical political sense of *ekklēsia* would have been attached to any group bearing that name both by those outside and inside the group.

Karl Ludwig Schmidt, "*Ekklēsia*," *TDNT* 3:501–36.

Achaia

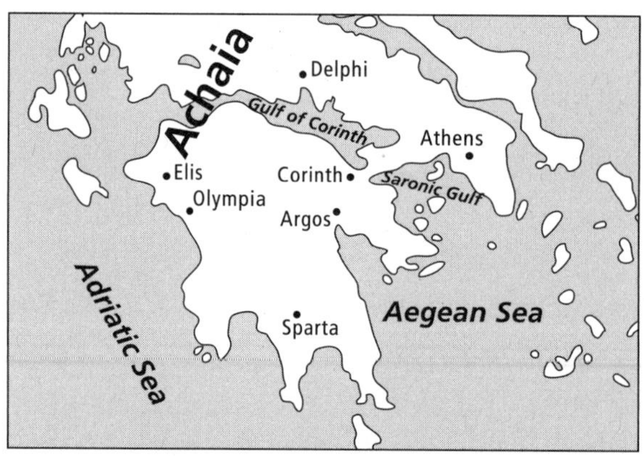

Achaia, an ancient term sometimes used to refer to all of Greece, was the name given by the Romans to the province they forged in 27 BC that included roughly the southern third of the mainland area that constituted the Greece of antiquity. The city of Corinth, which had been largely destroyed by the Romans in 146 BC in retaliation for Corinth's leadership in the revolt of the Achaean League, had been reconstituted as a Roman colony by decree of Julius Caesar around 44 BC. (See the section titled "Corinth: A Tale of Two Cities" in the introduction.) Exactly when, or even if, Corinth became the official capital of the new province of Achaia is unclear, but the city clearly became the dominant city in southern Greece. Paul's extension of the address in 2 Corinthians to include "the whole of Achaia" indicates the prominence and centrality of Corinth for the entire region, though the only 1st-century evidence for Christian communities in the province of Achaia beyond Corinth itself pertains to Cenchreae (the eastern port of Corinth) and Athens. Because Paul refers to the household of Stephanas as the "first converts in Achaia" (1 Cor 16:15), while 1 Thess 3:1 places Paul in Athens apparently prior to his first visit to Corinth and Acts 17:34 indicates that he had some converts there, it is unclear whether Paul's references to Achaia in 1 Cor 16:15 and in 2 Cor 1:1 and 9:2 should be taken in the provincial sense, as is apparently the case in 1 Thess 1:7-8, or only as pertaining to the region around Corinth (including Cenchreae). If in the provincial sense, then either Paul's recollection about early conversions was foggy (which he seems to acknowledge in 1 Cor 1:14-16) or a slight discrepancy exists between 1 Cor 16:15 and Acts 17:34. If the regional sense holds for 1 Cor 16:15 (and possibly 2 Cor 1:1 and 9:2), then Paul seems to have used the term Achaia differently at different times.

2 Thessalonians) identifies the recipients as "the church of the Thessalonians." Even Philemon, which names Philemon, Apphia, and Archippus as individual recipients, also includes the address "to the church in your house." Only in 1 and 2 Corinthians does Paul identify the recipients as *the church* in a particular city. (Note, however, that in Rom 16:1 Paul refers to the church *in* Cenchreae.) The address in 2 Corinthians also includes "all the saints in the whole of Achaia."

The singularity of the addressees as "the church which is in Corinth" is perhaps significant. By identifying his recipients as *the church* (singular) *in Corinth* (singular), and not as "the church *of the Corinthians*" (cf. 1 Thess 1:1, and 2 Thess 1:1) or as *the churches* in Achaia (cf. Gal 1:2), Paul may already be moving toward resolving two issues he must confront in the body of the letter: (1) *the church* is divided, and (2) the divisions are rooted in life *in Corinth.* Furthermore, he identifies them as "the church *of God* in Corinth" (also in 2 Corinthians, but not in Galatians; 1 Thessalonians has "the church *in* God the Father and the Lord Jesus Christ"). The genitive form "of God" indicates possession here. The church, as a whole, belongs to God, not to those powerful persons within the church who would exercise an inappropriate proprietary influence based on their external social status or internal display of "wisdom" or "spiritual" gifts.

This singularity of identity as the church of God moves toward a double plurality in the extension of the address. The Corinthians are both (1) collectively "sanctified in Christ Jesus" and "called to be saints" and (2) numbered with "all those calling on the name of our Lord Jesus Christ in every place." Thiselton has noted the significance of this transition to the plural here: "The singular stresses the solidarity of the readers as one united corporate entity; the plural calls attention to the individual responsibility of each member to live out his or her consecrated status in Christ."[6] The terms translated "sanctified" and "saints," the first a perfect passive participle (*hagiasmenois*) and the second an adjective used substantivally (*hagiois*), share the same root, which generally conveys the sense of something "set apart" or "dedicated" for a sacred purpose. [Holy] The perfect tense of "sanctified" signals a present reality stemming from a past action, while the passive voice carries a reminder that the performer of this action was God, not the Corinthians. The phrase *en Christō* could be taken instrumentally as "through Christ," signifying the means of God's work, but most translations take it as a dative of sphere/place, hence "in Christ." The phrase "called [to be] saints" suggests that the full realization of God's action on their behalf lies before them, summoning them onward. They do not pursue their calling in isolation; rather, they are joined "with all those who call upon the name of our Lord Jesus Christ in every place." The object of the possessive pronouns at the end of v. 3 (theirs and ours) has been disputed. While several ancient commentators understood it to refer to "place" and, thus, saw it as a counter to the geographical separateness of local congregations, most modern versions take it to refer to "our Lord Jesus Christ" and, thus, as a counter to possible Corinthian assumptions that they held a special relationship with Christ.[7]

Holy

AΩ Bible translators typically use the English word "holy" to translate the Hebrew (*qodesh*) and Greek (*hagios*), terms that mean something "set apart" or "dedicated" for a sacred purpose and, hence, "different" from what is common, profane, or ordinary. Both in regard to Israel in the Old Testament and the church in the New, the idea is clearly present that the people of God are to be different. They are called to a high purpose that obligates them to a higher standard. The English word "holy," however, roots in the German word *heil*, which refers to something that is unbroken, healthy, or complete. The word "whole" comes from the same root. "Holiness," as it is often used, seems to carry the sense of "wholeness" conveyed by *heil*, and thus is inferred to mean "complete" or even "pure." While Paul acknowledged that the Corinthians were "complete" in their speech, knowledge, and spiritual gifts (1 Cor 1:5-7), he also observed that they were not "different" enough from those around them. Thus, his use of *hagios* ("set apart," "different") in reference to the Corinthians appears optimistically and strategically generous.

(3) The Greeting, 1:3

Most of Paul's letters contain the greeting, "Grace to you and peace from God our/the Father and the Lord Jesus Christ." In the whole body of letters attributed to Paul, Colossians and 1 Thessalonians omit the reference to "our Lord Jesus Christ," and 1 and 2 Timothy uncharacteristically add "mercy" to "grace and peace." In typical Greek letters, the greeting consisted of a single word, *charein* (greetings) (cf. Jas 1:1). Paul seems deliberately to have altered the stock, perfunctory greeting with a theologically significant play on words by using *charis* (grace) instead of *charein.* To this he has added, in Greek, the standard Jewish greeting, *shalom* (Gk. *eirēnē*). Paul may have developed his customary greeting in the context of conflict over his status as an apostle in order to make two important statements. (Note the undeveloped form in 1 Thessalonians, which predates serious challenges to his apostolic authority.) First, the assertion that grace and peace come from God the Father (and the Lord Jesus Christ) places the discourse that follows in a theocentric (and christocentric) context. Second, as the one announcing the grace and peace that come from God, Paul asserts his role as God's agent (apostle). The influence of Paul's epistolary pattern on later Christian letters is evident in the form of greeting contained in all other true letters in the New Testament. (Note the exception of the somewhat anti-Pauline and nonepistolary "letter" of James.)

The Prayer of Thanksgiving, 1:4-9

Paul's revisionist use of the standard epistolary form is clearly evident in his prayer of thanksgiving that stands between the greeting and the body of the letter. Most letters written in Greek in antiquity simply moved from the letter opening to the body. Some letters, especially those written to members of one's family, might also include a brief prayer for the health of the recipient or a short prayer of thanksgiving for safe travel or good fortune. Among the letters attributed to Paul, however, most include a prayer of thanksgiving or blessing that constitutes a significant transition from the opening to the body. [Paul's Epistolary Prayers]

Paul's Epistolary Prayers

Eight of the letters attributed to Paul (Rom, 1 Cor, Phil, Col, 1 Thess, 2 Thess, 2 Tim, and Phlm) express thanksgiving. Four, including 1 Corinthians, have the formula *eucharistō* = "I give thanks"; two have the plural *eucharistoumen*; and two use different phrases to express thanksgiving. Two other letters (2 Cor and Eph) have prayers of blessing (using *eulogētos* = "Blessed be"). While most commentators think Paul omitted the prayer entirely in Galatians, Gal 1:4-5 actually contains a truncated prayer attached to the greeting. Only 1 Timothy contains no prayer at all between the opening and the letter body.

As has often been noted, Paul's thanksgiving prayers did more than merely fill a niche in the prescribed letter format. [Studies of Paul's Prayers] They subtly introduced themes that Paul would address in the body of the letter. In this regard, they functioned *rhetorically.* Ancient rhetoric was a developed art of persuading one's audience (either through speech or writing) to believe, feel, or behave in certain ways. Paul exhibited skillful use of rhetorical conventions in his letters. (Whether he acquired such skills through formal education is debated.) Clearly in 1 Corinthians, Paul was trying to persuade his audience to refrain from certain behaviors and cultivate other behaviors and attitudes.

His thanksgiving in this letter appears oriented toward fulfilling the rhetorical objective of securing the good will of his readers in regard to the issues he must confront more sharply in the extended body of the letter. In ancient rhetoric, this was the purpose of the exordium. (See the section titled "1 Corinthians as Rhetoric" in the Introduction.)

Studies of Paul's Prayers

The importance of Paul's thanksgivings/prayers in his letters was made evident foremost in Paul Schubert's *Form and Function of the Pauline Thanksgiving* (BZNW 20; Berlin: Alfred Töpelmann, 1939). The most complete recent treatment of Pauline thanksgivings is that of Peter T. O'Brien, *Introductory Thanksgivings in the Letters of Paul* (NovTSup 49; Leiden: Brill, 1977). Significant discussions of the form of Greek letters in general and Paul's thanksgivings in particular may also be found in William G. Doty, *Letters in Primitive Christianity* (GBS; Philadelphia: Fortress, 1973); Jerome Murphy-O'Connor, *Paul the Letter Writer: His World, His Options, His Skills* (GNS 41; Collegeville MN: The Liturgical Press, 1995); Stanley K. Stowers, *Letter Writing in Greco-Roman Antiquity* (LEC; Philadelphia: Westminster, 1986); and John L. White, *Light from Ancient Letters* (FF; Philadelphia: Fortress, 1986). The most thorough recent analysis of Greek letter forms and the particular elements of New Testament letters is Hans-Josef Klauck's *Ancient Letters and the New Testament: A Guide to Context and Exegesis* (Waco TX: Baylor University Press, 2006).

Paul's thanksgiving exordium here seeks to establish a favorable hearing for himself as an authoritative teacher through a two-pronged focus. The first is a carefully worded celebration of a present reality (vv. 4-6): God's gift of grace in Christ Jesus resulting in an abundance of grace-gifts (*charismata*) for the Corinthian believers, especially speech (*logos*) and knowledge (*gnōsis*). The second is a pointing toward the future (vv. 7-9), wherein the gifts bestowed might realize their intended purpose. Syntactically, all of vv. 4-8 comprise one sentence in Greek, but thematically v. 7 marks a transition from the "already" to the "not yet."

The thanksgiving makes several points that Paul develops later. First, Paul expresses his abiding concern for and pride in his Corinthian converts. They are in his prayers "always," and he is grateful that God has "graced" them in Christ (v. 4). Furthermore, he acknowledges that God's giving to them has been rich (v. 5); they are not lacking in grace-gifts (v. 7). He especially notes their richness in all speech and knowledge. As becomes clear later in the letter, eloquence in speech and privileged knowledge are two matters that Paul must confront. Later, he challenges their understanding and valuation of these gifts, but here Paul affirms their presence among his readers.

Second, Paul immediately places these signs of grace within a theocentric, even christocentric, context. They are *gifts of God.* God is the benefactor, not someone else. Pride in possessing signs of grace is undermined by the reminder that they are gifts, not accomplishments. Furthermore, the grace of God has been given *in Christ.* Paul refers to Christ no fewer than six times in his thanksgiving (vv. 4, 5, 6, 7, 8, 9; perhaps twice in v. 8). These references highlight Paul's concern that his readers recognize the "Christ-like" nature of their existence and experience. They exist in Christ, and they experience God's grace *in Christ.* God's grace has not been bestowed on individual believers in isolation; they experience it through incorporation into the one through whom God has acted gracefully. The fact of their existence as church is confirmation of the effectiveness of the *witness* (*martyrion*) of Christ (v. 6). What Paul had, in fact, "witnessed" to the Corinthians through his preaching was the message of the cross of Christ (1:17–2:5). To the extent that the message of the cross both created them by calling them into the "communion" of Christ (v. 9) and shaped their existence, that witness was confirmed.

Third, while the Corinthian believers do not "lack" or "fall short" in the grace gifts lavished on the church, all is not complete. The "not lacking" is joined to the "not yet." They hold these gifts while waiting for the revealing (*apokalypsis*) of the Lord Christ (v. 7). This "revealing" is joined to the "end" and the "day of our Lord Jesus Christ" in v. 8. An association with eschatological judgment is apparent in Paul's assurance that his readers will be confirmed as "blameless" on that day (whether by God or by Christ is unclear). [Confirmation] This confident word seems somewhat odd in light of the numerous problems Paul seeks to correct in the rest of the letter. Perhaps, in order to secure a fair hearing from his audience, Paul engages here in heightened compliment. Perhaps, though, he proleptically announces what he hopes his letter will accomplish: the correction of the Corinthian church so that it will truly realize its calling *into* (*eis*) the communion (*koinōnia*) of Christ.[8]

Fourth, the corporate nature of their existence *in Christ* is stressed, as in the address in v. 2b, by repeated use of plural pronouns (esp. *hymas* = "you all" and *hēmōn* = "our"). As a corporate body they have been graced by a God who has lavished grace-gifts upon them, so that they are not lacking as they wait corporately for the revealing of the one who is not only *their* Lord

Confirmation

ΑΩ The NRSV renders *bebaiōsei hymas* in v. 8 as "will strengthen you," while NIV has "will keep you strong." NAB and Thiselton have "will keep you firm." Most other English versions render it "will confirm you" in consistency with the rendering of *ebebaiōthē* in v. 6. Schlier argued that the legal sense of "declare valid" or "validly declare" generally lurks behind the use of this word in the NT. Conzelmann thought this view too narrow. One issue here is whether or not that which is "declared" valid actually has been "proven to be genuine." Webster's *New World College Dictionary* (4th ed.), 306, distinguishes between (1) *confirm*, the establishing as true what was doubtful or uncertain; (2) *validate*, the official confirmation of the validity of something; and (3) *verify*, the proving of something as true or correct after investigation. Thiselton states that the "blamelessness" of Paul's readers stems from God's *verdictive* action (i.e., "God *pronounces a verdict*; issues of the human moral condition remain secondary."), which more nearly aligns with Webster's "validate." Still, Thiselton prefers to render *bebaiōsei* in a nonverdictive sense ("keep firm"). Since the response of the Corinthian church would determine whether or not Paul's confidence in the final outcome was justified, "confirmation" appears to be the best translation. His trust that their blamelessness would be "verified" and "validated" by God awaited "confirmation."

Hans Conzelmann, *1 Corinthians* (Hermeneia; trans. James W. Leitch; Philadelphia: Fortress Press, 1975) 27.

Heinrich Schlier, "βέβαιος," *TDNT* 1: 600–603.

Anthony C. Thiselton, *The First Epistle to the Corinthians: A Commentary on the Greek Text* (NIGTC; Grand Rapids: Eerdmans, 2000) 101–102.

but also *our* Lord. Through *our Lord* the Corinthians believers have been called into the communion of *our Lord*, a communion that transcends individual possession or participation and the local collective body of believers in Corinth. Realizing the full nature of this communion in our Lord Jesus Christ constituted the fundamental challenge faced by the Corinthian church and the foremost challenge of Paul as he "strained upon the start" in penning the letter we know as 1 Corinthians.

CONNECTIONS

Sweetening the Ears

One ancient commentator on 1 Corinthians, Theodoret of Cyrrhus (AD 393–466), observed of Paul's opening lines in this letter, "Paul takes care to sweeten their ears before starting to admonish them."[9] Another commentator, John Chrysostom, suggested that Paul inserted words of praise for the Corinthians here at the start in order to prepare them for the strong criticism that would follow. Chrysostom noted, "Whoever starts out with unpleasant words antagonizes his hearers."[10] To begin with sweet words of praise was a stock convention of ancient rhetoric, and several modern scholars have argued that Paul was consciously following rhetorical convention in these opening verses.[11] Speakers and writers felt compelled by convention and the needs of the occasion to create an atmosphere of good will between themselves and their audience. To motivate the hearers/readers to feel good about the speaker/writer, the latter was obliged first to lead the former to feel good about themselves. Even in antiquity, some writers, such as Petronius, criticized speakers for thinking "first about what is calculated to please their audience."[12]

For Paul to have adopted such tactics makes him appear on one level as duplicitous and contradictory. Clearly in several places in 1 Corinthians 1–2 he downplayed the value of "eloquent wisdom" (1:17) and "lofty words or wisdom" (2:1). In fact, in several of his letters he went to great lengths to point out that he had not preached the same ways that teachers were expected to do. Yet, here at the start of his letter, and indeed throughout, he seems to have employed the very rhetorical devices he criticized. Was Paul guilty of playing "spin doctor" and using his language to accomplish exactly what he claimed not to be doing?

Perhaps! For a modern audience accustomed to the tactics of politicians and public relations experts who manipulate language to ensure that their "speaking points" are always heard and who deride the competition for doing the same, such maneuvering comes as no surprise. It does come, however, with a price, namely the loss of integrity in discourse in the public forum. From advertisements that deliberately distort to official public releases that present half-truths, modern society is bombarded with language designed to deceive, so much so that it has come to be accepted as the norm. ["Swift Boat" Controversy] Justifying the practices of dishonest language by contending that the rules of the game have already been established and players must simply follow suit if they are to survive does nothing to rehabilitate the integrity of the process. Nor does it redeem Paul simply to say that he had to adopt the established methods of discourse in order to be taken seriously by his audience, especially if those methods embodied the very values he sought to criticize.

"Swift Boat" Controversy

The 2004 presidential election in the United States witnessed what many political commentators considered a new "low" in electoral politics. A conservative veterans' group (Swift Boat Veterans for Truth) sponsored television, Internet, and print ads targeting Democratic candidate John Kerry, who had received several medals for his service in Viet Nam aboard a swift boat. The ads and the book *Unfit for Command* claimed that Kerry was undeserving of his military honors. Numerous men who served with Kerry on the swift boat in question substantiated Kerry's version of his record and criticized the veterans' group that maligned him. Even the Republican candidate, George W. Bush, called for the ads to stop.

On another level, however, Paul's praising of the Corinthians may be seen in a more positive light. Paul may have used the rhetorical device of praise here with integrity, if, as Thiselton has argued, it expressed "his own and sincere convictions."[13] In an insightful analysis of the rhetorical situation of 1 Corinthians, Stephen Pogoloff has argued that Paul rejected the cultural values that Greco-Roman society had wedded to rhetoric but not rhetoric itself.[14] As will become clear later in the letter, I think, Paul deliberately employed the rhetorical strategy of "status reversal" in regards to himself. That is, he stressed that his message had not been couched in eloquent words of wisdom but rather in the foolishness of the cross. By that he did not mean that he had muttered and stumbled his way along in preaching, but rather that he had as his agenda the very saving of his listeners' lives instead of the winning of their praise, the latter being exactly what most ancient speakers strived to achieve. In praising his Corinthian readers in regard to their speech, knowledge, and grace-gifts, Paul was subtly and subversively placing them among the ranks of those who valued such attributes precisely for their status-enhancing qualities. Yet, even in acknowledging those qualities they cherished, he embedded his praise for them in the language of a thanksgiving prayer to God, thereby reminding them that they were gifts of grace and not marks of achievement.

On still another level, Paul's use of seemingly self-serving flattery may be viewed positively if one notes the eschatological tone in which it is cast. His readers had been given what they needed to be found blameless in the end, and Paul expressed confidence that such would, indeed, ultimately prove to be true. That confidence, strained to be sure, undergirds the scathing criticisms that follow. As a parent confronting children whose behavior has proved disappointing, Paul offered correction in the persistent trust that those who had been born into life by the grace of God and nurtured with love would ultimately realize their God-given potential and become the persons he knew them to be. In doing so, he was embodying the character of persistent and hopeful love one finds repeatedly in the biblical portrayal of God. Modern messengers of that same hopeful love would do well to mimic the apostle in affirming the often yet-unrealized potential of their audience.

The Devil's Weapons

In his *Homilies on the Epistles of Paul to the Corinthians*, delivered while he was a presbyter in the church in Antioch (AD 386–398), John Chrysostom attributed the divisions in the church at Corinth to the devil. [Chrysostom on Devilish Divisions] The devil, Chrysostom pointed out, was able to use the wealth and wisdom of the Corinthian believers as weapons for dividing them. Clearly, Paul confronts the "wisdom" of the Corinthians later in chapter 1, though here in the letter opening he mentions only their "knowledge." As for wealth, however, Chrysostom most likely based his assessment of the affluence of the Corinthians on the long-standing reputation of Corinth as a wealthy city and not on the text of the letter itself.[15] While the question of the general socioeconomic status of the Corinthian believers is hotly debated today, and decisions regarding the matter greatly affect how one reads 1 Corinthians, Paul's language in this opening section suggests that the "wealth" he acknowledged the Corinthians possessed was not material.[16] He used a term (*eploutisthēte*) that was often used in reference to economic wealth to describe the way God had lavishly enriched the Corinthians in "everything," but he quickly defined the "everything" in terms of speech and knowledge (v. 5). Material wealth may have contributed to the divisions that developed in the church (and probably did),

Chrysostom on Devilish Divisions

The devil, seeing that a great city had accepted the truth and received the Word of God with great eagerness, set about dividing it. He knew that even the strongest kingdom, if divided against itself, would not stand. He had a choice weapon for doing this in the wealth and wisdom of the inhabitants, which made them exceedingly proud.

John Chrysostom, *Homilies on the Epistles of Paul to the Corinthians, Proem*, in Gerald Bray, ed., *1–2 Corinthians* (vol. 7 of ACCS NT; ed. Thomas C. Oden; Downers Grove IL: InterVarsity Press, 1999) 2.

but Paul appears not to have attacked that kind of wealth as directly as he did the surplus of speech and knowledge that Chrysostom insightfully noted had made the Corinthians "exceedingly proud."

Commenting on speech and knowledge, the great third-century biblical scholar Origen wrote, "Knowledge shows what there is to know. Speech goes further and explains it."[17] Theology is the discipline that seeks to explain what believers think they know about God. At least since the fourth century, Christian theologians have labored to express in precise words what Christians should believe about God. Prior to that time, more effort was given to explaining to outsiders who Christians were, how they lived, and why. [Pagels on Belief] Since the great christological controversies that prompted the Council of Nicea (AD 325) and continued for several centuries, however, matters of correct belief have been at the forefront of Christian debate. Knowledge has been enshrined in speech, and acceptance of particular statements of belief has often determined whether one is included or excluded. The result, especially within Protestantism, has been relentless multiplication by division.

Pagels on Belief

In describing her return to active participation in the life of the church after decades of absence, Princeton University professor of religion and noted author Elaine Pagels wrote, "What matters in religious experience involves much more than what we believe (or what we do not believe)."

Elaine Pagels, *Beyond Belief: The Secret Gospel of Thomas* (New York: Random House, 2003) 6.

According to Chrysostom, the Corinthians' wealth and knowledge made them exceedingly proud, and thus the devil could use those objects of pride as weapons to divide them. In western societies the affluence of the church has sometimes separated it from less affluent elements in the surrounding society. One could point to the isolation of wealthy monasteries in medieval times and to the establishment of certain types of private elementary and high schools by churches in the modern period. Within churches, too, the divisive power of socioeconomic status has lingered. But the more pervasive weapon of division has been found in knowledge and in the speech that explains it. Asserting sufficient knowledge about the God of Mystery to require submission to their speech that defines God, powerful groups have leveraged control of churches and denominations. Correct knowledge articulated in creeds and confessions of faith has been the weapon of choice to wage war against those who claim allegiance to Christ but who fail the litmus test of "speaking" as a true Christian. This knowledge, which makes us, too, exceedingly proud, has continued to divide us.

Undoubtedly, the rigid pecking order found in the socioeconomic stratification of ancient Corinth had a negative impact on relations within the church. Paul had to address some of the problems this situation created, and so must we address the divisions our own affluence creates. [Luther on Divisions] We should not overlook, however, the greater attention Paul gave in 1 Corinthians to the divisive power of speech and knowledge. Theological boxes designed to exclude rather than include sustain the devilish divisions Chrysostom identified and Paul labored to remove.

Luther on Divisions

Behold here, if the great Apostle, the most eminent teacher among the Gentiles, had to hear of, and see, in his day, the factions and sects which sprang up in his own parish, during his own life. Through security, and ingratitude for the Gospel; is it any wonder, if the same thing occurs now, when no such eminent preachers and pious Christians exist, as did at that time?

Martin Luther, "Eighteenth Sunday after Trinity," in *Luther to Massillon: 1483–1742* (ed. Clyde E. Fant Jr. and William M. Pinson Jr.; vol. 2 of *20 Centuries of Great Preaching: An Encyclopedia of Preaching*; Waco TX: Word Books, 1971) 67.

Calling and Vocation

First Corinthians begins as a letter from an individual "called to be an apostle" (1:1) to a community "called to be saints" (1:2) who were further "called into the communion" of Jesus Christ (1:9). The language of calling reappears in 1:26, where Paul urges his readers to remember their status prior to their calling. It becomes prominent later in chapter 7, where Paul addresses concerns about marriage, divorce, remarriage, circumcision, and slavery by advocating the basic principle of each person remaining in the state in which she or he was when called by God (7:20). (See [Call and Calling in 1 Corinthians] above.) Several observations about the way Paul articulated his concept of calling may inform present-day discussions about vocation.

First, we should observe what Paul did not say. He did not give anything resembling a treatise on his ideas about one's calling. His references to "calling" and "being called" pepper his treatment of other matters. Lurking somewhere behind the text of this letter seems to be a solid, well thought out, and much reflected on vision of individual and corporate calling.[18] The scope of that vision remains elusive. Paul's language and bits of his thinking here may reflect discussions about calling in vogue in his day. The primary milieu for his view undoubtedly resided in the story of Israel found in the scriptures and traditions of his Jewish heritage. All of these influences, however, were fitted into a scheme that took its shape from what Paul believed God had done in Christ. We are privileged only to those portions of his vision that Paul brought to bear in addressing other issues.

What is apparent in his allusions to God's calling is foremost his focus on God's action and intent. God is the agent doing the calling; humans are the recipients of God's action. The God who called the world into being (cf. 2 Cor 4:6) has called human beings into a new relationship with the creator. Thus, for Paul, calling was fundamentally a theocentric concept.

For Paul, God's calling also had a christocentric dimension. One is called "in the Lord" (7:22) and "into the communion" of Christ (1:9). Leading the "life which the Lord [Jesus] has assigned" is paralleled to that "[life] in which God called one" (7:17). The "lordship" of Christ defines the shape of that calling.

By stating that the Corinthians were "called into the communion" of Christ (1:9), Paul pointed to the corporate nature of God's calling. The church is a people "called together." (See [*Ekklēsia*] above.] One's "calling" is not merely a private matter.

Yet, as Paul made clear later in the letter, God's calling does have a personal component. God calls a person who exists in a specific state in life (7:17, 20, 24). Persons are called *into* corporate communion, but they are called *in* their individual station in life.

The term "vocation" may help us correlate these several observations about Paul's concept of calling and connect it in a meaningful way to our own experience. The word "vocation" derives from the Latin verb *vocare* (to call), which in turn stems from the noun *vox* (voice). While the root idea of vocation pertains to "hearing a voice that calls," vocation in common usage often refers to the career one has chosen to pursue. It is a matter of human choice. Also, in common usage vocation may refer to the type of career that involves more of the hand than the head. That is, one goes to *vocational* school to learn skills that may help one get a job that involves primarily physical labor. One may choose this route rather than go to college where the training may be primarily intellectual and the resultant "profession" one pursues may be less physically inclined. In either case, however, the *vocation* pursued is perceived as a matter of human volition.

In his book *Let Your Life Speak*, Parker Palmer has challenged this common perception of vocation as a career one chooses. [Parker Palmer on Vocation] "Vocation does not come from willfulness. It comes from listening," writes Palmer. "Vocation does not mean a goal that I pursue. It means a calling that I hear."[19] Hearing the voice that calls us from within faces enormous challenges, argues Palmer. Listening to your life speak proves difficult. "The difficulty is compounded by the fact that from our first days in school, we are taught to listen to everything

Parker Palmer on Vocation

Before I can tell my life what I want to do with it, I must listen to my life telling me who I am. I must listen for the truths and values at the heart of my own identity, not the standards by which I must live—but the standards by which I cannot help but live if I am living my own life.

Parker J. Palmer, *Let Your Life Speak: Listening for the Voice of Vocation* (San Francisco: Jossey-Bass, 2000) 4–5.

and everyone but ourselves, to take all our clues about living from the people and powers around us."[20]

Leo Tolstoy's *The Death of Ivan Ilyich* portrays the life and death of a late-eighteenth-century Russian judge who attained his ambitions of material success and social prestige. His misgivings about the questionable morality of the upper classes gave way as he conformed to social expectations and reaped the benefits of following the script prescribed for success. While suffering painfully for months from an accidental injury, he reflected on his life and came to an agonizing possibility: "What if my whole life has really been wrong?" In his agony, he repeatedly heard an inner voice that had long ago been suppressed, saying, "What is it you want?" Only as death pressed in upon him did he surrender to the voice of his own life.[21]

From Paul's theocentric perspective, the voice that calls us to our life is God's voice. One's vocation is that life to which one is called by God. But does this not mean that once again we are listening to some other power and not to our own voice? Would heeding this voice not be following a prescribed script? Though the metaphors of sound and sight become mixed, Paul's words in 2 Corinthians 4:6 suggest a way beyond the contradiction. The God who called the world into being has "shone in our hearts the light of the knowledge of the glory of God." The beacon beckons from within. For Paul, the heart, as the locus of reflection and intention, may be seen as the center of human volition.[22] In the heart God calls/shines, and in the heart God's volition may become human vocation.

The personal nature of vocation is evident in Paul's references to God's calling one *in* a station in life. His principle that persons should stay in the station in which they were called probably reflects his eschatological expectations, but here it is important to note that their calling did not prescribe that they leave one station for another. They were not called to follow a script; they were called to *be* someone. Brian J. Mahan, in his book *Forgetting Ourselves on Purpose*, has observed that depicting vocation as a calling to some ideal life of selflessness and compassion, as embodied in the Ghandis and Mother Teresas of the world, renders the whole matter of calling largely irrelevant to most people. He also contends that, despite the slim possibility of immolating such saintly servants, "we carry within us a 'shadow government' of compassion and idealism," and "most of us wish nothing more than to liberate our shadow government from exile and to incarnate in the routines of work and play and worship the deepest longings of our heart."[23] *In* our routines, *in* our stations in life, we are called to *be* who we really are. [Vocation and Ambition]

For Paul, this calling *in* life was also a calling *into* a certain quality of life. One is called "into the communion of Christ." Corporately speaking this is a calling into the body of "called together" persons, those "called to be saints together with all those who in every place call upon the name of our Lord Jesus Christ" (1:2). Christocentrically speaking, this is a call into the communion *of Christ.* The christocentric dimension shapes the corporate nature of the communion. Reverting again to 2 Corinthians 4:6, the light/voice that shines/calls in the heart is "of the knowledge of the glory of God *in the face of Christ.*" The face of Christ Paul presented to the Corinthians was of a crucified lord (1 Cor 2:2). The life one is called to reflects the cruciform shape of the Christ who gave his life for others. As Frederick Buechner has put it in an oft-quoted statement about vocation, "The place God calls you to is the place where your deep gladness and the world's deep hunger meet."[24] [Buechner on Vocation]

Vocation and Ambition

In ambition, the prestige of the achievement often seems to depend more on the dignity of the role itself than on the dignity of the one who fills it. This is not the case with vocation. Vocation speaks of a gracious discovery of a kind of interior consonance between our deepest desires and hopes and our unique gifts, as they are summoned forth by the needs of others and realized in response to that summons.

Brian J. Mahan, *Forgetting Ourselves on Purpose: Vocation and the Ethics of Ambition* (San Francisco: Jossey-Bass, 2002) 11.

Buechner on Vocation

There are all kinds of voices calling you to all different kinds of work, and the problem is to find out which is the voice of God rather than of Society, say, or the Superego, or Self-Interest.

By and large a good rule for finding out is this. The kind of work God usually calls you to is the kind of work (a) that you need most to do and (b) that the world most needs to have done.

Frederick Buechner, *Wishful Thinking: A Theological ABC* (New York: Harper & Row, 1973) 95.

Lectionary Connections

The whole section of 1 Corinthians 1:1-9 appears in the Revised Common Lectionary among the readings in Year A for the second Sunday after Epiphany. The same section, minus the first two verses, also is used in Year B for the first Sunday in Advent.

The longer reading in Year A is joined to Isaiah 49:3-6 and John 1:29-34. The Isaiah passage contains one of the "Servant Songs." This one identifies the servant as one the Lord will send as a light to the nations. In John, John the Baptist identifies Jesus as the lamb of God who takes away the sins of the world. Paul's focus in the opening verses of 1 Corinthians is narrower in that he focuses mostly on the ways God has spiritually enriched the lives of the Corinthians. Nonetheless, this longer reading that includes v. 2 reminds the recipients of this letter that they are part of the worldwide community of those sanctified in Christ. The universal scope of God's work in Jesus is, thus, a common thread in these texts.

The shorter selection in Year B is joined with Isaiah 63:16–64:4 and Mark 13:32-37. In keeping with the Advent theme of watchful preparation for Christ's coming, the Isaiah text and the final slice of the Markan "Apocalypse" depict a people anticipating the arrival of God. Isaiah stresses hope; Mark stresses being prepared; Paul stresses confidence that the God who has already begun to accomplish the longed-for dream of salvation shall bring it to final fruition in the day of our Lord Jesus Christ.

NOTES

1. William Shakespeare, *King Henry the Fifth*, Act 3, Scene 1, line 32.

2. See, for example, the "connections" between the thanksgiving in 1 Cor 1:4-9 and the rest of the letter made by Ben Witherington III, *Conflict and Community in Corinth: A Socio-Rhetorical Commentary and 1 and 2 Corinthians* (Grand Rapids: Eerdmans, 1995) 75, 88–89.

3. See the discussion of this matter in the companion commentary on 2 Corinthians by Mitzi Minor (Macon GA: Smyth & Helwys, 2009).

4. I am not persuaded by Murphy-O'Connor's creative suggestion that Sosthenes had a major role in the composition of 1 Cor 1:18-31 and 2:6-16. See Jerome Murphy-O'Connor, *Paul the Letter-Writer: His World, His Options, His Skills* (Collegeville MN: Liturgical Press, 1995) 23–24.

5. See the discussion of the use of fictive familial terms by non-Christian religious groups in Philip A. Harland, "Familial Dimensions of Group Identity: 'Brothers' (Ἀδελφοί) in Associations of the Greek East," *JBL* 124 (2005): 491–513.

6. Anthony C. Thiselton, *The First Epistle to the Corinthians: A Commentary on the Greek Text* (NIGTC; Grand Rapids: Eerdmans, 2000) 76–77.

7. See those noted by Thiselton, *The First Epistle to the Corinthians*, 77–78.

8. I am deliberately translating *koinōnia* as "communion." I agree with Thiselton's assessment that the use of "fellowship" in church parlance today is sufficiently removed from what *koinōnia* meant in Paul's time to render it impotent in conveying the significance of the term for Paul and his readers (Thiselton, *The First Epistle to the Corinthians*, 104). His rendering "communal participation," however, while substantially accurate, seems overly cumbersome to me.

9. *Commentary on the First Epistle to the Corinthians*, in Gerald Bray, ed., *1–2 Corinthians* (vol. 7 of ACCS NT; ed. Thomas C. Oden; Downers Grove IL: InterVarsity Press, 1999) 6.

10. *Homilies on the Epistles of Paul to the Corinthians* 2.5, in Bray, *1–2 Corinthians*, 7.

11. On this see especially Margaret M. Mitchell, *Paul and the Rhetoric of Reconciliation: An Exegetical Investigation of the Language and Composition of 1 Corinthians* (Louisville: Westminster John Knox, 1991) 194–97, and Witherington, *Conflict and Community in Corinth*, 44–48.

12. *Satyricon* 3.

13. Thiselton, *The First Epistle to the Corinthians*, 94.

14. Stephen M. Pogoloff, *Logos and Sophia: The Rhetorical Situation of 1 Corinthians* (SBLDS 134; Atlanta: Scholars Press, 1992) 121.

15. See J. B. Salmon, *Wealthy Corinth: A History of the City to 338 B.C.* (Oxford University Press, 1984) for a thorough discussion of Corinth's proverbial wealth.

16. For issues in the debate over the status of the Corinthians, see Bengt Holmberg, "The Methods of Historical Reconstruction in the Scholarly 'Recovery' of Corinthian Christianity," and Margaret Y. MacDonald, "The Shifting Centre: Ideology and the Interpretation of 1 Corinthians," in *Christianity at Corinth: The Quest for the Pauline Church* (ed. Edward Adams and David G. Horrell; Louisville: Westminster John Knox, 2004) 255–71, 273–94.

17. Origen, *Commentary on I Corinthians*, 1.2.29-30, in Bray, *1–2 Corinthians*, 6.

18. The question of how developed Paul's "theology" was has been greatly debated. J. Christiaan Beker has argued that Paul had a coherent core of basic theological convictions that were developed in specific ways depending on the contingent circumstances addressed in particular letters (cf. *Paul the Apostle: The Triumph of God in Life and Thought* [Philadelphia: Fortress, 1980] esp. 11–19). Ben Witherington III, however, has argued for a more complete theological narrative lying behind the contingent expressions contained in given letters (cf. *Paul's Narrative Thought World: The Tapestry and Tragedy of Triumph* [Louisville: Westminster/John Knox, 1994] esp. 1–5).

19. Parker J. Palmer, *Let Your Life Speak: Listening for the Voice of Vocation* (San Francisco: Jossey-Bass, 2000) 4.

20. Ibid., 5.

21. Leo Tolstoy, *The Death of Ivan Ilyich and Other Stories* (New York: New American Library, 1960) 147, 152.

22. Scott Nash, "Heart," *Mercer Dictionary of the Bible*, ed. Watson E. Mills (Macon: Mercer University Press) 360.

23. Brian J. Mahan, *Forgetting Ourselves on Purpose: Vocation and the Ethics of Ambition* (San Francisco: Jossey-Bass, 2002) 14.

24. Frederick Buechner, *Wishful Thinking: A Theological ABC* (New York: Harper & Row, 1973) 95.

HEARING THE WORD OF THE CROSS: DIVISIVENESS IN THE CHURCH

1 Corinthians 1:10–3:4

"Old religious factions are volcanoes burnt out."[1]

The Place of 1 Corinthians 1:10–4:21 in the Whole Letter

The section 1 Corinthians 1:10–4:21 marks Paul's first effort to address the several problems he learned existed in the Corinthian church. The extended attention he gives here to the problem of divisions, as well as the fact that he deals with this matter before confronting the other issues, suggests that Paul considered this particular problem to be the most urgent item on his agenda. [*1 Clement* on 1 Corinthians] The problem of divisions within the ranks of the church clearly arises again in 1 Corinthians 11:18-34, and one may detect hints of its presence lying less obviously beneath other problems addressed in this letter. Furthermore, in this first major section Paul lays out basic principles that he utilizes in addressing some of those other problems. Nonetheless, the nature and focus of those divisions related to other problems appear to differ somewhat from the particular issue here. Hence, despite the recurrence of attention to various divisions at different points in the letter, the problem of divisions *per se* may not have been the over-arching matter that Paul sought to correct throughout the letter.[2] Problems of almost any type involve some division of opinion, but divided opinion may not always be the main problem. In fact, Paul acknowledged the necessity of different opinions in order to discern the truth (11:19). The main problem with the divisions dealt with in

1 Clement on 1 Corinthians

The letter known as *1 Clement* was sent from the bishop of Rome to the church in Corinth c. AD 95 to deal with division within the church that had apparently led to the deposition of the appointed presbyters. Toward the end of the letter, Clement refers his readers to Paul's earlier experience with divisions in the church.

> Take up the epistle of the blessed Paul the Apostle. What wrote he first unto you in the beginning of the Gospel? Of a truth he charged you in the Spirit concerning himself and Cephas and Apollos, because that even then ye had made parties. Yet that making of parties brought less sin upon you; for ye were partisans of Apostles that were highly reputed, and of a man approved in their sight.

1 Clement 47:1-4 in J. B. Lightfoot and J. R. Harmer, eds., *The Apostolic Fathers: Revised Greek Texts with Introductions and English Translations* (Grand Rapids: Baker Book House, 1984) 77.

1:10–4:21 was that their existence stemmed from a perspective that Paul considered contrary to his basic message and his vision for the *ekklēsia* in Corinth.[3]

The urgency given to addressing this particular problem, beyond the danger it presented to the well-being of the church and Paul's relationship to it, stemmed both from the necessity of resolving this issue and the opportunity it afforded Paul to establish certain fundamental elements of his overall approach in resolving the several problems he understood to exist in Corinth.

First, the divisions addressed were rooted in the question of which authority figures the Corinthian Christians would recognize. Specifically, would they recognize Paul as their authoritative guide for matters of belief and behavior? The fact that the church had written to Paul for counsel regarding several of the matters addressed in the letter indicates that some significant portion of the church recognized his authority. Yet obviously not all in the church considered Paul in this way, since the primary focus of the divisions seemingly concerned confessed loyalties to different authorities ("I am of Paul," "I am of Apollos," "I am of Cephas," "I am of Christ," 1:12). In order to speak to the several other problems reported to him, Paul had first to reestablish (or establish for the first time for some of the Corinthians) his status in relation to the church. Nils Dahl has argued that Paul found it necessary to reassert his apostolic authority since some in the church had begun to consider other authority figures.[4] Elisabeth Schüssler Fiorenza, however, has argued that Paul never previously exercised the degree of authority that 1 Corinthians was designed to establish.[5] Dahl is probably correct in holding that the weightier element in the church had already recognized Paul as the principal authority. Fiorenza is probably correct in holding that the authority Paul sought to establish in 1 Corinthians was of a degree he had not held before. If so, then Paul's eventual success may have served as precursor to the strengthening of episcopal authority in the early church decades later. [*1 Clement* on Later Divisions] That does not mean, however, that Paul saw himself exerting the same level of authority that later

1 Clement on Later Divisions

Clement's letter was aimed not only at quelling the dispute in the Corinthian church near the end of the 1st century AD but also at gaining recognition of the authority of the church in Rome to address such matters. It reveals both that division had again occurred in the Corinthian church and that the resolution of the problem was sought through solidifying the authority of the established ministerial leadership. Part of the strategy of the letter was to appeal to the good reputation the Corinthian church had earned since the time of Paul's ministry there. At the beginning of the letter, Clement wrote,

> By reason of the sudden and repeated calamities and reverses which are befalling us, brothers and sisters, we consider that we have been somewhat tardy in giving heed to the matters of dispute that have arisen among you, dearly beloved, and to the detestable and unholy sedition, so alien and strange to the elect of God, which a few headstrong and self-willed persons have kindled to such a pitch of madness that your name, once revered and renowned and lovely in the sight of all people, hath been greatly reviled.

1 Clement 1:1 in J. B. Lightfoot and J. R. Harmer, eds., *The Apostolic Fathers: Revised Greek Texts with Introductions and English Translations* (Grand Rapids: Baker Book House, 1984) 57.

bishops exercised. Nonetheless, the occasion indicated to Paul that he had to assert firmly his right to guide the church through treacherous waters. Indeed, without a convincing argument that he had that right as an apostle called by God (1:1), Paul could not hope to speak to the other problems plaguing the church.

Secondly, Paul saw the challenge to his recognized authority as a challenge also to the message he proclaimed. One issue was the proclaimer of this message. That is, Paul's status as an authoritative apostle was weakened when his rhetorical skills where measured by the eloquence of more skillful teachers. He was deemed inferior in comparison to the type of teacher generally admired. But for Paul, the more critical matter was not how well he measured up to accepted criteria but rather the encroachment of such criteria into the thinking of the church. The questioning of his status on the basis of such criteria represented the overpowering of his message by what he deemed to be an inferior, contra-gospel perspective. Though buttressed by the environment of Roman Corinth in which eloquent sophists were esteemed and perhaps articulated through persuasive preaching by that perspective's proponents in the church, Paul saw the threat such a view presented for the realization of his message in the life of the church. To counter this view that had found a following within the church in Corinth, Paul moved to redirect the church's thinking toward his "word of the cross." As Alexandra Brown has put it, "In Corinth, Paul encounters the faith he founded gone astray, captured by the world."[6] Correcting their distorted thinking about the faith was crucial to correcting the other problems since his strategy for dealing with those problems rested on an appeal to his fundamental message about the cross.

Thirdly, the convergence of message and messenger enabled Paul to probe and articulate the ethical implications of his "word of the cross." Paul's own

Alexamenos Graffito

(Credit: http://upload.wikimedia.org/wikipedia/en/0/0b/AlexGraffito.jpg)

This early graffito was scratched into the wall of a guardroom on the Palatine Hill near the Circus Maximus. Dating to c. AD 200, the graffito depicts a man (Alexamenos) apparently worshiping a crucified figure that bears the head of an ass. The crudely etched inscription reads ALE • XAMENOS • SEBETE • THEON ("Alexamenos worships his God"). Probably drawn by a critic of Christians, the graffito embodies the "foolishness" that outsiders often saw in the message of a crucified God.

"The Alexamanos Graffito, Rome (c.200)," ReligionFacts. 12 January 2006. Accessed 20 August 2009 (http://religionfacts.com/jesus/image_gallery/200_alexamanos_graffito.htm).

manner of proclaiming the message became an occasion for demonstrating the kind of life called for by the "word of the cross." As Paul labored to defend his preaching and message, he correlated his "style" with his "substance." His own ministry incarnated his message, so much so, Paul believed, that near the conclusion of his extended argument in 1:10–4:21 he exhorted his readers to become "imitators of me" (4:16). This final request (*parakalō*) statement in 4:16 joins with the initial appeal (*parakalō*) to unity in 1:10 to form an *inclusio* around the whole section. At issue was not simply the problem that divisions existed or that some were questioning Paul's authority. Those matters were symptoms of the deeper problem. The more fundamental dilemma was the misconstrual of the gospel that prevented an authentic living of its ethical consequences. The underlying issue in this section, then, was whether or not the church could be united together and united with Paul in living out the implications of his "word of the cross." Unless concord could be achieved on that issue, then Paul's attempts to resolve the other problems he addressed would be futile.

The Structure of 1 Corinthians 1:10–4:21

The arrangement of 1:10–4:21 calls for some comment. The individual units within this section are easily identified, but the relationship between the units is less evident. Thematically, one can identify six major segments within the whole section, three in the passage commented on in this chapter and three in the next chapter's commentary. In 1:10–3:4 the thematic segments are (1) 1:10-17, the initial indictment of divisional strife; (2) 1:18–2:5, a contrast between worldly wisdom and the word of the cross; and (3) 2:6–3:4, a discussion of Paul's difficulties in communicating the wisdom of God to the Corinthians. [A Thematic Outline of 1 Corinthians 1:10–3:4] The commentary on this section below will follow this thematic outline, but it will also incorporate useful insights from literary and rhetorical analyses.

One of the most insightful literary studies of 1 Corinthians is that by Charles Talbert.[7] Observing certain literary clues in the text, Talbert has noted that Paul's request for unity in v. 10 is followed by (1) a report from Chloe's people that a problem exists

A Thematic Outline of 1 Corinthians 1:10–3:4

I. Indicting the Corinthians for Divisional Strife (1:10-17)
  A. Identifying the Problem (1:10-12)
  B. Initial Argument against Divisions (1:13-17)
II. Contrasting Worldly Wisdom and the Preaching of the Cross (1:18–2:5)
  A. The Cross as Foolish Wisdom and Power (1:18-25)
  B. God's Choice of the Foolish and Weak (1:26-31)
  C. Proclaiming the Cross as God's Power (2:1-5)
III. Communicating the Wisdom of God (2:6–3:4)
  A. Wisdom Revealed through the Spirit (2:6-13)
  B. Wisdom Incomprehensible to the Unspiritual (2:14-16)
  C. The Corinthians as Unspiritual (3:1-4)

(vv. 11-12) and (2) a series of three rhetorical questions that exposes the non-Christian character of their behavior (v. 13). Talbert sees the three questions providing the organizational key for 1:14–4:7. According to Talbert, Paul addressed the questions in reverse sequence. The third question about baptism is quickly resolved in 1:14-16(17). The second, about crucifixion, is addressed in 1:17–3:4, with 1:17–2:5 and 2:6–3:4 comprising distinct parts of Paul's answer. The first question ("Is Christ divided?") is addressed in 3:5–4:7, with 3:5-23 and 4:1-7 forming two distinct units. The remainder (4:8-21) serves as a conclusion to the entire section.[8]

Talbert's scheme seems to hold true for the third question in 1:13 ("Were you baptized in the name of Paul?") since Paul immediately responds to his own question in 1:14-17. The scheme also seems to be partly in play in regard to the second question ("Was Paul crucified for you?") since Paul transitions from discussing baptism to preaching about Christ's crucifixion in 1:17. In fact, the section 1:18–2:5 can be seen as a unit on the cross as the power of God with three concentric parts.[9] [The Structure of 1 Corinthians 1:18–2:5]

The Structure of 1 Corinthians 1:18–2:5

A—the cross as foolish wisdom and power (1:18-25)
B—God's choice of the foolish and powerless (1:26-31)
A'—proclaiming the cross as God's power (2:1-5)

Talbert's scheme seems not to hold as well for 2:6–3:4, however. Paul's focus moves from the message of the cross to the difficulties of communicating God's wisdom. Still, another three-part concentric pattern is visible. [Concentric Pattern in 1 Corinthians 2:6–3:4] The concentric nature of the unit is evident the *inclusio* in 2:6 where Paul asserts, "Yet among the mature we do impart wisdom," and 3:1 where he declares that he could not impart such wisdom to the Corinthians because they were "babes in Christ." The unit draws a contrast between God's wisdom and the world in a way that is parallel to 1:18–2:5. The wisdom of 2:6–3:4, however, is not explicitly stated to be the wisdom displayed in the cross but rather is cast as a secret wisdom revealed by the Spirit to the mature. The absence in the Corinthians of such maturity is evident, Paul argues, in their divisive claims of allegiance to particular leaders (3:4). The whole unit marks a transition back to Paul's main concern in this section: the divisions in the church.

Concentric Pattern in 1 Corinthians 2:6–3:4

A—wisdom revealed through the Spirit (2:6-13)
B—wisdom incomprehensible to the unspiritual (2:14-16)
A'—the Corinthians as unspiritual (3:1-4)

In regard to the third question in 1:13 ("Is Christ divided?"), the section that Talbert identifies as the answer (3:5–4:7) only addresses the question indirectly. Nowhere does Paul directly refer to Christ as divided, and he alludes to the issue of division only in three instances (3:5, 21; 4:6). Nevertheless, that issue does lie behind the argument in this section, as it does in all of 1:10–4:21. Paul's approach to dealing with that problem here takes the form of a series of arguments about identity, that of Paul and Apollos and that of the Corinthians. Paul alternates between "We are . . ." and "You are . . ." statements throughout the section. He brings his discussion of identities to a climax with a stinging contrast between the lowly apostles and the "puffed up" Corinthians in 4:8-13 before reminding them of his identity as their "father." (We will look at the details of this section more closely in the next chapter.)

Other scholars have conducted rhetorical analyses of 1 Corinthians 1–4, using the conventions of ancient rhetoric as a guide. (See the section titled "1 Corinthians as Rhetoric" in the Introduction.) In separate studies, both Rudolf Pesch and Helmut Merklein have identified 1:10-17 as an *exordium* and 1:18–2:16 as a *narratio*. They have also argued that 3:1-17 and 4:1-13 are proofs, each followed by its own *peroratio* (3:18-23 and 4:14-21).[10] Their analyses, however, completely ignore the function of 1:4-9 as the *exordium*, not 1:10-17, which actually functions more as a *narratio*. Their identification of 1:18–2:16 as the *narratio*, furthermore, overlooks the fact that this section is a part of Paul's actual argument.

More on target, it seems to me, is Margaret Mitchell's assessment.[11] (See [Mitchell's Rhetorical Scheme for 1 Corinthians] in the Introduction.) As pointed out in the Introduction to this commentary, Mitchell has identified the epistolary thanksgiving prayer in 1:4-9 as the *prooimion* (*exordium*). In her rhetorical scheme, 1:10 functions as the *prothesis* (*propositio*) for the entire letter, not only for 1:10–4:21. The *diēgēsis* (*narratio*), also for the whole letter, appears in 1:11-17. Then follows a series of four extensive proofs, the first of which is 1:18–4:21. For Mitchell, this first proof is a censure of the Corinthian factionalism that draws on the stock Greco-Roman *topos* about factionalism as a human failing.[12] [Mitchell's First Proof] Since Mitchell sees all of 1 Corinthians as a deliberative rhetorical argument for concord in the Corinthian church, she holds that the rest of the

Mitchell's First Proof

Though Mitchell does not provide a detailed outline of the proof she sees in 1:18–4:21, her discussion indicates these components:

(1) 1:18–2:8, a contrast between human and divine wisdom;

(2) 2:10-16, a contrast between the spirit of the world and the spirit that comes from God;

(3) 3:1-4, a severe application of the contrasts to the Corinthians;

(4) 3:5-17, an appeal to the example of the concord between Paul and Apollos;

(5) 3:18-23, a challenge to the Corinthians' wisdom;

(6) 4:1-13, a comparison of the Corinthians and the apostles; and

(7) 4:14-21, a summary and elucidation of the purpose of this proof.

Margaret M. Mitchell, *Paul and the Rhetoric of Reconciliation: An Exegetical Investigation of the Language and Composition of 1 Corinthians* (Louisville: Westminster John Knox, 1991) 202–25.

letter after 4:21 also contains proofs designed to persuade the Corinthians to overcome their disunity.

Mitchell's understanding and discussion of the forms of ancient rhetoric is extensive, and she has comprehensively applied those forms in her analysis of 1 Corinthians. Nevertheless, I cautiously venture to offer different views about the *possible* rhetorical scheme of this section. Since I do not see the whole letter as an argument aimed at the one basic problem of discord, I see 1:10 as a possible proposition only for this section (1:10–4:21).[13] (But see [Parakalō] below.) I also think that Paul's argument in support of his call for unity begins in 1:13, so I would limit the *narratio* to 1:11-12.[14] Furthermore, I think Talbert has correctly seen the importance of 1:13 as an organizational clue for what follows, even though the third section he identifies (3:5–4:7) does not directly address Paul's first question in 1:13. In ancient rhetoric, if the thesis to be argued contained several parts, a *partitio* identifying those parts might be given following the *propositio*.[15] The *partitio* might also signal the arrangement of a complex proof.[16] The three questions posed in 1:13 may have served this purpose. The argument proceeds, then, with three movements (1:14-17; 1:18–3:4; 3:5–4:5). Within the second movement, 2:6–3:4 may have served as a *digressio*, that is, a departure from the main topic at hand (the call for unity) to discuss a related matter (the difficulty of communicating the wisdom of God). As pointed out above, however, the contrast between God's wisdom and the world in 2:6–3:4 parallels the similar contrast in 1:18-31. Furthermore, 2:6–3:4 leads toward the third movement that begins in 3:5 with a clear connector in 3:4. Thus, the identification of this section as a *digressio* is tentative. At any rate, I cannot see 2:7-8 as a part of the argument in 1:18–2:5 (as Mitchell does), and I think the *inclusio* of 2:6 and 3:1 shows that 2:6–3:4 is a unit. The third movement (3:5–4:5) argues for unity through a definition of identities. The section 4:6-21 (not including 4:1-5, which Mitchell joins with 4:6-13) may be seen as a summary (*peroratio*). Here Paul may have been recapitulating the gist of his argument by employing a device known as *indignatio* in which he sarcastically blasted the Corinthians' pomposity and another device

A Rhetorical Outline of Paul's Argument in 1 Corinthians 1:10–4:21

Propositio: 1:10—Paul's request for unity
Narratio: 1:11-12—The report of the problem
Partitio: 1:13—Three questions indicating errant thinking
Argumentatio: 1:14–4:21—Arguments based on the three questions in reverse order
- 1:14-16(17)—The question of baptism
- 1:18–3:4—The question of crucifixion
  - 1:18–2:5—Human wisdom and the word of the cross
  - 2:6–3:4 (*digressio?*) Wisdom for the mature
- 3:5–4:5—The question of division
  - 3:5-15—Paul and Apollos united in Christ
  - 3:16-23—The Corinthians united in Christ
  - 4:1-5—Paul and Apollos as servants and stewards

Peroratio: 4:6-21—Recapitulation and final appeal
- 4:6-13 Contrast of Corinthians and apostles (using indignatio and conquestio)
- 4:14-21—Appeal to imitate their father, Paul (using pathos)

(*conquestio*) in which he presented himself and other apostles in a pitiable light (4:6-13).[17] The final appeal in 4:14-21 may have employed the rhetorical element of *pathos* (an appeal to the emotions) by reminding the Corinthians of Paul's paternal relationship to them.

I make these suggestions regarding the rhetorical scheme of this section acknowledging that Paul's argumentation at points resists a neat fit. Thus, the main use of such a scheme is to try to aid the reader's understanding, not to prescribe Paul's argument. [A Rhetorical Outline of Paul's Argument in 1 Corinthians 1:10–4:21]

COMMENTARY

Indicting the Corinthians for Divisional Strife (1:10-17)

The body of the letter begins in 1:10 with the request formula *parakalō* ("I ask") followed by Paul's relaying of the problem reported to him by Chloe's people (1:11-12). [Ancient Request Letters] This is followed by a series of three questions (1:13), the first of which is addressed in the balance of this unit (1:14-17). Verse 17 provides a key word (*stauros* = cross) for transition to the crucial argument about the "word of the cross" in the next section (1:18–2:5).

Paul's use of *parakalō* here should be seen in light of the ancient parenetic tradition. [*Parakalō*] On the basis of his close relationship to the Corinthian believers, which Paul later casts as that of a father to

Ancient Request Letters

Letters of request were among the most common in the ancient world since people often wrote letters asking for something. The most common letter (now replaced by email and text messages) sent home from college not long ago might have begun: "Dear Mom and Dad, please send money." Requests fill the letters of the New Testament as well, especially the letters of Paul (cf. Rom 12:1; 15:30; 16:17; 1 Cor 4:16; 16:15; 2 Cor 6:1; 10:1; 13:11; Phil 4:2; 1 Thess 4:1, 10; 5:14; Phlm 9, 10). In antiquity, the body of such letters of request often included the term *parakalō*, but more frequently they used *erōtō* ("I request"). The 1st-century BC letter of Hilarion to his wife Alis (whom he calls his "sister") given below contains both *parakalō* and *erōtō* in a disturbing appeal.

Hilarion to his sister Alia many greetings,
likewise to my lady Berous and to Apollonarion.
Know that we are even yet in Alexandria.
Do not worry if they all come back (except me) and I remain in Alexandria.
I urge (*erōtō*) and I entreat (*parakalō*) you, be concerned about the child
and if I should receive my wages soon, I will send them up to you.
If by chance you bear a child, if it is a boy, let it be, if it is a girl, cast it out.
You have said to Aphrodisias, "Do not forget me." How can I forget you? Therefore I urge you not to worry.
(Year) 29 of Caesar, Payni 23.

John L. White, *Light from Ancient Letters* (FF; Philadelphia: Fortress, 1986) 71–72.

his children (4:15), Paul asks them to pursue a course of behavior different from that which he learned they were following. In making his case for a change in behavior, Paul presents his word of the cross as the appropriate model and himself and his coworkers, including especially Apollos, as examples of that model. True to the parenetic fashion, Paul does not advocate a new teaching but rather calls them back to the traditions that he has already presented to them (4:17). Their failure to realize the full implications of his previous teaching had led to the emergence of divisions among them.

> ***Parakalō***
>
> AΩ Paul's use of *parakalō* (from *parakaleō*) in 1 Cor 1:10 signifies more than a simple request. Stanley Stowers has shown that *parakalō* had a long history as a semi-technical term in letters of exhortation, especially parenetic letters. Parenesis was a type of instruction that called persons to act in ways considered appropriate for a particular group or for humanity in general. Its appeal was not to some new teaching but to values and ideas held in common by the instructor and those instructed. A parenetic letter required that the author and recipient(s) be related in a positive way (e.g., as friends, parent-child, teacher-student). Also, according to Stowers, "The writer recommends habits of behavior and actions that conform to a certain model of character and attempts to turn the recipients away from contrasting negative models of behavior." This is exactly what Paul was trying to do in 1 Corinthians.
>
> Stanley K. Stowers, *Letter Writing in Greco-Roman Antiquity* (LEC; Philadelphia: Westminster, 1986) 24, 96.

In making his request, Paul refers to them as *adelphoi*, which should be understood generically to mean "brothers *and* sisters." As noted in chapter 1, Paul frequently employed fictive familial terms to refer to believers.[18] First Corinthians, however, contains the term *adelphos* in the plural far more frequently than any other letter (compare 27 times in 1 Corinthians to 13 times in Romans). Repetition of this term signifying familial bonds was part of Paul's strategy for restoring those bonds.

Paul makes his request "through the name of our Lord Jesus Christ." As Thiselton points out, the name of our Lord Jesus Christ "invokes the *character and reputation* of Jesus Christ as publicly known."[19] Paul is the person making the request, but that request carries the authorization of Christ in that Paul has been authorized by Christ to speak on his behalf. Thus, in a similar fashion, Paul will pronounce judgment "in the name of Lord Jesus" on the member guilty of immorality (5:4). What appears in many respects to be a human problem, namely divisions, is immediately elevated from the anthropocentric realm to the theocentric.

The content of the request contains two pairs of appeals: (1) "that all of you be in agreement *and* that there be no divisions among you," and (2) "that you be united in the same mind *and* the same purpose" (NRSV). The language of these appeals is politically charged and reflects ancient discussions regarding the dangers of communal division. [Political Language in Paul's Request] Together the terms signify the seriousness of the threat to the cohesiveness of the community and the urgency of restoring harmony.

Political Language in Paul's Request

AΩ Long ago, J. B. Lightfoot observed that the language of Paul's request resembles that of ancient Greek politics. Welborn and other scholars have shown how heavily the terms reflect the concerns of ancient rhetoric regarding civic concord. The first phrase, *to auto legēte pantes*, literally reads "everyone should say the same thing," but Mitchell has shown clearly that the sense here follows the use of such phrases regarding political concord, namely that they "be in agreement." The second phrase, "[that] there not be splits (*schismata*) among you," also reflects language concerning ruptures to the healthy body politic. The second pair of appeals flows from the periphrastic construction *ēte de katērtismenoi*, which resembles ancient appeals for the restoration of civic harmony and which would best be rendered here "[that] you be reunited." The phrase *en tō autō noē* (lit., "in the same mind") parallels the politically charged term for "harmony" (Gk. *homonoia*; Latin *concordia*) and might best be rendered "mind-set" or "perspective." The final phrase, *en tē autē gnōmē*, is often rendered "of the same opinion/judgment/purpose," but given the decidedly political flavor of Paul's total appeal, it might better be translated "of common consent."

J. B. Lightfoot, *Notes on the Epistles of St. Paul* (London: Macmillan, 1895) 151.

Margaret M. Mitchell, *Paul and the Rhetoric of Reconciliation: An Exegetical Investigation of the Language and Composition of 1 Corinthians* (Louisville: Westminster John Knox, 1991) 65–183.

L. L. Welborn, "Discord in Corinth: First Corinthians 1-4 and Ancient Politics" as revised in his *Politics and Rhetoric in the Corinthian Epistles* (Macon GA: Mercer University Press, 1997) 1–42.

The basis for Paul's concern stems from the report he had received from Chloe's people (v. 11) that "contentions" (*erides*) existed in the church. Welborn asserts, "*Eris* is hot dispute, the emotional flame that ignites whenever rivalry becomes intolerable."[20] Chloe was possibly a woman of some means in Corinth since she had sent some of her agents, possibly slaves, to report the problem to Paul. As such, she and her people may have been involved in the quarrels.

Paul continues his brief narration of the reported problem in v. 12. Several questions arise regarding the nature of the personal labels he names ("I am of . . . "). Were members of the church in Corinth actually using these slogans? Did four such factions exist, or three, or only two, or none? What was the basis for identification with one leader over against another?

Addressing these questions in reverse order, we focus first on the most significant issue, namely what lay at the heart of the divisions. In the Introduction, I have argued that the root of the problem lay in Corinthian challenges to Paul's leadership. (See the section titled "The Occasion for 1 Corinthians" in the Introduction.) They had begun to evaluate Paul's position on the basis of the same kind of criteria used to judge other similar teachers, in particular sophists. Paul's sophistic skills were lacking, in their opinion. They were accustomed to teachers who demonstrated their superior status through eloquent speaking. In 2 Corinthians 10:10, Paul would later quote his critics as saying of him, "His letters are weighty and strong, but his bodily presence is weak, and his speech contemptible" (NRSV). [A Description of Paul] Their contempt of his speaking had increased by the time he wrote those words, but hints that the issue was already present lurk in Paul's criticisms of such criteria in 1 Corinthians. The same competitive spirit that permeated Corinthian society had crept into the church and was affecting relationships of various sorts in various ways. In this section Paul deals with its effect on his relationship with the church.

The question of factions (and how many there were) has received numerous answers, from the suggestion that no factions actually existed to various efforts to describe the particular factions in detail. [Factions in Corinth] Factions probably did exist, but they were not clearly defined, at least not by theology. Questioning Paul's role as apostle-teacher would naturally have involved some persons showing preference for those they considered superior teachers. Very likely, if the report in Acts that Apollos was an eloquent and wise speaker is accurate, then some may have preferred to look to him for guidance. That does not mean, however, that Apollos in any way fostered that kind of following. Even less likely is the possibility that Cephas had cultivated a group of disciples in Corinth. The teachers some in the church preferred to Paul may have been "home grown" in that they were unnamed members of the church who were exercising their spirit-gifts of wisdom and knowledge in the assembly (12:8, 28-29; 14:29). Their interpretation of such talents not as gifts of the Spirit but as marks of superior leadership status receives Paul's sharp rebuke in 4:7ff. Paul's theological response to the problem suggests that, even though its manifestation was political, its origin lay in their ideological perspective that teachers who exhibited more excellent speaking gifts deserved higher respect. A significant portion of the members may have voiced strong prefer-

A Description of Paul

The late 2d-century apocryphal writing *Acts of Paul and Thecla* contains the earliest extant description of Paul. Several features of the description, especially his baldness, became conventional in later artistic portrayals of Paul.

> And he [Onesiphorous] went along the royal road which leads to Lystra, and stood there waiting for him [Paul], and looked at (all) who came, according to Titus' description. And he saw Paul coming, a man small of stature, with a bald head and crooked legs, in a good state of body, with eyebrows meeting and nose somewhat hooked, full of friendliness; for now he appeared like a man, and now he had the face of an angel.

Acts of Paul (3:3) in *New Testament Apocrypha: Volume Two: Writings Relating to the Apostles, Apocalypses, and Related Subjects* (ed. Wilhelm Schneemelecher; Eng. ed. trans. and ed. R. McL. Wilson; Philadelphia: The Westminister Press, 1964) 353–54.

Factions in Corinth

Many interpreters have assumed that the slogans Paul seems to recite in 1 Cor 12 signify that distinct groups with professed loyalty to different leaders actually existed in the Corinthian church and that those groups held differing theological positions. While harmony about what the disharmonious theologies were eludes such scholars, certain general characterizations have gained fairly wide acceptance. Many see the Paul group consisting of those persons who remained loyal to his leadership and who agreed with his supposedly anti-Jewish perspective about the Torah. The Peter group, then, is often characterized, largely on the basis of Gal 2 and Acts 15, as the more "Jewish" group, with a higher regard for Torah observance. The Apollos group is often seen as more inclined toward philosophical speculation, especially the type evidenced in Hellenistic Jewish wisdom traditions. The Christ group remains more difficult to categorize, with characterizations ranging from "Judaizing" to "ultraspiritual pneumatics." The Corinthian church was undoubtedly divided, and those divisions seem to have rooted in preferences for certain leaders. We do not have clear evidence, however, of formal "parties," nor do we have sufficient information to know what theological ideas may have defined such factions. Paul's major concern seems to be not that they have adopted erroneous theologies but that they have allowed nontheological, worldly perspectives to shape their thinking and behavior.

For a thorough discussion of the different characterizations of the groups and their theologies, see Anthony C. Thiselton, *The First Epistle to the Corinthians: A Commentary on the Greek Text* (NIGTC; Grand Rapids: Eerdmans, 2000) 123–33.

ence for Apollos on this basis, while another significant portion espoused loyalty to Paul. Others probably expressed their higher regard for other teachers. For Paul, the problem was not so much that they preferred one particular teacher over another but that the existence of such preferences at all revealed a deep error in their thinking.

As to the third question of whether members in the church were actually using the slogans Paul attributes to them in 1:12 (also 3:4 and implied in 3:21-22), Hall has identified three types of answers: the literal, the semi-literal, and the cryptic.[21] The literal view holds that distinct factions existed and that the members of those factions clearly identified themselves as followers of either Paul, Apollos, or Cephas (and perhaps Christ). The semi-literal view sees some distinct factions with clear allegiances expressed for two leaders (Paul and either Cephas, Apollos, or Christ). The cryptic view, which Hall favors, holds that Paul fabricated the slogans as part of his rhetorical strategy against unnamed leaders of factions. Mitchell has argued that, since the slogans are in the "language of slave ownership and childish dependence," Paul invented them to caricature groups that had "galvanized" around Paul, Apollos, and Cephas.[22] Paul may have coined the slogans himself to ridicule the practice of aligning one's self with certain teachers on the basis of sophistic skills. The slogans and other parts of 1 Corinthians 1–4 may reflect Paul's cryptic use of a device known as "covert allusion" as he attacked such alignments.[23] As Thiselton points out, however, the use of "covert allusion" does not mean that no tensions existed between those loyal to Paul and those who preferred Apollos.[24] Paul's great effort to show that no such tension existed between himself and Apollos may have served to attack the competitive spirit of those Corinthians who had

Paul and Peter

Though no evidence exists that Peter (Cephas) ever visited Corinth, the tradition (based on 1 Cor 1:12) that he did is maintained in the Catholic and Orthodox churches. By placing the two apostles flanked by Corinthian column capitals, Bagnacavallo may have intended his drawing to depict their joint ministry there.

Bagnacavallo (dit), Ramenghi Bartolomeo l'Ancien (1485–1542). *St. Peter and St. Paul*. Pen & brown ink, wash, black chalk on beige paper. Louvre, Paris, France. Photo: Jean-Gilles Berizzi. (Credit: Réunion des Musées Nationaux/Art Resource, NY)

aligned themselves behind unnamed leaders they considered superior to Paul. In light of Apollos's reputation, however, it seems likely that he also would have attracted, willfully or not, a following of those who valued his skillful preaching. Paul may have applied much of what he said figuratively to himself and Apollos (4:6), but behind the figurative language may have been actual strains in their relationship.[25]

The brief narration of the reported problem in 1:11-12 is followed in 1:13 by three questions that highlight the incredibility of the situation from Paul's perspective. The first ("Has Christ been divided?") raises an unthinkable possibility in a physical sense, but it also brings out the lunacy of the actual fractures that are occurring in Christ's body, the church. The second ("Was Paul crucified for you?") clearly contradicts reality in that Paul had not been crucified, but more importantly it interjects into the discussion by inference the important affirmation that Christ was. The third question ("Were you baptized in the name of Paul?") not only reminds the audience through indirection in whose name they were baptized but also challenges the situation in Corinth where loyalties to human figures have become so important. Paul draws out the implications of these questions in reverse sequence as his argument unfolds.

Regarding baptism (1:14-17), Paul displays a somewhat fuzzy memory in recalling whom he had baptized. The fuzziness contributes to his diminishing of the significance of the act as a signifier of status on the basis of the administrator of the rite. Admittedly, the persons Paul acknowledges having baptized were members with whom he appears to have been especially close (cf. 16:15; Rom 16:23). Despite these concessions to having baptized some, however, his

The Baptistry at the Lechaion Basilica in Corinth

(Credit: Scott Nash)

Paul dismisses the importance of his role as a baptizer of converts, but the ritual itself may have held great importance for the Corinthians. Richard DeMaris has recently suggested that the Corinthians may have even created the practice of "baptism for the dead" (1 Cor 15:29) out of a concern for the proper transition of the dead from this world and a high regard for the efficacy of the baptismal ritual. Clearly, in subsequent centuries, the rite of baptism held a high place in Corinthian liturgy, as is evidenced by the prominence given to baptisteries in the architectural design of church buildings. The excavations of two large basilicas in the vicinity of Corinth have uncovered rather elaborate baptismal edifices adjoining the main structures. The Kraneion basilica, built in the early 6th century, had a large but fairly shallow octagonal baptismal pool enclosed in an octagonal building on the north side of the basilica near the west end. Also, the huge basilica at Corinth's port Lechaion, the largest church building yet found in Greece, had a similarly designed baptistery located to the north toward the western end of the basilica. The basilica at Lechaion was constructed either a decade or so before or after AD 500, but the baptistery, which sits at a slightly different orientation to the main structure, was already in use before being attached to the enormous basilica and seems to have continued to be used even after the larger complex's destruction by earthquake in the middle of the 6th century.

Richard E. DeMaris, *The New Testament in Its Ritual World* (New York: Routledge, 2008) 71.

Richard M. Rothaus, *Corinth, the First City of Greece: An Urban History of Late Antique Cult and Religion* (Leiden: Brill, 2000).

point is that baptism by anyone pales in comparison to the greater calling to preach the gospel.

Stating this enables Paul in 1:17 to make a transition to his important discussion of the content of that gospel and the corresponding nature of his proclamation. His preaching was not in sophisticated speech (*en sophia logou*), for that would "empty" (*kenōthē*) the cross of Christ. This first mentioning of *sophia* (usually translated "wisdom") sets the stage for understanding its meaning in subsequent verses. Paul has a particular "wisdom" in mind, exactly the kind that the Corinthians have been valuing so highly—namely, that *sophist*icated speaking displayed by successful sophistic figures.[26] The juxtaposition of *sophia logou* with the cross of Christ accentuates the consequence of trying to merge the two: sophisticated speech *empties* the cross. How? Such speech reveals a regard for, a reliance upon, and an enslavement to a system of valuation that holds no place for the power of God at work in the world through the self-defaming cross of Christ and its proclamation. [Pogoloff on Values] Highly regarding the practitioner of sophistic eloquence and the practice itself engenders the spirit of competitiveness, which renders genuine community unattainable. Relying upon the power of speech to manipulate thought and action closes the door to the transforming work of God's Spirit. The end result is a perpetual enslavement to a system dominated by those who have learned the art of manipulation through language.

Pogoloff on Values

"Thus, Paul is responding not to division itself, but to the values which lie behind it."

Stephen M. Pogoloff, *Logos and Sophia: The Rhetorical Situation of 1 Corinthians* (SBLDS 134; Atlanta: Scholars Press, 1992) 119.

Contrasting Worldly Wisdom and the Preaching of the Cross (1:18–2:5)

In turning to address directly his second question ("Was Paul crucified for you?"), Paul focuses on the power of the cross by drawing a contrast between worldly wisdom and the word of the cross. The section falls into three parts in the concentric pattern noted above (A—1:18-25, B—1:26-31, A'—2:1-5). Rhetorically, the first part (and perhaps the second) may have functioned as a discussion of a *topos* on foolishness (*mōria*).[27]

1:18-25. The catchword *stauros* (cross) connects this part to the previous section. Here, "the word of the cross" (*ho logos gar ho tou stauros*), which is considered foolishness (*mōria*) to some, contrasts with the *sophia logou* (lit., "wisdom of speech") of 1:17, which is valued so highly by those same persons. The contrast in perception has a corresponding contrast in result: those who perceive the cross as foolishness are perishing, while those who see it as the power of God are being saved. The force of the present participles here (*apolymenois* = "are perishing"; *sōzomenois* = "are being saved") should not be overlooked. Paul does not speak here of salvation as an event accomplished in the past but rather as one in process awaiting future consummation.

While a sophist at this point may have appealed to some classical author in support of the point made, Paul appeals (as he does at least 14 times in 1 Corinthians) to the Hebrew scriptures (in their Greek translation). Though his audience for this letter appears to have been predominantly Gentile, Paul draws on the traditions of Israel and applies them to the church. In so doing, he connects the activity of God in the life of the church to the prior narrative of God's activity on behalf of the covenant people. His quotation of a part of Isaiah 29:14 in 1:19 follows the LXX except for the last word; Paul has *athetēsō* ("I will thwart" NRSV) instead of *krypsō* ("I will hide). Perhaps "nullify" or "make vanish" captures the intended force of *athetēsō* here as well as the term of its LXX source. [Isaiah 29:14 in Context] Those whom God has "nullified" now come into focus in 1:20: the wise (*sophos*), the scribe (*grammateus*), and the debater (*syzētētēs*) of this world (lit., "age"= *aiōn*). While *grammateus* may suggest association with Jewish scribes and given that *syzētētēs* appears nowhere else in the New Testament, these should be taken as three labels for the same figure: the sophist who claims to possess worldly wisdom and who demonstrates it in learned writing and contentious speaking. Such was the intellectual all-star of the day. What has come of such a person? God has made this person's wisdom mere foolishness.

Isaiah 29:14 in Context

The context of the passage from Isaiah that Paul cites in 1 Cor 1:19 is significant in that it probably refers to the time when Hezekiah was being counseled by his advisors to pursue a policy of liberation from Assyrian control. Rather than a policy that relied on the exercise of strength, Isaiah advocated one of weakness: submit to Assyrian domination. God's word to Judah through Isaiah was that the wisdom of the esteemed political experts would be nullified, while God's own plan of apparent weakness would result in eventual renewal. The context of the passage meshes with Paul's use of it in his argument pitting the apparent wise counsel of the world against the apparent weakness of God in the cross.

Anthony C. Thiselton, *The First Epistle to the Corinthians: A Commentary on the Greek Text* (NIGTC; Grand Rapids: Eerdmans, 2000) 161.

Verse 21 makes clear that wisdom (*sophia*) in itself is not the problem, for God has wisdom too. God's wisdom, however, takes a different course than that of the sophist so highly valued by this world. In God's wisdom, such sophistic wisdom does not lead to knowledge of God (1:21). Rather, such knowledge comes through the foolish "word of the cross." To both Jews and Greeks, God's wisdom runs counter to their aspirations and expectations. It is scandalous to one and foolish to the other (1:23). To those who believe, however, the word of the cross is both the power of God and the wisdom of God (1:24). The supposed foolishness of God, which appears as a sign of weakness in those who accept it, is in reality both wiser and stronger than the world's so-called wisdom (1:25).

This important unit establishes a fundamental element in Paul's argument. Things are not as they seem. What appears foolish and weak is actually wise and strong. What appears wise and strong is actually foolish and weak. The problem lies in perception. Part of the barrier to clear perception lies with the tunnel vision of the viewers, since their seeing has been shaped by the world. But part of the astigmatism comes from the lens needed to correct their vision: the cross. This lens blocks the vision of those who cannot see beyond it. It does not grant light for seeing in this world (*aiōn*) because it refracts a light from another world (*aiōn*), the "age" to come that has dawned in the cross of Christ. Paul's apocalyptic *view*point is evident here. The cross marks the inauguration of a new age, but unless one is living in that new age one's vision is still controlled by the old age. From the vantage point of the new age, the foolishness of this age's wisdom is apparent. To get to that vantage point, one's old lens must be shattered by the shocking impact of the spectacle of the cross. This occurs in the encounter with the proclaimed word of the cross, a message so characteristically foolish in the view of worldly wisdom that it calls into question the presuppositions of that wisdom. In regard to the capacity of the proclaimed word to effect this radical reorientation of vision, Alexandra Brown has written, "This is one aspect of its dynamic apocalyptic nature; by this power to dislocate, the Word begins to create the conditions under which readers may be transformed and transferred into a new world."[28] As Richard Hays has put it, "For anyone who grasps the paradoxical logic of this text, the world can never look the same again."[29]

1:26-31. As a paradigmatic proof of the counterintuitive nature of God's wisdom revealed in the word of the cross, Paul asks the Corinthians to look at themselves at the point of their calling. (See [Call and Calling in 1 Corinthians] in chapter 1.) When they do, they are reminded of the status (or lack of it) for the majority of members: "Not many were wise according to the flesh (*sophoi kata sarka*), not many were powerful (*dynatoi*), not many were well born (*eugeneis*)." This verse has been taken as an indication that a few in the church did possess such social attributes. While it does suggest that, the emphasis here is that most of them lacked those laudable assets.[30] Wisdom "according to the flesh" is wisdom from a human perspective. This is the main contrast Paul wishes to draw at this point since his argument thus far has focused on the difference between God's wisdom and the worldly wisdom they cherish. Paul expands his focus here, however, introducing two other qualities to form a triad that he will refer to again in 4:10. [Paul's Triad] There he sharply contrasts the Corinthians with the foolish, weak, and disreputable apostles such as himself. Here the focus is on contradictory values of worldly wisdom and of God's wisdom.

The point of Paul's reminder of their status at the time of their calling is not primarily to belittle them or to put them back in their place, though that is partly his purpose, but rather to stress the radical nature of God's wisdom. God acts counter to the world's norms. God chose the foolish, powerless, and lowly. The second term is *asthenē*, which is usually translated "weak" and thus contrasts with the "strong" (*schyra*) whom God has not chosen. The "strong," though, parallel the "powerful" of 1:26, so *asthenē* may be read "powerless." The last term, *agena*, contrasts with the *eugeneis* of 1:26, but Paul adds a qualifier (*ta exouthenēmena* = "the despised") to bring out the significance of the social attribute of being "well born": they are esteemed, while the lowly are not. The foolish, weak, and lowly are counted as "nothings" (*to mē onta*) in the perspective of worldly wisdom. Yet, God had chosen such nobodies to render the "somebodies" nothing (1:28). In fact, God's calling entails a reversal of the total order of the values of worldly wisdom. Paul asserts that God's purpose in calling was to subvert all human boasting before God. His target here is not only the world outside the church but also the point where the world's standards for boasting have penetrated the church. That those standards have done so is evident in 4:6-7 where Paul accuses the Corinthians of being puffed up and boasting. If his words were intended for the whole church and not simply for an elite that carried their external status into the assembly, then even the

> **Paul's Triad**
>
> The source for Paul's triad of social attributes in 1:26 and 4:10 was probably twofold. On the one hand, the wise, powerful, and well born were the status leaders in Roman Corinth. Whether any of the church members came from their ranks or not, the church as a whole seemed to accept such status indicators as legitimate. Such is the way of worldly wisdom. Furthermore, even those who did not come from those ranks behaved as if their inclusion in the church endowed them with wisdom, power, and honor, if 4:6-10 is to be understood as addressed to the whole church and not simply to an elite. Thus, the situation in the church made the triad appropriate.
>
> On the other hand, the triad was also suggested by Paul's OT texts. This unit concludes in 1:31 with the quotation, "Let one who boasts, boast of the Lord" (1:31). Most commentators take this to be a reference to Jer 9:23-24 (LXX 9:23), though some think it comes from an addition to the Song of Hannah that appears in the LXX (1 Kgdms [= 1 Sam] 2:10). Jer 9:23 (LXX 9:22) and 1 Kgdms 2:10 both reject the boasting of the wise, the powerful, and the wealthy. LXX Jer 9:22 has *sophos*, *ischyros*, and *plousios*, while 1 Kgdms 2:10 reads *phronimos*, *dynatos*, and *plousios*. In 1 Cor 4:10, Paul refers to the Corinthians as wise (*phronimos*), powerful (*ischyroi*), and honorable (*endoxoi*). In the LXX, the Wisdom of Sirach (Sir 10:22) associates the honorable (*endoxoi*) and the rich (*plousios*); this text, which praises the "fear of the Lord," may have also been in Paul's mind.
>
> J. Ross Wagner, "'Not Beyond the Things Which are Written': A Call to Boast Only in the Lord (1 Cor 4:6)," *NTS* 44 (1998): 279–97.
>
> Richard B. Hays, *First Corinthians* (IBC; Louisville: John Knox Press, 1997) 34–35.

foolish, weak, and lowly were guilty of boasting. Of what? One answer often proposed is that they were glorying in their experience of spiritual gifts. Another is that they were boasting of the superiority of the leader of their faction, which signified that their own status was superior to members of other factions. Both views can be supported, and both may have been true. An eschatological (or noneschatological) perspective different from Paul's was also likely involved. Paul saw the church as a "work in progress." The Corinthians relished what they had already accomplished, and from the perspective guiding their assessment, they had accomplished much. That perspective was shaped, however, by worldly wisdom and its competitive standards. Paul again interjects his theocentric perspective asserting that before God no one can boast.

This God is the sole source of their life in Christ Jesus, who is always the crucified Christ (1:30). This crucified one has become wisdom for us from God (recalling 1:24). Three other aspects of God's activity in Christ are added in 1:30: righteousness, sanctification, and redemption. Together with wisdom, these terms may form a fourfold contrast to the foolish, weak, lowly, and discounted nobodies of 1:27-28.[31] Or, the last three terms may define the results of God's peculiar wisdom.[32] The terms may also reflect the influence of Paul's source for the quotation that follows in 1:31: "Let one who boasts, boast in the Lord." [Jeremiah 9:24] The reference to God's action as steadfast love, justice, and righteousness may have led Paul to give a threefold explication of God's wisdom enacted in the cross of Christ. In any case, the stress is on the fact that they are *from* God. They are gifts, as Paul reminds them in 4:7, and thus boasting is precluded, except for boasting in what God has done.

Jeremiah 9:24

The text from Jer 9:24 that probably lies behind Paul's quotation reads, "But let those who boast boast in this, that they understand and know me, that I am the Lord; I act with steadfast love, justice, and righteousness in the earth, for in these things I delight says the Lord" (NRSV).

A Sophist's Start

Bruce Winter has described the way sophists typically began their careers in a new city. They would announce their intention to speak in a public setting and, when the crowd had gathered, would usually begin with a flowery encomium about the city and its citizens that was designed to flatter the audience. Then, to demonstrate their skill, they would declaim on a topic of the audience's choosing. If successfully proving their worth, the sophists would then be granted citizenship, enter into a public career of speaking on behalf of the city, establish a "school" of disciples, and display their success through public benefactions.

Bruce W. Winter, *Philo and Paul among the Sophists: Alexandrian and Corinthian Responses to a Julio-Claudian Movement* (2d ed.; Grand Rapids MI: Eerdmans Publishing, 2002) 141–79.

2:1-5. After directing the Corinthians' attention to their own status as a proof for his argument about the counterintuitive nature of God's wisdom, Paul directs their attention to himself, specifically his manner of proclaiming God's wisdom embodied in the cross. If their odd calling is a sign of God's unconventional working, then so is Paul's odd, unconventional preaching.

His recollection of his initial visit ("When I came to you") is probably designed to draw a contrast between his own style of preaching from the start and the usual pattern for sophists. [A Sophist's Start] His description of his preaching stresses its un*sophisti*c character. He asserts that he did not preach to them "in preeminence of speech or cleverness (*hyperochēn logou ē sophias*)" (2:1) and that he decided to know nothing among them "except Christ and him crucified" (2:2). He did not try to convince them of his superior rhetorical skill, nor did he claim to be an expert on any topic—only on the cross. Unlike self-assured sophists who would impress with their flair and earn an audience's adulation, he exhibited weakness and much fear and trembling (2:3). His rhetoric (*logos*) and his message (*kērygma*) were not in "persuasive words of wisdom (*peithois sophias logois*)" but in "clear proof (*apodeixei*) of the Spirit and of power" (2:4). [A Textual Matter in 1 Corinthians 2:4] He sought not to offer plausible arguments they would accept but rather to let the working of the Spirit and the manifestations of God's power among them prove the truth of his message. His aim was that their conviction (*pistis*) not be based on human rhetorical skill (*sophia anthrōpōn*) but on the power of God. Several of the terms he uses here suggest a deliberate contrast with sophistic rhetorical conventions, including the term *pistis*. While the word is usually translated as "faith" or "faithfulness," in this context the focus is on how the hearers become convinced of the truth of the message. For Paul, hearers are convinced (convicted) by the power of God, not by the successful manipulation of their thinking by skillful speakers.

This unit, then, flows naturally from 1:31 where Paul draws on Scripture to support his contention that the only boasting allowed is boasting in what God has done. Paul describes his own preaching as an embodiment of this. What he proclaimed to them was the "mystery of God" (2:1), not in the sense of a secret divulged to a select few but rather a message that originates with God and is not the result of human creativity. [The Text of 1 Corinthians 2:1] This mystery of what God has done in the crucified Christ is the only message conveyed by Paul. This message does not depend on the speaker's skill in manipulating language and emotions to convince an audience to

A Textual Matter in 1 Corinthians 2:4

Eleven different variant readings of *peithois sophias logois* can be found in ancient biblical manuscripts and in quotations by early church authors. The oldest manuscript (P^{46}) omits *logois*, while several add *anthrōpinēs* after *peithois*. The addition of *anthrōpinēs* is easily rejected as a later gloss, but the word *peithois* is problematic in that it appears nowhere else in any ancient Greek text. Since *peithois sophias logois* is supported by the early uncial texts ℵ*, A, C, D, and most ancient commentators and translations, it is accepted here.

The Text of 1 Corinthians 2:1

Several ancient manuscripts read *martyrion* instead of *mystērion*, leading many modern translations and commentators to prefer "testimony" over "mystery." The oldest papyrus (P46) appears to read *mystērion*, as do three of the oldest uncial texts (ℵ* A C) and some early translations (it^r syr^p). A copyist of ℵ altered it to read *martyrion*, thereby bringing it in line with other old uncials (B D) and several early translations ($it^{d,g}$ vg syr^h cop^{sa} eth). Since *mystērion* may be considered the more difficult reading and since one can understand how later copyists may have borrowed *martyrion* from 1:6 to avoid association with pagan mystery religions, *mystērion* is the preferred reading here.

Bruce M. Metzger, *A Textual Commentary on the Greek New Testament* (3rd ed.; Stuttgart: United Bible Societies, 1971) 545.

Anthony C. Thiselton, *The First Epistle to the Corinthians: A Commentary on the Greek Text* (NIGTC; Grand Rapids: Eerdmans, 2000) 207–208.

The Holy Trinity

El Greco (1541–1614). *The Trinity*, 1577–1579. Museo del Prado, Madrid, Spain. (Credit: Erich Lessing/Art Resource, NY)

El Greco's depiction of the crucified Christ in the arms of God the Father with the Holy Spirit hovering above them in the form of a dove enshrouded in brilliant light captures the threefold emphasis of Paul in 1 Cor 2:1-5. As the image of the crucified Christ fills the central portion of the painting, Paul's preaching centered on the message of Christ crucified. That message was delivered in demonstration of the power of the Holy Spirit to the end that faith might rest not in human wisdom but in the power of God.

accept it. Rather it has its clear proof in the working of God's Spirit and the demonstrations of its power to lead hearers to the conviction that the message is true. Thus, it is the power of God at work in the word of the cross, a foolish message from the perspective of human wisdom, that is saving those who believe it. The last phrase closes the loop of this section as an *inclusio* with 1:18 as Paul has come full circle in this unit, beginning and ending with the "power of God."

Communicating the Wisdom of God (2:6–3:4)

The next section poses something of an enigma. Paul has been arguing that the word of the cross eclipses human wisdom. In fact, the word of the cross is the only true wisdom. But now Paul seems to acknowledge that there is another wisdom that may be imparted to the mature. Since Paul does not directly relate this wisdom to the word of the cross, one might understand him to be saying that there is a body of teaching beyond the basic message of the cross that is reserved for those who are capable of receiving it. For this reason, some commentators have viewed Paul as rather Gnostic here since he holds in reserve for the mature a "secret and hidden wisdom of God" (2:7). Others have concluded that 2:2-16 must be an interpolation since Paul would not have written something that undercuts his previous argument.

Richard Hays has argued against viewing the passage as an interpolation or as a sign of Paul's incipient Gnosticism.[33] He contends that Paul is being ironic here. He offers no new, secret wisdom but rather cleverly subverts his readers' understanding of what constitutes wisdom and who possesses it. In response to criticism by the Corinthians that Paul has not taught them those higher teachings that other teachers have stepped up to provide, Paul asserts that he does, in fact, give such instruction—but only to the mature! In 3:1, he delivers the blow: they are not among the mature.

Paul may have employed irony here, but something else may also be at work. Paul confronts the difficulty of communicating God's wisdom. The truth of the word of the cross is not self-evident; in fact, on the surface it appears to be foolishness. Its truth, and the consequences of that truth for human behavior, becomes evident only through the working of God's Spirit. The Spirit's work in teaching "the things given by God to us" (2:12) occurs only among the "persons of the Spirit" (*pneumatikoi*). Paul labels the *unspiritual* as "merely human" (*psychikos anthrōpos*, 2:14), "humanly" (*sarkinos*; 3:1), "only human" (*sarkikos*; 3;3), and people who "live only in a human way" (*kata anthrōpon peripateite*; 3:3).[34] The Corinthians, who should be included among the *pneumatikoi*, have shown by their behavior that they are living as *unspiritual* humans. Thus, the full consequences of God's wisdom revealed in the cross remain incomprehensible to them. [Paul's Differentiating Terminology]

Paul's Differentiating Terminology

Paul uses a range of anthropological terms in his characterization of the Corinthians, but it would be presumptuous to view his intention to be that of presenting an anthropology per se. His objective was rhetorical, not educational, in that he was trying to expose the error of their current thinking and practice in order to convince them to change. His terminology, therefore, operates to draw strong contrasts between who they think they are, what their behavior says they are, and who they should be. They think that they are mature (*teleios*); Paul informs them that they are babies (*nēpioi*). They think they are spiritual (*pneumatikos*); Paul considers them to be "humanly" (*sarkinoi*) and "only human" (*sarkikoi*). Note that he does not actually call them "merely human" (*psychikoi anthrōpoi*). The *psychikos anthrōpos* does not have the Spirit of God, only the life force that invigorates the body. The sarkinos experiences the normal drives characteristic of human beings..The *sarkikos*, however, is completely oriented toward those drives as the defining features of human life. One's being *psychikos* and *sarkinos* is excusable, at least prior to conversion, since all persons are born into this mode of existence. Being *sarkikos*, however, is not, especially for those who are part of the church to which God's Spirit has been given. Paul's strongest contrast, then, is between the *pneumatikoi* and the *sarkikoi*. The Corinthians assume they are the former (and they should be), but their behavior is that of the contra-spiritual *sarkikoi*.

See David E. Garland, *1 Corinthians* (BECNT; Grand Rapids: Baker Academic, 2003) 109.

Paul's argument unfolds in the three-part concentric patter noted above (A—2:6-13; B—2:14-16; A'—3:1-4). Rhetorically, the section may be seen as a *digressio* since Paul takes a step back from the argument he has been pursuing to address a related matter, perhaps one presented to him by the Corinthians' criticism, as Hays suggests.

2:6-13. Paul's apocalyptic perspective again surfaces as he moves to discuss the role of the Spirit in communicating the wisdom of God. The wisdom that Paul communicates (*laloumen*) to the mature (*teleiois*) is not a wisdom of this age (*aiōnos*) nor of the rulers (*archontōn*) of this age. Some interpreters have seen in *archontōn* a reference by Paul to the kind of supernatural forces depicted in Ephesians 6:12. [Ephesians 6:12] Apocalypticism did frequently cast the political powers governing the world in otherworldly guise as an indication that the struggle between the faithful and their human adversaries was an expression of a supernatural contest between good and evil powers. But here, Paul probably means simply "the powers that be" in the sense of human rulers who call

Ephesians 6:12

For our struggle is not against enemies of flesh and blood, but against the rulers [*archas*], against the authorities, against the cosmic powers of this present darkness, against the spiritual forces of evil in the heavenly places. (NRSV)

the shots in the governance of world affairs on the earthly plane. They are the persons at the apex of the human pyramid of status and power. Paul speaks here in temporal terms, not spatial.[35] The time of their dominance is coming to an end as this age hurls toward its demise.

The wisdom that Paul imparts to the mature is not of this age. It remains hidden and unfathomable to those controlled by the mind-set of this age, even those who seem to control this age. This wisdom precedes this present age and even the age to come: "God decreed [it] before the *ages* for our glorification" (2:7; NRSV). That this wisdom should not be seen as a secret body of teaching disconnected from God's wisdom revealed in the cross becomes evident in God's purpose: "for our glorification." Through the cross, God is transforming the "things that are not" (1:28) into saints who will rule and judge the world (3:8; 6:2). The rulers of this age cannot understand this wisdom; otherwise they would not have crucified Christ. Why not? Either they would have known better than to have opposed the purposes of God revealed in Christ by crucifying him, or they would have known that the very act of crucifixion would launch the inauguration of the new age and the demise of that age in which they rule. Paul probably intended the latter here. The rulers unwittingly have contributed to their own end. So much then for worldly wisdom! If those at the top of the pyramid are clueless about what is really going on, then why trust in the wisdom of this world?

Isaiah 64:4

From ages past no one has heard,
No ear has perceived,
no eye has seen any God besides you,
who works for those who wait for him. (NRSV)

What remains incomprehensible to the powerful of this age has been revealed to the church through God's Spirit (2:10). What has been revealed is the glorification God has prepared for the saints. In support of this Paul cites Scripture ("But as it is written") in 2:9, but which Scripture is unclear. The nearest parallel is Isaiah 64:4 (LXX 64:3), but the wording there is different. [Isaiah 64:4] Origen thought Paul quoted the *Apocalypse of Elijah,* which is no longer extant.[36] Paul probably paraphrased Isaiah 64:4 to make his point that human wisdom cannot even glimpse what God is actually doing. An important emphasis in his paraphrase is that God has prepared something great for "those who *love* him." One might expect Paul to have written "those who *know* him." For Paul, knowledge of God is inseparable from love both for God and for others, as he will stress later in the letter.

The quotation leads into Paul's description of the work of the Spirit. The Spirit "searches" everything, including the "depths" of God (2:10). This "searching" is not so much "investigating" or "inquiring into" the unknown so as to discover the truth, but rather it is a "looking for" or "hunting for" what is at the heart of God so as to disclose it. Only God's Spirit can bring to light what lies in God's depths, much as a only a person's "spirit" can uncover that person's true self. Incredibly, Paul asserts, we have received God's own Spirit from God so that we might know those things given to us by God (2:12). What things? Paul does not refer here, nor in 2:14, to spiritual gifts (*pneumatika*), as he does later in 12:1 (as the NRSV incorrectly suggests). "The things of the Spirit" in 2:12 and 2:14 are the fuller consequences of the true wisdom of God. God's work in the cross of Christ has been oriented toward our "glorification," toward God's transformation of ourselves, including our transition from the competitive value-system of this age that divides us and keeps us enslaved to the dictates of this world's wisdom. Thus, Paul contends, we communicate (*laloumen*) these "things of the Spirit" in the "teachings of the Spirit" (*didaktois pneumatos*), not in the "teachings of human wisdom" (*didaktois anthrōpinēs sopias*). If some of the Corinthians thought they had received higher insight beyond what Paul had preached, either through advanced teaching by "wiser" preachers or through their own inquiry, they were mistaken, Paul held. [Dangerous Sight] Rather it is by the teachings of the Spirit, not human wisdom, that the things of the Spirit are *interpreted* to persons of the Spirit (*pneumaikoi*; 2:13). Most likely, this interpreting consists of the Spirit's opening up the person's understanding to the meaning of the word of the cross for identity in relation to God and behavior in relation to others.

Dangerous Sight

God gave us a mind in order that we might learn and receive help from him, not in order that the mind should be self-sufficient. Eyes are beautiful and useful, but if they choose to see without light, their beauty is useless and may even be harmful. Likewise, if my soul chooses to see without the Spirit, it becomes a danger to itself.

John Chrysostom, *Homilies on the Epistles of Paul to the Corinthians* 7.9, in Gerald Bray, ed., *1–2 Corinthians* (vol. 7 of ACCS NT; ed. Thomas C. Oden; Downers Grove IL: InterVarsity Press, 1999) 25.

2:14-16. The previous unit has stressed that understanding the wisdom of God, which Paul communicates to the mature, comes only through the working of God's Spirit. The Spirit's role here is to bring understanding to persons of the Spirit (*pneumatikoi*), that is to persons teachable by the Spirit. Not all persons are. For some persons, the "things of the Spirit" remain as foolishness. Such a person Paul calls *psychikos anthrōpos* ("merely human"). The noun from which the adjective *psychikos* is derived (*psychē*) is often translated "soul," but its basic meaning generally has to do with the *animating* force that brings a body to life. Thus, the Latin rendering is *animalis homo.* To draw from this the inference that Paul was referring to a subhuman "animal person," however, is to miss his point. The *psychikos anthrōpos* is not abnormal but rather one in the natural state of being human. Paul's terminology here has a parallel in 1 Corinthians 15:44 where he describes the body that dies as a *sōma psychikon.* This is not a negative or evil condition, but neither is it a sufficient one. The *psychikos anthrōpos* is empowered only by the life force common to all living beings; the Spirit (*pneuma*) of God does not dwell in that person. One who is "merely human" does not *accept* (*ou dechetai*) the things of the Spirit for they appear to be foolishness. Indeed, such a person cannot understand such things since they are discerned (or appraised) only from the perspective of the Spirit (*pneumatikōs* = spiritually). Resisting the Spirit's eye-opening activity, the *psychikos anthrōpos* remains unteachable and, therefore, bound to the normal human perspective from which God's wisdom appears foolish.

The person of the Spirit (*pneumatikos*), on the other hand, is able to appraise (*anakrinei*) all things (2:15). The distinction is not between "spiritual" people who have an innate capacity to appreciate "spiritual" things and those who lack this capacity. It is between those who will be taught by the Spirit and those who resist ("They do not accept"; 2:14). The *pneumatikos* is one to whom the Spirit is actively present, not one who is endowed with greater *spirituality.* One who is open to the Spirit's teaching can come to an understanding of what otherwise would appear foolish, namely the saving activity of God in the cross and its consequences for the believer. Since this person is guided by the Spirit's teaching, then that person is subject to no one else's appraisal (2:15). [Telling the Truth]

Telling the Truth

Who can condemn a man who tells the truth? When such a person states that all the enemies of the faith regard falsehood as true, their accusations are reduced to nothing because they are condemned by the judgment of the truth.

Ambrosiaster, *Commentary on Paul's Epistles* (CSEL 81.30-31) in Gerald Bray, ed., *1–2 Corinthians* (vol. 7 of ACCS NT; ed. Thomas C. Oden; Downers Grove IL: InterVarsity Press, 1999) 26.

To support this contention, Paul truncates a quotation from Isaiah 40:13: "For who has known the mind of the Lord so as to instruct him?" He has already pointed out that the Spirit searches even the depths of God (2:10). The one who is taught by the Spirit to appraise and understand spiritual things cannot be appraised by others any more than one could presume to instruct the Lord. The phrase "mind (*noun*) of the Lord" in the quotation leads Paul to affirm, "We have the mind (*noun*) of Christ." What the Spirit searches out and instructs the believer about is nothing other than that which is revealed in the cross of Christ. To have the mind of Christ is to see what God has done in Christ from the Spirit-led perspective that transforms the word of the cross from foolishness into the wisdom of God.

3:1-4. But to which group do the Corinthians belong, the *pneumatikoi* or the *psychikoi anthrōpoi*? Are they empowered only by the common life force, or are they empowered by the Spirit of God? On the one hand, they clearly belong to the *pneumatikoi*. The Spirit is not an individual possession but rather a corporate gift. As members of the church, they have received the Spirit. While some of them may have claimed to be more spiritual than others and, thus, to have become *teleios* (mature), they have missed the communal nature of the Spirit. On the other hand, they have not been behaving as *pneumatikoi*; thus Paul could not communicate with them as such (3:1). Paul had to approach them as being *sarkinoi* ("humanly"), which for one in Christ is an infantile state ("as babies"; *hōs nēpois*). The sting of this rebuttal to any claims that they were mature would have been sharp. Paul contends that he is still unable to address them as *pneumatikoi* for they are, in fact, "only human" (*sarkikoi*; 3:3). Being "only human" is worse than being "merely human" (*psychikoi*) or being "humanly" (*sarkinos*). Being "merely human" is the natural state of a living person. Being "only human" is to determine willfully that all things can be appraised only from the perspective of human wisdom. Paul asks whether the existence of jealousy (*zēlos*) and strife (*eris*) among them confirms that they are "only human" and "living only in a human way" (*kata anthrōpon peripateite*). Do not claims of exclusive loyalty to Paul or Apollos prove that they are the same as other humans (*anthrōpoi*) bound by the same lust for status and power and engaging in the same competitive struggles for its acquisition (3:4)?

Paul's language here regarding the contrast between *pneumaikoi* and *sarkikoi* (and related terms) should be viewed in context. (See [Paul's Differentiating Terminology] above.) Paul is not unpacking his anthropological understanding of human nature. He is arguing about perspective. God's wisdom, which cannot be understood from the perspective of human wisdom, does not lead persons to pursue the same agendas prescribed by worldly wisdom. Persons who pursue those agendas, even persons in the church (which has received the Spirit for instruction in God's wisdom), will be engulfed in competitive power struggles. The focal point, though not the origin, for such struggles in the Corinthian church has been the challenge to Paul's leadership on the basis of the criteria prescribed by worldly wisdom. This challenge betrays the underlying enslavement to worldly wisdom's system of evaluation on the part of those persons who should have known better. Thus, Paul concludes this section with two pointed questions to which he assumes the Corinthians know the correct answers. Yes, their quarreling over leaders reveals that they have been viewing things only from the perspective of human wisdom. How, then, should they see leaders? To that matter Paul now turns, and so shall we in the next chapter.

CONNECTIONS

The Devastation of Divisions

Paul's decision to confront the problem of divisions in the church at Corinth before addressing any other problems faced by that congregation is understandable. Beyond those reasons given in the commentary above for Paul's choosing to deal with this problem first, there is the simple truth that divisiveness appears to be endemic to Christianity. In fact, practically every religion that bases its beliefs and behaviors on revealed truth struggles with the problem of its adherents disagreeing about what has been revealed to be true. In the case of the Corinthians, it does not appear that their divisiveness was rooted in disagreements about doctrine. Instead, the source of their disagreement lay in their perspective toward the way God works in the world and the values they held. Paul's contention was that they misunderstood the working of God and that they held the wrong value system. Their perspective was too informed by the views and systems of valuation operative in their culture. The values of wealth, status, and social ranking shaped their perception of the gospel. According to Paul, they could not see that God's value system, as revealed in the cross of Christ, was contrary to their own. Their problem was, therefore, theological, though it manifested itself sociologically.

Undoubtedly, sociological differences have contributed to the divisions within the church throughout its history. The most glaring disruptions of the church's unity, however, have come from blatant theological disagreements. Such theological differences, often about the minutia of belief, have had a devastating effect on the church's presence and witness to the world. We are, in short, a divided people. The body of Christ is not merely broken; it has been shattered like broken glass into hundreds of pieces.

The reality of the fractured nature of the church was brought home to me in the summer of 1990 when I spent time traveling alone in Israel. I stayed for much of that time at the Maronite monastery in the Old City of Jerusalem. One morning I was joined by a former professorial colleague who had taught math at the college where I was employed. He was a Palestinian Maronite Christian who had spent his early childhood living in the Old City. After the "Six Day War" in 1967, his family had been forced to leave their home in the Old City, and his only visits back there were to attend worship services at the Maronite monastery near the Jaffa Gate. That morning we toured the Old City. As we entered areas with which I was familiar, but which he had never been allowed to visit as an Arab child, oddly I became something of an impromptu tour guide for him. We visited the Western Wall with its incredibly huge stones erected by Herod the Great as a retaining wall for his temple complex. We passed through security check points into the temple mount area and saw the Al Aksa mosque and the Dome of the Rock. I was impressed by his childlike wonderment as we viewed places this former resident of the Old City had never seen up close before. As we exited the mount complex and made our way down the Via Dolorosa, he told me that he had always been impressed by the emphasis Muslims and Jews placed on justice. He said, "One thing we surely need in this land is justice for everyone." "But," he then said, "Jews and Muslims do not have the key to solving our problems. We Christians with our emphasis on love hold the key." As we were talking, we entered the Church of the Holy Sepulchre, arguably the most sacred place in the world for Christians. Within that edifice, the reality of Christian division is strikingly evident in the centuries-old struggle between the various branches of the faith that have zealously claimed and protected their own areas within the one church building. The competition for space has been intense and at times violent. In microcosm, the Church of the Holy Sepulchre mirrors the fractured nature of the body of Christ. If Christians hold the key to reconciling the brokenness of the world, I thought in reflection on my colleague's remarks, then we had better learn how first to love one another. Paul appealed to his "word of the cross" in an attempt to resolve divisions within the church. The continuing challenge for the church is to pay attention to that word. [Hays on Division]

Church of the Holy Sepulchre

(Credit: Scott Nash)

Hays on Division

The division of the Christian communions is a scandal, and we should hear in Paul's letter to Corinth a reproach to ourselves for perpetuating this tragic state of affairs.

Richard B. Hays, *First Corinthians* (IBC; Louisville: John Knox Press, 1997) 25.

The Foolishness of God

The theological "heart" of 1 Corinthians is exposed in 1:18–2:5. In contrast to the prevailing cultural ethos that valued eloquence of speech and demonstration of personal power, Paul confronted his audience with a simple message of Christ crucified. To the church in Corinth, consisting mostly of persons whose personal lives were largely devoid of power over their own well-being, that message may have appeared odd in light of the way their society worked, but it at least offered some hope. If the crucifixion of Jesus, a scandalous event, was the evidence of God's power, then perhaps those political and religious forces that engineered his crucifixion, the same kind of forces that mostly shaped their day-to-day existence, were not ultimately in control after all. If, as they had already experienced to some degree, persons such as they could be called by God (1:26-28) to be a part of God's revolutionary transformation of the world's order, then perhaps they actually possessed more power than they had conceived was possible. And if the messenger of that word of power could be one such as Paul, whose presence and presentation left much to be desired (2:3-4), then perhaps the message was itself true.

Paul and the Cross

Statue of Saint Paul, in Saint Paul Cathedral garden, London. (Credit: Mathieu BOIS. http://commons.wikimedia.org/wiki/File:London_Statue_of_Saint_Paul_imgp3600.jpg)

Seeing its truth, however, required viewing the world differently. It required rejecting the definition of reality that had been given to them at birth and cultivated by nearly everything they had previously experienced. It required believing that things are not as they appear. Might does not make right, and the one who simply ends up with the most "toys" does not win. For the powerless, the word of the cross is a message of hope.

To the powerful, of course, that message is more hopeless than hopeful, and there apparently were some persons of relatively greater power within the Corinthian church, though probably not many. The radical reshaping of vision that the word of the cross calls for and actualizes in those who "get *it*" makes little sense to those who have benefited more from the ways and means of the prevailing culture and already "have *it*." The "*it*," of course, is different for the two groups. For the ones who "have *it*," the standards by which the world operates make sense in that they have been able to negotiate the channels successfully enough to have a piece of "*it*" for themselves. For those who "get *it*," however, those prevailing standards have been exposed as false, and the "*it*" that matters is no longer the prize one receives for playing the game well. For them, "*it*" is a radically different way of seeing the world whose "form is passing away" (7:31), and a vision of the new world that is already coming in those who understand that "those who save their life will lose it, and those who give their life will save it" (Mark 8:35).

Into which of the two groups should we place the church today? Perhaps for the vast majority of the world's approximately 2.1 billion Christians who do not "have it," God's foolish word of the cross is still a message of hope, for it still speaks a strong word of liberation from bondage to the world's power systems and offers a promise of transformation not only of the person but also of the person's world. [Transformation Is the Promise] For the majority of Christians in more affluent nations (where the percentage of Christians in the population is in decline) who do largely "have it" (and more!) the word of the cross may generate more discomfort than hope. For them of course, that word offers the very personal and individualistic hope of forgiveness of sins and eternal life in the next world, but none of that requires radically reassessing the standards by which this world operates, let alone trying to transform them. Why should they want to change a world order that has been good to them and for them?

Transformation Is the Promise

Transformation is the promise at the heart of the Christian life. . . . Christianity for the rest of us is not about personal salvation, not about getting everybody else saved, or about the politics of exclusion and moral purity. Christianity for the rest of us is the promise of transformation—that, by God's mercy, we can be different, our congregations can be different, and our world can be different.

Diana Butler Bass, *Christianity for the Rest of Us: How the Neighborhood Church Is Transforming the Faith* (San Francisco: HarperSanFrancisco, 2006) 281.

For those ensconced in the world's wisdom, both those outside and inside the church, the word of the cross still appears foolish. Its message of radical reversal and transformation is no longer necessary, except perhaps in the narrow, domesticated sense of the enhancement of one's self esteem. For such persons, the Christ of the cross is an "awesome God" who looks out for us now and will take us home to be with him one day. He is not the one in whom the wisdom and ways of this world are challenged, convicted, and changed by the foolishness of God. [The Perfect Fool]

The Perfect Fool

What God says, on the other hand, is "The life you save is the life you lose." In other words, the life you clutch, hoard, guard, and play safe with is in the end a life worth little to anybody, including yourself, and only a life given away for love's sake is a life worth living. To bring his point home, God shows us a man who gave his life away to the extent of dying a national disgrace without a penny in the bank or a friend to his name. In term's of men's wisdom, he was a Perfect Fool, and anybody who thinks he can follow him without making something like the same kind of fool of himself is laboring under not a cross but a delusion.

There are two kinds of fools in the world: damned fools and what St. Paul calls "fools for Christ's sake" (1 Cor 4:10).

Frederick Buechner, *Wishful Thinking: A Theological ABC* (New York: Harper & Row, 1973) 28.

People of the Spirit, 2:6–3:4

Some of the Corinthian believers had apparently become disenchanted with Paul as a teacher and leader. He seemed to lack those rhetorical gifts that were normally associated with esteemed teachers. His speech lacked the eloquence speakers such as the Sophists sought to develop and exhibit. Since eloquent rhetoric was viewed as an essential part of making a convincing argument, the content of his message was also seen to be lacking in wisdom as it was commonly understood, that is, as *sophisti*cation. Paul's initial response to such evaluations was to charge the Corinthians with using the wrong criteria for evaluating wisdom. The wisdom of God is not presented through eloquent rhetoric or sophisticated arguments. The wisdom of God comes through the demonstration of the Spirit and of power (2:4).

In the section 2:6–3:4, Paul turns the tables on his audience. In truth, *he* is not the person lacking in wisdom; *they* are. He has a wisdom from God, but he has been unable to communicate that wisdom to them because of their immaturity. Since such wisdom is taught and understood through the Spirit, their failure to recognize his wisdom is an indication that they are not sufficiently people of the Spirit. They have received the Spirit, in as much as it is a communal gift to the whole church. Their growth in the Spirit, however, has been arrested. Their divisive behavior is evidence that they are still babies in Christ (3:1). Paul asserts that he and his associate teachers have the mind of Christ (2:12, 16), which would be impossible without the Spirit's presence in them (2:11). Later in 7:40, he asserts that he has the Spirit of God and, thus, is qualified to instruct them.

Paul's autobiographical references in both 1 Corinthians and 2 Corinthians indicate that he would be one of those persons that Marcus Borg has labeled a "spirit person." [Spirit Persons] According to Borg, such persons become mediators of the reality beyond this world that they have experienced. They are "funnels or conduits for the power or wisdom of God to enter this world."[37] As one who possessed (or was possessed by) the Spirit of God, Paul saw himself called to interpret the Spirit-taught truths to those who themselves possessed the Spirit (2:13). His contention that he had been hampered in fulfilling this role for the Corinthians was an indictment of their lack of spirituality. Paul may not have expected that every believer would have the same kind of intense experience of the Spirit that he did, for "everyone has their own special gift from God" (7:7),

Spirit Persons

Marcus Borg has characterized Jesus and Paul as "spirit persons," that is one for whom the Spirit is an experiential reality. According to Borg,

> What all persons who have these experiences share is a strong sense of there being more to reality than the tangible world of our ordinary experience. They share a compelling sense of having experienced something "real." They feel strongly that they know something that they didn't know before. Their experiences are noetic, involving not simply a *feeling* of ecstasy, but a *knowing*. What such persons know is the sacred. Spirit persons are people who experience the sacred frequently and vividly. (author's italics)

Marcus J. Borg, *Meeting Jesus Again for the First Time: The Historical Jesus and the Heart of Contemporary Faith* (San Francisco: HarperSanFrancisco, 1994) 32–33.

but he did expect them to heed his instruction as a Spirit-called apostle.

For Paul, each person might experience the Spirit of God in a distinctive way (12:7), but none would be led by the Spirit to do anything detrimental to the temple of God's Spirit, the church (3:16). The spirit of divisiveness that plagued them was, clearly to Paul, not of the Spirit. While the Spirit had been given to them as a community of faith, not everyone in that community was working toward the edification of the body of Christ. Not every one of the Corinthians would necessarily be defined by Borg as a "spirit person," but collectively, as the church, they were a people of the Spirit. As such, they needed to grow up in the Spirit and build up the community.

Spirituality

Spirituality, seen naked of God, is a place of unknowing: the domain of the soul where image is as language is to the body within the physical world and where a glowing presentness is as the body is in the world of human affairs; where silence is musical and light without source is everywhere in the numen; where instruction comes without words and slips in as revelation; where forces flow so powerfully and in so foreign a coursing that, coming to the window of consciousness in order all the better to see them, the mind must name them instead, calling them like phantasmagoria by their roles and not their essence—spirits, angels, demons, and devils; where, timeless and boneless, every reconfiguring soul wanders in communion with what is, and wisdom is as logic is to the mind.

Phyllis A. Tickle, *Re-Discovering the Sacred: Spirituality in America* (New York: Crossroad, 1995) 101.

In recent times, persons have increasingly expressed interest in "spirituality." [Spirituality] At the same time, persons who identify themselves as "spiritual" also often quickly confess that they are not "religious." "Religion," which is often defined as "organized," appears to them to be restrictive and uninviting. "Spirituality," however, is seen as liberating, empowering, and fulfilling. Paul, who was in on the beginning stages of what became the world's largest religion, would have argued, I think, that the church was supposed to be liberating, empowering, and fulfilling. I suspect Paul would also argue that the quest for these goals cannot

be satisfied in isolation from fellow seekers. *Community* is an essential part of human *fulfillment.* "Religion," as a word, comes from the Latin terms *re* and *ligio* (*ligare*) and means to "tie together again." Etymologically speaking, religion is intended to tie us to God and to each other. The experience of many persons, however, has been that religion ties them *down* or ties them *up*, and so they have rejected it. Leaving the community of religion, though, has not always led to spiritual fulfillment. Isolation from and ignoring the needs of the community may lead to the deterioration of the community *and* the stunted fulfillment of the individual. Ideally, religion and spirituality overlap, much as the individual quest for spiritual fulfillment overlaps with the experience of a religious community. The church, which consists of individual souls united to Christ through the Spirit to form a community, is to be about the building up of the body of Christ for the transformation of God's world.

Lectionary Connections

Several readings from this section are included in the Revised Common Lectionary. First Corinthians 1:10-17 is read on the third Sunday after Epiphany, along with Isaiah 9:1-4 and Matthew 4:12-23 in Year A. The Isaiah text is partially quoted in the Mark passage in connection to the preaching of Jesus. The selection from 1 Corinthians has to do mostly with the problem of divisions, but a point of contact may be found in Paul's assertion that he had not been sent to baptize, but rather to preach the gospel.

First Corinthians 1:18-25, in Year C, is read on the second Sunday after Christmas, while a portion of the same text (1:22-25) is also used in Year B on the third Sunday in Lent. The longer reading is joined with Job 28:20-28, which speaks of God's wisdom, and Luke 2:36-40, which ends with a reference to Jesus' being filled with wisdom. The connection with Paul's discourse on the wisdom of God is fairly obvious. The shorter reading is joined to Exodus 20:1-3, 7-8, 12-17, and John's description of Jesus' condemnation of the Jerusalem temple cultus (John 2:13-25). Since John's account includes the Jews demanding a sign of Jesus, the tie to Paul's reference to Jews' demanding a sign is clear. Not so clear is the connection of either New Testament text to the Exodus passage, which concerns the Decalogue.

On the fourth Sunday after Epiphany, 1 Corinthians 1:26-31 is read in Year A in association with Zephaniah 2:3; 3:11-13, and Matthew 5:1-2. All three texts announce God's choice of the humble and lowly over the proud and arrogant.

First Corinthians 2:1-5 is read on the fifth Sunday after Epiphany in Year A, along with Isaiah 58:7-10 and Matthew 5:13-16. The Isaiah passage admonishes the help of the lowly and needy and promises that God's light will go with those who perform such deeds of service. The Matthean excerpt from the Sermon on the Mount identifies Jesus' listeners as the salt of the earth and the light of the world. Paul's words reflect the stance of one who gives light to the world through humble proclamation of the cross.

On the next Sunday after Epiphany in the same year, 1 Corinthians 2:6-10 is joined with Deuteronomy 30:15-20 and Matthew 5:27-37. The text from Deuteronomy presents the two ways: one way leads to death, while God's way leads to life. The Matthean passage includes some of Jesus' "Antitheses" in the Sermon on the Mount. Jesus calls for going beyond the way spelled out in the Torah of old. Paul indicates that the way of God involves a wisdom that is not of this world. It summons one beyond reason and the normal patterns of behavior.

NOTES

1. Edmund Burke, *Speech on the Petition of the Unitarians* (1792).

2. While I agree that various kinds of divisions existed in the Corinthian church, I disagree with Mitchell, Witherington, and others that the whole letter should be seen primarily as a unified argument for concord. See Margaret M. Mitchell, *Paul and the Rhetoric of Reconciliation: An Exegetical Investigation of the Language and Composition of 1 Corinthians* (Louisville: Westminster John Knox, 1991) and Ben Witherington III, *Conflict and Community in Corinth: A Socio-Rhetorical Commentary and 1 and 2 Corinthians* (Grand Rapids: Eerdmans, 1995). I agree with L. L. Welborn, "Discord in Corinth: First Corinthians 1–4 and Ancient Politics," as revised in his *Politics and Rhetoric in the Corinthian Epistles* (Macon GA: Mercer University Press, 1997) 1–42, that concord was the aim of Paul in 1 Cor 1–4, though I think he overly stresses the purely political nature of the divisions.

3. Whether Paul was ultimately successful in bringing an end to the divisions in the Corinthian church during his time or not, the propensity of the Christian community to foster divisiveness is evident at the turn of the first century in *1 Clement*. See the discussion of the situation addressed in *1 Clement* by Barbara Ellen Bowe, *A Church in Crisis* (HDR 23; Minneapolis: Fortress Press, 1988).

4. Nils Dahl, *Studies in Paul: Theology for the Early Christian Mission* (Minneapolis: Augsburg Press, 1977) 49ff.

5. Elisabeth Schüssler Fiorenza, "Rhetorical Situation and Historical Reconstruction in 1 Corinthians," *NTS* 33 (1987): 157.

6. Alexandra R. Brown, *The Cross and Human Transformation: Paul's Apocalyptic Word in 1 Corinthians* (Minneapolis: Fortress, 1995) 30.

7. Charles Talbert, *Reading Corinthians: A Literary and Theological Commentary on 1 and 2 Corinthians* (rev. ed.; Macon GA: Smyth & Helwys, 2002).

8. Ibid., 16–22.

9. The concentric pattern given here is different from the one Talbert, *Reading Corinthians*, 16–17, sees in 1:18-31.

10. Rudolf Pesch, *Paulus ringt um die Lebensform der Kirche. Viere Briefe an die gemeinde Gottes in Korinth* (Freiburg: Herder, 1986) 73–100, and Helmut Merklein, *Der erste Brief an die Korinther. Kapitel 1-4* (ÖTK 7/1; Gütersloh: Mohn, 1992) 109–13.

11. Mitchell, *Paul and the Rhetoric of Reconciliation*.

12. Ibid., 185–225.

13. I agree with Murphy-O'Connor, who holds that 1 Cor "does not contain an overarching *propositio*" (*Paul the Letter-Writer: His World, His Options, His Skills* [Collegeville MN: Liturgical Press, 1995] 85).

14. Limiting the *narratio* to 1:11-12 is supported by the noted scholar of ancient rhetoric, George Kennedy, *New Testament Interpretation*, 25, who, however, sees 1:10 as the proposition for the whole letter.

15. Mitchell, *Paul and the Rhetoric of Reconciliation*, 199, points out that a *partitio* is not required, especially with a single proposition.

16. Hans-Josef Klauck's *Ancient Letters and the New Testament: A Guide to Context and Exegesis* (Waco TX: Baylor University Press, 2006) 219.

17. See Murphy-O'Connor, *Paul the Letter-Writer*, 77.

18. See Philip A. Harland, "Familial Dimensions of Group Identity: 'Brothers' (Ἀδελφοί) in Associations of the Greek East," *JBL* 124 (2005): 491–513.

19. Anthony C. Thiselton, *The First Epistle to the Corinthians: A Commentary on the Greek Text* (NIGTC; Grand Rapids: Eerdmans, 2000) 115.

20. Welborn, "Discord in Corinth: First Corinthians 1–4 and Ancient Politics," 3.

21. David R. Hall, *The Unity of the Corinthian Correspondence* (JSNTSup 251; London: T & T Clark Int., 2003) 6.

22. Mitchell, *Paul and the Rhetoric of Reconciliation*, 81–83.

23. Benjamin Fiore, "'Covert Allusion' in 1 Cor 1–4," *CBQ* 47 (1985): 85–102.

24. Thiselton, *The First Epistle to the Corinthians*, 349–51.

25. See Donald P. Ker, "Paul and Apollos–Colleagues or Rivals?" *JSNT* 77 (2000): 75–97, and Joop F. M. Smit, "Epideictic Rhetoric in Paul's First Letter to the Corinthians 1–4," *Bib* 84 (2003): 184–201.

26. See Stephen M. Pogoloff, *Logos and Sophia: The Rhetorical Situation of 1 Corinthians* (SBLDS 134; Atlanta: Scholars Press, 1992) 108–13.

27. Suggested by François Bavon in a seminar on 1 Corinthians at Harvard Divinity School on 8 February 2001.

28. Brown, *The Cross and Human Transformation*, 76.

29. Richard B. Hays, *First Corinthians* (IBC; Louisville: John Knox Press, 1997) 27.

30. See the discussion of "The Corinthian Congregation" in the Introduction.

31. Thiselton, *The First Epistle to the Corinthians*, 190–91.

32. Gordon D. Fee, *The First Epistle to the Corinthians* (NICNT; Grand Rapids: Eerdmans Publishing, 1987) 85.

33. Hays, *First Corinthians*, 39–46.

34. The difficulty of adequately translating these terms is thoroughly discussed by Thiselton, *The First Epistle to the Corinthians*, 267–71, 288–93.

35. Henrik Tonier, "The Corinthian Correspondence between Philosophical Idealism and Apocalypticism," in *Paul beyond the Judaism/Hellenism Divide* (ed. Troels Engberg-Pederson; Louisville: Westminster John Knox Press, 2001), 182–86, argues that Paul is speaking primarily in a spatial sense here in that Paul is striving to lead the Corinthians to interpret their earthly reality from the perspective of God's heavenly wisdom rather than that of worldly wisdom. He fails to note sufficiently, however, the temporal dimension of Paul's language in contrasting the knowledge of the rulers of this age with the knowledge imparted by the Spirit whose presence is a sign of the in-breaking of the new age.

36. Thiselton, *The First Epistle to the Corinthians*, 251.

37. Marcus J. Borg, *Meeting Jesus Again for the First Time: The Historical Jesus and the Heart of Contemporary Faith* (San Francisco: HarperSanFrancisco, 1994) 33.

SERVING TOGETHER FOR THE GOOD OF THE CHURCH

1 Corinthians 3:5–4:21

All service ranks the same with God,
With God, whose puppets, best and worst,
Are we; there is no last or first.[1]

Paul's argument takes a different turn at 3:5. He begins to focus more directly on the problem first identified in 1:10-12. His response to the problem of divisions has followed a threefold, inverted response to the rhetorical questions with which he began his argument in 1:13. "Is Christ divided? Was Paul crucified for you? Or were you baptized in the name of Paul?" Finally, after having addressed the third question in 1:14-17 and the second in 1:18–2:5, he takes up his first question. [A Thematic Outline of 1 Corinthians 3:5–4:21]

A Thematic Outline of 1 Corinthians 3:5–4:21

I. Rightly Perceiving the Servants of the Lord (3:5-17)
- A. Cultivating the Field of God (3:5-9)
- B. Building on the Foundation of Christ (3:10-15)
- C. Caring for the Temple of God (3:16-17)

II. Appraising with Godly Wisdom (3:18–4:5)
- A. Rightly Discerning One's Self (3:18-23)
- B. Rightly Regarding Christ's Servants (4:1-5)

III. Applying God's Wisdom to the Church (4:6-21)
- A. An Argument against Boasting (4:6-7)
- B. Apostles as Spectacles and Refuse (4:8-13)
- C. Admonishment from a Father (4:14-21)

As pointed out previously, however, he does not directly speak to the issue of Christ's being divided. (See the section titled "The Structure of 1 Corinthians 1:10–4:21" in ch. 2.) Instead, he focuses on the question of identity. Since the problem of divisions has manifested itself in terms of loyalty to leaders, Paul presents an understanding of leadership that is very different from the one that has created the problem in Corinth. Clarifying the role and function of leaders leads to his defining the identity of the Corinthians themselves, again over against the one that seemed to prevail among them. Thus, his argument contains a series of statements cast in the first person ("We are . . .") or second person (You are . . ."). [Identity Statements in 1 Corinthians 3:5–4:21] His exhortations or admonishments typically appear in the third person throughout the section until near the end when he states, "Therefore, do not judge anything before the time, until the Lord comes" (4:5). This eschatologically grounded exhortation leads into the concluding section of his argument regarding divisions (4:6-21).

Identity Statements in 1 Corinthians 3:5–4:21

In this section Paul uses the first- and second-person voice to make statements of identity and third-person voice for exhortation and admonition. The exceptions, where he exhorts directly or indirectly in the second person, are noted in bold type below.

First Person	Second Person	Third Person
3:5-6 We are servants	3:9b You are God's field	3:7-8 Those who plant and water are equal
3:9a We are God's fellow workers	3:16 You are God's temple	3:10b-15 Let one be careful how one builds
3:10 I laid a foundation as a master builder	3:21b-22 You possess all things	3:17 If anyone destroys God's temple
4:1b [We are] as servants and stewards	3:22 You are Christ's	3:18a Let no one be deceived
4:3-4 I am judged only by God	4:5a **(You) should not judge before the time**	3:18b Let one become a fool
4:6a I have applied this to Apollos and myself	4:6b so that **You might not be puffed up**	3:21a Let no one boast of humans
4:9 We are a spectacle to the world	4:7b You have received a gift	4:1a Let one regard us thusly
4:10 We are fools, weak, in disrepute	4:7c **Why do you boast?**	4:2 Stewards must be trustworthy
4:11-13 We hunger, thirst, etc.	4:8 You are filled, rich, ruling.	4:5b Everyone will receive their commendation from God
4:15 I am your father in Christ	4:10 You are wise, strong, esteemed	
	4:14 You are my beloved children	
	4:16 **Imitate me**	

Even in his conclusion, though, he continues to focus on identity. First, he sarcastically attacks the arrogance of the Corinthians with a series of "You are" statements that contrasts their claims for boasting with the comparably inferior status of himself and other apostles (We are . . ."). Then, he explains that his purpose in arguing as he has is rooted in his identity as their father and theirs as his beloved children (4:14-15). He then brings the two sets of identities together when he urges them, "Be imitators of me." The section comes to an end with his brief projection of travel plans for himself and Timothy, plans designed to confirm the result he intended his letter to accomplish.

The concluding section (4:6-21) may be seen rhetorically as a summary (*peroratio*). The high level of *pathos* in his sarcastic description of their arrogance, in his depiction of the apostles as their lowly counterparts, and in his final portrayal of his paternal relationship to them would all have served to appeal to the emotions, as the *peroratio* was typically designed to do. Mitchell has identified numerous epideictic elements in Paul's deliberative rhetoric in this section as Paul uses the traditional device of blame to indict the Corinthians' present behavior.[2] (See the section titled "1 Corinthians as Rhetoric" in the Introduction.) His objective remains the correction of future behavior, however, as his final question about the nature of his eventual visit indicates (4:21). (See [A Rhetorical Outline of Paul's Argument in 1 Corinthians 1:10–4:21] in chapter 2.)

COMMENTARY

Rightly Perceiving the Servants of the Lord (3:5-17)

The section opens with a clear connection to 3:4 in the repetition of the names of Paul and Apollos. Agricultural and architectural metaphors abound as Paul strives to present the Corinthians with a different lens for viewing these two leaders and themselves.

One significant matter for interpretation concerns the place of Apollos in the argument of this section. Paul appears keenly bent on dispelling any idea that he and Apollos are competitors. No direct criticism of Apollos appears. They are both servants and fellow workers of God. Yet at the same time, Paul describes his work in relation to Apollos as being prior in time and, by implication, superior in some way. That Paul understood, and wanted the Corinthians to understand, that his role was unique eventually comes out clearly in the conclusion to the whole section in which Paul asserts that he is their *only* father (4:15).

So, did some tension exist between Paul and Apollos or not? Commentators, of course, are divided. Did Paul use the example of Apollos because he and Apollos served as models of the kind of unity Paul wished to prevail among the Corinthians? That is, by demonstrating that the two preachers most prominent among and best known to the Corinthians were united in their ministries, was Paul undermining the existence of factions that had lined up behind unknown leaders present in the church in Corinth?[3] Or, did Paul depict their relationship as more unified than it actually was in order to counter the preference some Corinthians had for Apollos? That is, was the basic division in Corinth between those loyal to Paul and those loyal to Apollos, and was Paul trying to defuse the Apollos faction by affirming the equality of the two preachers while subtly asserting his own dominant role?[4]

Paul and Apollos

Sir Edward Poynter. *Paul and Apollos*. 1872. Fresco on plaster. Tate Collections. (Credit: © Tate, London 2009)

The position taken here is a combination of the two options. Most of what Paul wrote in regard to Apollos was, as Paul suggests in 4:6, a metaphorical application to himself and Apollos intended to expose the error of unnamed sophistic leaders in the church. At the same time, his subtle diminishing of Apollos's role appears aimed at those who favored him over Paul. Whether Apollos consciously contributed to the competitive way the Corinthians viewed the two remains debated and unsolvable.

3:5-9. The way Paul frames his opening questions here is significant. He asked, "*What* then is Apollos? *What* is Paul?" He did not ask, "*Who* is . . . ?" The use of the neuter interrogative *ti* rather than the masculine/feminine *tis* places the two men in the category of *things.* The two men are instruments used by God. The low status this implies is confirmed in his answer to his questions: "We are servants" (*diakonoi*). Rather than a reference to the later office of deacon, the term suggests a lowly, menial figure who does the master's bidding. The questions and the answer also move the focus into the realm of function, as Andrew Clarke has observed, and out of the competitive realm of personalities.[5] Thus, in contrast to the personality contests of sophists' jockeying for superior position, Paul claims for himself and Apollos the function of lowly service. Paul only planted and Apollos only watered, and neither is anything (3:6-7). This reversal of status becomes important later in Paul's argument (4:9-13).

We should not miss, however, the high status also affirmed by Paul's language. As *diakonoi,* they are the servants through whom the Corinthians' faith began, as the Lord assigned. Furthermore, their planting and watering were followed by God's giving the growth. The focus is on God's activity, but their functions are a part of what God is doing. The planter and the waterer are equally fellow workers (*synergoi*) of God, and each will receive appropriate wages from the employer (3:8). On the one hand, this equality reduces the status of both Paul and Apollos to that of hired hands. On the other hand, the fact that they render this menial service for God elevates the status of such service.

Paul extends the agricultural language to include the church: "You are God's field" (3:9) A connection with Old Testament imagery depicting Israel as God's vineyard may have been intended by Paul (esp. Isa 5:1-7). [Isaiah 5:7] In any case, the identification of the church in this way also suggests a two-pronged point. (1) The church as field is passively cultivated by God; God alone gives the growth. The field cannot boast of its accomplishments. (2) Nevertheless, it is the field of God. For both the laborers and the field, the only aspect of identity that carries any significant status is the fact that they belong to God.

Isaiah 5:7

For the vineyard of the Lord
of hosts
is the house of Israel,
and the people of Judah
are his pleasant planting;
he expected justice,
but saw bloodshed;
righteousness,
but heard a cry!

(NRSV)

3:10-15. In 3:9, Paul also introduces an architectural metaphor that he will expand in the following verses: "You are God's building." [The Church as Building] Verses 10-11 have a concentric pattern:

A—I laid a foundation
B—another is building on it
B'—let one take care how one builds upon it
A' — the foundation is . . . Jesus Christ

In such chiasmic arrangements, the emphasis often falls on the central elements (B and B'), and that is the case here. Paul switches his metaphorical identity from lowly servant to skilled master-builder (*sophos architektōn*), but he prefaces this by acknowledging that this role was "according to the grace of God that was given to me." The translation of *sophos* as "skilled" here does not mitigate its ironic association with the wise (*sophos*) of 1:20 (and elsewhere) but rather heightens the contrast between those who are wise in a worldly sense and the skilled builder who contributes to the edification of God's building. As the chief architect in this building's construction, Paul has laid the foundation, which he points out is none other than the Jesus Christ (crucified) that he proclaimed. In between these two statements about the foundation appears Paul's acknowledgment that another is building on his foundation and his admonition that anyone doing so should exercise caution. This word of caution is the main point of the unit.

The Church as Building

In addition to 3:9-17, Paul uses building imagery in 1:6, 8; 4:1; 6:19, 8:1, 10; 9:17; 10:23; 14:3-5, 12, 17, 26; and 15:58. Margaret Mitchell has observed the frequency of terms associated with building in 1 Corinthians and has labeled the metaphorical reference to the church as a building "the predominant image of the epistle." She has further noted the use of this imagery in ancient appeals to unity for divided groups. Later in the letter (14:3-4), Paul stresses the use of spiritual gifts for the "building up" of the church.

Margaret M. Mitchell, *Paul and the Rhetoric of Reconciliation: An Exegetical Investigation of the Language and Composition of 1 Corinthians* (Louisville: Westminster John Knox, 1991) 99–111.

Paul elaborates on his warning about careful building on the foundation through a series of contrasts. One can build with durable materials (gold, silver, expensive stones) or with perishable ones (wood, hay, straw) (3:12). The quality of what is built will be revealed at the eschatological judgment (*hē hēmera* = the Day [of the Lord]; 3:13). The devastating fire to which ancient buildings, and even cities, were vulnerable often becomes, in apocalyptic language, the vehicle of God's judgment, as it does here. While in actuality all of the materials mentioned by Paul would have been ruined by fire, his point is that careful, costly construction stands the test while shoddy building with cheaper, inferior materials does not. As the materials of construction suffer different fates, so do the building contractors. The one whose construction survives will receive the appropriate "wages" (*misthon*), while the one whose work is consumed "will suffer a penalty" (*zēmōthēsetai*).[6] Paul adds that the contractor using poor materials would not suffer destruction but would be saved by "the skin of his/her teeth" (i.e., "as through fire").

In this unit the subtle hint of the priority of Paul's work over that of his successors becomes more pointed. Planting and watering may be essentially equal tasks blessed by God's giving the growth. By laying the only acceptable foundation (Christ), however, the master-builder Paul has given a blueprint from which later builders depart at their own peril. The Corinthians are, therefore, warned that any would-be contractors (preachers) who differ from Paul in the basis of their work (preaching) are practicing shoddy construction, however appealing their edifice may appear. The juxtaposing of "I have laid a foundation" and "another one is building upon it" in 3:10 may parallel Paul's planting and Apollos's watering in 3:6. If so, it may be taken as an indirect criticism of Apollos (or, at least, of his supporters). Some commentators, however, stress the present tense of the verb *epoikodomei* ("is building upon") in 3:10 and argue that this excludes Apollos since he was not in Corinth at the time.[7] Paul's admonition that "each one take care how one is building upon it," however, seems inclusive of anyone building on the foundation, including Apollos and Paul.[8]

Paul's language of rewards and punishments here poses problems for some readers since it seems to run counter to his emphasis elsewhere on salvation by grace. Note, however, that Paul does not refer to heavenly rewards or hellish punishments for the saved or the lost but rather to the results of the final scrutiny of a building contractor's work. The metaphor stresses that one who builds well gets paid while one who does not pays a penalty, in accordance with the building contract. Applied to the church, the metaphor suggests that preachers who actually do harm to the church (God's building) are liable for the damages, though they themselves may be spared bankruptcy.

3:16-17. The theme of responsibility for the well-being of God's edifice is intensified when the

Jerusalem Temple

(Credit: Scott Nash)

In Paul's time, the magnificent temple of Herod in Jerusalem was the center of Jewish devotion. The book of Acts depicts the followers of Jesus going regularly to the temple. Acts also describes a visit by Paul to the temple and the ensuing riot that led to his arrest (Acts 21:27-36). While the Jews had only one temple, temples were among the most common public buildings in the Gentile world. Corinth certainly had its share. Most pagan temples, like the Jerusalem temple, were oriented facing east with an altar in front on the east. Pagan temples typically had a cult statue or some other image representing the deity in the western end of the main temple building, facing the altar to the east. While the Jerusalem temple was the only one that held any legitimacy for Paul, his readers would probably not have envisioned that temple, but rather one with which they were more familiar, when Paul described the church as a temple (3:16-17).

nature of that edifice is cast in the metaphor of a temple. In declaring, "you are God's temple," Paul is clearly moving in a different direction from his assertion earlier that they were "merely human," "only human," and "living only in a human way" (3:1-3). Here Paul affirms that they are, in fact, people of the Spirit (*pneumatikoi*), since God's Spirit dwells in them. To account for Paul's apparent change in disposition toward the Corinthians we must consider a few features of the metaphor.

First, Paul uses here the term *naos*, which usually pertained to the main building in a temple complex, rather than *hieron*, which usually referred to the entire sanctuary complex. [Lanci on *Naos*] The *naos* housed the cult statue or symbolic relics, as well as many of the votive gifts donated by devotees. While the *hieron* may have designated sacred space, the *naos* housed the divine presence. Though Paul's Corinth contained numerous temples, the only other temple (besides the church) that Paul would have acknowledged as actually indwelt by the presence of God in any sense would have been the Jerusalem temple. Any association with the Jerusalem temple, however, should not be pressed beyond his basic point, that the church constitutes a place where God's Spirit dwells.

Lanci on *Naos*

John Lanci correctly points out that *naos* typically referred to the actual building that housed the statue or other object representing the deity and that the term *hieron* was usually used to mean all of the sacred area within the boundary (*temenos*). Technically, only the section of the building that housed the cult object was the *naos* proper, but since the other parts of the building (e.g., *pronaos* and *opithodomos*) were under the same roof as the *naos*, the entire building could also be called the *naos*. Thus, Lanci is correct in his criticism of NT scholars who take *naos* to refer only to the Holy of Holies, which was actually only a part of the *naos*. Lanci also argues that the terms *naos* and *hieron* were more interchangeable than NT commentators typically acknowledge, citing Josephus as an example. His main evidence that Josephus used *naos* and *hieron* interchangeably (*Bell*. 5.207), however, can be read otherwise. Josephus seems to have maintained a distinction between the temple building (*naos*) and temple precinct (*hieron*). So does Paul. As Lanci points out, Paul's only reference to *hieron* (1 Cor 9:13) refers to a temple complex, not a *naos* (main building). Josephus and Paul did not use *naos* to refer only to the Holy of Holies, as Lanci observes. Since *naos* often did refer to the total building that contained the symbol of the divine presence, and not exclusively to the part of the building that housed the symbol (the *naos* proper), Paul's use of *naos* for the church can legitimately be taken as referring to the place where God's Spirit dwells without specific reference to the Holy of Holies. Lanci's point that *naos* does not have to refer to the Holy of Holies is correct, but the implication that Paul did not mean for *naos* to refer to the place where God's Spirit dwells in incorrect.

John R. Lanci, *A New Temple for Corinth: Rhetorical and Archaeological Approaches to Pauline Imagery* (StBL 1; New York and Bern: Peter Lang, 1997) 66, 91–93.

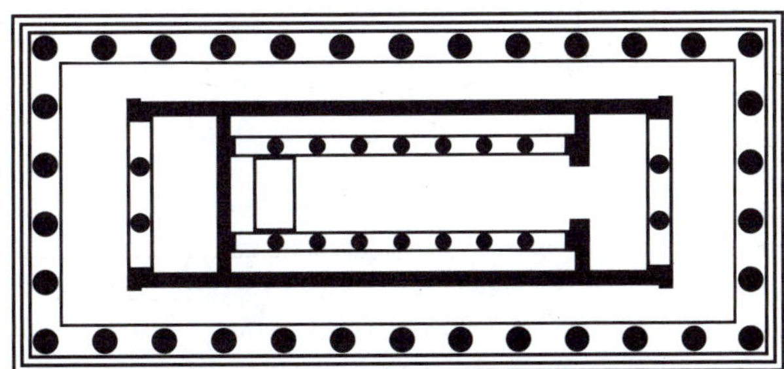

(Credit: Scott Nash)

Secondly, they are God's temple as a community, not as individuals ("you [pl.] are God's temple"; "God's Spirit dwells in you" [pl.]). When jealousy and strife exist among them, they are not a dwelling place for God's Spirit. When they exist as true community, however, their status rises.[9] (See [God's Temple in Ephesians] below.)

Whether they will ultimately to be a suitable dwelling place for God's Spirit depends on their overcoming the differences that divide them. Much as Paul proleptically affirmed their abundance of gifts and knowledge in his opening thanksgiving (1:4-9), here he retrojects what he hopes they will ultimately prove to be into their present situation.

Thirdly, the danger that they may not be what they truly are lurks perilously in their current condition. Thus, the warning Paul gives regarding those who endanger the temple of God is more severe than his admonition to secondary builders in the previous unit: "If anyone ruins (*phtheirei*) God's temple, God will ruin (*phtherei*) that one" (3:17). The warning is given in inverse symmetry:

A—If [ ] the temple of God
  B—[anyone] ruins
  B'—[ ] will ruin this one
A'—God

The verb *phtheirō* could mean "destroy," as it is often translated. More often, in Paul's time, however, the verb meant "to damage."[10] To translate it as "ruin" captures the seriousness of Paul's intent here and avoids the difficulty of seeing any human capable of "destroying" God's temple (church). The language is deliberately intense: those who endanger God's temple risk their own endangerment. The heightened metaphor of "temple" carries with it an increased culpability for those who prevent God's church from being the temple it is supposed to be. In the previous unit, builders were to be held accountable for poor construction. Here, actual damage to the church's well-being carries more serious consequences.

The activity of those who threaten the well-being of the church contrasts sharply with that of Paul and Apollos who planted and watered and of Paul who laid a good foundation. While those apostles had the best interests of the church as God's special possession in mind, someone else is actually working to do harm, though they and their followers may not realize it. In fact, in their self-promotion as the truly wise, they probably think they are surpassing the good accomplished by Paul. Paul has tried to expose their true identity and the consequences of their actions here in veiled metaphor. He becomes more explicit in the next unit.

Appraising with Godly Wisdom, 3:18–4:5

In the section of his argument that began at 3:5, Paul has been focusing on the matter of identity. He has tried to correct misconceptions through metaphors designed to illuminate the proper way to view leaders and the church as a whole. In the final two units before his conclusion to his whole argument in 3:18–4:21, he approaches the issue of proper identity more directly.

3:18-23. He first turns the spotlight on his readers, with those among them who have been viewing themselves from the perspective of human wisdom especially in view. Clarity of vision begins in the mirror. His opening imperative, "Let no one be self-deceived," calls to mind the Delphic inscription cited by Plutarch: "Know thyself." [Pope on Self Knowledge] Paul has in mind the self-deception that leads to competitive boasting on the basis of human achievement and that fails to see what is lost when God is overlooked.

Another well-known Delphic oracle, cited by Plato (*Apology* 23B), commended Socrates as the wisest of persons because he was aware of his own ignorance. Paul's admonition that those who think they are wise in this age should become fools in order to become wise similarly exposes the deception that the self-professed wise inflict on themselves. It also recalls the earlier argument in 1:20-25 where the world's value system is reversed. Those "wise in this age" must adopt the foolish perspective of the age to come in order to be truly wise. Whereas in the earlier reversal the world deemed God's wisdom as foolishness, here God considers the world's wisdom to be foolishness.

As he did in his earlier indictment of the world's wisdom, Paul cites Scripture. The first quotation is from the LXX version of Job 5:13, with two changes in the wording that may reflect Paul's recollection of the Hebrew text. [Job 5:13] God traps the wise in the very exercising of their so-called deceptive wisdom! The second quotation is from Psalm 94:11 (LXX 93:11). Paul substitutes the word "wise" (*tōn sophōn*) for the LXX's "humans" (*tōn anthrōpōn*). His change reflects the context in Psalm 93 where God considers the scheming of Israel's best minds to be futile. Those the

Pope on Self-Knowledge

Alexander Pope's poem, *Essay on Man*, published in 1734, was an attempt to justify "God's ways to humanity" philosophically. He has captured, in the excerpt below, the tension between the Corinthians' claim to be wise and Paul's contention that their wisdom is actually foolishness. Ironically, the church members in the city on the isthmus found themselves intellectually in a narrow stretch between two competing ways of viewing reality.

"Know then thyself, presume not God to scan
The proper study of Mankind is Man.
Placed on this isthmus of a middle state,
A Being darkly wise, and rudely great:
With too much knowledge for the Sceptic side,
With too much weakness for the Stoic's pride,
He hangs between; in doubt to act, or rest;
In doubt to deem himself a God, or Beast;
In doubt his mind and body to prefer;
Born but to die, and reas'ning but to err;
Alike in ignorance, his reason such,
Whether he thinks to little, or too much;
Chaos of Thought and Passion, all confus'd;
Still by himself, abus'd or disabus'd;
Created half to rise and half to fall;
Great Lord of all things, yet a prey to all,
Sole judge of truth, in endless error hurl'd;
The glory, jest and riddle of the world."

Alexander Pope, *Essay on Man*, Epistle 2, 1

Job 5:13

ΑΩ Paul cites Job 5:13 in 1 Cor 3:19, but he changes two words from that found in the LXX. The LXX reads *ho katalambanōn sophous en tē phronēsei*, but Paul has *ho drassomenos tous sophous en tē panourgia autōn*. While *katalambanōn* may mean "overcome" or "seize," *drassomenos* more effectively conveys the sense of "capture" or "trap" suggested by the Hebrew *qamats*. Likewise, *panourgia* expresses more precisely the idea of "craftiness" or "cunning" implied in the Hebrew *'armah* than does the LXX's *phronēsei* (= "understanding").

Anthony C. Thiselton, *The First Epistle to the Corinthians: A Commentary on the Greek Text* (NIGTC; Grand Rapids: Eerdmans, 2000) 322.

Corinthians have been regarding as their greatest "thinkers" are mental midgets compared to God! So why would anyone boast in such merely human intellectuals (3:21)?

Why, indeed, would the Corinthians be deceived into priding themselves in the preaching and teaching of such would-be *sophist*icated leaders when, in fact, they themselves already possess "all things"? Paul may have been taking up a Corinthian slogan here ("We possess all things") that they may have used to indicate the superior status of the wise among them. It reflects a maxim current among some ancient philosophical groups, especially the Stoics, that held that "to the wise, all things belong." In Stoicism, the saying emphasized the freedom and self-sufficiency of the wise. For Paul, the saying, now hurled back at the Corinthians, speaks not of self-sufficiency but of interdependence and mutuality. Together, they already possess all the leaders (Paul, Apollos, Cephas; 3:22), so why would they divide themselves into groups lauding one particular leader as the best, as if their leaders possessed them ("I belong to Paul," etc.). Priding themselves in their choice of the wisest leader to follow, they are actually depriving themselves of the full benefit of a plurality of ministerial leaders. Furthermore, what they already possess in Christ is everything: the world, life or death, things present or things to come. Whereas, each of these entities may have been seen as threatening powers (as in Rom 8:38), in Christ these entities, along with the leaders, have become vehicles for God's building up the church, not tearing it apart. [Romans 8:38-39]

Romans 8:38-39

For I am convinced that neither death, nor life, nor angels, nor rulers, nor things present, nor things to come, nor powers, nor height, nor depth, nor anything else in creation, will be able to separate us from the love of God in Christ Jesus our Lord. (Rom 8:38-39; NRSV)

Since 3:9, Paul has been moving away from the negative portrayal of the Corinthians that he gave in 3:1-4. He has elevated their status as God's field, building, and temple. He has urged them to see themselves as they really are and not through the self-deceptive lens of worldly wisdom. If they do, they will see that they are truly more than wisdom's competitive evaluation criteria tells them they are, for they possess all things. But there is more. They belong to Christ. As surely as they possess all things, they and all they possess belong to Christ. Dale Martin has argued that the identity of belonging to someone, as a slave belongs to the master, could confer a sense of high status.[11] Certainly, Paul has asserted the exalted status of the Corinthians throughout this section, but only to the degree that they truly belong to Christ. The stress here is no longer on what the Corinthians possess but rather on who possesses them. The one to whom they belong is the same crucified Lord that Paul proclaimed when he first preached among them (2:2). Being the property of one crucified projects low status from the world's perspective, but that perspective is foolishness. From God's perspective, the only one that counts for Paul, belonging to Christ brings the highest status possible. It also, however, brings the responsibility of living in a way defined by the cross, not by human wisdom.

Still, there is more Paul wants them to see: "Christ belongs to God." The subordination of Christ to God indicated here also appears later in 11:3 and 15:28. In chapter 11, Christ's subornation is a part of Paul's attempt to regulate head coverings in worship. In chapter 15, it is a part of his eschatological vision that culminates in God's becoming "all in all." Here, it brings to a climax everything stated previously. *Who* we are, and therefore what we are to do, is determined by whose we are. From the anthropocentric perspective fostered by human wisdom, competition and conflict are the avenues to success. From the theocentric perspective championed by Paul, belonging to God calls persons to travel a different road. This conviction shapes the balance of Paul's argument against divisions.

4:1-5. From a rhetorical perspective, 4:1-5 represents the final element of Paul's proofs in his argument against divisions before his summation in 4:6-21. Thematically, the unit continues the focus on correctly appraising identities. Here Paul returns to the question of the identity of Apollos and himself that he broached in 3:5, but he does so in a more direct way that reveals the nature of the Corinthians' challenges to his leadership.

In light of Paul's acclamation in 3:23 that everything ultimately belongs to God, how should the Corinthians really see himself and Apollos? They should see them as assistants (*hypēretas*) of Christ and managers (*oikonomous*) of God's mysteries, Paul insists. Both terms suggest persons entrusted with significant responsibilities yet clearly subordinate to their superiors. The "mysteries" to which Paul refers are not esoteric teachings or secret rites, as in the mystery religions, but rather the same mysterious gospel of the crucified Christ that baffles the wise of this world. [Paul's "Mysteries"] As managers of God's mysteries, Paul and all apostles like him (not that any other apostle was exactly like Paul!) must be found trustworthy (*pistos*).

But who determines whether or not Paul is a trustworthy manager? Paul makes it clear that the determination will not be made by the Corinthians or any human "court" (4:3). [Court] Paul speaks directly to Corinthian criticism of his ministry when he says, "It is the very least thing that I should be appraised (*anakrithō*) by you." He uses the same verb here (*anakrinō*) that he used in 2:14-15 to describe those persons of the Spirit who could appraise the things of the Spirit. The word suggests being able to evaluate and determine the "worth" of something or someone. Paul insists that the evaluation of his performance as God's manager does not lie in the domain of his human critics. In fact, even Paul cannot grade himself on job performance.

Paul's words here give us the clearest indication yet in the letter that some persons in the Corinthian church had found fault with Paul. In fact, their evaluation of him on the basis of the criteria normally applied to sophists had led some of them to gravitate toward more impressive leaders. Paul has already addressed the shortcomings of the criteria they have used, and now he exposes the inappropriateness of the practice of appraising leaders at all. Their evaluation of him simply does not matter, at least not in an ultimate sense. Paul obviously does care about the Corinthians' perception of him; otherwise he would simply ignore their criticisms. Still, he refuses to be bound by their views, partly because he thinks they are wrong and basically misunderstand him. More importantly, however, he trusts that the decisive judgment about his ministry lies not with them but with God. With that judge, Paul has good reason to feel confident of a fair judgment.

From Paul's perspective, he has done nothing that would merit a negative assessment; his conscience is clear (4:4). Whatever criticisms they may have made of him, he stands by his record. He quickly adds, however, that he is not therefore in the clear. His conscience may be clear, but his conscience is no more the final judge than is theirs. The right and responsibility of evaluating his work belongs to the Lord.

Paul's "Mysteries"

AΩ The term "mystery" (*mystērion*) appears more frequently in 1 Corinthians (6 times) than in any other of the letters generally accepted as having been written by him. It appears also in Romans (11:25; 16:25). The term appears in four of the six letters attributed to Paul but is widely considered as pseudonymous: Ephesians (6 times), Colossians (4 times), 2 Thessalonians (once), and 1 Timothy (twice). Only in 1 Corinthians (4:1; 13:2) does Paul use the plural "mysteries." Paul uses the singular form to refer to different things, such as the hardening of Israel that opened a door for the Gentiles (Rom 11:25) or the transformation of the living and the dead that will occur at Christ's coming (1 Cor 15:51). Thus, the content of any particular mystery may differ from another, but every mystery is something that has previously been hidden and has now been revealed to the church through a recipient such as Paul. When Paul uses the plural form in 1 Cor 4:1, he is stressing that these divinely revealed mysteries have been entrusted to him and his associates, such as Apollos. As stewards (*oikonomoi*) of the mysteries, Paul and Apollos both guard them (from outsiders) and interpret their meaning.

Court

AΩ The word typically translated as "court," "judgment," or "tribunal" is actually the word for "day" (*hēmera*). While "day" is sometimes related to "judgment" in Greek, Paul probably uses it here to draw a distinct contrast between the "Day of the Lord" (3:13) when true judgment will be rendered by God on all things and the "day" of Paul's human critics, whose judgment Paul considers ultimately inconsequential.

The Last Judgment

Fra Angelico. *The Last Judgment*. c. 1431. Tempera on wood. Museo de San Marco, Florence, Italy. (Credit: Scala/Art Resource, NY)

He then issues his first direct exhortation in this section: "Do not pass judgment (*krinete*) on anything before the time when the Lord comes" (4:5). Since they cannot appraise (*anakrinō*) his work, they certainly cannot render a verdict (*krinō*). Furthermore, the time for such judgment still lies in the future. Judgment is an eschatological event best left to the *eschaton.* At that time, a valid judgment can be made because the Lord will uncover whatever is hidden in darkness and expose the true intentions of those being judged. In Luke's Gospel, in a similar context where the scribes and Pharisees were scrutinizing Jesus to try to "catch" him in something, Jesus responded by saying, "Nothing is covered up that will not be uncovered, and nothing secret that will not be known" (Luke 12:2). Paul contends that judgment lies in the domain of the Lord and that when the Lord carries out this task, it will be done thoroughly. Their nit-picking focuses on external matters of appearance and performance, but the Lord's judgment will probe deeper into those internal matters of the heart, about which the Corinthians (or any human judge) are clueless.

Furthermore, the Lord's judgment will extend beyond the examination of leaders such as Paul; it will include the Corinthians, too. At that time, to each one will come the appropriate recognition from God. Perhaps a not-so-veiled warning is implied here by Paul: "If you would evaluate me and the other apostles, remember that in the end it will be God who recognizes what we all really are, including you folks in Corinth." Paul's last word in the previous unit (3:18-23) on how the Corinthians should see themselves was *God. God* is also the last word in this unit about how the Corinthians should see Paul and other leaders. God will have the last word regarding the evaluation of any person, Paul reminds them. So, from Paul's perspective, what is of ultimate consequence is not how we see each other but how God sees us.

Applying God's Wisdom to the Church, 4:6-21

This section provides the conclusion to Paul's argument against divisions in the church. Rhetorically, it constitutes a *peroratio* in which Paul sums up his preceding argument and makes his final appeal. He first explains what he has been doing thus far and to what end (4:6-7). He then engages in his most forceful criticism of Corinthian attitudes in a blast of sarcasm (4:8-13). After the storm, he moves more gently to affirm his affection for them and to reinforce his argument through the sending of Timothy and to assure them of his own future visit (4:14-21).

4:6-7. Paul begins his conclusion with a statement designed to clarify the nature of his argument. Unfortunately, his statement contains two of the most enigmatic elements in the letter, as the adjoining sidebar shows. [Paul's Enigmatic Statement] The explanation of his strategy (a) is followed by the two purpose clauses (b) and (d). The challenges to interpretation come in the meaning of "applied all this" in (a) and the intent of the slogan in (c).

Paul's Enigmatic Statement

1 Cor 4:6 contains several perplexing features. The enigmatic elements are presented below in italics.

(a) I have *applied all this* to Apollos and myself for your benefit, brothers and sisters,

(b) so that you may learn through us the meaning of the saying,

(c) *"Nothing beyond what is written,"*

(d) so that none of you will be puffed up in favor of one against another. (NRSV)

The word usually translated "applied" is *meteschēmatisa*. Some commentators insist that the word means that Paul was using himself and Apollos as "examples" of how they should behave.[12] Others argue that the word indicates "covert allusion." That is, Paul indicates that his argument has been *disguised* as if it applied to Apollos and himself while it was actually directed at unnamed persons in Corinth.[13] Still others hold that while the term does suggest some figurative allusion to unnamed persons, Paul did not exclude its application to himself and Apollos.[14] This last view allows for Paul to have addressed both those factions in Corinth that had lined up behind leaders currently operating there and those factions expressing a similar kind of competitive loyalty to Apollos and himself.

But what did Paul "allusively apply" to himself and Apollos? Does the word *tauta* ("all this") refer only to the metaphorical images and other devices in the immediately preceding section (3:5–4:5)? Or does it refer to the whole of his argument beginning in 1:12? Since it is likely that Paul invented the slogans he attributes to factions in Corinth in 1:12, it is probable that figurative allusion has been a part of his whole argument. "I have been focusing on Apollos and myself," Paul might have said, "but understand that everything I have written applies to you, too."

Even greater difficulty surrounds the interpretation of (c). In Greek, it reads, *to mē hyper ha gegraptai* ("Not beyond what is written") The awkward wording has led some to propose that the text has been corrupted, but most interpreters reject such arguments.[15] The use of the neuter article *to* suggests that Paul is quoting some saying known to the Corinthians; thus, he is probably not simply referring to what he has written above in his own letter (as Calvin suggested). Some suggest that the slogan was drawn from the early education of children and that Paul, who has told the Corinthians they are still "babes in Christ," is essentially now telling them to follow his and Apollos's example and "not color outside the lines."[16] [Seneca on Teaching Children] Others suggest that Paul drew the motto from known discussions of civic concord and that he is basically urging the Corinthians to "abide by the law" in overcoming their differences.[17] Paul uses *gegraptai* in his letters (30 times) always to refer to Scripture, however, so his meaning here is probably: "Do not go beyond the Scriptures." Does he mean all of Scripture (the OT), or does he mean only the parts he had quoted in this letter, or does he mean only certain Scriptures quoted in the letter?[18] Probably he means the teachings of all of Scripture (OT) as he has taught it to them not only in this letter but previously. Paul (and perhaps other missionaries) may have even articulated the principle of basing belief and behavior on the proper interpretation of Scripture in the form of a maxim. For Paul, the proper reading of Scripture took the gospel of the crucified Lord as its starting point. His argument against divisions includes exactly the type of interpretation of Scripture that he advocated in his preaching. He applied that interpretation figuratively to himself and Apollos in such a way that the Corinthians would be reminded of the principle "Do not go beyond the Scriptures."

Seneca on Teaching Children

Boys study according to direction. Their fingers are held and guided by others so that they may follow the outlines of the letters; next, they are ordered to imitate a copy and base thereon a style of penmanship. Similarly the mind is helped if it is taught according to direction.

Seneca, *Epistle* 94.51 (trans. Richard M. Gummere; 3 vols. LCL; Cambridge MA: Harvard University Press, 1917–1925) 3:45.

The second purpose clause in 4:6, (d), gets to the heart of the problem for which Paul has been offering a solution: "so that none of you will be puffed up in favor of one against another." A key text cited by Paul earlier in 1:31 reads, "Let one who boasts, boast in the Lord." In 3:21, Paul asserted, "Let no one boast in humans." Boasting in their human leaders was exactly what they were guilty of doing. In fact, Paul says they were being "puffed up" (*physiousthe*) in this. The use of the genitive *tou enos* (of one) with *hyper* (in behalf of) here, along with the phrase *kata tou heterou* (against the other), shows that the various groups were raving over the superiority of their leaders. In doing so, they were behaving the same as the disciples (a.k.a. "groupies") of celebrity sophists. The end result was a tumultuous and divided church.

In 4:7 Paul asks three questions that prick their inflated egos. He pointedly asks, "Who differentiates you?" That is, who determines who is superior and inferior and on what basis? His second question takes the air out of their sails: "What do you have that you did not receive?" That is, did you achieve something great on your own, or was it given to you (by God)? The third question brings them down to earth: "If you received it as a gift, then why do you boast?" The grounds for their boasting is, therefore, demolished. Their "puffed up" attitude has no basis. [Augustine on Boasting]

Augustine on Boasting

The people who boast imagine that they are justified by their own efforts, and therefore they glory in themselves, not in the Lord.

Augustine, *Letter to Valentine*, in Gerald Bray, ed., *1–2 Corinthians* (vol. 7 of ACCS NT; ed. Thomas C. Oden; Downers Grove IL: InterVarsity Press, 1999) 26.

From their anthropocentric perspective, the Corinthians found it logical and normal to evaluate their leaders on the basis of the criteria used in their society to discriminate between superior and inferior sophists. Successful sophists drew adoring crowds who relished in the glorious achievements of their favorite sophist and who took pride in their correct choice from among the competing candidates for their loyalty. Paul moves once again to change their perspective to a theocentric one. His blunt questions challenge their practice of distinguishing between their leaders on the basis of their sophistic gifts. Their choosing "one against the other" and being "puffed up" in their choice ignores the central place of God, the one who has given "all things" to them, including their leaders (3:21-22). Since God's gifts had been received, not achieved, their boasting was idle and ill informed.

4:8-13. To drive home his point, Paul engages in the most caustic comments of his whole argument. Once again he casts his comments in terms of identity language ("You are"). His depiction of the Corinthians' presumed status employs the rhetorical device of *indignatio* in an ironic fashion. The image of the Corinthians he projects may have been exactly the one that they proudly claimed, but it was also one completely alien to the life of the true follower of Christ and, thus, was an unacceptable option. In contrast, he presents the apostles, including himself, in a much less admirable light ("We are"). This could be seen as the employment of the rhetorical device known as *conquestio*, in which one sought to obtain the pity of the target audience. Paul uses the device, however, not simply to win their sympathy but to convince them that his word of the cross finds confirmation in the way of the cross and that those who appear so lowly in the eyes of the world are actually the ones whose lives reflect the truth of the gospel.

His sarcasm here brings out the irony of his opening thanksgiving prayer (1:4-9). There he affirmed the grace of God given to them that "enriched" (*eploutisthēte*) them in all speech and knowledge to the point of lacking nothing. Here he chides them that they are filled (lit., "bloated") and that they "have become rich" (*eploutēsate*); in fact, they have come to rule as kings! The contrast between the passive *eploutisthēte* in 1:5 and the active *eploutēsate* in 4:8 reinforces the fact of their failure to acknowledge what they have as God's gift. The reference to "ruling as kings" may reflect the philosophical idea common to Cynics and Stoics of the time that only the truly wise truly ruled since the wise person had mastered the one greatest threat to self-sufficiency—the self. [Cynic and Stoic Views of the Wise Person as King] Paul may be reacting here to claims made by the Corinthians, but it is more likely that he is caricaturing their attitude with common philosophical images.

Two of the three derisive statements begin with *ēdē* ("already"), and the third begins with *chōris ēmōn* ("without us"). The adverb *ēdē* is often taken as a sign that the Corinthians held a "realized eschatology."[19] That is, they believed that they had *already* experienced the full manifestation of their salvation and that they were *already* living in the fullness of the kingdom of God. The Corinthians may not have held such a view, however. In fact, it seems more probable that their view was noneschatological and that Paul himself inter-

Cynic and Stoic Views of the Wise Person as King

The maxim, "I alone am rich; I alone reign as king," which was quoted by Stoics in various forms, has been traced to the legacy of Diogenes, a Cynic philosopher of the 4th century BC who may have lived in Corinth at one time. According to Pausanias, the burial site of Diogenes was still identified just within the eastern city wall of Corinth in the 2d century AD. Though Cynicism and Stoicism were extremely diverse, a common idea found in their numerous varieties was that through wisdom one could master the self, which posed the greatest threat to self-sufficiency, and thus live as a king in the world among others who were still enslaved to their passions. The Stoic philosopher Seneca, who was a contemporary of Paul's, is often credited with the saying, "Most powerful is he who has himself in his own power."

Pausanias, *Guide to Greece 1: Central Greece* (trans. Peter Levi; New York: Penguin Books, 1971) 134.

Area near Corinth's eastern wall.
(Credit: Scott Nash)

jected the eschatological element of future fulfillment to counter their perspective.[20] The phrase "without us" in the third statement suggests that the Corinthians had come to their perspective of such high status through the instruction of teachers active after Paul's time in Corinth. In demonstration that their presumptuousness was hollow, Paul asserts that he wishes it were true so that he could piggyback on their status and rule with them. The irony here is the irony of dissimulation. They are, in fact, not filled, not rich, and not ruling as kings.

In contrast to the high status that the Corinthians believe they have attained, Paul presents the plight of himself and the other apostles. Two images of Paul's day may lie behind his imagery in 4:9. Hays suggests that the Roman "triumph" is in view.[21] Victorious generals were celebrated with a parade through the streets of Rome, their entourage consisting of their armies and the spoils of battle, including lastly the losing enemy leaders as prisoners. Paul may be comparing the apostles "as the ones God has exhibited last" to the vanquished captives. As such, they have become a "spectacle" (*theatron*) to the whole world, the earthly (*anthrōpois*) and the heavenly (*angelois*). Thiselton envisions the gladiatorial contests, at which condemned prisoners were often executed, as the intended image.[22] The spectators, including the Corinthians, watch as those "condemned to death" (*epithanatious*) meet their fate. [Paul and the Death Sentence] In either case, the apostles appear as a contemptible group, the opposite of the Corinthians.

Paul and the Death Sentence

Paul picks up the theme of being sentenced to death again in 2 Cor 4:10-12.

[We are] always carrying in the body the death of Jesus, so that the life of Jesus may also be made visible in our bodies. For while we live, we are always being given up to death for Jesus' sake, so that the life of Jesus may be made visible in our mortal flesh. So death is at work in us, but life in you. (2 Cor 4:10-12; NRSV)

To heighten the contrast even further, Paul gives a series of "We are" and "You are" statements that draws on the triad he introduced in 1:26. There Paul contrasted the foolish, weak, and lowly esteemed whom God has called with those considered worthy of adulation by the world's wisdom. Here Paul depicts the Corinthians as wise, strong, and honorable, thus among those to be admired and envied in this world order. The apostles, however, epitomize the opposite: "We are fools, . . . weak, . . . and dishonorable." The point is clear: the apostles with their perceived lowly status are actually living out the calling of God; the Corinthians, to the degree to which they depend upon the indicators of high status for their identity, are not living out their calling.

Paul continues his description of the apostles with a catalog of hardships that resembles similar lists in both Hellenistic literature and apocalyptic Jewish writings (4:11-12). In both Cynicism and

Stoicism, the endurance and overcoming of hardships was a sign of the truly wise. [Stoics on Hardships] If Paul had such Hellenistic traditions in mind, then his words may be taken as an admonition to the Corinthians that though they considered themselves wise, it was actually the apostles who exhibited the true signs of wisdom.[23] On the other hand, however, Paul seems throughout to want to distinguish clearly between the judgments of human wisdom and the wisdom of God. To appeal here to the apostles as examples of *true* human wisdom would seem to undermine his argument elsewhere. His overarching approach has been to challenge the assumptions of human wisdom by juxtaposing them to the wisdom of God revealed in the cross.[24] The catalog of hardships he gives here, then, continue that approach. If Paul had in mind (perhaps in addition) the depictions of the suffering of the righteous in the traumatic birthing of the new age in Jewish apocalyptic writings, then he would have understood the hardships of the apostles to be further confirmation of the coming of the end. The afflictions imposed upon them would have been consistent with the scenario of evil's increased resistance to God's impending triumph, as well as consistent with that form of life prescribed by the cross.[25]

Stoics on Hardships

Two Stoic writers from near Paul's time, Seneca and Epictetus, viewed the endurance of hardships as signs of the validity of one's status as a truly wise person.

> Thus no fortune, no external circumstance, can shut off the wise man from action. For the very thing which engages his attention prevents him from attending to other things. He is ready for either outcome: if it brings good, he controls them; if evil, he conquers them. So thoroughly, I mean, has he schooled himself that he makes manifest his virtue in prosperity as well as in adversity, and keeps his eyes on virtue itself, not on the objects with which virtue deals. Hence neither poverty, nor pain, nor anything else that deflects the inexperienced and drives them headlong, restrains him from his course. Do you suppose that he is weighed down by evils? He makes use of them. (Seneca, *Moral Epistles*, Ep. 85.29)

> Talk not of that ["How I make my dialogues"], but rather be able to say, "See how I accomplish my purposes; see how I avert what I wish to shun. Set death before me; set pain, a prison, disgrace, doom, and you will know me." This should be the pride of a young man come out from the schools. Leave the rest to others. (Epictetus, *Dissertations* 2.1.35)

The actual hardships named by Paul appear to be a mixture of traditional sufferings and some peculiar to his own experience. His description of the apostles as hungry, thirsty, poorly clothed, roughly treated, and homeless resembles the conditions Paul "boasts" of in 1 Corinthians 12:23-27. The description also has parallels in the hardship catalogs of other ancient writers. (The "homelessness" of the apostles also reminds one of Jesus' saying regarding the son of man in Matt 8:20.) Nonetheless, the full image this list gives is of apostles who suffer on the edge of mere survival as servants of Christ. The last item, "working with our own hands," refers to a condition that caused Paul special difficulty in Corinth. (He addresses this problem more directly in 1 Cor 9.) [2 Corinthians 11:7-9] He also identifies three ways that the apostles respond to the hardships they encounter. They reply to verbal abuse with "good words" (*eulogoumen*); they "put up with"

2 Corinthians 11:7-9

Did I commit a sin by humbling myself so that you might be exalted, because I proclaimed God's good news to you free of charge? I robbed other churches by accepting support from them in order to serve you. And when I was with you and was in need, I did not burden anyone, for my needs were supplied by the friends who came from Macedonia. So I refrained and will continue to refrain from burdening you in any way. (2 Cor 11:7-9; NRSV)

(*anechometha*) persecution; and they return "encouragement" (*parakaloumen*) for slander against them. Together the responses portray persons with no claim to power or self-assertion. They are people who bear the insults and abuse of the powerful. They appear as helpless nobodies in a world order where status is determined by the ability to manipulate others. The final self-description puts Paul and the other apostles in the most pitiable light imaginable: they have become the scum (*perikatharmata*) and scrapings (*peripsēma*) of everyone (or everything). Both terms suggest something scrubbed off and thrown away as unwanted filth.

The powerful imagery used by Paul in his description of the apostles draws a clear contrast between their status and that kind of status so important to the Corinthians. It also calls into question the Corinthians' understanding of the apostles and of themselves. By belittling himself so completely and so beyond what any of those to whom he is writing presumably would have done, Paul is attempting to subvert their whole system of evaluation. In a sense, he is subjecting himself to a kind of humiliation that constitutes psychological and social crucifixion. His purpose in doing so is to arouse the same kind of transforming self-reflection that his word of the cross was intended to effect when he first proclaimed Christ crucified in Corinth.[26]

4:14-21. The final unit in Paul's extended argument against divisions draws attention to the purpose of the letter, the reason for Timothy's visit, and the question of the nature of Paul's impending visit. Robert Funk has noted that Paul often prepared churches for his arrival through a pattern of "ascending order of significance."[27] First came the letter, then the emissary as Paul's representative, and finally the apostle himself. Here the feature that binds the three together is Paul's disclosure of his identity as their "father" (4:15). The harsh tone of his letter actually serves the father's instructional purpose. The sending of the "beloved and faithful child" serves to reinforce the father's intentions for his other "beloved children." The father's visit will involve paternal disciplining or a happy reunion, depending on the response of the church.

In 1:14, Paul explains that he has written as he has not to *shame* them but to *admonish* them. His language here held special implications for these residents of Corinthian society in which matters of status were so intense. Honor came to those whose aspirations of status were recognized by society. Shame came to those whose aspirations were rejected. [Honor and Shame] In one sense, Paul *has shamed* them because he has rejected their aspirations to status as defined by worldly wisdom. In another sense, however, Paul *honors* them by recognizing their status as his children who, despite their low worldly status (1:26), have been called by God to imitate Paul and the apostles, the ones who hold the highest ranks in the reversal of status in God's wisdom.[28] Furthermore, his admonishing them demonstrates that they are *beloved* children of this father. Not to warn them of error or correct their misbehavior would indicate not only a lack of concern for their well-being but also a lack of recognition of their high place in the family.

Honor and Shame

Bruce Malina has identified honor and shame as "pivotal values of the 1st-century Mediterranean world."

> [In that society] people acquire honor by personally aspiring to a certain status and having that status socially verified. On the other hand, people get shamed (not have shame) when they aspire to a certain status and this status is denied them by public opinion. At the point a person realizes he is being denied the status, he is or gets shamed, he is humiliated, stripped of honor for aspiring to an honor not socially his. Honor assessments thus move from the inside (a person's claims) to the outside (public validation). Shame assessments move from the outside (public denial) to the inside (a person's recognition of the denial). To be shamed or get shamed, thus, is to be thwarted or obstructed in one's personal claim to worth or status, along with one's recognition of loss of status involved in this rejection.

Bruce J. Malina, *The New Testament World: Insights from Cultural Anthropology* (rev. ed.; Louisville: Westminster John Knox, 1993) 51–52.

As their father, Paul claims a unique relationship to this church. He acknowledges that in Christ they might have "thousands of guardians" (*myrious paidagōgous*), but they have only one father (*patēr*). The *paidagōgos* was essentially a servant or hired "babysitter" entrusted with the supervision and protection of the child. The *paidagōgos* might discipline the child but only because that was a part of the job, unlike the parents' disciplining, which presumably would be motivated by love and concern for the child. Perhaps Paul intends a veiled reference to the teachers in whom the Corinthians have placed so much trust. If so, then he is demoting them to the status of hired hands. Paul became their father in Christ through his preaching that established the church.

On the basis of his paternal relationship to the church, Paul issues his second direct appeal in this section: "Be imitators of me." [Imitation] As noted previously, this *parakalō* statement forms an *inclusio* with the appeal of 1:10. The first appeal to "agree" finds its corresponding method in this second appeal to "imitate" their father. The combination of paternal identity with the call to imitation could be viewed as overbearing. Paul may be seen here as seeking to impose a totalitarian control upon the church. As noted above (see [*Paterfamilias*] in the Introduction), the authority of the father in a Roman family was essentially absolute. In respect to this concern, two observations are in order.

First, the idea of imitating one's parents, teachers, or good persons is found as a sound ethical principle in Hellenistic litera-

Imitation

In Euripides' play *Helen*, Helen was not taken to Troy by Paris but rather fled to Egypt where she longed to be reunited with Menelaus. The Egyptian king (pharaoh) wanted her for himself, and Menelaus's arrival in Egypt threatened Helen's fate. In her appeal to the king's sister not to divulge Menelaus's arrival, Helen urges her to imitate her father, the former king. Her appeal has some semblance to that of Paul in 1 Cor 4:15-16.

> Ah! Not that, maiden, I beseech you: grant me this favor, and imitate the character of a just father; for this is the fairest glory for children, when the child of a good resembles its parents in character.

In Xenophon's *Memorabilia*, Antiphon tries to steal away Socrates' students. Socrates chides Antiphon for living such a miserable life, rather than finding joy in philosophy. Given, the hard life that Paul lived as an apostle, the Corinthians may have had reservations about imitating him.

> Besides you refuse to take money, the mere getting of which is a joy, while its possession makes one more independent and happier. Now the professors of other subjects try to make their pupils copy their teachers; if you too intend to make your companions do that, you must consider yourself a professor of unhappiness.

Euripides, *Helen*, l. 940, in *The Complete Greek Drama* (2 vols.; trans. E. P. Coleridge; ed. Whitney J. Oates and Eugene O'Neill Jr.; New York: Random House, 1938).

Xenophon, *Memorabilia*, I.6.3 (4 vols.; trans. E. C. Marchant; LCL; Cambridge MA: Harvard University Press, 1923).

ture.[29] Furthermore, the Corinthians lacked other concrete examples to follow. Theirs was a young church drawn predominantly from non-Jewish elements that lacked the benefit of a deep grounding in that ethical tradition. One cannot say that Greeks and Romans did not also aspire to ethical ideals that promoted harmony and service, but the ideals that prevailed in the church in Corinth were drawn from principles of behavior that encouraged competition and division, not unity. Clearly they needed a better model than the ones they were then imitating.

Secondly, the image of "father" that Paul has already defined in his argument is of one who does not assert preeminence over others but rather one who submits to menial service on behalf of others. It was also noted above that in Paul's portrayal of God as "father," the sovereign dimension of the *paterfamilias* recedes into the background in order to highlight the gracious aspect of God. (See the section titled "God as the Sovereign and Gracious Father" in the Introduction.) So, too, Paul's identity as "father" emphasizes the self-giving, other-serving way of life called for by the word of the cross. What Paul asks them to imitate here is the cross-shaped life that he has described throughout his argument, not the strict self-assertion of the *paterfamilias.*

In order to help them learn to imitate their "father," Paul promises to send Timothy to visit them (4:17; see also 16:10-11). He describes Timothy as "my beloved and *faithful* child in the Lord." Perhaps they would have rather received another visit from the eloquent Apollos, but the emissary they will receive is one who faithfully embodies the apostle's teaching. In his letter to the Philippians (2:19-21), Paul describes Timothy as one who is genuinely concerned about others' well-being, unlike "those who only look after their own interests." Timothy will, Paul hopes, remind the Corinthians of Paul's "ways (*hodoi*) in Christ." The term *hodoi* may bear connotations of the Hebrew term *halakhah* ("walk") and thus indicate proper ethical behavior.[30] Paul points out that he teaches the same "ways" in every church. This is not so much to indicate that he wants to bring the Corinthian congregation in line with other churches simply to promote uniformity of belief and practice. Instead, Paul insists that what he is trying to develop among the Corinthians is consistent with what he is doing elsewhere, which is simply to preach and live out the word of the cross.

St. Timothy

Michael Burghers. *St. Timothy*. Engraving. Published in 1687 in *Apostolici (The History of the Lives, Acts, Deaths, and Martyrdoms of the Apostles)* by William Cave. Courtesy of the Pitts Theology Library, Candler School of Theology, Emory University.

Paul's final word in the long section is a last warning to those who are "puffed up" (4:18). His delay in visiting to Corinth apparently has emboldened some to assume he will not return and thus to pursue their own ascendancy to leadership. He will, indeed, return and discover whether their rhetoric (*logon*) contains substance (*dynamin* = "power"). Or will they prove to be nothing more than "windbags" after all? Empty rhetoric, however grandiose, is not the substance of the kingdom of God (one of Paul's few references to the kingdom); power is. Perhaps Paul intends here a contrast between the "kingly rule" he said the Corinthians claim (4:8) and the authentic rule of God evidenced in self-giving service. The real test, after all, is not the persuasive power of eloquent rhetoric and its skilled practitioners but the end result. Does such rhetoric produce the kingdom of God by transforming persons into Christ-centered, cross-shaped servants, or does it ultimately damage the kingdom by promoting competition and disunity? How Paul approaches them on his return is in their hands. He will come to them either with open arms to embrace them in a "spirit of gentleness," or he will come holding in his hand the rod of discipline. The choice is theirs.

CONNECTIONS

The Temple of God

In 1 Corinthians 3:9c-17, Paul likens the church to a building. In vv. 10-15, he uses this metaphor to stress the care the constructors of this edifice must exercise as they build upon the foundation of Christ. In vv. 16-17, however, the imagery shifts to the nature of the building itself: it is the temple of God. The transition from building to temple in the use of architectural metaphors resembles that of Ephesians 2:19-22 where the household of God morphs into a holy temple. [God's Temple in Ephesians] In both texts, the language of "church as temple" stresses that it is a place where God dwells. Later, in 1 Corinthians 6:19, Paul applies the same metaphor to the individual, reminding his readers that their bodies are a temple of the Holy Spirit.

The temple metaphor aptly caps the movement of the section 1 Corinthians 3:5-17. Paul begins with the agricultural imagery of planting and watering and moves toward the metaphor of the church as God's field. He immediately switches to the metaphor of the church as God's building. With both metaphors the point is the same, though the switch from one to the other permits a nuanced refinement of the point. In the field, some plant, some water, but it is God who gives the growth to God's field. The servants are simply workers who do the mundane tasks. God brings about the miracle of growth. The emphasis is on God.

God's Temple in Ephesians

The communal image of the temple as the dwelling place of God's Spirit was later captured by the author of Ephesians:

> So then you are no longer strangers and aliens, but you are citizens with the saints and also members of the household of God, built upon the foundation of the apostles and prophets, with Christ Jesus himself as the cornerstone, in whom the whole structure is joined together and grows into a holy temple in the Lord; in whom also you are built together spiritually into a dwelling place for God. (Eph 2:19-22; NRSV)

In Ephesians, Christ has been moved from the foundation to the cornerstone, but otherwise, the implications of Paul's temple metaphor in 1 Corinthians have been appropriately amplified. "The whole structure is joined together and . . . *built together spiritually* into a dwelling place for God."

With the change to the building metaphor, the emphasis leans more to the quality of the work of the builders. We never lose sight of the fact that the building is God's, just as the field is God's, but we now see that what the workers do is more crucial to the welfare of the building. Paul claims to have laid the foundation (Christ) himself, yet it is the grace of God given to him that made that possible. [The Church's One Foundation] Once again the most essential task remains in the purview of God, but the role of the "*master* builder" (Paul) is larger than that of the "planter." The planter (Paul), of course, had good seed, but no mention is made of his horticultural expertise. In contrast, the master builder has seen to it that the good foundation (Christ) has been laid well. Watering the seed is a simple-enough task, but building upon the well-laid foundation requires skill and attention to the project. Failing to follow the blueprint can result in disaster for the post-Paul shifts of builders—and for the building. Since the building is none other than the temple of God, then any damage done to the building will be taken most seriously. In fact, God will return damage for damage (3:17).

On the one hand, we could view these metaphors primarily in terms of Paul's objective. Some rivalry with Apollos, or at least between those who favored Apollos and those who favored Paul, lies behind this section. While affirming the role of Apollos, and of any others who sought to contribute to the welfare of the Corinthian church, Paul still subtly asserts his own priority as the planter and master foundation layer. He and Apollos are simply servants of the God who owns the field, and they are all working to construct God's building, the temple. Any workers who deviate from Paul's template, however, risk endangerment to themselves and to the church. All of this, of course, can be seen merely as an attempt on Paul's part to reestablish (or establish) his authority over the church in Corinth. Any such reading of Paul's objective as simply a power play to gain authority, however, ignores the real purpose behind Paul's efforts to counter the claims of other authority figures. He was concerned not so much that some of the Corinthians were following other leaders but that they were following them in the wrong direction. At issue here is not Paul's welfare but rather that of the church.

On the other hand, we can look beyond the context in which Paul wrote these words and the purpose they may have served for him and focus on what the section reveals about Paul's understanding of the interaction between God and the church of God. Clearly, Paul stresses that the church belongs to God and that those who work in the church work for God. The importance of the church as God's possession becomes clearest in Paul's portrayal of the church as God's temple. God Spirit dwells within the temple-church. "Temple" is a metaphor; "God's Spirit dwelling within the church" is intended to be more than metaphor. Of course, metaphors themselves should not be belittled as being *mere*

The Church's One Foundation

Samuel Stone's classic hymn takes its opening cue from 1 Cor 3:11 where Paul identifies Christ as the only foundation for the church. Echoes of other parts of 1 Corinthians abound in the hymn, especially the reference to being bought by Christ's death (6:20; 7:23). The frequently omitted fourth verse (vv. 1 and 4 are below) also observes that the kinds of divisions Paul faced have not disappeared.

The church's one foundation
Is Jesus Christ her Lord;
She is his new creation,
By Spirit and the Word;
From heav'n he came and sought her
To be his holy bride,
With his own blood he bought her,
And for her life he died.

Though with a scornful wonder
Men see her sore oppressed,
By schisms rent asunder,
By heresies distressed:
Yet saints their watch are keeping,
Their cry goes up, "How long?"
And soon the night of weeping
Shall be the morn of song!

Samuel J. Stone, "The Church's One Foundation" (1866).

metaphors, for all theology, all God-talk, must be metaphorical to a degree. If we take the image of the church as temple beyond the range of metaphor and see it as pointing to a concrete reality, however, the implications are both terrifying and empowering.

As temple, the church "houses" the very presence of God on earth. The foundation of this temple, laid in the self-giving death of Christ, indicates that the God who dwells in this temple via the Spirit is a God who is *for* us. The God whose Spirit we experience within the context of the church is a God who has already demonstrated sacrificial action on our behalf. Thus, this God is working both for us and through us. The Spirit comforts us by confirming through the Spirit's presence our identity as the people, the place, where God dwells. The Spirit also empowers us to be that suitable dwelling place for God's Spirit; that is, the Spirit works in us to make us that people who faithfully represent the God whose Spirit dwells among us, a God whose self-giving nature has been exposed in Christ. All of this is comforting, encouraging, and empowering.

Still, we can never forget that it is the Holy Spirit of a Holy God who dwells within the church. Isaiah's vision of the Lord in the Jerusalem temple cannot be expunged from our perception of the presence of God among us. That vision of God's presence was terrifying for Isaiah; so it should be for us. Especially should this be true since the Spirit that dwells within God's temple, the church, works through the persons who make up the church to complete the construction of the dwelling place. We cannot forget that Paul's use of the metaphor of church as temple comes in the context of a warning. Those who build upon the foundation must build well, for they will be held accountable. Those who damage the temple will be damaged. This may be metaphorical language, but it points to "concrete" action by "flesh-and-blood" human beings and "concrete" consequences. What we do *as* the church *to* the church matters. This is acutely the case for those who would be leaders in

Isaiah 6:1-5

The Lord Sitting upon His Throne. From *Figures de la Bible.* Illustrated by Gerard Hoet, and others. Published by P. de Hondt in The Hague (La Haye). 1728. Image courtesy Bizzell Bible Collection, University of Oklahoma Libraries.

In the year that King Uzziah died, I saw the Lord sitting on a throne, high and lofty; and the hem of his robe filled the temple. Seraphs were in attendance above him; each had six wings: with two they covered their faces, and with two they covered their feet, and with two they flew. And one called to another and said:

"Holy, holy, holy is the LORD of hosts;
the whole earth is full of his glory."

The pivots on the threshold shook at the voices of those who called, and the house filled with smoke. And I said: "Woe is me! I am lost, for I am a man of unclean lips, and I live among a people of unclean lips; yet my eyes have seen the King, the LORD of hosts!" (Isa 6:1-5; NRSV)

the church, those who build upon the foundation. Action that creates division injures the church. Power struggles undertaken to promote one view (and those who profess it) and suppress another view (and its supporters) inflict damage on the church's image and work. Unfortunately, much of the history of the church has been one of conflict aimed not at a unified attack on our common problems but aimed rather at those groups within the church with whom we disagree.

Fortunately (however frustrating it may be), the place where God has chosen for the Spirit to dwell is not a finished edifice. That is, God has chosen to dwell here, in this world, among an imperfect people, not in some pneumatically perfect, unearthly realm. The people Paul identified as the temple of God were beset with problems. Paul took seriously the tasks of building and being the temple of God, and so should we. He also did not write off the Corinthians as so hopelessly entrapped in a state of internal bickering and personal agenda-seeking that they could not still be considered the dwelling place of God's Spirit. Neither should we dismiss the abiding presence of God's Spirit among us, despite our equally debilitating penchant for infighting. They were, and we are, God's temple, as unlikely as that may seem. [Küng on the Church as Temple]

Küng on the Church as Temple

To refer to the Church as temple, therefore, does not mean referring to the Church in a spiritualized sense. These people, this community with all its evident human failings, is the temple of God. Although it must be admonished to live according to the Spirit, this Church is nonetheless in the Spirit, or rather, the Spirit dwells in it; God's moulding power and life-giving strength has through Christ taken possession of it, has overwhelmed and penetrated it in its entire existence. In the Spirit, God himself and the Kyrios are effectively present in the community of believers despite all their human weaknesses.

Hans Küng, *The Church* (Garden City NY: Image Books, 1976) 225.

Exercising Wise Judgment

In 1 Corinthians 3:18–4:5, Paul focuses on personal judgment in terms of how persons should assess themselves and how they should assess others. The immediate problem he confronted was that some of the Corinthians thought too highly of themselves and too lowly of him. Because their criteria for judging was based on the standards of their competitive society, and not on the word of the cross, they held themselves in high regard and considered Paul to be lacking in those qualities that their society valued in a teacher. Paul urged them to take the stance of a fool rather than a wise person in passing judgment (3:18). [Chrysostom on Fools] The fool views matters from the vantage point of God's foolishness, which subverts the value assumptions by which persons normally live. He further urged them to avoid exercising judgment *before the time* (4:4), before that day when the full truth is revealed. Paul realized that the human capacity to assess matters and persons truthfully is too limited to permit complete reliance upon it.

In the interim *before the time*, however, we find it both inevitable and necessary that we pass judgment on ourselves and others and that we, in turn, are judged by others. Evaluating our own thoughts and actions is an essential part of improvement. Assessing the motives, character, and behavior of others is a vital part of deciding whom we can entrust with our love and companionship and whom we should not. Scrutinizing other persons is a valid part of responsibly deciding who should be our political and religious leaders.

Paul's words caution us to apply the right criteria in our judgments and to be cautious about passing judgment too hastily. For Paul, the word of the cross provides a new criterion for assessing who should be highly regarded. The usual signs of success and power do not count; another standard informed by the example of the One who suffered and died for others is in play. Even the methods of assessment have been changed. We cannot rely completely on our own reasoning or even on the "eye-witness" testimony of others, as the recent exposure, through DNA evidence, of erroneous convictions of innocent persons should remind us. [Faulty Evidence] Human judgment is always to be considered provisional, waiting for the validation or correction of that time when the truth shall be made fully known.

Chrysostom on Fools

Paul asks us to become dead to the world, and this deadness is of benefit to us, because it is the beginning of new life. So also he bids us become foolish toward the world, thereby introducing us to true wisdom. You become a fool to this world when you despise earthly wisdom and are persuaded that it contributes nothing to your understanding of the faith. For Christians, everything is just the opposite of what it seems.

John Chrysostom, *Homilies on the Epistles of Paul to the Corinthians* 10.2, in Gerald Bray, ed., *1–2 Corinthians* (vol. 7 of ACCS NT; ed. Thomas C. Oden; Downers Grove IL: InterVarsity Press, 1999) 36.

Faulty Evidence

Numerous convictions have been overturned in recent years because of DNA evidence, which is now considered the most reliable forensic technique available to connect a person to certain crimes, especially rape. The high incident of wrongful convictions based on other forensic methods and on eyewitness testimony has led to a national reassessment of the techniques used and of the right to DNA testing on the part of those charged with serious crimes. In March 2009, the U.S. Supreme Court was to rule on the right of the accused to demand a DNA test. The problem of reliable evidence is not always resolved as redemptively as in the case described below.

In 1984, Jennifer Thompson-Cannino testified that Ronald Cotton was the man who had raped her. Eleven years later, DNA evidence cleared him of the crime. Ronald was filled with anger toward the woman whose testimony wrongly imprisoned him and toward the man who had actually committed the crime. Jennifer was filled with hatred toward Ronald for eleven years, and then, upon learning of her error, she was filled with remorse and shame. When they met, Jennifer asked for Ronald's forgiveness. He told her that he had forgiven her long ago and that he had let go of his anger toward the true perpetrator. Jennifer found forgiveness not only for herself but also for her actual assailant. Jennifer stated, "Without Ronald, I would still be shackled to that moment in time, and it would own me forever. I soon discovered that I could even forgive the man who had raped me—not because he asked me to, nor because he deserved it—but because I did not want to be a prisoner of my own hatred." Cotton and Thompson-Cannino have been working together for reform in the prosecution system.

Ronald Cotton and Jennifer Thompson-Cannino, "Finding Freedom in Forgiveness," National Public Radio's *All Things Considered* (5 March 2009).

Imitation and Spiritual Direction

The section 4:6-21 begins with a disclosure of the real point of Paul's veiled argument and ends with a passionate appeal for the Corinthians to imitate their father, Paul. Sandwiched between the beginning and end is a sarcastic and caustic rebuttal of the Corinthians' arrogant attitude. Paul's portrayal of his ministry and that of Apollos in 3:3–4:4 as the complimentary and cooperative effort of Christ's servants was designed to teach the Corinthians "in us" (i.e., "by our example"; 4:6) not to be "puffed up" through competitive jockeying for position. The tongue-lashing that Paul unleashes on them exposes the immature understanding they have of the Christian life and the role of its leaders. Those who would be kings understand little about the kingdom of God. [An Example of Greatness] They are as children wrestling over toys in the sandbox, with the winners proudly taking their seats as kings of the hill on thrones that stand on a mound of sifting sand. Meanwhile, the apostles, those who have been sent by God, wallow in the dirt of a "life and death" world, bearing that world's reproach as a foolish spectacle and being treated as the scum of the earth. The contrast could hardly be starker, and for those guilty parties who get the point, hardly more deflating of their exaggerated egos.

An Example of Greatness

Mark 9:33-37 captures in a humorous way the short-sightedness of those who would compete for power in the kingdom of God. On this occasion, Jesus exposes the presumptuous attitude of his disciples regarding "greatest" through the example of a child. A little later, in Mark 10:24, Jesus calls his disciples "children" and warns them that it is hard to enter the kingdom of God. Paul, likewise, calls the Corinthians his children and warns them that power, not childish bantering, characterizes the kingdom of God.

> Then they came to Capernaum; and when he was in the house he asked them, "What were you arguing about on the way?" But they were silent, for on the way they had argued with one another who was the greatest. He sat down, called the twelve, and said to them, "Whoever wants to be first must be last of all and servant of all." Then he took a little child and put it among them; and taking it in his arms, he said to them, "Whoever welcomes one such child in my name welcomes me, and whoever welcomes me welcomes not me but the one who sent me." (Mark 9:33-37, NRSV)

Paul assures them that such a reprimand is not intended for shame but for instruction. Children such as they sometimes need a dose of "tough love." Nonetheless, they are *beloved* children of the father who sired them in Christ. As their father, Paul urges them to imitate him. Children such as they also need a healthy model. The motif of imitation (*mimēsis*) was common in philosophical writings of the time, especially in works devoted to training rhetoricians. The kind of model Paul proposes, however, was not. One might be encouraged to emulate a successful Sophist who had wooed the crowds with his eloquence and charm. One would hardly be pointed to a person such as Paul, especially not the Paul who presented himself so ignobly in 4:10-13.

To criticize Paul for encouraging his parishioners to look to him as a model as if he were guilty of putting himself on a pedestal, so to speak, or for directing them to imitate him rather than Christ directly is to miss the point of his model. [Witherington on Imitation] Paul believed that he was faithfully following the example of Christ himself, especially in the way Paul tried to incarnate his word of the cross into his very manner of being an apostle. Furthermore, he considered himself responsible for the well-being of his converts. Teaching by example was instrumental to enabling them to learn his "ways in Christ." Undoubtedly, his assurance that he would send Timothy to them stemmed from this (and not simply from an attempt to gain control) in that Timothy exhibited those "self-giving" qualities that were so lacking among the Corinthians.

Witherington on Imitation

Paul is not interested in keeping the Corinthians in a state of perpetual infancy. He wants them to grow up. He would like nothing better than if they truly imitated Christ and did not cause him so much work and heartache. He is not threatened by the presence of other mature Christians, such as his coworkers, both male and female, or by other *apostoloi*. Whatever sort of hierarchy Paul presupposes, it entails an inverted pyramid where leaders are enslaved, belong to the community, and must serve it from below.

Ben Witherington III, *Conflict and Community in Corinth: A Socio-Rhetorical Commentary and 1 and 2 Corinthians* (Grand Rapids: Eerdmans, 1995) 145.

Throughout the history of the church, Christians have often found the practice of imitation to be crucial in the cultivation of spiritual growth. [Thomas à Kempis] The role that Paul was claiming for himself as a father who should be imitated could be considered along the lines of what has sometimes been called in Christian tradition a "spiritual director." Christianity, of course, is not unique in recognizing the great value of spiritual direction embodied in persons who, by their example as well as their wise counsel, enable others to progress toward greater spiritual maturity. In Hinduism, the role of the *guru* is crucial for the maturation of the student, as is the role of the *rōshi* in Zen Buddhism. In Christianity, however, the practice of looking to models of the faith who *embody* in their person the ideals of the gospel would seem to be only natural in light of that gospel's proclamation of a God who became *incarnate* in human form. [Thomas Merton]

Thomas à Kempis

The classic devotional work *Imitation of Christ* was composed in the early 15th century by Thomas à Kempis, a member of a Dutch association of priests known as the Brethren of the Common Life. The book contains his reflections as well as those of other members of the association. The passages below come from a section in which the imitation of Christ is intimately connected to submission to a spiritual guide.

> My child, he who attempts to escape obeying withdraws himself from grace. Likewise he who seeks private benefits for himself loses those which are common to all. He who does not submit himself freely and willingly to his superior, shows that his flesh is not yet perfectly obedient but that it often rebels and murmurs against him. (pt. 1)
>
> Learn to obey, you who are but dust! Learn to humble yourself, you who are but earth and clay, and bow down under the foot of every man! Learn to break your own will, to submit to all subjection! Be zealous against yourself! Allow no pride to dwell in you, but prove yourself so humble and lowly that all may walk over you and trample upon you as dust in the streets! (pt. 4)

Imitation of Christ, bk. 3, ch. 13 (trans. Harold Bolton and Aloysius Croft).

Oddly, though, except for the monastic tradition, Christianity as it is commonly practiced has placed more emphasis on the cerebral comprehension of doctrine and obedient adherence to a prescribed ethical code than it has on the cultivation of personal character and spirituality through emulation of examples of the faith. We should not be surprised, then, when persons who seek such models turn to other religious traditions. The models of the faith for modern Christians are too seldom cut from the mold of St. Francis or Mother Teresa. Instead, they are the successful preachers of the affluent megachurches, who themselves are patterned after those victorious embodiments of what may be modern America's true religion: financial success.

Thomas Merton

It must not be forgotten that the spiritual director in primitive times was much more than the present name implies. He was a spiritual father who "begot" the perfect life in the soul of his disciple by his instructions first of all, but also by his prayer, his sanctity and his example. He was to the young monk a kind of "sacrament" of the Lord's presence in the ecclesiastical community.

Spiritual Direction and Meditation (Collegeville MN: Liturgical Press, 1960) 17.

In his influential book, *Celebration of Discipline*, Richard Foster discusses the discipline of "Guidance" in a section on "Corporate Disciplines."[31] According to Foster, spiritual direction by example is a responsibility of the whole community of faith. Perhaps one reason that responsibility has been so seldom assumed, especially by Protestant churches, is that we have an aversion to allowing anyone to usurp that priestly role that is the property of every believer. Perhaps, though, it is also because we lack spiritual directors who would dare echo Paul's instructions to "imitate me." [Spiritual Directors]

Spiritual Directors

Richard Foster has described spiritual directors in this way:

> They can absorb the selfishness and mediocrity and apathy around them and transform it. They are unjudging [sic] and unshakable. They must have compassion and commitment. Like Paul who thought of Timothy as his "beloved child," they must be prepared to take on certain parental responsibilities. Theirs must be a tough love that refuses to give approval to every whim. They should also know enough of the human psyche that they will not reinforce unconscious and infantile needs for authoritarianism.

Richard J. Foster, *Celebration of Discipline: The Path to Spiritual Growth* (rev. ed.; San Francisco: Harper & Row, 1988) 186.

Lectionary Connections

Two texts from this section are included in the Revised Common Lectionary. First Corinthians 3:16-23 is read in Year A in conjunction with Leviticus 19:1-2, 17-18, and Matthew 5:38-39 on the seventh Sunday after Epiphany. The accompanying texts have two main points of connection with 1 Corinthians 3:16-23. Leviticus's stress on holiness and Matthew's emphasis on true righteousness mesh with Paul's depiction of the church as God's temple. All three texts also speak of refraining from doing harm to another.

First Corinthians 4:1-5 is also read in Year A on the eighth Sunday after Epiphany, along with Isaiah 49:14-18 and Matthew 6:24-34. A point of connection between the three texts is the theme of trusting one's destiny to God alone.

NOTES

1. Robert Browning, *Pippa Passes*, pt. 4.

2. Margaret M. Mitchell, *Paul and the Rhetoric of Reconciliation: An Exegetical Investigation of the Language and Composition of 1 Corinthians* (Louisville: Westminster John Knox, 1991) 213–25.

3. This position is well represented by David R. Hall, *The Unity of the Corinthian Correspondence* (JSNTSup 251; London: T & T Clark Int., 2003) 19–25.

4. A notable argument for this view is given by Donald P. Ker, "Paul and Apollos – Colleagues or Rivals?" *JSNT* 77 (2000): 75–97.

5. Andrew D. Clarke, *Secular and Christian Leadership in Corinth: A Socio-Historical and Exegetical Study of 1 Corinthians 1-6* (*AGJU* 18; Leiden: E. J. Brill, 1993) 119.

6. See the discussion of *zēmia* and *zēmioō* in the context of penalties for poor construction in Jay Shanor, "Paul as Master Builder: Construction Terms in First Corinthians, *NTS* 34 (1988): 461–71, and John R. Lanci, *A New Temple for Corinth: Rhetorical and Archaeological Approaches to Pauline Imagery* (*StBL* 1; New York and Bern: Peter Lang, 1997) 66.

7. Hall, *The Unity of the Corinthian Correspondence*, 8; Gordon D. Fee, *The First Epistle to the Corinthians* (NICNT; Grand Rapids: Eerdmans Publishing, 1987) 138–39.

8. Anthony C. Thiselton, *The First Epistle to the Corinthians: A Commentary on the Greek Text* (NIGTC; Grand Rapids: Eerdmans, 2000) 309.

9. See Dale B. Martin, *The Corinthian Body* (New Haven: Yale University Press, 1995) 64–65.

10. See Shanor, "Paul as Master Builder," 171–72, and Lanci, *A New Temple for Corinth*, 66–68.

11. Dale B. Martin, *Slavery as Salvation: The Metaphor of Slavery in Pauline Christianity* (New haven: Yale University Press, 1990).

12. See Johan S. Vos, Der μετασχημάτισμος in 1 Kor. 4.6," *ZNW* 86 (1995): 154–72.

13. See David R. Hall, "A Disguise for the Wise: ΜΕΤΑΣΧΗΜΑΤΙΣΜΟΣ in 1 Corinthians 4.6," *NTS* 40 (1994): 143–49, and Benjamin Fiore, "'Covert Allusion' in 1 Corinthians 1-4," *CBQ* 47 (1985): 85–102.

14. Thiselton, *The First Epistle to the Corinthians*, 348–51.

15. See John Strugnell, "A Plea for Conjectural Emendation in the New Testament, with a Coda on 1 Cor 4:6," *CBQ* 36 (1974): 543–58, and Jerome Murphy-O'Connor, "Interpolations in the 1 Corinthians," *CBQ* 48 (1986): 81–94.

16. Ronald L. Tyler, "First Corinthians 4:6 and Hellenistic Pedagogy," *CBQ* 60 (1998): 97–103.

17. Laurence L. Welborn, "A Conciliatory Principle in 1 Corinthians 4:6," as reprinted in *Politics and Rhetoric in the Corinthian Epistles* (Macon GA: Mercer University Press, 1997), 43–75.

18. Charles K. Barrett, *A Commentary on the First Epistle to the Corinthians* (2d ed.; London: A. & C. Black, 1971), 106–107, argues for all the OT; Morna D. Hooker, "Beyond the Things That are Written? St. Paul's Use of Scripture," *NTS* 27 (1980-81): 295–309, argues for those OT texts quoted by Paul in 1 Corinthians; J. Ross Wagner, "'Not beyond the Things Which Are Written': A Call to Boast Only in the Lord (1 Cor 4.6)," *NTS* 44

(1998): 279–87, thinks Paul means only the Scripture quoted in 1 Cor 1:31, which he argues was 1 Kgdms 2:10 (LXX).

19. See the argument that *ēdē* may, in fact, mean "now" here rather than "already" by Hall, *The Unity of the Corinthian Correspondence*, 79–85.

20. See Richard A. Horsley, *1 Corinthians* (ANTC; Nashville: Abingdon Press, 1998) 69–70, and Richard B. Hays, *First Corinthians* (IBC; Louisville: John Knox Press, 1997) 70.

21. Hays, *First Corinthians*, 71.

22. Thiselton, *The First Epistle to the Corinthians*, 359.

23. This is the argument of John T. Fitzgerald, *Cracks in an Earthen Vessel: An Examination of the Catalogues of Hardships in the Corinthian Correspondence* (SBLDS 99; Atlanta: Scholars Press, 1988).

24. This different assessment of the significance of the Hellenistic parallels is made by Karl A. Plank, *Paul and the Irony of Affliction* (SBLSS; Atlanta: Scholars Press, 1987).

25. This is the view of Wolfgang Schrage, "Leid, Kreuz und Eschaton. Die Peristasenkataloge als Merkmale paulinischer theologia crucis und Eschatologie," *EvT* 34 (1974): 141–75. The different readings of Paul's catalog of hardships in 1 Corinthians are reviewed by Thiselton, The First Epistle to the Corinthians, 36–568.

26. See Alexandra R. Brown, *The Cross and Human Transformation: Paul's Apocalyptic Word in 1 Corinthians* (Minneapolis: Fortress, 1995) 163.

27. Robert W. Funk, "The Apostolic *Parousia*: Form and Significance," in *Christian History and Interpretation: Studies Presented to John Knox* (ed. W. R. Farmer, C. D. F. Moule, and R. Niebuhr; Cambridge: Cambridge University Press, 1967) 248–68.

28. See Dale B. Martin, *The Corinthian Body*, 103.

29. W. Michaelis, "μιμέομαι κτλ," *TDNT* 4:660–61.

30. Thiselton, *The First Epistle to the Corinthians*, 374.

31. Richard J. Foster, *Celebration of Discipline: The Path to Spiritual Growth* (rev. ed.; San Francisco: Harper 7 Row, 1988) 175–89.

DISCIPLINING THE BODY

1 Corinthians 5:1–6:20

From all inordinate and sinful affections; and from all the deceits of the world, the flesh, and the devil, Good Lord, deliver us.[1]

At first glance, the portion of the letter beginning in 1 Corinthians 5:1 may appear to have little connection to the preceding section in which Paul has presented an extended argument for unity in the church. Remember, however, that the focus of the church's disunity regarded challenges to Paul's authority to lead based on comparisons of his rhetorical skills with those of sophistic teachers. In responding to those challenges, Paul has attacked the evaluative standards by which he was deemed inferior by articulating a different understanding of authority rooted in his word of the cross. The error in the church's value system has resulted not only in divisiveness but also in other attitudes and behavioral practices that threaten its integrity as God's holy temple (3:17; 6:19). Having concluded his argument for unity with a warning that his next visit might find him wielding a rod of discipline (4:21), Paul turns immediately to apply discipline firmly to an especially egregious case of immorality. Thus, Fee is somewhat on target in seeing the problem addressed in 5:1-13 as a kind of "test case" for Paul's reestablishment of his authority against those he classified as "arrogant" (4:18-19; cf. 5:2).[2] [A Thematic Outline of 1 Corinthians 5:1–6:20]

A Thematic Outline of 1 Corinthians 5:1–6:20

- I. Disciplining an Incredible Case of Immorality (5:1-13)
  - A. Removing the Guilty Party (5:1-5)
  - B. Removing Impurity within the Church (5:6-8)
  - C. Clarifying Earlier Instruction (5:9-13)
- II. Exercising Judgment within the Church (6:1-11)
  - A. Disciplining Fellow Church Members (6:1-8)
  - B. Excluding the Unrighteous from God's Kingdom (6:9-11)
- III. Keeping Immorality out of Christ's Body (6:12-20)
  - A. Misunderstanding Liberty in Christ (6:12-14)
  - B. Realizing the Significance of the Body (6:15-20)

More is involved, however, than a trial run to see if Paul's attempt to assert his authority will succeed. The particular problem addressed in 5:1-13, as well as the attitudes criticized in 6:1-11 and 6:12-20, posed significant threat to the church's inner well-being and its perception by outsiders. Having already demonstrated that they are vulnerable to the encroachment of the value system of their Corinthian environment, the church also shows signs of succumbing

Boundaries

Margaret Mitchell sees 1 Cor 5:1-11:1 as "entirely concerned with the integrity of the social/political boundaries of the church" (228). In 5:1–7:40, she thinks that Paul focuses on group solidarity and the threat of outside defilement posed to it by *porneia*. While Mitchell's concern is social/political boundaries, Dale B. Martin associates Paul's "boundary building" with Paul's anthropological perspective. "For Paul," Martin writes, "firm boundaries must be drawn between the church and the world precisely because firm boundaries do not exist between flesh and spirit, body and spirit, divine spirit and human spirit" (174).

Margaret M. Mitchell, *Paul and The Rhetoric of Reconciliation: An Exegetical Investigation of the Language and Composition of 1 Corinthians* (Louisville: Westminster John Knox, 1991).

Dale B. Martin, *The Corinthian Body* (New Haven: Yale University Press (1995).

to behaviors encouraged by that environment. The first problem Paul addresses here, however, exceeds even the influence of the external environment. The incredible situation of immorality he addresses in 5:1-13 would have stretched the limits of acceptability in Roman Corinth and risked public scorn for the church. Paul expected the church to be different from its surrounding culture, but he did not expect that difference to reside in flaunting the moral sensitivities of that culture.

Thus, part of Paul's approach beginning in 5:1 is to draw the proper boundaries between the church and "those outside," as Mitchell and others have argued.[3] [Boundaries] As Paul clearly indicates in 5:10, such boundaries were not intended to isolate the church from interaction with the outside world. Rather, they were intended to differentiate between who was "inside" and who was "outside" the community by defining behavior appropriate for this distinctive community. Paul presupposed interaction with those "outside," but he also assumed that those "outside" would recognize that those "inside" were different in a positive, even admirable, way. To engage in behavior considered disreputable by "outsiders" jeopardized the church's ability to interact positively with the outside world and placed the church in a position of justifiably being scrutinized in a negative light.

Sacred Boundaries

Temenos of sanctuary of Poseidon at Isthmia (highlighted by ellipse). (Credit: Scott Nash)

Ancient sanctuaries were typically surrounding by a *temenos*, a visible boundary that marked where the sacred space began. In the photograph, one can still view (in the lower section) a portion of the foundation for the western *temenos* wall of the temple of Poseidon on the isthmus of Corinth. In Paul's view, the church is a holy temple (1 Cor 3:16; 6:19) and should be sharply differentiated from the outside world. His boundaries, however, are not physical markers but rather distinctive behavior.

The topics addressed in chapters 5 and 6 indicate that Paul was concerned with boundary definition and protection of the well-being of those inside the boundaries. He calls on those "inside" to exercise sound judgment in guarding the boundaries. Purging the inner community of endangering immorality requires strict discipline (5:1-13). Those who exercise such discipline should also be able to adjudicate differences between fellow church members (6:1-8) and recognize which behaviors are acceptable within the community (6:9-11). They should also be able to determine when they are crossing the line in exercising their freedom in Christ (6:12-20). Thus, Paul begins with a particular case of immorality that demands clear judgment, in his opinion. He then urges the church to exercise its responsibility to handle all problems between members. He finally returns to the issue of immorality in a more general way, urging members to understand that their liberty in Christ is not a license to engage in behaviors that are not advantageous to one's self or to the church. The result is an apparent A-B-A' pattern:

A—immorality (5:1-13)
B—judgments (6:1-11)
A'—immorality (6:12-20)

While many interpreters view these three parts as distinct units with little connection between them, the position taken here is that items B and A' serve to reinforce A. Item A involves a particular instance of actual behavior in the church addressed by Paul. Item B is also widely understood to involve an actual practice as well, namely, church members pursuing lawsuits against one another in the civil courts. Paul, however, may refer only to a possibility, not an actual practice. He may have used a hypothetical situation to carry forward his insistence that the church address the particular case of 5:1-13 as well as other problems involving the behavior of church members. Item A' is also often understood to involve another practice actually occurring among the membership (some are visiting prostitutes), but again such is not necessarily the case. Paul may be raising another hypothetical situation to argue for the seriousness with which the church should consider immoral behavior. Paul's argument in the two chapters both picks up phrases and ideas articulated earlier in the letter and connects with pieces of his arguments regarding other problems later in the letter. These will be identified below in the commentary on the three parts of this section.

COMMENTARY

Disciplining an Incredible Case of Immorality, 5:1-13

Paul learned from an oral report by Chloe's people that the church was disunited (1:10), though the church did not mention that in their letter to him. That letter, to which he responds in chapter 7 and probably elsewhere, also did not mention another situation that came to Paul's attention by word of mouth. A man in the church was "having" (*echein*) his father's wife. The case involved the double taboo of adultery and incest. Though the woman in question was apparently not the man's biological mother, Roman law held that sexual relations between such parties was incestuous and that it was adulterous if the woman's husband (the man's father) was still living.[4] Paul labels the situation as *porneia*, a term that typically covers various forms of sexual immorality. Furthermore, he asserts that it is immorality of a kind "not among the gentiles." ["Not among the Gentiles"] Paul's dismay is that the church is *tolerating* immorality within its ranks of a scale not tolerated by those outside.

The obvious question of *why* begs for an answer. Several proposals have been offered to explain the extraordinary tolerance of the Corinthian church in this matter. A common one has been to blame the moral laxity of the persons involved and the congregation in its acceptance of their behavior on the alleged rampant immorality of ancient Corinth. As pointed out in the Introduction, however, this position is based on a misreading of ancient texts and a misapplication of the supposed reputation of the Greek city-state of Corinth to the Roman colony of Paul's time. However popular this view may have become, it lacks substance in light of the evidence. Furthermore, as Paul clearly states, the problem was not the immoral environment of the church but rather the church's willingness to tolerate a situation not tolerated in the larger society.

Another, more defensible, view is that the situation was rooted in some kind of *spiritual elitism.* Paul's sarcastic assault on the Corinthians' smugness in 1 Corinthians 4:8-13 might suggest that certain members of the congregation believed that in

Roman Law Regarding Adultery and Incest

Adulterous wife appearing in court: conjugal law. Justinian in fortiatum. 14th C. Biblioteca Real. Escorial. Madrid, Spain. (Credit: Bridgeman-Giraudon/Art Resource, NY)

Roman law identified illicit relationships that constituted both adultery and incest. The 6th-century Roman emperor Justinian, who is depicted as judge in the painting, codified Roman law in *The Digest*. That work defined such relationships on the basis of a code originating in 18 BC and titled "*ad Iuliam de adulteriis et de stupro*." That code held that sexual relations between a man and his stepdaughter, daughter-in-law, or stepmother were both adulterous and incestuous and that both parties should suffer similar punishments.

Bruce W. Winter, *After Paul Left Corinth: The Influence of Secular Ethics and Social Change* (Grand Rapids MI: Eerdmans, 2001) 46.

"Not among the Gentiles"

AΩ The NRSV rendering "not *found* among the *pagans*" (italics added) may correctly convey Paul's distinction between those in the church and those outside (i.e., translating *ethnesin* as "pagans" rather than simply "gentiles"), but it misses the force of Paul's point. Adulterous, even incestuous, liaisons were sometimes *found* in Roman society, but the seriousness with which they were viewed found expression in specific rules of Roman law that prescribed the most serious of penalties for the guilty parties.

some sense they had already "arrived" at the glorious state Paul's eschatological vision held they were to attain.[5] This proposal holds that they subscribed to an "over-realized eschatology" or a "triumphalism" that celebrated, prematurely, the attainment of eschatological freedom from the evil forces controlling this world. These spiritually elite persons within the church were viewed as already living above the constraints of earthly life, including such restrictive conventions as marriage. Their freedom to flaunt conventional morality in some sense confirmed their existence on a higher plane. This proposal carries the benefit of connecting the problem of immorality in 1 Corinthians 5 with the exaggerated exaltation in spiritual gifts in 1 Corinthians 12–14 and the discounting of the bodily resurrection in 1 Corinthians 15. The Corinthians' arrogance in regard to the *porneia* of 1 Corinthians 5, then, would have been based on their affirmation of the "spiritual" advancement of the persons involved.

In light of the pervasive Corinthian concern for matters of status, however, a more satisfactory explanation understands the situation as one of *social elitism*, as several scholars have recently argued.[6] The man in question may have been one of some prominence, at least in relation to the status of most of the church members. Dependence on the patron-client network of Corinth may have made those members of lower status (the majority of the church) hesitant to address the situation. In fact, the man's inclusion in the membership of the church may have enhanced their own status. Their arrogance, then, would not have lain so much in their pride in his extramarital affair but in his position in the larger community. To have this person in the church and to maintain cordial ties with him, including table fellowship, would have appeared more advantageous than risking their association with him by reprimanding him for his illicit behavior. Furthermore, even though the relationship between the man and the woman was illegal and subject to severe penalties according to Roman law initiated by the emperor Augustus and even though the official stance of Roman public ethics was to condemn such relationships, numerous cases of deliberate defiance of what some considered to be excessive governmental intrusion in private affairs occurred.[7]

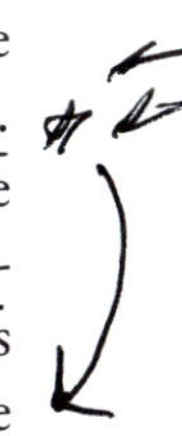

[Ovid on Morals] The man's open violation of Roman law may have suggested to the rest of the church, not that he was spiritually mature, but that he was socially and politically powerful enough to risk public censure. If he possessed sufficient clout to rebuff Roman convention,

Ovid on Morals

The Roman poet Ovid (43 BC–AD 17), in regard to adultery committed by Roman wives, wrote sarcastically in his *Amores* (3.4), "A man is really a bumpkin who takes her unfaithfulness seriously; he does not know enough about the morals of Rome."

then surely those church members who otherwise benefited from his association could overlook his improper relationship with his stepmother. This view that the basic problem rooted in social elitism also connects with other problems addressed by Paul in the letter, namely the issue of divisions in 1 Corinthians 1–4, civil court cases and perhaps attitudes toward immorality in chapter 6, eating meat offered to idols in chapters 8–10, head gear for men and women and the divisions at the Lord's Supper in chapter 11, and perhaps a matter of patronage in chapter 16.

Dale Martin has added another element to the discussion about why the church tolerated the man's immoral behavior.[8] He argues that Paul differed from the more elite members of the church in his understanding of the dangerous, polluting effects of such immorality in regard to the individual's body and the church body. Paul saw the presence of *porneia* within the church as a tangible, even physical, threat to the church's well-being. The counter view in Corinth, especially among those of relatively higher status (according to Martin), was that such instances of moral misbehavior did not actually affect the inner self, let alone damage the essential life of the congregation. Thus, while the man's behavior might be deplorable, it did not corrupt his true self or pose any tangible threat to the church. Paul's concern for protecting those within the boundaries of the church led him to demand the expulsion of the corrupting agent—the guilty man. It also led him to argue in the conclusion to 1 Corinthians 6 that *porneia* did, in fact, corrupt the body. The failure of the congregation to recognize and eradicate this threat prompted Paul to advocate severe disciplinary action, even at the risk of losing an influential church member. [Flesh's Threat to the Spirit]

Another element also deserves consideration in trying to understand Paul's argument here. In pointing out that such incredible immorality is not tolerated among the *Gentiles*, Paul seems to imply that those inside the boundary of the church are not Gentiles. Assuming that most of the Corinthian converts were, in fact, Gentiles and in view of Paul's insistence in other letters that Gentile believers did not have to convert to Judaism to enter the church, this appears a little odd. Paul's letter to the Romans, which he later

Flesh's Threat to the Spirit

According to Dale Martin (171), Paul's views about the flesh's threat to the purity of the spirit differed significantly from those of the higher-class, educated members of the church. He contends, "Even if they were willing to grant that *sarx* might somehow pollute *pneuma* within someone's body, Paul's cultured despisers would have scoffed at the idea that the mere presence of a 'polluted' man within the social group could lead to infection of the *pneuma* of other people in the group" (173).

Justin Meggitt, however, argues that Martin has erred in attaching the different views of the body to socioeconomic status. He points to evidence that shows members of both high and low status could have held both views. Some may even have subscribed to elements of both views, even though they were ideologically incompatible.

Dale B. Martin, *The Corinthian Body* (New Haven: Yale University Press, 1995) 168–74.

Justin J. Meggitt, "Sources: Use, Abuse, Neglect. The Importance of Ancient Popular Culture," in *Christianity at Corinth: The Quest for the Pauline Church* (ed. Edward Adams and David G. Horrell; Louisville: Westminster John Knox, 2004) 248–49.

wrote from Corinth, clarifies Paul's view of the relationship of Gentiles and Jews (Rom 9–11). Through Christ, the Gentiles have been "grafted" into Israel (Rom 11:17). Thus, though they remain ethnically Gentile and do not have to take on the yoke of the Torah, they have become a part of that community of faith that is distinguished from the larger Gentile world. As such, they have inherited the Scriptures of Israel, which, as Paul points out later in 1 Corinthians 10:11, was written to instruct the church. His argument here, though cognizant of the expectations and penalties of Roman law, appeals to the guidance of those Scriptures especially in its use of Paschal imagery (5:6-8) and its direct appeal to the command of expulsion from Deuteronomy 17:7 (5:2, 13). Even the catalogs of vices Paul employs in 5:11 and later in 6:9-10 draw from nearby sections of Deuteronomy (esp. Deut 5:18; 17:3, 7; 19:18-19; 21:20-21; 22:21-2; 23:2-9; and 24:27), as Brian Rosner has noted.[9] Thus, while Paul may have been concerned about the moral reputation of the church in the outside community and while he may have viewed the immoral person in question as a tangibly corrupting influence, his overall concern seems to have been that the church was falling short of the life prescribed for God's called community in the Scriptures.

5:1-5. In his argument, Paul indirectly confronts the man guilty of *porneia* and directly criticizes the church's inappropriate response. The woman seems not to have been the focus of Paul's concern, perhaps reflecting that she was not a part of the church. Paul specifically indicts the church for having become "puffed up" (*pephysiōmenoi este*; cf. 4:6 *physiousthe*) regarding this matter. He then asks, "Should you not rather have mourned?" This question is directly connected by a *hina* clause calling for the man's removal from the church. [*Hina* Clause] The church has not done as it should have done; it should have expelled the guilty party. Paul expects the church to act decisively should the man fail to leave voluntarily, as his quoting of Deuteronomy 17:7 at the conclusion of this unit (5:13) makes clear: "Drive out the wicked person from among you!"

Hina Clause

AΩ In Greek, the word *hina* is often followed by a verb in the subjunctive mood in a clause that expresses purpose. In rare instances, however, the *hina* clause may denote result rather than purpose. In 5:2, if purpose is intended, then the church's mourning is intended to achieve the man's departure. If result is expressed here, then the grieving is because such a situation has occurred.

Daniel B. Wallace, *Greek Grammar beyond the Basics: An Exegetical Syntax of the Greek New Testament* (Grand Rapids: Zondervan, 1996) 473.

In contrast to the Corinthians who have tolerated the situation, Paul asserts that he has already judged the perpetrator of the offense (5:3). The phrase "in the name of [our] Lord Jesus" in 5:4 probably belongs with Paul's pronouncement in 5:3, though some understand it to qualify the guilty man's action: He has openly

In the Hands of Satan

Dieric Bouts the Elder (c. 1415–1475). *The Fall of the Damned*, detail. 1450. Oil on wood. Photo: J. G. Berizzi. Palais des Beaux-Arts, Lille, France. (Credit: Réunion des Musées Nationaux/Art Resource, NY)

In this detail of a side panel of a triptych depicting the Last Judgment, which was designed as an altarpiece for the town hall of Leuven, the Flemish painter Dieric Bouts has captured the hopelessness of one who is turned over to the hands of Satan. In this instance, the helpless victim is being carried by one of Satan's grotesque demons to be deposited before the opening to the fiery cave of Hell. There, before being carried below, he is to be tortured, along with other damned persons, by serpentine demons.

sinned *in the name of the Lord Jesus* (see NRSV footnote).[10] Though absent, Paul envisions his spirit being present when the church assembles and when, with the power of the Lord Jesus, they hand the offender over to Satan (5:5). The result (*eis*) of this handing over will be the destruction of the flesh, but the purpose (*hina*) will be the saving of the spirit in the day of the Lord. Note that Paul refers to the flesh and *the* spirit, not *his* flesh and spirit. He was probably describing, primarily at least, not the fate of the man but rather that of the church.

Exactly what Paul saw happening to the man, beyond excommunication, is unclear. If "spirit" and "flesh" in v. 5 refers to that of the man, Paul probably did not mean the physical destruction of the man's material being and the salvation of his eternal spirit. [Flesh and Spirit in Paul's Letters] Perhaps Paul understood that the man's inevitable suffering, once he was removed from the protective realm of the church and delivered into that fleshly realm where Satan's destructive power was at work, would also lead to the purification of his own spirit, but that was probably not his concern.[11] If v. 5 is about the man's fate, then it is more likely that Paul was referring to his eventual, eschatological destruction since he would no longer stand within the kingdom of God (6:9).

Flesh and Spirit in Paul's Letters

When Paul refers to flesh and spirit in a contrasting way, he does not pit the physical over against the nonmaterial. Generally, he portrays flesh-in-opposition-to-spirit as that realm of worldly existence that is opposed to God. In that realm, sin, death, and evil hold sway. The realm of the spirit, however, is the sphere where God's grace, salvation, and life prevail.

See Eduard Schweizer, "πνεῦμα, πνευματικος, κτλ.," *TDNT* 6:428–30, and "σάρξ, κτλ.," TDNT 7:126–28. Schweizer takes *sarx* in 1 Cor 5:5 to refer to the man's "earthly being as a whole" (6:126).

Verse 5, however, may not concern the man's fate at all. More likely, Paul is referring to "flesh" and "spirit" in terms of the church. The "flesh" is the man himself in that he represents (or rather manifests) danger to the well-being of the church. The spirit in the church is that vital force proceeding from God's Spirit. The flesh-in-opposition-to-spirit is that force at work corrupting and destroying the life of the spirit. If the flesh itself is to be destroyed, then its destructive powers are nullified, and the spirit is purified of its presence. Paul here sees the removal of the guilty man as important for the purification of the *church's* spirit. The removal of this "fleshly" danger protects the church's "spiritual" well-being. Paul's concern for the safety of the church guides his instruction, not his concern for the individual man.[12]

5:6-8. In 5:6, Paul returns to his criticism of the church's "puffed-up" attitude that he identified in 5:2. He specifically condemns their "boasting" (*kauchēma*), though it is not "boasting" in itself that is his target. Paul has acknowledged proper boasting in 1:31 and will do so again in 9:15-16 and 15:31. The problem here is the basis for their boasting, which derives from their acceptance of a value system that takes pride in human accomplishment. He argues against their false pride by using the metaphor of leaven, that portion of old, yeast-energized dough that bread-makers through the ages have used to cause a new batch of dough to rise. Some commentators have suggested that Paul's reference to leavened and unleavened bread here may stem from the fact that he wrote this letter during the Passover season since he indicates in 16:8 that he would be staying in Ephesus until Pentecost, which came fifty days after Passover.[13] Perhaps so, but the imagery of swelling dough also fits the Corinthians who are "puffed up" with false pride.

The Passover practice of removing all the old leaven from houses in preparation for observing the seven-day feast of unleavened bread (Exod 12:15) seems to lie behind Paul's call to "cleanse out the old leaven" in 5:7. [Exodus 12:15] Just as the ancient ritual signaled an annual fresh beginning rooted in Israel's deliverance from slavery to begin their life as God's covenant community, the church must purge itself of those remnants of the old life that stand in the way of becoming what God has called them to be: an unleavened, new people. Paul affirms that this unleavened state is what they truly are, for their Passover lamb (Christ) has already been sacrificed. While, technically, the Passover lamb was not a sacrifice of atonement, the symbolism of a new beginning carries the connotation of liberation from the bonds of the past. Paul considers this to have happened in the death of Christ; thus the church lives perpetually in the season of Passover, as Chrysostom later observed. [Chrysostom on Passover] The celebration of new life in Christ calls for the

Exodus 12:15

"Seven days you shall eat unleavened bread; on the first day you shall remove leaven from your houses, for whoever eats leavened bread from the first day until the seventh day shall be cut off from Israel." (Exod 12:15; NRSV)

Christ as Lamb

Jan van Eyck (c. 1390–1441). *Adoration of the Lamb*, lower center panel, The Ghent Altarpiece. 1432. Oil on panel. Cathedral of St. Bavo, Ghent, Belgium. (Credit: Scala, Art Resource, NY)

In van Eyck's work, Christ as a lamb stands on the altar of sacrifice but not as victim. The once-slaughtered lamb has been raised and is now surrounded by worshipers (cf. Rev 5:8-13).

removal of the old leaven of evil and malice and the enjoyment of the new leaven that is pure and true (5:8).

Sandwiched between his earlier call to cast out from their fellowship the man guilty of egregious immorality and his admonition not to associate with such persons within the church, Paul's instructions to "cleanse out the old leaven" can be taken as applying specifically to the discharging of the individual in question. His focus seems to have broadened, however, to include anyone or anything that bears the marks of their previous life. Thus, his real target here appears to be their "puffed up" attitude that has led them to tolerate not only one particular case of immorality but also has made them susceptible to other leavening influences. They cannot view themselves as they did previously, nor can they accept within this new, unleavened body the same attitudes and behaviors as before.

5:9-13. Paul apparently had expressed similar ideas in an earlier letter, but his point seems to have been missed, or his appeal may have gone unheeded. His earlier attempt to draw boundaries between the church and those outside, he explains, was not intended to be isolationist. In fact, he acknowledges, extreme isolation from the outside world is impossible (5:10). Recognizing that the church must exist within a world where immorality is present, however, does not mean tolerating immorality within the church. Paul expands his definition of immorality in 5:10 to include sexual immorality, greed, robbery, and idolatry, and further expands it in 5:11 to include slandering and drunkenness. Placing sexuality first in his list may

Chrysostom on Passover

The present time, then, is a time of festival. When Paul said, "Let us celebrate the festival," he did not say this because Passover was at hand, or the feast of Pentecost, but to show that all time is a festal time for Christians, because the abundance of blessings bestowed on them. What blessing has not come to pass? The Son of God has become man for your sake. He has delivered you from death and called you to the kingdom. Since you have received and are receiving such things, how should you not celebrate the festival throughout your whole life?

John Chrysostom, *Homilies on the Epistles of Paul to the Corinthians* 15:6 (NPNF[1] 12:86).

reflect the concern of the specific case at hand, while the placement of greed second may be influenced by the discussion that comes next in 6:1-8.[14] The list of unacceptable behaviors resembles catalogs of vices given by numerous Greek and Roman writers, especially Stoics[15]. Often, such lists might be employed without a direct connection to the context at hand. Paul, however, seems to have selected behaviors that were relevant to his Corinthian context and expands on most of them in other places in the letter.[16] Furthermore, the discussion of acceptable and unacceptable behaviors for the covenant community of Israel found in Deuteronomy seems to have influenced his list (see above). Deuteronomy prescribes stiff penalties, including exclusion, for community members found guilty of violating these prohibitions. Just as Israel was called to exercise judgment on its members, Paul calls on the church to judge and discipline those inside. Outsiders are left to the judgment of God. Paul does not prohibit association with outsiders who may be guilty of the named behaviors, as long as that association occurs outside the boundaries of the church. Within those boundaries, such behavior cannot be tolerated and those members who do them are to be excluded. Paul's double standard roots in his conviction that the church represents a new, different community that must interact with the world outside without permitting that world to shape the identity and nature of those inside. Severe discipline of insiders may even lead the church to "drive out the wicked from among you" (5:13). This stern admonition recalls Paul's instruction in 5:2 and forms an *inclusio* around the unit.

Exercising Judgment within the Church, 6:1-11

Chapter 6 appears to present an abrupt switch to different topics. The first eight verses seem to address the problem of church members' taking fellow believers to public courts rather than resolving their differences within the confines of the community. The last section in the chapter (6:12-20) moves back to a discussion of immorality that is more general than the specific case addressed in chapter 5. Verses 9-11 are generally understood to relate to 6:1-8, but thematically they have much in common with 6:12-20. Thus, the unit 6:1-8 stands out from the rest of chapters 5–6. If, as it appears to most commentators, Paul has completely changed his focus in 6:1, then he has suddenly chosen to address other, unrelated issues that the Corinthians apparently had not mentioned in their letter to him. As we shall see, however, the issues addressed in chapter 6 may not be unrelated to the topic in chapter 5.

6:1-8. Several different options exist for understanding the function of this unit within the total context of the letter. Most interpreters accept that Paul is apparently disturbed that some of the Corinthian believers have chosen to bring lawsuits against fellow church members in the civil courts. If so, then Paul's concern may have rooted in the notorious reputation such courts had for dispensing "justice" only to citizens of higher standing and wealth.[17] [Crooked Lawyers] In fact, persons lacking citizenship could not bring charges at all, and persons of lower status were hindered in suing those of higher rank. The result was a system that provided a means for persons of power to take advantage of those possessing less or no power. Thus, Paul can be viewed here as criticizing those higher-status members of the church who used the corrupt court system to press claims against other members, resulting in "wronging" and "defrauding" their "brothers" (6:8). The term Paul uses in 6:7-8 (*apostereō*) can be used to mean "rob" or "deprive financially." Paul's inclusion of the "greedy" and "robbers" in his list of unacceptable behaviors in 5:10-11 and again in 6:10 may reflect his concern with more powerful members using the courts to exploit those of lesser status.[18]

Crooked Lawyers

A reference to "lawyers innumerable perverting justice" among the other hucksters of their goods at the Isthmian games in Dio Chrysostom's 8th Discourse (*Or.* 8.9) has been cited as evidence that Corinth's courts were unjust. While Dio's inclusion of lawyers in his derision of jugglers, poets, and peddlers may simply reflect the age-old custom of "lawyer bashing," the court system in Corinth was probably plagued with the same propensity to unfairness that has been documented for Roman courts in general in the early imperial period.

Bruce W. Winter, *After Paul Left Corinth: The Influence of Secular Ethics and Social Change* (Grand Rapids MI: Eerdmans, 2001) 60–64.

Perhaps, though, it was not the reputation of the courts that concerned Paul as much as the damage such court cases might inflict upon the reputation of the church. Even if legitimate grievances were handled in a just fashion, the fact that church members sought justice in the public arena could tarnish their identity as a different kind of community. Paul's argument focuses on the capacity and responsibility of this community to handle its own affairs. Conceivably here, Paul may have in mind a specific instance rather then a recurring practice.[19] The "defrauding" of one member by another may have preceded and precipitated the resorting to the courts. If such were the case, then Paul has three targets: (1) the person guilty of the initial action, (2) the person who chose to seek justice through the court, and (3) the church as a whole for allowing this matter to be taken outside its boundaries rather than resolving it within.

Another possibility is that the case or cases taken to court involved personal enmity between rivals rather than financial matters.[20] The courts could become the arena for persons of comparable status to pursue vendettas against their opponents. [Personal Enmity] In the political contentions of Roman society, personal enmity might find its way into the courtroom where the proceedings offered opponents an opportunity to smear each other's reputations. If this is Paul's concern here, then one can find possible connections to the divisions already addressed in chapters 1–4. Those divisions seemed to have crystallized around eloquent teachers in the church who competed for the loyalty of the members. The strife (*eris*) that had come to characterize their behavior inside the church (1:11) may have spilled over into the public forum as teachers sought competitive advantage through legal means. The end result of such cases was typically increased enmity between the parties involved and their supporters.[21] Paul's view, if this is his concern, is that such litigation results in a "lose-lose" situation for all involved: "In fact, to have lawsuits at all with one another is already a defeat for you" (6:7a, NRSV). Instead, they should willingly endure being wronged or defrauded rather than inflict the same on another believer (6:7b).

Personal Enmity

The late 2d-century AD writer Athenaeus described the kind of litigation that might follow public embarrassment. In his *Deipnosophists* ("The Learned Banquet"), the character Epicharmus states, "But after drinking comes mockery, after mockery filthy insults, after insult a lawsuit, after a lawsuit verdict, after the verdict shackles, the stocks, and a fine" (2.36).

Cited by Bruce W. Winter, *After Paul Left Corinth: The Influence of Secular Ethics and Social Change* (Grand Rapids MI: Eerdmans, 2001) 64–65.

Each of the above views is plausible and fits with the pattern of divisiveness that existed in the Corinthian church, a divisiveness that appears to have been rooted in status competition. None of the views, however, adequately connects 6:1-8 with chapter 5 or with the balance of chapter 6. [The Relationship of 1 Corinthians 5 and 6] Therefore, other interpreters have argued that the cases being taken to the civil courts involved sexual issues, not instances of financial exploitation or personal enmity. Paul's inclusion of the sexually immoral (*pornos*) in his lists of prohibited behaviors in 5:10-11 is expanded to four types of sexual immorality in 6:9, suggesting that sexual behavior ranked high in his concerns. Furthermore, the only other time that Paul uses *apostereō* (1 Cor 7:5) clearly has reference to sexual intercourse.[22] The "defrauding" or "stealing" in question, then, may have involved sexual rights. Possibly, the man guilty of the immorality Paul condemned in 5:1-13 had been taken to court by members of the church who objected to his behavior on the grounds of his viola-

The Relationship of 1 Corinthians 5 and 6

Most interpreters see only a loose connection between 1 Cor 5 and 1 Cor 6, especially 6:1-8. The first to argue for a close connection between 6:1-8 and the case of immorality in 5:1-13 was apparently J. H. Bernard, "The Connexion between the Fifth and Sixth Chapters of 1 Cor," *ExpTim* 7 (1907): 433–43, who held that the lawsuit in question involved the case of incest. His proposal has been developed more recently in different ways by Will Deming, "The Unity of 1 Corinthians 5-6," *JBL* 115 (1996): 289–312, and Peter Richardson, "Judgment in Sexual Matters in 1 Corinthians 6:1-11," *NovT* 25 (1983): 37–58. Antoinette Clark Wire, *The Corinthian Women Prophets: A Reconstruction through Paul's Rhetoric* (Minneapolis: Augsburg Fortress, 1990) 74–75, has also suggested that the two sections involve the same issue.

tion of his father's sexual rights in regard to the woman involved. Presumably, their efforts had been unsuccessful, and the man had received some kind of favorable ruling, perhaps accounting for the arrogance of his supporters that Paul addressed in 5:2, 6. If so, then Paul has now shifted his target audience from the members of the church who have supported the guilty man to those who opposed him. Having condemned the arrogance of those who condoned the immoral person, Paul now assails those who took the man to court rather than settling the matter within the church.

A variation of this view is to consider the case or cases in question to have involved sexual issues but not to have been directly connected to the particular situation in 5:1-13.[23] According to this view, all of chapters 5–6, as well as chapter 7, deal with matters related to sexual morality and family relationships. Paul moves from dealing with a specific case of sexual immorality in chapter 5, which the church has not addressed, to other cases in 6:1-11 involving sexual "defrauding," which the church again has not addressed but which were instead taken to public courts, to the more general discussion of sexual morality in 6:12-20, and finally to specific issues regarding sexual relations and related matters in chapter 7, which the church had written about in their letter to Paul. A parallel structure may exist between Paul's treatment of the issues in 5:1-13 and 6:1-11. In both instances, Paul (1) names a specific case or cases, (2) calls for community action in the present with a reference to eschatological judgment, (3) discusses purity within the church, and (4) includes a listing of unacceptable behaviors, many of which regard sexual relations.[24] The inclusion of nonsexual behaviors in the lists (esp., "greedy," "robbers," and "thieves") may indicate that some of the cases in 6:1-11 involved financial matters associated with marriage such as dowries.[25]

Despite the almost universal acceptance of the view that Paul addresses here an actual practice, the evidence of such in these verses is surprisingly slim. Paul may have actually used a hypothetical example to shame the church into assuming the responsibility for internal discipline of members' behavior. Numerous scholars have noted that chapter 6 contains elements often found in a diatribe, a popular literary device in which the writer debates an imaginary opponent in a way that exposes, even ridicules, the opponent's error.[26] The first word in 6:1 (*tolma* = "Do you dare?") and the repeated use of the expression "Do you not know?" (6:2, 3, 9) suggest a diatribal style here [*Tolma*]. Paul has just asked the church, "Is it not those inside [whom] you [are to] judge?" (5:12). The question assumes an affirmative answer. In 6:1, Paul asks a

Tolma

ΑΩ Paul uses the present, active, third-person form of the verb *tolmaō* in 6:1. Most interpreters and translators assume that Paul uses the indicative mood here and that he intends the question this verb introduces to be only rhetorical. Thiselton argues that "the question carries the force of an exclamatory expression of censure" and could be rendered "How dare you!" Since the other questions Paul asks in 6:1-8 are not usually understood to be rhetorical, one should exercise caution in assuming this first question in 6:1 is merely rhetorical. The possibility that Paul asks an actual question, but about a hypothetical situation, is strengthened if the mood of *tolma* is subjunctive rather than indicative. The subjunctive form is the same as the indicative. If subjunctive, then one might translate the opening words, "Would any one of you dare?" If indicative, however, the rendering "Does any one of you dare?" still may introduce a hypothetical situation.

Anthony C. Thiselton, *The First Epistle to the Corinthians: A Commentary on the Greek Text* (NIGTC; Grand Rapids: Eerdmans, 2000) 423.

question about judging that assumes a negative reply. Rather than forcefully challenging an actual practice, Paul may have presented an unthinkable possibility: "Would you dare do such a thing?" "Of course not!" A series of questions follows, some of which assume an affirmative answer while the others call for a negative reply. [Paul's Questions in 1 Corinthians 6:1-9]

If the answers that seem to be implied by the questions are given their due force, then much of the evidence that Paul was addressing

Paul's Questions in 1 Corinthians 6:1-9

The entire unit of 6:1-9 consists mainly of questions Paul asks of his readers. The assumed answers to the questions suggest that overall Paul was addressing a hypothetical situation. The questions are given below with their probable answers in bold-faced type.

v. 1 Would any one of you, having a matter (*pragma*) against the other, dare (*tolma*) to be judged (*krinesthai*) by the unrighteous (*adikōn*) and not by the saints? **No!**

v. 2a Do you not know that the saints will judge (*krinousin*) the world? **Yes!**
v. 2b And if the world will be judged (*krinetai*) by you, are you unworthy of adjudications of minor matters (*kritēriōn elachistōn*)? **No!**

v. 3a Do you not know that we will judge (*krinoumen*) angels? **Yes!**
v. 3b Not to mention everyday matters (*biōtika*)? **Yes!**

v. 4 If then you have such everyday matters (*biōtika*) for adjudication (*kritēria*), do you seat [for judgment] (*kathizete*) those who are least esteemed in the church? **No!**

v. 5b Is it such that there is no one among you wise who will be able to arbitrate (*diakrinetai*) between a fellow believer? **No!**

v. 6 But rather must a fellow believer be judged (*krinetai*) against a fellow believer, and this before unbelievers? **No!**

v. 7b Why not rather be wronged? **Yes!**
v. 7c Why not rather be defrauded? **Yes!**

To this string of questions in 6:1-8 can be added the question that opens 6:9-11.

v. 9a Do you not know that the wrongdoers will not inherit God's kingdom? **Yes!**

Only three statements in the section 6:1-8 break the pattern of questions that presuppose a "yes-or-no" answer.

v. 5a To shame you I say [this].

v. 7a Already then it is completely a defeat for you that you have judgments (*krimata*) with one another.

v. 8 But you wrong and you defraud, and this [you do to] fellow believers.

an actual practice disappears. Among the questions, only vv. 1, 2b, 4, and 6 may be read as indicators that believers were using the courts to resolve disputes. Each of these questions, however, may be read as implying a negative answer. Thus, they more likely depict a situation that did *not* exist. Believers would not dare to take matters before the unrighteous (v. 1). The church was not unworthy of making judgments in small matters (v. 2b). The church was not putting into places of judgment those least esteemed by the church (v. 4). [Translating 1 Corinthians 6:4] It was not true that no one in the church was wise enough to arbitrate between believers (v. 5b) to the extent that they had to be judged by unbelievers (v. 6). To the degree that the church's inaction in matters such as the one discussed in 5:1-13 gave the appearance that the community lacked such wise persons, Paul's questions shamed them (v. 5a). Paul's question about their apparent lack of wisdom receives added sharpness in light of his earlier sarcastic recognition that they are wise (4:10). He pointed out in 4:14 that his barrage of sarcasm in 4:8-10 was not intended to shame them. Here, however, their inaction in self-discipline brings shame, not because they lack the wisdom needed, but because they have not exercised it.

Translating 1 Corinthians 6:4

AΩ The RSV renders 6:4 "If then you have such cases, why do you lay them before those who are least esteemed by the church?" The "why" adds the insinuation that they were, in fact, doing this. The NRSV, correctly observing the absence of "why" in the Greek text, has "If you have ordinary cases, then, do you appoint as judges those who have no standing in the church?" This version can allow for the possibility that Paul is using a hypothetical situation.

The terms that have typically been understood to signify actual lawsuits may also be read differently. The word *pragma* (6:1), which could refer to a lawsuit in a clearly legal context, more frequently meant simply a "problem" or "dispute" in a context of conflict. [Lawsuits?] Likewise, *krima* (pl. *krimata*, 6:7) usually referred either to a "decision"(perhaps, but not necessarily, made by a judge) or a "matter for judgment," and not specifically "lawsuits."[27] While *kritērion* (6:2, 4) regularly referred to the place of adjudication, it could also mean the act of adjudication or the body that performed such action.[28] Paul probably used the term to refer to a body within the church that would engage in adjudication, not to an outside court.[29] Very likely, his thinking here bears some influence from the prescriptions for internal adjudication given to Israel in Deuteronomy 1:9-17 and Exodus 18:13-26.[30] The verbs pertaining to "judging" (*krinō, diakrinō, kathizō*) do not require that a body outside the church has

Lawsuits?

AΩ Though scholars often cite James H. Moulton and George Milligan, *The Vocabulary of the Greek Testament* (Grand Rapids: Eerdmans, 1960) 532, in support of translating *pragma* as "lawsuit," that work actually gives more examples of *pragma* as "matter" or "problem." If one does not presuppose a legal setting for 1 Cor 6:1-8, the more natural way to translate *pragma* would be "problem" or "dispute." For examples of selective citing of MM, see Gordon D. Fee, *The First Epistle to the Corinthians* (NICNT; Grand Rapids: Eerdmans Publishing, 1987) 231 n9, and Anthony C. Thiselton, *The First Epistle to the Corinthians: A Commentary on the Greek Text* (NIGTC; Grand Rapids: Eerdmans, 2000) 424 n11.

actually engaged in adjudicating matters between church members. Paul may refer to those outside bodies only hypothetically. Would the church allow something unlikely to happen; that is, would it leave disputes and other problems to the judgment of outsiders, or would it assume that task itself? Since the saints will judge both the world and the angels in the future, the church should exercise its capacity and responsibility to adjudicate its internal affairs in the present. The problem Paul addresses is the failure of the church to perform this responsibility at all, not its "passing of the buck" to an outside body.

The church's failure to exercise judgment is evident not only in the egregious case of 5:1-13 but also in the case of internal disputes that have gone unresolved. Paul considers the existence of such disputes already to be a loss for the church (6:7). In fact, he considers it better to be wronged (*adeikeisthe*) or defrauded (*apostereisthe*) than to engage in disputes. [Philosophers on "Wronging Others"] Instead of bearing the wrong inflicted by others, however, the Corinthians are themselves wronging (*adikeite*) and defrauding (*apostereite*) fellow believers (6:8). Their behavior toward one another necessitates the development and implementation of an internal method of adjudication.[31]

This understanding of 6:1-8 removes the appearance of an abrupt change in focus from chapter 5. In 5:12 Paul asked, "Is it not those inside [whom] you [are to] judge?" In 6:1-8 he urges the church to assume this responsibility by shaming them with the embarrassing prospect of members' having to have their disputes settled by outsiders. Most likely, such outsiders are the ones labeled "those least esteemed by the church" in 6:4. In using such language, Paul does not necessarily consider the public legal system to be corrupt. In fact, Paul would undoubtedly have affirmed that system's jurisdiction in criminal matters. For matters of everyday life (*biōtika kritēria*), however, the church itself holds superior judiciary wisdom. Those who would one day participate in eschatological judgment (6:2a, 3a) operate under a different "law code" in that their fundamental principles are informed by God's redemptive activity in Christ. According to this code, one should prefer to suffer wrong rather than inflict it. But when wrong is

Philosophers on "Wronging Others"

Richard B. Hays has observed the similarities between Paul's preference regarding "wronging" in 6:7 and the teaching of some Greek and Roman philosophers.

> There is, however, a very strong echo here of a well-known teaching of Socrates as reported by Plato: "If it were necessary either to do wrong or to suffer it, I should choose to suffer rather than do it" (*Gorgias* 469C and passim, using exactly the verbs Paul employs in 1 Cor 6:7-8, *adikein* and *adikeisthai*). The maxim is repeated by philosophers such as Epictetus and Musonius Rufus; the latter actually wrote a treatise arguing that the philosopher should never prosecute anyone for personal injury, not only because it is disgraceful to inflict wrong on another person but also because the Stoic should never concede having been harmed by anyone in the first place.

Richard B. Hays, *First Corinthians* (IBC; Louisville: John Knox Press, 1997) 95–96.

committed within the church, the church should resolve the matter. Not to do so is shameful.

6:9-11. Paul's argument for severe discipline in the extreme case of 5:1-13 includes near the end lists of unacceptable behaviors (5:10-11). In concluding his argument that the church should exercise discipline, Paul also includes a list of unacceptable behaviors (6:9-10), which he introduces with the same diatribal question found in 6:2 and 6:3: "Do you not know?" Having just pointed out in 6:8 that some of the Corinthians are guilty of wronging (*adokeite*) fellow believers, he reminds them that "wrongdoers" (*adikoi*) will not inherit God's kingdom. [Paul's List of Wrongdoers] The earlier lists served to urge the church to take severe action in excluding the man guilty of incest. The list here emphasizes the incompatibility of certain behaviors with identity as a member of God's kingdom. Paul's purpose in doing this seems to be twofold. On the one hand, he wants the church to become responsible in disciplining its members. Thus, his call for severe discipline in chapter 5 is broadened in chapter 6 to include matters of everyday life. On the other hand, he wants to prevent those behaviors that make such discipline necessary. Thus, he reminds the church that their wrongdoing toward fellow believers, which leads to disputes, is characteristic of those wrongdoers who have no share in God's kingdom. The Corinthians, who are called to share in that kingdom, are called to a quality of living that surpasses that of the unrighteous (*adikoi*).

Paul's List of Wrongdoers

Paul's delineation of vices in 6:9-10 has grown beyond the lists in 5:10-11 to include adulterers (*moichoi*), passive homosexual men (*malakoi*), active homosexual men (*arsenokoitai*), and thieves (*kleptai*) along with the sexually immoral (*pornoi*), idolaters (*eidōlolatrai*), greedy (*pleonektai*), drunkards (*methysoi*), revilers (*loidoroi*), and robbers (*harpages*) named previously.

The Fate of the Immoral

Taddeo di Bartolo (1363–1422). *The Last Judgment*, detail, *Sodomite and Adulterer*. Collegiata, San Gimignano, Italy. (Credit: Alinari/Art Resource, NY)

This particular part of Bartolo's work on the last judgment may have been informed by Paul's list of those who will not inherit the kingdom of God in 1 Cor 6:9-10. Instead of the kingdom, those who commit sodomy and adultery receive punishment at the hands of demons.

Paul's list of unrighteous persons in 6:9-10 includes four clear references to sexual immorality. The first of these is *pornoi*, which in general can refer to any kind of illicit sexual activity (as in 5:9-10) but in particular can signify heterosexual activity by an unmarried person. Since Paul also includes adulterers (*moichoi*) in his list, thereby indicting those married persons who are guilty of sexual misbehavior, *pornoi* here should probably be seen in the more narrow sense. To this pair of terms regarding illicit heterosexual activity

Paul adds two terms denouncing homosexual intercourse (*malakoi* and *arsenokoitai*). The precise meaning of these terms has received much discussion. [Views on the Meaning of *Malakoi* and *Arsenokoitai*] The term *malakoi* basically means a "soft person." Despite significant attempts to restrict the term to effeminate young men or to boys who voluntarily or for pay became the subordinate party in pederastic relationships, the word most likely referred to any male who was the passive partner in a homosexual relationship.[32] The penetration of a Roman male citizen by another male was considered a punishable offense, and to be penetrated by another male was considered shameful.[33] To be the active male who penetrated another male was neither punishable nor shameful, unless the passive male was a Roman citizen. Paul apparently considered the active homosexual partner also to be guilty of prohibited behavior. Though some have taken *arsenokoitai* to mean a "male prostitute" (heterosexual or homosexual), Paul seems to have meant a homosexual male who penetrates another male.[34] [*Arsenokoitai*] Thus, Paul condemns both the passive and active partners in homosexual activity, just as he condemns illicit heterosexual activity by married and unmarried persons.

In the discussions of the particular types of vices condemned by Paul, his larger objective is sometimes lost. Paul's focus is not merely on condemning specific behaviors nor those who engage in them. His main focus is on reminding the Corinthians who and what they have become. Yes, some of them were formerly included among the wrongdoers he names. But something has happened to change that. They were washed, sanctified, and justified in the name of the Lord

Views on the Meaning of *Malakoi* and *Arsenokoitai*

Extensive discussions of the meanings of these terms can be found in the following works.

Boswell, John. *Christianity, Social Tolerance, and Homosexuality*. Chicago: University of Chicago Press, 1980.

Hays, Richard B. "Relations Natural and Unnatural." *JREth* 14 (1986): 184–215.

Petersen, William L. "Can *arsenokoitai* Be Translated by 'Homosexuals'?" *VC* 40 (1986): 187–91.

Scroggs, Robin. *The New Testament and Homosexuality*. Philadelphia: Fortress Press, 1983.

Thiselton, Anthony C. "Vice Lists, Catechesis, and The Homosexuality Debate," in *The First Epistle to the Corinthians: A Commentary on the Greek Text* (NIGTC; Grand Rapids: Eerdmans, 2000) 440–53.

Winter, Bruce W. "Roman Homosexual Activity and the Elite (1 Corinthians 6:9)," in *After Paul Left Corinth: The Influence of Secular Ethics and Social Change* (Grand Rapids MI: Eerdmans, 2001) 110–20.

Wright, David F. "Homosexuals or Prostitutes? The Meaning of *arsenokoitai* (1 Cor 6:9; 1 Tim 1:10)." *VC* 38 (1984): 125–53.

———. "Translating ΑΡΣΕΝΟΚΟΙΤΑΙ: 1 Cor 6:9; 1 Tim 1:10." *VC* 41 (1987): 396–98.

de Young, James B. "The Source and NT Meaning of *arsenokoitai*, with Implications for Christian Ethics and Ministry." MSJ 3 (1992): 191–215.

Arsenokoitoi

ΑΩ The term *arsenokoitoi* does not appear in any Greek literature prior to Paul's use of it in 1 Cor 6:9. One cannot be certain that Paul himself coined the term since "gutter talk" did not always make its way into written texts. If Paul did create the term himself, however, he probably drew from the language of the LXX for Lev 18:22 and 20:13 where the word for male (*arsenos*) and the word for "lying with" in a sexual sense (*koitēn*) appear together. Leviticus considers the act of a male having sexual intercourse with another male to be an "abomination" punishable by death. Paul considers it to be an offense that excludes one from the kingdom of God.

David F. Wright, "Homosexuals or Prostitutes? The Meaning of ἀρσενοκοίται (1 Cor 6:9; 1 Tim 1:10)," *VC* 38 (1984): 125–53, and "Translating ΑΡΣΕΝΟΚΟΙΤΑΙ: 1 Cor 6:9; 1 Tim 1:10," *VC* 41 (1987): 396–98.

Jesus Christ and in the Spirit of God (6:11). The overwhelmingly positive intent of 6:11 should not be missed for it underlies the purpose of the argument that began in 6:1. The Corinthian believers have been transformed. They *are* capable of exercising self-discipline, both as a community resolving disputes between its members and as individuals who are called to a manner of living that makes wrongdoing against fellow believers as unthinkable as seeking the judgment of outsiders for the resolution of differences.

Keeping Immorality out of Christ's Body, 6:12-20

Another abrupt shift in topic seems to occur at 6:12 as Paul challenges an attitude of permissiveness regarding behaviors pertaining to the body. The attitude is expressed in one slogan ("All things are permitted for me," 6:12) and supported by another ("Food is meant for the stomach and the stomach for food," 6:13). Paul's argument against this attitude utilizes three "Do you not know?" questions that focus on the body (6:15, 16, 19). His reference to a prostitute (*pornē*) at the center of his argument (6:15-16) suggests to many interpreters that engagement with prostitutes is the problem that concerns Paul here. More probably, Paul's concern is that the church in general is not taking matters of immorality seriously enough to confront them. The church has not dealt with the particular case addressed in 5:1-3. It has not assumed its responsibility to "police" the membership in such matters. Thus, Paul has argued in 6:1-11 that the church can and should exercise internal judgment of even trivial matters, as well as major ones. This failure to perform such discipline as Paul has called for (5:2b, 4b-5, 12-13) seems to root in the perspective that matters of the body are not of spiritual consequence. Paul attacks this perspective by affirming a different view of the body. In doing this, he points to the extreme, and unthinkable, example of joining Christ's body with that of a prostitute.[35]

6:12-14. Most commentators take the statement "All things are permitted for me" (*panta moi exestin*) as a Corinthian slogan that Paul quotes and qualifies both in 6:12 and later in 10:23. Many interpreters also see the origin of the slogan in the discussions of Greek and Roman philosophers, especially the Stoics, regarding freedom and the limits of what is permissible.[36] [Legally or Morally Permitted?] One did not have to be a student of any particular school of philosophy to have some awareness of their basic ideas since they were widely dispensed through public oratory and by "street teachers" such as the Cynics. Kernels of philosophical teaching,

Legally or Morally Permitted?

Ancient moralists discussed the issue of the difference between legal freedom and moral freedom. In his fourteenth Discourse, Dio Chrysostom (c. AD 40–110) engages an interlocutor (*Int.* below) regarding what is permitted for the wise person to do. Greek phrases resembling Paul's language in 1 Corinthians have been added in parentheses.

Int. Then I say that the one to whom it is permitted to what he wishes (*exestin ho bouletai prattein*), in regard to those matters which are not forbidden by the laws or enjoined by them, is free, and that the man who on the contrary lacks that power is a slave.

Dio. Well then, do you think that it is permitted to *you* to do all things, which, while they are not expressly forbidden by the laws, yet are regarded as base and unseemly by mankind? I mean, for example, collecting taxes, or keeping a brothel, or doing other such things.

Int. O no, indeed. I should say that it is not permissible for the free to do such things either. And indeed for these acts the penalty fixed is to be hated or abominated by men.

Dio. Well then, in the case of intemperate men, whatever acts they commit by reason of their intemperance, and in the case of the ignorant all that they do owing to their ignorance in neglecting either their property or their person or in treating their fellows unjustly and inconsiderately, do not all these things impose a penalty upon those that do them? For they are injured either in their person (*eis to sōma*) or in their property or, most serious of all, in their own soul.

Int. What you now say is true.

Dio. Therefore it is not permissible to do these things either?

Int. No, certainly not.

Dio. In a word, then, it is not permissible to do mean and unseemly and unprofitable things, but things that are just and profitable and good we must say that it is both proper and permissible to do?

Int. It seems so to me at any rate.

Dio Chrysostom, *Or.* 14–16.

especially pertaining to ethics, were encapsulated also in aphorisms, many of which were engraved in inscriptions.[37] If the Corinthian church included sophistic teachers, as has been argued earlier, then they may well have included such aphorisms in their teaching. In philosophical discussions regarding freedom and its limits, those powerful persons who "did as they pleased" were typically contrasted negatively with the virtuous wise person who exercised restraint. If Corinthian believers were using such a slogan, however, it was intended not as a sign of virtuous restraint but of freedom to engage in certain behaviors that convention considered to be prohibited.

Some interpreters think the slogan, or at least some version of it, originated with Paul himself in his preaching about freedom in Christ.[38] According to some, Paul had taught that Gentile believers were free from the Jewish law. In his absence, some in the Corinthian church expanded the range of this freedom-principle to include other non-Jewish laws and conventions. Thus, they were asserting their "God-given" right to flaunt certain moral prescriptions. Or perhaps, Paul's message of freedom from sin had become distorted to the point that some persons believed that they were free to sin without consequences.[39] Another possibility is that the statement is not actually one used by the Corinthians or by Paul in his earlier preaching but rather one that Paul has composed in this letter to counter the Corinthian perspective that has led them to take immorality so lightly.[40] The fact that Paul does not flatly repudiate the slogan but rather qualifies it in both 6:12 and 10:23 lends support to the idea that Paul had articulated some version of it in his preaching.

Whatever the source of the slogan, it enables Paul to move from his reminder that the Corinthians have been transformed into new persons (6:11) to his repudiation of their attitude regarding the inconsequential nature of immoral behavior. Even if "all things are permitted for me," he asserts, "not all things benefit (*sympherei*)." Margaret Mitchell has shown that in deliberative rhetorical arguments, one sought to demonstrate how one course of action was to the advantage (*to sympheron*) of the audience while others were not.[41] Paul, here, appeals to what is *beneficial.* In 10:23, he will repeat this appeal and add another to that which *builds up.* The thrust of his appeal here is a call to a way of life that proves beneficial to the church. Liberty, especially the liberty that Paul affirms for himself and the Corinthians in Christ, must be tempered by the memory that this liberty has come through great cost (6:20). Paul's word of the cross lies in the background here as he pleads for a lifestyle that is rooted in the principle of giving up one's liberty or right for a larger good. Those who exercise their liberty without "cross-guided" constraint, furthermore, risk losing their liberty. Thus, he repeats the slogan, "All things are permitted for me," but adds, "I will not be dominated (*exousiasthēsomai*) by anything." [*Exestin* and *Exousia*]

Exestin* and *Exousia

ΑΩ The words for "permitted" and "dominated" stem from the same root in Greek (*ek* + *eimi*) and permit Paul to convey a serious pun. The unconstrained exercising of one's right (*exousia*) communicated in the slogan "All things are permitted (*exestin*)" can lead to one's being dominated (*exousiasthēsomai*).

For Paul, the danger of domination that can occur through unconstrained exercising of one's liberty is especially acute in matters pertaining to the body. Thus, he quotes another slogan that seems to have been used by the Corinthians to support their idea that indulging the needs of the body without constraint was normal: "Food [is meant] for the stomach, and the stomach [is meant] for food" (6:13a). In chapters 8–10 Paul will take up the matter of food and will also argue for constraint in doing "what is permitted." Here, however, the point of the slogan seems to pertain not specifically to food but rather to indulging the body, especially in regard to sexual behavior.

One significant issue in understanding the intent of the slogan is determining exactly where it ends. Most translations punctuate the slogan as beginning and ending with the word "food," thereby making the rest of the sentence ("and God will destroy both one and the other") Paul's rebuttal. If the point of the slogan is that eating (and by extension, sexual activity) is a normal function of the body and should not be constrained, then Paul's rebuttal would serve as a reminder that the body, along with its needs, is temporary and not of ultimate consequence since God will destroy it. The Corinthians' error, then, would lie in placing too much emphasis on satisfying the body's needs.

This way of understanding the slogan, however, probably misconstrues the Corinthians' perspective, and it clearly misconstrues Paul's. Paul did not denigrate the body as being of ultimate inconsequence, especially not in this section. Instead, his argument affirms the importance of the body now and in the future. The Corinthians' error lies in their taking the body too lightly. If Paul responded to the slogan about food and the stomach with the words "and God will destroy both one and the other," he would have essentially affirmed their cavalier perspective on the body. Rather, the statement about God's destruction of food and the stomach appears to have been a part of the slogan or at least the principle that lay behind it. Thus, several commentators understand the statement "and God will destroy both one and the other" to have been made by the Corinthians, not Paul.[42] Paul's rebuttal of the Corinthians' position begins with "But the body [is meant] not for immorality, but rather [is meant] for the Lord, and the Lord for the body" (6:13b). [The Structure of 1 Corinthians 6:13] The Corinthians, then, were probably of the mind that what one did regarding the body had no negative effect on one's ultimate destiny since the body was transitory. As the "house of the soul," the body was endowed with senses that enabled one to enjoy the pleasures of this life. To deprive the senses of their enjoyment was to go against nature. When the body has served its purpose, the soul will pass on to its blissful state with God, unaffected by the natural indulgences of its "house."[43]

The Structure of 1 Corinthians 6:13

The Corinthians' view quoted by Paul in 6:13 and his rebuttal have a parallel arrangement.

The Corinthians	Paul
"Food for the stomach,	"The body not for immorality, but for the Lord,
and the stomach for food;	and the Lord for the body;
and God will destroy both one	and God also raised up the Lord
and the other."	and will raise us up by his power."

(1 Cor 6:13; NRSV)

Paul's rebuttal to the Corinthian slogan mimics its pattern but affirms the significance of the body. It is not for *porneia* but for the Lord. That is, the body's purpose is not to indulge in its senses but to enable one to use those senses for the Lord. Christ's investment in the bodily existence of believers is reinforced by the additional statement, "And the Lord [is] for the body." Rather than serving its temporary purpose and being sloughed off as unnecessary baggage in the end, the body shall be resurrected (as Paul will stress in ch. 15). The Lord who is for the body and for whom the body is meant is none other than the resurrected Lord. Those whose bodies are the Lord's share in his resurrection though their own "raising up" lies ahead. [The Text of 1 Corinthians 6:14]

The Text of 1 Corinthians 6:14

AΩ The tense of the verb in the clause, "and [God] will raise us up," appears as future (exegerei) in many ancient manuscripts, but many also have either the aorist (*exēgeiren*) or present (*exegeirei*) forms. The oldest papyrus (P[46]) appears to have originally had the present form, which was corrected by a later scribe to read as a future form. Still later, another scribe altered it to read as an aorist, possibly to correlate it with the other aorist form earlier in the verse or, perhaps, under the influence of Col 3:1 where the resurrection of believers is depicted as a past event.

Bruce M. Metzger, *A Textual Commentary on the Greek New Testament* (3rd ed.; Stuttgart: United Bible Societies, 1971) 552.

6:15-20. The rest of Paul's argument that matters pertaining to the body should be taken seriously is framed in terms of three "Do you not know" questions. The first and third of these questions affirm the importance of the body as "members of Christ" (6:15) and as a "temple of the Holy Spirit" (6:19). These two affirmations frame the second "Do you not know" question, which asserts the union of bodies that occurs in sexual intercourse (6:16). Each of the three questions is followed by an exhortation. These exhortations are easily seen for the second and third questions: "Flee immorality!" (6:18) and "Glorify God in your body!" (6:20). The first question also has an accompanying exhortation, but its structure as a question somewhat obscures its hortatory nature: "Should I therefore take the members of Christ and make (*poiēsō*) them members of a prostitute?" [Poiēsō] The powerful exclamatory expression "May it not be!" clarifies that such action is unthinkable.

Poiēsō

AΩ Thiselton observes that *poiēsō* could be taken as a future active indicative or an aorist active deliberative subjunctive. He considers the latter possibility, even if Paul's question is rhetorical, to be inappropriate for the tone of Paul's strong language in 6:15, and so he favors the future indicative.

Wallace, however, notes that the future indicative may be used in deliberative questions, though the subjunctive is more common. He gives a definition of a "Deliberative Rhetorical Subjunctive" that makes it not only appropriate but likely that *poiēsō* should be taken as such in this instance. According to Wallace,

> As the name implies, the *rhetorical* question expects no *verbal* response, but is in fact a thinly disguised statement, though couched in such a way as to draw the listener into the text. In the speaker's presentation, there is uncertainty about whether the listener will heed the implicit command. Unlike the interrogative indicative, it does not ask a question of fact, but of *obligation*. It is supremely a question of "oughtness." (author's italics)

Anthony C. Thiselton, *The First Epistle to the Corinthians: A Commentary on the Greek Text* (NIGTC; Grand Rapids: Eerdmans, 2000) 465.

Daniel B. Wallace, *Greek Grammar beyond the Basics: An Exegetical Syntax of the Greek New Testament* (Grand Rapids: Zondervan, 1996) 465.

Interpreters often see Paul addressing here the problem of Corinthian believers actually engaging in sexual relations with prostitutes. As usual, the alleged immoral climate of Corinth is appealed to in support of this view. Fertile imaginations may even envision members of the church furtively making their way up Acrocorinth's slopes to visit one of Aphrodite's sacred

women. (See [Strabo] in the Introduction.) Somewhat less whimsical is the idea that some church members were continuing their pre-Christian habit of frequenting the city's brothels. More plausible is the proposal of Bruce Winter that the presumed sexual liaisons were taking place not in brothels but at banquets (*convivia*) where the host might provide "after dinner" sexual companions for the guests.[44] His argument that the problem centered on the young men in the church who had reached the age when attendance at such banquets had become their "right," in accordance with Roman custom, connects well with Paul's discussion about "what is permitted" in 6:12 and with his countering of the slogan about "food for the stomach" in 6:13. Winter's proposal, though, depends largely on accepting the idea that the church included a significant number of high-status young males. Unfortunately, insufficient evidence exists to verify this. (See the Introduction.)

"After Dinner" Companions

Young man and a courtesan. Wall painting from Pompeii. Museo Archeologico Nazionale. Naples, Italy. (Credit: Erich Lessing/Art Resource, NY)

Professional courtesans (*heterai*) who provided pleasurable companionship to men at banquets were often a part of Greek and Roman culture. In his lengthy work describing one such banquet (*Deipnosophists*), Athenaeus devoted a section (*Deip*. 13) to describing both the allure and the danger of such companions.

One also has to wonder why, if members of the church were actually visiting prostitutes, Paul does not directly condemn such behavior and those who engage in it. His stern position regarding the man guilty of incest in 5:1-13 demonstrates Paul's willingness to take on perpetrators of immoral behavior. Yet, in 6:12-20 he does not accuse or indict anyone of having actually engaged in relations with prostitutes. Rather, his reference to a prostitute in 6:15-16 serves as an extreme example of the seriousness of sins pertaining to the body.[45] Moralists such as Dio Chrysostom, Seneca, Musonius, and Epictetus often used prostitutes and those who visited them as examples in their discussions of freedom and morality.[46] [Musonius Rufus on Sexual Relations] Paul appears to be doing exactly that in his argument against permitting immorality to exist among the members. The fact that the word for prostitute (*pornē*) shares its root with the word for immorality (*porneia*) also makes the prostitute an appropriately stark example of immorality.

Musonius Rufus on Sexual Relations

The 1st-century AD Stoic philosopher Musonius Rufus argued that all sexual intercourse outside of marriage was shameful, including that with prostitutes. The excerpt below involves an exchange with an imaginary debater (diatribe).

So no one with any self-control would think of having relations with a courtesan or a free woman apart from marriage, no, nor even with his own maid-servant. The fact that those relationships are not lawful or seemly makes them a disgrace and a reproach to those seeking them; . . .

> "That's all very well," you say, "but unlike the adulterer who wrongs the husband of the woman he corrupts, the man who has relations with a courtesan or a woman who has no husband wrongs no one for he does not destroy anyone's hope of children."
>
> I continue to maintain that everyone who sins and does wrong, even if it affects none of the people about him, yet immediately reveals himself as worse and a less honorable person; for the wrong-doer by the very fact of doing wrong is worse and less honorable.

Musonius Rufus, *Frag. 12* (*On Sexual Indulgence*).

Paul has already pointed out that the body belongs to the Lord and that it has more than transient significance. His three framing questions carry this point further. First, do they not know that their bodies are bodily parts of Christ? In chapter 12, he will develop the concept of the church as the body of Christ more fully. Here, it is important to see that this concept is more than a metaphor for Paul. A union exists between the body of the believer and the resurrected body of Christ, for their bodies share one spirit (6:17).[47] It is unthinkable, then, to take (lit., "take away") a part of Christ and place it in the body of a prostitute.

Secondly, do they not know that such an inconceivable act results in a bodily union with a prostitute? For Paul, sexual intercourse is not simply a momentary act but rather one that creates an enduring bond between the two persons. He quotes a part of Genesis 2:24 to support his view of the oneness of being that sexual intercourse causes: "The two shall become one flesh." [Genesis 2:24] While the Genesis text speaks to the union of wife and husband, Paul sees it applying to any sexual union. "Flesh" in the quotation does not seem to carry the negative sense that Paul often attributes to it (see above), but rather it appears to be synonymous with "body" here. He does, however, refrain from using the word flesh in describing the union between believers and Christ. Instead, they become "one spirit" with him. To unite one's self with the epitome of immorality (*porneia*), the prostitute (*pornē*), is to defile the body that should belong exclusively to Christ. Whether Paul also thought that becoming one with a prostitute makes Christ in some sense one with her and the realm of *porneia* that she represents, as Martin contends, is unclear.[48] The tone of his rhetorical question ("Shall I take away [*aras*] the members of Christ and make them members of a prostitute?") supports the idea, but the "tearing away" implied in the participle *aras* suggests that Paul means that something has been taken away from

Genesis 2:24

Paul cites the LXX text of Gen 2:24, which has "the two (*hoi dyo*) will be one flesh," rather than the "they become one flesh" of the Hebrew text. The NRSV translation of Gen 2:24 reflects the Hebrew original: "Therefore a man leaves his father and mother and clings to his wife, and they become one flesh."

Christ and joined with another.[49] The horror of Paul's example, then, probably lies not in the unimaginable thought of uniting Christ with *porneia* but of tearing out what should be a part of Christ's body and merging it with *porneia*. Unlike other sins, intercourse with *porneia* via a *pornē* is a sin against (lit., "into") one's own body because the physical union enables a penetration of *porneia* into the one who penetrates the *pornē*.[50] [Sinning against the Body] Thus, Paul's exhortation regarding this danger in 6:18 is short and clear: "Flee *porneia*!"

Sinning against the Body

AΩ Paul's language of "sinning against one's own body (*eis to idion sōma*)" is similar to the language of Dio Chrysostom. An excerpt from the passage given in fuller form earlier is repeated below.

Dio. Well then, in the case of intemperate men, whatever acts they commit by reason of their intemperance, and in the case of the ignorant all that they do owing to their ignorance in neglecting either their property or their person or in treating their fellows unjustly and inconsiderately, do not all these things impose a penalty upon those that do them? **For they are injured either in their person (*eis to sōma*)** or in their property or, most serious of all, in their own soul.

Dio Chrysostom, *Or.* 15 (bold-faced type and Greek transliteration added).

Thirdly, do they not know that the body is a temple of God's Holy Spirit? Earlier, Paul referred to the church as God's holy temple (3:16-17) and issued a severe warning to anyone who might damage it. Here, Paul locates the dwelling place of God within the body of the believer. The body is not the "prison of the soul" nor the temporary "house of the spirit." Embodied existence is the sphere of God's activity, not some immaterial realm of spiritual bliss nor some nonphysical world of the mind. In the realm of embodied existence God has acted tangibly and physically to claim the body of believers as God's own—at great cost (6:19). Though Paul does not mention it here, undoubtedly he has in view the cross as the act by which God has "bought" (*agorazō*) them. In that culture, persons who were "bought" became the property (slaves) of their owners.[51] In 1 Corinthians 7:22-23, Paul exhorts that those who have been "bought with a price" are God's slaves and should not become the slaves of human beings. Paul's final exhortation makes clear that it is *in* these "bought bodies" that one is called to glorify God (6:20).

In summary, chapters 5–6 constitute a sustained argument for the church to take immorality seriously and to exercise discipline when it arises. The church's failure to handle the egregious case of incest has exposed its lack of responsibility in such matters and its cavalier attitude toward immorality. The root of the problem is seen to lie in a view of the body that considers such behavior to be inconsequential for one's spiritual well-being. Paul's approach to resolving the problem has been first to deal decisively with the specific case of immorality that has alarmed him so, secondly to shame the church into assuming its responsibility to deal with such matters, and, finally, to correct their thinking about the body and the disastrous effects immorality can have on it.

CONNECTIONS

Shocking Behavior

Chapter 5 contains a shocking exposé of a matter the Corinthians had apparently "swept under the rug" in their cavalier attitude toward certain types of behavior. Displaying what must have appeared to some of them as a rather unsophisticated and antiquarian morality, the apostle Paul berated them for exercising too much tolerance. From his perspective, they were guilty of overlooking a grievous case of immorality that even those outside the church would have condemned. The immoral behavior was bad enough, but their refusal to oppose it was unacceptable, in his view. Thus, he called on them to expel from their ranks the scoundrel who had committed the offense.

What about this incident is shocking to the modern church? Certainly, the fact that someone in the church could commit such an offense is not. We do not have to go on very long in the litany of recent sexual scandals by church leaders (Jim Bakker, Jimmy Swaggert, Ted Haggard, etc.) before the "shock factor" of such behavior gives way to the numbness of familiarity. We are no longer surprised at new revelations of inappropriate sexual misconduct by those who would be leaders of the church today. In fact, the particular offense that shocked Paul appears to us rather mild in comparison to the escapades of many recently dethroned (at least temporarily) Christian ministers.

The fact that the Corinthian congregation did not directly confront the offender is also not all that shocking to the church today. [Minister Found Guilty of Immorality] We are accustomed to churches' striving to prevent leaks of delicate information about the sexual exploits of their leaders. The image of the Roman Catholic Church has recently been tarnished in the eyes of many not only by the exposure of the sexual exploitation of children and young persons by some of its priests, but also, and perhaps even

Minister Found Guilty of Immorality

On 1 March 1884, the *New York Times* ran a story on a Methodist minister in Chicago who was found guilty by a church committee of immorality. The committee deliberated only fifteen minutes before voting to sustain five of seven charges brought against their pastor. They found him guilty of maintaining an improper relationship with the wife of the church's sexton and of other matters relating to a cover-up of the affair. The committee also expressed sympathy for the sexton and for his wife, both of whom they considered to be victims of the minister's manipulations.

The committee's action may appear somewhat quaint in the current context of ministerial misconduct, but from the perspective of the apostle Paul, the committee was faithfully fulfilling its charge.

"A Minister in Trouble," *New York Times*, 1 March 1884.

more so, by the sad story of systemic cover-up. Keeping the dark secret of sexual abuse within the church, as well as hiding it from outsiders, is so common that efforts to expose the truth are often criticized as too zealous and too judgmental.[52] The Corinthians' response, or lack of it, does not surprise us.

What is shocking to the modern church about this incident, frankly, is Paul's reaction to it. Paul not only condemned the behavior, he also condemned the person who committed it. In fact, he verbally spanked the church for failing to take action against the man sooner. The tardy action that Paul demanded the church take was to "deliver the man to Satan." That, indeed, is shocking behavior! Where was the good apostle's compassion for the sinner? Where was his understanding of the foibles of human nature? Where was his appreciation for the delicate position in which the Corinthians found themselves given the probability that the man was of substantial status in their community? Where was Paul's concern for dealing with the man redemptively? In short, none of these issues mattered to Paul. The man's very presence was a threat to the holiness and purity of the church. Their toleration of his behavior was a threat to their integrity. The man was, in Paul's eyes, a cancer that needed to be cut out of the body (and quickly) before further metastasis occurred.

Paul's blunt refusal to tolerate the situation in the least may strike us as severe. His call for radical removal of the offensive member may appear callous. His willingness to hand the man over to Satan may even appear to us as "un-Christian." The apparent radicalness of Paul's behavior to the modern mind-set, however, may say more about us than about Paul. It may reveal our own blunted sensitivity to the total inappropriateness of sexual misconduct. It may at least suggest that the modern church is not all that uncomfortable in a culture where sexual promiscuity has become the norm. [Ambrosiaster on Sin] Our reluctance to follow Paul's lead in exercising discipline in such matters may not be due as much as we might like to think to our compassion or respect for privacy. It may, instead, reveal our own cavalier attitude toward the importance of the church in general and its integrity in particular.

Ambrosiaster on Sin

Just as the sin of one person contaminates many, if it is not dealt with once it is known, so also does the sin of the many who know what is happening and either do not turn away from it or pretend that they have not noticed it. Sin does not look like sin if it is not corrected or avoided by anybody.

Ambrosiaster, *Commentary on Paul's Epistles* (CSEL 81.55), in Gerald Bray, ed., *1–2 Corinthians* (vol. 7 of ACCS NT; ed. Thomas C. Oden; Downers Grove IL: InterVarsity Press, 1999) 47.

Shameful Behavior and Saintly Identity

The position usually taken in regard to 1 Corinthians 6:1-11 is that Paul has suddenly shifted his focus from the specific case of immorality addressed in chapter 5 to the problem, as he saw it, of Corinthian believers' suing one another in secular courts. While that may, in fact, be Paul's concern in these verses, the position taken here is that this section actually continues Paul's major concern in chapter 5, namely, that the church has failed to exercise judgment in a serious matter involving one of its members. When the text is read without the assumption that members were actually taking one another to court, then it begins to appear doubtful that such was the case. Instead, Paul appears to use what seems, to him at least, an improbable situation in which believers would turn to outsiders to resolve their problems as a way of shaming them for failing to handle matters such as the one addressed in chapter 5 (cf. 6:5). It is their lack of attention to discipline and judgment, not their reliance on outsiders, that bothers Paul. [Origen on the Corinthians' Failure] The next section (6:12-20) reveals the source of their inaction: they did not consider matters of the body to be of ultimate consequence.

Origen on the Corinthians' Failure

Paul attacks the Corinthians because, although they are right in the middle of Greece, they have no truly wise people in their midst, even though many had gone to preach wisdom to them.

Origen, *Commentary on 1 Corinthians* 2.27.20–22, in Gerald Bray, ed., *1–2 Corinthians* (vol. 7 of ACCS NT; ed. Thomas C. Oden; Downers Grove IL: InterVarsity Press, 1999) 51.

Whether 6:1-11 involves actual court cases, as most commentators suppose, or only hypothetical ones, as suggested here, the overriding point of the section is the same, though it can be easily missed. Paul states that his critique of their failure to act responsibly is intended to *shame* them, but shame is not the ultimate goal of this section. The shame stems from their failure to be who they are. Stimulating them to re-envision their identity is Paul's real objective in 6:1-11, and that aim underlies his discussion in 6:12-20, too. To that end, Paul begins in 6:1 by calling them "saints" and reminding them that as saints they will judge the world and the angels one day. Paul concludes the section by affirming that they have, indeed, been "washed," "sanctified," and "justified." Toward the end of the section that follows, he reminds them that their very "body" is a temple of God's Holy Spirit. He aims to help them *re*-envision who they are because they have lost sight of their true identity. Their vision has become constricted. Their shame comes not from thinking too much of themselves (as was the case in chs. 1–4) but from thinking too little of themselves. Paul's solution to their inaction in exercising discipline is to spur them, even by shaming them, to regain a true sense of their identity.

Interpreters of this section may find it rather easy to focus on Paul's catalog of what he considered shameful behavior in 6:9-10.

After all, Paul did cover a wide range of what he considered unacceptable behaviors, and, since all of the practices he named are still with us in some form, one has much to choose from in connecting his denunciations to our own favorite criticisms of current morals. Add to his list of unrighteous persons Paul's own assault on the Corinthian church's failure to take on immorality within its ranks and we practically have a mandate to loose the cannons on the shameful and shameless persons we detect today, both outside and inside the church. To reduce Paul's words here to a summons to attack immorality in its myriad forms, however, is to overlook his larger purpose in the section. Furthermore, Paul's strategy of shaming his readers may have worked in an ancient Mediterranean honor-shame culture, but its effectiveness would be lessened greatly in modern society. [Shameless Behavior]

Shameless Behavior

In September of 2008, the U.S. federal government expended $85 billion to "bail out" the giant private insurance company American International Group (AIG). In March 2009, it was revealed that millions of the tax-payer-funded bail-out money was designated for bonuses to AIG's executives, who were, in the opinion of many, responsible not only for AIG's financial woes but also for weakening the world economy. The Pulitzer-prize-winning political cartoonist David Horsey captured the public's outrage at AIG's behavior in a cartoon entitled "Pirate Ethics" (viewable at http://www.seattlepi.com/horsey/viewbydate.asp?id=1918). The cartoon shows two pirates opening a treasure chest labeled "Bonuses." A third pirate approaches them and says, "Aarrggh! The captain says we have to give back the treasure 'cause the way we got it was shameful." Another pirate, with AIG on his shirt, replies, "What's shame?" Horsey's cartoon suggests shame is not completely extinct as a negative epitaph in modern society. (See **[Honor and Shame]** in ch. 3.)

Instructional and homiletical purposes are better served by this text when the focus is on Paul's efforts to arouse the church to re-envision its identity. In the first part of this section (vv. 1-6), Paul's passionate rebuttal of their behavior seeks to awaken within them the awareness that they are more than capable of exercising wise judgment. Their failure to do so is irresponsible *because* they can do it, not because they are not up to the task. In the last part (vv. 9-11), his catalog of behaviors and persons not to be tolerated within the church is couched in the context of reminding them that *they* have been transformed into persons who no longer behave these ways. Preaching and teaching that calls on the church to remember that it is a new creation can empower church members to behave as such. Confronting the church with its own immorality may be necessary at times, but to do so without reminding the church of God's power to transform those who have been trapped in such immorality may only perpetuate the enslavement rather than promote liberation from it.

Buechner on Freedom

A man has freedom to the degree that the master whom he obeys grants it to him in return for his obedience. He does well to choose a master in terms of how much freedom he gets for how much obedience.

To obey the law of the land leaves him his constitutional freedom but not the freedom to follow his own conscience wherever it leads.

To obey the dictates of his own conscience leaves him freedom from the sense of moral guilt but not the freedom to gratify his own strongest appetites.

To obey his strongest appetites for drink, sex, power, revenge, or whatever, leaves him the freedom of an animal to take what he wants when he wants it but not the freedom of a man to be human.

The old prayer speaks of God "in whose service is perfect freedom." The paradox is not as opaque as it sounds. It means that to obey Love himself, who above all else wishes us well, leaves us the freedom to be the best and gladdest that we have it in us to become. The only freedom Love denies us is the freedom to destroy ourselves.

Frederick Buechner, *Wishful Thinking: A Theological ABC* (New York: Harper & Row, 1973) 29–30.

Freedom and the Body

Many commentators understand Paul to be turning to still another topic in 6:12, after briefly dealing with lawsuits in 6:1-11. Upon careful a reading of chapters 5–6, however, one may ascertain that Paul stays on subject throughout, rather than switching from topic to topic. The section 6:12-20 reveals why the church failed to act in the case under discussion in chapter 5 and why Paul had to remind them of their ability and responsibility to exercise discipline in 6:1-11. They considered matters of the body, such as sexual immorality, to be within the purview of personal liberty, especially since they believed that actions affecting the body had no ultimate consequence. Paul's response to this underlying perspective is to challenge their view of personal freedom and to point out that the bodies with which they were prone to take such liberties in actuality belong (indeed, are even joined) to Christ.

In regard to personal freedom, Paul simply counters that while all things may be *permitted*, not everything is *beneficial*. In fact, exercising freedom without regard for what is beneficial may lead to enslavement. [Buechner on Freedom] When Paul discusses the limits to personal freedom in 1 Corinthians 10:23-24, he urges consideration of how one's actions may affect someone else. That communal dimension of freedom also lies in the background here. Those who exercise their freedom indiscriminately, without regard for what is beneficial to others, may introduce a kind of contamination into the church. Their actions affect the whole body of believers. Paul's great concern with the specific case of immorality in chapter 5 stemmed from his conviction that such offenses contaminate the whole church. Thus, he prescribed radical surgery to remove the dangerous tissue. Here, he advocates sifting the freedom to do all things through the sieve of what is beneficial.

The effect certain behaviors have on others and on the whole church may lie in the background of Paul's instructions here, as well as in much of 1 Corinthians, but the foreground here belongs to the consequences such actions have for the individual. One who enjoys the privilege of liberty may unwittingly (or wittingly) engage in behavior that hurts other persons. That possibility, for Paul, is enough to prompt one to reconsider whether certain actions are permissible after all. What is distinctive in this passage (and is the primary point Paul was trying to make here) is that such action also harms the person engaging in it, as well as the Lord to whom that person is joined. For Paul's culture, consideration of how certain actions affected the group to which one belonged may have received primary consideration. For our culture, however, the first consideration may more likely be "How does this affect me?" In such a culture, Paul's warning may resonate more clearly than appeals to be mindful of how one's behavior affects others. Thoughtless actions pursued in the quest for personal satisfaction and fulfillment may, in fact, do more harm than good to the person who does them.

To counter the perspective that what one does with the body holds no lasting negative consequences, Paul introduces a new way of understanding the significance of one's body. In contrast to the Corinthian viewpoint that God would *destroy* the body (v. 13), Paul asserts that God will *resurrect* the body (v. 14). The full explanation of this view comes later in chapter 15, but it already underlies Paul's understanding here. The body is not temporary, and what one does in the body matters. Furthermore, one's body is a member of Christ's body. Christ, thus, has a claim on one's body, a claim that precludes misusing the body, as would be the case in the extreme example of joining one's body to a prostitute. Since Paul understands sexual union to involve a merging of bodies in some sense, he sees sexual immorality as a kind of contamination of one's actual body. Finally, since the body of the individual in actuality, as well as the "body" of the church, is the locale where God's Spirit dwells, the body must be kept free from such contamination. The only appropriate use of the body that houses God's Spirit is to glorify God in the body (v. 20).

All of this clashes not only with the Corinthian perspective that held the body to be of no lasting significance but also with the modern tendency to draw a sharp contrast between the inner self (whether this be called the soul or the spirit), which is the domain of spiritual matters, and the outer self, which connects us to the realm of everyday, practical matters. [Sallust on the Body] Both the ancient and the modern views smack of a dualism that Paul rejected. Likewise, the current infatuation with taking care of the body through exercise and diet, while

Sallust on the Body

The demeaning of the body's significance that affected the Corinthians' thinking and that of many modern persons is reflected in this 1st-century BC quotation from the Roman historian Sallust: "All our power, on the contrary, lies in both mind and body; we employ the mind to rule, the body rather to serve; the one we have in common with the Gods, the other with the brutes."

Sallust, *The War with Catiline* 1.2 (trans. John C. Rolfe; LCL; Cambridge: Harvard University Press, 1931).

good practices in their own right, seldom pursues good health with much regard for the body's spiritual significance. Good health may simply be another tactic for enjoying as much of the sensual pleasures of life as possible. "Glorifying God" in the body means more than seeking to have the best body possible. Rather, it should lead believers to consider their bodies as vessels in which God's Spirit dwells and through which God works in the world.

Lectionary Connections

The only portion of chapters 5–6 included in the Revised Common Lectionary is 5:6-8. In Year C, the brief text is read on Maundy Thursday in conjunction with the prescription for Passover preparations in Numbers 9:1-3, 11-12, and the description of Jesus' observance of Passover in Mark 14:12-26. If one chooses to focus on this text, one would do well to emphasize, as Paul did, the need to purge from one's life whatever impurities are there that would prevent a true celebration of Christ's sacrifice.

NOTES

1. "The Litany," *The Book of Common Prayer* (New York: The Church Pension Fund, 1945) 54.

2. Gordon D. Fee, *The First Epistle to the Corinthians* (NICNT; Grand Rapids: Eerdmans Publishing, 1987) 194.

3. Margaret M. Mitchell, *Paul and The Rhetoric of Reconciliation: An Exegetical Investigation of the Language and Composition of 1 Corinthians* (Louisville: Westminster John Knox, 1991) 225–37.

4. For a thorough discussion of the legal issues involved, see Bruce W. Winter, *After Paul Left Corinth: The Influence of Secular Ethics and Social Change* (Grand Rapids MI: Eerdmans, 2001) 44–57.

5. Probably the most complete articulation of this kind of view is that by Anthony C. Thiselton, "Realized Eschatology at Corinth," *NTS* 24 (1978): 510–26, reprinted in *Christianity at Corinth: The Quest for the Pauline Church* (ed. Edward Adams and David G. Horrell; Louisville: Westminster John Knox, 2004) 107–18. Thiselton has more recently expanded his view to allow for the influence of competing status concerns.

6. See John K. Chow, *Patronage and Power: A Study of Social Networks in Corinth* (JSNTSS 75; Sheffield: Sheffield Academic Press, 1992); Andrew D. Clarke, *Secular and Christian Leadership at Corinth* (Leiden: E. J. Brill, 1993); and Bruce W. Winter, *After Paul Left Corinth: The Influence of Secular Ethics and Social Change* (Grand Rapids MI: Eerdmans, 2001) 44–57.

7. Winter, *After Paul Left Corinth*, 126.

8. Dale B. Martin, *The Corinthian Body* (New Haven: Yale University Press, 1995) 168–74.

9. Brian S. Rosner, *Paul, Scripture and Ethics: A Study of 1 Corinthians 5–7* (Leiden: E. J. Brill, 1994) 61–93.

10. This has been argued by Adela Yarbro Collins, "The Function of 'Excommunication' in Paul," *HTR* 73 (1980): 251–63.

11. Martin, *The Corinthian Body*, 172–74, argues against drawing an ontological dichotomy between the individual man's flesh and spirit and that of the church.

12. Richard E. DeMaris, *The New Testament in Its Ritual* World (New York: Routledge, 2000) 00–00, approaches this passage from the perspective of ritual studies. He sees Paul criticizing the church for failing to perform the necessary funeral rite of mourning to accomplish the removal of the immoral man. Paul, therefore, commands them to conduct another rite of expulsion. DeMaris correctly stresses that Paul's concern was for reestablishing the purity of the church.

13. See Phillip Carrington, *The Primitive Christian Calendar* (Cambridge: Cambridge University Press, 1952) 42, and John C. Hurd Jr., *The Origin of I Corinthians* (Macon GA: Mercer University Press, 1983) 139.

14. This is suggested by Richard B. Hays, *First Corinthians* (IBC; Louisville: John Knox Press, 1997) 88.

15. See Hans Conzelmann, *1 Corinthians: a Commentary* (Hermeneia; trans. James W. Leitch; Philadelphia: Fortress Press, 1975) 100–101.

16. See Peter S. Zaas, "Catalogues and Context: I Corinthians 5 and 6," *NTS* 34 (1988): 622–29.

17. For descriptions of the advantages held by persons of higher status in the courts, see Peter Garnsey, *Social Status and Legal Privilege in the Roman Empire* (Oxford: Clarendon Press, 1970).

18. See Alan C. Mitchell, "Rich and Poor in the Courts of Corinth: Litigiousness and Status in 1 Cor 6:1-11," *NTS* 39 (1993): 562–86, and John K. Chow, *Patronage and Power: A Study of Social Networks in Corinth* (JSNTSS 75; Sheffield: Sheffield Academic Press, 1992) 123–41.

19. This is the view of Fee, *The First Epistle to the Corinthians*, 228–29, and of Hurd, *The Origin of I Corinthians*, 86.

20. See Bruce W. Winter, "Civil Litigation in Secular Corinth and the Church: The Forensic Background to 1 Cor 6:1-8," *NTS* 37 (1991): 559–72, and his revised and expanded argument in *After Paul Left Corinth*, 58–75.

21. Winter, *After Paul Left Corinth*, 66–67.

22. Peter Richardson, "Judgment in Sexual Matters in 1 Corinthians 6:1-11," *NovT* 25 (1983): 45–46.

23. This is the argument of Richardson, "Judgment in Sexual Matters in 1 Corinthians 6:1-11."

24. See Richardson, "Judgment in Sexual Matters in 1 Corinthians 6:1-11," 42.

25. This is suggested by Antoinette Clark Wire, *The Corinthian Women Prophets: A Reconstruction through Paul's Rhetoric* (Minneapolis: Fortress Press, 1990) 75, as well as Richardson, "Judgment in Sexual Matters in 1 Corinthians 6:1-11," 54.

26. See Hans Conzelmann, *1 Corinthians*, 104; Fee, *The First Epistle to the Corinthians* 232; Deming, "The Unity of 1 Corinthians 5-6,"305; and William F. Orr and James Arthur Walther, *I Corinthians* (AB 32; New York: Doubleday, 1976), 193.

27. See "κρίμα," *LSJ*, 995, and Friedrich Büschel "κρίνω, κρίσις, κρίμα κτλ," *TDNT* 8:921–54. Büschel, who renders *krimata* as "lawsuits" in 1 Cor 6:7, acknowledges that "there are no other known instances of this usage," 942.

28. See Anthony C. Thiselton, *The First Epistle to the Corinthians: A Commentary on the Greek Text* (NIGTC; Grand Rapids: Eerdmans, 2000) 427–28, and Fee, *The First Epistle to the Corinthians*, 234.

29. See Thiselton, *The First Epistle to the Corinthians*, 428, who prefers the translation "tribunals."

30. See Brian S. Rosner, "Moses Appointing Judges: An Antecedent to 1 Cor 1–6?" ZNW 82 (1990): 275–78.

31. Several scholars have noted some similarity between Paul's understanding of how the church should resolve such matters and the teaching about church discipline attributed to Jesus in Matt 18:15-17. See esp., J. Duncan M. Derrett, "Judgment and 1 Cor 6," *NTS* 37 (1991): 22–36.

32. Robin Scroggs, *The New Testament and Homosexuality* (Philadelphia: Fortress Press, 1983), and John Boswell, *Christianity, Social Tolerance, and Homosexuality* (Chicago: University of Chicago Press, 1980), among others, have argued for restricting *malakoi* to "call boys" in pederastic contexts. Fee, Thiselton, Winter, and numerous other commentators consider the historical and lexicographical evidence to support understanding the term to refer to passive homosexual men.

33. Winter, *After Paul Left Corinth*, 110–13.

34. See David F. Wright, "Homosexuals or Prostitutes? The Meaning of ἀρσενοκοῖται (1 Cor 6:9; 1 Tim 1:10)," *VC* 38 (1984): 125–53, and "Translating ΑΡΣΕΝΟΚΟΙΤΑΙ: 1 Cor 6:9; 1 Tim 1:10," *VC* 41 (1987): 396–98. See also Winter, *After Paul Left Corinth*, 118–20, and Thiselton, *The First Epistle to the Corinthians*, 447–51.

35. Wayne A. Meeks, *The First Urban Christians: The Social World of the Apostle Paul* (New Haven: Yale University Press, 1983),129, suggests that Paul may have used a *reductio ad absurdum* here.

36. See esp. Winter, *After Paul Left Corinth*, 81–85, and Deming, "The Unity of 1 Corinthians 5–6," 299–303.

37. Winter, *After Paul Left Corinth*, 76, 81.

38. Ben Witherington III, *Conflict and Community in Corinth: A Socio-Rhetorical Commentary and 1 and 2 Corinthians* (Grand Rapids: Eerdmans, 1995) 167–68; Archibald T. Robertson and Alfred Plummer, *A Critical and Exegetical Commentary on the First Epistle of Paul to the Corinthians* (ICC; 2d ed.; Edinburgh: T & T Clark, 1914) 121; and Conzelmann, *1 Corinthians*, 108–109.

39. See Richard B. Hays, *First Corinthians* (IBC; Louisville: John Knox Press, 1997) 101–102.

40. Deming, "The Unity of 1 Corinthians 5-6," 310–12, argues that Paul composed the slogan to parody the Corinthians' conduct. He considers all of chs. 5–6 to be dealing with the single case of immorality first mentioned in 5:1. Though the slogan belongs to Paul, Deming holds, it expresses the basis on which the guilty man excused his

conduct. While I agree that chs. 5–6 are a unity, I do not think Paul's focus is on the one case in question. In all of ch. 6 especially, Paul's attention appears to be focused on the church's failure to consider such offenses serious enough to exercise discipline.

41. Margaret M. Mitchell, *Paul and the Rhetoric of Reconciliation: An Exegetical Investigation of the Language and Composition of 1 Corinthians* (Louisville: Westminster John Knox, 1991) 28, 232–33.

42. See Thiselton, *The First Epistle to the Corinthians*, 462–63; Fee, *The First Epistle to the Corinthians*, 255; Hays, *First Corinthians*, 103–104; and Charles Talbert, *Reading Corinthians: A Literary and Theological Commentary on 1 and 2 Corinthians* (rev. ed.; Macon: Smyth & Helwys, 2002) 46.

43. Winter, *After Paul Left Corinth*, 77–80, points to a passage from Philo's discourse "The Worse Overcomes the Better" (*Det.* 33–45) in which he demonstrates how sophists argued, on the basis of Platonic anthropology, that the body's senses should be enjoyed.

44. Winter, *After Paul Left Corinth*, 86–93.

45. Interpreters who consider this a valid understanding of Paul's reference to a prostitute here include Deming, "The Unity of 1 Corinthians 5-6," 290, 304; Meeks, *The First Urban Christians*, 129; Hurd, *The Origin of I Corinthians*, 86–87, 164; and J. Paul Sampley, "The First Letter to the Corinthians," *The New Interpreter's Bible* (12 vols.; Nashville: Abingdon Press, 2002) 10:863.

46. See Deming, "The Unity of 1 Corinthians 5-6," 299–304 for examples and discussion.

47. Martin, *The Corinthian Body*, 176–78, gives an extended discussion of the significance of this bodily union for Paul.

48. Martin, *The Corinthian Body*, 176–78.

49. Archibald T. Robertson and Alfred Plummer, *A Critical and Exegetical Commentary on the First Epistle of Paul to the Corinthians*, 125, hold that *aras* here means "take away." Also, Thiselton, *The First Epistle to the Corinthians*, 465.

51. Dale B. Martin, *Slavery as Salvation* (New Haven: Yale University Press, 1990) 63.

52. One effort to identify sexual abuse within the church and to help both victims and offenders is that of "Speaking Truth in Love Ministries," whose stated goal is to "stop sexual abuse in the body of Christ." See www.speakingtruthinlove.org.

REMAINING AS YOU ARE: SEX, DIVORCE, AND MARRIAGE

1 Corinthians 7:1-40

"Marriage, if one will face the truth, is an evil, but a necessary evil."[1]

Chapter 7 marks a significant transition in Paul's letter to the Corinthians in several respects. First of all, it is clear from 7:1 that Paul is turning to address matters about which the Corinthians have written to him. The other two problems addressed by Paul thus far (divisions in chs. 1–4 and a case of sexual immorality in chs. 5–6) came to his attention via oral reports from visitors from the Corinthian congregation (cf. 1:11; 5:1). That the church had written to Paul about more than one matter is evident from the plural relative pronoun *hōn* ("of which") in v. 1, but exactly what topics their letter included is not so easily determined. The phrase *peri de* in the opening clause of v. 1 ("*Now concerning* [the matters] about which you wrote") reappears five more times (7:25; 8:1; 12:1; 16:1; and 16:12) and has often been taken as an indicator of the topics from the letter to which Paul responds. [Topics Introduced by *peri de*] The fact that the only other two instances of this phrase in Paul's letters (1 Thess 4:9; 5:1) and the similar phrase *peri gar* (1 Cor 9:1) all involve references to the writing (or not writing) of letters supports the view that Paul uses the phrase in 1 Corinthians to mark those points where he takes up a topic from the Corinthians' letter to him. In general, however, the phrase was used by other writers to signify a simple change in topic, so one cannot be certain that Paul only uses the phrase when he is responding to issues they raised in their letter. (See [The Phrase *peri de* in 1 Corinthians] in the Introduction.) While it is reasonable to take the topics addressed in the contingent section of 7:1–11:1 and introduced by *peri de* (7:1, 25; 8:1) as matters included in the

Topics Introduced by *peri de*

Paul introduces the following six topics with the phrase *peri de* (= "Now concerning . . ."):

7:1 "Now concerning the matters about which you wrote,
"It is good for a man not to touch a woman"

7:25 "Now concerning the virgins"
8:1 "Now concerning the foods offered to idols"
12:1 "Now concerning the spiritual gifts"
16:1 "Now concerning the contribution for the saints"
16:12 "Now concerning the brother Apollos"

Whether all of these topics were matters raised in the letter Paul received from the Corinthians is debatable, but probably the first three were included in that letter.

Corinthians' letter, extending the list to encompass every later use of *peri de* (12:1; 16:1, 12) is less tenable. Even less supportable is the expansion of this list to include topics not introduced by the phrase.[2] We should concede that we cannot know all the topics raised in their letter nor all of them that Paul chose to address in 1 Corinthians.

Chapter 7 also marks a transition in regard to Paul's style of argumentation. As Hurd has pointed out, Paul's tone becomes calmer, his treatment of issues is more even-handed and less one-sided, and there is less criticism of their past behavior.[3] In general, he appears more compassionate and less harsh. Of course, exceptions exist to this "kinder, gentler" Paul after 7:1, especially in his rebuke of their behavior in connection with the Lord's Supper in 11:17-34. Furthermore, his argument regarding head attire in 11:2-16 could hardly be classified as even-handed, and the first part of his argument regarding bodily resurrection in chapter 15 ends in a stinging pronouncement of shame (15:34). Apart from 11:17-34, however, the argumentation from 7:1 through 15:58 appears designed to persuade his audience through comprehensive and delicately argued proofs.

Despite the reorientation toward issues raised in the Corinthians' letter to Paul (at least in 7:1–11:1) and the change in tone, connections can be found in chapter 7 to the previous chapters. Obviously, the concern for immorality expressed in 7:2 and 7:5 (and perhaps 7:36) calls to mind elements of the discussions about immorality in 5:1, 6:9, and 6:13-20. Paul's use of the plural with the article (*tas porneias* = "the [situations] of immorality") in 7:2 may be taken, in fact, as pointing back to the particular instances of immorality under consideration earlier.[4] Less obvious, but perhaps more significant, is the connection between his earlier references to "calling" (1:1, 2, 9) and his principle of "remaining in the state in which one was called by God" (7:17-24). Paul began this letter with numerous reminders to the Corinthians' existence as a community called by God. They have been called together corporately to be a people shaped by the one through whom they have been called, namely Christ. That call affects not only their communal life as a church but also their individual, personal lives. Thus, his instructions here about such personal matters as sexual intimacy between married persons, marriage for the unmarried, and divorce for the married are placed in a decidedly theocentric context with a christocentric focus through his use of the language of "calling." (See [Call and Calling in 1 Corinthians] and the section titled "Calling and Vocation" in chapter 1 above.) Finally, his earlier reference to sending Timothy to remind them of "my ways in Christ" (4:17) connects to his appeal in 7:17 to the practice he has established in all his churches here. He makes a similar appeal to traditional teachings or established practices later in 11:2, 16, 17; 15:1-8; 16:1, and perhaps 14:33.

Structurally, chapter 7 falls into two easily detectable parts, vv. 1-24 and vv. 25-40. [A Thematic Outline of 1 Corinthians 7:1-40] The first part deals with the topics of sexual intimacy within marriage (vv. 1-9) and divorce (vv. 10-24). In the section on sexual intimacy, at least the first five verses address celibacy within marriage (perhaps vv. 6-7 also), while the last two (and perhaps vv. 6-7) address remarriage for those previously married persons who cannot live celibate lives. There is some question as to which of these sections vv. 6-7 belong. The section on divorce advocates remaining married, if possible, and bases this on the principle of remaining in the state in which one was called. The argument based on this principle incorporates the matters of circumcision and slavery (vv. 17-24), though these do not seem to be problems in the church, only illustrations of the principle. The second part of the chapter, beginning in v. 25, deals with marriage for those who have not previously been married. The argument includes Paul's reasons for advocating once again that persons remain in the state in which they were called. The final two verses in this section speak to the possibility of remarriage should those who are not presently married lose their future spouse, if they decide to marry at all.

A Thematic Outline of 1 Corinthians 7:1-40

- I. Counsel Regarding Sexual Relations and Divorce (7:1-24)
  - A. Sexual Relations Should be Maintained in Marriage (7:1-9)
    - 1. Regarding Married Persons (7:1-7)
    - 2. Regarding Unmarried Persons (7:8-9)
  - B. Persons Should Remain Married, If Possible (7:10-16)
    - 1. Regarding Marriage with a Believer (7:10-11)
    - 2. Regarding Marriage with an Unbeliever (7:12-16)
  - C. One Should Remain in One's State When Called (7:17-24)
    - 1. Regarding Circumcision (7:17-19)
    - 2. Regarding Slavery (7:20-24)
- II. Counsel Regarding Marriage for Unmarried Persons (7:25-40)
  - A. The Unmarried May Marry, or Not! (7:25-38)
    - 1. A Preference for the Unmarried Life (7:25-28)
    - 2. The Case for the Unmarried Life (7:29-35)
      - a. The Passing of This World (7:29-31)
      - b. Freedom from Anxiety (7:32-35)
    - 3. The Concession for Marriage (7:36-38)
  - B. Widows May Marry, or Not! (7:39-40)

Scholars have not been inclined to identify any particular rhetorical scheme in this chapter.[5] [A Rhetorical Scheme for 1 Corinthians 7] Understandably, the fact that Paul is responding here to questions raised or positions taken in the Corinthians' letter to him leads his discussion to be guided somewhat by their agenda. As we might expect from Paul, however, the agenda quickly bears the mark of his own concerns as he seems to carry the discussion beyond the matters they raised. One could argue that the statement in v. 1, "It is good (*kalon*) for a man not to touch a woman," presents a

A Rhetorical Scheme for 1 Corinthians 7

Propositio—"It is good for a man not to touch a woman," v. 1

Argumentatio I—about what is "good" regarding sex and marriage, vv. 2-24

Refutatio I—Qualification of *propositio* on basis of *porneia*

Husbands and wives should engage in sex due to danger of immorality, vv. 2-5/6

Widowed persons may marry if they cannot exercise restraint, vv. 6/7-9

Refutatio II—Expansion of argument to issue of divorce, vv. 10-17

Marriage to believers should remain married, vv. 10-11

Marriage to unbelievers should be maintained, if possible, vv. 12-16

Remain in the state in which one was called, v. 17

Digressio—Extension of argument to circumcision and slavery, vv. 18-23

Peroratio—Remain in the state in which one was called (principle), v. 24

Argumentatio II—About what is "good" regarding the unmarried

Confirmatio—Affirmation of *principle* in view of this present distress, vv. 25-37

Remain in one's present state, vv. 26-27

Marriage brings anxieties, vv. 28-35

Marriage is permissible, if necessary, vv. 36-37

Peroratio—One who marries does well; one who does not does better, vv. 38-40

—Restatement of principle, v. 40

propositio for at least some of what follows. The presumed affirmation of celibacy of this statement provides the focal point at least for the first seven verses, the ones that seem to speak directly to one issue the Corinthians had raised. The question of marriage for widowed persons (vv. 8-9) may or may not have been raised by the Corinthians, but Paul includes it in his discussion of what is good regarding sexual behavior by affirming remaining celibate as "good" while allowing marriage as "better" than being aflame with passion. Paul's teaching regarding divorce that follows appears to be his own addition to the discussion, prompted not by their letter but by his extension of the matter of sexuality within marriage to the issue of remaining married. The question of what is "good" returns in v. 25, however, as he takes up what was probably another of their questions, namely what to do about the not-yet married, in particular, those identified as virgins. Twice in v. 26 he refers to what is "good" in this matter, and in v. 35 he asserts that his argument is based on what is "beneficial" to them. In the end, he concedes that those who marry one's betrothed and those who do not both do "well" (*kalōs*). His conclusion, however, is that choosing not to marry is "better" (v. 38), both for those not yet married and for those who might face the decision to remarry (v. 40).

Paul's discussion of marriage and celibacy in this chapter has led to two very opposite views about Paul's position on human sexuality, just as his words about slaves in vv. 21-24 were used by both proslavery advocates and abolitionists in nineteenth-century America.[6] On the one hand, Paul's conditional affirmation of celibacy was used in the early church to support the view that those of a higher calling followed the path of asceticism, including celibacy. While Protestant scholars in general have seen the trend toward asceticism in the early centuries after Paul as a distortion of Paul's views rather than a logical development of them, some modern studies have argued that Paul himself shared the inclination toward asceticism found in other philosophical or religious movements of his time.[7] On the other hand, some scholars have interpreted Paul here not only as an advocate of sexual intimacy within marriage but as a champion of marriage as the normal state of calling, with celibacy being seen as somehow abnormal. As with his words about slavery, his teaching about marriage and celibacy has proven pliable enough for persons to embrace and use them in accordance with their own predispositions. In all probability, Paul was neither an ascetic, in the sense in which this is usually taken, nor an advocate of sexual fulfillment within marriage, in the way in which this is usually viewed. His preference for celibacy was motivated primarily by his eschatological perspective, and his affirmation of sexual intimacy in marriage seems not to have been concerned with personal enjoyment or fulfillment.

In examining his teaching here we should remember first of all that Paul was not a person of the twenty-first century. His views regarding marriage, sexuality, and intimacy were not shaped by modern perspectives (or obsessions), thus he may not have been addressing the same concerns that modern persons bring to these verses. Secondly, we should keep in mind that he *was* addressing specific issues raised in a specific context. Even though we cannot recover all of that context or know all of those issues, we can appreciate that his argument was tied to that context and occasion. We do not have access to Paul's full perspective on marriage, sexuality, celibacy, or divorce. We only have his attempt to resolve certain problems faced by the Corinthian believers. Thirdly, we can recognize that as Paul dealt with those problems, he exhibited tremendous flexibility in applying his basic principles. He offered no "one size fits all" solution to their problems. Modern interpreters would do well to exercise the same flexibility in applying his teachings to the problems they address.

COMMENTARY

Counsel Regarding Sexual Relations and Divorce, 7:1-24

7:1-9. The opening section of this chapter addresses two issues: sexual relations within marriage and remarriage for widowed persons. The connection between the two parts lies in Paul's identification of the grounds for permitting widowed persons to marry again, namely, that they cannot otherwise exercise control over their sexual inclinations. Exactly where Paul turns from one part to the other is unclear because of the ambiguity of v. 6. If v. 6 is taken as referring to what Paul has already discussed, then the second part begins in v. 8. If, however, v. 6 points forward, then it signals the beginning of the second part.

As noted above, in v. 1 Paul begins to address certain matters included in a letter to him from the Corinthian church. Perhaps their letter to him was in response to the earlier letter Paul had sent to them, the one mentioned in 5:9. If so, then their letter may have contained elements of resistance to instructions he gave in that letter, or it may have asked for clarification on certain points. Also possible is a scenario in which they wrote to him seeking his guidance on certain matters not covered in his earlier letter and about which they were uncertain or divided in opinion. The probability that Paul's reply to their letter incorporates statements they made suggests that they argued for certain viewpoints that Paul does not find totally acceptable. The first of these is probably what appears to be a quotation in v. 1: "It is good for a man not to touch a woman."

Since "touch" here obviously signifies more than merely physical contact, the maxim espouses a positive view of celibacy: "It is good for a man not to engage in sexual relations with a woman." While many early interpreters, viewing Paul as an advocate of celibacy for all fully committed believers, understood the statement to be Paul's own words, practically all modern interpreters accept the statement as a quotation from the Corinthians. The main point of continuing debate is the degree to which Paul agreed or disagreed with the statement.

Another point of contention, however, is the question of the motivation behind the statement. The maxim expresses the view of at least some of the Corinthians that husbands and wives should refrain from sexual relations. The obvious question, for which we do not have the Corinthians' answer, is why. The numerous answers to this question offered by interpreters generally fall into three major groups.

Some commentators see the root of the Corinthians' inclination toward celibacy in some kind of negative view of sexual activity. In the second century and beyond, many Christians developed the idea that sexual activity was essentially evil since it originated in sinful desire and led to indulgence in the flesh. That idea, however, was largely fueled by a body-soul dualism that Paul and the

Corinthians seem not to have held. Even so, numerous Greek and Roman writers closer in time to Paul did express the view that sexual activity not only stemmed from desire but also intensified it. Desire itself was frequently depicted as a burning, devouring disease.[8] (See [Burning Passion] below.) Paul, too, refers to "burning" in v. 9 in a context where he clearly means sexual passion. Controlling sexual desire within marriage through celibacy may have seemed to certain Corinthians to be a logical way to cultivate purity, holiness, and health. Paul, however, argues for sexual engagement by married partners as a way of controlling desire associated with sexuality.

Other interpreters find a basis for the Corinthians' position in their conviction that curtailing sexual activity was necessary in order to achieve a greater good. They did not necessarily view sex as inherently evil, but they did see it as a hindrance. Whatever impetus there may have been toward sexual asceticism in Hellenistic and Jewish thought during Paul's time seems to have been motivated by concerns about the limitations on pursuing a higher calling posed by involvement in marital life. Stoic writers addressed this issue, with some Stoics arguing for a more traditional view of assuming one's societal roles, including marriage, and some arguing for a more "Cynic" position in which one should seek freedom from such responsibilities in order to pursue the life of a philosopher.[9] [Epictetus on Marriage and the Philosopher] If women in the Corinthian church were the primary advocates for refraining from sexual intimacy with their husbands, then their aim may have been to free themselves from sexual obligations, and the subsequent child-rearing that such activity almost always entailed, in order to give themselves more fully to their sense of calling as followers of Christ.[10] If the advocates of celibacy were men, or at least included men, then freedom from certain marital responsibilities may have been seen as desirable, and even necessary, in order to pursue a higher calling. Paul himself advises the single life for those not married, and his reasons resemble those of the Cynic-Stoics who sought freedom from entanglement in worldly affairs.

Epictetus on Marriage and the Philosopher

The Stoic philosopher Epictetus (c. AD 50–c. 135) presented arguments both for and against marriage by one devoted to philosophy. He depicted the true Cynic as one called to healing the world in a difficult time and, thus, too committed to his vocation to be distracted by marriage. His language about the present time as a "battlefield" and his characterization of marital obligations resembles Paul's concern about the distraction (*aperispastos*) marriage creates for one devoted to the service of the Lord.

> But in such an order of thing as the present, which is like that of a battlefield, it is a question, perhaps, if the Cynic ought not to be free from distraction (*aperispastos*), wholly devoted to the service of God, free to go about among men, and not tied down by the private duties of men, nor involved in relationships which he cannot violate and still maintain his role as a good and excellent man, whereas, on the other hand, if he observes them, he will destroy the messenger, the scout, the herald of the god, that is he. For see, he must show certain services to his father-in-law, the rest of his wife's relatives, to his wife herself; finally, he is driven from his profession, to act as a nurse in his own family and to provide for them. To make a long story short, he must get a kettle to heat water for the baby, for washing in a bath-tub; wool for his wife when she has had a child, oil, a cot, a cup (the vessels get more and more numerous); not to speak of the rest of his business, and his distraction (*aperispastos*).

Epictetus, *Discourses* 3.22.69-71 (LCL).

He does not, however, advocate becoming single by divorcing one's spouse, and he does not support husbands' and wives' refraining from sexual activity in general. For some Corinthians to have advocated celibacy in marriage as a way of achieving the goal of freedom from entanglement would have only gone so far toward this end, considering all the other obligations they would have had to maintain.

Finally, some scholars argue that the Corinthians' position and Paul's reaction to it were not based on any general view about sexuality or its possible limitations on attaining some other end but rather stemmed from specific circumstances faced by the Corinthian church. Paul's contention that remaining unmarried is good "because of the present distress" (v. 26) may indicate that the Corinthian church was facing difficult circumstances that caused members to question the advisability of marriage or of sexual activity within marriage. Marital responsibilities may have appeared daunting in light of economic and/or social hardships. Paul agrees that during such "hard times" marriage should be avoided if possible. Persons already married may have considered it unwise to risk conceiving children in such circumstances. Paul may not have favored allowing married couples to practice preemptive birth control through a moratorium on sexual relations, but he does not indicate that such was his reason for arguing against celibacy in marriage. He does concede that sexual activity may be postponed for a while for purposes of prayer, but only when both partners are in agreement (v. 5). At least one scholar has suggested that prayer for the welfare of the city was the driving motive behind the Corinthians' desire for celibacy.[11] Since prayer was understood to be performed effectively when the pray-er was in a state of consecration to the task, and since sexual relations with one's spouse resulted in distraction from this goal, the urgency of praying in such difficult times meant that one should avoid sexual activity. Paul allows for seasons of prayer, without the obligations of sex, but he limits their dura-

Temptation

Lovis Corinth (1858–1925). *Paradise*, 1911–1912. Oil on canvas. Private Collection. (Credit: Visual Arts Library/Art Resource, NY)

In Lovis Corinth's depiction of Adam and Eve in Paradise, the serpent waits in the background for the chance to tempt the couple and destroy their blissful existence. The primordial image of Satan's taking advantage of moments of weakness, especially in matters of sex, lies in the conceptual background of Paul's concern about prolonged abstinence in marriage.

tion. He considers the prospect of lifelong devotion to such prayer to be dangerous because of the sexual temptations that might arise.

Understandably, each of these approaches to explaining the Corinthians' motivation for celibacy has merit, but none of them resolves every question. What is clear is that Paul disagrees with their position but only in certain respects. Their statement gives Paul a launching point for discussing what is "good" in regard to a spectrum of issues pertaining to sex and marriage. He quotes their viewpoint about avoiding sexual contact and then issues two pairs of imperatives to the contrary, calling for married couples to engage in sexual activity. Because of "opportunities for sexual immorality" (*porneias*), he instructs husbands to "have" their own wives and wives to "have" their own husbands (v. 2). The imperatives to "have" refer to engaging in sexual intimacy with spouses, not to getting married, and restrict such relations to one's spouse ("each one . . . his/her own").[12] The second pair of imperatives employs terminology frequently used in reference to the payment of debts, but it is also found in contexts referring specifically to marital obligations (v. 3, "Let the man/woman give what is owed to the wife/husband").[13] The reason stated for this "having" and "giving what is owed" comes in v. 4 in a balanced assertion of each party's "not having authority" over their own body. Together the imperatives and reason form an A-B-A-B-B-A pattern. [The Pattern of 1 Corinthians 7:2-4]

The Pattern of 1 Corinthians 7:2-4

A—"Let each [husband] have his own wife," v. 2b
B—"Let each [wife] have her own husband," v. 2c
A—"Let the husband give the due to the wife," v. 3a
B—"Let the wife [give the due] to the husband," v. 3b
B—"The wife does not have authority of her own body, but the husband," v. 4a
A—"The husband does not have authority of his own body, but the wife," v. 4b

Two aspects of Paul's argument here are especially noteworthy. First of all, his language removes sexual intimacy from the sphere of individual, private privilege and places it in the sphere of shared experience and obligation. The focus is on the "other" in the marriage relationship. Sex is presented more as something one *gives* than as something one *receives.* He accepts it as a given obligation of the marital relationship. Paul does not explain why the married partner should "give what is owed." He does not associate sex with pleasure, need, or procreation. The only hint at purpose in the section is the initial admonition against *porneias.* His explanation does not focus on the effect such instances of *porneia* might have on the person who indulges in them, but rather he puts the emphasis on the partner who would not receive what is her or his due. Each married partner has responsibilities to the spouse that preclude using his or her body for personal gratification in extramarital encounters. To do such is to rob the spouse of that to which he or she alone is entitled. Thus, Paul insists in v. 5a, "Do not defraud (*apostereite*) one another," using a term that has connotations of robbing or taking what belongs to another. Lurking behind his admonition in v. 5a may be the LXX rendering of Exodus 21:10, which uses the same verb (*aposterēsei*) in reference to the wife's sexual rights. [Exodus 21:10] To withhold sexual intimacy is to rob the spouse of what is rightfully hers or his.

The other noticeable element of Paul's argument is the complete mutuality of the wife and husband in regard to sexual intimacy. Paul's statement in v. 4a that the wife does not have authority over her own body would not have struck his first-century audience as odd. His assertion in v. 4b that the same holds true for the husband, however, would not have been universally recognized. That is not to say that Paul was unique or radical in his affirmation of equality between the sexes, at least in sexual matters, for similar expressions of the mutuality between husbands and wives regarding their bodies can be found in several contemporary, or nearly contemporary, sources.[14] [Mutuality of Bodies] If one supposes that the persons who were inclined toward celibacy in marriage were women, then one might argue that Paul's affirmation of mutuality in regard to sexual obligations was intended not to foster equality but rather to pull the women back into a relationship of submission to their husbands' sexual demands.[15] Paul's use of the maxim, "It is good for a man not to touch a woman," and his direction of the first imperative in each pair in vv. 2-3 to the men, however, may indicate that his target group was predominately or exclusively male. If so, then his affirmation of mutuality in marital rights was subversive not of the women who were seeking celibacy but of the men. Men must "have" their own wives, must give them their "due," and do not "have authority" over their own bodies. While a few philosophers may have espoused views about certain husbands and wives sharing everything, including their bodies, Paul's argument that this pattern of relationship should

Exodus 21:10

The LXX version of Exod 21:10 uses language similar to Paul's injunction against depriving the spouse of sexual rights. The Exodus passage prevents the husband from withholding various marital rights from a first wife should he add another wife. The LXX version reads, "He will not deprive her intercourse" (*tēn omilian autēs ouk aposterēsei*). 1 Cor 7:5a reads, "Do not deprive one another" (*mē apostereite allēlous*).

David E. Garland, *1 Corinthians* (BECNT; Grand Rapids: Baker Academic, 2003) 258.

Mutuality of Bodies

Paul's argument that husbands and wives have mutual rights and responsibilities in regard to their bodies resembles the perspective expressed in some philosophical writings of the period.

Musonius Rufus (AD 30–100) wrote in his *What Is the Chief End of Marriage?*, "The husband and the wife, he used to say, should come together for the purpose of making a life in common and of procreating children, and furthermore of regarding all things in common between them, and nothing peculiar or private to one or the other, not even their own bodies."

Hierocles, a Stoic philosopher from the time of Hadrian (AD 117–138), according to an excerpt from the 5th-century anthologist Johannes Stobaeus, wrote. "Whereby they agree with one another to such an extent and have everything in common even to the point of their own bodies—even more, their own souls themselves."

M. Eugene Boring, Klaus Berger, and Carsten Colpe, eds., *Hellenistic Commentary to the New Testament* (Nashville: Abingdon Press, 1995) 409.

hold within a social community, the church, went beyond what was customary. Though at times Paul retreats from the high affirmation of Galatians 3:28 that in Christ "there is neither male nor female," he does not do so here.

In v. 5, Paul is willing to allow for an exception to the claim that one spouse has on the other's body but only in cases of mutual consent (*ek symphōnou*) and then only for an agreed period (*pros kairon*). The language Paul uses for the conditions under which such refraining from sexual engagement may occur (*ei mēti an*) suggests vague possibility, not probability. The mutual agreement of abstinence for a season has a distinct purpose: "So that you may devote time to prayer *and* may be together again." Both of the verbs (*scholasēte* = "may devote time" and *ēte* = "may be") are joined with *hina* ("so that") in a purpose clause. [Leisure Time] The mutual agreement is for a time devoted to prayer and to returning to normal marital relations.[16] Scholars have noted the similarity of language and thought here with that of the pseudepigraphical work *Testament of Naphtali* (dated 100 BC–AD 100), in which the patriarch Naphtali instructs his sons about God's ordering of commandments in the end times. In that work, the season for sexual intercourse and the season for prayer are sharply separated and the boundary between them should not be violated [*Testament of Naphtali*] Paul, however, sees the rigid separation of sexual activity and prayer as an unlikely practice that should be undertaken only in rare instances and only when both spouses agree that it is necessary. The positive purpose of the agreement for temporary abstinence (to pray) is joined by a negative purpose, namely to prevent Satan's power to tempt them because of a lack of self-control (*akrasian*). The allowance for time devoted exclusively to prayer carries with it the caveat that such a time of abstinence must end before Satan has had opportunity to exploit it. The caveat recognizes that what they intend as a period of consecration to a good end may actually lead in another direction. The initial imperative in this verse is given

Leisure Time

AΩ The verb *scholasēte* in 1 Cor 7:5 is related to the noun *scholē*, which typically was used to refer to "leisure time." The word "school" is based both on the Greek word and the concept behind it. Such time was unfettered by work, family, or social obligations. For the philosopher, leisure time enabled one to devote one's self to study and personal development. In Cynic-Stoic debates about marriage, the Cynic position was that the sexual responsibilities of marriage interfered with one's leisure time. The Cynic *Epistle of Diogenes* 44 states that sexual activity, in general, jeopardizes leisure: "But incessant liasons with women—leave these alone altogether, as they require a lot of spare time (*scholē*)." The verb *scholazō*, however, conveys more than simply "making leisure time." It expresses the idea of using time for a special purpose. Thus, it is aptly rendered as "devote," as in "devote yourself to prayer."

Will Deming, *Paul on Marriage and Celibacy: The Hellenistic Background of 1 Corinthians 7* (SNTNMS 83; Cambridge: Cambridge University Press, 1995) 112–13.

Anthony C. Thiselton, *The First Epistle to the Corinthians: A Commentary on the Greek Text* (NIGTC; Grand Rapids: Eerdmans, 2000) 508–509.

Testament of Naphtali

For the commandments of the Law are double,
and they are fulfilled with a regularity.
There is a time for having intercourse with one's wife,
and a time to abstain for the purpose of prayer.

Testament of Naphtali 8.7-8, from "Testaments of the Twelve Patriarchs: A New Translation and Introduction by Howard Clark Kee," in *The Old Testament Pseudepigrapha*, vo. 1: *Apocalyptic Literature and Testaments* (ed. James H. Charlesworth; Garden City NY: Doubleday & Company, 1983).

The Mishnah on Sexual Abstinence

The issue of temporary abstinence between couples is addressed by Jewish scholars in the Mishnah, which reached its final form about AD 200.

> If a man vowed to have no intercourse with his wife, the School of Shammai say: [She may consent] for two weeks. And the School of Hillel say: For one week [only]. Disciples [of the Sages] may continue absent for thirty days against the will [of their wives] while they occupy themselves in the study of the Law; and labourers for one week. The duty of marriage enjoined in the Law is: every day for them that are unoccupied; twice a week for laborers; once a week for ass-drivers; once every thirty days for camel-drivers; and once every six months for sailors. So. R. Eliezer.

m. Ketuboth 5.6 (Danby translation).

with a present-tense verb that indicates the cessation of something already occurring ("Stop depriving one another"), as is the warning regarding Satan ("So that Satan might not keep on tempting you"). This suggests that some of the Corinthians were already practicing abstinence in marriage and that some of them were experiencing problems with self-control. Paul's solution is to recognize the problem of abstinence and to limit it to stipulated instances. [The Mishnah on Sexual Abstinence]

As noted above, vv. 6-7 either conclude Paul's counsel on celibacy in marriage or mark a transition to a slightly different topic. The crux is how one understands the first word of v. 6. The verse is deceptively simple: "This I am saying according to a concession not according to a command." But to what does "this" refer? Most commentators view the "this" as pointing backwards to something he has already discussed in vv. 1-5.[17] Early interpreters who were inclined toward asceticism understood Paul to be "conceding" sexual intimacy between spouses. His preference, as they viewed it, was for all persons to be celibate in accordance with Paul's own example (v. 7). Since his instructions regarding sexual intercourse are cast clearly as imperatives in vv. 2-5, however, it is not likely that Paul would label his counsel as concession rather than command. Furthermore, his whole argument up to this point has been to encourage the maintenance of normal sexual relations; to cast such activity as "concession" would significantly weaken his case. The most likely referent in vv. 1-5 is the concession regarding temporary abstinence by mutual consent in v. 5. Only in this particular instance will Paul concede that those who advocate that it is good not to engage in sex have a point. He makes it clear, however, that such a practice is in no way to be considered the rule. Verse 7, then, would be Paul's acknowledgment that celibacy is simply not a feasible lifestyle for most persons. Not everyone has the gift (*charisma*) to control sexual desire. While Paul might wish that others were like him in possessing this gift, he concedes that not everyone does. Instead, they have other gifts from God. Thus, those who are married should give sexual intimacy the full attention it deserves and not endanger their relationship by trying to practice abstinence, except in the one stipulated circumstance.

Some commentators are not satisfied with this understanding of vv. 6-7. They see the "this" of v. 6 pointing forward to what Paul says in v. 7 (or beyond), not backwards.[18] [The Text of 1 Corinthians 7:7] What Paul is conceding but not commanding is that he wishes everyone could be as he is, presumably in being able to control sexual impulses and thus be celibate. He does not command this because he recognizes that people have different gifts. They should exercise the gifts they have and not try to emulate those who have other gifts. If this view about the forward referent of "this" is correct, then vv. 6-7 provide a rather smooth transition to Paul's instructions in vv. 8-9. They also set up the argument in vv. 10-24 in that his main premise for staying married is that everyone should remain in the state to which the Lord has assigned and in which God has called them (v. 17ff.). One's station in life is given by God in the same way that the gifts one has for living that life come from God.

The Text of 1 Corinthians 7:7

The textual evidence strongly supports the reading of postpositive *de* ("but") in 7:1, with the earliest papyrus (P^{46}) and uncials (ℵ* A C D*) in agreement. An alternative reading *gar* ("for") also appears in several early manuscripts (inc. $ℵ^c$ B $D^{b,c}$ and several translations). The change from *de* to *gar* can be explained as due to the scribes' view that the *touto* ("this") of v. 6 pointed forward to v. 7. While the scribes' view may have been correct, their alteration of the text cannot itself support that reading (contra David E. Garland, *1 Corinthians* [BECNT; Grand Rapids: Baker Academic, 2003] 275).

Bruce M. Metzger, *A Textual Commentary on the Greek New Testament* (3rd ed., Stuttgart: United Bible Societies, 1971) 554.

Paul turns to a different target group in v. 8, but his focus is still on what is "good" regarding marriage and sex. While some see two very different groups in v. 8, the not-yet-married (*agamois*) and those whose spouses have died (*chērais*), most likely only one major group is intended, namely those formerly married. The masculine noun *agamois* probably refers to widowers, while the feminine noun *chērais* refers to widows. Paul's instructions to the never married come later in vv. 25ff. Paul seemingly includes himself in this group in that his instructions encourage them to remain as he is, that is, single and celibate. This is what is "good" for persons who no longer have a spouse. Later, in his instructions to the never married, Paul explains why he considers it good for them to remain single. He wants them to be free from worldly concerns so that they can devote themselves fully to the Lord (v. 32). Furthermore, his eschatological perspective, in which the world as it now exists is quickly passing away (v. 31), argues against entering into long-term commitments. None of that explanation is found here, but one can assume that Paul could have employed similar arguments for the formerly married had the dissuasion of those who wanted to marry have been his primary concern. His focus here, instead, seems to be on controlling sexual passion. He wishes everyone could be as he is

Burning Passion

According to Dale Martin, "The reference to burning [in 1 Cor 7:9] could be taken to refer to both the fire of desire and the fire of judgment; one could read both senses in Sirach 23:16: 'Hot passion that blazes like a fire will not be quenched until it burns itself out; one who commits fornication with his near of kin will never cease until the fire burns him up' (NRSV). Although it is not entirely clear what the second 'burns' refers to (and it could simply be a parallel to the first), it could have been read, especially by an apocalyptic Jew, as promising the fires of eschatological judgment."

Dale B. Martin, *The Corinthian Body* (New Haven: Yale University Press, 1995) 292 n39.

in this regard. That is, he wishes they could exercise self-restraint. He thinks that it is good for the formerly married to follow his example in this. But if they cannot, if they cannot exercise self-control (*ei de ouk egkrateuontai*), then they should marry. The instruction about getting married is a third-person imperative (*gamēsatōsan*), as were the instructions to the married in vv. 2-3. Celibacy is what is "good" for such persons, but marriage is "better" than "burning." [Burning Passion] While some commentators have seen this "burning" as an allusion to eschatological judgment as a result of unchaste behavior, the term should be taken in the metaphorical sense of "passionate desire." This was the sense in which the metaphor was frequently used in antiquity, and this use makes the best sense of Paul's point here. Rather than seeing Paul's command here as one rooted in the idea that marriage is simply a control on sexual passion, we should observe that Paul consistently presents marriage as the appropriate place for sexual fulfillment. Sufficient opportunities existed then, as now, for finding outlets for sexual energies outside of marriage, but Paul does not consider any such options as valid.

In both his instructions to the married and to those who were formerly married, practicality seems to guide Paul's counsel. He does not appeal to a theological basis for his argument. Within marriage, spouses should recognize the legitimacy of sexual claims by the other spouse. Practicing abstinence beyond temporary, mutual agreement puts one or both spouses at risk. For those widowers and widows who find celibacy beyond their God-given gifts, then marriage is to be preferred to perpetual frustration. Celibacy may be "good," but it is not an ultimate good. Celibacy may bring certain freedoms to those gifted for it and for those who are free from marital obligations, but for those who are not, trying to pursue a celibate lifestyle can prove disastrous to the married and problematic to the unmarried.

7:10-16. The principle of "remaining as you are" connects Paul's instructions to the formerly married in the previous section to his instructions to the already married in the next section. Those who have lost a spouse should remain single, if possible. Those who have a spouse should keep them, if at all possible. As we shall see, the "if at all possible" dimension of Paul's instructions regarding remaining married practically precludes divorce as an option except in a situation where it is a de facto reality and cannot be changed.

Beyond the principle of "remaining as you are," do other connections exist between v. 10ff. and the previous instructions? Or has Paul simply extended the discussion of sexual intimacy in marriage to the larger question of marriage itself? Some commentators think that the issue of divorce addressed here is directly tied to the matter of celibacy in the previous verses.[19] According to this view, the preference for a celibate lifestyle may have led some persons to leave their spouses altogether, presumably because one of the spouses did not agree to sexual abstinence. Otherwise—that is, if they had been in mutual agreement regarding abstinence—it is difficult to see why divorce would have been considered. One does not have to see Paul's teaching about divorce here as a direct counter to those who saw divorce as another route to celibacy, however. The connection between the two may be more indirect. Questions about sexual intimacy between spouses may also raise general questions about being married altogether. For Paul to extend his discussion in this direction, either on his own initiative or in response to questions posed in the Corinthians' letter, is quite understandable.

To those who "have gotten married" (the perfect active verb *gegamēkosin* indicates a present condition), Paul issues a clear command (*paragellō*): "Do not divorce!" The clarity of this command stems not from Paul's apostolic authority but from the declaration that it is the Lord's own charge. Many interpreters see an allusion here to the teaching of Jesus found in Mark 10:11-12 or to an underlying tradition on which the Markan account was based. Others favor the Q version found in Matthew and Luke as the tradition behind Paul's reference. [Synoptic Teachings on Divorce] Paul does not quote the saying from the Lord; he only alludes to it. One can assume that the Corinthians were sufficiently familiar with the teaching for Paul not to have to recite it. The fact that he charges *both* the husband and the wife not to divorce lends support to the Markan tradition as the basis, but we should observe that Paul's use of the tradition is not to lay blame for adultery on either spouse, which is the focus of Mark 10:11-12, but rather

Synoptic Teachings on Divorce

The Synoptic Gospels contain slightly different versions of Jesus' teaching on divorce and remarriage. The Markan version places equal blame on the divorced husband and wife for committing adultery if either marries another person. The Matthean and Lukan accounts place the blame for adultery on the husband who remarries and the man who marries the divorced woman.

Mark 10:11-12—He said to them, "Whoever divorces his wife and marries another commits adultery against her, and if she divorces her husband and marries another, she commits adultery."

Matt 5:32—But I say to you that anyone who divorces his wife, except on the ground of unchastity, causes her to commit adultery; and whoever marries a divorced woman commits adultery.

Luke 16:18—Anyone who divorces his wife and marries another commits adultery, and whoever marries a woman divorced from her husband commits adultery. (NRSV for all texts)

to exclude divorce as a possibility. If the Markan tradition, or some precursor to it, lies behind Paul's words, it may come from the earlier passage in Mark 10:5-9 in which Jesus responds to the Pharisees' question about the legality of divorce. Jesus asserts that Moses' provision for divorce was due to the human "hardness of heart," but God's intention was for the husband and wife to become one flesh and for no one to separate what God has joined. The language of "separation," and Jesus' implied censure of it, is echoed in Paul's prohibition.

What Paul commands, as the Lord commands, is expressed as two infinitives that function as imperatives: "The wife [is] not to separate herself (*mē chōristhēnai*) from [her] husband" (v. 10), and "The husband [is] not to send away (*mē aphienai*) [his] wife" (v. 11). The verb used of the husband's action, *aphiēmi* (lit., "I send away"), was commonly used in ancient Greek in reference to divorce since, in essence, when a husband divorced his wife, he sent her away.[20] In modern society we may distinguish between "separation" and "divorce" as two different phases in the dissolution of a marriage, but such was not the case in antiquity. The different verbs used of the two parties simply reflect the different orientations of their action. The wife who divorced her husband left his house; that is, she separated herself physically from him and was no longer a part of his household. The husband, on his part, could simply make his wife leave the home; that is, he sent her away. The act of sending away was legally sufficient; no formal charges or legal proceedings were necessary. In Roman society, all the husband had to do was utter the formula *tuas res tibi habeto* ("Take your things!").[21] The Roman wife could also initiate divorce from her husband, unlike in Jewish marriages, even accomplishing the act in his absence and without notifying him beforehand. The frequency of divorce apparently grew during the early empire, a condition lamented by many ancient writers.[22]

The first part of v. 11 contains Paul's parenthetical corollary to his basic prohibition against divorce. It consists of two third-person imperatives directed to the wife. If she does leave her husband, she has only two options, according to Paul. She can either remain single or be reconciled to her husband. Paul's perspective regarding remarriage here probably reflects the view connected with Jesus in Mark 10: those who remarry after divorce commit adultery. The fact that Paul only addresses the parenthetical prohibition against remarriage to the wife should not be pressed as evidence that he was targeting women. Throughout this section, he alternates between addressing the husbands and wives first, but he gives essentially the same commands to each. The parenthesis in v. 11 should be understood as addressing the men too: they should either take the wife back or remain unmarried.

When Paul turns to address a slightly different situation, namely, divorce from an unbelieving spouse (these are "the rest" to whom Paul turns in v. 12), he acknowledges that he has no directly pertinent saying from the traditions connected to Jesus: "I say, not the Lord." One could read this as if Paul were presenting himself as an authority in juxtaposition to Jesus or that he was asserting his right to qualify the teachings of the Lord when situations called for it. Instead, his words indicate his admission that he is now treading on ground not covered by the teachings of Jesus.[23] Overall, his instructions to those in mixed marriages is the same as to those in marriages to fellow believers: "Do not divorce!" Thus, even though he does not have a saying of Jesus that directly speaks to the situation of mixed marriages, his counsel is still guided by that underlying tradition.

In Roman society, the problems for a believer married to a nonbeliever were different for husbands and wives. For husbands, the problem would have been viewed as insubordination. Plutarch's "Advice to Bride and Groom" summarizes the common perspective in directing the wife "to worship and know only the gods that her husband believes in."[24] [Plutarch on Marriage and Religion] For the wife to forsake the worship of those gods acknowledged by her husband would have been perceived as a failure to submit to her husband's authority in an arena in which he was expected to dictate the direction of the household, namely, religion. Roman criticisms of certain cults, in particular those of Dionysos and Isis, for enticing women to stray from their husbands' religious devotion were often extended to Judaism.[25] Ovid included Jews with other deviant cults in his criticism of Roman women who were seduced by "the Jewish walk, where the foul drove on sabbaths rest from everything but love."[26] In his *Histories*, Tacitus accused Jews of "regard[ing] as profane all that we hold sacred" and "permit[ing] all that we abhor."[27] He extended his criticism to Jewish family life. Apologetic responses to such accusations by Jewish scholars such as Philo and Josephus stressed that the Law of Moses called for wives to be submissive to their husbands in all things.[28] Other New Testament writings (Ephesians, Colossians, 2 Timothy, 1 Peter) affirm wifely submission to their husbands, perhaps in response to

Plutarch on Marriage and Religion

A wife ought not to make friends of her own, but to enjoy her husband's friends in common with him. The gods are the first and most important friends. Wherefore it is becoming for a wife to worship and to know only the gods that her husband believes in, and to shut the front door tight upon all queer rituals and outlandish superstitions. For with no god do stealthy and secret rites performed by a woman find any favor.

Plutarch, *Moralia* 140.

similar criticisms voiced against Christians, who would generally not have been distinguished from Jews by Romans.

For the male spouse in a mixed marriage, the refusal of the wife to submit to his religious leadership would have been perceived as insubordination on her part and a failure of household management on his. Thus, the husband would have suffered a loss of status for not controlling the wife. Roman custom allowed, even expected, the husband to send away such an insubordinate wife. Paul disagrees with Roman custom here in two respects. First and foremost, he does not permit the husband to divorce the unbelieving wife. Though he has no saying of Jesus that speaks directly to this situation to back him up, he applies the same principle to mixed marriages that he applied to marriages between believers. The husband should not divorce his unbelieving wife, provided she consents to live with him. Secondly, he does not follow the example of Jewish apologists and later Christian writers in asserting that the wife should subordinate herself to the wishes of the husband in religious matters. He may hope for the conversion of the unbelieving wife, but he does not command it. The wife's consent to live with her husband, while not adopting his religion, is sufficient for the marriage to continue.

The situation for the believing wife married to an unbelieving husband was somewhat different and much more difficult. Subordination, a grounds for divorce both for Romans and some Jews, was not the only issue. [Sirach on an Insubordinate Wife] The wife confronted suspicion as well. As the Roman writers cited above, especially Plutarch, indicate, women were considered more easily seduced by deviant religions. Part of the concern expressed regarding Judaism, and by association Christianity, was that it led women astray into practices that were considered improper for upstanding Romans and injurious to the state. Thus, wives who became believers and participated in the life of the church in Corinth, apart from their husbands, not only posed a challenge to their husbands' authority and status but also a threat to the city's welfare. The impetus for the unbelieving husband to divorce such a wife was strong, provided he could not coerce her into forsaking her new faith.

Paul's instruction to wives in mixed marriages is the same as that to husbands: "Do not divorce, if your husband agrees to live with you!" His words reflect the Roman situation in which the wife could initiate divorce. His perspective, however, is reflective of the

Sirach on an Insubordinate Wife

The Jewish sage Jesus Ben Sira (c. 180 BC) prescribed divorce for a disobedient wife: "If she does not go as you direct, separate her from yourself" (Sir 25:26; NRSV). The Greek version on which the NRSV translation is based literally reads, "cut her off from your fleshes." Some Hebrew versions clarify the meaning of the statement by adding, "take and divorce her."

more restrictive position of some Jews (e.g., Shammai) and of Jesus. [The Mishnah on Divorce] Divorce is not an option, unless the unbelieving husband imposes it on the believing wife. Undoubtedly, the believing wife's situation was more precarious than the believing husband's in a mixed marriage, considering the coercive pressures her husband might place upon her to recant and the pressures society placed on the unbelieving husband to send her away.

The Mishnah on Divorce

The Mishnah includes several discussions of the grounds for divorce. In the tractate on "Bills of Divorce" (*m. Gittin*), this famous disagreement between the schools of Shammai and Hillel appears.

> The School of Shammai say: A man may not divorce his wife unless he has found unchastity in her, for it is written, "Because he hath found in her indecency in anything." And the School of Hillel say: [He may divorce her] even if she spoiled a dish for him, for it is written, "Because he hath found in her indecency in anything." R. Akiba says: Even if he found another fairer than she, for it is written, "And it shall be if she find no favour in his eyes."

m. Gittin 9.10 (Danby translation).

Paul's command to believing couples was grounded in the teaching of Jesus ("the Lord"). Though Paul applies the same teaching to those in mixed marriages, he acknowledges that he has no teaching of the Lord that speaks directly to them. His instructions to them, therefore, require more justification. Paul provides this substantiation of his position in v. 14a. The believing wife should feel no compulsion to leave her unbelieving husband, and the believing husband should not feel pressured to send away his unbelieving wife because the unbelieving partner in marriage is *made holy* by the believing spouse. In v. 14b he provides a proof to support his contention in v. 14a by pointing out that the children resulting from mixed marriages are holy. If both spouses were not holy, then the children would be "unclean" (*akatharta*). Since they are, in fact, not unclean, then both spouses must be considered holy. The unbelieving spouse has been made holy in the believing spouse.

Paul's argument here suggests that the primary impetus for dissolving mixed marriages may have been concerns about "uncleanness" rather than, or in addition to, the matters of insubordination and suspicion discussed above.[29] At the beginning of this letter (1:2), Paul addressed his audience as "those *sanctified* (made holy) in Christ Jesus, called to be saints (holy ones)." Paul's concern for their holiness is clearly expressed in chapters 5–6, in which he severely criticizes them for tolerating immorality within their ranks. In his criticism he finds it necessary to clarify what he wrote to them earlier (5:9) about not associating with immoral people. They had apparently taken his earlier instruction to mean that they should close their ranks and not associate with outsiders. Such a strategy would have been intended to protect them from corruption through contact with those considered "unclean." A section of 2 Corinthians (6:14–7:1), which appears to be either a

2 Corinthians 6:14–7:1

Do not be mismatched with unbelievers. For what partnership is there between righteousness and lawlessness? Or what fellowship is there between light and darkness? What agreement does Christ have with Beliar? Or what does a believer share with an unbeliever? What agreement has the temple of God with idols? For we are the temple of the living God; as God said,
"I will live in them and walk
among them,
and I will be their God,
and they shall be my people.
Therefore come out from them,
and be separate from them, says
the Lord,
and touch nothing unclean;
then I will welcome you,
and I will be your father,
and you shall be my sons and
daughters,
says the Lord Almighty."

Since we have these promises, beloved, let us cleanse ourselves from every defilement of body and of spirit, making holiness perfect in the fear of God.

later interpolation or a misplaced section from another letter from Paul (perhaps part of the earlier letter mentioned in 1 Cor 5:9), clearly argues against marriage to unbelievers, quoting a passage from Isaiah (52:11) that prohibits touching anything unclean. [2 Corinthians 6:14–7:1] While it is doubtful that 2 Corinthians 6:14–7:1 represents an authentic Pauline composition, since it flatly contradicts his argument here, it may well reflect a view held by some of the Corinthians.[30] In fact, they may have developed the view on the basis of Paul's warning about associating with immoral people. Marriage certainly constitutes close association, so some may have worried that maintaining their marriages, especially if sexual contact was involved, would result in contamination. They were in danger of becoming unclean through association with their unclean, unbelieving spouse.

Paul disagrees. In fact, he sees the opposite happening. Instead of being contaminated by their unbelieving spouses, the believing spouses extend holiness to those who otherwise would be considered unclean. In light of Paul's earlier warning about sexual immorality affecting one's very body (6:18), his contention that the unbelieving spouse is made holy *in* the believing spouse is remarkable. In 6:15, Paul argued that one who had been joined to Christ should not want to defile Christ by joining sexually with a prostitute. Here, he argues that one who is in Christ may be joined to an unbeliever without defilement. Indeed, the union of the two results in the "making holy" of the unbeliever and of the children who come from their union. In a sense, the holy partner cleanses the unclean partner. Christ's "holiness" present in the believer neutralizes the contaminating effect of an unbeliever and actually overcomes their own uncleanness.

The change from "uncleanness" to "holiness," however, should not be mistaken as salvation. Paul does not say that the unbeliever is "saved" through marital union with a believer. He holds out the possibility that the unbelieving spouse may be saved (v. 16), but he does not say that it happens through marriage alone. The language of "holiness" and "uncleanness" refer not to salvation but to distinguishing between what is "inside" and what is "outside" certain boundaries. Paul was certainly concerned about maintaining boundaries, but he was also pragmatic in recognizing how tightly boundaries could be drawn. He was concerned that immorality not creep into the church from outside, but he did not advocate isolationism. In chapter 5, Paul argues that it is simply impractical to think that all association with the "immoral" world of outsiders can be avoided (5:10). Here, he argues that it is even more impractical to think that one has to divorce an "unclean" spouse to avoid contamination. Furthermore, it is unnecessary since that spouse has become holy (i.e., within the boundaries) in God's eyes. For validation of this position, he points to the holiness of their children, which the Corinthians apparently accepted without argument. Thus, Paul does not argue *for* the holiness of the children but rather argues *from* it. Since the children are holy, the unbelieving parent is confirmed to be holy too.

Having stated clearly that believers should not divorce their unbelieving spouses, Paul acknowledges, in v. 15, that such divorces may happen anyway. The divorced party has no control over the other party. The marriage can be maintained only with the other person's consent, and if that person refuses to continue the relationship, the believer is helpless to prevent its dissolution. Paul's view here is realistic, given the ease with which divorce could occur in Roman society. The divorce could not be disputed; the only dispute to be resolved was that of the dowry. In such cases, the believer is not "enslaved" (*dedoulōtai*), according to Paul. The word *dedoulōtai* is often translated "bound" (so NRSV) and, thus, frequently understood to mean that the believing spouse is no longer under any obligation to the unbelieving spouse and is, therefore, free to remarry. This is sometimes referred to as the "Pauline Privilege," since he otherwise seems to forbid remarriage for women whose divorced spouse is still alive (cf. v. 39; Rom 7:2-3). While certain restrictions regarding remarriage might have applied to divorced women, such was not the case with men, and Paul addresses both when he says "the brother or sister is not *enslaved*." Others consider "not bound" to mean that the spouse is no longer obliged to remain in a disastrous marriage. Remaining in the marriage was not an option, however, since the divorced partner had no control over the other spouse's decision. Furthermore, Paul does not use the word for "bound" here, as he does in v. 39; he uses the word for being "enslaved." Deming has argued that the term should be

Marriage as Slavery

Deming argues that marriage was often depicted as a form of slavery in Cynic and Stoic philosophical traditions. As an example, he cites the well-known saying of Menander: "Having married, know that you are a slave for life" (*Sentences* 529J). He suggests that such thinking was influential among the Corinthians and that Paul's language and argument in 1 Cor 7 reflects an attempt to counter their association of marriage with slavery.

Will Deming, *Paul on Marriage and Celibacy: The Hellenistic Background of 1 Corinthians 7* (SNTNMS 83; Cambridge: Cambridge University Press, 1995) 152.

viewed in the context of Stoic and Cynic depictions of marriage as slavery.[31] [Marriage as Slavery] Paul, was saying, then, that the divorced spouse is no longer enslaved. Instone-Brewer contends, however, that Jewish divorce legislation was based on the law of the slave wife in Exodus 21:10-11, with the result that being released from marriage was likened to being released from slavery.[32] He thinks this background lies behind Paul's language, not the idea that marriage itself was a form of slavery. In general, Paul uses slavery imagery in a positive sense, so it is unlikely that he intended here to depict marriage negatively as a form of enslavement from which the divorced spouse has been set free. We cannot assume, however, that those to whom he wrote did not view marriage as a form of slavery. His choice of *dedoulōtai* here, therefore, may have served a double purpose. To those who saw marriage as enslavement, Paul asserted that the brother or sister is "not enslaved." To those whose spouses insisted on divorce, Paul gave assurance that they had been "released" from their marital obligations to their former spouse.

The final part of v. 15 gives rise to several questions. First of all, what does the sentence actually say? It reads, "But (*de*) in (*en*) peace God has called you." [The Text of 1 Corinthians 7:15c] Many translators and commentators take the conjunction *de* in a causal sense and render it "for." They also treat the proposition *en* as if it were *eis* ("unto" or "for") and make the sentence function as a justification for Paul's contention that the believing spouse should not resist the unbeliever's movement toward divorce since that would lead to conflict and a disruption of the peace to which God has called believers. The view assumes that the believer actually could resist the divorce, which was not the case. The preposition *en* should also be given its normal sense of "in" here. God has called the believer *in* a state of peace, not *for* peace.

The Text of 1 Corinthians 7:15c

The textual evidence slightly favors the reading *hēmas* ("us") rather than hymas ("you"), but the committee for the third edition of the United Bible Societies' Greek New Testament decided in favor of hymas on the basis of scribal tendency to generalize aphorisms. The committee for the fourth edition upgraded the probability of hymas as the original reading from {C} to {B} ("almost certain").

Bruce M. Metzger, *A Textual Commentary on the Greek New Testament* (3rd ed.; Stuttgart: United Bible Societies, 1971) 555.

This leads to a second question: Does v. 15c follow the thought of the rest of v. 15, or does it belong with the following verse? Those who take it with the preceding sentence typically understand that it refers to maintaining peaceful relations in a marital breakup. The divorced spouse should let go of the relationship and not engage in hostile and stressful attempts to hold on to the other person. But again, this wrongly presupposes that one spouse could actually keep the divorce from occurring. The sentence makes better sense if it is viewed in the context of the larger argument in vv. 12-16 in which Paul argues against a believer's divorcing an unbelieving spouse. The lack of peace that may occur comes not from vain attempts to hold a marriage together but from believers' creating turmoil in otherwise healthy marriages by deciding that the unbelieving partner's lack of belief constitutes a grounds for divorce. "You were *in* peace when you were called," Paul states. His concern is that this peace be maintained by maintaining the marriages. The underlying principle that guides much of his argument in this chapter lurks beneath the surface here: "Remain as you are."[33] They were presumably in a harmonious relationship when they became a believer; their new status as a believer should not lead to the turmoil of a marriage broken on their initiative.

If, as suggested here, v. 15c should be seen in the larger context of Paul's argument to preserve marriages between believers and nonbelievers, then it promotes an optimistic reading of v. 16.[34] Often v. 16 is taken pessimistically. That is, Paul allows for divorce with an unbeliever because one has no assurance that he or she could convert his or her spouse anyway. In fact, according to this view, Paul seems rather doubtful that conversion will occur. Such a reading leaves Paul with a less-than-hopeful attitude toward the possibility of converting nonbelievers, which is difficult to correlate with his usual missionary thrust. The question he poses directly to the husband and wife married to unbelieving spouses could be rendered, "For what do you know [but that] you will save the spouse?" Of course, the believer is unlikely to have a positive, transformative impact on the unbeliever if the relationship is disrupted by divorce. If the believer holds on to the marriage with a nonbeliever, however, then the conversion of the spouse remains a real possibility. For Paul, that possibility is sufficient grounds to maintain the marriage, provided the unbelieving spouse will let it continue.

7:17-24. The section that begins in v. 17 forms a continuation of the preceding argument, not a transition to different topics. Rhetorically, vv. 17-24 are a *digressio*, but not a departure from the main topic at hand. In these verses Paul elucidates the basic principle that undergirds his argument throughout chapter 7, namely, that one should remain in the state in which one was called. He has urged married couples to maintain sexual relations with their spouses, not to engage in some ill-advised pursuit of celibacy. He has advised widowed persons to remain single, provided they can practice self-control. He has commanded married couples to stay married. He has told those married to unbelievers to stay in their marriages, if at all possible. In this *digressio*, he finally brings to the forefront for explicit discussion the premise implicit in his other instructions. It functions as a *propositio* within the subsection. As a crucial piece of his total argument, this unit has its own structure. It begins with a statement of his principle in v. 17a. In v. 17b, as a proof to support the *propositio*, he identifies the principle as one having universal application in all the churches. Then, he employs two examples to illustrate both the force and the intention of the principle. The first example (vv. 18-19) is circumcision versus uncircumcision. The second (vv. 21-23) is slavery versus freedom. In between each example (v. 20), he restates his principle (*peroratio*), and at the end (v. 24), he restates it again. [The Structure of 1 Corinthians 7:17-24]

The Structure of 1 Corinthians 7:17-24

Propositio—"Let everyone lead the life the Lord has assigned and in which God has called him/her." v. 17a

Confirmatio—

- 1st Proof—"This is my rule in all the churches." v. 17b
- 2d Proof—The Example of Circumcision/Uncircumcision. vv. 18-19
  - Question—"Were you circumcised/uncircumcised when called?"
  - Answer—"Do not change!"
  - Reason—"Neither circumcision nor uncircumcision matters."

Peroratio—"Everyone should remain in the state in which he/she was called." v. 20

- 3rd Proof—The Example of Slavery/Freedom. vv. 21-23
  - Question—"Were you a slave when called?"
  - Answer—"Do not worry!"
  - Exception—"But if you can gain your freedom, . . ."
  - Reason—"A slave is a freed person/a free person is a slave (in the Lord)."
  - Answer—"Do not become slaves of people!"

Peroratio—"Let each one remain in the state in which he/she was called." v. 24

Two matters must be addressed before examining Paul's argument. First of all, we have no indication that Paul has deviated from the general focus of the rest of chapter 7 in order to speak to problems the church was facing in regard to circumcision and slavery. First Corinthians and 2 Corinthians do not suggest in any way that the church in Corinth was troubled by the issue of circumcision that created such havoc in the Galatian churches. Evidence exists that both Jews and Gentiles were in the Corinthian church, but none of the problems the church faced seem to have rooted in Jew-Gentile relations. Slaves and freedpersons (former slaves) made up a majority of the residents of Corinth, and most likely of the church too, but we have no evidence that the behavior of slaves or the question of their emancipation created problems for the city or the church. Paul introduces the subjects of circumcision and slavery here as examples in an argument directed toward problems associated with marriage. He may have been drawn to these two examples in particular because they were already tied in his traditional teaching to the issue of male and female relations. Some have suggested that the formula found in Galatians 3:28 may lie behind the introduction of circumcision and slavery here.[35] [Galatians 3:28] Hays has even described 1 Corinthians 7 as "Paul's own explication of Galatians 3:28."[36] Whether that is the case or not, we should recognize that circumcision and slavery function here only to help Paul deal with problems associated with marriage.

Secondly, it would be a mistake to read Paul's principle of "remaining as you are" simply as his endorsement of the status quo. Paul's concern was not to stabilize an established social structure by putting a lid on those who threatened it. He was not simply trying to keep people in their places. Much of his counsel in this chapter actually went against the grain of accepted social practices. His call for mutuality and consensus between married partners in regard to sex may resemble the views of some philosophers, but it hardly fits the pattern of actual practice. His strong prohibition against divorce could not have been more drastically different from the social norm for a Roman city. Even his argument in this section regarding circumcision and slavery would have appeared odd in his social context. People had themselves circumcised or uncircumcised to improve their social standing within their primary social group. People gained their freedom or became enslaved voluntarily as a way to improve their social or economic standing. For Paul to urge people to remain as they were was out of synch with the kind of jockeying for status and upward mobility that characterized a place such as Corinth. Rather than reinforce the status quo, Paul was challenging the importance of the accepted social markers. Whether one was circumcised or not, enslaved or not did not determine one's status or standing before God, Paul argued. Such social markers, which were all-important in Roman society, were not, for Paul, of primary significance. Changing one's social marker has no bearing on one's relationship with God. That does not

Galatians 3:28

Richard Hays makes the following correlations between 1 Cor 7 and Gal 3:27-28.

As many of you were baptized into Christ have clothed yourselves with Christ.
There is no longer Jew or Greek
[cf. 1 Cor 7:18-19]
there is no longer slave or free,
[cf. 1 Cor 7:21-23]
there is no longer male and female;
[cf. The rest of 1 Cor]
for all of you are one in Christ Jesus.
(Gal 3:27-28)

Richard B. Hays, *First Corinthians* (IBC; Louisville: John Knox Press, 1997) 123.

The Circumcision

Luca Signorelli (1441–1523). *The Circumcision*. (c.1490–1501) Oil on canvas, mounted on board, transferred from wood. National Gallery, London, Great Britain. (Credit: © National Gallery, London/Art Resource, NY)

render such markers meaningless, but it does reduce them to a place of secondary importance.

Paul states his overarching principle in the form of two "as" (*hōs*) clauses, followed by a "likewise" (*houtōs*) clause with an imperative. "As the Lord has apportioned to each one" and "as God has called each one" form the basis for the command, "likewise live." In 1 Corinthians 1:13, Paul asked the question, "Has Christ been divided (or "apportioned")?" The assumed answer there was, "No!" Christ has not been divided or apportioned out to competing groups, but each person has been apportioned or "sorted out" to a particular place in life. Where one has been assigned is not insignificant. One's place in life is not insignificant. Indeed, it was "*in* the assigned place" that God called each one. Note that Paul does not say that God called the individual *to* the assigned place. The person had an assigned place when God's call came. God's calling was not to an assigned place, as if God called a slave to be and remain a slave. God called the slave *as* a slave. The calling of God is not the same as the person's place in life, but it does come within that place. Certain places do not put one in a preferred position to receive God's calling. Therefore, Paul's principle is that one should remain and live out God's call within the place one already has. His point is not to discourage one from exercising any particular gifts for ministry that God may have bestowed but rather to encourage persons to see their present position in life as a proper place for exercising those gifts. One does not have to change places to serve God.

In support of the principle espoused, Paul adds that he has "ordered" (*diatassomai*) "likewise" (*houtōs*) in all the churches. His principle, then, has universal applicability. His ruling to the Corinthians is the same as that to churches elsewhere. This identifies the principle as more than an instruction tailored to the specific situation in Corinth. Other churches follow the principle. It would be "disorderly" for the Corinthians to see themselves as exceptions and follow a different route. The statement also subtly suggests to the Corinthians that Paul's principle has been recognized as authoritative in other churches, with the implication that they should abide by it, too. Finally, the statement ties the principle to that body of teaching that Paul referred to as "my ways in Christ" in 4:17.

Paul then states his example in a diatribal form. (See [Diatribe] in ch. 10 [1 Cor 15].) He identifies a condition in which one was called (circumcision/uncircumcision) and then gives an imperative negating the importance of the condition.[37] If one [while] circumcised was called, he should not seek to have the marks of circumcision removed (v. 18a). Though the practice was not widespread, some Jews, usually for reasons of social acceptance and status enhancement, underwent a painful surgical procedure (*epispasm*) to reverse the marks of circumcision. [*Epispasm*] Likewise, one called [in a state of] uncircumcision should not undergo the procedure of circumcision (v. 18b). While some of Paul's contemporaries viewed circumcision as an essential element in becoming a part of the Jewish-based movement that recognized Messiah Jesus as Lord, Paul staunchly argued against the necessity of Gentiles' being circumcised. Here he relativizes both circumcision and uncircumcision as nonessentials in determining one's status before God. What counts, according to Paul, is "keeping the commandments of God." In light of Paul's arguments elsewhere (especially Galatians) against the need for Gentiles to become observers of Torah, his statement here appears a little odd. Since the Torah included the command to be circumcised, it is doubtful that Paul meant that the Corinthians, who were mostly Gentiles, should observe all of the Torah *except* circumcision. Also doubtful is the suggestion that he may have been referring to the so-called Noachian covenant that Jews understood God had made with all peoples.[38] Most likely, Paul simply means the requirements of God as presented in Paul's teachings, some of which were rooted in Torah. His point is basically that doing God's will takes priority even over that most fundamental of all religious status markers that distinguished the people of the covenant from those outside, circumcision. Changing one's status from "outsider" to "insider" in the traditional way does not really matter. What does matter is living as an insider, that is, being faithful to God's will.

Paul repeats his basic principle in v. 20 and then gives his second example in v. 21, again in the form of a diatribe. Whereas he addressed the matter of circumcision in v. 18 in the third person ("anyone called . . ."), here he uses the second person "you were called . . ."). The difference may indicate that the matter of slavery was more directly personal to his audience than was the issue of circumcision. Paul used both circumcision and slavery as examples to reinforce his argument about staying in the same marital state in which one was called. In using slavery as an example, however, he

Epispasm

A medical handbook written by Aulus Cornelius Celsus during the reign of Tiberius describes the surgical procedure known as *epispasm*.

> If the glans is bare and the man wishes for the look of the thing to have it covered, that can be done; but more easily in a boy than in a man; in one in whom the defect is natural, than in one who after the custom of certain races has been circumcised; and in one who has the glans small and the adjacent skin rather ample, while the penis itself is shorter, rather than in one in whom the conditions are contrary.

De Medicina 7.25 (trans. W. G. Spencer; Loeb Classical Library; Cambridge MA: Harvard University Press, 1938) 3:421.

could not ignore the fact that many of the persons in his target audience were or had been slaves. Estimates about the percentage of persons who were slaves in the Roman Empire, of course, cannot be confirmed, but one may confidently assume that the majority of persons in Corinth were either slaves or former slaves (freedpersons).[39] Much of the early population of the Roman colony of Corinth consisted of freedpersons who remained in a client-patron relationship with their former owners. Many of the former slaves of Corinth prospered because the new city offered greater opportunities for upward mobility than were present elsewhere. Persons might choose to become slaves temporarily as a means to improve their economic circumstances, and if they became slaves to the right persons, they could even enhance their social status. Still, slaves were denied most of the privileges held by citizens. Freedom was generally preferred to slavery. Paul had to be sensitive, therefore, to the hopes that the slaves in his audience might have about gaining their freedom.

The special circumstances regarding the slaves in the church accounts for Paul's wording here. He does not say, "If you were called as a slave, do not become free." Instead, he says, "Do not let it worry you!" The issue of social status (slave/free) is no more determinative than the issue of ethnic identity (circumcised/uncircumcised). In terms of one's relationship to God, there was no need to change from being a slave to being free, much as there was no need to change one's circumstances regarding circumcision. Freedom, however, held significant advantages both for persons' well-being (usually) and for their unrestricted attention to the "affairs of the Lord" (v. 34). Paul's recognition of that can be found in the notoriously problematic second part of v. 21: "But if ever you are able to become free, rather use ________!"[40] Paul does not name *what* should be used. If one assumes that "slavery" should be put in the blank, then Paul is understood to have told the slaves not to worry about gaining their freedom. Instead, they should use their slavery in the best ways possible as they live out their calling. This would fit with his basic principle of remaining as one is. If Paul intended to tell slaves not to become free, however, then he would have done so in the first part of v. 21 rather than tell them "not to worry." The fact that he did not follow the pattern of v. 18 in v. 21 strongly suggests that his instruction regarding slavery is somewhat different from his instructions about circumcision. The use of the strong adversative *alla* (hard "but") rather than *de* (soft "but") furthermore indicates that Paul is drawing a contrast to his instruction "not to worry." As he does numerous times elsewhere in

Freedman Inscription

Market near Corinth's forum. (Credit: Scott Nash)

The inscription below has been reconstructed from thirteen fragments found at the forum in Corinth. It has been dated to the late Augustan or Tiberian period. Originally affixed to a fish market lying to the north of the forum on the main road from Lechaion, the inscription identifies as one of the builders of the market a certain Maecius Cleogenes, freedman (L = *liberti*) of Quintus Maecius.

Q • CO[r]N[elius • [.] • f • a[EM • SECVNDVS • et
MAEC[ia • q]• F • VXOR • [eius • [.] • cornelius • secundus •
M[A]e[CIANVS •F • Q • CORN[elius
SECV[nd]VS • F • [co]RN[elia • secunda • f • eius • uxor • q •
m]A[e]CI • Q • L • **CLEOGEN[is**
MACELL

Quintus Cornelius, son of [——], of the tribe Aemilia, together
with his wife Maecia, daughter of [Quintus Maecius], his son
[Cornelius Secundus] Maecianus, his son Quintus Cornelius
Secundus, his [daughter] Cornelia [Secunda, the wife of Quintus]
Maecius Cleogenes, the freedman of Quintus [Maecius], [built?] the
meat-market [——] along with [——] and a fish-market [———].

John Harvey Kent, *The Inscriptions 1926–1950* (*Corinth* VIII.3; Princeton: American School of Classical Studies at Athens, 1966) 127–28, n321.

this chapter (7:5, 8-9, 10-11, 13-15, 27-28, 39), Paul allows for an exception to his stated principle. If one puts "freedom" in the blank, then, Paul would be understood not as discouraging slaves from gaining their freedom but rather encouraging them to use their freedom well, should it come.

With this exception allowed, Paul nevertheless is making the same point. One's status as a slave is not to be viewed as negatively affecting one's relationship to God. In fact, one who is a slave when called becomes a freedperson of the Lord (v. 22). Former slaves generally remained connected to their former owners in a patron-client relationship and continued to render certain services to that person. Manumission from slavery might (but not necessarily) result in improved financial circumstances, but it always signaled an improvement in status. The freedperson had rights withheld from the slave. The true status of the freedperson largely depended on the status of the patron to which they were joined, as was the case with clients who had never been slaves.[41] The pride with which certain freedpersons viewed their alliance to prestigious patrons is evident from many funeral and dedicatory inscriptions.

Paul's terminology here draws from the patron-client system when he identifies the slave as a freedperson "of the Lord." Within the household of God, the slave has a new status that transcends the slave's status in the world. In fact, the status of a slave "called in the Lord" ranks above that of the free person who is called, for that person is a "slave of Christ." [Martin on a Slave's Status] Paul's objective in stating this is not to devise a new ranking system within the church that simply reverses the one in play outside the church. His aim is to subvert social ranking entirely. The radical reversal of slaves "in Christ" to a position above free persons "in Christ" discredits the normal scheme that determined social intercourse. That scheme holds no authority within the household of Christ, though it may still shape the political, economic, and social lives of those who are in Christ.

Martin on a Slave's Status

[Paul] took the highest-status person, the free man, and placed him in the lowest-status position of the household. Then he took the lowest-status person, the slave, and gave him a status above his fellow Christian, though still without making him an *eleutheros*, a free man. Paul thereby keeps both persons within the household of Christ, yet within the hierarchy of that household, he reverses their normal status positions. Freedom is not the issue here; status is.

Dale B. Martin, *Slavery as Salvation* (New Haven: Yale University Press, 1990) 66.

The relevance of Paul's example of slavery to his larger discussion becomes especially apparent in v. 23. The statement, "You were bought with a price," recalls Paul's similar language in 6:19-20, where he stressed the importance of glorifying God in one's bodily existence. Both slaves and free persons have been brought into the household of Christ as the result of a tremendous payment. They now belong to a new master (*kyrios*), the Lord (*kyrios*). The new Lord now assumes responsibility for their well-being, and they now assume their roles as his servants. Doing his bidding ("keeping the commandments of God," v. 19) is their new calling. Whether they be free or slave, circumcised or uncircumcised, married or single, they are called to live their lives in their bodily existence, in the state in which they find themselves, for the Lord.

The second part of v. 23 carries a double meaning. Those who are free persons should not become slaves to other persons. This instruction applies first to people who are not presently enslaved. They should not become enslaved. They should remain as they are. While Paul allows for the exception of slaves' gaining their freedom, he does not want free persons to become enslaved, probably for the reasons he uses in arguing for staying single in vv. 28-35. Slavery entangles one in worldly affairs. One has to please a human master, and this can create hindrances to serving the Lord. The words also have applicability, however, to both slaves and free persons, that is, to all those who are in Christ. Slaves called by God are freedpersons of the Lord, and free persons called by God are slaves of Christ. Both groups are servants of the Lord. He is their master, and his will is their calling. Their calling is not to the slave-master system of their society, nor to the status-determining hierarchy that tried to define their identities. "Not becoming slaves to people" also means not being defined and shaped by the wisdom of this world that identifies worth, meaning, and purpose on the basis of social status.

Each one has been called *in* a place in life (v. 24). As a rule, Paul would have them remain in that place. Exceptions are permitted: temporary sexual abstinence between married couples for prayer, marriage for the formerly married who cannot practice self-control, divorce for the believer whose unbelieving spouse demands it, and freedom for the slave who happens to receive it. Ultimately, however, these changes are inconsequential. One does not have to change one's place to serve God. Being celibate, single, married, divorced, circumcised, uncircumcised, slave, or free does not ultimately define who one is. It is not the place that determines who one is; it is God's calling that determines who one is. The person who is called by God is a different person, whether their place changes or not. Each one is in his/her place *with* God (v. 24).

Counsel Regarding Marriage for Unmarried Persons, 7:25-40

The target audience changes somewhat in the next section, but Paul's basic principle does not. Because he is still espousing that principle, the continuation of his argument supporting it proceeds with one eye still on his first audience. Much of what he says to his second audience applies to the first. The preceding section was directed to the married or formerly married, while the rest of the chapter addresses those not yet married (including vv. 39-40). Paul's instructions to the two groups stem from the same principle of remaining as one is. This is his counterpoint to the statement he has quoted from the Corinthians' letter, that "it is good for a man not to touch a woman." Their position has some merit, as his argument acknowledges, but his counterpoint carries more weight. In certain circumstances, refraining from marriage that leads to sexual intimacy is to be preferred. Those already married, however, should not try to emulate the celibacy of the unmarried. They should remain as they are, fully married, and maintain sexual relations with their spouses. Those not yet married, however, represent that group for whom Paul's principle and the Corinthians' statement converge. For them, remaining as they are entails refraining from sexual relations. Paul expresses the same sensitivity to this group, though, that he expressed to the formerly married who could not control their sexual impulses. If the unmarried find themselves unable to control themselves, then they, too, should go ahead and marry their betrothed. Neither the formerly married nor the never married persons commit a sin in getting married. Yet, they do choose a route that is less than ideal.

The rhetorical structure for the rest of the chapter begins with Paul's restatement of his principle and an allusion back to the original *proposito* about what is "good" (vv. 25-26). Each of the proofs Paul employs in support of his principle begins with a verb of assertion expressing Paul's view: "I consider" (v. 26), "I declare" (v. 29), and "I wish" (v. 32). At the end of the first and third proofs, both of which focus on "worldly troubles," Paul concedes that marriage is permissible, if necessary (v. 28a, vv. 36-37). The middle proof is a *digressio* about the shortness of time (vv. 29-32). The *peroratio* (vv. 38-40) includes counsel about what is good and better for men and about what women who may become widowed may/should do. The statement of principle (*gnōmēn*) appears at the beginning (vv. 25-26) and ending (v. 40) of the section, each time accompanied by a christological attestation of the validity of Paul's view. [The Structure of 1 Corinthians 7:25-40]

The Structure of 1 Corinthians 7:25-40

Argumentatio II—about what is "good" regarding the unmarried
Restatement of *principle* and support—"It is good for a person to remain as he/she is." vv. 25-26
- *Confirmatio*—Affirmation of *principle* in view of this present distress, vv. 25-37
  - Application: Remain in one's present state, but marriage allowed. vv. 26-28a
  - Reason: Marriage brings anxieties, vv. 28b-35
- *Digressio*—The shortness of time, vv. 29-31
  - Application: Marriage is permissible, if necessary, vv. 36-37
- *Peroratio*—Affirmation of *principle;* allowance of exceptions, vv. 38-40
  - – A man who marries does well; one who does not does better. vv. 38
  - – A widow may marry in the Lord; one who does not is happier. vv. 39-40
  - – Restatement of *principle* and support. v. 40

7:25-40. As noted previously, the phrase *peri de*, with which this section opens, does not necessarily indicate that Paul is turning to another topic raised in the Corinthians' letter to him. Since Paul did indicate in 7:1, however, that he was going to address the *matters* (plural) about which they wrote, it is likely that what follows pertains to issues included in their letter. Thus, they had apparently asked him about the marriage of virgins. But exactly who were "the virgins" (*tōn parthenōn*) named in v. 25? [The Virgins] The major options suggested are (1) unmarried young women in general, (2) unmarried young men and women in general, (3)

The Virgins

AΩ In 1 Cor 7:25 Paul uses the genitive plural form of the word *parthenos*, which is usually translated as "virgin." The plural form of the word makes it impossible to know without question whether it refers to men and women or only to women. While the word typically refers to a young woman of marriageable age, the term could also be used of young, unmarried men. The usage of the word for these groups generally assumes that they have never had sexual intercourse. When Paul uses the singular form of this word in vv. 28, 34, 36, 37, and 38, the presence of the feminine definite article signifies that he means young, unmarried women. In v. 34 he refers to "the unmarried woman" (*hē agamos*) and "the virgin" (*hē parthenos*), indicating a distinction between the two. The *agamos* could be a woman formerly married or an older (?) woman never married, while the *parthenos* could simply mean a never-married woman or (more probably) an unmarried girl of young (?) age. The clear usage of the word *parthenos* in reference to women in the other verses, however, does not settle the question of the meaning of the plural term in v. 25. The fact that Paul addresses men directly in vv. 27-28 and only addresses the *parthenos* indirectly in v. 28 may suggest that the primary thrust of the section is to offer direct guidance to men about how to deal with the young women (*tōn parthenōn*) to whom they are engaged. Since the men addressed, however, have probably never been married, the section may legitimately be viewed as instructions for the "not yet married," both women and men.

young women who are engaged, (4) young women and men who are engaged, and (5) married persons who refrain from sexual relations (so-called "spiritual marriages").[42] Though not without some problems, the least difficult of these options in light of Paul's use of the term *parthenos* elsewhere in the chapter is option (3). His instructions here focus primarily on directing the young men about what to do in regard to the young women to whom they are engaged.

In giving his instruction, Paul acknowledges once again that he has no command (*epitagēn*; cf. v. 6) from Jesus that directly addresses the situation (cf. v. 12). Nonetheless, as one who has been "mercied" (*ēleēmenos*) by the Lord to be trustworthy (*pistos*), he offers his "principle" (*gnōmēn*). In 2 Corinthians 4:1, Paul uses a similar passive form of the verb *eleeō* ("show mercy") in reference to God's entrustment of ministry to himself and others. Paul's "trustworthiness," then, is not rooted in his own character or achievement but in his calling to be an apostle. Having been called as such, his *gnōmēn* is more than an "opinion," as the term is usually translated.[43] Paul identified his principle in v. 17 as what he had "ordered" (*diatassomai*) in all the churches. The noun "command" (*epitagēn*) and the verb *diatassomai* are based on the same root verb (*tassō*). In effect, then, Paul considers his *principle* to be nearly as authoritative as a command of the Lord.

Paul's principle carries the weight of his apostolic authority; it also presents a reasonable approach "because of the present distress"). The Corinthians argued, "It is good for a man (*kalon anthrōpō*) not to touch a woman" (v. 1). With their slogan still in mind, Paul states what he considers (*nomizō*) "good." "Because of the present distress," he reasons, "it is good for a person (*kalon anthrōpō*) to remain as he/she is." A point of contention between scholars is the referent for the phrase "the present distress" (*tēn enestōsan anankēn*). Many see here an allusion to Paul's eschatological perspective in which increasingly difficult conditions should be expected before the coming of the end. They sometimes argue that *enestōsan* should be translated "impending," thus signifying imminent apocalyptic woes.[44] They connect "the impending distress" to Paul's assertion that the "time has grown short" in v. 29. Paul typically uses *enestōsan*, however, to refer to present circumstances (cf. 1 Cor 3:22; Rom 8:38; Gal 1:4). Therefore, others think that Paul has in mind here something more immediate, that is, certain distressful circumstances faced by the church in Corinth. Bruce Winter has pointed to the significant evidence in Roman writings that the Roman Empire experienced severe grain shortages and resultant famines several times in the middle of the first century, especially in the years around the time that Paul founded the church in Corinth.[45] The famine was severely felt throughout Greece. The archaeological evidence from Corinth indicates that during the Claudian period, extensive, government-sponsored construction of warehouses within the city and major improvements in Corinth's harbor at Lechaion were undertaken to improve the transit and storage of grain and other foodstuffs roughly during the same time that Paul wrote 1 Corinthians.[46] Winter thinks that those harsh conditions were partly behind the Corinthians' inclination toward celibacy in that

Construction in Corinth

Lechaion's Inner Harbor (Credit: Scott Nash)

Horrea in Corinth (Credit: Scott Nash)

During the reign of Claudius (AD 41–54), significant building projects were undertaken in Corinth related to the problems of grain shortages and famine. The shipping facilities at Lechaion, Corinth's port to the west, were improved by dredging out the inner harbor. Large warehouses (*horrea*) were constructed in the western part of the city. Claudius experienced pressure during his early years from riots caused by grain shortages in Rome. Maintaining food supplies throughout the empire became a priority of his administration.

Charles K. Williams II, "Roman Corinth as a Commercial Center," in *The Corinthia in the Roman Period* (ed. Timothy E. Gregory; JRASup 8: Ann Arbor MI: Journal of Roman Archaeology, 1993) 24–25.

they were trying to avoid conceiving children in such hard times.[47] Paul agrees that it is good for the unmarried to stay single, but he does not hint at birth control as a reason. He does, however, indicate that the avoidance of additional troubles (v. 28b) influences his preference for the single life in "this present distress." Most likely, Paul viewed the present hardships as evidence that the current world order had already entered into its demise (cf. v. 31b). So, even though he may have had present difficulties in mind, those circumstances signaled the unraveling of the power structures that held sway.

After stating his principle, Paul applies it to the matter at hand by posing two questions and answering them on the basis of his principle. The questions are addressed directly to the men: "Have you been bound (*dedesai*) to a woman?" "Have you been released (*lelysai*) from a woman?" The word for woman in each question (*gynē*) is typically used to refer to a wife, whereas we might expect Paul to have used *parthenos* to refer to a fiancée. Still, the verbs used suggest an engagement rather than a marriage. Both verbs are perfect passives, indicating in each case that the man's present condition is a result of past action. The first question addresses the man who has become engaged; the second addresses a man who has been released from an engagement, not one who has never been engaged. Paul has already addressed the issue of remaining married. Here he speaks to persons who are betrothed but not yet married. If one has been bound (i.e., made a commitment to marry), one should not seek to dissolve the arrangement. If, however, one has already been released from an engagement, one should not seek another commitment. "And" (not "But"), Paul adds, "if you do go ahead and marry your fiancée, you have not sinned, and the fiancée (*parthenos*) has not sinned if she marries" (v. 28a). The fact that Paul's principle is not an iron-clad rule gives the couple permission to consummate their engagement if they choose to do so. Paul's preference that they simply remained engaged is evident, however, later in vv. 37-38. His preference stems from practical reasons, not moral ones, so he assures them that they have not sinned if their own preference is to marry.

Verse 28b begins Paul's explanation of his preference to remain single in the present distress. The explanation continues to v. 35, with a *digressio* (vv. 29-31) about the "shortness of time" sandwiched within the larger argument. (We will look at the larger argument and then return to the *digressio*.) Those who do marry can expect hardships "in the flesh." By "flesh" here, Paul does not mean life inflicted with temptation or the onslaught of evil but

Anxiety

AΩ In 1 Cor 7:32 Paul expresses his wish that the Corinthians be free from anxiety (*amerimnous*). The adjective amerimnous is derived from the verb *merimnaō*, which can mean "to be excessively concerned" (i.e., "anxious") or "to be properly concerned" about something. Paul plays on the nuanced difference between these two meanings. The unmarried man or woman may be "properly concerned" (*merimna*) about the affairs of the Lord, specifically how to please the Lord, but the married man or woman will be "excessively concerned" (*merimna*) about worldly matters, specifically how to please their spouse. What makes the concern for the spouse excessive is that it is added to the person's concern for the Lord. The husbands and wives in question are believers. They are devoted to the Lord. As married persons, however, they are also devoted to one another. Thus, they have excessive concerns, that is, concerns in addition to their *proper* concern for the Lord. That is why Paul describes the married man as "divided" (v. 34). Their concern for one distracts from their concern for the other. Paul's wish is that they have "undistracted devotion" to the Lord (v. 35).

Anthony C. Thiselton, *The First Epistle to the Corinthians: A Commentary on the Greek Text* (NIGTC; Grand Rapids: Eerdmans, 2000) 586–93.

rather, more neutrally, life as it is experienced in everyday human existence. Marriage always brings increased responsibilities, but marriage *in the present distress* brings intensified hardships. If Paul has in mind specific economic and social pressures affecting the Corinthians at the time, then his counsel presents a realistic appraisal of the strains married couples would face in those conditions. His aim is to lessen the hardships, not increase them. Part of the hardship comes from external pressures, but much of the strain comes from internal anxiety. Thus, in v. 32 Paul adds to his desire that they be "spared" hardships (v. 28b) his wish that they be free from anxiety (*amerimnous*). [Anxiety] The anxiety stems from being pulled in two directions. Married persons seek to please their spouses and, thus, are necessarily concerned about the things of the world. Paul does not condemn the concern to please one's spouse, nor does he characterize a concern for the things of the world as evil. He does, however, depict them as problematic. They necessarily interfere with being concerned about the things of the Lord. They result in a person's being "divided" (v. 34). [The Text of 1 Corinthians 7:34]

Paul's characterization of the different concerns of the married and the unmarried follows a consistent pattern, except for two places (as the accompanying sidebar shows). [The Pattern of 1 Corinthians 7:32b-34] The portrayal of married men versus unmarried men juxtaposes a concern for the affairs of the Lord (A1) and pleasing the

The Text of 1 Corinthians 7:34

The ancient texts have numerous differences in the reading of v. 34. Many of them are minor and simply involve the movement, repetition, or omission of the feminine article he and the adjective *agamos* ("unmarried"). The major difference involves the conjunction *kai* ("and") before the verb *memeristai* ("is divided"). The verse-numbering system used for most versions reflects the omission of *kai* in many ancient texts, with the result that memeristai is understood to begin a new sentence in v. 34 rather than conclude the sentence that is found in v. 33. The KJV, thus, renders it "There is difference also between a wife and a virgin. The unmarried woman careth for the things of the Lord. . . ." This reading strains the meaning of *memeristai* and misses the parallel structure of the previous verses. The multiplicity of variants may have stemmed from the difficulty of the compound subject *hē gynē hē agamos kai hē parthenos* ("the unmarried woman and the virgin") used with a single person verb *merimna* ("is anxious"). Such a construction, however, is not uncommon. Since *memeristai* also has a singular personal ending, the problem of the compound subject is not resolved by placing it with *hē gynē and hē parthenos*.

Bruce M. Metzger, *A Textual Commentary on the Greek New Testament* (3rd ed.; Stuttgart: United Bible Societies, 1971) 555.

Anthony C. Thiselton, *The First Epistle to the Corinthians: A Commentary on the Greek Text* (NIGTC; Grand Rapids: Eerdmans, 2000) 588–89.

Lord (B1) with a concern for the affairs of the world (A2) and pleasing the wife (B2). Likewise, the portrayal of unmarried women versus married women juxtaposes a concern for the affairs of the Lord (A3) with a concern for the affairs of the world (A4) and pleasing the husband (B4). The pattern is broken in the portrayal of the men with the additional statement that the married man is divided (C2). In the portrayal of the unmarried women, Paul does not repeat his statement about pleasing the Lord (B1) but, instead, says that her concern for the Lord's affairs is so that she may be holy in body and in spirit (B3). The additional statement regarding the "division" of the married man (C2) probably reflects the fact that Paul is directing his words primarily to men in this section since men were the ones who generally initiated marriages. Married women would be equally "divided" in their concerns. The difference between B1 and B3 has led interpreters to offer various explanations. Some see here a subtle defense on Paul's part of the sanctity of the single state for those women who choose it in a culture where marriage was generally thrust upon a woman.[48] Others see an allusion to a part of the argument the Corinthians were making for celibacy.[49] Celibate women could devote both body and spirit to the Lord. If the Corinthians were making such an argument and if Paul intended an allusion to it, then he could hardly be charged with trying to impose marriage on the unmarried women, as he has sometimes been accused.[50] Probably, though, no such allusion is intended, and B3 should be viewed as a fuller explication of B1. Paul would have argued that men, too, can devote themselves fully (which is what "body and spirit" means) to the Lord. That is, unmarried men, as well as unmarried women, may do so; the married find it more difficult because of their divided concerns.

The Pattern of 1 Corinthians 7:32b-34

A1—The unmarried man is concerned about the affairs of the Lord
B1—how to please the Lord, v. 32
A2—The unmarried man is concerned about the things of the world
B2—how to please his wife, v. 33
C—and he is divided, v. 34a
A3—The unmarried woman or virgin is concerned about the affairs of the Lord
B3—so that she may be holy in body and spirit, v. 34b
A4—The married woman is concerned about the things of the world
B4—how to please her husband, v. 34c

In several places in 1 Corinthians, Paul distinguishes between what one is free to do and what is to one's or another's *advantage* (*symporon*) to do. [Advantage] In 6:12, where Paul argued for taking the actions of

Advantage

Arguing on the basis of what was to the advantage (*to symphoron*) of the audience was a standard feature of deliberative rhetoric. In such rhetoric, the speaker tried to convince the audience that engaging in a certain course of action would serve their self-interest. Paul does appeal to self-interest, but he also often redirects the church from individual self-interest to what is to the community's advantage. In 1 Cor 7:35, by pointing out that his instructions regarding marriage are not intended to restrict his readers, but rather to promote what is proper and conducive to their devotion to the Lord, he is subtly redirecting their attention from private self-interest to a concern for God. Once again, then, he tries to move them from an anthropocentric perspective to a theocentric one.

Margaret M. Mitchell, *Paul and the Rhetoric of Reconciliation: An Exegetical Investigation of the Language and Composition of 1 Corinthians* (Louisville: Westminster John Knox, 1991) 33–39.

the body seriously, he countered the Corinthian slogan "All things are permitted for me" with his own contention that not all things are *advantageous.* In 10:23f, he again refutes the argument that all things are permitted in regard to eating meat by arguing that one should seek to do what is *advantageous* to others, pointing out at the end of his argument (10:33) that his own policy is to seek the *advantage* of others rather than his own. In 12:7 he argues that spiritual gifts are imparted to the church for the *advantage* of all. Here in v. 35, Paul insists that what he says is intended for their own *advantage* (*symporon*), not his. He has no intention of "throwing a rope around their necks," which is what the Greek *brochon hymin epibalō* visually suggests. He is not trying to enslave them; rather, he is trying to free them for unfettered service to the Lord. His goal is to enable them to exercise appropriate conduct (*euschēmon*) and devotion (*euparedron*) to the Lord without distraction (*aperispastōs*). (See [Epictetus on Marriage and the Philosopher] above.)

Nestled into his explanation of why he thinks marriage brings worldly troubles and anxiety is a *digressio* (vv. 29-31) that on the surface might be seen as contradictory to much that Paul has argued for in this chapter. It begins with the second of Paul's three assertions in this section: "This I thus declare" (*touto de phēmi*). What he declares emphatically is that the "appointed time (*kairos*) has been shortened (*synstalmenos estin*)." The use of *kairos* here, which typically conveys a season of opportunity, rather than the normal word for chronological time (*chronos*), indicates that Paul is referring to a special period of time and not merely to the length of time. The *kairos*, the season between the resurrection of Christ and his return, the season of opportunity for responding to the gospel and for doing the Lord's work, has been "shortened" or "constricted" or "limited." His basic point is not so much that the Lord's return is imminent in that it could happen "any time now" but that the final clock has, in a sense, started ticking. For the rest of this critical season that remains, believers should have a radically different perspective about those features of everyday life that typically occupy their thoughts and energies.

He names five features of normal life that call for reorientation: marriage, weeping, rejoicing, consumption, and entanglement. Taken literally, without regard for the rest of his argument in the chapter and without due regard for the nuances of his eschatology, Paul's instructions read as if he is calling for complete withdrawal from involvement in the normal elements of everyday life. If in regard to marriage, for example, he actually means that those who have wives should

Romans 12:15

Rejoice with those who rejoice; weep with those who weep.
(Romans 12:15, NRSV)

live as if they do not, then the rest of his argument in this chapter about couples staying married and engaging in full sexual intimacy would be completely undermined. If he means that no one should rejoice or weep, then his instructions written from Corinth to Rome about weeping and rejoicing would be a classic case of opportunistic doublespeak. [Romans 12:15] His polarities are designed to depict the paradoxical nature of the church as an eschatological community. Later, in 2 Corinthians 6:10, Paul describes himself and his coworkers as those who "are sorrowful, yet always rejoicing; as poor, yet making many rich; as having nothing, yet possessing everything." The same paradoxical perspective should guide the church in this "shortened time." Marriage and the other aspects of normal life (weeping, rejoicing, buying, consuming) must be viewed from the vantage point of the kingdom of God, the importance of which transcends all other commitments and ties. The last two items Paul names typify the contrast between the eschatological vision under which the church should live and the myopic vision that occupies the earth-bound. Those who buy should be as those who do not possess, for the greater one's possessions are, the more one is possessed by what he/she has bought. Those who engage the world (and Paul assumes that they will continue to engage the world; cf. 5:10) should not become entangled in the world. That is, they must use (*chrōmenoi*) the world without making such full use (*katachrōmenoi*) of it that they are too entangled in it to be free of dependence on it.

The shortness of the time signals that the outward structure (*shēma*) of this world is passing away (*paragei*). The word *shēma*, in Greek literature, always denotes the outward form or appearance of something. It could be used of the "role" that one plays in a drama, as indicated by the costume one wears. It could also be used of the "constitution" of a city-state, that is, the "form" of its government.[51] Paul's stress here is on the outward form by which the world is currently known and under which guise it operates. The structures of power, which at his time were predominately those designed and dictated by Rome, and those systems of social arrangement, which determined one's place in the world, are already diminishing (as the present tense of *paragei* indicates).

The image of the world's structures' passing away has an eschatological cast to it and ties together Paul's principle for living in the "present distress" (v. 26) with his *digressio* (vv. 29-31) about the perspective one should have in the "shortened time" (v. 29). As noted above, Paul may well have had certain pressures faced by the Corinthian community in mind when he referred to the "present

An Ominous Year

Regarding the year AD 51, the Roman historian Tacitus wrote, "Many prodigies occurred during the year. Ominous birds took their seat on the Capitol; houses were overturned by repeated shocks of earthquake, and, as the panic spread, the weak were trampled underfoot in the trepidation of the crowd. A shortage of grain, again, and the famine which resulted, were construed as a supernatural warning."

Tacitus, *Annals* 12.43.

distress." Paul and his readers may also have seen those pressures as signs of eschatological "shortness of time." If so, they were not the only ones to interpret the signs of the time as "ominous." The year AD 51 saw numerous natural disasters, famine, social unrest, and disruptions in international relations, including threats to Rome's tenuous relationship with its most feared enemy, the Parthians. Tacitus reported that some Romans saw these crises as supernatural signs.[52] [An Ominous Year] Paul's insertion of his eschatological *digressio* into his argument about the practicality of the single life in stressful times reframes their present distress in light of his apocalyptic vision of the transformation of the world's structures at the coming of Christ. The apparent "unraveling" of the empire's proud promise to provide eternal peace and prosperity signaled, for Paul, the empire's inevitable passing away. Hence, life for the believer should be rooted in an orientation toward the coming kingdom, living as if it were already present, for to a certain degree, it was (is) already present.

Verses 36-37 constitute an application of Paul's principle with an allowance for the same kind of exception provided for in vv. 5, 9, 15, 21, and 28. The allowance here most closely resembles the one in v. 9. If one cannot exercise self-control, then marriage is an acceptable alternative to the principle of staying as you are. If the young man, in this case, cannot control his sexual urges toward his fiancée, then he should go ahead and marry her. At least this is the most likely understanding of the matter in these verses. Numerous ancient interpreters read the passage quite differently, taking the subject of the action in vv. 36-37 to be the father of an unmarried daughter (*parthenēn autou*) rapidly approaching her prime marrying age (*hyperakmos*).[53] The main support for this ancient interpretation in the text itself is Paul's use of the verb *gamizō* at the end of v. 36, whereas he typically uses *gameō* throughout the chapter. Verbs ending in *-izō* often had a causative effect, at least in Classical Greek, so *gamizō* could mean "I give in marriage." In the Koine period, however, many *-izō* verbs no longer carried a causative force, and Paul may have switched to it here because, unlike in the instances where he uses *gameō*, the verb has a direct object (*parthenēn*).[54] Taking Paul's instructions here to be given to fathers of marriageable daughters interjects a completely different topic into the discussion, as well as a host of interpretive problems. Likewise, understanding the passage to refer to persons who are

Hyperakmos

AΩ The term *hyperakmos* in 1 Cor 7:36 has occasioned much debate among commentators. Many analyze it according to its parts, the preposition *hyper* ("above" or "beyond") and the noun *akmē* (lit., "point" or "edge"). Since *akmē* is often used in reference to the "prime" or "climax" of something, they take the combined form *hyperakmos* to mean "past one's prime." Thus, they see the problem addressed in vv. 36-37 as one faced by fathers whose daughters are approaching the end of the ideal time for marriage. Should the fathers "marry them off," or should they resign themselves to maintaining their single daughters for life, which could be an economic strain if the Lord's return should be long delayed? Analyzing words by their etymology, or by the meaning of their parts, is always suspect, however. Combined forms take on meanings beyond those of their parts. The term *hyperakmos* was sometimes used to signify the onslaught of puberty in young women or to refer to the strong sexual passion of young men. Sometimes the word was used in a context indicating sexual promiscuity. Paul's use in 1 Cor 7:36 seems most likely to indicate that the young men in question may be experiencing intense sexual passion toward their fiancées.

Bruce W. Winter, *After Paul Left Corinth: The Influence of Secular Ethics and Social Change* (Grand Rapids MI: Eerdmans, 2001) 246–49.

living in some kind of celibate "marriage-like" relationship strains the text. Paul has already argued against celibate marriages in vv. 1-5; to sanction such a relationship at this point, as this view holds he does in v. 37, would be to contradict his earlier stance completely.

The simplest and most satisfactory reading of the passage is to understand Paul as advising young couples to marry if they feel strong urges to do so, even though his preference is that they simply remain engaged. This reading takes *aschēmonein* ("to act improperly"), *hyperakmos* ("heightened passions"), and *houtōs opheilei ginesthai* ("thus it is bound to happen") in v. 36 all to refer to sexual feelings or behavior.[55] [Hyperakmos] Also, in v. 37, the terms *anankē* ("necessity") and *thelēma* ("wish" or "desire") can denote sexual feelings. Paul recognizes the reality of such urges and does not try to force young persons into a life of

Marriage Contract

Jan Steen. *Marriage Contract*. c. 1650s. Oil on canvas. The State Hermitage Museum, St. Petersburg, Russia. Photograph © The State Hermitage Museum.

Steen's painting captures the different reactions of men and women to the sealing of a marriage agreement. The men in the painting, with the noticeable exception of the groom, appear joyous, while the women seem somber or even worried. The bride, in particular, appears saddened by the prospect of the marriage.

celibacy when they have not been "gifted" for it (cf. v. 7). He stresses that those who do marry under such circumstances do not sin. Those who feel no urgent pressure and have control of their desire, however, do *well* if they refrain from marriage.

The summation (*peroratio*) of Paul's argument that began in v. 25 comes in vv. 38-40. It includes a rehearsal of his guiding principle in reference to the question of whether young men should marry their fiancées and in reference to what women should do if they lose their husbands. Paul's over-arching perspective is clear. If a man decides to marry his fiancée, in this present distress, that is well (*kalōs*). If one decides not to marry her, that is better (*kreisson*). Marriage in such circumstances is no sin; one can do it with a clear conscience. For practical reasons (not moral), however, not marrying is a better choice for men to make. Paul's instructions have been directed primarily to men throughout this section because men were typically responsible for making decisions regarding marriage. Fathers negotiated marriages with the husband-to-be, or with his father. Women typically exercised more responsibility when and if their husbands died. Then, as widows, they could decide whether or not to enter into another marriage. Thus, Paul here addresses women who might face that choice in the future. He addressed women who were already widows previously in vv. 8-9; he is not repeating that instruction here, though most commentators assume he is. The man may decide to marry now, if he chooses, and it is well. The woman whom he marries is bound to him as long as he lives. If he dies, the woman may marry again, if she chooses, but "only in the Lord." The phrase "only in the Lord" may mean simply that the woman should remember that she is a believer and should enter into any future marriage mindful of her obligations to the Lord. More likely, though, it means that she should only marry another believer. Paul did not call for believers to break their marriages to nonbelievers, but he did allow for the break-up of those marriages if the unbelieving partner insisted (v. 15). Since the husband's own religious identity would create pressures on the wife to conform, entering into such a mixed marriage would have been inadvisable for a widow. Paul's view is that the woman will do better not to remarry, in the same way that the man will do better not to marry. He expresses this, though, not in terms of what is good or better but in terms of what will make her "happier." The word *makariōtera* is the comparative form of the term found in beatitudes of the Sermon on the Mount (Matt 5:3ff.). It can simply mean "happier," or it may carry the connotation of "more blessed." She would be happier in the same way that the single person would experience fewer of the worldly troubles caused by married life (v. 28). She would also be more blessed by having fewer anxieties to distract her from the Lord's work (v. 34).

The section began with Paul stating his principle (*gnōmēn*) about remaining as one is and affirming his identity as one "mercied" by the Lord (v. 25). He ends in v. 40 by repeating his principle (*gnōmēn*) and asserting his possession of the Spirit of God. The two verses form an *inclusio* around the whole section that reinforces the weight of Paul's principle. He offers not simply his opinion about the question of getting married. He offers a guiding principle for living in the present distress. That it is a principle and not a law is evident in the several exceptions he recognizes as legitimate. Paul has stated his principle and supported it with reasoned arguments and practical applications. He has also sensitively respected the needs of his audience that would lead them to deviate from his principle. Such a manner of addressing what were very urgent and personal matters for the Corinthians reflects a leader guided more by the Spirit of God than by the letter of the law.

CONNECTIONS

Human Sexuality and Marriage

Commentators have often pointed out that Paul's instructions regarding sex and marriage in 1 Corinthians 7:1-9 do not constitute a Pauline theology of marriage.[56] That is certainly true. Paul's teaching here reflects his focused response to a particular problem that arose among a particular group of people in a specific time and place. The same can be said, of course, in regard to much of his teaching in this letter. Nonetheless, interpreters are charged with discovering that part of the apostle's response to a particular situation that might still speak across the centuries and beyond the immediate context addressed by Paul. Perhaps nothing else in this letter touches upon matters more at the center of person's lives in the twenty-first century than the very personal issues of sex and marriage. We can acknowledge that Paul did not give counsel that covers every conceivable problem that persons today might face regarding sex and marriage, but we can also listen attentively to what he did say.

One thing Paul did in these verses was to embrace human sexuality as a vital part of the relationship between a wife and husband. Rather than hold sex at arm's length as if it were an unspeakable

Pastor Issues Sex Challenge

(Credit: Image Courtesy of Fellowship Church, Grapevine, TX)

Ed Young, pastor of Fellowship Church in Grapevine, Texas, challenged his married members to have sexual relations every day for one week.

matter for the church, Paul addressed the issue candidly and openly. After centuries of guarded treatment of human sexuality, the modern church has been forced by an oversexed culture to place sex back on the agenda of topics that are not taboo. Still, many in the church today are uncomfortable with frank discussion of such matters.

The Reverend Ed Young, pastor of the evangelical Fellowship Church in Grapevine, Texas, received extensive media attention when, on November 16, 2008, he issued a challenge to the married members of his 20,000-member congregation to have sex with their spouses for seven straight days.[57] The timing of the challenge was intended to make Thanksgiving Day 2008 a truly memorable celebration. Critics charged Young with simply using sex as a marketing ploy to attract more members. Even some members of his congregation raised their eyebrows when Young issued his challenge from a bed instead of a pulpit. Young, however, insisted that his aim was not to sell his church to a market that responds to sexual advertisements but rather to strengthen marriages and give people something positive to experience during gloomy economic times. Citing 1 Corinthians 7:5 in support of his challenge, Young proclaimed, "It is time for the church to put God back in the bed."

Young's approach might strike some as inappropriate, even crude. One wonders, however, if the Apostle Paul would be among Young's critics. Paul's candid discussion of sex in 1 Corinthians 7 has made some readers, influenced in part by Victorian-era aversion to open discussion of sexual matters, uncomfortable. The same attitude that drove open discussion of sex underground also generated modern infatuations with pornography. The objectification and dehumanization of sex that pornography and the underground sex industry have produced is part of the legacy of the church's reluctance to embrace healthy sex and talk about it openly. The attempt to silence such talk has been unsuccessful in preventing the perversion of sex and the disruption of marriages caused by infidelity and sexual addiction. The flourishing of sex trafficking and sexual slavery in the early twenty-first century is further evidence that when sex is not confronted candidly and affirmatively in the church, it becomes the tool of those who recognize its potential for exploitation. In the first century, Paul refused to ignore the issue of sexual intimacy. He frankly observed that those who deny the importance of sexual relations between married persons run the risk of sexual urges manifesting themselves in unhealthy ways.

Paul also made what, for some people in his culture, would have appeared to be radically egalitarian statements about the mutual needs and rights of both women and men. He may not have been unique in his claims that both husbands and wives had the same consensual rights regarding sex, but he was out of step with the dominant cultural *ethos*. Some interpreters think otherwise. They charge Paul with forcing sexual relations on wives who were trying to assert their freedom to devote themselves more fully to the Lord by avoiding sexual intimacy and the possibility of childbirth. It seems more likely, however, that it was men who were denying sexual intimacy to their wives. By insisting that the men honor their sexual obligations to their wives, and doing so by asserting the wife's ownership of the husband's body, Paul was actually elevating the role and status of married women in a culture that often considered women to be essentially the property of men.

S.T.O.P.

Credit: Mercer University Sex Trafficking Opposition Project

During the spring semester of 2008, a group of students and professors from Mercer University in Macon, Georgia, became concerned about the rising number of "health spas" in their city. The spas were suspected of being centers for prostitution. Believing that these spas were largely staffed by victims of sex-trafficking, they formed the organization S.T.O.P. (Sex Trafficking Opposition Project). Their drawing attention to the problem led city police to raid many of the spas, resulting in numerous arrests and some rescues of the exploited workers. Among the many activities sponsored by S.T.O.P. was a conference held in March 2009 to raise consciousness and explore ways to combat sexual exploitation.

Recognition of mutuality in sexual relationships still runs counter to prevailing social mores. Lip service is often paid to the idea, but women yet face a world where they are viewed as objects of sexual gratification for men. "Respectable" women are those who silently serve their husband's sexual needs while hiding their own. Women who flaunt their sexuality may become celebrities, but they tend to be viewed as "disreputable" by the very society that adulates them. True equality between men and women remains elusive as long as the most basic of differences between the sexes, namely their sexuality, remains under the domination of one sex.

Marriage and Divorce

Paul's instructions regarding divorce in 1 Corinthians 7:12-16 contain two affirmations that stand in some degree of tension with each other, and one affirmation also stands in tension with certain values of modern society. On the one hand, he clearly affirms the binding nature of marriage. [Augustine on Divorce] In a culture, not unlike our own, in which divorce was common, Paul advocated remaining married.[58] The pervasiveness of this tradition within the early church is attested to by the appearance of teachings to that effect by Jesus in all of the Synoptic Gospels, as well as by Paul's reference to the same in 1 Corinthians 7:10. Marriage was considered a lifelong, binding commitment. Paul even considered this commitment to override his personal preference for the single life. While the single life was free from the anxieties and responsibilities that could hinder one's giving complete devotion to the Lord, Paul did not want people to break up their marriages in order to gain this freedom. In short, the commitment trumped the freedom.

Augustine on Divorce

We are given here to understand that neither spouse may divorce the other if both are believers.

Augustine, *Questions* 83, in Gerald Bray, ed., 1–2 Corinthians (vol. 7 of ACCS NT; ed. Thomas C. Oden; Downers Grove IL: InterVarsity Press, 1999) 64.

In a culture such as ours, where personal freedom is valued as an unquestioned "good," the binding nature of marriage presents challenges. In marriage, persons agree to limit personal freedom, undoubtedly in the belief that such restraint will lead to certain fulfillment that could not be realized as a single person. The high level of divorce in modern societies is an indication that such beliefs are often unfulfilled. Herein lies the tension with Paul's affirmation of the binding nature of marriage. Paul's own dominant culture esteemed the value of longevity in marriage, yet divorce was widely practiced. Our own culture values stability in marriage, yet for many persons that ideal appears unrealistic in light of the centrifugal forces that drive persons apart, not to mention the numerous extraneous forces that tug at the seams of tenuous marriage bonds.

Paul's tactic in confronting the forces that divide from within and without was to appeal to an external authority to hold the couple together, namely the charge of the Lord that husband and wife should not separate. That charge is sufficient for some, even for some persons who find themselves in abusive marriage relationships. For many others, however, the external authority of biblical imperative is not adequate to overcome the forces that divide. For such persons, the need is for a centripetal force that pulls together from within the marriage bond. Paul's assurance to persons married to nonbelievers that their spouse is made holy, despite their unbelief, might hold some promise for believers and unbelievers alike that being united in body and spirit with another person produces a level of sacredness in life that does not exist in solitude. The God made known in Christ may be served more efficiently by the single person, but that God who engages the world in Christ, even exposing supreme vulnerability in that engagement, is perhaps best known through our costly, self-limiting engagement with the other. No human relationship exposes one to the depth of personal vulnerability and self-limitation more than marriage. Likewise, no other relationship offers the deep potential for personal enrichment through intimate knowledge of the self, the other, and perhaps even God than marriage.

Paul's affirmation of the binding character of marriage stands in tension with his sensitivity to certain circumstances that make remaining married unworkable. Somewhat reluctantly, he recognizes that holding a marriage together may lie beyond the control of the believing spouse (7:15). The unbelieving partner may simply refuse to let the marriage continue. Paul's willingness to recognize the possibility of exceptions to his policy of remaining as you are, as reluctant as it may be, at least opens a door for being sensitive to insurmountable problems that may arise in marriages. For Paul, the believing spouse's helplessness in the face of a forced divorce leads him to declare that the injured sister or brother is not "enslaved." In affirming that they have been released from the untenable relationship, Paul is also affirming the dignity and continuing worth of the divorced person. That affirmation of dignity and worth offers the beginning of healing for those who find they cannot uphold the binding character of marriage. Divorce, even in the most understandable of circumstances, inevitably brings pain and self-doubt. Enabling such persons to begin the healing process through the affirmation of their dignity may begin with the simple affirmation that they have been released. [Woman, Thou Art Loosed!]

Woman, Thou Art Loosed!

The African-American minister T. D. Jakes echoes the sensitivity of Paul to the traumatic effects of divorce in his best-selling book, *Woman, Thou Art Loosed!*

> Approximately five out of ten marriages end in divorce. Those broken homes leave a trail of broken dreams, people, and children. Only the Master can heal these victims in the times in which we live. He can treat the long-term effects of the tragedy. One of the great healing balms of the Holy Spirit is forgiveness. To forgive is to break the link between you and your past. Sadly enough, many times the person hardest to forgive is the one in the mirror. Although they rage loudly about others, people secretly blamed themselves for a failed relationship. Regardless of who [sic] you hold responsible, there is no healing in blame! When you begin to realize that your past does not necessarily dictate the outcome of your future, then you can release the hurt. It is impossible to inhale the new air until you exhale the old.

T. D. Jakes, *Woman, Thou Art Loosed!* (Shippensburg PA: Treasure House, 1993) 6.

Remaining As One Is

Paul's main premise in arguing for the continuation of sexual relations in marriage, the maintenance of marriage for the married, and the maintenance of the single life for those not married is his principle that one should remain as he/she was when called by God. This principle provides the cornerstone of his argument throughout the whole chapter, though he only introduces it about one third of the way into his argument (v. 17). As his argument proceeds, it becomes evident that his principle roots at least partly in his eschatological perspective about the impending demise of the prevailing world order as he knew it. Viewed from the vantage point of almost two millennia later, that perspective can legitimately be questioned as a viable operative principle for framing responses to the issues Paul faced. To put the matter bluntly, would Paul himself offer the same instruction in light of the fact that the world order as he knew it has not yet seen its demise? In regard to remaining married, he undoubtedly would. In regard to remaining single, he probably would not. In regard to circumcision and slavery, which he only brought into the discussion as illustrations of his principle, he would probably affirm his principle for the former but not, we would hope, for the latter. Though he did allow, according to the interpretation held here, that slaves might avail themselves of freedom should the opportunity arise, he did not challenge the institution itself. Acknowledging that the experience of slavery for most people in his time was different from that known in more recent centuries only goes so far in redeeming Paul's view. Likewise, pointing out that the practice of slavery was such an ingrained element in the ancient world that Paul could not have effectively challenged it even if he had tried only partially exonerates his acquiescence to a dehumanizing institution. Sadly, similar arguments about the humane treatment of slaves and the economic necessity of the "peculiar institution" were all too common in early nineteenth-century debates about slavery, a debate that was ultimately settled only by the most costly war known to the world up until that time. Yet, Paul's position, which was fueled by his conviction that such institutions would not be a part of the coming kingdom, is not really the issue. The more important question is whether those of us who have seen the endurance of this world order for another two millennia can justify continued acquiescence to dehumanizing institutions and practices. Living in the light of the imminent triumph of God, as Paul did, is one thing. It can enable us to question the legitimacy of any structures that are inconsistent with our vision of God's coming kingdom. Using the delay of that coming as a sign of the futility of our action or relying on that coming to remedy what we do not even attempt to challenge, however, are not excusable positions.

Paul's principle of remaining as you are was only partly shaped by his eschatological perspective. It was informed by his affirmation of one's new status in the coming order of God, an order that reduced the ultimate significance of those social markers that gave structure to his world. But it was also informed by his affirmation of one's participation in God's *current* creation. The call of God comes to persons in their place in life, however that is defined by the prevailing social structures. One does not have to be in one place rather than another in order to be called, nor does one have to change places to live out that call faithfully. Paul's perspective, therefore, has a bipolar focus. On the one hand, any person, positioned wherever the prevailing status system places him or her, may receive the call. All places in life are thereby affirmed. The slave as well as the master may be called. All places are also relativized. The master holds no higher standing in God's order than does the slave. In fact, as a signal that the old structures have been transcended already in God's order, Paul actually elevates the slave to the position of God's freedperson while the free person holds the position of "slave of Christ" (v. 22). [John Taylor] Unfortunately, the centuries have taken their toll on both aspects of Paul's bipolar vision. Churches have not only sustained the old orders of social differentiation; they have also created their own hierarchies that propagate distinctions of personal importance on the basis of wealth, education, and social status. Thus, they have given only token recognition to Paul's conviction that all are one in Christ, and they have been reluctant to let go of the privileges that competing skillfully in the old order can bring.

John Taylor

John Taylor (1752–1833) was the founder and pastor of several Baptist churches in pioneer Kentucky. A mostly self-educated farmer-preacher, Taylor wrote three books, including *A History of the Ten Churches*. In his account of his ministry at the Clear Creek Baptist Church in Woodford County (where I was the pastor from August 1978 until June 1983), Taylor described the conversion of many slaves. He himself owned as many as fifteen slaves at one time. In recalling one particular baptismal service, Taylor described the equality that he believed existed for master and slave in Christ.

> One of these poor, black men by the name of Essex, soon as his head was raised above water, began to praise God aloud and enquired for his dear master, who was then weeping on the shore. He wanted to give him his hand, which he soon did. Here master and servant meets [sic] on perfect equality. James says, "Let the brother of low degree rejoice that he is exalted, and the rich in that he is made low" [Jas 1:9-10]. Jack and Harry [two of Taylor's slaves] or Essex has a master in the shop or on the farm but not so in the church of Christ. There they all have a Master, and only one Master—Jesus Christ. And there they are all Christ's free men and [are] on perfect equality with each other. There as in the grave the servant is free from his master, and the oppressor's voice [is] not to be heard. There [they] call no man master or father on earth. There conscience is free.

Undoubtedly, Taylor was sincere in his belief that true equality existed between slave and master *in* the church, but the illusory nature of that perspective would have been clear once the owner and the "owned" passed through the church's doors, returning to their everyday world. The inability of Taylor and his parishioners to see the contradiction in their perspective is evident from their arraignment before the church of one member, John Sutton, for vigorously advocating emancipation.

Chester Raymond Young, ed., *Baptists on the American Frontier: A History of the Ten Baptist Churches of Which the Author Has Been Alternately a Member by John Taylor* (annotated 3rd ed.; Macon GA: Mercer University Press, 1995) 210, 220.

Lectionary Connections

Two selections from chapter 7 are included in the Revised Common Lectionary. First Corinthians 7:29-31 is read in Year B on the third Sunday after Epiphany, along with Jon 3:1-5, 10, and Mark 1:14-22. Both Jonah and Jesus call for repentance in light of the impending working of God. Paul's words can be used to flesh out the nature such repentance can take as one lives in the light of the impending transformation of the old world order.

First Corinthians 7:32-35 is read the following Sunday in Year B with Deuteronomy 18:15-22 and Mark 1:21-28. Deuteronomy speaks of the prophet like Moses who is to come, and Mark presents Jesus as a prophet-teacher unlike any his audience was accustomed to hearing. The main point of connection with Paul's words may be found in Jesus' exorcism of the tormented man with the unclean spirit and Paul's reference to being undivided in one's devotion to the Lord.

NOTES

1. Menander, *Unidentified Fragments* 651.

2. The classic case of conjecture (though well argued) about the contents of the letter from the Corinthians is that of John C. Hurd Jr., *The Origin of I Corinthians* (Macon GA: Mercer University Press, 1983) esp. 83–94.

3. Ibid., 74, 82.

4. Anthony C. Thiselton, *The First Epistle to the Corinthians: A Commentary on the Greek Text* (NIGTC; Grand Rapids: Eerdmans, 2000) 501.

5. An exception is the study by Rollin A. Ramsara, "More Than an Opinion: Paul's Rhetorical Maxim in First Corinthians 7:25-26," *CBQ* 57 (1995): 531–41, but he focuses mostly on the second part of Paul's argument in ch. 7.

6. See the discussion of 19th-century usages of 1 Cor 7:17-24 by Brad Ronnell Braxton, *The Tyranny of Resolution: I Corinthians 7:17-24* (SBLDS 181; Atlanta: Society of Biblical Literature, 2000) 237–74.

7. See, in particular, Vincent L. Wimbush, *Paul the Worldly Ascetic: Response to the World and Self-understanding according to 1 Corinthians 7* (Macon GA: Mercer University Press, 1987).

8. See examples in Dale B. Martin, *The Corinthian Body* (New Haven: Yale University Press, 1995) 213.

9. Will Deming, *Paul on Marriage and Celibacy: The Hellenistic Background of 1 Corinthians 7* (SNTNMS 83; Cambridge: Cambridge University Press, 1995).

10. This is essentially the argument of Antoinette Clark Wire, *The Corinthian Women Prophets: A Reconstruction through Paul's Rhetoric* (Minneapolis: Fortress Press, 1990),

and of Margaret Y. McDonald, "Women Holy in Body and Spirit: The Social Setting of 1 Corinthians 7," *NTS* 36 (1990): 161–81.

11. Bruce W. Winter, *After Paul Left Corinth: The Influence of Secular Ethics and Social Change* (Grand Rapids MI: Eerdmans, 2001) 215–322. Winter also sees the avoidance of pregnancy involved in their reasoning.

12. For a discussion of the meaning of the verb "to have," see especially David E. Garland, *1 Corinthians* (BECNT; Grand Rapids: Baker Academic, 2003) 256.

13. Deming, *Paul on Marriage and Celibacy*, 117.

14. See Hans Conzelmann, *1 Corinthians: A Commentary* (Hermeneia; trans. James W. Leitch; Philadelphia: Fortress Press, 1975) 116–17, and Deming, *Paul on Marriage and Celibacy*, 119–21.

15. Wire, *The Corinthian Women Prophets*, 84.

16. Garland, *1 Corinthians*, 260, argues that the second subjunctive verb (*ēte*) has the force of an imperative here, but subjunctives typically have such force only in negative prohibitions, as in 7:29. Subjunctives with *hina* sometimes express imperatives but only rarely and not when joined with another subjunctive denoting purpose. See Gordon D. Fee, *The First Epistle to the Corinthians* (NICNT; Grand Rapids: Eerdmans Publishing, 1987) 282.

17. See the discussions of options by Thiselton, *The First Epistle to the Corinthians*, 510–11, and Fee, *The First Epistle to the Corinthians*, 283.

18. In particular, Winter, *After Paul Left Corinth*, 233–40, argues that *touto* used with verbs of saying, seeing, knowing, or thinking points forward to the substance of the verb. This is clear when *hoti* immediately follows such verbs, but Winter presents evidence of *hoti* being omitted yet understood. He believes such is the case here. Garland, *1 Corinthians*, 268–70, agrees.

19. See Jerome Murphy-O'Connor, "The Divorced Woman in 1 Cor, 7:10-11," *JBL* 100 (1981): 601–606; Fee, *The First Epistle to the Corinthians*, 296.

20. Thiselton, *The First Epistle to the Corinthians*, 520.

21. Ben Witherington III, *Conflict and Community in Corinth: A Socio-Rhetorical Commentary and 1 and 2 Corinthians* (Grand Rapids: Eerdmans, 1995) 171.

22. See Paul Veyne, "The Roman Empire," in *From Pagan Rome to Byzantium* (ed. Paul Veyne; trans. Arthur Goldhammer; vol. 1 of *A History of Private Life*, ed. Philippe Ariès and George Duby; Cambridge: Harvard University Press, 1987) 34.

23. Here I agree with the assessment of Thiselton, *The First Epistle to the Corinthians*, 525–26.

24. Plutarch, *Moralia* 140D.

25. See David L. Balch, *Let Wives Be Submissive: The Domestic Code in 1 Peter* (SBLMS 26; Chico CA: Scholars Press, 1981), 65–80.

26. Ovid, *The Art of Love*, I.75.

27. Tacitus, *Histories*, V.4.

28. Philo, *Apology for the Jews*, 7.3; Josephus, *Against Apion*, II.199.

29. See Martin, *The Corinthian Body*, 218.

30. Deming, *Paul on Marriage and Celibacy*, 137.

31. Ibid., 148–57.

32. David Instone-Brewer, "1 Corinthians 7 in the Light of the Jewish Greek and Aramaic Marriage and Divorce Papyri," *TynBul* 52 (2001): 238–39.

33. This perspective is effectively argued by Garland, *1 Corinthians*, 290–94.

34. Thiselton, *The First Epistle to the Corinthians*, 537–39, and Garland, *1 Corinthians*, 291–95, give detailed analyses of the "optimistic" and "pessimistic" views.

35. See Scott S. Bartschy, *MALLON CHRESAI: First Century Slavery and the Interpretation of 1 Cor. 7:21* (SBLDS 11; Missoula: Scholars Press, 1973); Dale B. Martin, *Slavery as Salvation* New Haven: Yale University Press, 1990); Deming, *Paul on Marriage and Celibacy*, 153–73.

36. Richard B. Hays, *First Corinthians* (IBC; Louisville: John Knox Press, 1997) 123.

37. See Deming, *Paul on Marriage and Celibacy*, 159, for a discussion of the diatribe here. Deming, however, wrongly insists that Paul begins with rhetorical questions in vv. 18 and 21 (so NRSV). The syntax does not require translation as questions.

38. Garland, *1 Corinthians*, 306.

39. Orlando Patterson, *Slavery and Social Death: A Comparative Study* (Cambridge MA: Harvard University Press, 1982) 105, estimates that 85% of the residents of Rome were slaves or former slaves and that in provinces such as Achaia the percentages were only somewhat less.

40. Braxton, *The Tyranny of Resolution*, esp. 220–34, argues that Paul deliberately left his instruction about gaining freedom ambiguous because he did not know what to do about church members who were slaves.

41. This is a major point made by Martin, *Slavery as Salvation*.

42. Extensive discussion of these options, and others, may be found in Thiselton, *The First Epistle to the Corinthians*, 568–71.

43. Garland, *1 Corinthians*, 321–22, is on the right track in translating *gnōmēn* as "maxim," but that term carries the connotation of a "saying" taken from tradition rather than a principle formulated by Paul himself.

44. Conzelmann, *1 Corinthians: A Commentary*, 132.

45. Winter, *After Paul Left Corinth*, 215–32.

46. Charles K. Williams II, "Roman Corinth as a Commercial Center," in *The Corinthia in the Roman Period* (ed. Timothy E. Gregory; JRASup 8: Ann Arbor MI: Journal of Roman Archaeology, 1993) 24–25.

47. Winter, *After Paul Left Corinth*, 231.

48. James Moffatt, *The First Epistle of Paul to the Corinthians* (MNTC 7; London: Hodder & Stoughton, 1938) 95.

49. Charles K. Barrett, *The First Epistle to the Corinthians* (HNTC; New York: Harper & Row, 1968) 181.

50. See Margaret Y. McDonald, "Women Holy in Body and Spirit: The Social Setting of 1 Corinthians 7," *NTS* 36 (1990): 161–81; Wire, *The Corinthian Women Prophets*.

51. Johannes Schneider, "σχῆμα, μετασχηματίζω," *TDNT* 7:954.

52. See the discussion by Winter, *After Paul Left Corinth*, 222–23.

53. See the discussions of the views of ancient and modern interpreters in Thiselton, *The First Epistle to the Corinthians*, 594–98, and Garland, *1 Corinthians*, 336–43.

54. This point is made by Garland, *1 Corinthians*, 338.

55. Bruce W. Winter, "Puberty or Passion? The Referent of Ὑπέρακμος in 1 Corinthians 7:36," *TynBul* 20 (1998): 71–89.

56. Richard B. Hays, *First Corinthians* (IBC; Louisville: John Knox Press, 1997) 111; Garland, *1 Corinthians*, 242; Thiselton, *The First Epistle to the Corinthians*, 294–95.

57. "Pastor's Advice for Better Marriage: More Sex," *New York Times*, 24 November 2008, New York ed., A13.

58. On the unusual nature of the Christian prohibition against divorce, see Carolyn Osiek and David L. Balch, *Families in the New Testament World: Households and House Churches* (*The Family, Religion, and Culture,* ed. Don S. Browning and Ian S. Evison; Louisville: John Knox Westminster, 1997) 62–63.

EATING FOOD OFFERED TO IDOLS

1 Corinthians 8:1–9:27

"If a little knowledge is dangerous, where is the man who has so much as to be out of danger?"[1]

In 1 Corinthians 8:1–11:1, Paul clearly turns to another topic. Hardly anything else about the long section, however, is so clear. The general subject has to do with some type of participation in eating practices that could be associated with pagan religion in some form. Beyond this, the particular situation addressed by Paul has been the subject of much scholarly disagreement. Paul's argument also is somewhat difficult to follow in places, giving rise to numerous suggestions that the section contains parts of different letters. Greater attention to the features of ancient rhetoric has enabled many modern scholars to affirm the literary integrity of the section, but even then, parts of Paul's rhetoric do not exhibit an obvious coherence. Perhaps the most challenging hurdle the section presents to interpretation for preaching and teaching purposes is the question of relevance. Whereas the problems addressed by Paul earlier in the letter (divisions, immorality, marriage, divorce, and sex) are still at the forefront of the church's concerns today, few twenty-first-century Christians (at least in North America and Europe) ever face a dilemma over eating food associated with pagan religion.[2]

In this commentary, I take the position that these three chapters do form a single literary and rhetorical unit free of insertions from other letters. I also think that we can identify the structure and flow of Paul's argument, though some parts are not easily fitted into any neat and tidy outline. I also think that when we can move beyond the specific problem that Paul addressed and focus on the basic premises of his argument, we can discover some of the most relevant principles 1 Corinthians has to offer for the church and individual Christians today.

Because this is a long section, we will examine it in two chapters. The present chapter covers 1 Corinthians 8 and 9; the next chapter deals with the rest of the section, which includes all of 1 Corinthians 10 and the first verse of chapter 11. Introductory matters regarding the historical context and the literary/rhetorical structure of the

A Thematic Outline of 1 Corinthians 8:1–11:1

I. The Problem of Eating Food Associated with Idols (8:1-13)
   A. Introduction to the Problem (8:1-6)
   B. The Danger of Hurting a Person of Weak Conscience (8:7-13)
II. The Example of Paul as a Guide to Solving the Problem (9:1-27)
   A. Paul's Relinquishing of His Right as an Apostle (9:1-18)
   B. Paul's Subservience Designed to Win Others (9:19-27)
III. The Theological Danger of Eating Food Offered to Idols (10:1–11:1)
   A. Israel's Example as a Warning to the Corinthians (10:1-13)
   B. The Lord's Supper as Sign of Exclusive Devotion to God (10:14-22)
   C. Eating or Drinking without Offense (10:23–11:1)

section are a part of the present chapter. [A Thematic Outline of 1 Corinthians 8:1–11:1]

The Issue in 1 Corinthians 8:1–11:1

What exactly was Paul trying to correct in this part of the letter? He begins the section in v. 1 with the phrase "and/now concerning idol sacrifices (*eidōlothytōn*)." The precise meaning of the term *eidōlothytōn* calls for clarification, but that will come later. In v. 4, Paul narrows the focus somewhat in his repetition of the topic: "then concerning the eating (*brōseōs*) of idol sacrifices." The issue at hand concerns eating. As noted previously, the phrase *peri de* ("and/now concerning") may simply indicate movement to another topic, but since Paul seems to enter here into a debate that has a prehistory to this letter, it is reasonable to conclude that the Corinthians had addressed the subject in their letter to Paul. It is also not unreasonable to suppose that Paul may have already addressed the matter himself in the letter he had sent to them earlier (cf. 1 Cor 5:9). That earlier letter had dealt with the issue of with whom the Corinthian believers should associate. While Paul clarified in 5:10-11 that his earlier concern had not really been association with outsiders but rather toleration of immorality within their own ranks, the fact that he mentioned idolaters twice in those verses suggests that he had earlier warned them against affiliation with idolatry. He had not advised them to discontinue all relations with idolaters, for, as he acknowledged, that was impossible. Undoubtedly, however, both in his earlier preaching and communications he had warned against the dangers of close affinities with the idolatrous practices that permeated their culture. His response to their response to that warning here further suggests that they had offered some defense of the practice of associating with idolaters in ways that they considered safe but which Paul considered seriously harmful. That practice seems to have involved eating food connected to some extent with idols or images.

Two matters that have divided scholars are (1) *what* they were eating and (2) *where* they were eating it. At the center of the debate are the meanings of the terms *eidōlothytōn* (8:1, 4, 7, 10; 10:19) and *eidōliō* (8:10), the latter of which indicates a place where the eating may have occurred. Another divisive issue is whether Paul strictly forbade the practice or gave contradictory instructions that actually condoned the consumption of *eidōlothytōn* in certain circumstances or settings.

What did Paul mean by *eidōlothytōn*? [*Eidōlothytōn*] While some commentators try to define the term narrowly, the full range of evidence suggests that Paul and other New Testament writers used it to refer broadly to "food sacrificed to idols." That is, it was the residual portion of the food dedicated to a deity. Usually a small

Eidōlothytōn

ΑΩ The term *eidōlothytōn* (genitive form) does not appear in Greek literature outside the realm of Jewish and Christian writings. It appears first in the noncanonical Jewish work called 4 Maccabees (5:2), which has been dated anywhere from the last quarter of the 1st century BC to the first quarter of the 2d century AD. Its appearance in Pseudo-Phocylides 31 (dated early 1st century to mid-2d century AD) is probably a Christian interpolation. In the New Testament, in addition to 1 Corinthians, it appears in Acts 15:29; 21:25; and Rev 2:14, and it is in the early Christian writing known as the *Didache* (6:3). In all of these writings (besides 1 Corinthians), the term refers to the eating of food associated with idolatry. The first part of the word, *eidōlon*, was frequently used in Greek literature to refer to a "phantom," an "unsubstantial form," or a "copy" of something. Only Polybius (31,3,13-15), among pagan Greeks, used the word to mean "idol." The usual Greek term for an idol was *agalma*. In the LXX, *eidōlon* is regularly used both of idols and of the "fake" gods they represent. Jewish and Christian writings in Greek typically use *eidōlon* in the same derogative sense. The second part of the word, *thysōn*, is rare, but it stems from the noun *thysis* and the verb *thysō*, which almost always have to do with "sacrifices." The stock Greek term for the "food associated with sacrifices" was *hierothyton*, which indicates that the food in question was *sacred* (*hieros*) in that it was dedicated in some way to a deity. The term *eidōlothyta* (nominative plural) appears to be a derogatory label applied to such sacrificial food by Jews and Christians.

Charles Kennedy contends that the term *eidōlothyta* applied only to "memorial meals for the dead," which often involved a meal eaten in the presence of some "likeness" of the deceased. His view does fit the more common Greek meaning for *eidōlon* of "copy," but it ignores the regular Jewish/Christian pejorative meaning of a "fake god" or "idol." Furthermore, *thytōn* cannot be restricted to the idea of a "meal," as Kennedy at times suggests. Meals were typically involved in the sacrifice of foods, but a meal involving no sacrifice would not have been called a *thytōn*. The kind of funerary meal Kennedy points to would have involved a sacrifice to the dead as one who had entered the realm beyond that of mortals. The Mishnah tractate on idolatry, *Abodah Zarah* (2.3), forbids the eating of meat taken from an idol after being dedicated to it and likens this to "sacrifices for the dead." The expression is based on Ps 106:28, which refers to the transgression of some Israelites while passing through Moab. The account in Num 25, however, describes the transgression as worshiping the Baal of Peor. The "dead" of Ps 106:28 may be a pejorative allusion to the dead gods of the Moabites, not to their ancestors, as Kennedy argues. Kennedy appeals to the later writings of Origen (*Celsus* 7.21) and Tertullian (*De spect*. 13) to support the identification of *eidōlothyta* as "meals offered to images of the dead," but what those writers actually show is that Christians came to prohibit partaking of pagan funerary meals *as well as* "food sacrificed to idols." Tertullian carefully distinguishes between the two, calling the former necrothytis and the latter *eidōlothytis*.

Paul's prohibition may have included such funerary meals since they would have represented to him a kind of offering to a being other than God, but we cannot restrict his reference only to such meals. Nor can we restrict *eidōlothyta* as a term absolutely to *meat* since various foodstuffs were offered as sacrifices. Meat was the focus of many (but not all) Jewish prohibitions not only because of its association with idolatry but also because of concerns that it had not been prepared according to kosher standards. Paul's assertion in 8:13 that he would forgo eating meat altogether if it caused a fellow believe to fall may indicate that meat was the focus of the debate about *eidōlothyta* in Corinth, but this cannot be determined with the certainty that many commentators assume.

Johannes Behm, "θύω, θυσία, κτλ.," *TDNT* 3:180–90.

Friedrich Büchsel, "εἴδωλον, εἰδωλόθυτον, κτλ.," *TDNT* 2:375–79.

Charles A. Kennedy, "The Cult of the Dead in Corinth, in *Love and Death in the Ancient Near East: Essays in Honor of Marvin H. Pope* (ed. John. H. Marks and Robert. M. Good; Guilford CT: Four Quarters, 1987) 227–36.

portion of the food was actually burned on the altar, a portion was given to the priests and attendants, and a portion was consumed by the persons offering the sacrifice. In the case of large sacrifices by wealthy patrons, especially during festivals, the leftovers available for consumption might be considerable, and the partakers might be large in number. The portion given to the priests might find its way into the marketplace for later sale. Such food was typically referred to as *hierothyton* ("sacred sacrifice") by pagans, but Jews and Christians referred to it pejoratively as *eidōlothyton* to indicate it was "food offered to *fake* gods." Because the food was connected to pagan worship, eating it was prohibited for Jews and Christians. For Paul, it was this connection to idolatry that mattered; it was not anything inherently evil or dangerous about the food itself. If the connection to idolatry disappeared, the food could be consumed. If the connection should be reestablished, however, then the food became taboo again.

Apparently some of the Corinthian believers held that eating such food was not a problem. Their reasoning was that since the deities to whom the food was sacrificed did not actually exist, then the food was not really connected to those deities. Besides, participation in the various meals at which such food was served was a normal part of life in a place such as Corinth. The large religious festivals held on numerous occasions throughout the year were important times for social interaction. One's civic responsibility was to participate in such activities. Any members of the church who may have belonged to relatively higher social ranks may have found it socially troublesome to decline invitations to special banquets associated with the festivals. If they did attend, as they would normally have done before becoming a believer, then participating in the affairs only partially by refraining from eating the food connected to the sacrifices of the occasion would have created certain social tensions. For these reasons, many interpreters think that the people who were inclined to eat the *eidōlothyton* were of higher social status. The tension regarding eating such food, however, was not necessarily restricted to those of higher status. For the members of the church who would not have been privileged to attend the special banquets anyway, curtailing their participation in those activities provided for the masses, including feasts, would have meant missing out on major cultural and social events, especially the opportunity to eat foods that were probably not a part of their regular diet. Persons of lower status could as easily have justified partaking of food associated with sacrifices on the basis of their knowledge that the gods to whom those sacrifices were made did not exist. While the higher-ranking members of the church may have experienced more social pressure to partake of such food and to have been inclined to assert their "right" to do so ((8:9), the lower-ranking members would have also felt both pressure and attraction to partake.[3]

Paul disagreed with their reasoning. Their premises, that "an idol has no real existence" and "there is no God but one" (8:4), were accurate enough. Their conclusion that the premises permitted partaking of *eidōlothyton*, however, overlooked two important points, according to Paul. One was the effect that such action might have on persons who were not fully convinced of the premises (8:9-12; 10:28-29). Seeing those with knowledge eat, persons who did not have that knowledge might also eat as if the gods were real, thus leading to their downfall. The other was the effect such action would have on the partaker of that food. True enough, Paul agreed, idols have no real existence, but the demons to whom those idol sacrifices are unwittingly made are real (10:20). The believer who participates in a meal of food offered to demons becomes a partner with those demons. As long as the food had a clear connection to the worship of fake gods, Paul prohibited it.

Where would such food have been eaten? Paul only mentions one specific place: an idol's temple (*eidōleion*: 8:10). It is unclear, however, that all of the dining referred to in this long section occurred in this setting. The invitation to dinner mentioned in 10:27 may have been to a meal in a temple precinct or (more probably) in the home of an unbeliever. The exact meaning of *eidōleion* is also uncertain. [Tomb Shrines] Most take it to be a pejorative term for a pagan temple. Rather than refer to such a structure by the usual Greek terms of *hieron* or *naos*, Paul follows the Jewish custom

Tomb Shrines

Charles Kennedy has argued that the term *eidōleion* should be seen in reference to a grave shrine, some of which were quite elaborate. Many tombs of the affluent were designed to accommodate the funeral meals that were often held there by surviving family members. Kennedy's argument that *eidōleion* can only mean a grave shrine and that *eidōlothyta* can only mean a funerary meal at such a shrine, however, is not supported by the meaning given to these terms in other writings. In 1 Macc 1:47 and Bel 10, the term clearly refers to a particular deity's temple. Furthermore, Paul does not indicate in any other way in this section that he is addressing funeral rituals. Still, one cannot exclude from consideration meals held at a tomb shrine as well as meals held in a temple precinct. Both involved eating a kind of sacrificial food, and, in Paul's view, both would have constituted participation in idolatry. We should give *eidōleiō* a broad meaning, referring to any pagan religious structure including tomb shrines.

Charles A. Kennedy, "The Cult of the Dead in Corinth, in *Love and Death in the Ancient Near East: Essays in Honor of Marvin H. Pope* (ed. John. H. Marks and Robert. M. Good; Guilford CT: Four Quarters, 1987) 231–34.

National Archaeological Museum, Athens, Greece. (Credit: Scott Nash)

of calling a pagan temple an "idol place." We do not have to restrict such an application of the term by Paul to a large temple complex that had specific rooms designated for dining. Even smaller shrines that housed idols, including some tomb shrines, could accommodate space for reclining to eat from the food sacrificed on the altar. Nor must we insist that an idol actually had to be present in the temple or shrine in order for it to have been called an *eidōleion.* Any monument of any size might have been referred to as such since it would have been the location for sacrificial rituals to pagan deities.

In debating the question of the setting for the consumption of *eidōlothyton,* many argue for seeing three different settings involved. The first, the one addressed in 8:1-13, they argue, occurred in the dining area of a temple precinct but not in a specifically religious context. [Temple Dining in Corinth] This view holds that meals could be held in a religious place but not have a religious purpose, such as a birthday celebration.[4] According to this understanding of the setting, Paul's prohibition against eating *eidōlothyton* came into play only if a believer with a weak conscience should see the fellow believer eating the food. In 10:1-22, however, Paul directly addresses another setting, one in which a believer might actually

Temple Dining in Corinth

Significant recent studies on the possible settings for the temple dining addressed by Paul in 1 Corinthians include the following works.

Nancy Bookidis, "Religion in Corinth: 146 B.C.E. to 100 C.E.," in *Urban Religion in Roman Corinth: Interdisciplinary Approaches* (ed. Daniel N. Showalter and Steven J. Friesen; *HTS* 53; Cambridge: Harvard University Press, 2005) 141–64.

Alex T. Cheung, *Idol Food in Corinth: Jewish Background and Pauline Legacy* (JSNTSup 176: Sheffield: Sheffield Academic Press, 1999).

John Fotopoulos, *Food Offered to Idols in Roman Corinth: A Socio-Rhetorical Reconsideration of 1 Corinthians 8:1–11:1* (Tübingen: Mohr Siebeck, 2003).

Peter D. Gooch, *Dangerous Food: 1 Corinthians 8–10 in Its Context* (Studies in Christianity and Judaism 5; Waterloo, Ont.: Wilfred Laurier University Press, 1993).

Derek Newton, *Deity and Diet: The Dilemma of Sacrificial Food at Corinth* (JSNTSup 169; Sheffield: Sheffield Academic Press, 1998).

Richard E. Oster Jr., "Use, Misuse and Neglect of Archaeological Evidence in Some Modern Works on 1 Corinthians (1Cor 7,1-5; 8,10; 11,2-16; 12,14-26)," *ZNW* 83 (1992): 69–73.

Wendell Lee Willis, *Idol Meat in Corinth: The Pauline Argument in 1 Corinthians 8 and 10* (SBLDS 68; Chico CA: Scholars Press, 1985).

Bruce W. Winter, *After Paul Left Corinth: The Influence of Secular Ethics and Social Change* (Grand Rapids MI: Eerdmans, 2001) 269–86.

Ben Witherington III, "Not So Idle Thoughts about *Eidolothuton,*" *TynBul* 44 (1993): 23–754.

Khiok-Khng Yeo, *Rhetorical Interaction in 1 Corinthians 8 and 10: A Formal Analysis with Preliminary Suggestions for a Chinese, Cross-Cultural Hermeneutic* (BIS 9; Leiden: E. J. Brill, 1995).

partake of food in a religious context by eating food taken from the deity's table, a practice he completely forbids. In 10:23–11:1, as this view holds, Paul refers to a nonreligious meal in a private home in which food formerly involved in temple sacrifices has been bought at the market and served. Unless someone makes an issue of the food's connection to the temple, then the believer should have no qualms about eating it. Advocates of this view that three different settings are envisioned also tend to see the main issue being whether or not believers could buy from the market and eat food that was formerly connected to temple sacrifices. They see a "weak" group in the church that advocated avoiding *eidōlothyton* in any form in debate with a "strong" group that not only affirmed eating such food but also flaunted their enlightened right to eat it by frequenting both temple sacrifices and secular dinners in temple precincts.[5] According to this view, Paul sought to maintain unity by seeking certain concessions from both parties.

Several problems exist for this understanding of the settings, the groups involved, and Paul's instructions. First of all, the modern distinction between religious and secular hardly fits the ancient context. Celebrations of a nonreligious purpose may have been held for private groups in a temple precinct, for the dining facilities at those venues could be rented for such occasions. To describe those venues simply as the "restaurants" of antiquity, however, ignores the abundance of evidence that purely secular eating facilities of various types did exist and the fact that no matter how secular the affair might be, any dining conducted in a temple precinct automatically held religious connotations for the participants.[6] The inevitable association with idolatry for any meals held in a temple precinct led Jews of Alexandria who belonged to

Corinthian Eateries

(Credit: Scott Nash)

Excavations of buildings 1 and 2 on the east side of the north-south street running east of the theater in Corinth uncovered two structures with large ovens designed apparently for commercial use. The large number of animal bones found in one of the buildings has led the excavator, Charles Williams, to conclude that both buildings were used by butchers to sell cooked meat to neighborhood residents and especially to persons attending the theater across the street. The buildings were not designed to serve wine or host seated customers and so were not *tabernae*, *popinae*, or *cauponae* (contra Witherington, 191) but rather were "carry-out" restaurants with the cooked meat sold through windows facing the street.

Charles K. Williams II and Orestes H. Zervos, "Corinth, 1985: East of the Theater," Hesperia 55 (1986): 147–48.

Ben Witherington III, *Conflict and Community in Corinth: A Socio-Rhetorical Commentary and 1 and 2 Corinthians* (Grand Rapids: Eerdmans, 1995) 191–95.

certain guilds to refrain from participating in guild banquets when they were held in a temple.[7] Paul shared their aversion to any association with idolatry, actual or perceived. The view that Paul condones Christian participation of a nonreligious type in a temple setting in 8:1-13, except when a believer of weak conscience might witness the act, but forbids consumption at an overtly religious meal in the same setting in 10:1-22 wrongly assumes that Paul differentiated between the two occasions and types of meals. By virtue of location, both kinds of meals had a religious dimension of an idolatrous nature. The setting for the meals of 8:1-13 and the meals of 10:1-22 are the same, and Paul's instructions are the same in both chapters ("Do not partake!"), though his reasons in each case are different. The setting for 10:23–11:1, however, is different. Food that was formerly *eidōlothyton* may be bought in the market for consumption at home, or one may eat it when invited to dine at an unbeliever's home. Even in this private setting, however, if the food's former connection to the temple is reestablished, it is forbidden. Paul was not concerned only about eating in a temple setting, as some argue; he was also concerned if the temple's idolatrous significance was brought into another setting.[8]

Secondly, the view that Paul was negotiating between two groups in the church that were divided on this issue and asking for certain concessions from both groups overlooks the fact that the division is clearly between Paul and those who advocate eating *eidōlothyton*. This view holds that Paul essentially agreed with the so-called "strong" party in regard to the harmlessness that such eating entailed, but that he urged them to forgo the harmless practice out of consideration for the "weak." The supposition of two parties arguing the issue probably reflects the influence of the different situation addressed by Paul in Romans 14–15.[9] In that letter, Paul was negotiating acceptance of one group's views by another, but the "strong" and "weak" groups were those who held different views about Torah observance. Paul never addresses any "weak" group in 1 Corinthians, and he never refers to those he does address as "strong." He uses the example of a believer who might have a "weak conscience" in his argument to convince those who are advocating eating *eidōlothyton* not to do it.

Thirdly, the view that Paul permits eating *eidōlothyton* on some occasions but not others overlooks Paul's consistent objection to the practice. This view contends that Paul acknowledges the "right" of the advocates to eat *eidōlothyton* in a nonreligious setting but advises refraining from exercising this "right" when a believer of weak conscience is present (8:9). Coye Still contends that Paul's argument in 1 Corinthians 9 about forgoing his rights as an apostle

Sacrifice to Aesclepius

Il Riccio (Andrea Briosco) (1470–1523). *Sacrifice to Aesclepius.* One of eight reliefs from the Della Torre Tomb. Bronze. Louvre, Paris, France. Photo: Daniel Arnaudet. (Credit: Réunion des Musées Nationaux/Art Resource, NY)

requires that Paul recognized the theological legitimacy of the Corinthians' right to eat such food since it was not really idol-tainted.[10] Otherwise, he argues, Paul would not have been asking them to give up anything. Bruce Winter is more on target in arguing that the "right" referred to was that political right that belonged to citizens of Corinth to attend such events.[11] Everyone was eligible to attend temple sacrifices and public feasts, but citizens had the "right" (and obligation) to attend festival dinners sponsored by the city's administrators. Jewish citizens were exempted from the obligation this "right" carried, and since Christians were still viewed in Corinth as a Jewish group, they could have claimed exemption, too (cf. Acts 18:12-17). Paul is not referring to a "right" of conscience based on knowledge about the nonexistence of pagan deities; he means a special privilege that some members of the church wanted to exercise. Paul urges them not to do so, and his hypothetical example of the "weak" believer who might see them is simply one of his arguments against the practice. He does not acknowledge the legitimacy of their "right" to participate. Nor does he suddenly grant an exemption to his prohibition when he permits the consumption of food bought in the market or served by a host in 10:23–11:1. That food is no longer *eidōlothyton.* It may be eaten. If someone reconnects it to idolatry by identifying it as *hierothyton,* then it is once again off limits.

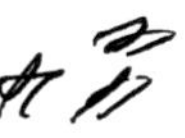

To summarize the issue, then, Paul completely rejected the argument that eating *eidōlothyton* was acceptable. Any food associated with idolatry was off limits. Whether the person ate the food at an official, religious observance or at a less religiously charged (but still religiously tainted) private banquet in a temple precinct did not matter. Whether the location was actually a temple or a tomb did not matter. These differences in possible contexts and locations are ultimately of no consequence. The food was connected to idolatry and could not be consumed by a Christian. Once the connection disappeared, the food was acceptable. If the connection should be reestablished, the food was again forbidden. It was the association with idolatry that mattered to Paul. The extent to which it mattered to him is evident from the attention he gave to the subject in 1 Corinthians and from the careful design of his argument.

The Structure of 1 Corinthians 8:1–11:1

Doubts about the structural integrity of this long section focus on two aspects: (1) the supposed contradiction in viewpoint on Paul's part between 8:1-13 and 10:1-22 and (2) the supposed incongruity of chapter 9 with what precedes and follows. As for (1), some contend that Paul adopts the same lenient policy toward consuming *eidōlothyton* in 8:1-13 that he does in 10:23–11:1 but espouses a different, intolerant stance in 10:1-22. According to this view, Paul accepts the argument of those in Corinth who claim that eating such food is not problematic since it is not actually devoted to any nonexistent deities. The only caveat Paul gives pertains to the conscience of others. In 8:1-13, one should consider the effect such action might have on a believer of weak conscience who sees the fellow believer reclining in a temple. In 10:23–11:1, one should consider the conscience of an unbelieving informer who knows the cultic connection of the food. This same view holds that Paul inconsistently reverses his stance in 10:1-22 and considers eating *eidōlothyton* to be dangerous for the partaker. Some try to resolve the apparent discrepancy by positing different settings for all three sections, but others conclude that resolution is impossible and the only explanation is that an editor has pasted together incompatible arguments from different letters. The position taken here is that 8:1-13 and 10:1-22 deal with the same setting and present the same stance on Paul's part in regard to eating *eidōlothyton*. In 10:23–11:1, the setting is different and Paul's position is different *because* the food is no longer considered *eidōlothyton.*

As for (2), many interpreters see 9:1-27 addressing a completely different matter, namely Paul's apostolic status. They understand Paul to be defending his position as an apostle against claims that he has not behaved in certain ways in which the other apostles are known to behave. In short, he is charged with being less than an apostle since he has not made use of recognized apostolic rights. None of this argument, contend adherents of this view, has anything to do with the matter of eating *eidōlothyton* and thus it does not belong to the section. At best, it is an irrelevant digression; at worst, it is a misplaced interpolation. This assessment of chapter 9 overlooks the point of Paul's argument and, therefore, fails to see the clear connection that it has to 8:1-13.

Rhetorical analysis has enabled several scholars to detect an underlying structure to this section. All rhetorical analysis should proceed cautiously given the fact that most discussions of rhetoric in antiquity concerned oral communication rather than written. (See the section titled "1 Corinthians as Rhetoric" in the Introduction.) Furthermore, Paul should not be expected to have followed ancient rhetorical conventions slavishly since the immediate problems he sought to resolve largely dictated his approach rather than any established rules of argumentation. Nonetheless, rhetorical convention itself in many respects simply mirrored what experience taught were effective methods of argumentation. We should not be surprised to find Paul's arguments reflecting generally accepted principles of rhetoric since those principles tended to hold promise for achieving the desired result and since both Paul and his audience lived in an environment with certain rhetorical expectations. Unpacking the parts of his argument in 8:1–11:1 using rhetorical analysis enables us to understand much better the flow of his argument.

As have several other scholars, Joop Smit has undertaken an extensive rhetorical analysis of this section in several published studies. [Joop Smit's Rhetorical Analysis of Paul's Argument] Overall, I think Smit has most effectively demonstrated the literary integrity of the

Joop Smit's Rhetorical Analysis of Paul's Argument

Partitio 8:1-6	Statement of the principles on which the bipartite argument is based
	8:1-3 The principle: "Knowledge puffs up; love builds up."
	8:4-6 The principle: "There is no God but one."
Argumentatio I 8:7–9:27	Discussion of the social aspect of the problem
Narratio 8:7	Statement of the facts of the situation
Propositio 8:8	Statement of two theses
Refutatio 8:9-12	Refutation of the Corinthians' practice
Confirmatio 8:13–9:23	Recommendation of Paul's example
Peroratio 9:24-27	Summary of argument with an emotional appeal
Argumentatio II 10:1–11:1	Discussion of the theological aspect of the problem
Refutatio 10:1-13	A warning based on the example of Israel
Confirmatio 10:14-22	An appeal to the example of the Lord's Supper
Anticipatio 10:23-30	
Recapitulatio 10:31–11:1	Summary of the argument with reference to two other situations

The rhetorical scheme given above is based on several publications by Joop F. M. Smit, all of which have been republished in Joop F. M. Smit, *"About the Idol Offerings": Rhetoric, Social Context and Theology of Paul's Discourse in First Corinthians 8:1–11:1* (BET 27; Leuven, Belgium: Peeters, 2000).

entire section and has isolated the major movements in Paul's argument, though I disagree with his analysis on a few details. A key to his identification of the rhetorical structure is his understanding the opening verses (8:1-6) as a two-part *partitio* that sets the stage for the two major components of Paul's argument in what follows.[12] He sees vv. 1-3, with its differentiation between knowledge that puffs up and love that builds up, as the premise for the first part of Paul's argument in 8:7–9:27. In this section, Paul focuses on the social consequences of the problem of eating food offered to idols. Paul urges those with knowledge to consider the effects of their behavior on others in the church. In 9:1-27, Paul offers his own behavior as an example of one who forgoes his rights in order to build up others. Smit takes vv. 4-6, with its affirmation of the oneness of God, as the basis for the second part of Paul's argument, which focuses on the theological implications of the affirmation. In this section (10:1-22), Paul uses the examples of Israel and the Lord's Supper to warn about the dangers of being connected to demons through eating food offered to idols. In both arguments, Paul first presents a negative proof (*refutatio*) and then a positive proof (*confirmatio*). Smit takes 10:23-30 to be a different, brief argument (*anticipatio*) added at the end that both addresses a different situation and offers some concession to those with whom he has been arguing.

Much of Smit's analysis is attractive. I suggest, however, that throughout the section Paul is seeking to counter the "knowledge" that his target audience thinks it has and that they believe enables them to partake of food offered to idols. This knowledge is the subject of vv. 4-6 as well as vv. 1-3, so it seems to me that all of vv. 1-6 constitutes a *propositio*, though the division between the two sections does function as a *partitio*, as Smit contends. Much as the Corinthian slogan "It is good for a man not to touch a woman" forms the basis for Paul's discussion of what is "good" throughout 1 Corinthians 7, their assertion that "We all have knowledge" (8:1) provides Paul with the launching pad for countering their perspective throughout 8:1–11:1. In both vv. 1-3 and vv. 4-6, Paul states the propositions of the Corinthians and his initial qualifications of their views.[13] Verse 7, the *narratio*, briefly describes the problem with this knowledge, namely, that all do not actually have it. The first argument comes in 8:8–9:27, and, much as Smit contends, focuses on the social dimension of the problem, which is the emphasis of that part of the *propositio* found in 1:1-3. Smit downplays too much, though, the theological undergirding of this section. In 8:9-13, Paul describes the negative consequences of knowledge that puffs up rather than builds up. In three stages in 9:1-27 (1-18, 19-23, 24-27), he offers his own behavior as an example of seeking to build up. The part of the *propositio* in vv. 4-6 provides the basis for Paul's second argument that begins in 10:1. Here Paul's concern is not for the "other" who might be affected by the action of those who think they have knowledge but rather for the "knowers" themselves. The argumentation here is more theological than in 8:7–9:27, as Smit holds, but theology is not the only concern. Paul wants those who think they can eat food offered to idols safely to know that they endanger their own well-being. The first part of chapter 10 (vv. 1-13) gives the negative example of Israel's experience with idolatry as a warning. Verses 14-22 contain Paul's main argumentative point about the danger of eating food offered to idols, namely its connection with demons. I take 10:23-30 to be a recapitulation (*peroratio*) of Paul's basic points in the first two arguments. He repeats the point he made in 6:12 regarding the distinction between what is "allowed" and what is "helpful" and couples it with a similar contrast regarding what "builds up." Then, he expands the application of this principle to other contexts. The last four verses (10:31–11:1) summarize Paul's main points and provide a conclusion to his argument. [A Rhetorical Scheme for 1 Corinthians 8:1–11:1]

A Rhetorical Scheme for 1 Corinthians 8:1–11:1

Propositio	8:1a	Basic thesis: "All have knowledge."
	8:1b-3	Qualification of thesis: true knowledge and love
	8:4-6	Definition of thesis: identifying what is "known"
Narratio	8:7	The problem with the thesis
Argumentatio I		Directed toward concern for those with a "weak" conscience
Refutatio I	8:8-13	The danger of exercising one's "right"
Confirmatio I	9:1-23	The example of Paul
	9:1-18	Paul foregoes his "right."
	9:19-23	Paul foregoes his "freedom."
	9:24-27	Paul "abstains" from everything.
Argumentatio II		Directed toward concern for those who "know"
Refutatio II	10:1-13	The example of Israel
Confirmatio II	10:14-22	An appeal based on the Lord's Supper
Peroratio	10:23-28	Recapitulation of both arguments
Conclusio	10:31–11:1	Summary and final appeal

COMMENTARY

In 1 Corinthians 8:1, Paul turns to a subject about which it appears that he and the Corinthians have already had some discussion. While the opening phrase *peri de* ("Now concerning") does not in itself mean that Paul was taking up another topic that the Corinthians had written to him about, the nature of his remarks strongly suggest that they had communicated to him their own position on the matter. In their letter to him, the Corinthians had probably articulated why they thought his earlier caution regarding eating food offered to idols was unnecessary. Paul seems to repeat at least three parts of their argument in favor of eating this food in v. 1 and v. 4. His response in chapter 8 involves a subtle qualification of their assertions and a demonstration of one of the negative consequences of their thinking. In chapter 9, he offers a positive example of the kind of behavior that should follow from an appropriate understanding of the knowledge they profess to have. In chapter 10, he pursues his qualification of their assertions and points out other negative consequences of their erroneous thinking.

The Problem of Eating Food Associated with Idols, 8:1-13

For Paul, eating food offered to idols (*eidōlothytōn*) was a problem; for at least some of the Corinthian believers, it was not. Paul's words throughout 8:1–11:1 are best understood as addressed to those who disagreed with him. His objective in this section is to convince them to change their behavior by changing their thinking on the matter. To do this, he isolates the basis of their perspective and shows were it is lacking. He then urges them to consider the effects their actions might have on fellow believers.

8:1-6. The basis of the Corinthians' view that eating food offered to idols was not a problem is evident in Paul's opening words in this section. In all probability, when Paul states in v. 1, "We know that *we all have knowledge*," he is repeating a claim made by the Corinthians. Whether their statement "We have knowledge" also included the word "all" is debated.[14] Some commentators think that Paul added the word "all" to counter an assertion by some of the Corinthians that they possessed a special knowledge that was not available to or not understood by certain others within the church.[15] Thus, they were claiming an esoteric knowledge that gave them enlightenment regarding idols that less informed Christians did not have. In response to their smugness then, Paul began by affirming that *all* Christians actually possessed the knowledge that certain believers considered to belong only to them.

At least two problems emerge for this view, however. For one thing, Paul seems to claim in v. 7 that not everyone does, in fact, have this knowledge. It would be odd for Paul to affirm universal Christian possession of the knowledge in question in v. 1 and then admit in v. 7, as his opponents in this issue supposedly claimed, that other believers did not actually possess the knowledge they had. Furthermore, the content of this knowledge does not appear to have been esoteric (much less "Gnostic") at all. When Paul apparently defines this knowledge in v. 4, he seems to use his opponents' own words: "No idol exists in the world" and "No God exists except one." This is hardly secret information belonging to the enlightened few within the church! Undoubtedly, Paul's preaching in Corinth had included an affirmation of the oneness of God and the nonexistence of pagan deities. Whether all of the converts understood the full implications of monotheism may be seriously doubted. That any converts (or outsiders) were unaware of the early Christian movement's claims regarding one true God, however, is highly doubtful. It was a basic tenet of the faith and the chief concept that differentiated the movement from practically every other religion of the time known to them except Judaism. In all probability then, the Corinthians addressed by Paul here had affirmed a basic position that they took for granted every believer shared. In addition to the conclusions that his opponents drew from this general knowledge, Paul challenged their assumption that all believers really did understand the basic concept of monotheism.

Before discussing the content of this knowledge, though, Paul attacks the problem that arises from allowing knowledge to be the determinative criterion for behavior. Knowledge may simply "puff up." Four times before in this letter (4:6, 18, 19; 5:2) Paul charged the Corinthians with being "puffed up." [The Frog and the Ox] In each of the previous instances, his charge was that their self-inflation was groundless and detrimental. Here again, Paul's use of the term *physioō* is intended to deflate pretentious claims to status. "Knowing" in and of itself is inadequate; what one does with what one knows determines one's true standing. Status claimed on the basis of knowledge leads to a ballooned ego that is easily pricked by a greater knowledge. In contrast, Paul asserts that "love builds up." The juxtaposing of "puffing up" and "building up" highlights the emptiness of claims to status based on knowledge. *Substantial* enlargement (i.e., edification) comes by way of love. Later in 10:23, when Paul begins to summarize his argument for the whole section, he makes the point that while "all things are allowed, not all things build up." He follows that with an appeal: "Let no one seek his/her own [edification] but that of the other" (10:24). The basis for that later appeal is already being laid here in v. 1.

The Frog and the Ox

Paul's repeated use of the term *physioō* (to be "puffed up") conveys a humorous belittling of arrogance, which is judged to be nothing more than empty self-inflation. Aesop's often-told fable captures the danger of "puffing up" one's self.

> There was once a frog who noticed an ox standing in the meadow. The frog was seized by a jealous desire to equal the ox in size so she puffed herself up, inflating her wrinkled skin. She then asked her children if she was now bigger than the ox. They said that she was not. Once again she filled herself full of air, straining even harder than before, and asked her children which of the two of them was bigger. "The ox is bigger," said her children. The frog was finally so indignant that she tried even harder to puff herself up, but her body exploded and she fell down dead.

Aesop's Fables: A New Translation by Laura Gibbs (World Classics; Oxford: Oxford University Press, 2002).

The Text of 1 Corinthians 8:2-3

The UBS Greek NT 4th ed. includes the longer reading of both verses as the preferred text. The oldest manuscript (P^{46}), however, omits *ti* ("something") from v. 2 and both *ton theon* ("God") and *hyp' autou* ("by him") from v. 3. The early church fathers Tertullian and Origen both agree with P^{46} for v. 2, while Clement of Alexandria agrees for v. 3. The inclusion of *ti* in v. 2 and *ton theon* in v. 3 is supported by the early papyrus P^{15} (3rd cent.) and by the early uncials ℵ A B D and several other Greek manuscripts and translations, most of which also support *hyp' autou*. The original ℵ agrees with P^{46} in omitting *hyp' autou* from v. 3, but the second corrector added the phrase.

Fee favors the shorter reading for both verses. He argues that in v. 2 the issue is not knowing *something* (*ti*) but thinking that one has real knowledge. He argues that in v. 3 it is not loving *God* that is at issue but rather loving fellow Christians. Also, loving is not tied to *being known by God* but to true knowing. This reading is supported by taking *egnōstai* in v. 3 as middle voice ("has come to know for oneself") rather than passive. He thinks reading the verb as a passive led scribes to insert of *ton theon* and *hyp' autou*.

Besides the unlikelihood that *egnōstai* is in the middle voice, Fee's contention that the shorter reading better fits Paul's argument misconstrues Paul's main objective. He was concerned about the effect "unloving" behavior might have on others, but he was primarily concerned about unwitting participation in idolatry both by persons who lacked full knowledge about the nonexistence of pagan deities and by persons who thought they could safely eat food offered to idols. As Garland observes, loving God and being known by God entails exclusive devotion to the one God. The longer reading, which has far superior textual support, does fit Paul's argument.

Gordon D. Fee, *The First Epistle to the Corinthians* (NICNT; Grand Rapids: Eerdmans Publishing, 1987) 367–68.

David E. Garland, *1 Corinthians* (BECNT; Grand Rapids: Baker Academic, 2003) 370–71, 376–77.

In v. 2, Paul continues his initial challenge of their assumptions about the importance of knowledge. If the maxim "A little knowledge is a dangerous thing" had been available to Paul, he might have used it at this point. Instead, he subverts their reliance on knowledge by subtly raising a question about the extent of their knowledge. He uses two parallel conditional statements that continue his contrast between knowledge and love. Some questions exist about the actual wording of vv. 2-3, but the longer reading given in the UBS Greek New Testament fourth edition is usually accepted. [The Text of 1 Corinthians 8:2-3] Based on that text, the verses read:

v. 2, "If anyone supposes (*dokei*) to know something, he/she does not yet know as it is necessary to know"; v. 3, "but if anyone loves God, this one is known by God."

Paul typically uses *dokeō* to indicate presumptuous knowing that is unsubstantiated (cf. 3:18; 10:12). What they *know* (namely, that there is only one God) is correct, but this is insufficient knowledge. What is "necessary to know" is the proper role for knowledge. Knowledge itself is incomplete and impermanent (cf. 13:8, 12). Love, by contrast, is the "better way" that never "falls" (cf. 12:31b; 13:8a).

Since Paul has just said that love builds up and since he will soon go on to warn about tearing down another believer (v. 11), we might expect at this point for Paul to urge his audience to show love to fellow believers. Instead, he recasts the issue in terms of loving God (cf. Deut 6:5). From this vantage point, what one knows is no longer in the picture. Rather, the focus is on "being known." Paul does not say here that one who loves others knows God, nor that one who loves God knows God, but that one who loves God *is known* by God. Loving the neighbor is, of course, of concern to Paul, and he will quickly address this

matter. The more fundamental issue, however, and the one that drives his argument in the end, is exclusive love for the one God. Love for the God who knows us, not what we know, is the prior issue. This love for God frames Paul's argument about loving the fellow believer who might be harmed by the "knowers'" action. By acting unlovingly, they hinder the weaker believer's exclusive love for God.

The language here is similar to that of Galatians 4:9. There, Paul first states that the Galatians had come to *know* God, but then he rephrases his words by qualifying that, rather, they had come to *be known* by God. [Galatians 4:8-9] The context in the Galatian letter is similar, too. There Paul is concerned that those who were formerly in bondage to beings who were not gods are returning to their enslavement. Here Paul is concerned that the Corinthians will become entrapped, unwittingly through their reliance on their knowledge, to beings who are not gods. In both instances, being known by God places believers in a state that calls for exclusive allegiance to the one God.[16]

Galatians 4:8-9

Formerly, when you did not know God, you were enslaved to beings that by nature are not gods. Now, however, that you have come to know God, or rather to be known by God, how can you turn back again to the weak and beggarly elemental spirits? How can you want to be enslaved to them again? (Gal 4:8-9, NRSV)

Paul restates the topic in v. 4 with a refined focus on the *eating* (*brōseōs*) of food offered to idols. As he did in v. 1, he quotes here from the Corinthians: "No idol [exists] in the world," and "No God [exists] except one." These two statements define the knowledge claimed in the quotation in v. 1. Their dismissal of the existence of "idols" and acknowledgment of the existence of only one God give them, they believe, the freedom to eat food offered to nonentities. Scholars note that the confession of faith embodied in the *Shema* of Deuteronomy 6:4 lies behind the monotheistic claims of these quotations, especially the second one, and behind Paul's commentary on the quotations.[17] [Deuteronomy 6:4] Christianity originated within Judaism and shared its commitment to the concept of one God and the obligations of exclusive devotion this concept demands. Christianity also shared with Judaism an aversion to idolatry.[18] Equally influential, if not more so, to the theology embedded in the quotations were the first two commandments of the Decalogue forbidding the having of other gods and the making of graven images. The frequent use of graven

Deuteronomy 6:4

The RSV rendering of Deut 6:4 is, "Hear, O Israel: The LORD our God is one LORD." The NRSV reads, "Hear, O Israel, The LORD is our God, the LORD alone." The Hebrew syntax (and the Greek of the LXX that mimics the Hebrew) allows for either translation. The RSV reading stresses the unity of God, which may have been of concern to Israel in reaction to the Canaanite practice of seeing the gods of different places as interchangeable. The NRSV translation emphasizes relationship, which may reflect Israel's concern for exclusive allegiance to YHWH. While the first emphasis may to be present in Paul's contrast in 1 Cor 8:5-6 between the many "gods" and "lords" of pagans, the main stress is clearly on exclusive relationship.

Mark E. Biddle, *Deuteronomy* (Smyth & Helwys Bible Commentary; Macon GA: Smyth & Helwys, 2003) 125.

images in pagan worship provided a focal point for the criticism of such worship by Jews and Christians.

Idols signified more to Jews and Christians, however, than they actually did to the adherents of pagan religion. Most smaller Greek and Roman sanctuaries did not have a central cult idol. The images that might be found at such sites were typically of modest size and quality and represented gifts made to the deity to whom the place was dedicated. The temples of larger sanctuaries often did house statues of deities, along with other objects presented as gifts to the honored deity. Pagan temples were essentially storehouses for these donated treasures. In any case, the temple was not viewed as the place where the deity dwelled, and an idol was not considered an embodiment of the deity.[19] Idols were simply one of the several ways that a deity might be honored. The most important way, of course, was by means of the sacrifices burned on the altar. Temple buildings and idols were optional in a sanctuary, but an altar was essential. When the sacrifices were large enough, the portions not actually consumed on the altar could be eaten by those persons present in a banquet that further honored the deity. By eating the food in the precinct of the cult idol, the participants were reminded of whose food they were eating. For them, none of this activity was viewed as worshiping the idol. Rather, they were honoring the deity who might be represented by an idol.

For Paul, though, idols signified much more. The first two commandments of the Decalogue were essentially two sides of one coin. On the one side, exclusive allegiance to the one God was required; on the other side, the use of idols was forbidden. To violate the second commandment was to violate the first. Thus, Jewish and early Christian polemic against pagan religion regularly employed criticism of idolatry. In fact, idolatry in any form signified the forsaking of the commitment to exclusive allegiance to the one God. The anti-idolatry polemic of the Old Testament and other early Jewish writings at times focused on the perceived lunacy of worshiping lifeless images of nonexistent deities (e.g., Isa 44:9-17; Wis 13-15). At other times, though, the attack on idols focused on the evil beings actually being worshiped when one bowed down to an idol (e.g., Deut 32:17; Ps 106:36-37; *Jub.* 22:17). For the Corinthians who saw no problem eating food sacrificed to idols, the first type of polemic—that idols represented nonexistent deities—was determinative. For Paul, though, the second type—that idolatry involved the worship of demons—carried more weight.[20] Paul could agree with the Corinthians' position to an extent, but his own view saw a demonic danger lurking behind the lifeless idols.

Recognizing that some agreement and tension existed between Paul and the Corinthians in this matter aids an understanding of the confusing structure of 8:5-6. [Translating 1 Corinthians 8:5-6] Verse 5 is Paul's response to the statement "No idol exists in the world." "If there are so-called gods and lords either in heaven or on earth," Paul counters, "then in a sense there are many gods and many lords." As noted above, in Galatians 4:8 Paul refers to "beings who are not gods" and recognizes their power to enslave persons. In 1 Corinthians 10:20, Paul identifies the beings who actually receive the food offered to idols as demons. These beings are not gods. Pagans, however, call these beings gods and lords, and there are many of them. From Paul's perspective, these beings are misidentified as gods and lords, but they exist nonetheless. Asserting that Paul means here that these false gods exist in the pagans' minds and are thus real to them misses his point. They are real for Paul too, but they are not gods. Trying to identify which beings Paul understands as those in heaven or on earth or distinguishing between which ones he thinks are mislabeled as "gods" or "lords" is not really helpful. He uses these terms generically and interchangeably for all the beings people mistakenly think are gods. As a group, they stand in contrast to the one God and one Lord of believers.

Verse 6, then, is Paul's response to the statement "No God exists except one" in light of his qualification in v. 5. The Corinthians denied the reality of idols (and the beings idols represent) and affirmed the existence of the one God. Paul affirms the reality of the beings represented by idols but refuses to recognize them as gods. In contrast to the pagans who call these beings gods and lords, Paul (and fellow believers) recognize only God the Father as "God" and Jesus Christ only as "Lord." As recognized by several scholars, the titles "God" and "Lord" reflect the terminology of the *Shema* (Deut 6:4), but Paul has reconfigured this basic confession of allegiance to the one God to provide a crucial place for Jesus Christ as the one Lord. The role Jesus Christ has in Paul's reconfiguration closely resembles that of *Sophia* in Hellenistic-Jewish

Translating 1 Corinthians 8:5-6

AΩ The first half of v. 5 expresses the supposition of a conditional sentence: "For indeed, if there are so-called gods either in heaven or upon earth." A question arises as to the second half of the conditional sentence, that is, the fulfillment part of the "if, then" statement. Most translations and interpretations understand v. 6 to be the completion of the condition: "but for us [there is] one God the father. . . ." The second half of v. 5 ("as there are many gods and many lords") is taken as Paul's grammatically awkward insertion into the conditional sentence as a qualification of the supposition. Thiselton observes that the "but" with which v. 6 begins "strictly interrupts the syntax as if v. 5 had already functioned as a main clause." Still, he supports reading v. 6 as the fulfillment of the condition. The awkwardness of v. 5b and the rough beginning of v. 6 are removed if we follow Smit's suggestion that v. 5b is actually the fulfillment part of the conditional sentence. Thus, he translates all of v. 5 as "If indeed there are so-called gods either in heaven or on earth, then in that sense there are many gods and many lords." Verse 5, then, is Paul's response to the Corinthian quotation "No idol exists in the world." Verse 6 is Paul's commentary on their quotation "No God exists but one" in light of his qualification of their first statement.

Joop F. M. Smit, "1 Corinthians 8,1-6, a Rhetorical Partitio: A Contribution to the Coherence of 1 Cor 8,1-11,1," in *The Corinthian Correspondence* (BETL 125; ed. Reimund Bieringer; Leuven, Belgium: Peeters Press, 1996) 585.

Anthony C. Thiselton, *The First Epistle to the Corinthians: A Commentary on the Greek Text* (NIGTC; Grand Rapids: Eerdmans, 2000) 631.

wisdom literature and the *logos* in Stoicism and Philo (and what appears after Paul's time in John 1:1-3).[21] God the Father is the origin (*from* whom) and the destination (*to* whom) of all things, while Jesus Christ the Lord is the agent (*through* whom) both of the creation of all things and of the consummation of our arrival at the destination. The formulaic nature of v. 6 may indicate that Paul employs here some version of a creedal statement known to his readers.[22] In any case, the verse not only gives Jesus a crucial role in God's work but also firmly establishes the exclusivity of commitment to the one God and one Lord. No room is left for dabbling in activity associated with the many wrongly identified gods and lords represented by idols.

8:7-13. In the first six verses, Paul has laid out the basic issues to be argued. Certain Corinthians believe that the knowledge all Christians possess permits them to eat food offered to idols without any repercussions. The knowledge in question is the basic Christian conviction that only one God exists and that idols represent nonexistent deities. Paul has already made two qualifications regarding this knowledge. First, such knowledge in itself is insufficient. It must be subservient to love, both the love for God and for the neighbor. Second, their knowledge about nonexistent deities is only partly correct. Suprahuman beings who are not gods do exist, and idolatry is their medium for subverting the allegiance that believers should have exclusively for the one God. In chapter 10, Paul will take up his second qualification again and make it clear that all believers should avoid any kind of interaction with idolatry, no matter how safe it may appear to be. Before making that argument, he returns to his first qualification and argues for abstention from eating food offered to idols on the basis of love for other persons. This argument runs from 8:7 through the end of chapter 9.

Verse 7 establishes the first reason why the knowledge claimed in v. 1 is inadequate: this knowledge is not *in* everyone. The use of the article (*hō*) before the word "knowledge" specifies a particular knowledge, namely that claimed by the Corinthian opponents regarding the nonexistence of idols. The use of the preposition "in" suggests that while all believers may give assent to the belief that only one God exists, some do not understand the full implications of this belief regarding the deities represented by idols. In all probability, Paul is referring here to persons recently converted to the faith. As neophyte believers, they are not sufficiently distanced from their previous religious ideas to avoid perceiving their new religion through the lens of the old. Paul appears very sensitive here to a practical reality: it takes time to grow in the faith.

Paul further explains the problem. Since they have been accustomed to viewing the gods represented by idols as *real*, they would still see the food offered to idols as *really* dedicated to those beings. They have neither the perspective of the Corinthian "knowers" that those gods do not *really* exist nor the perspective of Paul that the *real* beings represented by idols are not actually gods. This deficiency in their perspective is the key to understanding what Paul means here by a "weak" conscience. [Conscience] They simply do not yet possess a sufficiently informed moral guidance system to refrain from eating such food *as if* it really were being offered to idols. For the "knowers," the food is innocuous, and they can eat it while sneering at those superstitious pagans who do not know the truth that their gods are nonexistent. For the believer whose conscience is still immature ("weak"), the food is charged with religious significance. If they eat it, they believe that they are participating in pagan worship of the gods represented by the idols. In doing so, their conscience (i.e., what moral guidance system they do possess) is "polluted" (*molynetai*) by their reverting back to idolatry. It is not that they would eat it against their better judgment or that they would reluctantly bow to the scorn of the "knowers" and eat under pressure; they would willingly eat it as an actual offering to a god because, following the example of the "knowers," they would erroneously conclude that such eating was permissible for believers. The full implication of the basic knowledge that all believers supposedly have, namely that "for us there is one God and one Lord," would be compromised by their conscious reversion to polytheism. Thus, they would be in violation of the commandment that follows the *Shema*, namely, to *love* God with undivided devotion. [Deuteronomy 6:5]

Conscience

AΩ The word translated "conscience" (*syneidēsis*) is often taken to mean either a person's consciousness of himself or herself in relation to others (Maurer) or one's inner moral convictions (Murphy-O'Connor, Gooch). In the first instance, a *weak* conscience would involve a person's sense of inferiority in comparison to others, a situation that could lead to caving in to pressure. In the second instance, a weak conscience would involve going against one's better judgment and engaging in some action believed to be wrong. Neither of these really fits Paul's concern in 1 Cor 8. The person of *weak* conscience does not possess the inner moral guidance system needed to make the correct decision (Garland's moral compass). Such a person is neither pressured to perform a certain action because of a sense of inferiority, nor is that person going against better judgment. He or she has poor judgment and simply follows the example of other believers who are eating food offered to idols.

David E. Garland, *1 Corinthians* (BECNT; Grand Rapids: Baker Academic, 2003) 383–84, 393–94.

Paul W. Gooch, "'Conscience' in 1 Corinthians 8 and 10," *NTS* 33 (1987): 244–54.

Christian Maurer, "*synoida, syneidēsis*," *TDNT* 7:899–919.

Jerome Murphy-O'Connor, "Freedom or the Ghetto (I Cor. viii, 1-13; x,23-xi,1)," *RB* 85 (1978): 543–74.

Deuteronomy 6:5

You shall love the LORD your God with all your heart, and with all your soul, and with all your might. (Deut 6:5, NRSV)

Having delineated the problem the behavior of the "knowers" might pose for those of "weak" conscience, Paul unfurls his argument designed to persuade the "knowers" to abstain from eating food offered to idols. Several interpreters take v. 8 to contain a verbatim or paraphrased quotation of an argument used by the Corinthians to defend their position.[23] Supposedly, they argue that food is neutral. It will not "bring us into God's presence" (either in the positive sense of "commending" one to God or in the negative sense of "bringing one into judgment before" God, depending on how one translates *parastēsei*). We are neither "better off" (*perisseuomen*) nor "worse off" (*hysteroumetha*) for eating. This verse makes better sense, however, if we see the statements as Paul's own words. Paul is not neutral about eating food offered to idols. It serves no recognizable, religious benefit. It will not "commend" us to God. We are not "lacking" (*hysteroumetha*) if we do not eat, and we are not "abounding" (*perisseuomen*) if we do.[24] One may argue that not eating the food may have harmed the Corinthians in some way regarding their social status since it was an *expected* practice of good citizens, but that is not Paul's concern.[25] He is concerned about their status before God. Eating food offered to idols does nothing to enhance one's relationship with God. In fact, as he will later show, it can destroy that relationship.

His primary argument at this stage, however, is not about the effects of eating on the "eater" but on the "weak observer." Thus, he issues a warning to the "knowers": "Beware lest this right of yours become a stumbling block for the weak!" The Corinthians presume they have a "right" (*exousia*) to eat such food. [*Exousia*] Paul does not challenge that presumption directly, perhaps because in some sense he does recognize the existence of a certain right. He does, however, challenge one's use of such a right. The right in question is not grounded in a theological conviction with which Paul partly agrees, for he does not accept their argument that the nonexistence of idols/gods negates any negative consequences of eating food offered to idols. He is not asking them to forgo a right based on conviction, though they may have argued on that basis that it was acceptable to use their right. More likely, it is a political right based on their status as Corinthian citizens.[26] They have a legal right (with accompanying social pressure) to eat such food. His argument in 10:1-22 makes little sense if Paul agrees with them theologically here, and his argument in chapter 9 loses its effect if they actually have no right of any kind.[27] They may have a political right, but for reasons of theology and ethics, Paul urges them not to exercise it.

Exousia

ΑΩ The term *exousia* is often translated "power" or "authority." Unlike the word *dynamis*, however, it does not mean "power" in the sense of having the innate ability to do something. It refers, instead, to a recognized capability of performing a certain action either because of no external deterrent or because of an "authorization" by an external source to do something. Hence, it is often translated "right," and this is the sense in which Paul uses the term in 1 Cor 8:8 and in ch. 9. The issue is "rights," not "power" (contra Garland *et al.*). The Corinthians are not claiming a power stemming from their supposed "knowledge," though this knowledge reinforces for them their "right" to eat food offered to idols.

Werner Foerster, "ἔξεστιν, ἐξουσία κτλ," TDNT 2:560–75.

David E. Garland, *1 Corinthians* (BECNT; Grand Rapids: Baker Academic, 2003) 386.

Paul then sets up a hypothetical situation in v. 10 in which the exercising of this right would prove detrimental to a believer with a weak conscience. Though the situation is hypothetical in context in that Paul does not claim that such an event has actually happened, it reflects a real danger. Paul asks a question that assumes a positive answer: If a person of weak conscience should see a "knower" reclining in an idol's temple (*eidōleiō*), would not that person be built up (*oikodomēthēsetai*) to eat food offered to idols? As noted above, the term *eidōleion* is a pejorative label applied to pagan religious structures including temples, temple complexes, and other shrines housing elements of pagan religion. (See [Tomb Shrines].) The reference to reclining (*katakeimenon*) indicates that some kind of banqueting is envisioned since that was the normal posture at such affairs. Hence, Paul portrays them as participating in a meal in a religious setting. Sarcastic irony is probably intended when Paul says that this setting would "build up" the weak-conscience person *so as to eat* (*eis to esthiein*) the food offered to idols.[28] As he soon shows, this knowledge-based, unloving behavior does not "build up" but, instead, leads to destruction.

Some commentators understand the situation envisioned to be one in which the "knowers" are actively *encouraging* (a possible meaning of *oikodomeō*) the weak believers to eat the food, perhaps as a way of enabling them to overcome their immature scruples and step up to the higher plane of spiritual enlightenment.[29] Nothing in the text, however, suggests that Paul is accusing the "knowers" of this. He is alerting them to a danger that they have not considered. If someone should see them participating in temple meals, that person will formulate the idea on his or her own that such participation is acceptable for a believer. Since that person's conscience is weak, he or she does not have the moral guidance system necessary for comprehending the dangers involved. Instead of actually "building up" a fellow believer, as the "knowers" would do if they were guided by love, their "up-puffing" knowledge is causing someone else to fall.

The seriousness of the consequences of the careless behavior in bringing about the destruction of the weak person is highlighted by identifying that person as "a *brother* for whom *Christ died*" (v. 11). This person is not simply some acquaintance or even a friend; this person is a member of the family of Christ. Christ died for the sake of this person, but that death is for naught because of the inconsiderate insistence by those who claim to have knowledge that eating food offered to idols is harmless. In actuality then, the offense is not only against a fellow believer; it amounts to sinning against Christ.

Reclining in a Temple

Dining Couches in the Corinthian Asklepieion. (Credit: Scott Nash)

Some commentators argue that since reclining was involved, the setting had to be one of the dining rooms found in a temple precinct. Many even point to specific sites in Corinth as possible locations, including the sanctuary of Demeter and Kore on the north slope of the Acrocorinth (Gooch) and the sanctuary of Asklepios (Fotopoulos) on the southern edge of the city. Though some dining on a small scale may have still occurred in the sanctuary of Demeter and Kore, the dining complexes often referred to were no longer used for such purposes in the Roman period. Oster misuses the published archaeological report when he insists that some of the dining rooms "were in use during the time of Paul's ministry in Corinth" (65). The buildings that formerly housed dining rooms were rebuilt—but not as dining rooms. Gooch (followed by Newton and Cheung) acknowledges the disuse of the dining rooms but still insists the archaeological evidence points to extensive dining in the sanctuary in the Roman period. The excavator, Bookidis (158 n. 81), grants that artifactual remains indicate that there "may have been dining on the site," but it had certainly diminished from the scale of previous periods.

As for the Asklepieion, the evidence is slightly more promising in identifying that site as a potential location for the kind of reclined dining Paul mentions. Some interpreters, including the excavator (Roebuck) downplay the connection between the dining rooms located directly below the temple and the temple cultus itself. Much of the reason for doing so stems from a misreading of Pausanias, who made reference to the temple of Asklepios and a fountain complex known as the Lerna. Thinking that the courtyard, fountain system, and dining chambers below the Asklepieion were the Lerna, some have insisted that this area had a nonreligious, public function. With the location of the Lerna now being identified elsewhere, the area in question is better seen as a part of the Asklepieion (so Fotopouolos, 51–69). The peripheral location of the Asklepieion and the rather restricted view of the dining rooms, however, makes it unlikely that it would have been the only site for the kind of dining that concerned Paul.

Winter (281) prefers to locate the dining questioned by Paul in the sanctuary of Poseidon on the Isthmus of Corinth about twelve miles to the east of Corinth. While the Isthmian Games, which were held every two years, do provide a likely setting for such dining, the return of the festival to its traditional home on the Isthmus may postdate 1 Corinthians (as Winters acknowledges).

The temples located in or near Corinth's forum offer other possible locations, though no exact location for ritual dining has been identified. The forum itself, the theater area to its north, or a host of other sites in Corinth may have been the place or places (more likely) where people could recline to dine at numerous festivals in honor of various pagan deities, including the emperor. No one site commends itself as *the* location or even the most probable place of reclined dining. (For references, see [Temple Dining in Corinth] above.)

Verse 13 both concludes the first part of Paul's argument and provides a transition to the second part. What follows in chapter 9 is an extended elaboration on the principle Paul interjects here. He has been addressing his audience in the second person. Now he switches to the first person. In contrast to their behavior, which fails to take into consideration its devastating effects on someone else, Paul espouses the principle of self-restraint out of regard for another's well-being. If what he ate should become a stumbling block (v. 9) that causes someone to fall (*skandalizei*), Paul would choose to forgo eating meat forever. The verb *skandalizein* could mean "to cause offense," but that meaning does not adequately capture Paul's intention here. The person of weak conscience is not *offended* by someone eating food offered to idols. As argued above, a *weak* conscience is not one having more scruples over food than one that is not weak. It is a conscience that is immature and cannot adequately guide the person to make the right decision. What is at stake here is not offense; it is destruction. The example of the supposed "knowers" causes the person to fall into sin. Paul's principle embraces the responsibility believers have for the well-being of fellow believers.

Paul's reference to meat here has led many commentators to see only meat in question in regard to the food offered to idols, but it is unlikely that Paul would have condoned eating other types of food offered to idols besides meat. More likely, Paul hypothetically renounces meat here for rhetorical impact. Giving up all food would be impossible. Giving up bread or cheese would hardly be impressive. Giving up meat, which for nonvegetarians is typically the food of choice, demonstrates the seriousness of making sacrifices for the sake of another person.

Types of Food Offered to Idols

The sanctuary of Demeter on the Acrocorinth. (Credit: Scott Nash)

In 1994 Nancy Bookidis led an archaeological excavation in the sanctuary of Demeter and Kore on the lower, north slope of the Acrocorinth that involved the analysis of flora and fauna finds. Having already determined in earlier excavations that the site contained numerous large dining facilities during the Classical and Hellenistic (but not Roman) periods, the aim of the analysis was to identify what was consumed. Most of the food eaten on site was similar to regular, domestic fare, but given the setting and what is known about the rituals of Demeter worship, it is likely that much of the food had religious significance even if it was not part of an actual sacrifice. Plant finds identified included wheat, barley, grape, fig, and olive. Animal finds included domestic pig, domestic sheep and goat, fish, and sea urchin. The numerous rodent and reptilian bones also found were from natural residents of the site presumably not used in meals. Except for the absence of bovine remains, the finds at the site are similar to what would be found in most religious settings where food was consumed. The focus of the analysis of flora and fauna remains at the sanctuary of Demeter and Kore was on the Classical and Hellenistic periods, the periods when ritual dining was known to have occurred on a large scale. The results, however, reinforce what is known about food offerings in all periods, including the early Roman. Food offered to idols included much more than meat.

Nancy Bookidis et al., "Dining in the Sanctuary of Demeter and Kore at Corinth," *Hesperia* 68 (1999): 1–54.

The Example of Paul as a Guide to Solving the Problem, 9:1-27

In 8:7-13, Paul has presented his first proof to counter the statement "We all have knowledge" that is being used by some of the believers in Corinth to justify their continued participation in meals involving food offered to idols. Such knowledge "puffs up" the possessor and, as Paul has shown, causes others to fall. The first proof focused on the harmful effects the "knowers'" exercising of their "right" might have on a believer with a weak conscience. Now Paul will offer a positive example of forgoing rights for the sake of others.

Many interpreters see Paul departing here from the main topic in order to give a defense of his apostleship. That view, however, misses the clear connection that chapter 9 has with what precedes it and what follows it. It also misconstrues what Paul is actually doing in chapter 9. He is not defending his right *to be* an apostle; he is explaining why he has not exercised his rights *as* an apostle. Furthermore, his explanation is not designed to defend his behavior but rather to convince others to follow his example.[30]

9:1-18. Paul begins with a series of four questions that presume a "yes" answer. The first two questions ("Am I not free? Am I not an apostle?") actually reveal the design of the whole chapter. The last two questions reinforce the second question. Paul will deal with the subject of freedom posed by the first question in vv. 19-23, but he will first address the matter of apostolic rights introduced by his second question.

Paul's assertion in 8:13 that he would give up eating meat rather than cause a fellow believer to fall takes on added significance in light of his identity. He is an apostle. The basis of his apostleship is his witness to the resurrected Lord. The confirmation of his apostolic calling is his founding of churches such as the one in Corinth. In fact, the Corinthian congregation is, as Paul put, the "certification" (*sphragis* = lit., "seal") of his apostolic status. For them, Paul contends, his status is unchallenged. They know who and what he is. The one who seeks to persuade them is a recognized apostle. While this status as an apostle should add weight to his argument, asserting apostolic authority is not his main objective. The emphasis is not so much on the status of the one who instructs them but on the status of the one who relinquishes apostolic rights for the sake of others.

Paul then unloads a barrage of questions that reflect the basic objection one might raise about the sacrificial behavior Paul espoused in 8:13.[31] The scenario envisioned is one in which someone might ask, "But Paul, why do you deprive yourself? Aren't you an apostle who is entitled to certain benefits?" He introduces the questions by describing them as the "answer" (*apologia*) he would give to anyone who might "evaluate" (*anakrinousin*) his behavior (cf. 4:3-4). The questions appear in three groups with three questions (or three pairs) in each group. [Paul's Questions in 1 Corinthians 9:4-12] Cumulatively, the questions build an imposing tower of support for the financial "rights" of an apostle. In the end, though, Paul pulls the rug from under the tower, and the whole edifice crumbles.

The first three questions focus directly on the "right" of an apostle to receive financial support. The question about food and drink should not be seen as a general statement about the freedom to eat and drink what one chooses, though it does relate to the larger matter at hand. Rather it concerns the right of an apostle to be fed by those to whom they minister. Likewise, the question about having a wife accompany them is not about permitting apostles to marry. [Apostolic Wives] The question actually concerns the obligation of the churches to provide support to the spouse who might travel with the apostle. Apparently, Paul's readers knew that other apostles, including the brothers of Jesus and Cephas, took advantage of this spousal benefit. Paul does not intend to distinguish between apostles and the brothers of Jesus, as if they were distinct groups. Rather he names from among the apostles the brothers of Jesus and Cephas because these apostles in particular were undoubtedly the best known.

The Corinthians must have also known that only Barnabas did the same as Paul in not depending on the financial support of their congregations. Both worked for a living. Later, in 2 Corinthians (11:7-12; 12:13), Paul will respond to criticism about his policy of supporting himself through physical labor rather than depending on the church, but we have no hint here that the practice was already causing anyone to question his apostolic status. Here, Paul's point is that even though he and Barnabas

Paul's Questions in 1 Corinthians 9:4-12

Paul's asks three groups of questions in this section, with each group consisting of three questions or three pairs of questions.

Group 1

v. 4—"Do we not have a right to eat and drink?"
v. 5—"Do we not have a right [for] a believing wife to accompany?"
v. 6—"Do only I and Barnabas not have a right not to work?"

Group 2

v. 7a—"Who soldiers always at his own expense?"
v. 7b—"Who plants a vineyard and does not eat its fruit?"
v. 7c—"Who shepherds sheep and does not eat from the milk of the sheep?"

Group 3

v. 8—"We do not say this according to a human standard, do we? or does the law not say this?"
vv. 9b-10a—"It is not about oxen that God is concerned, is it? or does it certainly speak concerning us?"
v. 11-12a—"If we have sown spiritual things in you, [is it] a great thing if we reap your physical things?"
"If others share this right of you, do not we even more [share this right]?"

Apostolic Wives

In 1 Cor 9:5, Paul refers to a "sister woman" (*adelphēn gynaika*) as one who may rightly accompany an apostle. Some early church interpreters balked at the idea of noncelibate apostles and understood the reference to be either to a Christian female attendant of the apostles or to an apostle's wife who lived with him in a celibate relationship. The term *adelphē*, however, is more appropriately taken to mean "believer" in the same way that male believers are often referred to as "brothers" (cf. 1 Cor 8:11-13). The "believing wife" who accompanies her apostle-husband is entitled to financial support from the congregations the same as the man.

Anthony C. Thiselton, *The First Epistle to the Corinthians: A Commentary on the Greek Text* (NIGTC; Grand Rapids: Eerdmans, 2000) 680.

Working for a Living

Paul seems to have adopted the practice of largely supporting himself as a bivocational minister by performing manual labor. While the opportunities for making a living at this trade may have been greater in Corinth than in some other places, given the ongoing need for leather products such as sails for the many ships passing that way and the tents needed by vendors and the temporary visitors to the various festivals, Paul states that he was frequently in need. Though he did accept financial support from other churches, he preferred to live at a subsistence level (or below) rather than receive money from the church to which he was ministering at the time. Working for a living was not in itself viewed negatively, but persons who plied trades and crafts involving manual labor were often looked down upon by the more leisurely classes. Paul's insistence on supporting himself in this way freed him from obligations to supporters and enabled him to offer the gospel free of charge. It did, however, cause some concern within the Corinthian church, at least by the time 2 Corinthians was written. Paul gives no signal that the rumblings of criticism were already present at the time of 1 Corinthians. In fact, his right to boast of such labor would have been lessened if he were already being criticized.

Ronald F. Hock, *The Social Context of Paul's Ministry: Tentmaking and Apostleship* (Philadelphia: Fortress Press, 1980).

support themselves, as apostles they have the same right to financial support as the others. [Working for a Living]

The second trio of questions (v. 7) draws on the common expectation of other professions to reinforce the practice of financial support for apostles. Who would ever serve as a soldier without provisions? Who would plant a vineyard without eating some of the grapes? Who would tend sheep and not benefit from some of the sheep's milk? All of these examples point to the normal expectation that workers will have their basic necessities taken care of from within the realm of their work. The policy of providing basic support for apostles, then, is in accordance with the widely accepted practice for other professions.

The final group of questions used to construct the basic point of apostolic rights includes three pairs of questions. The first pair in v. 8 moves beyond the human practice (*kata anthrōpon*) depicted in v. 7 and gives the policy of supporting apostles divine sanction ("Do I say this according to human standards or does not the law say this?"). Paul asserts that the Law of Moses also supports this policy, and in v. 9a he quotes Deuteronomy 25:4: "You shall not muzzle an ox while it is treading out the grain."

The second pair of questions pertains to how the quoted text should be applied: "Is God concerned about oxen or does [God] certainly (*pantōs*) speak for our sakes?" [Pantōs] Some commentators consider Paul to be using the Old Testament passage allegorically, without any consideration for its original meaning or context.[32] Hays has argued, however, that the larger context of the single verse in Deuteronomy has to do with issues of justice and provision for the needy. Given the focus of Deuteronomy 24–25, Hays thinks it would not have been surprising for Paul to assume this verse also had to do with human economic affairs.[33] Hanson argues, though, that Paul's analogical use of the text closely resembles the way rabbis later treated the passage. Without ignoring its original sense, they found in it a principle that could be applied to other situations not directly addressed in Scripture.[34] That does appear to be Paul's intention here. As the ox is allowed to eat from the grain

Pantōs

ΑΩ Some interpreters criticize Paul for ignoring the intention of Deut 25:4 in its original context. He seems to show no regard for the ox that the rule in Deuteronomy was intended to protect. Instead, according to this view, Paul rips the verse out of context and claims that it applies *only* to the situation he is addressing in 1 Cor 9, namely, the right of apostles to receive financial support from churches. This understanding is partly based on reading *pantōs* in 1 Cor 9:10 as "only," "entirely," or "altogether." As pointed out in BADG (614), however, *pantos* clearly has such a meaning only when used in a negative expression. In the only two instances where Paul uses *pantōs* with the negative particle *ou/ouk* (Rom 3:6; 1 Cor 16:12), it does mean "not at all." In 1 Cor 9:22, however, *pantōs* clearly cannot mean "only" or "entirely" because he is talking about saving *some*. Of the seventeen instances BADG lists for *pantōs* used in a positive sense, only in *Barnabas* 1:4 and the Shepherd of Hermas (*Similitude* 1:5) can it mean "altogether." Paul's intention, it seems, was to affirm that the passage from Deuteronomy *certainly* applies to the church, without dismissing its original application to the poor ox.

threshed through its efforts, the apostles should rightly feed from the threshing floor of their labors. For Paul, Scripture was alive and relevant for his own day, so from his perspective, he could say, "certainly God spoke [this] on our behalf."

In answering his own question, Paul affirms in v. 10b that the Scripture was written "on account of us" and then follows this affirmation in the rest of v. 10 with a proverb-like statement that some interpreters take to be a quotation from an unknown source.[35] The presence of *hoti* immediately after "it was written" (*hoti* often introduces the content of what was written or said) suggests to them that Paul has moved on to another quotation that he claims was also written "for our sakes." Fee points out, however, that Paul never uses the aorist passive form of *graphō* (which is what we have here in *egraphē*) as an introductory formula to a quotation.[36] The *hoti* is better rendered "because," and what follows is not a quotation from some unknown source but rather Paul's explanation of why Deuteronomy 25:4 applies to the situation he is discussing: "Because the plower ought to plow in hope and the thresher in hope of sharing." His point is that human workers likewise appropriately work in hope of receiving a share of the fruits of their labors. This point reinforces his main point in the argument so far, that the apostles have a right to be supported by the churches.

The final pair of questions Paul uses in constructing his edifice of apostolic rights comes in vv. 11-12. The "we" in these verses could be all the apostles, except for the last one in v. 12, which must refer only to Paul and his coworkers. As sowers of spiritual things, are they not entitled to their share of material things? Verse 12 puts the crowning touch on his tower of support for the rights of apostles: What is true of all the apostles who may have sown among the Corinthians is even more true in regard to Paul, given his special founding relationship to them. If anyone is entitled to a *share* of financial support, it is certainly he, is it not?

Then comes the swift kick that knocks the tower over and along with it any claims by the Corinthians to exercise their right to eat food offered to idols. Though Paul and his associates clearly have a "right," they have not taken advantage of it (v. 12b). They prefer to endure everything, including impoverishment, rather than give any kind of impediment (*enkopēn*) to the gospel of Christ. In 8:9, Paul charged the "knowers" with putting a stumbling block (*proskomma*) before the weak, and in 8:13, he asserted that he would forgo eating meat rather than cause a fellow believer to fall (*skandalizei*). Here he expands his willingness to incur personal loss to everything (*panta*) and his avoidance of harmful action to anything (*tina*). The contrast between those guided by knowledge (the "knowers") and those guided by love (Paul) is sharply drawn. Parallels with his description of giving up something previously considered significant in Philippians 3:4-9 also come to mind. [Philippians 3:4b-9]

Philippians 3:4b-9

If anyone has reason to be confident in the flesh, I have more: circumcised on the eighth day, a member of the people of Israel, of the tribe of Benjamin, a Hebrew born of Hebrews; as to the law, a Pharisee; as to zeal, a persecutor of the church; as to righteousness under the law, blameless.

Yet whatever gains I had, these I have come to regard as loss because of Christ. More than that, I regard everything as loss because of the surpassing value of knowing Christ Jesus my Lord. For his sake I have suffered the loss of all things, and I regard them as rubbish, in order that I may gain Christ and be found in him, not having a righteousness of my own that comes from the law, but one that comes through faith in Christ, the righteousness from God based on faith. (NRSV)

To remind his audience once again of how significant his self-sacrifice is, Paul returns for a moment to the edifice he has just toppled. This time, though, he draws his example of workers' being entitled to appropriate support from the realm of religious cult. The two clauses ("those who conduct the sacred things [*hiera*] eat from the temple [*hierou*]," "those who attend to the altar share in the altar") may signify two different groups, but the absence of a conjunction suggests that the second clause further refines the first. Those who conduct sacrifices are known to receive a portion of the sacrificial food. [Which Temple?]

Which Temple?

AΩ Whether Paul is speaking generally about temple sacrifices or specifically about the Jerusalem temple cannot be determined. The NT typically uses *hieron* in reference to the Jerusalem temple, but Paul never refers to that structure, unless he is doing so here. In the one instance where he refers to pagan temples without using the pejorative term *eidōleion* (Rom 2:22), he calls them *hierosyleis*. He prefers the term naos when referring to the church or believers as the temple of God (1 Cor 3:16-17; 6:19; 2 Cor 6:16). In light of his rigid rejection of any association with pagan temples or sacrifices in 1 Corinthians, it seems more likely to me that his neutral terminology here must refer to the Jerusalem temple.

In similar fashion, the Lord directed (*dietaxen*) those who proclaim the gospel to make their living out of the gospel (v. 14). Paul's appeal to this teaching of Christ reflects familiarity with some form of the tradition later embedded in the Synoptic Gospels (Mark 6:7-11; Matt 10:1-15; Luke 9:1-5; 10:1-12). Matthew's account (10:10b) has Jesus saying, "For the laborer deserves his food," while Luke (10:7) has, "For the laborer deserves his wages." Citing this tradition places the seal on Paul's defense of apostolic rights, which he has deliberately rejected. The verb *diatassō* typically means to "order" or "command" (as it does in 1 Cor 7:17 and 16:1, and perhaps 11:34b). Paul appears, then, to be defying a command of Christ by not accepting support from the church in Corinth. Paul interprets the provision for apostolic support not as a command, however, but as a *right.* He may take advantage of this right sanctioned by the Lord, or he may not. The choice is his. Then again, as he will now show, he is compelled to relinquish his apostolic rights not simply because of his choice but because of his understanding of his calling as an apostle of the gospel of Christ.

In the final part of his argument about forgoing his right as an apostle (vv. 15-18), Paul focuses not on how this sacrifice benefits others (as we might expect him to do) but rather on how it benefits him. The nature of this benefit, however, is not what his readers would have expected. He switches from the plural used in vv. 11-12 to the emphatic singular: "I myself have not made use of any of these [rights]." He quickly adds that he did not compose the preceding argument of support for apostolic rights in an effort to secure such rights either. Paul's passion in this matter becomes evident not only in the substance of what he writes but also in the broken sentence structure by which he expresses it: "For it would be good for me rather to die than . . . !—No one will void (*kenōsei*) my boasting!" (v. 15).

The only other time Paul used the verb *kenoō* in this letter was in reference to the cross of Christ (1:17); there is a connection to his use here. Paul stated early in this letter that he did not preach the gospel in eloquent words of wisdom so as not to "empty" (or "void") the word of the cross. He also referred to "boasting" in that context and insisted that the only grounds for boasting was "in the Lord" (1:31). Here Paul dares to boast, but his boasting is not grounded in his success as an apostle, nor even in the fact that he is an apostle with certain rights. Rather, his brief boasting here foreshadows the extended boasting that comes in 2 Corinthians 11:16–12:13 when he finds himself defending his apostleship from, among other things, criticism because he does not accept financial support from the Corinthians. [2 Corinthians 11:30] In both instances, his boasting consists of things his readers would have considered demeaning, not enhancing. For Paul, this was consistent with the very gospel he preached. The word of the cross proclaims one who "emptied himself, taking on the form of a slave" (Phil 2:7) for the sake of others. That word is "voided" when the one who proclaims it uses it for self-exaltation. It is proclaimed in power when the one

2 Corinthians 11:30

If I must boast, I will boast of the things that show my weakness. (NRSV)

who preaches it takes on the form of the self-giving, crucified slave of all. Paul will neither "void" the gospel nor his boasting in proclaiming it by using his preaching to enhance his status or financial well-being.

Paul explains that preaching the gospel in and of itself is no grounds for boasting (v. 16). He is only doing what he has to do; he cannot do otherwise. Much as the Old Testament prophets sometimes asserted, Paul states that he preaches under compulsion, even "necessity" (*anankē*). [Prophetic Compulsion] If he were preaching simply of his own free will, then he might expect to be paid for doing the job he agreed to do. He would be a hired hand, preaching for wages. In v. 17, Paul makes a play on words between "willingly" (*ekōn*) and "unwillingly" (*akōn*). With the wordplay Paul does not mean to suggest that he preaches the gospel reluctantly against his will. He means that he preaches not simply as a matter of choice. He did not enlist for duty; he was drafted. What he was drafted to, however, is "more than a job," to quote an advertisement for "today's" U.S. Army. Paul has been "entrusted" (*pepisteumai*) with a "stewardship" (*oikonomian*). In 4:1, he insisted that he and the other apostles should be viewed as "assistants" (*hypēretas*) of Christ and "managers" (*oikonomous*) of the mysteries of God. As the term *oikonomos* there suggests someone who has been placed in charge of the household, *oikonomia* here conveys the sense of responsibility placed on one so entrusted by the lord of the household (God).

Prophetic Compulsion

Paul's stated sense of preaching the gospel out of necessity resembles the sentiment expressed by some OT prophets.

The lion has roared;
who will not fear?
The Lord God has spoken;
who can but prophesy? (Amos 3:8; NRSV)

If I say, "I will not mention him,
or speak any more in his name,"
then within me there is something
like a burning fire
shut up in my bones;
I am weary with holding it in,
and I cannot. (Jer 20:9, NRSV)

With this language, Paul is already setting the stage for the second part of his argument in vv. 19-23, in which he answers his initial question about being free (9:1) by describing himself as a slave to all. For Paul, though, the language is not simply posturing for effect. His language reveals who and what he understands himself to be. His identity as an *oikonomos* of God means that he does not work for those to whom he ministers. He belongs to God. Any payment that comes to him comes from God, not them. So what is his payment? He answers this anticipated question candidly: "So that while preaching the gospel free of charge I may offer the gospel to the end that I do not take advantage of my right in the gospel" (v. 18).[37] Paul's manner of preaching the gospel allows him to give up the "right" that he has labored to convince his readers belongs to apostles. The whole aim of his argument is to persuade the "knowers" in Corinth to give up the right that they are convinced belongs to them. For Paul, giving up such rights constitutes living out the message of the gospel.

9:19-27. This section consists of two parts (vv. 19-23 and vv. 24-27) that provide two more stages in Paul's use of his own example as a positive counter to the Corinthian position refuted in 8:7-13. Both parts more directly address the question with which Paul began in 9:1: "Am I not free?" The first section brings to the forefront the "slave" motif that Paul lightly alluded to in vv. 17-18. The second appeals to the practice of athletes who bring their freedom under the control of abstinence in order to obtain a prize.

Verses 19-22 have a chiasmic arrangement.[38] [The Structure of 1 Corinthians 9:19-22] In the first and last lines (A, A'), Paul begins the same way: "To all I have. . . ." In the second and next to last lines (B, B'), he also begins the same way: "I have become to. . . ." In the two center lines (C, C'), he also begins the same way ("To the ones . . .") and includes an explanatory note qualifying his being "under" or "not under" the law. The juxtaposing of line B with B' and line C with C' aids our understanding of which group Paul refers to in C and C'.

The Structure of 1 Corinthians 9:19-22

The section has a clearly discernable chiasmic pattern.

A—v. 19, "To all people I have made myself a slave,
in order that I might gain the more."
B—v. 20a, "I have become to the Jews as a Jew,
in order that I might gain Jews."
C—v. 20b, "To the ones under the law as [one] under the law, . . .
in order that I might gain the ones under the law."
C'—v. 21, "To those not under the law as [one] not under the law, . . .
in order that I might gain the ones not under the law."
B'—v. 22a, "I have become to the weak ones weak,
in order that I might gain the weak ones."
A'—v. 22b, "To all people I have become all things,
in order that by all means I might save some."

Many interpreters identify four distinct groups named by Paul in these verses: the Jews, those under the law, those not under the law, and the weak.[39] The chiasmic structure of the verses, however, suggests only two groups are intended. The "Jews" (B) are paralleled to "those under the law" (B') and, thus, represent the same group. Those "not under the law" (C) are paralleled to the "weak" (C') and, likewise, represent the same group. Paul, then, has two groups in mind: Jews and Gentiles. Jews are under the law; Gentiles are not. Gentiles are also synonymous in some way with the "weak."[40] The "weak" here are not exactly the same as those with a "weak conscience" mentioned earlier, but there is some overlap. Those with a weak conscience were described earlier as those who formerly were accustomed to idols (8:7); that is, they were Gentiles. Paul's concern in chapter 8 is that those Gentiles who have become believers might be drawn back into idolatry by thinking that eating food offered to idols is acceptable for believers.

All Gentiles are "weak" in the sense that they are prone to idolatry. Idolatry is not as likely to be a problem for "those under the law" because they are guided by the first two commandments, which prohibit both the worship of other gods and the use of idols. The "weak" Gentiles, however, do not have this defense against "being led astray to dumb idols" (12:1).

To both of these groups, Paul has accommodated himself, within limits, in order to win them over to Christ. To the Jews (i.e., "those under the law"), Paul has become *as* a Jew under the law, though he is not under the law. [The Text of 1 Corinthians 9:20] To the Gentiles (i.e., "those not under the law"), he has become *as* one not under the law, though he is not outside the law of God but rather is subject to the law of Christ. How did the Jewish Paul become *as* a Jew? Without getting into the great debate about how much of his Jewish identity Paul retained after becoming a follower of Christ, we can at least observe that Paul still considered himself to be a part of Israel (Rom 12:1). He did not forsake his Jewish heritage. Unlike the division of labor between Paul and Peter suggested by Galatians 2:7, Paul affirms here his continuing mission to win over Jews. To do that, Paul at times had to subject himself to what was required by the Law of Moses for maintaining one's identity as a Jew, even to the point of enduring synagogue discipline (2 Cor 11:24).[41] Without disregarding the Jewish law, Paul nonetheless no longer considered himself to be living *under* it as the determining factor for living in faithful obedience to God.

The Text of 1 Corinthians 9:20

The overwhelming evidence from early manuscripts supports the presence of *hōs* before *Ioudaios* in v. 20, thus giving the reading "*as* a Jew." Only a few later texts (G* 6 1739) omit the *hōs*. Clement and Origen apparently cited earlier texts that omitted it. The absence of *hōs* would actually make v. 20 more exactly parallel to v. 23 where *hōs* does not appear before *asthenēs* ("weak") in most early manuscripts, including P[46], though it is in a few early texts. The desire for symmetry in sentence structure, however, cannot override the evidence. Conzelmann (159 n.5) observes that *hōs* is "superfluous" in v. 20 but still probably original.

Hans Conzelmann, *1 Corinthians: a Commentary* (Hermeneia; trans. James W. Leitch; Philadelphia: Fortress Press, 1975) 159.

In regard to Paul's accommodation to Gentiles, how did he become *as* one not under the law? As a Jew, Paul could not and did not forsake his Jewish heritage by flaunting the law and indulging in practices forbidden by the law, though he did at times stretch the law to its limits and in ways that some other Jews might not have approved. Still, he did consider himself not to be *under* the law (*anomos*) in the same way that Gentiles were not *under* the law. The adjective *anomos* does not mean "lawless" in the sense of "wild and wicked." It means living apart from the law. For Paul, Gentiles did not fall under the domain of the law at all, except in regard to those "laws of God" embedded in the Law of Moses that had universal applicability to all people, such as the prohibition against idolatry. Just as Gentiles lived outside that domain defined by the law, Paul lived in a realm where the law no longer defined one's relationship to God. The law still defined his identity as a Jew, but it did not define his relationship to God. Much as he could restrict his behavior under the dictates of the law to preserve his identity as a Jew so as to win over Jews, he could stretch his behavior as much as his Jewish identity defined by the law allowed in order to win over Gentiles. In doing so, he did not see himself as outside God's law; instead, he saw this as being ultimately defined and directed by the law of Christ to which he was totally subjected.

In what sense did Paul become "weak"? In one sense, Paul became "weak" by accommodating himself to "weak" Gentiles, who were "not under the law," to the degree that he could while maintaining his Jewish identity. His becoming "weak," however, suggests much more than this. Only in this last line of the chiasmic arrangement in vv. 20-22 does Paul omit the word "as" (*hōs*). Conzelmann is incorrect in claiming that the presence of "as" in v. 20 is "superfluous." Its absence in v. 22a is also not insignificant.[42] To the "weak" Gentiles, Paul *became* "weak" (not "*as* one who is weak") but not exactly in the same way in which they were weak. Paul was not prone to idolatry, nor did he lack the support of the law to guide him away from idolatry. Elsewhere in 1 Corinthians (1:27; 4:10), Paul includes "weak" among the status indicators that he contrasts with those who are "strong," "wise," and "powerful." God has chosen those of low status rather than those of high status, and God has chosen to work in ways that the world considers "weak." Paul has chosen both to identify with those of "weak" status and to work in the "weak" ways of God.[43] Paul's "weakness" is not only an identification with low-status persons but also an identification with the cross of Christ. He has become weak as Christ became weak, taking the path of self-sacrifice and lowly service.

The motif of being "enslaved to all" (v. 19) permeates the entire section of 9:21-23. The final line in the chiasmus, v. 22b, indicates what being a slave to all entails. It means becoming all things to all people so that by all means he might save some. This "becoming all things" is not simply a matter of employing the most effective tactics for winning people over; it involves putting one's self at the disposal of others, identifying with them, and enduring both the pain they experience and the pain they inflict on others. In short, it means living out the demands of the cross-shaped life. Indeed, it is Paul's enslavement to the gospel that drives him to become all things to all people (v. 23). Only by sharing in the pain of the cross can he truly *become* a partner (*synkoinōnos*) of the gospel. Paul's

Paul and the Isthmian Games

American-sponsored excavations at the sanctuary of Poseidon on the isthmus of Corinth began in 1952 under the direction of Scandinavian archaeologist Oscar Broneer. Broneer's interest in Paul took him to Corinth in the first place, so it is not surprising that two of his publications focused on Paul and Isthmia. In one article, Broneer offered an imaginative account of Paul's visit to Isthmia during the games. In all probability, however, Paul never visited Isthmia since the sanctuary appears to have been abandoned following the Roman destruction in 146 BC until at least the middle of the 6th decade of the 1st century AD. Corinth regained control of the biennial Isthmian games soon after its founding as a Roman colony in the 1st century BC. The games were held in the spring of the 2d and 4th years of the four-year Olympic cycle of pan-Hellenic contests. Under Augustus, a second set of games, the Caesarean, were added immediately following the Isthmian. Later, either during the reign of Tiberius or Claudius, a third festival honoring the living emperor (the *Caesarea Sebastea*) was added. During the time that Paul was in Corinth, these games would all have been held in the city of Corinth itself. Since the forum of Roman Corinth was built on the site of the stadium during the Greek period, it is possible that the foot races were still held there. In any case, though Paul did not visit Isthmia, he may have had opportunity to view these various games twice during his first, long tenure in Corinth.

Oscar Broneer, "The Apostle Paul and the Isthmian Games," *BA* 25 (1962): 1–31, and "Paul and the Pagan Cults at Isthmia," *HTR* 64 (1971): 169–87.

Elizabeth R. Gebhard, "The Isthmian Games and the Sanctuary of Poseidon in the Early Empire," in *The Corinthia in the Roman Period* (ed. Timothy E. Gregory; JRASup 8: Ann Arbor MI: Journal of Roman Archaeology, 1993) 87–88.

Starting gate at racetrack in the Corinthian forum. (Credit: Scott Nash)

hope to share in the gospel's blessings by sharing in its sufferings may lie in the background (cf. Phil 3:10-11), but his emphasis here is on becoming what the gospel of the cross requires.

The last section in chapter 9 (vv. 24-27) begins a transition toward the second main part of Paul's argument in chapter 10 where he directly warns the "knowers" in Corinth about the dangers they subject themselves to by participating in idolatry-related meals. These verses connect to the preceding parts of chapter 9 in that Paul is still offering himself as a positive example of relinquishing one's rights. In the first part of the example (vv. 1-18), Paul focused on forgoing his rights as an apostle. In the second part (vv. 19-23), he focused on forgoing his freedom by enslaving himself to all. Here, he focuses on "abstaining" in order to win the prize. The future orientation of those who labor toward the prize picks up the final element in Paul's second example where he explained that his enslavement was aimed toward *becoming* a partner in the gospel (v. 23). Paul still strives toward this goal; so should the Corinthians.

Paul's use of athletic imagery has spawned suggestions that the famous Isthmian games sponsored by Corinth inspired his language and imagery in vv. 24-27. [Paul and the Isthmian Games] One cannot rule out some influence on his choice of images, especially since the Isthmian games were probably held in the city of Corinth during Paul's tenure there (and not at the sanctuary of Poseidon on the isthmus some twelve miles to the east), but the frequent use of such athletic imagery by writers of the time makes it unnecessary to posit a direct connection.[44] One may suppose that Paul's Corinthian readers would have linked his imagery to their experience with the Isthmian games, but practically anyone in any large city in the Roman Mediterranean sphere would have witnessed athletic contests and could have related to his analogy. One may further surmise that the prominence of the Isthmian games prompted Paul to employ athletic imagery on this occasion, while he had not done so previously in those letters thought to have been written prior to 1 Corinthians.[45] Once again, however, the imagery would have been just as effective at this point in his letter even if the Corinthians did not have their own special pan-Hellenic contests. Even more unnecessary is the attempt to restrict the whole issue of eating food offered to idols to the banquets associated with the Isthmian games.[46]

Far more important than the question of what may have inspired Paul to use athletic imagery at this point in his argument is an understanding of the way he used it. Appealing to their shared knowledge about foot races, Paul reminds them that while all the runners in the stadium run, only one wins the prize. Then he urges them to run so that they might seize the prize. To do this, they must follow the example of the athlete who trains rigorously by "abstaining from" (*enkrateuetai*) all things. This is the main point of his imagery. Discipline is essential for the successful athlete, especially the discipline of abstaining. [Epictetus on Training] The athlete's arduous training is endured for the chance to gain a perishable crown (*phtharton stephanon*). In point of fact, the triumphant athletes in the esteemed pan-Hellenic contests were awarded great honors, sometimes including free meals for life. The most cherished prize, however, was the wreath (*stephanos*) of olive, laurel, pine, or celery placed upon their heads. [Perishable Crown] In contrast to these withering crowns, Paul reminds his readers that their own coveted prize is imperishable.

Epictetus on Training

The Stoic philosopher Epictetus used the imagery of an athlete in training who controls desire and abstains from everything as an example for those pursuing tranquility.

> There must be many who exercise themselves for the contest, many who call out to those who exercise themselves, many masters, many spectators.—But my wish is to live quietly.—Lament then and groan as you deserve to do. For what other is a greater punishment than this to the untaught man and to him who disobeys the divine commands, to be grieved, to lament, to envy, in a word to be disappointed and to be unhappy? Would you not release yourself from these things?—And how shall I release myself?—Have you not often heard, that you ought to remove entirely desire, apply aversion (turning away) to those things only which are within your power, that you ought to give up every thing, body, property, fame, books, tumult, power, private station? for whatever way you turn, you are a slave, you are subjected, you are hindered, you are compelled, you are entirely in the power of others.

Epictetus, *Discourses* 4.4.11.

Paul concludes his athletic analogy by applying it to himself. In doing so, he picks up both the stress on seizing the prize and disci-

Perishable Crown

The winners in the contests at all of the pan-Hellenic festivals received crowns of perishable materials. At Olympia the crown was of olive, at Delphi it was of laurel, and at Nemea it was of *selinon* (celery or parsley). At Isthmia, the crown was originally of pine, but in the early 5th century BC it was changed to *selinon*, probably because *selinon* was typically used for funerals and the Isthmian games came to be seen, like the Nemean, more as funerary contests. Evidence exists for the use of both pine and *selinon* in the 1st century AD.

While the wreaths of perishable materials were the most coveted prizes at these games, the victors actually also received more lasting rewards. In some cases, the winner's city would provide the champion with meals for life. In most cases, the victors were entitled to have a monument or statue in their honor erected in the sanctuary complex. The accompanying photograph shows a victory stele erected at Isthmia by L. Kornelios Korinthos, winner of the flute contests. The reliefs of victory wreaths on the stele portray the various places where Kornelius won this event.

Isthmia Museum, Greece. (Credit: Scott Nash)

Oscar Broneer, "The Isthmian Victory Crown," *AJA* 66 (1962): 259–63.

Elizabeth R. Gebhard, "The Isthmian Games and the Sanctuary of Poseidon in the Early Empire," in *The Corinthia in the Roman Period* (ed. Timothy E. Gregory; JRASup 8; Ann Arbor MI: Journal of Roman Archaeology, 1993) 81, 86.

plining the self. He does not run aimlessly but keeps his eye on the prize. He does not "shadow box" beating the air; instead, he bruises (*hypōpiazō*) and subdues (*doulagōgō*) his own body. The first verb literally means "I strike under the eye," while the second could be read literally as "I lead into slavery." He is capturing the imagery of physical training in a severe form and applying it to the total subjection of his life for the cause for which he has become enslaved, namely the gospel. He has no illusions about being exempt from the need for persistent vigilance on his own behalf. Paul may be an apostle, but he must still exercise due diligence in discipline, including abstaining from certain rights and privileges in order that he might not in the end become disqualified himself. If he, an apostle, is still striving toward the goal, then the Corinthians should also exercise the discipline required and forgo their perceived right to partake of food offered to idols. [Philippians 3:12-13]

Philippians 3:12-13

Not that I have already obtained this or have already reached the goal; but I press on to make it my own, because Christ Jesus has made me his own. Beloved, I do not consider that I have made it my own; but this one thing I do: forgetting what lies behind and straining forward to what lies ahead, I press on toward the goal of the prize of the heavenly call of God in Christ Jesus. (Phil 3:12-13; NRSV)

CONNECTIONS

Paul's Strategy

The section 8:1–11:1 is a long, sustained argument by Paul to dissuade the Corinthians from participating in pagan celebrations that involved food offered to idols. Though some interpreters see Paul steering a middle course between some of the Corinthians who saw no problem with this practice and some who thought it was wrong, in actuality Paul has only one target audience and his objective is to convince them to end a practice they considered acceptable. He does not want any of the Corinthians to partake of food offered to idols in any context where a connection between the food and idolatry is evident. He does not imply to those who consider themselves to be "in the know" about the nonexistence of the deities represented by idols that he agrees with their conclusions that such knowledge should permit them to participate. He does not indicate that such participation is acceptable as long as no one who does not share their "knowledge" is negatively affected. He wants them to forgo whatever right they think they have to eat the food that has any known connection to idolatry.

Faith Crushing Idolatry

Jean Baptiste Theodon (1646–1713). *Faith Crushing Idolatry.* Il Gesu, Rome, Italy. (Credit: Scala/Art Resource, NY)

Theodon's sculpture group titled *Faith Crushing Idolatry* adorns one side of an altar dedicated to St. Ignatius Loyola, the founder of the Jesuits, in a chapel of Il Gesu in Rome. His work represents a merging of Roman Baroque and French Neoclassicism and captures the zeal of Jesuit calls for total obliteration of paganism and heresy.

Before dealing directly with his target group and warning them about the dangers they are risking for themselves, Paul appeals to their more noble side (8:7-13). He asks them to consider the effects their actions might possibly have on someone who is not as informed about matters of faith as they. Eventually, in chapter 10, Paul will appeal to what is in their own best interests. First, however, he gives them a chance to think about someone other than themselves. Such a strategy was risky for Paul then, and it remains risky today. Overcoming self-interest has always been difficult. [Mahan on Self-interest] Paul was asking his readers to transcend the normal ways of thinking and behaving that guide persons to put themselves first, and adopt a new way of living that

Mahan on Self-interest

Let me be blunt: there is something approaching a consensus these days, at least in some quarters, that human motivation is self-interested without remainder. By *consensus*, I don't mean to suggest something consciously accepted, even less something recommended as ideal. I speak rather of something "in the air": a collective assumption of sorts.

Some, it is true, get really excited about the gospel of self-interest. Brandishing Ayn Rand's *Fountainhead* or some sociobiological or free-market facsimile, they wish to awaken the uninitiated to the virtues of egoism. . . .

Still, I have often noticed a kind of wistfulness. . . . It is as if we carry within us a "shadow government" of compassion and idealism.

In fact, I've come to believe that most of us wish nothing more than to liberate our shadow government from exile and to incarnate in the routines of work and play the deepest longings of our heart.

Brian J. Mahan, *Forgetting Ourselves on Purpose: Vocation and the Ethics of Ambition* (San Francisco: Jossey-Bass, 2002) 13–14.

puts others first and accepts certain restrictions on one's freedom to that end. For Paul, that is the new way of living defined by love. Even knowledge should be brought under the guidance of love.

For Paul's target audience, knowledge was liberating. Knowing that idols represented fake gods enabled them to indulge in certain pagan activities with a clear conscience. No god was really being honored by their participation. They could not be charged with worshiping deities that did not exist by enjoying banquets set in the sanctuaries of those deities. Anyone who knew the truth should have no problem with attending the feasts, eating the food, maintaining good ties with their pagan friends, and fulfilling their civic responsibilities.

For Paul, rather than liberating, such knowledge was falsely inflating ("puffing up"). It inflated the ego at the cost of social responsibility toward others in the new society (the *ekklēsia*) into which they had been called by God. Knowledge unfettered by compassion could be divisive and destructive. Such knowledge, unmindful of the consequences of egocentric behavior, was in reality defective knowledge.

Rather than tackle their presumed knowledge head on, Paul explores the ramifications of love. Does relishing in their knowledge and exercising their rights take precedence over compassion for the other? Can they really love the God they know to be the only god and contribute to the destruction of one for whom God's Christ died? Is the well-being of their sisters and brothers important enough to lead them to reel in the limits of their newly found liberty?

This tactic is not the only one in Paul's arsenal, but it is his first approach. It is a risky tactic, and Paul will eventually add to it a tactic geared more toward the persistent self-interest that holds us all. For this first tactic to work, his target audience must have within themselves some capacity for compassion that transcends self-interest. For it to work, something of the gospel's deepest core must have already become a part of their being. For it to work, Paul's idealistic notion of the word of the cross as a power at work in the world transforming the world and the lives of those who live in it must have some element of truth to it.

Paul's strategy in using this tactic first carries risk, but it is a good one to emulate. In fact, it is a tactic more in keeping with the word of the cross than is the more direct appeal to self-interest that Paul will make in chapter 10. There Paul will employ the age-old effective instrument of fear in his attempt to scare his readers away from pagan feasts. Here, he applies the less overtly scary instrument of love in seeking to woo his readers away from practices that may harm others. Only on the surface, however, is this approach actually less frightening, for if one gives in to the lure of love, the radical changes in cherished values and proven perspectives that will follow may prove terrifying indeed. [Buechner on the Gospel] The full implications of following the way of love may, in the end, scare us back toward the *known* security of self-interest. Knowledge may only "puff up," but it at least creates the illusion of being in control within the protective bubble of what we "know." Love pricks that bubble and leaves us exposed. The appeal to love can only work if, as Brian Mahan suggests, we really do carry within ourselves a "shadow government" of compassion and idealism.[47] Appealing to that "shadow government" carries risk, but such is the way of the cross.

Buechner on the Gospel

What is both Good and New about the Good News is the mad insistence that Jesus lives on among us not just as another haunting memory but as the outlandish, holy, and invisible power of God working not just through the sacraments (q.v.). But in countless hidden ways to make even slobs like us loving and whole beyond anything we could conceivably pull off by ourselves.

Thus the Gospel is not only Good and New but, if you take it seriously, a Holy Terror. Jesus never claimed that the process of being changed from a slob into a human being was going to be a Sunday School picnic. On the contrary. Childbirth may occasionally be painless, but rebirth never. Part of what it means to be a slob is to hang on for dear life to our slobbery.

Frederick Buechner, *Wishful Thinking: A Theological ABC* (New York: Harper & Row, 1973) 33.

The Right to Eat and Drink

In the first part of chapter 9 (vv. 1-18), Paul goes to great lengths to build up a defense for the right of apostles to receive financial support from the churches to which they minister. In doing so, he cites the practice of other apostles, such as Cephas and the Lord's brothers; the common practice of farmers, soldiers, and shepherds; the words of Scripture (Deut 25:4); the example of the Jerusalem priests; and the words of Jesus himself. It is a towering argument in support of ministerial right to basic support from congregations. In the end, though, Paul's objective is to point out that, however entitled he may have been to such support, he did not avail himself of it.

By presenting himself as an example of one who relinquishes a recognized right, he hopes to persuade his readers to give up what they consider to be their right in regard to eating food offered to idols. He does not question the existence of their right. In fact, his argument would lose much of its force if their claim to a certain right did not have some validity. That validity could not have simply been their presumed possession of knowledge about the nonexistence of idols, for Paul clearly undermines that knowledge in chapter 10. Their claim to a right must have been based on social and political factors rather than theological, though it was their theology that convinced them they could exercise their sociopolitical right. Whatever the legitimate basis of their perceived right, Paul wanted them to follow his example in forgoing that right out of concern for others.

The focus of their claimed right was on food and drink. They wanted to continue their preconversion practice of participating in the feasts and banquets connected to the cycle of festivals honoring pagan deities, including those that were a part of the imperial cult. As an apostle, Paul also had a right to eat and drink, not at the pagan festivals to which Corinthian citizens were entitled to share, but rather to eat and drink on the tab picked up by the church. Paul chose to pay his own food and drink bill.

The right to eat and drink as our circumstances permit is an assumed privilege of affluent western societies. For our time, the issue as Paul framed it cannot be reduced merely to a debate about *what* we can eat and drink. [To Drink or Not to Drink?] We would do better to cast it as a challenge to *how much* we consume. Affluence, and the accompanying power to eat and drink as much as we can afford, comes at a great cost to those people who are not so empowered. They often have to pick up our tab. Paul's example translated into our context might mean forgoing our assumed right to unchecked consumption.

To Drink or Not to Drink?

In the setting in which I grew up, the Bluegrass region of central Kentucky where most of the world's Bourbon whiskey is made, whether or not one drank alcoholic beverages was often a major criterion in determining one's status as a true Christian. Even though Bourbon had been developed by the famed pioneer Baptist preacher Elijah Craig, most Baptist churches included a statement in their church covenants that committed the members to total abstinence. The use of alcohol carried such a stigma that many churches excluded members who worked at a distillery from serving as deacons or in other positions of church leadership. Raised in this environment, I can still recall my shock upon seeing a newspaper photograph showing President Jimmy Carter, a good Baptist, sipping a glass of champagne at a White House dinner.

While I still believe that problems associated with the abuse of alcohol should not be taken lightly, a view regularly confirmed by my years as a college professor observing the disastrous consequences of binge drinking for students, I also think that we easily trivialize Paul's words in 1 Cor 8 and 9 by such a narrow application to the consumption of alcohol or any other particular food or drink. We would be more in tune with his concerns if we applied his discussion of rights to our presumed freedom to consume more than our fair share of the world's resources.

Becoming All Things to All Persons

One could read Paul's words about becoming all things to all people as a shrewd strategy of duplicity. Simply take on the appearance of similarity to those with whom you are engaged at the moment so that you can befriend them and get them to do what you want. Then move on to the next group and don another disguise. Chameleonic behavior works well enough in politics, but something smells "fishy" when we find it in religion. His claim to become all things to all people may make us wonder where the real Paul is behind all those masks.

The truth is that Paul was all the persons he became. He was much like the mythical Proteus, the changeling or shape-shifter, who could alter his appearance not by donning a mask or changing the hue of his skin but by becoming another creature. The clue to understanding Paul's metamorphoses is to be found not in the last verse of the section 9:19-22 but in the first: "Being free from all, I have enslaved myself to all." In this section Paul is taking up his initial question in 9:1: "Am I not free?" Yes, he is free, but his freedom is not the kind we normally cherish. His freedom is the kind spoken of in the prayer attributed to St. Augustine, the freedom of service. [Augustine's Prayer] In a context where one might expect Paul to elaborate on how free he is in Christ, he turns instead to describe his willing submission to the needs of his different audiences in order to gain them to (or gain for them) the gospel. Surrendering one's rights or submitting one's self to another person are usually not high on our list of preferred ways of relating. We have become sensitive enough to the exploitation of personal rights and the abuse of forced submission to authority figures that we tend to view skeptically any call to submission or enslavement. For Paul, however, addressing persons who relished their freedom to indulge in actions their minds told them were harmless, becoming enslaved to the needs of others was the greater freedom. [Foster on Submission]

Augustine's Prayer

O Lord God, the light of the minds that know you,
the life of the souls that love you,
and the strength of the hearts that serve you:
Help us so to know you that we may truly love you,
and so to love you that we may fully serve you,
whom to serve is perfect freedom;
through Jesus Christ our Lord. Amen.

Foster on Submission

I said that every Discipline has its corresponding freedom. What freedom corresponds to submission? It is the ability to lay down the terrible burden of always needing to get our own way. The obsession to demand that things go the way we want them to go is one of the greatest bondages in human society today. . . .

In submission we are free at least to value other people. Their dreams and plans become important to us. We have entered into a new, wonderful, glorious freedom—the freedom to give up our own rights for the good of others.

Richard J. Foster, *Celebration of Discipline: The Path to Spiritual Growth* (rev. and exp. ed.; San Francisco: Harper & Row, 1988) 111–12.

Lectionary Connections

Three readings from chapters 8–9 are assigned in the Revised Common Lectionary in Year B for the Fourth, Fifth, and Sixth Sundays after Epiphany. On the Fourth Sunday, 1 Corinthians 8:1-13 is joined with Deuteronomy 18:15-20 and Mark 1:21-28. The texts from Deuteronomy and Mark have an obvious point of connection in that the first looks forward to the coming of the "prophet like Moses" and the second describes the beginning of Jesus' ministry as one who teaches unlike the teachers the people have previously heard. The text from 1 Corinthians holds only remote possibilities for linkage to the other two texts. One could focus on what Paul says about Christ in these verses. He is the "one Lord from whom are all things and through whom we exist"(v. 6), and he is the one who died for the brother or sister (v. 11) who might be harmed by another believer's behavior.

The Fifth Sunday after Epiphany in Year B include Isaiah 40:21-31, 1 Corinthians 9:16-23, and Mark 1:29-39. The Gospel reading recalls Jesus' ministry to a variety of needs in Capernaum and environs. The chief tie to Isaiah 41 comes in v. 29: "He gives power to the faint, and strengthens the powerless." The 1 Corinthians reading depicts Paul as one who "made himself all things to all people" in a variety of ways.

The Sixth Sunday after Epiphany in Year B includes 1 Corinthians 9:24-27, which Paul writes about running the race and receiving a victory crown. The readings from 2 Kings 5:1-14 and Mark 1:40-45 both involve the healing of lepers and do not offer many points of contact with the 1 Corinthians text. If one chooses to focus on 1 Corinthians 9:24-27, Paul's emphasis on "abstaining" should receive attention, remembering that this is part of a larger argument in which he is trying to convince people to abstain from eating food offered to idols.

NOTES

1. Thomas Henry Huxley, *On Elemental Instruction in Physiology* (1877). The well-known maxim, "A little knowledge is a dangerous thing," to which Huxley refers, is probably based on Alexander Pope's line, "A little learning is a dangerous thing" (*An Essay on Criticism*, pt. 2, l. 15).

2. Several recent studies show the contemporary relevance of the ancient issue of food in polytheistic settings, especially Derek Newton, *Deity and Diet: The Dilemma of Sacrificial Food at Corinth* (JSNTSup 169; Sheffield: Sheffield Academic Press, 1998), and Alex T. Cheung, *Idol Food in Corinth: Jewish Background and Pauline Legacy* (JSNTSup 176: Sheffield: Sheffield Academic Press, 1999).

3. For a discussion of the "right" of certain members, see Bruce W. Winter, *After Paul Left Corinth: The Influence of Secular Ethics and Social Change* (Grand Rapids MI: Eerdmans, 2001) 269–86.

4. Proponents of the idea that persons could eat in a temple precinct without any religious significance being attached to the meals include Bruce N. Fisk, "Eating Meat Offered to Idols: Corinthian Behaviour and Pauline Response in 1 Corinthians 8-10," *TJ*

10 (1989): 49–70; E. Coye Still III, "Paul's aims regarding ΕΙΔΩΘΥΤΑ: A New Proposal for Interpreting 1 Corinthians 8:1-11:1," *NovT* 44 (2002): 333–43; and Richard E. Oster Jr., "Use, Misuse and Neglect of Archaeological Evidence in Some Modern Works on 1 Corinthians (1Cor 7,1-5; 8,10; 11,2-16; 12,14-26)," *ZNW* 83 (1992): 69–73.

5. For a discussion and critique of this "traditional" view, see Gordon D. Fee, *The First Epistle to the Corinthians* (NICNT; Grand Rapids: Eerdmans Publishing, 1987) 357–63, and Joop F. M. Smit, *"About the Idol Offerings": Rhetoric, Social Context and Theology of Paul's Discourse in First Corinthians 8:1–11:1* (BET 27; Leuven, Belgium: Peeters, 2000) 47–48. For a defense of the three-settings idea, see Still, "Paul's aims regarding ΕΙΔΩΘΥΤΑ, 333–43.

6. Numerous commentators accept the view that temple dining facilities were essentially restaurants, including Hans Conzelmann, *1 Corinthians: a Commentary* (Hermeneia; trans. James W. Leitch; Philadelphia: Fortress Press, 1975) 148, and Fee, *The First Epistle to the Corinthians*, 361.

7. Bruce W. Winter, "Theological and Ethical Responses to Religious Pluralism—1 Corinthians 8–10," *TynBul* 41 (1990): 218.

8. Ben Witherington III, "Not So Idle Thoughts about *Eidolothuton*," *TynBul* 44 (1993): 237–54, argues that Paul was only concerned about eating the food in a temple setting.

9. Gregory W. Dawes, "The Danger of Idolatry: First Corinthians 8:7-13," *CBQ* 58 (1996): 86–91.

10. Still, "Paul's aims regarding ΕΙΔΩΘΥΤΑ, 334–36.

11. Winter, *After Paul Left Corinth*, 269–86. Winter's argument is valid, but he limits his focus too narrowly by insisting that the problem pertained only to the Isthmian Games festivals.

12. Joop F. M. Smit, "1 Corinthians 8,1-6, a Rhetorical Partitio: A Contribution to the Coherence of 1 Cor 8,1–11,1," in *The Corinthian Correspondence* (BETL 125; ed. Reimund Bieringer; Leuven, Belgium: Peeters Press, 1996) 577–91. John Fotopoulos, *Food Offered to Idols in Roman Corinth: A Socio-Rhetorical Reconsideration of 1 Corinthians 8:1–11:1* (Tübingen: Mohr Siebeck, 2003) 208–20, argues that the *partitio* extends to 8:9.

13. Fotopoulos, *Food Offered to Idols in Roman Corinth*, 208–14, considers these qualifications to be refutations.

14. Wendell Lee Willis, *Idol Meat in Corinth: The Pauline Argument in 1 Corinthians 8 and 10* (SBLDS 68; Chico CA: Scholars Press, 1985) 67–70, argues that the whole clause "We know that all have knowledge" belongs to the Corinthians, but most scholars disagree.

15. David E. Garland, *1 Corinthians* (BECNT; Grand Rapids: Baker Academic, 2003) 366–67.

16. Garland, *1 Corinthians*, 371, makes exactly this point.

17. Garland, *1 Corinthians*, 373. It seems to me that both Deut 6:4 and 6:5 underlie Paul's argument.

18. Peter J. Tomson, *Paul and the Jewish Law: Halakha in the Letters of the Apostle to the Gentiles* (*CRINT* 3/1; Minneapolis: Fortress Press, 1990) 177.

19. Jon D. Mikalson, *Ancient Greek Religion* (Oxford: Blackwell, 2005) 18.

20. Richard A. Horsley, "Gnosis in Corinth: I Corinthians 8.1-6," in *Christianity at Corinth: The Quest for the Pauline Church* (ed. Edward Adams and David G. Horrell; Louisville: Westminster John Knox, 2004) 125–28.

21. For references to the relevant writings, see Richard A Horsley, *1 Corinthians* (ANTC; Nashville: Abingdon 1998) 119–20.

22. Horsley, *1 Corinthians*, 120, argues that Paul deliberately substituted Christ for Sophia in a formula espoused by the Corinthians, but such was not necessarily the case.

23. See, e.g., John C. Hurd Jr., *The Origin of I Corinthians* (Macon GA: Mercer University Press, 1983) 68; Khiok-Khng Yeo, *Rhetorical Interaction in 1 Corinthians 8–10: A Formal Analysis with Preliminary Suggestions for a Chinese, Cross-Cultural Hermeneutic* (BIS 9; Leiden: Brill, 1995) 192–93; Fee, *The First Epistle to the Corinthians*, 383–84.

24. See Joop F. M. Smit, "The Rhetorical Disposition of First Corinthians 8:7–9:27," *CBQ* 59 (1997): 480–81.

25. Contra Garland, *1 Corinthians*, 385 n.11.

26. Winter, *After Paul Left Corinth*, 269–86.

27. Still, "Paul's aims regarding ΕΙΔΩΘΥΤΑ, 335, argues persuasively that a genuine right must have been acknowledged by Paul, but he misidentifies the right as a theological basis rather than a political one.

28. The infinitive with *eis to* here indicates result.

29. Anthony C. Thiselton, *The First Epistle to the Corinthians: A Commentary on the Greek Text* (NIGTC; Grand Rapids: Eerdmans, 2000) 651–52.

30. See the discussion and criticism of the view that ch. 9 is a defense of Paul's apostleship by Garland, *1 Corinthians*, 396–401, and Thiselton, *The First Epistle to the Corinthians*, 661–63.

31. Smit, "The Rhetorical Disposition of First Corinthians 8:7–9:27," 485 and n. 34, refers to this rhetorical device as an *anticipatio* or *prokatalepsis* and notes discussion of it in Quintilian and Lausberg.

32. Conzelmann, *1 Corinthians*, 154–55; Walter Schrage, *Der erste Brief an die Korinther* (1 Kor 6,12-11,16) (EKKNT 7/2; Zurich: Benziger, 1995) 299–301.

33. Richard B. Hays, *First Corinthians* (IBC; Louisville: John Knox Press, 1997) 151.

34. Anthony T. Hanson, *Studies in Paul's Technique and Theology* (Grand Rapids: Eerdmans, 1974) 163–66; also Garland, *1 Corinthians*, 410–11.

35. Conzelmann, *1 Corinthians*, 155.

36. Fee, *The First Epistle to the Corinthians*, 409 n.68.

37. The infinitive with eis to in the phrase *eis to mē katachrēsasthai* could express either purpose or result.

38. See Garland, *1 Corinthians*, 427. I disagree, though, with Garland's identification of the "weak" in this chiasmus (433–34).

39. For example, Hays, *First Corinthians*, 153–54.

40. Garland, *1 Corinthians*, 434, argues that "weak" may refer theologically to the "condition of all humankind as ungodly" and cites Rom 5:6 where Paul does, in fact, depict all humankind as weak. In 1 Cor 9:22, however, Paul refers to *becoming* "weak"

by choice as a way of winning over the weak. "Becoming weak" here cannot mean the same thing as "being weak" in Rom 5:6.

41. See the discussion by Garland, *1 Corinthians*, 430.

42. Hans Conzelmann, *1 Corinthians: a Commentary* (Hermeneia; trans. James W. Leitch; Philadelphia: Fortress Press, 1975) 159 n5. Garland, *1 Corinthians*, 433–44, rightly points out that the absence of the word "as" in v. 22a is important, but he does not adequately note the difference between Paul's weakness and the weakness of the Gentiles.

43. Dale B. Martin, *Slavery as Salvation: The Metaphor of Slavery in Pauline Christianity* (New Haven: Yale University Press, 1990) 123–24, has noted Paul's deliberate lowering of his own status in order to identify with the "weak." Paul also has chosen to work through the kind of weakness displayed in the cross of Christ.

44. See Victor C. Pfitzner, *Paul and the Agon Motif: Traditional Athletic Imagery in the Pauline Literature* (Leiden: Brill, 1967).

45. Jerome Murphy-O'Connor, *St. Paul's Corinth: Texts and Archaeology* (Collegeville MN: Liturgical Press, 1983) 16–17.

46. As Winter, *After Paul Left Corinth*, 269–86, has done.

47. Brian J. Mahan, *Forgetting Ourselves on Purpose: Vocation and the Ethics of Ambition* (San Francisco: Jossey-Bass, 2002) 14.

FLEE THE WORSHIP OF IDOLS

1 Corinthians 10:1–11:1

"Those who take advantage of everything that is lawful rapidly deteriorate into doing what is not lawful."[1]

The section 1 Corinthians 10:1–11:1 is a continuation of the long argument Paul began in 8:1. Readers can consult the first part of the previous chapter on 1 Corinthians 8:1–9:27 for a discussion of the issue Paul addresses in this long argument and for an analysis of the argument's literary and rhetorical structure. In the first part of his argument (8:7–9:27), Paul focuses on the harmful effects the behavior of some Corinthians might have on other members of the church. After appealing to his own example as one who gives up his rights in many respects out of concern for others, Paul turns here to express his concern for those who actually engage in the practice of eating food offered to idols. We misread Paul here if we think that he has reversed his stance on this issue or that he is addressing a different situation. Paul is consistently against any believer's eating food offered to idols in any circumstances. The only exception to this comes when the food has been disconnected from its association with idolatry (10:25-27). If the connection is reestablished, however, then the food once again becomes forbidden.

Throughout his argument, Paul is contending with the assumption of some Corinthians that they possess a true knowledge that justifies their use of their right to eat food offered to idols. They know that the gods represented by idols do not exist. Therefore, they argue, eating food offered to them should have no negative consequences. Paul's initial counter-argument is that such knowledge is limited in its focus. It "puffs up" the possessors of such knowledge to the point of disregarding the harmful effects their behavior might have on others. Instead, they should be guided by a love for God and the well-being of those for whom God's love has been shown in the death of Christ. Having appealed to a loving concern for other persons, Paul now pushes the fuller implications of their knowledge. Knowing that only one God exists also means that one must be exclusively devoted to the one God. Any kind of participation in idolatrous activity, however innocent or inconsequential it may appear, has disastrous ramifications for one's relationship to the one God.

COMMENTARY

The first three verses of chapter 8 introduce the dimension of the Corinthians' knowledge that Paul counters in 8:7–9:27. Likewise, the next three verses (8:4-6) introduce the aspect that Paul argues against in chapter 10. The oneness of God for believers, especially in the context of a culture where polytheism is affirmed, demands that believers refrain from any activity that would compromise their exclusive relationship with the one God. To demonstrate the dangers of compromise, Paul recalls the previous history of God's people Israel, who suffered disaster for violating their exclusive bond to God, and applies it directly to the Corinthians' situation in some creative ways (10:1-13). Rhetorically, vv. 1-13 constitute a negative proof or *refutatio*. (See [A Rhetorical Scheme for 1 Corinthians 8:1–11:1] in the previous chapter.) He then exposes both the depths of exclusive communion with God and the true demonic danger lurking behind idolatry (10:14-22). Verses 14-22 comprise a positive proof or *confirmatio*. He then recapitulates (*peroratio*) the main points made in 8:7–9:27 and 10:1-22 and expands the issue of eating food offered to idols beyond the context of a religious setting (10:23-30). Finally, he sums up his argument (*conclusio*) with some basic appeals (10:31–11:1). [Detailed Outline of 1 Corinthians 10:1–11:1]

Detailed Outline of 1 Corinthians 10:1–11:1

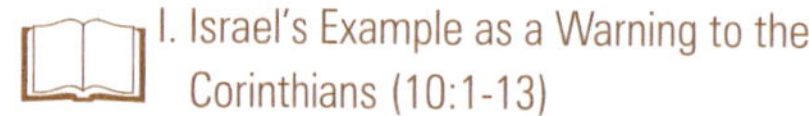

I. Israel's Example as a Warning to the Corinthians (10:1-13)
  A. Our Ancestors All Shared the Same Benefits, But Not All Made It (10:1-6)
  B. We Must Not Make the Same Mistake (10:7-13)
II. The Lord's Supper as Sign of Exclusive Devotion to God (10:14-22)
  A. We Participate in the Lord's Supper (10:14-18)
  B. Do Not Participate in the Table of Demons (10:15-22)
III. Eating or Drinking without Offense (10:23–11:1)
  A. Seek the Good of the Neighbor (10:23-24)
  B. Eat Whatever Is Sold in the Market (10:25-26)
  C. Eat What Is Set before You, Unless It Is Connected to Sacrifice (10:27-30)
  D. Do All to the Glory of God (10:31–11:1)

Israel's Example as a Warning to the Corinthians, 10:1-13

10:1-6. Paul transitions to his second main point of his long argument with a commonly used formula for beginning a discussion: "I do not want you to *ignore*." The verb *agnoein* could mean simply "to be ignorant of" or "to be unaware of," but in this context, it is better rendered "to ignore." Paul is not informing them of matters about which they have no knowledge; he is urging them not to ignore the significance of things they already know. What they already know is the story of Israel. Paul appeals to Scriptures that have their origin in the life of Israel because those Scriptures have become the Scriptures of the church. For Paul and for those who have heard his preaching, the church has itself become a part of the story of Israel. Thus, even though the Corinthians are predominately Gentile, the Israelites are their "ancestors." He is not introducing them to the story of Israel as if for the first time; that story has already begun to shape their identity. What they are in danger of ignoring, however, is the severe warning that Israel's story contains for them.

As he reminds them of Israel's story, Paul repeatedly uses the word "all." *All* of their ancestors (Israel) "were under the cloud," "passed though the sea," "were baptized into Moses," "ate the same spiritual food," and "drank the same spiritual drink." A deliberate linkage to the church's sacraments of baptism and the Eucharist is probably intended here. Those who were under the cloud and passed through the sea were baptized into Moses in the cloud and in the sea. The cloud was the visible sign of God's presence with the people and led them from the moment they were liberated from slavery in Egypt (Exod 13:21). The passage through the waters of the sea, and the resultant destruction of the Egyptian army, sealed their deliverance. Whether Paul intends here to imply a connection between the cloud of God's presence and the Holy Spirit, as many interpreters suggest, is uncertain, though it is quite possible.[2] Spirit and water came to be a seen as jointly involved in the baptismal experience in some Christian traditions (cf. John 3:5). Paul himself links Spirit to baptism and to the one "drink" (the "cup" of the Lord's Supper) in 1 Corinthians 12:13.

The phrase "baptized into Moses" is puzzling. [The Text of 1 Corinthians 10:2] Such an idea does not occur in Jewish literature, but we should be surprised. The concept of "being baptized into" someone is distinctively Christian. Believers are baptized into Christ (Rom 6:3). Paul is transposing the exodus story into a new key, one that is shaped by the gospel. Christ parallels Moses in that both were deliverers and both were the agents of God's covenant. So, as believers in the present episode of Israel's story are baptized into Jesus, from the vantage point of Paul, the Israelites of old could be depicted as being baptized into their deliverer and covenant agent Moses.

The Text of 1 Corinthians 10:2

The passive form *ebaptisthēsan* ("they were baptized") was preferred over the middle form *ebaptisanto* ("they baptized themselves" or "they accepted baptism") by the majority of the UBS NT 3rd ed. committee. Two committee members (Metzger and Wikgren) preferred the middle on the basis of the Jewish practice of self-baptism. The textual evidence slightly favors the passive over the middle, but the decisive factor in the committee's decision was the fact that Paul always uses the passive form when referring to the act of baptism. The minority apparently considered Paul to be describing an actual Jewish practice, but this is unlikely. The unease some scribes felt with applying Christian baptismal practice to OT characters probably accounts for the change to the middle form.

Bruce M. Metzger, *A Textual Commentary on the Greek New Testament* (3rd ed.; Stuttgart: United Bible Societies, 1971) 559.

Baptism, though, is not Paul's main concern here for that sacrament does not provide as direct a connection between Israel's experience and the Corinthians' in the same way that the Lord's Supper does. The "baptism" of ancient Israel simply points to their having been fashioned as a covenant community through the saving activity of God, the same way Christian baptism signals entrance into the community of those saved by the gracious act of God in Christ. Similarly, in the same way that the church receives the bread and cup in the Lord's Supper, Israel in the wilderness received food and drink from God. Paul identifies the food and drink as "spiritual" (*pneumatikon*), and he attributes the same "spiritual" quality to the rock from which the drink came. [Spiritual Food] By referring to the rock as "spiritual," Paul does not mean that it was immaterial or that it possessed magical powers, though the *moving* rock certainly had unusual properties. The rock was miraculously provided by God as the source for the water in the wilderness. Thus, both the rock and the drink were "spiritual," not natural. Likewise, the manna miraculously given by God was "spiritual" bread. Eating the manna and drinking the water from the rock did not provide the Israelites with any special powers or immunities. It simply enabled them to survive. Nonetheless, the stress is on the supernatural source (God) of these daily necessities.

The real point that Paul is making with his creative reading of the exodus story is that *all* of the Israelites had the same food and drink. That point is easily lost when we focus on the extent to which his creative reading led him in identifying the mobile rock as Christ (v. 4). The idea that the rock followed the Israelites in the wilderness does not come from a literal reading of the Old Testament, but it was a conclusion apparently drawn by other readers in addition to Paul. The earliest known reference to the water source's following the Israelites appears to be by Pseudo-Philo in *Liber Antiquitatum Biblicarum* (*Biblical Antiquities*) 11:15, a writing probably dating from around the time of Jesus.[3] The tradition of the moving rock, which also appears in later rabbinic writings, was at least known to some Jewish interpreters during Paul's time. [The Moving Rock] After all, they could easily suppose that the Israelites needed water more than only twice during their forty-year journey. Exodus 17:1-7 describes God's provision of water from a rock at the beginning of the journey, while Numbers 20:2-13 depicts a similar event occurring near the end of their trek. Both episodes involve the Israelites' "quarreling" with Moses (and thus also with God) about their lack of water. In both accounts, the name of the

Spiritual Food

The divine apostle also, in calling the Lord "spiritual food and drink," suggests that he knows that human nature is not simple, but that there is an intelligible part mixed with a sensual part and that a particular type of nurture is needed for each of the elements in us—sensible food to strengthen our bodies and spiritual food for the well-being of our souls.

Gregory of Nyssa, *On Perfection* 58:107, in Gerald Bray, ed., *1–2 Corinthians* (ACCS NT 7; ed. Thomas C. Oden; Downers Grove IL: InterVarsity Press, 1999) 92.

The Moving Rock

Some rabbinical commentaries (*midrashim*) on Scripture composed in the 5th century AD or later refer to the moving well or rock that accompanied the Israelites in the wilderness. The midrash *Sipre Numbers* (11:21), which dates before the year AD 300, refers to a brook following them but does not mention a well or rock. The earliest clear rabbinic reference to the rock well is in the Tosefta, a supplemental collection of mishnaic teachings that was composed sometime before AD 400. It reads, "So the well which was with Israel in the wilderness, was like a rock, traveling with them" (*t. Sukkah* 3:11).

place of the incident is given as Meribah ("quarreling"). In Exodus 17:7, it is also called Massah ("test"). Paul alludes both to their "quarreling" (or "grumbling") and to their "testing" of God later in vv. 9-10, so these texts were in his mind. For Jewish interpreters, it was not a far-fetched idea to conclude that since a rock provided water for the Israelites at the beginning and near the end of their journey, it must have been the same rock and it must have traveled with them as the cloud did.

To make the leap to the assertion that the moving rock was Jesus, however, as Paul did, moves far beyond any conclusion one might draw from the stories in Exodus and Numbers. Paul was not the first, though, to see in the rock more than a source for water. The Wisdom of Solomon (11:1-8) sees wisdom at work during the wilderness journey and mentions the water from the rock as one of the events by which wisdom "prospered" Israel. Philo identifies the rock allegorically as the wisdom of God. [Philo on the Rock] Paul may have been influenced by previous associations of the rock and wisdom, and if so, his assertion that Jesus was the wisdom of God could have led him to posit that Jesus was the rock (wisdom). Probably more influential for Paul's identification of the rock as Christ, however, is the song of Moses in Deuteronomy 32. In that song, God is repeatedly referred to as the "Rock" (Deut 32:4, 15, 18, 30, 31), and a strong contrast is drawn between God the true Rock and the false rock (idols) the people turned to for refuge (Deut 32:31, 37). The song also includes the indictment "They sacrificed to demons" (Deut 32:17), which Paul cites in 10:20. The first reference to God as the Rock in Deuteronomy 32 follows this statement in 32:3:

Philo on the Rock

Philo interpreted the rock allegorically as the wisdom of God: "For the flinty rock is the wisdom of God, which he marked off highest and chiefest of his powers, and from which he satisfies the thirsty souls that love God" (*Leg. All.* 2.86). For Paul, Christ is the wisdom of God (1 Cor 1:24, 30). It was not a large step for Paul to take, therefore, in identifying the rock as Christ.

For I will proclaim the name of
the Lord;
ascribe greatness to our God!

The next two verses read:

The Rock, his word is perfect,
and all his ways are just.
A faithful God, without deceit,
just and upright is he;
yet this degenerate children have
dealt falsely with him,
a perverse and crooked generation.

A Christian Image

Moses makes a source spring from the rock. 3rd C. AD. Relief from an early Christian sarcophagus. Museo Nazionale Romano, Rome, Italy. (Credit: Erich Lessing/Art Resource, NY)

The connection Paul made between Christ and the rock from which Moses drew water is reflected in the use of the story in early Christian art. The corner panel of a 3rd-century-AD sarcophagus indicates the extent to which Moses' rock had become a Christian image.

The LXX version alters the last part of Deuteronomy 32:4 to read, "A faithful God, and he is not wicked; a righteous and devout lord." The word "lord" (*kyrios*) is not in the Hebrew text of v. 4, but its presence in the Greek version opened the door for Paul to link the verse to Christ. The Old Testament text uses typical poetic parallelism here in describing God, but the pairing of "Lord" and "God" in v. 3 and v. 4b (LXX) may have allowed Paul to read "Lord" in both instances as references to Christ. The pairing of "Rock" with "God" in v. 4a would have facilitated his identifying the Rock as Christ. Thus, vv. 3-4 could be seen by Paul as containing three references to God and three references to Christ ("Lord" twice; "Rock" once).

The text of Deuteronomy 32 provided Paul with much more than an opportunity to connect Christ to the story of Israel's wilderness journey. The anti-idolatry polemic of Moses' song undergirds Paul's total aversion to any semblance of idolatry by the Corinthians. This brings us back to Paul's objective in 10:1-4, namely to set the stage for the "But" of v. 5: "But with most of them God was not pleased; for they were mowed down (*katestrōthēsan*) in the wilderness." All of the Israelites received the same miraculous provisions from God, *but* most of them failed to remain exclusively devoted to the God who provided them and as a result met disaster.

Paul reveals his hermeneutical agenda in recalling Israel's story in v. 6: "These things have become our examples (*typoi*)."[4] "These things" refer to the parts of Israel's story he has already mentioned, as well as their particular offenses that he will now relate. The word *typoi* ("types") is sometimes overloaded by interpreters with meaning drawn from the typological exegesis that developed later in the early church. [Type] Paul's usage of the noun *typoi* here and the adverb *typikōs* in v. 11 is not laced with the kind of allegorical overtones that usually accompanied typological interpretations. His use of the Old Testament is more analogical here. The translation "example" for *typos* is acceptable if we recognize exactly what kind of example the incidents of Israel's failure constituted for the Corinthians. Because of their propensity for idolatry, God *made an example* of them. They are, thus, a negative example. "Prototype" is another valid translation, if prototype is taken as "a person or thing that serves as a model for one of a later period."[5] In a sense, what the Corinthians are experiencing in their temptation to compromise their exclusive relationship with God by eating food offered to idols was already experienced by ancient Israel. Most of ancient Israel gave in to this temptation and experienced the disastrous consequences. What one may learn from a prototype is not to repeat the same mistakes. The Corinthians have an opportunity to avoid disaster. Israel as prototype, then, is not a model to be emulated in this regard but a negative example for learning how to respond more appropriately to the dangers of idolatry.

Type

AΩ The word *typos* has occasioned much discussion as to its meaning in 1 Cor 10:5. Paul clearly uses the word simply to mean an example to be followed in Phil 3:17 and 1 Thess 1:7. In Rom 6:17, it has more the sense of a "standard." In Rom 5:14, Paul uses the word in reference to Adam in a sense that cannot mean example or standard. Adam, the ancestor of the human race and the one through whom sin came into the world, is a kind of prototype of Christ who brings new life to the human race and replaces sin with righteousness. In 1 Cor 15:22, 45-49, Paul does not use the word *typos*, but he depicts Adam as a prototype of Christ. He even calls Christ the "last Adam" in 15:45. In both Romans and 1 Cor 15, Paul portrays Adam and Christ alike as progenitors of the human race, but his stress is on the different kinds of life they bring. Adam is not an example or model for Christ; he is more of a "version one" that needed replacement by the perfected "version two," Christ.

Is this the sense in which Paul refers to Israel's exodus experience as "types" for the Corinthians in 1 Cor 10:6? Yes and no. Ancient Israel resembles the Corinthians in that they received the blessings of God and faced temptation to turn away from God. In this sense, Israel "prefigures" the Corinthians much as Adam prefigures Christ as progenitor (Hays, 162). The Corinthians, or any other members of the church, however, do not bear the image of ancient Israel the way humanity "bears the image of the man of dust" (1 Cor 15:49). Israel did not "live out" or "prefiguratively represent" the experience of the Corinthians in OT times as if the Corinthians were somehow present in them or connected to them. Israel did experience the same kind of blessing and temptation, but their response to both was different from what Paul hopes the response of the Corinthians will be. Most of Israel failed the test of "version one." Paul wants "version two," the Corinthians, to pass the test. Israel endured the consequences of its failures "prototypically" (1 Cor 10:11) in that the disasters that came upon them function now for the Corinthians as "examples" of instruction. One supposedly learns from prototypes how to avoid repeating the same mistakes.

Richard B. Hays, *First Corinthians* (IBC; Louisville: John Knox Press, 1997) 162.

Paul indicates that this is the intended function of the examples by adding the purpose clause, "so that we will not be desirers of evil just as they also desired" (v. 6b). The references to "desiring" (*epithymētas*, *epethymēsan*) alludes to Numbers 11:4-35 where the "rabble" among Israel had a strong "craving" for something to eat other than manna. They fondly recalled their Egyptian fare, especially the meat. God became angry about their craving but sent them an overabundance of quail. Before they could consume the quail, however, God sent a plague that killed the cravers. Their burial site bore the ominous name "Graves of craving." For those Corinthians who were arguing for their right to eat food offered to idols, the point of the example should have been clear. Their desire to eat the food made them "cravers of evil" facing the prospect of similar disaster.

10:7-13. Paul follows his not-so-veiled warning about desiring evil (i.e., food offered to idols) with four exhortations for the Corinthians not to be like those members of ancient Israel who sinned against God and met their doom (vv. 7-10).[6] The four exhortations parallel the four gifts of God named in vv. 1-4 (under the cloud, through the sea, spiritual food, and spiritual water). The "some of them" who transgressed in each exhortation contrasts with the all-inclusive nature of the gifts. All were equally blessed, but some sinned and died.

The first exhortation in v. 7 is stated as a clear imperative: "Do not become (or "be") idolaters, as some of them!" This is Paul's central command in this section, and he repeats it when he begins the next section in v. 14. The issue at hand concerns idolatry plain and simple in Paul's view. The Corinthian "knowers," of course, do not see it that way. Because they know that the gods represented by idols do not exist, they do not view their participation in meals involving food offered to idols as tantamount to idolatry. Paul does, and to make his point forcefully, he cites the classic episode of Israel's tragic indulgence in idolatry: the golden calf incident in Exodus 32:6. The line from the story Paul chooses to quote has clear implications for the Corinthian situation: "The people sat down to eat and drink and they rose up to play." At the very moment that God had brought Israel through the desert to the foot of Mount Sinai, from which would come the sacred law specifying their obligations to the God to whom they were bound, they sacrificed to an idol and then celebrated with revelry. The eating, drinking, and "playing" of the Israelites parallels the activity advocated by some of the Corinthians. They are not contending with Paul for the right to make sacrifices to pagan gods; they are

The Golden Calf

Emil Nolde. *Dance of the Golden Calf.* 1910. Neue Pinakothek, Bayerische Staatsgemaeldesammlungen, Munich, Germany. © Nolde Foundation Seebuell (Credit: Erich Lessing/Art Resource, NY)

Emil Nolde (1867–1956) was a deeply religious German Expressionist painter. His rendition of the golden calf story uses deliberately crude drafting and dissonant colors in portraying the Israelites with demonic faces and dancing in erotic frenzy.

asserting their right to participate in the celebratory banquets held in conjunction with various pagan festivals. The word translated "to play" (*paizein*) probably has sinister overtones for Paul. [Playing] Jewish critics of Gentiles often correlated idolatry and immorality. Paul follows this pattern in Romans 1:18-32 when he depicts the depravity of the Gentile world by first indicting them for idolatry and then immorality. The eating, drinking, and playing of the ancient Israelites before the golden calf signaled their self-reduction to the deplorable state of those outside the covenant community who abandon themselves to idolatry and immorality. Paul wants the Corinthians to avoid the "partying" that is one step down the slippery slope to idolatry.

Playing

ΑΩ The term translated "play" (*paizein*) is related to the word for child (*paidion*) and in its simplest sense means something like "child's play." "Playing" may sometimes refer to rather innocent, fun behavior such as playing games or dancing. "Playing" may also be contrasted with taking something or someone seriously and have the connotation of "playing with" or even "making fun of." "Playing" also could be associated with religion. The term *paizein* in the LXX version of Exod 32:6 translates the Hebrew word *tsakhaq*, which could also be used to refer to pagan cultic activity. The "playing" of the Israelites before the golden calf probably involved dancing, perhaps of an erotic nature. Playing games and dancing were traditionally a part of the festivities at the religious festivals in Greece. Winter has noted the disdain expressed by Greek and Roman moralists over the excessive eating, drinking, and sexual indulgences that often accompanied festive occasions. Paul's use of Exod 32:6 may have been a deliberate pointer not only to the eating and drinking of pagan cultic festivals but also to the unbridled revelry that was often a part of such celebrations.

Georg Bertram, "παίζω, ἐμπαίζω κτλ," *TDNT* 5:625–30.

Bruce W. Winter, *After Paul Left Corinth: The Influence of Secular Ethics and Social Change* (Grand Rapids MI: Eerdmans, 2001) 76–109.

The next three exhortations recall both specific infractions of ancient Israel and the terrible consequences. The "let us not" form used in vv. 8-9 (and perhaps in v. 10) expresses a prohibition but not as forcefully as the command given in v. 7. Paul's primary concern is that they not slide into idolatry, hence the stronger exhortation in v. 7. We should not conclude, however, that the exhortations in vv. 8-10 are added merely for effect. The particular episodes Paul rehearses from Israel's story have points of contact with the Corinthians' present experience. The incident recalled in v. 8 involved immorality that led to idolatry. In Numbers 25:1-9, some of the Israelite men had sexual relations with Moabite women and then participated in sacrificing, eating, and bowing down to the Baal of Peor. As a result, God sent a plague that killed 24,000 Israelites. Paul's 23,000 may reflect a loose recollection or another way of reading the death totals in the different stories he cites.[7] In any case, his prohibition against immorality here is tied by the story he cites to idolatry. The story reinforces Paul's Jewish perspective that idolatry and immorality go hand in hand. Eating, drinking, and playing lead one down the dangerous road to idolatry.

The third exhortation also recalls an incident involving food but not idolatry directly. In v. 9, Paul exhorts, "Let us not put Christ to the test, as some of them did and were destroyed by serpents." [The Text of 1 Corinthians 10:9] The specific incident involving the ser-

The Text of 1 Corinthians 10:9

Several early manuscripts (inc. ℵ B C) read *kyrion* ("lord") in v. 9 instead of *Christon* ("Christ"). One early codex (A) reads *theon*. Important early witnesses such as P46 D F G, however, support *Christon* as original. The criterion of the "harder reading" also supports "Christ" as the term written by Paul. Several scribes understandably considered it odd that Paul would essentially place Christ in the OT story, so they altered the text to what they considered to be a more plausible reading.

Bruce M. Metzger, *A Textual Commentary on the Greek New Testament* (3rd ed.; Stuttgart: United Bible Societies, 1971) 560.

pents is found in Numbers 21:4-9. Once again the people complained about their diet, and God punished them by sending poisonous snakes to bite them. Psalm 78 may have provided Paul with a lens for reading the story in Numbers. In Psalm 78:18, the peoples' demand for better food is described as "testing God." The people are also said to have "tested" God in Psalm 78:41 and 56. Throughout Psalm 78, Israel is depicted as consistently craving something other than what God supplied and turning away from their covenant obligations. Even without the lens of Psalm 78, however, Paul would have seen that "testing" God is a persistent theme in Numbers. In Numbers 14:22-23, God states that the people have tested him already ten times and that, as a result, most of the people shall not live to see the promised land.

Numbers also portrays the people as repeatedly complaining or "grumbling" (*gongyzō*) against God. This is the focus of the fourth exhortation in v. 10: "Do not/let us not grumble as some of them grumbled." [The Form of the Exhortations] No specific Old Testament episode matches up with Paul's language in this verse involving a time when "they were destroyed by the Destroyer (*olothreutou*)." The LXX version of Psalm 106:23 (LXX 105:23), however, employs a similar term (*exolethreusai* = "to destroy") to describe God's intended reaction to the people's idolatrous worship of the golden calf. This psalm includes a litany of Israel's transgressions in the wilderness sojourn, using many of the same words that Paul employs here to describe Israel's sins.[8] Right after God's expressed intent to destroy the people in Psalm 106:23, v. 25 describes them as "grumbling" in their tents. God's reaction to this grumbling, in Psalm 106:26-27, is to decree that they shall fall in the wilderness and their descendants scattered among the nations. Psalm 106 is referring here to the episode in Numbers 14:22-23 mentioned above. In Numbers 14:16 (LXX), we find the same verb (*katastrōnnymi*) Paul used in

The Form of the Exhortations

AΩ Willis has argued that Paul's exhortations in 1 Cor 10:7-10 follow a A-B-B-A pattern in that the first and last begin with imperatives while the second and third begin with hortatory subjunctives. This holds only if "grumble" in v. 10 is in the imperative form (*gongyzete*), which is the preferred reading of the UBS Greek NT 4th ed. The 3rd ed. of the UBS text, however, listed *gongyzete* only as a {C} reading (considerable degree of doubt) over *gongyzōmen*, the hortatory subjunctive form found in important early witnesses such as ℵ and D. The UBS committee decided that *gongyzōmen* in these texts was influenced by the subjunctive form in the preceding verse. Scribes may, indeed, have altered *gongyzete* to conform to the subjunctive pattern of the verbs in vv. 8-9. In light of the fact that Paul's main prohibition in 1 Cor 10:7-10 is against idolatry (v. 7), however, it would have been appropriate for him to use an imperative in v. 7 and subjunctives in the following three exhortations.

Bruce M. Metzger, *A Textual Commentary on the Greek New Testament* (3rd ed.; Stuttgart: United Bible Societies, 1971) 560.

Wendell Lee Willis, *Idol Meat in Corinth: The Pauline Argument in 1 Corinthians 8 and 10* (SBLDS 68; Chico CA: Scholars Press, 1985) 147.

1 Corinthians 10:5 to describe the people's being "mowed down" in the wilderness.[9] Most likely, then, the "destruction" Paul refers to in 10:10 is that near annihilation of Israel that occurred during the forty-year sojourn in the wilderness as a result of their chronic lack of faithful obedience to God. In any case, Paul's exhortations draw on both specific and general indictments of Israel's behavior as narrated in the Pentateuch and as rehearsed in the Psalms.

Perhaps the Corinthians were guilty of grumbling about Paul's restrictive policy regarding eating food offered to idols.[10] [Grumbling] It is not necessary, however, to match every single element of Paul's Old Testament examples with a specific counterpart in the Corinthians' experience. The basic approach of those who supported the practice of eating food offered to idols was itself indicative to Paul of the shortsighted and fatal perspective of those ancient Israelites who failed the tests of obedience in the wilderness.

Grumbling

Theodoret of Cyr offered an interesting explanation of their grumbling. In his *Commentary on the First Epistle to the Corinthians*, he wrote, "Some of the Corinthians were grumbling that they had only received the lesser spiritual gifts, when they wanted them all" (227).

Published in Gerald Bray, ed., *1–2 Corinthians* (vol. 7 of ACCS NT; ed. Thomas C. Oden; Downers Grove IL: InterVarsity Press, 1999) 64.

Paul repeats his hermeneutical principle in v. 11: "These things happened to them as an example (*typikōs*), and they were written for our admonition." As prototype, Israel experienced numerous temptations to violate its exclusive relationship with God, and repeatedly many of the Israelites failed. We should not overlook the other side of their experience, however. Not all of them failed. Israel as a covenant people survived. Prototypically experiencing what is "common to humanity" (v. 13), namely the temptation to turn from God, Israel endured the disciplining experience of both exodus and exile. The written record of their experience, from Paul's perspective, has a special relevance for his audience. The symphonic story of Israel continues but in a new key. Through Christ, Gentiles have been brought into the covenant community. They have become a part of Israel's story. This inclusion of Gentiles into the covenant community is itself a signal of the final movement of the symphonic story. Those who have been brought into the story in its final movement are those upon whom the "ends of the ages" have come. [The End] The plural of *ta telē* ("the ends") should not be ignored. For Paul, the two ages, the old and the new, intersect in the current generation. The new age has begun, yet the old age has not ended. Israel has not yet reached its home, but it now knows where it truly lies. The story of tempta-

The End

Paul mentions the end of the ages in order to startle the Corinthians. For the penalties which come then will not have a time limit but will be eternal. Although the punishments in this world end with our present life, those in the next world remain forever.

Chrysostom, *Homilies on the Epistles of Paul to the Corinthians* 23.5, in Gerald Bray, ed., *1–2 Corinthians* (ACCS NT 7; ed. Thomas C. Oden; Downers Grove IL: InterVarsity Press, 1999) 64.

Much to learn

tion, discipline, and survival continues. The current generation has much to learn from the paradigmatic generation of wilderness wanderers. As some of them were idolaters, indulgers in immorality, testers of God, and grumblers, so are some tempted to become such in the current generation. One who ignores the lessons learned by prototypical Israel runs the risk of destruction in the new wilderness. One who presumes to stand should beware of the potential for falling (v. 12). Exclusive loyalty to the one God is still required; compromising that exclusivity jeopardizes one's standing with God.

Paul brings the first stage of his argument, his negative proof, to an end in v. 13 with a word of encouragement that carries overtones of warning. Very literally, it begins, "Testing has not come upon you except [what is] human." The term *peirasmos*, of course, may be rendered "temptation" as well as "test." [Bearing Temptation] In a sense, either meaning fits the occasion, if we view the matter simply from Paul's perspective. Some of the Corinthians were inclined to participate in meals associated with the worship of idols. For Paul, this could be considered either a temptation to commit idolatry or a testing of their faithfulness, or both. Conceivably, he may have also intended a twist on the "testing" referred to in v 9. As Israel put God to the test, so those who are determined to eat food offered to idols are "testing" God. But would the Corinthians have viewed their experience as either "temptation" or "testing"? They did not see their action as committing idolatry, nor did they consider it to be faithless disobedience. They saw nothing wrong with eating food offered to idols since they could do it knowing that the idols represented nonexistent gods. What they would have considered *peirasmos*, however, was the pressure and possible ostracism they may have experienced if they refused to eat the food. Eating the food held many advantages in terms of maintaining their old network of relationships and preserving their standing in the community of Corinth. Not eating the food, when it was the normal thing for residents of Corinth to do, could potentially cause them significant loss of social status and social ties. As citizens of Corinth, they had a right to eat the food. As informed believers, they thought they could justify exercising that right and, thereby, avoid the "trials" (*peirasmos*) that nonparticipation might bring.

Bearing Temptation

Many do not bear it but are conquered by temptation. What God gives us is not the certainty that we shall bear it but the possibility that we may be able to bear it.

Origen, *On First Principles* 3.2.3, in Gerald Bray, ed., *1–2 Corinthians* (vol. 7 of ACCS NT; ed. Thomas C. Oden; Downers Grove IL: InterVarsity Press, 1999) 64.

Paul's words in v. 13 assure them that their experience is not unique. Others have faced similar trials. He further assures them that the God for whom they may have to experience such trials is a faithful God. That God will not let them face trials beyond their ability but will make a way out so that they can endure. Notice that the "way out" is not an exit *from* the trials but a means for making it *through* the trials. If they are faithful, God will enable them to endure. This assurance is rooted in the faithfulness of God. The only two times in the Old Testament where God is actually called "faithful" are Deuteronomy 7:9 and 32:4. We have already seen that Deuteronomy 32 lies in the background of thought in Paul's reference to the rock in v. 4 and that it is the source for Paul's assessment that idolatry actually involves offerings to demons in v. 20. The passage from Deuteronomy 7:9 is even more informative for understanding Paul's statement here. [Deuteronomy 7:9-10] The verse comes in Moses' assertion of God's covenant faithfulness. God is loyal to those who keep the covenant and vengeful toward those who do not. The word of assurance, then, carries the caveat that God's faithful provision of a way to endure trial is contingent on their faithfulness.

Deuteronomy 7:9-10

Know therefore that the LORD your God is God, the faithful God who maintains covenant loyalty with those who love him and keep his commandments, to a thousand generations, and who repays in their own person those who reject him. He does not delay but repays in their own person those who reject him. (NRSV)

The Lord's Supper as Sign of Exclusive Devotion to God, 10:14-22

10:14-18. Verse 14 begins the second stage of Paul's direct challenge to those who wish to eat food offered to idols. He restates the imperative he issued in v. 6 in a form similar to his command in 6:18 regarding immorality. In 6:18 and here he uses the verb *pheugete* ("flee"). In chapter 6, Paul was concluding his argument begun in 5:1 about not tolerating or associating with immoral members within the church. They are to flee from immorality even when it exists in a fellow believer. Here they are to flee from idolatry. [Flee Idolatry] They do not think they are idolaters themselves, but they want to associate with idolaters in idolatry-laden activity. Instead, Paul urges them to flee from such associations.

Flee Idolatry

When the apostle says: "Flee from the worship of idols," he means idolatry whole and entire. Look closely at a thicket and see how many thorns lie hidden beneath the leaves!

Tertullian, *The Chaplet* 10, in Gerald Bray, ed., *1–2 Corinthians* (vol. 7 of ACCS NT; ed. Thomas C. Oden; Downers Grove IL: InterVarsity Press, 1999) 64.

In vv. 1-13, Paul directed their attention to the negative example of Israel. Now he appeals to their own judgment about his analysis of idol worship (v. 15). They are "sensible" people; they can appreciate the point he is about to make. Perhaps, as Hays notes, there is a touch of irony in Paul's reference to them as "sensible."[11] In 4:10,

he juxtaposed them as "sensible" to his being a "fool." In the other instances where Paul uses the term translated "sensible" here (*phronimois*), it has the connotation of being "conceited" (2 Cor 11:19; Rom 11:25; 12:16). If Paul intends any irony in this instance, though, it is certainly muted by his reference to them as "my beloved" in v. 14. Rather than offend them through a veiled jab at their presumptuous knowledge, Paul seems to be genuinely appealing to their better judgment.

In leading them to arrive at his own conclusion about the real danger of eating food offered to idols, Paul asks a series of questions about the "connecting" power of food and drink in vv. 16-18. He points to the elements of the Lord's Supper and the sacrifices made by Israel as examples of partaking that connects participants. He then exposes the connection that occurs when people partake of food offered to idols in v. 20. Several questions about these verses divide interpreters. For one thing, how many meals does Paul intend here? Many interpreters see three: the Lord's Supper, contemporary Jewish sacrificial meals, and pagan sacrificial meals. Others see only two: the Lord's Supper and the food consumed by ancient Israel when they made sacrifices to pagan gods. The crux of this division between scholars is v. 20a. In the NRSV, v. 20a reads, "No, I imply that what pagans sacrifice, they sacrifice to demons and not to God." "Pagans" in the NRSV is a translation of *ta ethnē* ("the gentiles"), which appears in most early manuscripts but not in several other significant early textual witnesses. [The Text of 1 Corinthians 10:20a] If *ta ethnē* belongs in the text, then Paul clearly names three different meals. If not, then the sacrifices of v. 20 appear to be the same as those made by Israel in v. 18.

Deciding between the two options about the number of meals intended by Paul is not easy. The large number of early witnesses including *ta ethnē* and the fact that Paul is concerned with Corinthian participation in pagan sacrificial meals support the first option. So does the present tense form of the verb *thousin* ("they sacrifice"). Two features of Paul's argument, however, support the second. In v. 18, Paul refers to "Israel according to the flesh (*kata sarka*)." This could simply mean "historical Israel" in the sense of Israel as it consisted of flesh-and-blood

The Text of 1 Corinthians 10:20a

Verse 20a includes *ta ethnē* according to P46 ℵ A C and several minuscules and ancient versions. Important witnesses omitting *ta ethnē* include B D F G. Some scribes apparently changed the plural form *thousin* to the singular *thyei*. Metzger (561) and Garland (484–85) see this as a response to the insertion of *ta ethnē* into the text since *ta ethnē* is a neuter plural noun, which generally takes a third person singular verb ending. If *ton Israēl* (a neuter singular) in v. 18 is the intended subject of *thyō* in v. 20 (as Metzger contends), one wonders why Paul did not use the singular form originally. The best answer, it seems to me, is that Paul did not intend to restrict his focus to ancient Israel. He used the plural form *thousin* because he was also thinking of *ta ethnē*. The scribes who added *ta ethnē* did not miss his point, as they are often accused of doing.

David E. Garland, *1 Corinthians* (BECNT; Grand Rapids: Baker Academic, 2003) 480, 484–85.

Bruce M. Metzger, *A Textual Commentary on the Greek New Testament* (3rd ed.; Stuttgart: United Bible Societies, 1971) 561.

human beings. But what would be the counterpart? Paul never refers to a "spiritual Israel." The phrase *kata sarka* can be purely neutral, but it can also be used to describe life given over to the "dark side," in a sense (cf. Rom 8:3-13; Gal 5:16-24).[12] Paul has described ancient Israel in exactly this sense in vv. 5-10. In the wilderness, they repeatedly lived according to the flesh in disobeying God. The second feature supporting option two is the recognition that Paul's words in v. 20a are based on Deuteronomy 32:17, which in its context refers to Israel's idolatry. [Deuteronomy 32:17] In this case, both v. 18 and v. 20 refer back to the examples of Israel's indulgence in idolatry and eating food offered to idols, especially the classic case of the golden calf cited in v. 7.

Deuteronomy 32:17

They sacrificed to demons, not God,
to deities they had never known,
to new ones recently arrived,
whom your ancestors had not feared. (NRSV)

This still leaves unresolved the matter of the present tense verbs in both v. 18 and v. 20. All of Paul's references to ancient Israel in vv. 5-10 involved past-tense verbs. Has he suddenly shifted his focus to contemporary Israel, and is he referring to consumption of the sacrifices in Jerusalem and to current instances of Jewish idolatry that are actually, though unknowingly, directed toward demons? This is highly improbable. If v. 18 and v. 20 are connected, then Paul would be identifying the Jerusalem sacrifices as demon worship. Much more probable is the view that both verses refer to ancient Israel's indulgence in idolatry, but v. 20 is not limited to that. Thiselton argues that Paul in v. 20 changes the past tense of the verb found in the LXX version of Deuteronomy 32:17 "to indicate a permanent axiom with a present application."[13] If so, then in both v. 18 and v. 20 Paul has moved beyond Israel as an example of ancient failure to the axiom that what Israel did in sacrificing to demons is what all people do who sacrifice to idols. [Enoch 19:1] All people who eat the food involved in such sacrifices become connected to the demons to whom those sacrifices are made. The division between option one and option two, then, essentially becomes inconsequential. The early scribes who added *ta ethnē* to the text were not so mistaken in their understanding after all![14] The "pagans" are doing what ancient Israel did, and the Corinthians are following in the mistaken ways of both if they consume the food offered to idols.

Enoch 19:1

In the book known as *1 Enoch*, Enoch is transported into the heavens where he sees, among other things, the prison house for the stars and the powers of heaven who disobeyed God. Uriel, his angelic guide, tells him that at the appointed time, those angels who transgressed God's design (Gen 6:1-4) shall be confined to this prison. Uriel explains that these angels are behind the world's idolatry: "They have defiled the people and will lead them into error so that they will offer sacrifices to demons as unto gods, until the great day of judgment in which they shall be judged till they are finished."

E. Isaac, "1 (Ethiopic Apocalypse of) Enoch: A New Translation and Introduction," in *The Old Testament Pseudepigrapha, vol 1: Apocalyptic Literature and Testaments* (ed. James H. Charlesworth; Garden City NY: Doubleday & Company, 1983) 23.

The meals to which Paul points have several features in common. First of all, they involve a sacrifice. This, of course, is clear in respect to the sacrifices mentioned in vv. 18-20. In regard to the Lord's Supper, however, Paul does not describe it explicitly as such. In 11:26, in his recitation of the tradition he had passed on to the Corinthians about the Lord's Supper, Paul concludes that eating the bread and drinking the cup constitute a proclamation of the Lord's death. The meal of the Lord's Supper, though depicted by Paul as instituted by the Lord Jesus before his death (11:23), is perpetually observed as a result of his sacrificial death. The consumption of the food and drink of the Lord's Supper is participation in a sacrificial meal, no less so than is eating the food associated with other sacrifices.

Secondly, the consumption of this food establishes a connection (*koinōnia*) between the consumers and the actual sacrifice. Believers who drink the cup and eat the bread of the Lord's Supper have a "sharing" (*koinōnia*) in the blood and body of Christ (v. 16). Those members of Israel who ate the sacrifices are "sharers" (*koinōnoi*) in the altar (v. 18). Those who offer sacrifices to demons become "sharers" (*koinōnoi*) with demons in the demon's table (vv. 20-21). Without speculating on Paul's understanding as to *how* consuming what was not actually sacrificed established a connection to what was sacrificed, we can at least observe that Paul assumed a connection. The food and drink not "destroyed" on the altar but consumed by persons remains tied to the portion physically sacrificed. Thus, those who consume the bread and cup, which was not really sacrificed, are connected to the body and blood of Jesus that was sacrificed.

Thirdly, the connection is communal in nature, hence the term *koinōnia*, which indicates that something is held "in common." Those who consume the elements tied to the actual sacrifice become connected to each other. They form a fellowship (*koinōnia*) of partners (*koinōnoi*). Paul stresses this communal aspect in relation to the Lord's Supper in v. 17: "Because [there is] one bread, we the many are one body, for all partake of the one bread." [One Bread] The communal aspect is also present for participation in other sacrifices. The consumption of food in the name of a deity binds together the consumers. For polytheistic Gentiles, these bonds of fellowship were not exclusive. One might belong to overlapping fellowships, being bound to those sacrificing to Poseidon and to those sacrificing to Asklepios.

One Bread

So by bread you are instructed as to how you ought to cherish unity. Was that bread made of one grain of wheat? Were there not, rather, many grains? However, before they became bread, these grains were separate.

Augustine, *Easter Sunday*, 227, in Gerald Bray, ed., *1–2 Corinthians* (vol. 7 of ACCS NT; ed. Thomas C. Oden; Downers Grove IL: InterVarsity Press, 1999) 64.

For Paul, however, being a part of the *koinōnia* of Christ's blood and body precluded becoming a "sharer" in another sacrifice.

Fourthly and most importantly, consuming food associated with a sacrifice connected people to the one in whose honor the sacrifice was made. This is Paul's crucial point and his major concern. Those who partake of the table of the Lord share in the blood and body of the Lord. They are connected to Christ. Those who partake of the table of demons are connected to demons.

10:19-22. Paul began his argument against eating food offered to idols by citing slogans of the Corinthians: "An idol is nothing in the world" and "There is no God but one" (v. 4). In v. 19, he rephrases the first slogan as a pair of questions: "What am I saying? That food offered to idols is anything or that an idol is anything?" His own answer, paraphrased, is that both are "not anything," but neither are they "nothing." There is no God but one, but there are demons lurking behind the idols. For Paul, these are real entities that enslave people even though these entities are not gods (cf. Gal 4:8). [Demons] Those who participate in meals involving food offered unwittingly to demons establish an unintended connection to demons.

For Paul's analysis of the situation to be convincing to "sensible" people, those persons must share Paul's view regarding connections between food, sacrifices, and demons. We have no reason to suppose that his target audience did not share his perspective on the connection between food consumed in meals and the sacrifices offered on the altars. Nor should we assume that they did not share his views about demons. In light of popular Greek and Roman ideas regarding malevolent spirits, we should rather assume that they held the same position Paul did on the existence and

Demons

AΩ What exactly did Paul understand the demons (*daimonioi*) to be? The term *daimonion* was originally an adjective based on the noun *daimōn*, which in Pre-Hellenistic Greek could refer to the gods or lesser deities, anything that overpowers humans externally (e.g., destiny or death), protective deities, the divine element in humans, the spirit or ghost of the dead, or "shady" beings inhabiting dark or desolate places and performing mysterious activities (Foerster, 2–8). The adjective *daimonion*, then, could describe anything that exhibited any of the characteristics of a *daimōn*. The LXX uses *daimonioi* mostly in a pejorative sense to refer to pagan deities. Intertestamental Jewish literature began, possibly under Persian influence, to portray demons as malevolent spirits aligned with a Satan-like figure against God and the angels and both tempting and harming humans (Reese, 140).

Since Paul only uses the term *daimonion* in 1 Cor 10:20-21, we cannot know his precise view regarding demons. Kennedy (235), who holds that the food offerings (*eidōthyton*) in question in 1 Cor 8–10 consisted of food consumed in funerary meals at grave shrines, argues that *daimonion* must be understood as the spirit of a dead person, but his supporting evidence from Origen's 3rd-century response to Celsus is questionable. Though Paul does not use the term in Gal 4:8-9, much of what he states there about enslavement to beings who are not gods may be applicable to his view of *daimonioi* in 1 Cor 10. In Galatians, he describes the "not-god beings" as weak and beggarly "elementary spirits" (*stoicheia*). This depiction of pesky, supernatural forces of a low order meshes with the animistic view of "demonic spirits" in Greek and Roman popular religion. For Paul, the *daimonioi* are certainly not gods, but they are dangerous and troublesome.

Werner Foerster, "δαίμων, δαιμόνιον κτλ," *TDNT* 2:1–20.

Charles A. Kennedy, "The Cult of the Dead in Corinth, in *Love and Death in the Ancient Near East: Essays in Honor of Marvin H. Pope* (ed. John. H. Marks and Robert. M. Good; Guilford CT: Four Quarters, 1987) 231–34.

David George Reese, "Demons: New Testament," *ABD* 2:140–42.

threat of demons. What is new for them in Paul's analysis is the contention that demons are connected to the sacrifices and the consumed food. Their knowledge about the nonexistence of pagan deities was correct but incomplete. They had overlooked the role played by lower-level demonic entities. Missing this piece of the puzzle, they had not seen that their actions violated their exclusive commitment to the one God.

Paul concludes this section of his argument with a stern warning. Participation in the Lord's Supper and eating meals associated with pagan sacrifices are incompatible (v. 21). They cannot do both. They cannot drink the Lord's cup and the cup of demons. They cannot eat from the Lord's table and the table of demons. [Table of Demons] Since meals both in public and private settings often included libations in honor of the god of wine Dionysos, who was sometimes referred to as the "good *daimōn*," the implications of the first prohibition were far-reaching.[15] The second prohibition effectively excluded all consumption of food offered to idols in any setting. Association with idolatry in any form will not be tolerated by the jealous God who demands exclusive loyalty.

Paul's final words in v. 22 recall the tragic story of those Israelites who failed to recognize and live out their exclusive relationship to God, but they are directed toward his present audience: "Shall we [continue to] make the Lord jealous?" The present tense of the verb *parazēloumen* ("make jealous") conveys the idea of continuing the provocative behavior. Will they persist in their view that eating food offered to idols is an innocent activity and run the risk of bringing God's wrath upon them? Drawing on a persistent theme of Deuteronomy 32 once again, namely the "strength" of God to act decisively in punishing idolaters, Paul ends this section with a threatening question that casts the issue of eating food offered to idols in a dazzling new light.[16] The social pressure to eat may be strong. The insidious deception of demons may be strong. The Corinthians may even be strong-willed themselves and confident that their stance is valid. But, Paul asks, "Are we stronger than [God]?" Any "sensible" person would know the answer.

Table of Demons

AΩ The table (*traezēs*) of demons may refer to the table upon which a portion of sacrificial offerings was placed during a sacrifice. Part of the sacrificed was burned, part was given to the priestly officiants and the worshipers, and part was placed on the table (and was referred to as the *trapezomata*). The officiants and the worshipers might eat of the *trapezomata* during the feast following the sacrifice, and some of it might find its way into the markets.

Paul's reference to the cup of demons and the table of demons in 1 Cor 10:21 may allude to the known customs of sacrifice involving the *trapezomata*, but it probably also reflects Paul's deliberate juxtaposing of partaking of pagan sacrificial food and partaking of the two elements of the Lord's Supper, namely the cup and the bread.

David H. Gill, "Trapezomata: A Neglected Aspect of Greek Sacrifice," *HTR* 67 (1974): 117–37.

Eating or Drinking without Offense, 10:23–11:1

10:23-24. Verse 23 appears to be an abrupt break in the flow of Paul's argument. Actually, he has concluded his main argument that consisted of two proofs (8:8–9:27 and 10:1-22) and is now moving into the recapitulation section. In this section, he draws together some of the main points previously made and answers certain objections he anticipates his audience might have regarding the rigid position he has taken in forbidding the eating of food offered to idols. He begins this section, in much the same way that he concluded his argument about not tolerating immorality in chapters 5–6 (cf. 6:12), by quoting a slogan that undergirds much of the Corinthians' stance in regard to such matters. In both 6:12 and 10:23, Paul twice quotes the slogan "All things are permitted" and offers qualifications. [1 Corinthians 6:12 and 10:23] From the ensuing discussion, it is apparent that Paul accepts the basic principle of freedom embedded in the slogan, but he holds that this principle must give way to the higher principle of obligation whenever the two principles collide.[17]

1 Corinthians 6:12 and 10:23

1 Cor 6:12 "All things are permitted for me," but not all things are beneficial.
"All things are permitted for me," but I will not be enslaved by anything.

1 Cor 10:23 "All things are permitted," but not all things are beneficial.
"All things are permitted," but not all things build up.

The two qualifiers that Paul gives to the principle of freedom focus on what "benefits" (*sympherei*) and what "edifies" (*oikodomei*). In 6:12, Paul's similar qualification of the freedom principle focused on what was in the best interests of the persons who wished to exercise their freedom. In his argument there he tried to convince the Corinthians to take the body seriously and to realize the harmful effects of immorality on it. Previously in chapter 5, he had discussed the communal consequences of immorality. Here in 10:23ff, his focus is on the effects one's freedom might have on other persons. Thus, he is returning to the point of his first proof in 8:8–9:27. In 10:1-22, he tried to convince his readers that any involvement in idolatry by eating food offered to idols carries serious consequences for the participant. In recapitulating his argument here, he shifts the focus once more to the "other." In his conclusion (10:31–11:1), he will again stress the importance of not harming others. He will also point to his own example once again, as in 9:1-27, of seeking the "benefit" (*symphoron*) for others rather than his own. Verse 24 gives Paul's guiding rule of conduct for resolving the conflict between the two principles of freedom and obligation: "Let no one seek the _____ of himself/herself, but rather the _____ of the other." Paul does not supply a noun for the

Makellon

The term Paul used for market in 1 Cor 10:25 was *makellon*, a word that appears to be a Greek transliteration of a Latin term *macellum*, although the Greek form also appears in inscriptions prior to the arrival of Roman influence in Greece. The Latin term is derived from a word meaning "to enclose." A *macellum* or *makellon*, then, was an enclosed market as opposed to the open-air market area called the *agora* (Greek) or *forum* (Latin). Since it was a permanent, ongoing market, it is to be distinguished from the *panēgyreis* (markets at religious festivals), *nundiae* (periodic markets), and *mercati* (fairs) (Spawforth, 926). Many scholars assume that only meat was available in a *makellon*, but actually a variety of foodstuffs was sold (Cadbury, 141).

Market north of Corinth's forum. (Credit: Scott Nash)

Despite numerous assertions to the contrary, the location of the *makellon* referred to by Paul is unknown. Probably in Paul's day, the most established *makellon* in Corinth lay just north of the forum on the east side of the road to Lechaion just past the Peirene Fountain (see photograph). Inscriptional evidence and the design of the structure, with a large tholos in the center over a drain, support identifying this as a *macellum* that included a fish market (*macellum piscarum*) (Williams, 39–40). The "Peribolos of Apollo," whose partial remains are still visible on this site, was constructed after the earthquake of AD 77. Thus, the idea that this market had some "sacred identity" associated with Apollo or another deity during Paul's time is unfounded (Fotopoulos, 142). Other so-called markets identified as possible candidates for Paul's *makellon*, such as the structure farther north on the west side of the road (Murphy-O'Connor, 33) or the "North Market" due north of the Temple of Apollo, were, in fact, office complexes, not retail establishments (Williams, 40–44).

Tholos of fish market. (Credit: Scott Nash)

Undoubtedly, Roman Corinth had many markets that sold food. In fact, Paul actually wrote, "Buy everything sold in *a* market." He did not seem to have a particular market in mind.

John Fotopoulos, *Food Offered to Idols in Roman Corinth: A Socio-Rhetorical Reconsideration of 1 Corinthians 8:1–11:1* (Tübingen: Mohr Siebeck, 2003) 139–42, 240–41.

Jerome Murphy-O'Connor, *St. Paul's Corinth: Texts and Archaeology* (Collegeville MN: Liturgical Press, 1983) 33.

Anthony J. S. Spawforth, "Markets and Fairs, *The Oxford Classical Dictionary* (3rd ed.; ed. Simon Hornblower and Anthony Spawforth; Oxford: Oxford University Press, 1996) 926.

Charles K. Williams II, "Roman Corinth as a Commercial Center," in *The Corinthia in the Roman Period* (ed. Timothy E. Gregory; JRASup 8: Ann Arbor MI: Journal of Roman Archaeology, 1993) 31–46.

---

blanks, but it is probable that he is referring back to the "benefit" and/or "edification" of v. 23. "Seek the other's good," is his point. Obligation trumps freedom.

10:25-26. But freedom is not a principle that Paul takes lightly. It is also a guiding rule of conduct whenever it does not result in harm for another. Thus, he points to two situations regarding food offered to idols in which freedom can be exercised. The first concerns the freedom to eat whatever is sold in a market (*makellon*). [*Makellon*] "Eat everything sold in a market," Paul instructs them, "asking nothing on account of the conscience." He will repeat the phrase "on account of the conscience" twice more in vv. 27-28. Earlier in 8:10-12, Paul urged abstention from eating food offered to idols in an obviously religious context out of concern for those who might have a weak conscience. We should not assume that Paul has suddenly reversed his position and is now advocating that one could disregard another's conscience. The conscience in question in 10:25-26 is that of the person eating, not an observer. In the market, whether or not the food in question was previously associated with a religious context may or may not be determinable. Paul essentially argues, "It does not matter." Whatever association the food may have had with idol worship has been removed by its dislocation from a religious context. One can eat such unidentified food in "good conscience." One's conscience, furthermore, should not compel one to try to discern the origin of the food. "Don't ask, don't tell," is Paul's policy.

The reason Paul can exercise such freedom in regard to market food is that food, itself, is not the issue. Thus, Paul can quote Psalm 24:1 to the effect that God has dominion over all things, even food. The quotation also calls to mind Paul's words in 8:6 that God is the one "from whom are all things." The food can be appreciated as a gift from God. The slogan "All things are permitted" had special application to food in debates between Gentile and Jewish Christians. It is quite possible, in fact, that Paul himself had used the slogan in Corinth to counter the efforts of some to bring Gentile believers under the yoke of the Torah.[18] Paul's attitude toward kosher food rules was similar to his stance on circumcision. Such external markers were not important for Gentiles who had been brought into God's covenant community through Christ. In Romans 14:14, written later from Corinth, Paul would go so far as to declare no food unclean. [Romans 14:14-15] Paul is making clear here that his argument against eating food offered to idols is not based on any inherent "uncleanness" in the food. It is based on the food's connection to idolatry. Eating the food in an idolatrous setting potentially harms the believer of weak conscience and possibly exposes the eater to demonic influence. Removed from that context, the food may be consumed without regard to anyone's conscience.

Romans 14:14-15

In his letter to Christians in Rome, Paul appears to affirm the cleanness of all food, but at the same time he urges Gentile believers to be considerate of Jewish Christians who have scruples about eating certain foods. Gentile believers are free from kosher rules, but they are not free to harm their more scrupulously inclined fellow believers.

"I know and am persuaded in the Lord Jesus that nothing is unclean in itself; but it is unclean for anyone who thinks it unclean. If your brother or sister is harmed by what you eat, you are no longer walking in love." (NRSV)

10:27-30. Paul also affirms freedom in regard to dining in the home of a pagan friend. "Eat everything set before you, asking

Eating

We must shun gluttony and eat only what is necessary. But if some unbeliever invites us to a banquet and we decide to accept, the apostle tells us to eat whatever is set before us. We do not need to abstain from rich foods completely, but we should not hanker for them either.

Clement of Alexandria, *Christ the Educator* 2.10, in Gerald Bray, ed., *1–2 Corinthians* (vol. 7 of ACCS NT; ed. Thomas C. Oden; Downers Grove IL: InterVarsity Press, 1999) 64.

nothing on account of the conscience" (v. 27b). [Eating] Once again, the policy is "Don't ask, don't tell." The food's possible former connection to idol worship no longer exists. Once again, however, obligation trumps freedom. If someone points out that the food comes from a religious context, then the connection with idolatry is reestablished and the food should not be eaten. The identity of the person raising the question and the source of their knowledge about the food's origins are much debated. Some see the questioner as a fellow believer dining with one of the "knowing" believers in a pagan friend's home. This is unlikely for at least two reasons. One is that the questioner refers to the food as *hierothyton* ("sacred-offering food"), which is what a pagan would probably call it, rather than the pejorative term *eidōlothyton* ("food offered to idols") one would expect a believer to use. Secondly, it is doubtful that a believer who had such scruples about eating food would have been in attendance at a dinner in a pagan's home. One wonders, too, how a fellow guest would know the origin of the food. The questioner is most likely the pagan host who, either out of respect for the guest's known religious commitments or, less likely, in an attempt to "test" the guest's convictions, points out to the guest the food's former connection to pagan sacrifices. The host may know the food's former religious ties because it has been brought directly from the temple, some inquiry about its origins was made when it was purchased in the market, or it is part of a sacrifice performed at home. In any case, the guest faces the dilemma of choosing whether or not to eat.

Paul's counsel is clear: "Do not eat the food!" Note, however, that the hypothetical situation posed by Paul in v. 28 is introduced with the word *ean* ("If it should possibly happen that . . .") rather than the word *ei* (simply "if") that he used in v. 27.[19] Regardless of the remoteness of the possibility of the food's being identified as *hierothyton*, however, the hypothetical case demonstrates how one should resolve the conflict between freedom and obligation. In such a setting, doing something "on account of conscience" means abstaining from the food. The believer's conscience is still not in question, but the unbeliever's conscience is. That is why Paul clarifies whose conscience he means in v. 29. Not knowing that the food was connected to pagan religion frees the believer to eat it, but learning about the connection places the believer under the prohibition once again. This time, however, it is not out of consideration for a fellow believer's conscience but the conscience of the unbeliever. Why? Several answers have been suggested, but the one most in keeping with Paul's general argument about doing what is good for the other is that the believer's partaking of the food damages the believer's integrity as an authentic witness to the unbeliever. The unbeliever's conscience and capacity to be won over to the one God are affected negatively by the believer's unfaithful action. [Christian Freedom]

Christian Freedom

What Paul means is this. God made him free and put him beyond harm's reach, but the Gentile does not understand his rule of life. He cannot see the nature of Christian freedom and will say to himself that Christianity is a lie, because although Christians shun demons, they are prepared to eat things which have been offered to them, so great is their gluttony. Such a judgement may be unfair, but it is better not to give the Gentile any room for judging at all.

Chrysostom, *Homilies on the Epistles of Paul to the Corinthians* 25.2, in Gerald Bray, ed., *1–2 Corinthians* (vol. 7 of ACCS NT; ed. Thomas C. Oden; Downers Grove IL: InterVarsity Press, 1999) 64.

The two questions that Paul interjects in vv. 29b-30 present an enigma for interpreters. Paul asks, "For why is my freedom judged by another's conscience? If I partake with thanksgiving, why am I slandered on account of that for which I give thanks?" The two questions express a position that seems to run counter to what Paul has just advocated in vv. 28-29a. Many different explanations of the apparent incongruity have been offered, but three views commend themselves the most. The first two views take the two questions to be expressive of Paul's own stance in regard to freedom and conscience. One view holds that v. 29b follows the train of thought begun in v. 27 and interrupted by the hypothetical parenthesis of vv. 28-29a.[20] In v. 29b, Paul resumes his argument as to why the believer should not ask any questions regarding the food on account of conscience. In essence, Paul would be saying, "I can eat the food in good conscience. My conscience is not subject to another's conscience, and my freedom to eat is not determined by their conscience. If I am thankful for this gift of food from God, then who has a right to slander me?" [Unjust Slander] The second view also sees the questions as defending the believer's freedom to eat without guilt or criticism, but it does not see vv. 28-29a as a parenthesis.[21] Instead, the two questions in vv. 29b-30 explain the distinction being made in v. 29a between the believer's conscience and the other person's conscience. In choosing to refrain from eating, the believer is not allowing someone else's conscience to judge the believer's freedom. Nor does the believer deserve criticism for eating with thanksgiving to God. Both views maintain the emphasis on freedom that Paul articulates in vv. 25-27. Neither view, however, adequately overcomes the stark difference of per-

Unjust Slander

Paul is saying that an idolater can have it both ways. On the one hand, he can glory in his idols, and on the other hand he can attack the apostle for eating what has been sacrificed to them, even if the latter does so after giving thanks to God. Such a person has an excuse for remaining in his error and sets a bad example to the brethren.

Ambrosiaster, *Commentary on Paul's Epistles* 81.118, in Gerald Bray, ed., *1–2 Corinthians* (vol. 7 of ACCS NT; ed. Thomas C. Oden; Downers Grove IL: InterVarsity Press, 1999) 64.

Possible Settings for the Meals

John Fotopoulos identifies five possible settings for the meals discussed in 1 Cor 10:27–11:1. He sees (c), (d), and (e) as possibilities; he favors (d) as the most likely context.

(a) Food sacrificed in a temple and eaten in a temple precinct.
(b) Sacrificial food purchased from the *macellum* and eaten in a temple precinct.
(c) Food sacrificed at a temple, taken home, and eaten in a home.
(d) Sacrificial food purchased from the *macellum* and eaten in a home.
(e) Food sacrificed in a home and eaten in a home.

John Fotopoulos, *Food Offered to Idols in Roman Corinth: A Socio-Rhetorical Reconsideration of 1 Corinthians 8:1–11:1* (Tübingen: Mohr Siebeck, 2003) 139–42, 241–42.

spective between what Paul states in vv. 23-24, as well as vv. 28-29a, and what the questions affirm. Freedom is important to Paul in this section, but, as we have already seen, obligation trumps freedom. It is difficult to see Paul arguing otherwise now as forcefully as he does if the questions express his own position.

The third view, therefore, understands the questions to be Paul's articulation of objections he anticipates his audience might make.[22] Having argued that one should eat everything bought in the market or served in a pagan host's home without regard for conscience, how can Paul compromise a believer's freedom to eat anything that is a part of the Lord's creation if they do so thankfully? How can someone else's conscience determine what a believer does if a believer is not even to let his or her own conscience be a factor? The two questions vividly express such understandable objections to Paul's apparent inconsistency. [Possible Settings for the Meals]

Two major problems present themselves for accepting this view. One has to do with the form of the questions. If Paul is here using the diatribe form of presenting the objections of an imaginary interlocutor, one would expect him to introduce the questions with a phrase such as, "Someone might say." Instead, we find Paul using the phrase *hinati gar* ("For why"). The word *gar* ("for") usually functions as a conjunction connecting what follows to the preceding as an explanation, inference, or cause, but not as an adversative, which is what we should expect here.[23] In certain questions, however, especially those expressing surprise or indignation (as in v. 29b), *gar* may be used to heighten the effect.[24] So the form of the questions does not present a real obstacle for this view. The other problem this view faces, however, is the apparent lack of an answer to these imaginary objections. If Paul is going to raise anticipated objections, we would expect him to respond to those objections. Perhaps Paul does respond in his conclusion.

10:31–11:1. The conclusion to Paul's entire argument about eating food offered to idols comes in 10:31–11:1, and it emphasizes exactly the counterpoints Paul has made throughout to those who think their knowledge about the oneness of God gives them the freedom to exercise their right to eat. These concluding verses pick up the theme of his first major proof in 8:8–9:27 and the thrust of his argument in 10:23-24. They also speak directly to the objections raised in the questions in vv. 29b-30. "Whether you eat or drink" relativizes the significance of either action in the light of the greater admonition to "do everything to the glory of God." Paul has been arguing long and hard against certain eating and drinking practices some Corinthians want to maintain. He has made allowances for those situations where the freedom to eat and drink pose no problems. In the end, however, the question of eating and drinking must surrender itself to the larger issue of living in such a way that glory rebounds to the God about whom the Corinthians claim to have such liberating knowledge. In the end, it is not about us; it is about God.

What does doing everything to the glory of God entail? Since the God involved is the God revealed in the cross of Christ, it means giving up claims to freedom and rights when they prove detrimental to others. Echoing his appeal to his own example of becoming all things to those under the law and those outside the law (9:20-21), Paul urges them to become a "non-damaging influence" (*aproskopoi*) for either Jews or Greeks.[25] The addition of "the church of God" to this pair echoes his warning in 8:9 about the damage those who exercise their right can inflict on the weak. Translating v. 32 as "Give no offense" fails to capture the impact of Paul's words. He is concerned about actually harming someone else by creating a barrier between them and the gospel (cf. 9:12b). That this is his concern is born out by Paul's stated aim in v. 33: "so that they may be saved." Likewise, when he refers to "pleasing" everyone in all he does, Paul does not mean getting on their good sides or receiving their approval. "Not harming" and "pleasing" are not matters of getting and staying in one's good graces. They are more tangible than that. They have to do with "benefiting" and "edifying," the themes with which Paul began his recapitulation in 10:23. Paul states this clearly when he says he does not seek his own "benefit" but that of those to whom he ministers.

Paul closes in 11:1 with the same call he gave in his first argument against divisions in 4:16: "Be imitators of me." This time, however, he adds, "as I am of Christ." The way of life Paul advocates relishes the freedom that the believer enjoys in Christ. It always recognizes, however, that freedom in Christ is shaped by the image and example of the Christ who gave himself fully for the sake of others. When that personal freedom collides with the obligation to do what benefits or builds up another,

Perfect Christianity

This is the rule of the most perfect Christianity, a landmark exactly laid down, the point that stands highest of all. Nothing can make a person like Christ more than caring for one's neighbors.

Chrysostom, *Homilies on the Epistles of Paul to the Corinthians* 25.3, in Gerald Bray, ed., *1–2 Corinthians* (vol. 7 of ACCS NT; ed. Thomas C. Oden; Downers Grove IL: InterVarsity Press, 1999) 64.

that freedom must give way. Paul has claimed this way of life, serving the other, as the example he has learned from Christ, and he has offered it once again as the pattern for all believers. [Perfect Christianity]

CONNECTIONS

Finding Ourselves in the Story

For interpreters trained to be sensitive to the historical context of a biblical text, Paul's use of the Old Testament in 1 Corinthians 10:1-13 may appear to be straining the literary and theological integrity of the Scriptures. After all, would either Moses or the composers of the exodus narratives have ever considered the passage through the sea as a type of baptism? Would they have understood the food and water provided by God in the wilderness as "spiritual" food and drink, much like the cup and bread of the Lord's Supper? Would they have seen that the rock from which God's gift of water gushed forth was a living, "spiritual" entity capable of following them around? Even more, would they have suspected that the rock was Christ? Paul seems to play fast and loose with these texts, allowing his creativity and desire to find some relevant connection to his experience and leading him to ignore the "meaning" of the texts in their own contexts.

For interpreters sensitive to finding their own "meaning" in biblical texts, however, Paul's approach may not appear so far fetched. For Paul, the "meaning" of a biblical text could not be reduced to discovering the "point" of a narrative or isolating the "timeless truth" of nonnarrative texts. For Paul, "meaning" lies in the interaction between the reader and the text. Rather than plumb the text to mine its "meaning," the text leads us to probe our lives to find our "meaning." Who are we? What do we "mean"? Where do we find ourselves in the Story?

When Paul began in 10:1 by saying, "I want you to understand that *our* ancestors," he was addressing Gentile believers who were not biological descendants of ancient Israel. Yet, the story of Israel in Scripture was also their story. [The Story] Indeed, they (we) are part of a Story that includes and transcends the story of Israel. Israel's story is the foundational narrative for understanding our Story, but our Story includes more than Israel's story. It also includes the story of Jesus and the story of the church. The story of Jesus shapes the way the church reads Israel's story. The church's story shapes the way we read the story of Jesus. Still again, the story of Israel and the story of Jesus shape the way we read the church's story. For Paul, the three fundamental stories are intertwined in the one Story. Each story informs the others. Israel's story is read in light of the church's encounter with Jesus' story and in light of the church's role in the larger Story. Thus, Paul can find Jesus and the church *in* the story of Israel. But the stories of Jesus and the church can only be understood in light of Israel's story. Likewise, the stories of Israel and the church derive their "meaning" from Jesus' story.

> **The Story**
>
> The Story is a tale as large as the universe and yet as small as an individual human being. It is, however, not a Story about everything, not even about all of human history. It is a Story that focuses on God's relationship to humankind, from the beginning of the human race in Adam to its climax in the eschatological Adam, and beyond. It is a Story about creation and creature and their redemption by, in, and through Jesus Christ. It is a Story about a community of faith created out of the midst of fallen humanity. It involves both tragedy and triumph, both the lost and the saved, both the first and the last. Its focus is repeatedly on divine and human actions on the stage of human history. It is out of this Story, which Paul sees as involving both history and His story (i.e., Christ's), that he argues, urges, encourages, debates, promises, and threatens.
>
> Ben Witherington III, *Paul's Narrative Thought World: The Tapestry of Tragedy and Triumph* (Louisville: Westminster/John Knox Press, 1994) 2.

Together, these three stories give us the floor and walls of our Story. The room is incomplete, however, until the ceiling of our own experience is placed atop the walls to form our Story. For that to happen, our personal story must become intertwined with the other three. We read our personal story in the light of the stories of Israel, Jesus, and the church to discover where we are in the Story. When we find ourselves in their stories, we reread our own story to find our place in the Story. Reading all of these stories as a part of the Story, we discover what these stories "mean," and we discover what we "mean."

But what does this imply about the way we approach the biblical texts? Does it lead us to ignore questions of historical context? No, but it does lead us to see that once we have arrived at an understanding of what the biblical texts may have meant in their own contexts, we have not yet arrived at the "meaning" of those texts. To do that, we have to enter the texts and become a part of the stories they embody. When Paul cited Exodus 32:6 in 1 Corinthians 10:7 about how the Israelites "ate and drank and rose up to play," he obviously had the Corinthians in mind. By reading them into the story of Israel's great failure, he was leading the Corinthians to see their own behavior in a new light. We can easily make the connection between Israel's behavior and that of the Corinthians, but do we see ourselves in their stories? Can we make the same kind of connection to our lives that Paul was trying to make between Israel and the Corinthians? When have we, as they did, dabbled in a little idolatry? When have we eaten, drunk, and played at the foot of the holy mountain, or when have we

Embodied Stories

He Qi. *Moses Striking Rock*. 2002. Watercolor on paper. (www.heqigallery.com)

Cultural differences may prevent one from easily entering into the stories found in Scripture. Sometimes the biblical story must be recast in the dress of one's culture before one can enter the story. Chinese artist He Qi has tried to overcome the foreignness of Christianity for Chinese culture by painting scenes from biblical stories using traditional Chinese techniques. His interpretation of Moses' striking the rock depicts Moses in traditional Chinese priestly attire.

courted the approval of our society by engaging in behaviors that compromise the claim on us made by the one God? Or, perhaps more accurately, when have we not?

Perhaps we should forgive Paul of his creative license with the biblical texts and indulge in a little more of it ourselves. Perhaps then the stories of Israel and of the Corinthians would appear less strange. Perhaps we would see that they are our ancestors, too. Perhaps, by entering more creatively into their stories, we will find our place in the Story.

Partners with Demons

In 1 Corinthians 10:20, Paul reveals his real concern about believers dabbling in idolatry in any form: they will become partners with demons. The pagan gods represented by the idols may not exist, but other powers do exist, and they can establish a partnership with unwary participants in pagan sacrifices. The possession of knowledge about the gods, the idols, and the sacrifices does not prevent the demons from using the perceived empty rituals of pagan religion to become partners with believers. Though Paul does not mention this threat of demons elsewhere in his writings, he does depict the worship of beings who are not gods as enslavement (Gal 4:8-9). Nonbelievers are under the power of demons, and believers who engage in pagan activity, however slight, are not immune.

Belief in demons as powerful beings who occupy a place between the divine and human have been a part of most ancient cultures. In fact, one can find this belief in demons throughout much of human history, including the present time. In his book, *The Demon-Haunted World*, scientist Carl Sagan argues that the old belief in demons has been transformed by many people today into stories of abduction by aliens. In the Middle Ages, demons were believed to visit unsuspecting men and women in the night to engage in sexual activity. This partnership of sorts was explained by St. Bonaventure as involving the seduction of men by female demons (*incubi*) who, upon receiving the male semen, were allowed by God to change into male demons (*succubi*) and deposit the semen into their female victims.[26] With the rise of modern science and the concurrent scientific explanation of many acts previously blamed on demons, demons were replaced in the modern psyche by aliens, who are believed by many people to have abducted them in order to perform sexual experiments on them. Of course, in some circles, the aliens are thought to be the same creatures as the demons of old. [Hal Lindsey] Sagan attributes this persistent belief in malevolent beings who are out to harm people to shared delusions based on the way humans are constructed biologically and on their common cultural expectations.

Demons at Dinner

In the manner of the Python Painter (4th C. BC). *Young men at a Symposium, with Bacchic demons.* Krater painting. Museo Gregoriano Etrusco, Vatican Museums, Vatican State. (Credit: Alinari/Art Resource, NY)

Demons were thought to live in the air above human beings and below the dwellings of the gods. On this Classical Period Greek Red-face krater, the faces of demons appear above the young men who are dining.

Hal Lindsey

I have become thoroughly convinced that UFOs are real. . . . They are operated by alien beings of great intelligence and power. . . . I believe these beings are not only extraterrestrial but supernatural in origin. To be blunt, I think they are demons . . . part of a Satanic plot.

Hal Lindsey, *Planet Earth—2000 A.D.: Will Mankind Survive?*, as cited by Carl Sagan, *The Demon-Haunted World* (New York: Ballantine Books, 1996) 129.

Walter Wink, however, argues that stories about demons or other malevolent forces do not necessarily reflect delusions that can be dispelled by science but may reveal insight into real powers that are work in the world both for good and evil. [Wink on Demons] He writes, "When a particular Power becomes idolatrous, placing itself above God's purposes for the good of the whole, then that Power becomes demonic."[27] He thinks we mistakenly assume that all ancients, including Paul, con-

Wink on Demons

No intelligent person *wants* to believe in demons, but the utter failure of our optimistic views of progress to account for the escalating horrors of our time demands at least a fresh start at understanding the source and virulence of the evils that are submerging our age into night, leaving us filled with such a sense of helplessness to resist.

Walter Wink, *Unmasking the Powers: The Invisible Forces That Determine Human Existence* (Philadelphia: Fortress Press, 1986) 41 (author's italics).

ceived of these Powers as "a variety of demonic beings flapping around in the sky, occasionally targeting some luckless mortal with their malignant payload of disease, lust, possession, or death."[28] Because our categories of thinking are shaped by the myth of materialism and because we assume that the ancients saw reality the same way, we reject their views as being unrealistic and unimportant. Demons as supernatural beings do not exist, for most of us, so the danger of becoming partners with demons is nonexistent.

When we approach the matter from this perspective, we are walking in the sandals of the Corinthians. They, not because of science but because of their newly found faith, possessed the knowledge that pagan gods do not exist. Hence, they had no need to fear any danger from idolatry. Armed with our scientific knowledge that demons do not exist, we have no need to fear them. Paul's response to the Corinthians' "knowledge" was that it was incomplete. His response to our "knowledge" would probably be similar. The Corinthians stood in danger not of possession by demonic beings but of seduction into the arms of idolatry. The fear that Paul wanted them to have was not of the demons themselves but of their partnership with demons and, more importantly, of God's response. Becoming partners with demons amounted to repudiation of their partnership with God. "You cannot have it both ways," Paul argued. "You are either bound exclusively to God, or you are not." What was demonic about their experience is that they believed they could live fully in the world where God is sovereign and in the world where other powers antithetical to God assert their sovereignty. We make the same mistake when we participate, however innocently, in the power structures and systems of the world that present the "goods" of this world as the highest good. When we give in to the lure of materialism and the commodification of life, believing that we can indulge in ways and means that ignore the will of God for the whole world but bring us personal benefit *and* still serve God faithfully, then we have unwittingly become partners with the demonic.

What "Did" Jesus Do?

For some time now, the letters WWJD have appeared on t-shirts and bracelets. The letters represent the question, "What would Jesus do?" Answering that question when faced with a decision about what to do in a given situation is supposed to guide one to make the correct decision. Would Jesus drive an SUV? Would Jesus buy stock in a company known to engage in actions that harm the environment? Would Jesus support an unjust war? Would Jesus watch R-rated movies? So on it could go. The positive intent of this question is that it recognizes Jesus as a model for ethical decision-making. The negative side is that it presupposes that we can think as Jesus thought and therefore know what Jesus would do if he were faced with our choices. Being unable to think as Jesus thought, we are left with a lot of wiggle room to fashion Jesus in our own image. He becomes a source of support for our decision, whatever *we* decide it should be.

WWJD

(Credit: www.istockphoto.com)

Paul does not appear to have touted a WWJD bracelet. Instead, he pointed repeatedly to what Jesus *did*. The most significant thing Jesus did, according to Paul, was to die on the cross. (Perhaps Paul would have worn a cross necklace, if one were available.) In 1 Corinthians 2:2, Paul stated that the only thing he wanted to know was "Jesus Christ and him crucified." Throughout the letter, when Paul mentions Christ, the cross is usually in the picture, most often front and center.

The last word in his long argument about eating food offered to idols in 1 Corinthians 11:1 is Christ. "Be imitators of me, as I am of Christ," he wrote in conclusion. This deceptively simple exhortation caps the concluding section of his argument (10:23–11:1). The section began with Paul quoting a slogan that typified the ethical filter used by the Corinthians: "All things are permitted." The mesh of that filter was not fine enough for Paul. Twice he chipped away at the apparent incontestable weight of this principle by adding, "Not all things are beneficial; not all things build up." Then he offered two other exhortations based on what Jesus *did*: "Let no one seek his/her own [benefit], but the [benefit] of the other person" (v. 24); "Whatever you do, do to the glory of God" (v. 34). What Jesus did was to die for the sake of others. The Lord of glory was crucified (2:8). For Paul, doing everything to the glory of God means following the way of the cross. That way is the way of sacrifice, not of offerings on an altar but of a life lived in service to others.

Richard Foster warns us, however, that service itself runs the risk of becoming "self-righteous."[29] [Self-righteous Service] Self-righteous service sees service as a way to impress God and other persons by doing large and noticeable acts. It seeks rewards for the servant and

Self-righteous Service

Self-righteous service fractures community. In the final analysis, once all the religious trappings are removed, it centers in the glorification of the individual. Therefore it puts others into its debt and becomes one of the most subtle and destructive forms of manipulation known. True service builds community. It quietly and unpretentiously goes about caring for the needs of others. It draws, binds, heals, builds.

Richard J. Foster, *Celebration of Discipline: The Path to Spiritual Growth* (rev. and exp. ed.; San Francisco: Harper & Row, 1988) 129–30.

is calculated to achieve visible results. It is service done not so much for the sake of the other person or to the glory of God but for the glory of the servant. True service seeks the benefit of the other. True service is a lifestyle. True service imitates Christ. True service means that every day, in some way, the servant is crucified.

Lectionary Connections

For the Third Sunday in Lent in Year C, the Revised Common Lectionary includes readings from 1 Corinthians 10:1-13, Isaiah 55:1-9, and Luke 13:1-9. The Gospel reading contains Jesus' words about the need for repentance and the parable of the fig tree that receives another, but last, chance. The Isaiah passage also stresses repenting and seeking the Lord's forgiveness. This correlates well with Paul's use of the punishment Israel experienced in the wilderness as a word of warning to the Corinthians. Lent is a season for soul-searching, for confession and repentance, and for seeking forgiveness. It is a time to remember the warning signs and to heed them.

NOTES

1. Clement of Alexandria, *Christ the Educator* 2.1.14, in Gerald Bray, ed., 1–2 Corinthians (vol. 7 of ACCS NT; ed. Thomas C. Oden; Downers Grove IL: InterVarsity Press, 1999) 100.

2. Richard B. Hays, *First Corinthians* (IBC; Louisville: John Knox Press, 1997) 160.

3. Daniel J. Harrington, "Pseudo-Philo," in *The Old Testament Pseudepigrapha* (ed. James H. Charlesworth; Garden City NY: Doubleday & Company, 1985) 2:299.

4. The genitive plural *hēmōn* (lit., "of us") could be taken as a genitive of reference and be translated "in reference to us" or "for us" (NRSV). The genitive of reference is very rare in the NT, however, and in this instance the more common sense of possession ("our") is probably intended.

5. *Webster's New World College Dictionary* (4th ed.; Foster City CA: IDG Books Worldwide, Inc., 2001) 1154.

6. The use of the ascensive conjunction *mēde* (sometimes meaning "not even," but here meaning "and not") before each of the four exhortations in vv. 7-10 indicates that they are additional, specific prohibitions that stem from the basic prohibition given in v. 6, "not to crave evil."

7. See David E. Garland, *1 Corinthians* (BECNT; Grand Rapids: Baker Academic, 2003) 462–63, for possible explanations of Paul's computations.

8. See discussion by Garland, *1 Corinthians*, 464.

9. See discussion by Gordon D. Fee, *The First Epistle to the Corinthians* (NICNT; Grand Rapids: Eerdmans Publishing, 1987) 450.

10. Suggested by many scholars, including Garland, *1 Corinthians*, 464. Hays, *First Corinthians*, 165, acknowledges the possibility but also recognizes that "grumbling" may represent a comprehensive judgment on unfaithful people.

11. Hays, *First Corinthians*, 166.

12. Eduard Schweizer, "σάρξ, σαρκικός κτλ," *TDNT* 7:127, argues that *kata sarka* has a negative connotation only when used with a verb, but he notes that in 1 Cor 10:20 it "carries with it an evaluation." In the context of 1 Cor 10, this evaluation can only be negative.

13. Anthony C. Thiselton, *The First Epistle to the Corinthians: A Commentary on the Greek Text* (NIGTC; Grand Rapids: Eerdmans, 2000) 775. Garland, *1 Corinthians*, 480, sees Paul contemporizing the language of Deut 32:17. Neither Thiselton nor Garland, however, explores the full import of this.

14. Contra Thiselton, *The First Epistle to the Corinthians*, 772–75.

15. John Fotopoulos, *Food Offered to Idols in Roman Corinth: A Socio-Rhetorical Reconsideration of 1 Corinthians 8:1–11:1* (Tübingen: Mohr Siebeck, 2003) 177.

16. See Brian S. Rosner, "'Stronger Than He?' The Strength of 1 Corinthians 10:22b," *TynBul* 43 (1992): 171–79.

17. See Joop F. M. Smit, *"About the Idol Offerings": Rhetoric, Social Context and Theology of Paul's Discourse in First Corinthians 8:1–11:1* (BET 27; Leuven, Belgium: Peeters, 2000) 140–41.

18. Ben Witherington III, *Conflict and Community in Corinth: A Socio-Rhetorical Commentary and 1 and 2 Corinthians* (Grand Rapids: Eerdmans, 1995) 167–68.

19. Observed by Garland, *1 Corinthians*, 494.

20. Garland, *1 Corinthians*, 499, favors this view.

21. Smit, *"About the Idol Offerings,"* 143–44, argues for this view.

22. Fotopoulos, *Food Offered to Idols in Roman Corinth*, 247–48, presents an argument for this view.

23. Daniel B. Wallace, *Greek Grammar Beyond the Basics: An Exegetical Syntax of the New Testament* (Grand Rapids: Zondervan, 1996) 673–74.

24. Herbert Weir Smyth, *Greek Grammar* (Cambridge MA: Harvard University Press, 1920, 1984) 638.

25. Thiselton, *The First Epistle to the Corinthians*, 794, translates the phrase as "avoid doing damage."

26. Carl Sagan, *The Demon-haunted World* (New York: Ballantine Books, 1996) 124.

27. Walter Wink, *Naming the Powers: The Language of Power in the New Testament* (Philadelphia: Fortress Press, 1984) 5.

28. Ibid., 4.

29. Richard J. Foster, *Celebration of Discipline: The Path to Spiritual Growth* (rev. and exp. ed.; San Francisco: Harper & Row, 1988) 128–30.

PROBLEMS IN THE CONTEXT OF WORSHIP

1 Corinthians 11:2-34

"What kind of god art thou, that suffer'st more of mortal griefs than do thy worshipers?"[1]

Chapter 11 marks a transition by Paul to a new set of behavioral issues involving the Corinthian church as it was gathered for worship. This new focus continues through chapter 14. The three issues Paul addresses are the proper head attire for men and women (11:2-16), the proper observance of the Lord's Supper (11:17-34), and the proper use of spiritual gifts (12:1–14:40). Only in the case of the last matter does Paul use the phrase *peri de* ("now concerning") to introduce the topic. Its use in 7:1, 7:25, and 8:1 indicate that he was responding to matters the Corinthians had raised in their letter to him. Its presence in 12:1 may or may not indicate that he is returning to the subjects of their letter after dealing with the problems addressed in chapter 11. (See [The Phrase *peri de* in 1 Corinthians] in the Introduction.) Paul apparently learned of the problem of discrimination in observances of the Lord's Supper from an oral report (11:18), but he does not divulge how he learned about the problem of head attire. Hurd argues that Paul's style of argumentation in 11:2-16 resembles more the calm, sympathetic style of chapters 7–10 than it does the confrontational, critical style of chapters 1–6, and so he considers it likely that the section concerns a topic from the Corinthians' letter.[2] If he learned about that matter also from an oral report, however, then we can detect a pattern in his approach. Paul addressed issues the Corinthians had written to him about in chapters 7–10 only after confronting the problems he had heard about from vis-

A Thematic Outline of 1 Corinthians 11:2-34

- I. Proper Head Attire When Praying and Prophesying in Worship (11:2-16)
  - A. Paul's Judgment about What Is Proper (11:2-12)
    - 1. Opening Commendation for Maintaining the Traditions (11:2)
    - 2. Argument Based on the "Head" (11:3-6)
    - 3. Argument Based on Creation (11:7-12)
  - C. Paul's Call for the Corinthians to Judge What Is Proper (11:13-16)
    - 1. Argument Based on Nature (11:13-15)
    - 2. Argument Based on Established Practice (11:16)
- II. Proper Observance of the Lord's Supper in Worship (11:17-34)
  - A. Paul's Description of the Problem (11:17-22)
  - B. Paul's Reminder of the Lord's Supper Tradition (11:23-26)
  - C. Paul's Prescription for Resolving the Problem (11:27-34)

iting messengers. Similarly, as he turns to a new set of problems in chapter 11, he first deals with what had been brought to his attention through word of mouth and then addresses matters from the Corinthians' letter once again. Either way, chapters 11–14 form a unit dealing with problems arising in the context of worship.

[A Thematic Outline of 1 Corinthians 11:2-34]

COMMENTARY

Beyond the context of the church at worship, the two problems Paul addresses in chapter 11 do not appear to be related to each other. If we give due consideration to the social dynamics of each problem, however, we may detect a common source for both.

The problem of head attire has to do with the public roles of women and men or, more specifically, wives and husbands. In Roman society, married women typically covered their heads in public. Men typically did not, except for certain men in religious settings. Paul clearly argues against the practice of women uncovering their heads when praying or prophesying in a worship assembly. Though it is less certain that it was an issue in Corinth, he also argues against men praying or prophesying with their heads covered. The women and men who were most likely to view the matter of head coverings differently from Paul were those of higher social status, or at least those who were influenced by the practices of higher-status persons. If his real concern is only with the women, as some interpreters argue, then Paul was still dealing with a social dynamic, namely the resistance of some women to the traditional markers of sexual differentiation.

The problem in regard to the Lord's Supper also concerns distinctions between groups in society, only in this case it has to do with socioeconomic differences. In short, church members of higher status and affluence were discriminating against members of lower status and means in connection with the food served in a worship setting. Whereas Paul calls for maintaining traditional symbols of sexual difference in regard to head attire, he opposes allowing traditional socioeconomic distinctions to be observed when the church is gathered for worship. Paul's arguments in both cases make some appeal to theological matters, but the problems themselves were social in nature.

Proper Head Attire When Praying and Prophesying in Worship, 11:2-16

In seeking to understand what Paul is trying to do in 11:2-26, we have to address several questions that have generated much study and discussion. These questions are four in number, with the first question involving two components.

(1) What exactly is Paul arguing against in these verses?
  (a) Is he concerned with "hairstyle" or "head attire"?
  (b) Is he concerned with both men and women or only women?
(2) Does he refer to "women" and "men" or "wives" and "husbands"?
(3) What does he mean by the word "head" (*kephalē*)? 
(4) Why did Paul consider this to be a problem?

These questions are all interconnected, with the answers for each one affecting how one answers the others. Rather than rehearse all of the scholarly debate regarding these questions, I will simply note the major options for answering them and focus on the ones I think have the most merit. One can consult the commentaries and special studies I mention for more thorough discussions of the details.

What exactly is Paul arguing against in these verses? This question necessarily breaks down into two related parts. *Is he concerned about "hairstyle" or "head attire"? Is he concerned with both men and women or only women?* To answer the question of what he was arguing against, we have to decide what the questionable behavior was and who was doing it.

Several interpreters have taken the position that Paul was concerned with hairstyles for men and women.[3] In the case of women, they argue that Paul was bothered that some women in the church were either (1) adopting hairstyles that too closely resembled the hairstyles of men (i.e., short hair) or (2) allowing their hair to fall down and become disheveled during worship in a way that resembled either the practice of prostitutes or the frenzied behavior of women involved in some pagan cults. In the first instance, the short hair of the women blurred the boundaries of sexual differentiation, and Paul wished to uphold the cultural norm of men and women being different in appearance. In the second instance, Paul was concerned that the loosed-hair women might be seen as "loose" women sexually and bring shame upon themselves, their husbands, and the church, or that their loosed-hair praying and prophesying would lead outsiders to see the church as a cult like those that

Roman Hairstyles

Archaeological Museum of Ancient Corinth. (Credit: Scott Nash)

National Archaeological Museum, Athens, Greece. (Credit: Scott Nash)

involved frenzied, ecstatic worship practices. In the case of men, some interpreters see Paul upset that some men were wearing their hair too long, which in Roman society signified effeminacy. They, like the loosed-hair women, were violating the cultural norms of differentiating between the outward appearances of men and women. In vv. 14-15, Paul argues that nature itself teaches us that men should have short hair and women long hair. These verses are then used to interpret v. 4, in which Paul says that a man who prays or prophesies with his hair "down from the head" (*kata kephalē*) dishonors his head (*kephalē*). This interpretation, in turn, leads to reading v. 5 as referring to women who pray or prophesy "loose-haired" (*akatakalyptō tē kephalē*) and thereby dishonor their head (*kephalē*). In my opinion, the interpretations that see hairstyles as the issue misread the phrases *kata kephalē* and *akatakalyptō tē kephalē* and miss the double meaning Paul gives to the word *kephalē*. They also misunderstand the function of vv. 14-15 in Paul's argument.

Paul is concerned about what one does or does not wear on her or his head during worship.[4] More specifically, he is concerned about the head attire of those who pray or prophesy in worship. He clearly opposes women who pray or prophesy with their heads "uncovered," which is the most natural reading of the phrase *akatakalyptō tē kephalē*. Why he opposed this practice will be discussed below. Though it may or may not have been an issue in the Corinthian church, he also opposes the practice of men praying or prophesying with their heads covered. The fact that he thought men should not have their heads covered in such circumstances shows that Paul was not trying to impose Jewish or oriental customs on the Corinthians, as many interpreters have assumed. If he were doing that, he would have insisted that the men cover their heads, not uncover them. Nor was he trying to overcome the resistance of Corinthian women to the imposition of the oriental practice of wearing a veil. He was not writing about veils in the sense of a face covering. He was writing about head coverings. He was writing to women and men who lived in Roman Corinth. He was writing about Roman customs, not Jewish or oriental.

But who was his real target group? Was he actually concerned about the head attire of both men and women or only the women? The traditional view is that he was only concerned about the women, and much in this passage suggests that such was the case. Paul clearly devotes more space to women than to men in this section. His references to men are always paired with references to women (vv. 3, 4-5, 7, 8-9, 11-12, 14-15), while he sometimes addresses women without any reference to men (vv. 6, 10, 13). One may argue that all the references regarding men are designed to support his argument about women.

Still, the fact that he does discuss what is proper regarding men and always mentions men first when paired with his words about women should not be overlooked. His greater attention to women may suggest that they were his primary target group, but what he writes about men could very well reflect a secondary concern. Paul argued that a man ought not to cover his head (v. 7), and he considered it to be dishonorable to the man's "head" to pray or prophesy with his head covered (v. 4). Why he might have considered this to be a problem will be discussed below. At this point, I would simply suggest that Paul was concerned about the head attire of both women and men.

But which women and men are the objects of Paul's concern? Is it all men and women or only some? His concern seems to focus on women and men who are praying and prophesying in a worship setting, but does he also intend for all women and men to heed the instructions he gives for these worship leaders? Answering this question involves considering what Paul means when he uses the terms *gynē* and *anēr*. The word *gynē* may be translated as "woman" or "wife," while the word *anēr*, likewise, may mean "man" or "husband." Unlike the more generic term *anthrōpos*, which may simply mean "person," *anēr* typically means a "male" and when joined with *gynē*, it frequently means "husband." In certain verses in this section, the general meanings of "woman/female" and "man/male" might be present, but in other verses the words indicate "wife" and "husband." In the case of *gynē*, the distinction between "woman" and "wife" is only significant in a few instances since the women actually dealt with by Paul would in all likelihood have been wives. Recognizing that Paul at times refers to wives and not women in general, however, is important for understanding the point he is making and why he makes it. By the same token, whether Paul meant "husband" or "male" is significant in only some cases, but in those cases, it is very significant to see that he meant "husband" and not "male." My position is that when Paul argues that a woman should cover her head, he specifically means

"wives." The issue of covering the head for women is determined by their relationship to their husbands. A wife should not pray or prophesy with her head uncovered. In the case of men, however, the issue of not covering the head is not determined by their relationship to their wives but by their relationship to Christ. No man should pray or prophesy with his head covered.

This leads to a consideration of the question about the meaning of the word for "head" (kephalē). [Chrysostom on the Head] The term obviously has both material and metaphorical meanings. Materially, *kephalē* means the part of the human body that sits atop the neck. One key to understanding Paul's instruction here is to recognize when he uses the term in the material sense and when he does not. Another key is to understand what *kephalē* means for Paul when he uses the term metaphorically. It is on this point that interpreters are the most divided.[5] The divisions root in different critical assessments of the metaphorical meanings of "head" in ancient writings, but they also reflect the inevitable bias of the interpreters. The options for metaphorical meaning that have the most support are (1) authority,[6] (2) source,[7] and (3) foremost part.[8]

Chrysostom on the Head

The word head is used in two different senses here, since otherwise absurdity would result. The distance between Christ and man is far greater than between man and woman, on the one hand, or between Christ and God on the other, and is of a different kind. Christ and God are equal in substance but different in relationship, and the same applies to man and woman. But between God and Christ the Son on the one hand and man [and woman] on the other, there is a vast difference of substance as well of relationship.

Chrysostom, *Homilies on the Epistles of Paul to the Corinthians* 26.3, in Gerald Bray, ed., *1–2 Corinthians* (vol. 7 of ACCS NT; ed. Thomas C. Oden; Downers Grove IL: InterVarsity Press, 1999) 105.

The idea of the "head" as the authority over something can be found in ancient Greek literature, but not nearly as often as one might suppose, that is, one accustomed to viewing the head as the control center for the body. Because we see the brain, which is housed in the head, as the part of the body "in charge" of the rest, we often use "head" to mean the person in authority, as in the department "head." Ancient anatomical views, however, typically located the control center in some other part of the body. Thus, "head" was not generally considered to be an appropriate metaphor for the person "in charge."

Identifying who is in charge, furthermore, has no real relevance for Paul's argument in 1 Corinthians 11, though many have used his references to "head" in this passage as a basis for asserting male "authority" over women. The meaning "source" may relate to what Paul wrote about the woman being made from the man in v. 8, but the use of "head" as "source" is practically nonexistent in ancient writings. That leaves "head" as the "foremost part." The "head" of something is the front part or the top part, that is, the part that ones sees first. The head is representative of the whole. This usage can be found in the ancient writings, and it fits the context of

1 Corinthians 11. The husband was the recognized representative of the family. He was its public face. The behavior Paul criticizes in this passage presents no challenge to a husband's "authority," but it does threaten to dishonor his public face. If we understand Paul's symbolic usage of *kephalē* in this way, then we can appreciate both the connection and contrast he makes between the material and metaphorical meaning of "head."

Finally, we can address the last question: *Why did Paul consider this to be a problem*? Some wives apparently were uncovering their heads when they prayed or prophesied in worship. Perhaps some men were covering their heads as they prayed or prophesied. Why was Paul concerned? In the case of the men, the covering of the head was accomplished not by the donning of a hat but by pulling the back of their togas up over their heads as a hood. The toga was hanging "down from the head," hence the meaning of *kata kephalēs* in v. 4. This was the regular Roman guise for the person leading a religious function, as significant statuary from Corinth shows. By following this custom in a church worship setting, the man was dishonoring his "head" (Christ) in two ways. First, he was incorporating pagan ritual into Christian worship. Understandably, the men of the church in Corinth were in a sense only following the patterns of piety they had witnessed and practiced all their lives before becoming a part of the church. It most likely seemed to them to be an appropriate way to express their devotion to Christ. But for Paul, it signified the intrusion of pagan idolatry into the church. Secondly, the man who covered his head in pagan worship was the leader of the ritual. He was the "head" of the ceremony as the one who stood in front of the others and represented them before the deity. For Paul, this signified that the man who covered his head was drawing attention to himself as the leader-representative of the church. He was dishonoring the true "head" of the church, Christ. If this situation actually existed in the Corinthian church, then one could suppose that the persons who adopted such a

Covered Heads

Two statues from Ancient Corinth show the emperors Augustus and Nero with their togas pulled up over their heads, which served to represent them both as pious and as religious leaders in their guise as Pontifex maximus.

Augustus Statue. Archaeological Museum of Ancient Corinth. (Credit: Scott Nash)

Marble Head of Nero. Archaeological Museum of Ancient Corinth. (Credit: Scott Nash)

practice were those who were accustomed to doing so prior to becoming a part of the church. That is, they were most likely the men of higher status. Thus, the covering of the head reinforced the same hierarchy of status that existed outside the church. To maintain their awareness that the church had only one head and that all members were equally a part of Christ's body, Paul instructed the men not to cover their heads.

In the case of the women, the uncovered head of the wife dishonored her "head" (husband). Only three kinds of women appeared in public with their heads uncovered in Roman society: virgins, widows, and prostitutes. Married women covered their heads in public. Married women who appeared in public without their heads covered were behaving as if they were not married; that is, they were giving the appearance of being prostitutes. This brought shame upon a woman's household and dishonor to the husband in particular. Evidence exists that some Roman women of means deliberately violated this custom as a way of exerting their right to engage in the same promiscuous behavior that Roman society allowed for men. The scandalous nature of their actions evoked criticism and scorn from many moralists of the period, and it also inspired certain social legislation under Augustus. Whatever the motives may have been for women in the church to follow this pattern, Paul saw it as a threat to the reputation of the church and possibly as a threat to its survival. Outsiders perceiving that the church tolerated or promoted scandalous behavior by the wives could conclude that the church was a subversive threat to society.

A Roman Woman

National Archaeological Museum, Athens, Greece. (Credit: Scott Nash)

To summarize the answers I would give to the four questions identified above, (1) Paul is arguing against the practice of women removing the head coverings that signified they were married and against the practice of men covering their heads during times when either would be praying or prophesying in church, (2) he is usually referring to wives and husbands in his discussion, (3) he uses the word "head" both to mean one's physical head and metaphorically to mean the foremost person in a relationship, and (4) he considered the practices to be detrimental to the health and reputation of the church.

11:2-12. Paul's argument falls into two basic parts. In the first part (vv. 3-12), he presents his reasons for opposing the customs of headdress practiced by some women, and probably some men, when the church is gathered for worship. In the second part (vv. 13-16), he calls upon the Corinthians to judge for themselves what is proper on the basis of "nature."

Before launching into his argument, though, Paul makes a transition from his long treatise on eating food offered to idols by extending a word of commendation to his readers. He ended his previous argument with a call for the Corinthians to imitate him (*mimētai mou*) as he imitates Christ (11:1). In v. 2, Paul commends them for remembering him (*mou memnēsthe*) in everything and for maintaining the traditions just as he transmitted them to the Corinthians. The similar sounding words suggest that remembering Paul is one way of imitating him, and he commends them for doing so. This verse seems out of place, however, in light of the argument that follows, in which he tries to convince them to stop doing something that is contrary to his teaching. Why does he commend them and then try to correct them? Some suggest that the verse is simply a rhetorical attempt to begin the argument on good footing by creating a sense of goodwill between Paul and his audience. Others see a cryptic criticism of their actual failure to maintain the traditions. Still others think that his compliment refers to a particular part of the practices he describes in the following verses, namely that they are allowing women to pray and prophesy in church as he had instructed them to do. What is clear is that Paul begins his argument in v. 2 in a much more positive way than he begins the next argument in v. 17. The contrast between the two beginnings and the similar terminology could hardly be accidental. Paul's criticisms in 11:17-34 are sharp and condemnatory. I suggest that Paul begins the first argument the way he does, with a soft pat on the back, in order to set the stage for the slap in the face that will follow.

Verse 3 functions somewhat as a rhetorical *propositio* in that it lays down a premise that Paul will appeal to in his argument. The statement in v. 3, however, is not a thesis that Paul wants to prove. He presents it as a given and uses it to support the first half of his argument. The premise specifies three pairs of relationships: (1) the head of every man is Christ, (2) the head of a wife [is] the husband, and (3) the head of Christ [is] God. If Paul was intending for this to represent a hierarchy of relationships, he would have stated them in a descending or ascending order. Instead, he gives the pair man-Christ first, then wife-husband, and then Christ-God. The first two pairs establish the premise he will use in his argument about the head attire of men and wives. The third comes into play only indirectly in v. 7. Notice that Paul refers to *all* men in the first pair but only to *a* wife in the second. All men are not the "head" of all women. Only in the relationship between husband and wife does the husband in any sense constitute the "head." Above I argued that "head" does not signify "having authority over" but rather "being the foremost part of" the relationship. In Roman society, the husband was the public face of the family. His basic point is that in each of these relationships, one member of the pair is the "head." The "head," as the foremost member in the pair, is entitled to honor in some sense from the other member.

Verse 4 follows the pattern established in v. 3 of mentioning the man (in relationship to Christ) before the wife (in relationship to the husband). Any man who prays or prophesies with uncovered "head" (material sense) dishonors his "head" (metaphorical sense). The man dishonors Christ. [Pelagius on the Men] In the context of Roman Corinth, a man who pulled the back of his toga over his head was signifying his role as leader in a religious ritual. This was a pagan custom; Paul did not want it to be practiced in church. Furthermore, no man had the right to assume the role of "head" of the church; that role was Christ's alone. Paul may have only begun with the example of a man to set up his application of the same principle to the case of a wife. I think it most likely, however, given the fact that the men of the church in Corinth grew up in a religious context in which the men who exercised leadership roles in ritual activity normally pulled their togas over their heads, that some of the Corinthian male believers considered this to be a proper way to express their piety in church. Paul wanted to correct their thinking and their practice.

Pelagius on the Men

Paul was complaining because men were fussing about their hair and women were flaunting their locks in church. Not only was this dishonoring to them, but it was also an incitement to fornication.

Pelagius, *Commentary on the First Epistle of Paul to the Corinthians* II, in Gerald Bray, ed., *1–2 Corinthians* (vol. 7 of ACCS NT; ed. Thomas C. Oden; Downers Grove IL: InterVarsity Press, 1999) 106.

The behavior of the wives, however, is probably Paul's main concern. In v. 5, he begins to address the wives the same way he addressed the men, but then he elaborates considerably beyond the simple point of similarity. The wife who prays or prophesies with her "head" (material sense) uncovered, dishonors her "head" (metaphorical sense). The wife dishonors her husband. The wife does not dishonor all men, nor does she dishonor Christ. She is not guilty of violating any divinely established hierarchy of male-female relationships in the church, nor is she assuming a leadership role that she ought not to have. She is also not claiming for herself a role that belongs only to Christ, as the man with covered head does. The wife is recognized by Paul to have the same right to pray and prophesy in the church as a man. The only boundary she has overstepped is that of proper deportment toward her husband. She has removed the social marker that identifies her as a married woman. From society's perspective, she is appearing unmarried, unattached, and available for sexual exploitation when she is, in fact, married to her husband. In a shame-honor culture, she is guilty of inflicting dishonor on her legal spouse.

The seriousness of this situation both for the married couple and for the church leads Paul to elaborate on the scandalous nature of such behavior. The wife is presenting herself as an unmarried woman by uncovering her head. This, Paul argues, is tantamount to having her head shaved. Why so? The shaving of a woman's head in Greco-Roman society signified sexual shame, either adultery or prostitution. [Shaving an Adulteress] Why does Paul think that the act of removing one's head covering qualifies one to be treated as a person guilty of sexual offense? He goes so far in v. 6 to argue that if the wife refuses to cover her head, then she should be shaved. Note that Paul is not accusing the women of wearing their hair too short. He is accusing them of behaving in a way that merits a complete shaving. Why does Paul consider her offense to be so great?

Shaving an Adulteress

In defending Fortune against unjust blame, Dio Chrysostom noted that Fortune had produced women of renown in the past, including Demonass, who gave to Cyprus certain laws, including one about adultery: "She [Demonassa] gave the people of Cyprus the following three laws: a woman guilty of adultery shall have her hair cut off and be a harlot—her daughter became an adulteress, had her hair cut off according to the law, and practiced harlotry."

Dio Chrysostom *Or.* 64.3 (LCL; trans. H. Lamar Crosby; Cambridge MA: Harvard University Press, 1951).

Winter has presented significant evidence that in Roman society a movement had begun among some higher-status married women that involved their assertion of their rights to engage in the same lifestyle permitted for married Roman men, including sexual promiscuity.[9] One of the practices of these "new" Roman women was to appear in public with their heads uncovered. The only women who were expected to appear with heads uncovered in a social setting that included dining were prostitutes. When married women appeared in such settings, they were viewed as intentionally presenting themselves as prostitutes. Since a desire for sexual freedom was apparently the primary motivation for their actions, they were essentially pursuing adultery. The penalty for a woman convicted of adultery sometimes included public humiliation by shaving her hair and reducing her status to that of a prostitute.[10] Whether the motives behind this early feminist movement were as sinister as they are depicted by ancient writers (men) or not, the reputation of these women was shameful and their husbands were dishonored for allowing it to happen.

If Winter has correctly analyzed the situation regarding the "new" Roman women, then it may enlighten us as to why Paul took the matter so seriously. The married women who appeared in a public setting that involved dining, as the worship services in Corinth described by Paul clearly did, were seen as emulating the behavior of those women that Roman society considered scandalous. The women may not have intended to project such an image. Since the worship services often took place in private homes, they may have thought it was quite acceptable to uncover their heads in the presence of "family." The fact that Paul only deals with a situation in which women are praying or prophesying may mean that the habit of removing the head covering is not in itself the main concern. Only when women attract attention to themselves by leading in worship does the issue become important. That is the point at which they become most visible and most susceptible to being viewed as scandalous women.

But who would view them in this way? Would the more devout members of the church frown upon these underdressed women daring to lead in the holy worship of God? Would male fellow worshipers read the uncovered heads of the women as permission to make sexual advances toward them? I am not convinced that Paul's concern is that the uncovered heads of the women would interfere with the ability of the men in the crowd to stay focused on worship, as some interpreters argue. That may or may not have been the case. Paul's concern is not so much that the bare-headed women will tempt the men to think improper thoughts or pursue improper liaisons. Rather, he is concerned that these women will be misread as advocates of the promiscuous behavior attributed to the "new" Roman women. If women are viewed this way when they are leading the church in worship, then the social stigma attached to such women in Roman society could be affect the way the church itself was seen by outsiders.

Syllogism in 1 Corinthians 11:6

If (a) a woman will not cover her head, then (b) she should be shaved.
If (c) being shorn or shaved is shameful, then (a) let her be covered.

Paul's attempt to convince the wives of how shameful the behavior is takes the form of a syllogism in v. 6. [Syllogism in 1 Corinthians 11:6] The syllogism assumes the connection between being shaved (or shorn) and shame. It also assumes that this assumption is widely shared. The association of shaved or shorn heads with adultery or prostitution was in all probability widespread. The syllogism is the climax of Paul's first effort to convince the women to stop uncovering their heads when they pray or prophesy. It is an act that brings dishonor to the husband and shame to the woman. Though Paul does not say so, the practice could also damage the church's reputation.

In vv. 7-12, Paul offers another reason why the practice should stop, one based on creation. The first proof in vv. 3-6 is simple in comparison to this second one. The first proof focuses on pairs of relationships and the dishonor one half of a pair may inflict on the other. The second proof is more theological in nature and offers reasons that may not have been self-evident to Paul's audience. Parts of his argument here are simply baffling, and one can easily see why such a thick forest of interpretation has grown up around these verses. As interesting as each thicket of issues in this forest may be, I prefer to pass through the woods as quickly as possible. One may consult the detailed commentaries by Fee and Thiselton for discussion of the intricacies of these verses.[11]

As in his first proof, Paul begins with the man: "For a man ought not to cover the head, being the image and glory of God." The second part of this sentence gives the basis for the first part. Since the man is the image and glory of God, his head should not be covered. Paul is obviously alluding to the creation account in Genesis 1:27. [Genesis 1:27] That text, however, says nothing about "glory" (*doxa*). Paul seems to have added it to his allusion to the Genesis account because he wants to draw a contrast between men and women in terms of glory. The story of the creation of human beings in Genesis 1 affirms that both male and female are made in the image of God. Paul does *not* want to say that the man is made in God's image and the woman is made in man's image, so he adds the word "glory" to the story. [Glory] Whatever Paul specifically means by "glory" here, his objective is to show that the differences in the glory of men and women lie behind the differences in head attire.

Genesis 1:27

So God created humankind in his image,
In the image of God he created them;
male and female he created them. (NRSV)

The structure of Paul's argument in v. 7 is unusual.[12] We might expect to see this arrangement:

A—A man ought not to cover his head
B—since he is the image and glory of God.
B'—A woman is the glory of man,
A'—[therefore she should cover her head.]

Surprisingly, however, the last element is missing. Instead, we find two statements explaining why woman is the glory of man in vv. 8-9. The woman was made *from* man (v. 8) and *for* man (v. 9). Here Paul is using the narrative of the creation of the man and woman in Genesis 2 to explain the differences in glories. God made man directly and then made the woman from man. The missing part of the sentence in v. 8 finally comes in v. 10, which is

Glory

AΩ The meanings given to the Greek word *doxa* in the NT are often influenced by the range of meanings for the Hebrew word *kabod* in the OT. The root idea of *kabod* is "weightiness." Metaphorically, one's "glory" is that "weighty part that impresses." This is what makes one distinctive in being in a positive way. Thus, in 1 Cor 15:40-41 Paul refers to the different kinds of "glory" of different kinds of beings. Terrestrial beings and celestial beings have different "glories," just as the different celestial beings (sun, moon, stars) each has its own "glory." In 1 Cor 11:7, Paul distinguishes between the "glory" of a man and a woman. Unlike in 1 Cor 15, however, in 1 Cor 11 the "glory" is not simply a distinguishing quality of a being but rather is a quality transferred in some sense from one being to another. The man is the glory *of* God, and the woman is the glory *of* man. The man in some sense exhibits or reflects God's glory, while the woman does the same for the man's glory. This distinction between "glories" for men and women is driven by Paul's attempt to give a theological basis for the different customs for women and men regarding head attire in church.

The Text of 1 Corinthians 11:10

Evidence that many ancient interpreters understood *exousia* in 1 Cor 11:10 to mean "veil" is given by the insertion of the word for "veil" (*kalymma*) in several early translations (cop[bo] arm? eth[ro]) and patristic writers (inc. Valentinians, Ptolemy, Iranaeus, Tertullian, Jerome, and Augustine).

Bruce M. Metzger, *A Textual Commentary on the Greek New Testament* (3rd ed.; Stuttgart: United Bible Societies, 1971) 562.

perplexing in content no less than form. "For (*dia*) this reason a woman ought to have authority (*exousia*) over/upon (*epi*) the head because (*dia*) of the angels." [The Text of 1 Corinthians 11:10] The statement contains two reasons why the woman should have "authority over the head." The first reason looks back to the preceding reference to the Genesis story and the explanation of why the woman's glory is a reflection of the man and not of God. The second reason looks forward to the angels as another cause for covering the head. In between the two reasons lies another riddle. What did Paul mean by "have authority over the head"?

Many interpreters understand Paul to be saying that the woman should have something on her head to signify that she is under a man's authority, but this gives to the word *exousia* a passive sense that it never has elsewhere. Others argue that the woman should have some "symbol" of authority *upon* her head to be recognized as having the "right" to pray and prophesy (NRSV). This corresponds to the probable meaning of *exousia* as "right" in 1 Corinthians 8:9. When *exousia* has the meaning of "right," however, it means having the power or permission to do something, not a "sign" of that right. Likewise, the idea that the word *exousia* is simply a substitute for a word meaning "head covering" does not match its use in any other instance (RSV). The phrase *exousia epi* elsewhere in the New Testament means having "authority *over*" someone or something. The most natural way to read the phrase in v. 10 is that the woman has "authority *over* [her own] head." That is, she has the power to decide for herself whether she will cover her head or not. This way of reading the phrase *exousia epi* fits its usage elsewhere, but it seems to clash with the thrust of the rest of the argument. Paul has not been affirming the right of women to do as they think best; rather he has argued that women should cover their heads. None of these readings is without problems, but (despite misgivings) it seems to me that the meaning that best fits the context is that the woman should have on her head a covering that signifies that she is married, since, in fact, she is.

The phrase *dia tous angelous* is even more puzzling. The word *angelos* means "messenger." Most commentators assume that supernatural messengers are intended here, thus "angels." [Angels as Bishops] A few argue that the *angeloi* here are human messengers. Winter suggests that they are outsiders who might see the women behaving improperly by appearing in a public place with their heads uncovered.[13] The *dia touto* at the beginning of the sentence, then, does not point back to the previous point but forward to the second *dia,* which concerns "messengers." These "messengers" might report their observations about unseemly behavior occurring in the church meetings to the authorities, with possible negative consequences for the church. This reading is very attractive and eliminates speculation about why "angels" are of concern to Paul. It seems odd, however, for Paul to insert this caveat into the middle of a theological argument about creation. It would fit better in his first proof or at the end of his argument.

Angels as Bishops

Some early interpreters argued that *angelos* refers to human messengers in the sense of ministers, based on their reading of Rev 2–3. Ambrosiaster stated that "the veil signifies power, and the angels are bishops."

Ambrosiaster, *Commentary on Paul's Epistles*, in Gerald Bray, ed., *1–2 Corinthians* (vol. 7 of ACCS NT; ed. Thomas C. Oden; Downers Grove IL: InterVarsity Press, 1999) 108.

I am afraid we are stuck with the enigma of *angelous* meaning "angels," even though the meaning "messengers" provides an attractive escape route. Why be concerned about the angels? Were they prone to being overcome by temptation at the exposed heads of the women? Some interpreters point to Genesis 6:1-4 as an instance of heavenly beings transgressing the boundary between heaven and earth in taking human women as wives. [Genesis 6:1-4] The Corinthians would certainly have been familiar with similar stories from their culture of gods abducting women and producing semi-divine offspring. But does Paul actually think the women in the church are vulnerable to such attacks? Others suggest that the problem is that if the women throw off the signs of submission to the divinely ordained hierarchy of relationships, the angels will be tempted to do the same and rebel against God. Intertestamental Jewish writings tell of that happening once before. Possibly, Paul's apocalyptic perspective could allow for some future angelic rebellion, but this would require that Paul believed some overly assertive women could compromise God's sover-

Genesis 6:1-4

When people began to multiply on the face of the ground, and daughters were born to them, the sons of God saw that they were fair; and they took wives for themselves of all that they chose. Then the LORD said, "My spirit shall not abide in mortals forever, for they are flesh; their days shall be one hundred twenty years." The Nephilim were on the earth in those days—and also afterward—when the sons of God went in to the daughters of humans, who bore children to them. These were the heroes that were of old, warriors of renown. (NRSV)

eignty over the angels. Perhaps the issue is that the angels, who may have been perceived as present during worship, would be offended by their behavior. Another take on this is that the angels serve as God's "police" and would report any infractions of proper decorum in worship. No view is without serious problems, given that Paul did not explain what he meant. Perhaps the least objectionable way to see the angels' involvement here is that Paul understood them to be present in some sense during worship and considered the uncovered heads of the women to signify a lack of respect for the angels.

In any case, v. 10 provides the missing piece of v. 7. Verses 8-9 explain why the woman is the glory of the man, as was asserted in v. 7. Verses 11-12 affirm the mutuality of men and women. Neither is "without" (*chōris*) the other, and while it is true that the woman originally came *from* the man, now the man comes *through* the woman. Both men and women come from God. The "nevertheless" (*plēn*) indicates that v. 11 follows in some way from what precedes it. If Paul was saying that the woman "has authority over her own head," then vv. 11-12 would be arguing that the woman should "nevertheless" exercise her "right" to uncover her head, mindful that her actions were not without impact on the man, namely her husband. If Paul was saying that the woman who is married should cover her head to indicate this, then vv. 11-12 would function to point out that this does not mean in any way that woman is inferior to man. On balance, and in light of the fact that Paul has been careful not to indicate that woman is made in the *image* of man, the latter understanding seems to me to fit the context better.

11:13-16. In moving to what constitutes his third proof in this argument, Paul appeals to the Corinthians to judge for themselves what is "proper" (*prepon*). Here he appeals to nature (*physis*) and assumes that the Corinthians have the same understanding as he about what nature teaches and can, therefore, draw the right conclusion. He presents a mutually recognized basis for determining what is right; he does not argue that nature teaches something other than what they already know. By "nature," of course, Paul does not simply mean *phys*iology, though his understanding of "nature" includes it. "Nature" is "the ways things are" as defined by physiology *and* convention.

The "natural order of things" in his day was for men to have short hair and women long. Epictetus, a Cynic-Stoic philosopher from shortly after Paul's time, argued that a man who removed his hair from his body was "complaining against nature."[14] By removing *body* hair (not from the head), the man was trying to appear as a woman. [Epictetus on Natural Hair] Paul acknowledges what was commonly accepted, that men with long hair were not appearing "manly." There were, of course, exceptions. Philosophers sometimes wore their hair long, and it was expected that farmers and barbarians would have long hair.[15] [Effeminate Barbarians?] Men who were considered civil and respectable, however, followed what had been the Roman pattern since the third century BC and kept their hair short. For such a man to wear long hair was considered "dishonorable" (*atimia*).

In contrast, long hair brings a woman "glory" (*doxa*). It was given to her as a "covering" (*perinolaiou*). Nature teaches, Paul was pointing out, that it is "natural" for a woman to be covered; that is why nature gave her long hair. Since it is "natural" for a woman to be covered, then women should cover their heads. He is not arguing that long hair "substitutes" for a head covering, as some interpreters suppose. Rather, he is arguing that nature itself teaches that a woman should be covered. Nor is Paul arguing that men must have short hair, as if he is targeting some men in the church who violated this convention. He only refers to the men by way of contrast with nature's provision for women. The fact that "nature," in the purely physiological sense, does not dictate that men have short hair and women long (since hair growth is determined by genetic ancestry, not sex) is irrelevant to the point Paul was making. Nature, as Paul understood it and as he was certain the Corinthians understood it, designed for women to be covered but not men. Paul is certain the Corinthians will concede to the irrefutable decree of nature.

Epictetus on Natural Hair

Come, let us leave the chief works of nature (*physis*) and consider what she does in passing. Can anything be more useless than the hairs of a chin? Well, what then? Has not nature used even these in the most suitable way possible? Has she not by these means distinguished between the male and the female? Does not the nature of each one among us cry aloud forthwith from afar, "I am a man; on this understanding approach me, on this understanding talk with me; ask for nothing further; behold the signs?" . . . Wherefore, we ought not, so far as in us lies, to confuse the sexes which have been distinguished in this fashion.

As cited in *Hellenistic Commentary to the New Testament* (ed. M. Eugene Boring et al.; Nashville: Abingdon Press, 1996) 426.

Effeminate Barbarians?

The Captives Façade that stood on the northern side of the forum in Corinth to the west of the main entrance included two gigantic statues of barbarians with long tresses. Barbarians were typically portrayed in statues as having long hair, but never with finely groomed locks. The point of depicting the colossal barbarians with "womanly" hair in this late 2d- or early 3rd-century statue group was perhaps to show how the powerful Roman Empire had subdued and domesticated the barbarians.

Archaeological Museum of Ancient Corinth. (Credit: Jim Pitts)

Josephus on the Contentious

In concluding one of his arguments about the antiquity of the Jewish people, Josephus used a tactic similar to Paul's in 1 Cor 11:16. Josephus wrote, "None but the most contentious of critics, I imagine, could fail to be content with the arguments already adduced." (*Ag. Ap.* 1.21)

The possibility that everyone may not see the obvious and may still hold out for the propriety of uncovered women praying and prophesying in worship leads Paul to his final point in v. 16. Only the "contentious" (*philoneikos*) could hold a different view. [Josephus on the Contentious] Paul already knows that the Corinthians are prone to dissension and quarreling (1:9-10). The rest of the churches, however, are in agreement with Paul in this matter. The final pitch is not simply a case of Paul's arguing, "Do it this way because that is the way we do it!" Nor is he exercising some parental perogative: "Do it because I say so!" He has just appealed to nature, to "the way things are." Church practice is another aspect of the natural order. Anyone who advocates a different practice is out of sync with the customary "nature" of church worship. The issue is not simply that some believers might refuse to follow the rule of conduct of the majority. The issue is more the problem of individual inclination taking priority over the common life to which believers are called. A church of individuals insisting on going their own ways is not the church of God.

Proper Observance of the Lord's Supper in Worship, 11:17-34

The problem of wearing or not wearing head coverings that Paul addressed in the previous section involved certain individuals violating social protocol and risking dishonor for themselves, their spouses, and the church. Paul's position was that married women should not pray and prophesy with their heads uncovered. He also opposed men performing the same worship functions with their heads covered, though it is not clear that such a problem existed in the church. Whatever may have prompted the behavior(s), Paul opposed them as a threat to the church's well-being. His concern for the whole church led him to call for submission to society's traditional markers of distinction between the sexes.

In 1 Corinthians 11:17-34, Paul sees a serious threat to the church unfolding within the context of worship. This time, there is no hint of violation of social protocol. In fact, it appears that what was happening in the church during the Lord's Supper was in keeping with expected behavior during other meals. Paul's resolution of the problem, therefore, is in the opposite direction of his instruction in 11:2-16. Instead of appealing to social expectations, he argues against them. The problem is rooted in cultural traditions; he seeks to uproot the problem by appealing to the distinctively Christian tradition of the Lord's Supper.

11:17-22. The first section gives Paul's description of the problem. Verse 17 signals not only that Paul has turned to a different topic, but that his whole demeanor has changed. He introduced the previous topic with a commendation; he cannot begin the same way in addressing this problem. In this case, their coming together does not result in something better occurring but rather something worse. The assembling for worship, the central event of their life together as church, is intended to move them from the plane of their old life into the new plane of existence as the people called of God. Instead, their life together is damaged by the very way in which they assemble.

In v. 18, Paul indicates that once again he is reacting to reports that he has heard regarding the affairs in Corinth. He has learned of divisions (*schismata*) among them. In 1:10, in response to reports that they were quarreling, Paul appealed that there be no divisions among them. Now he indicates that the presence of divisions has been confirmed. Translators often render his evaluation of the report about divisions as "and I partly believe it (*kai meros ti pisteuō*). More likely, however, Paul meant, "and I believe the report."[16] After all, why should Paul doubt the existence of divisions in Corinth? Verse 19 seems to have Paul say that such divisions are necessary for sorting out the genuine (*dokimoi*) from the false, but this conflicts entirely with his earlier appeal against divisions. [Genuine or Esteemed?] Verse 19 makes more sense in context if Paul is being ironic or sarcastic here and saying, "For it is also necessary that cliques be among you so that the 'esteemed ones' may be manifested." It is hard to see how any of the divisions could result in some of them being proven to be genuine, but it is understandable that their separation into cliquish groups based on social status would allow the persons of higher status and means to stand out. "This seems to be quite normal and necessary for you," Paul would be saying.

Beginning with a sarcastic tone would be in keeping with Paul's candid criticism of the church in v. 20: "When you gather at the same place, it is not the Lord's Supper that you eat." The earliest practice of the church seems to have

Genuine or Esteemed?

AΩ The adjective Paul uses in 1 Cor 11:19, *dokimos*, can mean "tested," "proven," or "genuine." It is related to the verb *dokimazō*, which means to "test," "prove," or "approve." Paul uses the adjective twice in both Romans (14:18; 16:10) and 2 Corinthians (10:18; 13:7). In Rom 14:18, *dokimos* clearly means "esteemed." In Rom 16:10, it could mean either "esteemed, "approved," or "proven." In 2 Cor 10:18, it could mean "esteemed," "respected," or "approved." In 2 Cor 13:7, where *dokimos* appears in proximity to *peirazō* ("test"), it is more likely to mean "proven." Even there, however, *dokimos* could mean "approved." It is contrasted with *adokimos*, which seems to mean "not approved" rather than "not proven." It certainly does not mean "untested." When Paul uses *dokimazō* in 1 Cor 11:28, it means "examine" not "put to the test." Overall, Paul seems to use *dokimos* in the sense of "approved" or "esteemed." The latter fits an ironic tone in 1 Cor 11:19, if that is what Paul intended.

been to observe the Lord's Supper in the context of a meal. It was not a separate ritual observed as part of a worship "service" that followed, nor was it a meal consisting only of bread and wine. The entire meal of the Lord's Supper was most probably modeled after the Passover meal.[17] It would have included, before the meal proper, a common cup of wine, entrée, and a second common cup. If the Passover was the model followed, then the Passover liturgy would have preceded the second cup.[18] The breaking of the bread would have signaled the beginning of the dinner, and the cup of blessing would have come at the conclusion. The event was both a full meal and a worship ritual. The Corinthians' behavior, however, was mocking any semblance of the meal they observed to the Lord's Supper. How so?

Verse 21 describes what was actually happening. "In the eating" (*en tō gagein*), each one devours (*prolambanei*) his or her own dinner, and "one is hungry and one is drunk." The verb *prolambanō* is often translated as "go ahead," giving the idea that some were not waiting for the others to arrive before eating. This rendering of *prolambanō*, which is an unusual meaning for the term, is partly based on reading *allēlous ekdechesthe* in v. 33 as "wait for one another." Reading v. 33 this way leads to the conclusion that the basic problem was that some members were going ahead and consuming more than their share before the others arrived. From this, a scenario is devised in which the wealthier members, who had more leisure time, arrived early in the evening, as their less demanding schedules permitted, and began drinking and eating, while the poorer members, who had to work longer hours, arrived to find the bulk of the food gone and the early birds drunk.[19]

While the above scenario is possible, *prolambanō* more likely has the meaning "I seize or grab," hence "devour" is an appropriate rendering in connection with food.[20] When Paul says "each one devours his/her own," we also have clues to the nature of the meal. Each person brought his or her own food in potluck style. This was one version of the Roman *eranos* ("subscription") dinner, which could involve the guests paying their share for the food or bringing their own food.[21] The latter kind of *eranos* dinner fits the Corinthian context. Each person brought food, but ideally that food would become community property and not be eaten only by the person who brought it. The persons of means were eating everything that they brought themselves; those of lesser means had more meager fare, if anything. What was supposed to have been a communal meal signifying the oneness of the community instead became another occasion for highlighting the differences between

The Anaploga Villa

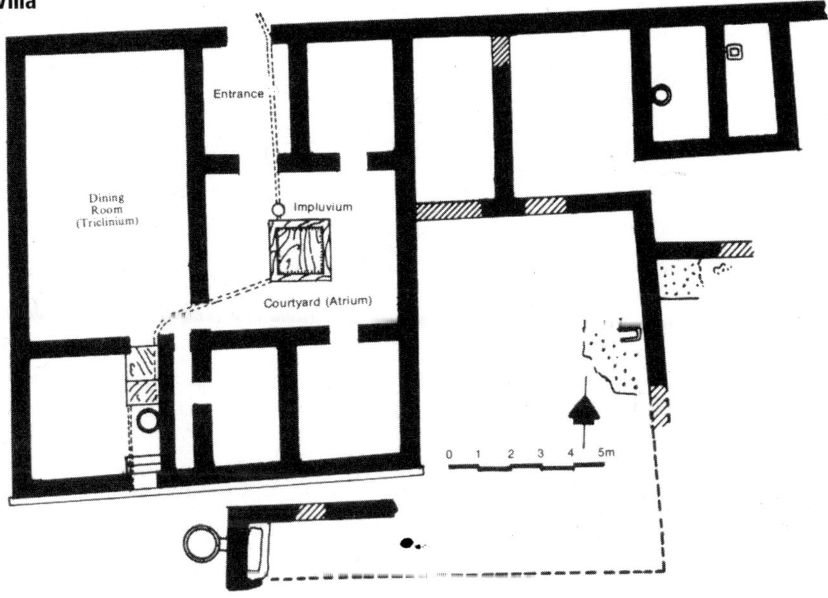

Stella G. Miller, "A Mosaic Floor from a Roman Villa at Anaploga," *Hesperia* 41 (1972): 332–54. Reproduced courtesy of the Trustees of the American School of Classical Studies at Athens, Greece.

members from different social strata. Paul contended that the meal as it was being conducted had nothing to with the Lord's Supper.

The social inequities of the occasion may have been exaggerated by two other factors. One was the location of the meals. In all probability, the meals were observed in private homes. There were no "church" buildings. Some gatherings of the church could have taken place outdoors. The climate of Corinth is actually not very conducive to outdoor meetings, unless there is a large protective cover to shield from the relentless Greek sun or from the severe winters. (I have endured both burning sun and freezing snow in Corinth.) The meals were most likely to have been observed indoors on all occasions, as were private meals in general. This means the church was dependent on the hospitality of those members, or sympathetic patrons, who had large enough homes to accommodate a gathering. Most private dwellings were quite small, providing space only for sleeping and storage. The largest private homes found to date by excavators in Ancient Corinth are villas located on the western edge of town near the present village of Anaploga.[22] They are considerably smaller than many of the private villas excavated at Pompeii.[23] Murphy-O'Connor has compared the two villas excavated in Ancient Corinth and similar structures in Pompeii and Olynthus and computed an average accommodation space for between thirty to forty persons.[24]

The most significant, and perhaps relevant, feature of these villas is their design. In typical Roman style, the entrance in to the home from the street led into an open-air atrium that usually had a pool (*impluvium*) in the center to catch the rainwater that drained from the roof around the sides. Most of the rooms were private family space, but the dining room (*triclinium*) was available to guests. *Triclinii* had rows of couches around three sides of the room to accommodate nine to thirteen reclining diners. The overflow of guests would be confined to the atrium. In such a setting, the social rank of guests would be noticeable since, in all probability, those guests who reclined with the host in the *triclinium* would have been persons of similar rank.

Another factor possibly contributing to the social inequality of meal observances by the church may have been a famine that occurred in the middle of the first century AD. Winter has accumulated considerable evidence that Corinth was affected by grain shortages during and after Paul's time there.[25] Both Winter and Blue think Paul's reference to "this present distress" in 1 Corinthians 7:26 is an allusion to the economic hardship caused by the famine. If so, it is understandable that the hard times would have fallen more severely on the poorer members of the church. Their inability to bring adequate food for themselves to the Lord's Supper would have exacerbated the inequality between them and the wealthier members. The insensitivity of the more affluent by hoarding and eating their own provisions would have made a mockery of what was supposed to be a holy meal celebrating the oneness of the members in the body of Christ. Thus, Paul decreed, "It is not the Lord's Supper that you are eating."

Paul concludes his presentation of the problem in v. 22 with a sharp indictment of the more affluent members. If eating and drinking are all that concern them, they should eat at home. More literally, Paul writes, "Do you not have houses for eating and drinking?" The Lord's Supper, though it involves eating and drinking, is not only about eating and drinking. Their discrimination against the lower-status members of the church reveals that they see the Lord's Supper no differently than they see other private meals that are intended for the enjoyment and pleasure of the participants. [Juvenal] Their behavior shows that they have no regard for the church of God; in fact, they are treating it despicably. They are humiliating those who do not have.[26] Nothing in their behavior merited commendation, and Paul refused to condone their activity.

11:23-26. Immediately after indicting them for their behavior, Paul cites the tradition that he had passed on to them. The language he used in doing so confirms that in 11:2 he was setting the stage for his rebuke in vv. 17-34. There he wrote, "I commend you because . . . just as I handed [them] over to you, you maintain the traditions." In v. 17, he states categorically that he does not commend them in regard to the Lord's Supper. He repeats his refusal to commend them in v. 22 and then recites the tradition (*paradosis*) about the Lord's Supper.

Juvenal

Satirical writers such as Juvenal (late 1st–early 2d century AD) vented vitriolic criticisms of Roman culture in ways that stereotyped and caricatured their targets. Nonetheless, comedic critics often expose the basic flaws in culture that more reserved writers fail to see. In the excerpt below, Juvenal unleashes his cynicism on a client who willingly suffers abuse from his patron at dinner.

> See now that huge lobster being served to my lord, all garnished with asparagus; see how his lordly breast distinguishes the dish; with what a tail he looks down upon the company, borne aloft in the hands of that tall attendant! Before you is placed on a tiny plate a crab hemmed in by half an egg—a fit banquet for the dead. The host souses his fish in Venafran oil; the sickly greens offered to you, poor devil, will smell of the lamp; for the stuff contained in your cruets was brought up the Tiber in a sharp-prowed Numidian canoe—stuff which prevents anyone at Rome sharing a bath with Bocchar, and which will even protect you from a black serpent's bite.

Juvenal, *Satires* 5 (trans. G. G. Ramsay; LCL; Cambridge MA: Harvard College, 2004).

The language Paul uses in reciting the tradition is also significant. "For I received (*parelabon*) from (*apo*) the Lord what also I handed over (*paredōka*) to you." The terminology of "receiving" and "handing over" is used by Paul in other instances in regard to the passing on of traditions or instructions, but he typically uses the preposition "by" (*para*) to refer to the human agents of transmitted teaching. He deliberately specifies that this tradition comes "from" (*apo*) the Lord. This does not mean that Paul was claiming he received the tradition directly from Christ but rather that the Lord is the source of the tradition, however Paul received it. "On the night in which he was *handed over* (*paredideto*), he *took* (*elaben*) bread." The tradition that Christ was "handed over (*paredideto*)" was itself "handed over" (*paredōka*) to them. Paul's "receiving" (*parelabon*) the tradition parallels Christ's "taking" (*elaben*) the bread. When Jesus had given thanks, he broke the bread and said (very literally), "This of me is the body the one on behalf of you." We would expect to find "my" (*mou* = of me) immediately after the word "body." Instead, Paul seems to have shifted the word order to stress that this body, which was handed over to be crucified, is "on your behalf." The command, "Do this for my remembrance," emphasizes that the eating of the bread is not intended to sate physical hunger; it is a remembrance of the Lord's giving of his body *on your behalf.* Likewise, the saying about the cup carries the command, "Do this, as often as you drink, for my remembrance." The wine of the Lord's Supper is not intended to quench thirst, much less to intoxicate; it is a remembrance of the shed blood that established the new covenant. [Synoptic Parallels]

The way Paul recites the tradition about the Lord's Supper stresses the theme of someone or something being "handed over."

Synoptic Parallels

The numerous differences between Paul's account of the Lord's Supper and those found in the Synoptic Gospels (John has no Lord's Supper) have led to much discussion about which version is more original or "authentic." I am not interested in that debate, but I do find it interesting that the Gospel writer whose account most resembles Paul's is Luke. Only Luke approximates Paul's language in having Jesus say of the bread, "This is my body *which is given for you*" (Luke 22:19). Again, only Luke matches Paul in having Jesus specify that the cup "is the *new* covenant" (Luke 22:20). I find it interesting also that in Luke 22:21, immediately after the words about the cup, Jesus says, "But behold the hand of the one handing me over (*paradidontos*) with me on the table!" In Luke 22:22, Jesus goes on to say that what is to happen (being handed over) to the Son of man has been determined. Perhaps this is relevant to the old debate about whether or not Paul was referring to Judas when he wrote "on the night in which he was handed over." From Luke's perspective, Judas was only one of the instruments involved in Jesus' being "handed over." Ultimately, God was behind it. Paul also depicts the "handing over" as something embraced by Jesus, not something inflicted on him by Judas or any other human agent. The Pauline flavor of Luke's Gospel is often apparent. Some would argue that this verifies the old tradition about Luke's getting his information from Paul. Others would observe that such points of similarity between Luke and Paul may have led the early church to associate the Third Gospel with a traveling companion of the apostle.

The tradition was "handed over *to you*," he reminds the Corinthians. The Jesus of the bread and cup was "handed over *for you*." Partaking of the Lord's Supper is a proclamation of the Lord's death, a death experienced *for* the church. In participating in this meal, the church shares in the ongoing proclamation of the word of the cross. They do it not simply looking back to that one determining moment when Christ died, however. They do it looking forward in faithful anticipation of that crowning moment when Christ's victory is complete. The coming of the Lord, however, also involves judgment (1:7-8; 3:8, 13-15; 4:5; 5:5). The message of hope is also a word of warning. The Lord's Supper is a testimony that the one whose body was broken and whose blood was spilled shall return in triumph and judge the world. The tradition is not being maintained, the church is not imitating Christ, the Lord's death is not being proclaimed when the Lord's Supper becomes an occasion for violating the word of the cross by turning it into a self-indulgent banquet in which selfishness, rather than self-giving, prevails. Paul's recitation of the Lord's Supper tradition, therefore, validates his refusal to commend the Corinthians.

11:27-34. The last three words of v. 26, "until he comes," flow into the final part of Paul's argument as he focuses on judgment. The language of "judgment" permeates vv. 27-32 as Paul employs several terms that have *krin-* (from *krinō* = "I judge") as their root.[27] [Judgment Language] The "judgment" theme is present even in verses where the words have no direct connection to *krinō*. The first verse of the section, v. 27, states that persons become "liable" (*enochos*) for profaning the body and blood of the Lord if they eat and drink "inappropriately" (*anaxiōs*). The frequently found translation of the adverb *anaxiōs* as "unworthily" conveys a sense not in keeping with the context. The problem Paul addresses is that some of the Corinthians treat the Lord's Supper as if it is a meal for their enjoyment and nutrition. Rather, it is a meal that proclaims Christ's death *for them.* To eat the meal as something else is to nullify the significance of Christ's having died for others. The "for others" message of the Lord's Supper is lost on those who partake of it thinking only of themselves. The message of the Lord's Supper demands that one be oriented toward others. The treat the meal in this selfish way makes one liable for the body and blood the meal represents. Eating the meal "appropriately" means embodying in their own behavior the same selflessness the meal proclaims.

Judgment Language

AΩ In 1 Cor 11:29-34, Paul employs four different terms that derive their root from the basic verb *krinō* ("I judge"), which appears in vv. 31 and 32. He uses the noun *krima* ("judgment") in vv. 29 and 34. In vv. 29 and 31, Paul has the compound form *diakrinō*, which can mean "evaluate," recognize," or "discern." The basic idea expressed by this form is that one "judges between" different things. In the case of v. 29, it has the sense of "discerning the truth" about the body. This idea is present in v. 31 also, where the sense is that persons must "discern the truth" about themselves. In v. 32, the compound form *katakrinō* conveys the sense of "judging against" or "condemning." The overall thrust of this "judgment" language is to express the warning that if persons cannot discern the truth about the nature and meaning of the Lord's Supper and do not "discern" the truth about themselves in relation to the meaning of the Lord's Supper, then they bring the Lord's judgment up themselves.

Anthony C. Thiselton, *The First Epistle to the Corinthians: A Commentary on the Greek Text* (NIGTC; Grand Rapids: Eerdmans, 2000) 892, 897.

In v. 28, Paul calls on his readers to "examine" (*dokimazeō*) themselves. The verb *dokimazō* can mean "put to the test," and it does have something of that sense here. They are not simply to examine or put themselves to the test, however; they are to evaluate themselves against the standard embodied in the Supper of the Lord who gave himself for others in order to determine if they are "approved" to partake. This is not simply a call to recognize that they are behaving incorrectly. It is a summons to see the truth about what it means to be who they are, a people who have been called by God through the crucified Christ to be a Christ-like people. If they can determine that they are, in fact, the people they have been called to be, then (and only then) may they eat the Lord's Supper. Otherwise, they are actually eating some other meal (v. 20), one that has no connection to the Lord's Supper, and their behavior proclaims a message exactly the opposite of that proclaimed by the Lord's Supper itself.

Exactly what Paul meant by "not discerning the Lord's body" in 11:29 is unclear. Some see it referring to the actual body of Christ. Not to "discern" it would be not to recognize the significance of his death. Some see it referring to the elements of the Supper. If one fails to see that they really are the body or blood of Christ, then one physically ingests spiritual judgment. Others see it referring to the church as Christ's body. If one fails to appreciate the value of all of the persons who make up the church, then one brings judgment on one's self. Very probably, Paul means both Christ's physical body given on the cross, as proclaimed in the bread and cup of the meal, *and* the church as his continuing body. For Paul, the two are joined together. Christ's suffering was for the sake of the church. Those who indulge in his Supper without regard for his broken, bloody body *or* for that body of the redeemed for which he died are guilty of profaning his body (11:27). Eating and drinking "without discerning the body" means missing the message that "Christ [really] died for [all of] us." That is, we are united into the body of Christ through his death. If we dishonor a part of his body (as the rich Corinthians were dishonoring the poor), we dishonor the meaning of his death and bring judgment on ourselves.

Paul seems to consider this such a serious offense that he asserts that many persons in the Corinthian church have become weak or ill; some have even died (v. 30). Paul could conceivably mean that, because of the discrimination at the table, some of the "have nots" in the church have suffered from the lack of food, even to the point of death.[28] The possibility that hard economic conditions were severely affecting the poorer members makes this interpretation less implausible than it may appear at first. [*Shepherd of Hermas*]

Shepherd of Hermas

The mid-2d-century apostolic writing, *Shepherd of Hermas*, includes in the sections known as the Visions a call for wealthier members of the church to share their food with the poorer members. *Hermas* does not refer to the Lord's Supper in this context, but what it says about the fate of those who are discriminated against in regard to food may support the idea that Paul was referring to a similar situation in which the poor were suffering from the selfishness of the rich in Corinth.

> Now then hear me and be at peace among yourselves, and have regard one to another, and assist one another, and do not partake of the creatures of God alone in abundance, but share them also with those that are in want. For some men through their much eating bring weakness on the flesh, and injure their flesh: whereas the flesh of those who have nought to eat is injured by their not having sufficient nourishment, and their body is ruined. This exclusiveness is hurtful to you that have and do not share with them that are in want. Look ye to the judgement that cometh.

Her. *Vis*. 3.9.3-5a in *The Apostolic Fathers* (ed. J. B. Lightfoot and J. R. Harmer; Grand Rapids: Baker Book House, 1984) 416.

Most interpreters, however, understand Paul to refer to the physical consequences some of the Corinthians have experienced because of their own failure to discern the Lord's body. For some, these words suggest that Paul saw the Lord's Supper as magical. If one misused the magic, there could be harmful effects.[29] Martin suggests that Paul had in mind the properties of medicine as it was understood in antiquity. The ancients knew then, as we know now, that medicine, if abused, can become deadly. In fact, many medicines contained poison that could become lethal if not used properly. Martin argues that Paul was explaining to the Corinthians that what was supposed to heal them (the Eucharist) was, in fact, harming them because they were misusing it.[30]

One may be inclined to reject the notions of the Lord's Supper as magical or medicinal. We should keep in mind, however, that Paul did not radically separate the spiritual from the physical. In

1 Corinthians 6:12-20 he went to great lengths to argue that what one does with the body affects one's spiritual self. The reverse is also true. What one does spiritually has an impact on one's physical self, for human beings are psychosomatically whole. Thus, if Paul does mean that the illness of many and the death of some results from abuse of the Lord's Supper, then the church as a whole should take this as a warning sign, especially those who are guilty of the abuse.

Moreover, Paul urges in v. 31, Christians should take pains to discern (*diekrinomen*) the truth about themselves so as not to be judged (*ekriometha*). Readers typically understand the call for self-examination in v. 28 and the statement about discerning ourselves in v. 31 to be two ways of referring to the same act of individual soul-searching. The two verses may be connected, but we should recognize the plural form of v. 31: "If *we* discern *ourselves* truly." The church as a whole is called to examine itself, to judge itself, to correct itself whenever it has distorted the proclamation of Christ's death through divisiveness within or discrimination without against those for whom Christ died. Individually and collectively, the church should examine and judge its practice to determine whether it actually proclaims the Lord's death or belongs among those who are to be condemned (*katakrithōmen*) by Christ "when he comes." Paul indicates in v. 32, that judgment inflicted on the church by the Lord is for disciplinary purposes rather than condemnation (11:32). Verse 34, however, indicates that the failure to "discern ourselves truly" may yet result in the Lord's condemnation.

In closing his argument (vv. 33-34), Paul urges them to "receive one another" (*allēlous ekdechesthe*). His words are often translated as "wait for one another," in conjunction with reading v. 21 to mean that some were eating before (*prolambanei*) the others arrived. I argued there that *prolambanō* can mean "devour." Simply waiting for the poor to arrive would not solve the problem. The problem is not schedule; it's selfishness. Waiting for the poor to arrive before diving in to compete for the food will not restore the Lord's Supper to its intended significance. In Romans 14:1-7, Paul urges the "strong" in the church at Rome to be considerate of and helpful to the "weak." In Romans 14:7, he urges, "Receive one another as Christ has received you." The word for "receive" (*proslambanesthe*) in Romans 14:7 is not exactly the same word as in 1 Corinthians 11:33, but the intention seems to be the same. Those who "have" are to share with those who "have not," guided by the example of the one whose death is proclaimed in the Lord's Supper. Not to receive the poorer members completely, that is, by not sharing their food, is to bring condemnation on their very act of coming together. Paul apparently has more to say about the matter, but he decides to wait until his next visit to say it.

CONNECTIONS

Symbols of Sexual Differences

Paul's discussion of head coverings in 1 Corinthians 11:2-16 presents challenges to the interpreter both in understanding the substance of Paul's argument and in applying his conclusions to the life of the church today. [Hays on 1 Corinthians 11:2-16] The sad history of the interpretation and application of his instructions has often resulted in severe restrictions on the role of women both within the church and society at large. His opening words about pairs of relationships in which one party is the head have been used to force subordination of all women to all men, or at least to impose a rigid hierarchy within the family wherein the husband dominates the wife. Without question, that kind of male-dominated hierarchy existed in Paul's own culture, and it is often assumed that Paul simply acquiesced to the cultural expectations either because he agreed with them or because he did not want to rock the boat. To some degree, of course, he did acquiesce. He embraced the cultural symbols that distinguished men from women in that he insisted that married women should have their heads covered in public and that men should have short hair. To be fair to Paul, however, we should observe what he did not say as well as what he did. He did not use the language of subordination, submission, or obedience that we find elsewhere in the New Testament in the household codes (Eph 5:21–6:9; Col 3:18–4:1). Instead, he discussed honor, glory, and social propriety. He expressed concern that women should not dishonor themselves or their husbands and that men should not dishonor themselves or Christ. Behind this, one suspects that he was also concerned that neither women nor men dishonor the church.

Hays on 1 Corinthians 11:2-16

More than any other passage in this letter, 1 Corinthians 11:2-16 presents severe problems for the interpreter. The first principle that should be applied to our readings of this text is the principle of hermeneutical honesty: we should never pretend to understand more than we do. In the case of this passage, the teacher or preacher should be prepared to acknowledge that we can neither understand it entirely nor accept it entirely (the latter perhaps follows from the former). Telling the truth about such matters will do much to clear the air, and it may help members of our congregations recognize more clearly the great cultural distance between 1st-century Corinth and our world.

Richard B. Hays, *First Corinthians* (IBC; Louisville: John Knox Press, 1997) 190.

His solution to this problem focused primarily on persuading the wives to abide by the social custom of covering their heads in public. While some interpreters believe that Paul was concerned because the women were trying to take on the appearance of men by wearing short hair, that does not appear to be what Paul was addressing. Still, he was concerned that the boundaries between male and female were becoming indistinct. On the one hand, this is a legitimate concern. Calls for equality between the sexes that involve removing all hints of sexual differences rob either sex of their particular gifts. Equality does not require extinguishing sexual identity. Androgeny is an ancient myth that does not need to become a present goal. [Androgeny] Paul's words in Galatians 3:28 to the effect that "in Christ there is neither male nor female" do not nullify the words of Genesis 1:27: "male and female created God them." Being in Christ does not signal a divine sex change or neutering operation. Equality, yes, but androgeny, no. In our own culture, where sexual identity is increasingly blurred in the name of equality, the church can still affirm the God-givenness of femaleness and maleness while championing sexual equality.

Androgeny

The myth of androgeny has been created by men, and its design is the co-option, incorporation, and subjection of women: in seeking "feminine" elements with which to complete himself, the man reduces the woman to merely symbolic stature, plays parasite, and paradoxically demands from the creature he has mentally enslaved his own freedom.

Barbara Charlesworth Gelpi, *Feminist Theory: A Critique of Ideologies* (ed. Nannerl Keohanne et al.; Chicago: University of Chicago Press, 1982) 145.

On the other hand, Paul's counsel to the women raises serious questions about true equality. Paul seems to have worded his argument from creation carefully. He describes men as the image and glory of God, on the basis of Genesis 1:27, while he describes women (wives) as the glory, but not image, of men (husbands). The distinction he makes between male and female is not based on Genesis 1:27 but rather on the creation account in Genesis 2, in which the male is made first and the female is made from the male. He may have been trying to avoid any semblance of inequality, but a degree of inequality is, nevertheless, inherent in his depiction of the woman's being made out of and for the man. It did not take the early church long to pick up on this and begin to exclude women from the very acts of praying and prophesying that Paul took for granted. The return to the functional equality of both sexes in the church that Paul embraced has been impeded by the church's use of Paul's own words.

One may argue, of course, that Paul's instructions regarding the need for women to maintain the cultural symbols of distinction between men and women reflect not only his cultural context but also his eschatological perspective. In the eschaton all differences between men and women may disappear, but despite the church's present entrance into the new age, the church still lives in the here and now. One should not, therefore, live as though one were already completely in the new age by removing all worldly signs of sexual differentiation. The old age is ending soon, but until it does, one should abide by the cultural symbols distinguishing men from women. Again, on the one hand this is a healthy affirmation of God-given femaleness and maleness. But, on the other hand, those cultural symbols may have a built-in message of inequality. Paul may have been primarily concerned that women in the church not be seen as disreputable women and, thus, should wear the sign of respectability, especially when serving in a visible capacity. That sign of respectability, the covered head, however, essentially meant that the woman was visibly under the domain of the man. Cultural signs of domination are hard to square with the gospel message of equality. Perhaps the women were more sensitive to this incongruity than was Paul. His eschatology told him that, since the form of this world is passing away, women could (should) tolerate the symbols of inequality without any detriment to their functional equality within the church. Two thousand years later, we have to wonder if continuing to tolerate those symbols, if they also betoken inequality, does not, in fact, nullify the functional equality.

Benazir Bhutto

Benazir Bhutto, former prime minister of Pakistan. (Credit: © Olivier Mathys/epa/Corbis)

Christine Amjad-Ali, a Pakistani biblical scholar, has raised this issue in her own cultural context in which women are expected to wear the *purdah* (veil).[31] She points out that Benazir Bhutto, when she was the prime minister, functionally disregarded the traditional, cultural, and religious understanding of the subordination of women but, to avoid criticism from conservative quarters, deferred to the cultural symbols of subordination by wearing the traditional attire. Amjad-Ali questions whether Bhutto could substantially transform the substance of inequality as long as she maintained the symbols of inequality. The recent assassination of Bhutto shows that respecting the cultural signs of subordination brings no protection when one is still perceived as a threat to a status quo that maintains the functional inequality of women.

What we cannot know and can only speculate about is why the women were removing their head coverings. Perhaps they were doing it for the wrong reasons, and Paul knew that. Perhaps, though, they had right reasoning behind their actions. If so, then we have to allow that perhaps Paul knew that they had good reasons but still believed that the time had not yet come for the church to take that big a step in the right direction. He certainly had to dig deep into his trunk of arguments to counter their position, even bringing the mysterious angels into the picture. His position may have been the right one for the moment. Now, however, we need to hear the women's voices, without trying to cover them with symbols of inequality.

The Real Picture

Paul's instruction to the church at Corinth about the Lord's Supper in 1 Corinthians 11:17-34 appears in a long section of the letter in which he addresses several problems that arose whenever the church was gathered for worship (1 Cor 11:2–14:40). We should keep in mind, therefore, that his words regarding the ordinance are framed in the context of problem solving. Paul was not trying to outline his theology of the Lord's Supper; he was trying to correct a Corinthian practice that was dishonoring the meal and its message.

Because Paul was confronting real problems experienced by the Corinthian church in worship, we have a snapshot of sorts of their corporate life in that setting. The picture we have of their life together around the table of the Lord is not a flattering one. The root of their problem regarding the Lord's Supper was that the Supper itself was not at the center of their communal experience. Instead, their own wants and needs took priority over the message of the meal. It is not accidental, then, that in confronting their misbehavior, Paul inserted into the center of his argument a recitation of the Lord's Supper tradition that he had earlier delivered to them. Returning their focus to the centrality of the meal itself was Paul's main strategy for resolving the situation.

The word "tradition" refers to a teaching, practice, or custom that is handed down from one person or group to another. The purpose of the tradition is to keep alive an important belief or action. It also serves to unite later generations to the generation that began the tradition. Some traditions eventually fall by the wayside because they no longer speak meaningfully to later generations. Sometimes, letting go of a tradition is necessary for following the Spirit's lead into new vistas of awareness and service. Sometimes, however, the demise of a tradition means the loss of something vital to the faith and a loss of connection with the larger family of faith through the ages.

In 1 Corinthians 11:23-26, Paul calls the Corinthians' attention back to the tradition he had received from the Lord and "handed

Bread and Cup

Carlo Dolci (1616–1686). *Christ Blessing Bread and Wine*. c. 1670. Oil on canvas. Gemaeldegalerie Alte Meister, Staatliche Kunstsammlungen, Dresden, Germany. (Credit: Bildarchiv Preussischer Kulturbesitz/Art Resource, NY)

over" to them. Paul reminded them that on the night when Jesus was "handed over," he gave them bread to eat and said, "Do this in remembrance of *me*." Likewise, he gave them the cup to drink "in remembrance of *me*." In doing this, Paul wrote, "you proclaim the Lord's *death* until he comes" (11:26). Paul's words stress that the Lord's Supper is to be focused on the Lord, not on filling the belly. The gospel of the crucified Lord who gave himself for us is message of the meal. To treat the dinner as one of self-indulgence, especially without regard for the "have nots," means that it is no longer the Lord's Supper (11:20).

Some traditions are so central to the Christian faith that to lose, neglect, or distort them is catastrophic to the integrity of faith itself. To neglect or distort the tradition of the Lord's Supper is to lose contact with the central message of the gospel that through Christ's death we have been united to each other and to God.

The Lord's Supper proclaims the "oneness" of Christ's body. Though his body was broken and his blood was spilled, his death has united believers together and to him by the saving grace of God. Although many churches observe the Lord's Supper today by serving individual portions of bread and drink, the early church appears to have used one loaf of bread and a common cup. The significance of the "oneness" of the body of Christ represented by the single loaf and cup can sometimes be lost when we pass around "a pan full of cracker crumbs and thimbles full of grape juice," as the late New Testament scholar Frank Stagg used to describe it. The greatest threat to the message of "oneness" that the Lord's Supper proclaims, however, comes when the body of Christ is divided.

What divided the Corinthian church can be boiled down to selfishness. What was supposed to be a sacred meal was reduced to the status of a pagan banquet. The more affluent members were gorging themselves, while the poorer members went without. Any semblance of oneness was destroyed by this discrimination and insensitivity. The visual message of the meal about one who gave himself for others was mocked by persons essentially pushing others away from the table in order to satisfy their own cravings for food and drink. It was not a pretty picture.

Decadence of the Romans

Thomas Couture Thomas (1815–1879). *The Decadence of the Romans.* 1847. Oil on canvas. Musee d'Orsay, Paris, France. (Credit: Erich Lessing/Art Resource, NY)

The old saying, "One picture is worth a thousand words," could be applied both to the snapshot we have of the Corinthians' life together and to the Lord's Supper itself. We have seen that the picture we have of the Corinthians is unsettling, much as a snapshot of particular moments in the life of the church today might be disturbing. For example, if one were to photograph a modern church at worship, the initial impression we have of that church might be shaped by the beauty of the sanctuary or the attractive appearance of the worshipers. Closer inspection might reveal, however, that there is a sameness about the worshipers. They may all resemble one another in the stylishness of their cloths or the same color of their skin. Their attire and appearance in all likelihood will be consistent with the level of affluence portrayed by the decorations and furnishings of the sanctuary. It may appear from a close examination of the picture that only those persons of similar socioeconomic standing belong in this picture. Others have been pushed away from the table, so to speak. This, too, is not as pretty a picture as we supposed on first glimpse. If we were to take our camera away from the setting of the church at worship and photograph other moments in the church's life, we might find those snapshots to be even less flattering. We might be disturbed by the church's general lack of concern for the "have nots" who have pushed away from the table, as expressed in those activities that the church considers important enough to give its time and resources to support. The modern church may not experience the kind of discrimination against the poor that occurred within the Corinthian church simply because the poor are not present to experience the discrimination.

If we turn our camera away from the church and focus it on the Lord's Supper, we may see a different kind of picture. We may see a simple meal that proclaims a deceptively simple message about one who died for all persons, rich or poor. We may see one bread and one cup that bind all persons of all stripes together to the one Lord. We may see a model for how the church is supposed to look.

My grandmother went to art school and began to paint landscapes and portraits after she retired from nursing. After finishing a painting, she would spend hours trying to find exactly the right frame. She explained that her attention to the frame was because the frame "makes or breaks" the picture. What applied to her paintings applies to the picture Paul gave us of the Lord's Supper. For better or worse, the only frame we have to put around that picture is the church. Ideally, the church is not the picture itself, only the frame. The Corinthians' problem was that they put themselves in the picture in place of Christ's death and the Supper that proclaims it. Thus, they could not serve as the appropriate frame for the real picture. The message of the Supper is complimented or distorted by the quality of unity and the degree of compassion for those in need that exists within the body of Christ. A healthy, harmonious, caring church frames the picture well. A sick, contentious, selfish church obscures the picture so that its message cannot be seen. It takes the right frame to do the real picture justice.

The Lord's Supper

Salvador Dali (1904–1989). *The Sacrament of the Last Supper.* 1955. Oil on canvas. National Gallery of Art, Washington D.C. (Credit: © DACS/The Bridgeman Art Library)

Lectionary Connections

The only part of 1 Corinthians 11 that appears in the Revised Common Lectionary is Paul's account of the Lord's Supper that appears in vv. 23-26. This passage is read on Maundy Thursday for all three years in the cycle. The Old Testament reading is the account of the first Passover in Exodus 12:1-14. The Gospel lesson is from John 13:1-17, 31b-35. John's Gospel describes Jesus' last meal with his disciples within the context of Passover, but it omits any reference to the Lord's Supper. Instead, the focus in the lectionary reading is on the washing of the disciples' feet by Jesus and the giving of the new commandment to "love one another." There is a brief reference to Judas's impending betrayal of Jesus in John 13:2, which sets up the exchange between Jesus and Judas in the verses omitted from the reading. The usual emphasis in Maundy Thursday messages is either on the foot washing or the new commandment. One could, however, choose to focus on the theme of betrayal in the omitted verses. Since the word for "betray" is also translated "hand over," a dual connection can be made between the Johannine text and Paul's words in 1 Corinthians 11:23-26. Paul stresses that he had "handed over" to the Corinthians the tradition that begins, "The Lord Jesus on the night in which he was handed over." This stress on Jesus' being "handed over" can, in turn, be related to the Exodus account of the "passing over" of the death angel. Instead of death "passing over" Jesus, he was "handed over" to die.

NOTES

1. William Shakespeare, *King Henry the Fifth* (1598–1599), IV, i, 256.

2. John C. Hurd Jr., *The Origin of I Corinthians* (Macon GA: Mercer University Press, 1983) 90.

3. Scholars who think the issue is hairstyle include Richard A. Horsley, *1 Corinthians* (*ANTC*; Nashville: Abingdon Press, 1990); J. B. Hurley, "Did Paul Require Veils or the Silence of Women? A Consideration of 1 Cor 11:2-16 and 1 Cor 14:33b-36," *WTJ* 35 (1973): 190–220. Jerome Murphy-O'Connor, "Sex and Logic," *CBQ* 42 (1980): 482–99.

4. This view is favored by Joël Delobel, "1 Cor 11:2-16: Towards a Coherent Explanation," in *L'Apôtre Paul: Personalité, style et conception du ministére* (ed. A. Vanhoeye; Leuven: Peeters, 1986) 369–89; David E. Garland, *1 Corinthians* (BECNT; Grand Rapids: Baker Academic, 2003) 518–22; and Bruce W. Winter, *After Paul Left Corinth: The Influence of Secular Ethics and Social Change* (Grand Rapids MI: Eerdmans, 2001) 121–41, and *Roman Wives, Roman Widows: The Appearance of New Women and the Pauline Communities* (Grand Rapids MI: Eerdmans, 2003) 77–96.

5. Anthony C. Thiselton, *The First Epistle to the Corinthians: A Commentary on the Greek Text* (NIGTC; Grand Rapids: Eerdmans, 2000) 812–22, gives a thorough, critical review of the major views.

6. Joseph A. Fitzmyer, "Another Look at Κεφαλή in 1 Corinthians 11:3," NTS 35 (1989): 32–59, and "*Kephalē* in 1 Cor. 11:3," *Inter* 47 (1993): 32–59; Wayne Grudem, "The Meaning of *kefalē* ('Head'): A Response to Recent Studies," *TrinJ* 11 (1990): 3–72; and Archibald Robertson and Alfred Plummer, *First Epistle of St Paul to the Corinthians* (2d ed.; *ICC*; New York: Charles Scribner's Sons, 1914) 229–30.

7. Gordon D. Fee, *The First Epistle to the Corinthians* (NICNT; Grand Rapids: Eerdmans Publishing, 1987) 503; Jerome Murphy-O'Connor, "Sex and Logic"; and Robin Scroggs, Paul and the Eschatological Woman," in *The Text and the Times: New Testament Essays for Today* (Minneapolis: Fortress Press, 1993) 69–95.

8. Garland, *1 Corinthians*, 515–16; A. C. Perriman, "The Head of a Woman: The Meaning of κεφαλή in 1 Cor 11:3," *JTS* 45 (1994): 602–22.

9. Winter, *Roman Wives*, 17–76.

10. Winter, *After Paul Left Corinth*, 128.

11. Fee, *The First Epistle to the Corinthians*, 512–24; Thiselton, *The First Epistle to the Corinthians*, 833–43.

12. See Fee, *The First Epistle to the Corinthians*, 513–23.

13. Winter, *After Paul Left Corinth*, 133–38.

14. Epictetus, *Diss*. 1.26 (LCL).

15. Cynthia L. Thompson, "Hairstyles, Head-coverings, and St. Paul: Portraits from Roman Corinth," *BA* (1988): 104.

16. The evidence for *meros ti* meaning "some report" and not "partly" is given by Winter, *After Paul Left Corinth*, 159–63. Garland, *1 Corinthians*, 537–38, accepts Winter's argument.

17. Luise Schottroff, "Holiness and Justice: Exegetical Comments in 1 Corinthians 11:17-34," JSNT 79 (2000): 56–57.

18. Winter, *After Paul Left Corinth*, 150.

19. Gerd Theissen, *The Social Setting of the Pauline Churches: Essays on Corinth* (trans. and ed. John Schütz; Philadelphia: Fortress Press, 1982) 151–55.

20. Winter, *After Paul Left Corinth*, 144–47.

21. The idea that the Lord's Supper was like a Roman *eranos* dinner was first proposed by Peter Lampe, "The Eucharist: Identifying with Christ on the Cross," Int 48 (1994): 36–49. Winter, *After Paul Left Corinth*, 154–55, considers the Lord's Supper to be a particular type of *eranos* dinner, namely the *asybolon deipnon* ("private dinner"), which was potluck.

22. James Wiseman, "Corinth and Rome I: 228 B.C.–A.D. 267," *ANRW* 7/1 (1979): 528.

23. Andrew Wallace-Hadrill, *Houses and Society in Pompeii and Herculaneum* (Princeton: Princeton University Press, 1994) 67–89.

24. Jerome Murphy-O'Connor, *St. Paul's Corinth: Texts and Archaeology* (Collegeville MN: Liturgical Press, 1983) 163–64.

25. Winter, *After Paul Left Corinth*, 216–25. See also Bradley Blue, "The House Church at Corinth and the Lord's Supper: Famine, Food Supply, and the *Present Distress*," *Criswell Theological Journal* 5 (1991): 221–39.

26. Paul does not say specifically what it is that the "have nots" (*tous mē echontas*) do not have. Most interpreters understand him to mean that they are simply poor, or that Paul is referring specifically to "food." The nearest referent, however, is *oikias* ("houses"). It is possible that Paul is accusing those who have houses of looking down on those who do not.

27. Pointed out by Garland, *1 Corinthians*, 550.

28. The possible interpretation is tentatively offered by Garland, *1 Corinthians*, 553. He also points out the parallel in the Shepherd of Hermas.

29. Johannes Weiss, *Der erste Korintherbrief* (KEK; 9th ed.; Göttingen: Vandenhoeck & Ruprecht, 1910) 290–91.

30. Dale B. Martin, *The Corinthian Body* (New Haven CT: Yale University Press, 1995) 191–94.

31. Christine Amjad-Ali, "The Equality of Women: Form or Substance (1 Corinthians 11.2-16)," in *Voices from the Margin. Interpreting the Bible in the Third World* (new ed; ed. R. S. Sugirtharajah. Maryknoll NY: Orbis Books, 1995) 185–93.

SPIRITUAL GIFTS AND LOVE

1 Corinthians 12:1–14:40

"Any truth spoken by anyone is spoken by the Holy Spirit."[1]

In chapters 12–14, Paul addresses the matter of "spiritual things" (*pneumatikōn*). For the most part, however, he rarely refers to what is "spiritual" in this section (only in 14:1, 37), though his discussion is clearly focused on the Spirit (*pneuma*). Rather than refer to manifestations of the Spirit as *pneumatika,* he calls them "services" (*diakonia*), "workings" (*energēmata*), and especially "gifts" (*charismata*). Whereas referring to such manifestations as "spiritual things" may place the emphasis on the possessor of those manifestations, his preference for "gifts" places the emphasis properly on the Spirit as the source. Furthermore, his abundant use of words related to "knowing" (e.g. *oida, ginōskō, gnōrizō, epiginōskō,* and *agnoeō*) seems to be aimed at challenging what some of the Corinthians think they know about "spiritual things."

The section follows a pattern we have observed elsewhere in 1 Corinthians (chs. 8–10; 11:17–12:1) in which Paul inserts what appears on the surface to be a digression of sorts into his main argument. In his discussion of eating food offered to idols, chapter 9 gives a lengthy example of Paul's own practice of giving up his apostolic rights in order to help others. While some interpreters misread this as a detour into an unrelated topic, namely a defense of his apostleship, it is apparent that this section informs the whole of his argument. Likewise, in 11:17–12:1, the central section (11:23-26), in which he recites the tradition about the Lord's Supper, provides the basis of his resolution of the problem. Here in chapters 12–14, the central section (ch. 13) does not mark a temporary aside to discuss the merits of love but rather represents the model that should guide the exercise of "spiritual things" in the church. [A Thematic Outline of 1 Corinthians 12–14]

A Thematic Outline of 1 Corinthians 12–14

- I. The Gifts of the Spirit (12:1–13:13)
  - A. The Same Spirit Gives All Gifts (12:1-12)
  - B. The Church Is the Body of Christ (12:12-31)
  - C. The Way of Love Is the Best Way (13:1-13)
- II. The Gifts of Prophecy and Tongues (14:1-40)
  - A. Prophecy Edifies More Than Tongues (14:1-25)
  - B. Order Should Prevail in the Church (14:26-40)

COMMENTARY

The Gifts of the Spirit (12:1–13:13)

While the phrase " now concerning" (*peri de*), as we have noted, need not necessarily indicate that Paul is taking up another one of the topics mentioned in the Corinthians' letter to him, what he goes on to discuss suggests that is the case here. We seem to be entering into a conversation that has a prehistory. Some of what he says here (or does not say) indicates that he is reacting to a situation that is already present in the church, one that he most likely learned about from their letter. Our inability to know precisely what that situation was stems from Paul and the Corinthians already sharing some knowledge about the situation, with the result that certain bits of information that might be useful to our reconstruction go unrevealed.

Garland on Biased Reading

David Garland issues a caveat that is worth heeding as one begins interpreting 1 Cor 12–14.

> Commentators should not pretend that they approach 12:1-3 as completely objective observers. Those who have experienced the gift of tongues find it to be far more significant and tend to offer more sympathetic interpretations of the phenomenon than those who have not experienced it. . . . On the other hand, these chapters deal with a more basic phenomenon that is no respecter of denominational breeding. All will have experienced church conflict that is rooted in the hunger for status and recognition. Many will have been in communities where the more cerebral gifts have become the gifts of choice and are exalted over others. Many will have witnessed impatience with other "benighted souls," a lack of kindness, inflated self-importance, ill-mannered dismissal of fellow Christians who are judged as less gifted or wrongly gifted, and burning envy (cf. 13:4-7). Paul gives specific instructions to solve a specific problem in Corinth but calls for Christian charity as the way to prevent the conflict from arising in the first place.

David E. Garland, *1 Corinthians* (BECNT; Grand Rapids: Baker Academic, 2003) 573.

Based on what Paul does reveal about the situation, we may surmise that the Corinthians' experience of the workings of the Spirit among them created some problems. [Garland on Biased Reading] Apparently these experiences had created some disorder during worship. More importantly, though, the manifestations of the Spirit seem to have provided another opportunity for the Corinthians to engage in their favorite sport of competing for status. Certain manifestations of the Spirit seem to have been valued more than others, especially those that were more dramatic in appearance and more unusual. Speaking in tongues, especially, seems to have created one more type of pecking order in which those who practiced the phenomenon claimed superior status to those who did not. Paul's approach to the problem did not lead him to discredit that particular manifestation of the Spirit. Instead, he affirmed it as a valid gift. He did, nonetheless, affirm it as one among many gifts and went so far as to place it among the lower gifts. The criterion he applied to the ranking of gifts was different from that of the Corinthians, but it was consistent with Paul's approach throughout the letter. Whatever builds up the church is superior to whatever edifies or "puffs up" the individual. Then, as now, the gift of speaking in tongues could become divisive. Paul's answer to the problem of its use in the church, though sound and sensible, even now does not satisfy the practice's most ardent supporters or opponents.

12:1-12. Paul's introduction of the matter in v. 1 follows a common formula for broaching a new topic: "I do not want you to be ignorant." What he does not want them to be ignorant of are "spiritual things" (*pneumatikōn*). The word *pneumatikōn* could be a masculine substantive adjective ("spiritual person"), but in light of his use of *pneumatika* in 14:1 (which is clearly neuter), the reference is undoubtedly to "spiritual matters," not persons. His statement following this introduction continues to puzzle interpreters. Very literally, v. 2 reads, "You know that when Gentiles you were to dumb idols as ever you were led being led away." The syntax of the statement is confusing. Also unexpected is his implication that the persons to whom he is writing, who are predominately Gentiles, are in some sense no longer such. "When you were Gentiles" implies that they should no longer regard themselves as Gentiles. The opposite of Gentiles would be Jews, or at least Israel. This correlates with Paul's reference in 10:1 to the Israelites as the "ancestors" of his Gentile readers. It also reinforces their identity as persons who have become a part of the community of God (Israel) and who have become separated from their pagan (Gentile) past.

His description of that past is brief and enigmatic. I interpret the force of his statement to mean, "When you were Gentiles, however it was that you were led to dumb idols, you were being led astray." It is tempting to see a contrast between his reference to "silent idols" and his discussion of "speaking" in church that follows, but the term "dumb idols" is simply his use of a typical Jewish criticism of idolatry. It is also tempting to find in his reference to their "being led to idols in some way" and to "being led astray" a criticism of those fantastic features of paganism that had intrigued them. The connection of this implied criticism to what follows would conceivably be that they are still being overly influenced by the sensational element in religion. Once they were drawn by the dramatic processions, mysterious rituals, and oracular utterances of pagan cult, and now they are impressed by extraordinary manifestations of divine power in the church. If Paul intended to make that connection, he did so rather vaguely. His point, instead, seems to be that, whatever drew them to idolatry, they were on the wrong track.

Now they are on the right track, but they still have much to learn. So Paul informs them in v. 3 of something that is elementary but also fundamental for their new faith: "No one speaking by the

Anathema Jesus

The statement "*Anathema Iēsous*" has generated much speculation not so much about its meaning but about the context in which such words might be uttered. The statement has no verb, so it could be rendered "Jesus is cursed" or "Let Jesus be cursed." Winter suggests that it be read "Jesus curse" and be taken as an instance of someone invoking Jesus to place a curse on someone. Several artifacts inscribed with curses have been found by excavators in Ancient Corinth and vicinity, including the remarkable lead curse tablets (pictured here) found in the sanctuary of Demeter and Kore on the north slope of the Acrocorinth. Four lead curse tablets were also found in the "Cave of the Lamps" near the city's northern edge. Winter points to these pagan examples of curses and notes the present of curse inscriptions on some later Christian graves. He does not, however, discuss some of the lamps found in the "Cave of the Lamps" that bear Christian graffiti. One lamp (L 4607) has an inscription that could be read as a curse: "I invoke you by the great God Sabbaoth, by Michael, by Gabriel, in order that you . . ." (Rothaus, 264). Winters correctly observes that Christians sometimes employed the pagan custom of invoking curses, but he does not sufficiently explain the parallel structure between "*Anathema Iēsous" and Kyrios Iēsous*" in v. 3. Both statements contain simply a noun and the name Jesus, and it is most likely that both are indicative assertions that assume the verb "is."

Inscribed lead cursed tablet, 1st C. AD, in Nancy Bookidis and Ronald S. Stroud, *Demeter and Persephone in Ancient Corinth* (American Excavations in Old Corinth; American School of Classical Studies at Athens: Princeton, 1987) 31. Reproduced courtesy of the Trustees of the American School of Classical Studies at Athens, Greece.

But who would say "Jesus is cursed"? Thiselton discusses eight different proposals. They include (1) the confession a Christian might be compelled to make under persecution, (2) the acclamation of a Christian who got carried away by uncontrolled ecstasy in worship, (3) a Jewish pronouncement that Jesus is cursed, (4) a statement by a Christian under demonic influence, and (5) a hypothetical situation. I am more inclined toward the hypothetical view, but I would carry it further. Paul does not say that anyone has uttered such a statement, nor does he hypothesize that someone might. His point is that the Spirit of God does not lead one to pronounce Jesus as cursed; rather the Holy Spirit, and only the Holy Spirit, enables one to pronounce Jesus as Lord.

Richard M. Rothaus, *Corinth: the First City of Greece, An Urban History of Late Antique Cult and Religion* (Leiden: Brill, 2000) 130.

Anthony C. Thiselton, *The First Epistle to the Corinthians: A Commentary on the Greek Text* (NIGTC; Grand Rapids: Eerdmans, 2000) 918–27.

Bruce W. Winter, *After Paul Left Corinth: The Influence of Secular Ethics and Social Change* (Grand Rapids MI: Eerdmans, 2001) 164–83.

Spirit of God says, 'Jesus is cursed,' and no one is able to say, 'Jesus is Lord,' unless [one does so] by the Holy Spirit." The last part of this statement is clear enough, but the first part is not. How could anyone in the church possibly utter such words? [Anathema Jesus] Despite several attempts by scholars to envision a setting in which a Christian might pronounce that Jesus is cursed, the possibility that Paul was referring to such an actual occurrence is extremely remote. If that is what he intended, then we might expect Paul to have attacked the practice forcefully. It is the impossibility of such a thing happening that Paul stresses. The Spirit of God would never lead one to do such a thing, but the Holy Spirit (and only the Holy Spirit) would and does lead persons to confess "Jesus is Lord." By whatever means the Corinthians may have previously been drawn to idols, it is only by the Holy Spirit's work that they have entered into the community of faith and confessed the lordship of Jesus.

Paul's List

In 1 Cor 12:8-10, Paul lists eight manifestations of the Spirit. The list falls into a threefold pattern determined by his use of different terms for the phrase "to another" (*heterō* and *allō*). This pattern sets the first two manifestations in v. 8 as one group, the five listed in vv. 9-10b as another, and the last two in vv. 10c as a third group.

Group 1:	v. 8	To one is given . . . the speech of wisdom
		to another (*allō*) the speech of knowledge
Group 2:	vv. 9-10b	to another (*heterō*) faith
		to another (*allō*) gifts of healings
		to another (*allō*) workings of miracles
		to another (*allō*) prophecy
		to another (*allō*) discernment of spirits
Group 3:	v. 10c	to another (*heterō*) kinds of tongues
		to another (*allō*) interpretation of tongues

This Spirit that began their lives as believers works within the church in a variety of ways. There are many different gifts, services, and workings in the church, but the same Spirit of God inspires them all (vv. 4-6). Paul's emphasis is twofold: (1) There is a diversity of ways the Spirit works, but (2) there is only one and the same Spirit behind the diversity. Each person receives something individually from the Spirit, but the purpose of these individual endowments or abilities is for the common good (v. 7). Paul will reiterate the emphasis on the common good later. Paul next lists, but not exhaustively, some of the different ways the Spirit works. [Paul's List] At the top of the list in v. 8, Paul puts "word of wisdom" (*logos sophias*) and "word of knowledge" (*logos gnōseōs*). Since Paul is not focused on the possession of wisdom and knowledge but on their communication, we should translate *logos* in each instance as "speech" rather than "word." In his opening thanksgiving prayer, Paul noted in 1:5 that "in every way you were enriched in all speech (*logos*) and all knowledge (*gnōsis*)." In much of chapters 1–4, Paul contrasted the wisdom of the world with God's wisdom expressed in the cross of Christ. In 4:10, he sarcastically described the Corinthians as "wise." At the top of his list, then, Paul places the two very attributes that the Corinthians have indicated they value most highly. The wisdom and knowledge that he lists here, however, are not of the same stripe as what they cherish. They are the wisdom and knowledge given by the Spirit. As he has indicated before, there are legitimate forms of both, but neither is cast in the mold of worldly attainment. As gifts of the Spirit, they do not give one a basis for personal boasting or glorying.

Coming next in Paul's list (vv. 9-10b) are five manifestations of the Spirit that, for the most part, make evident contributions to the common good. These are the gift of healing, working of miracles, prophecy, and the discernment of spirits. The one that does not have an obvious community orientation is the first one named, faith. Since all believers have faith in some sense, then when Paul describes this faith as being apportioned to some, he must mean a special kind of faith. Most likely faith is named in this second tier because it is related to the other four.

Included in his list, but at the bottom, are tongues and the interpretation of tongues (v. 10c). The placement of tongues and their interpretation last points forward to chapter 14 where we see that speaking in tongues has generated some problems, stemming mostly from valuing this particular manifestation of the Spirit too highly. In other listings in chapter 12 (vv. 28-30), Paul also places tongues and their interpretation at the bottom. Not to be overlooked as well is the fact that Paul never directly refers to tongues or their interpretation as a *charisma* ("gift"), which is ironic in light of what has come to be emphasized among "charismatic" Christians. Also not to be overlooked is the fact that Paul refers here to "kinds" or "species" (*genē*) of tongues. This suggests that the Spirit does not give to every person the same *kind* of "tongue." Scholars have offered numerous understandings of what the different kinds of tongues might be.[2] Some contend that the "speaking in tongues" discussed in chapter 14 constitutes only one type of tongue. I would argue, instead, that the tongues of 12:10c are the same as the tongues mentioned throughout these three chapters. They are of different *kinds* because they are given to different people. Each person who receives the gift of tongues receives his or her own special tongue. Each tongue reflects the unconscious verbalization of the unconscious of each speaker. Since no two persons are exactly alike, no two tongues are the same; they are each a different kind (*gynos*). That is part of the problem in communicating them. If each person spoke in the same tongue, someone could eventually devise a language code for their interpretation. Paul is clear, however, that the interpretation of tongues is itself given by the Spirit to those the Spirit chooses.

When I say that tongues is an unconscious communication of the person's unconscious, do I mean that the person is in an ecstatic trance? Forbes has effectively argued against seeing the phenomenon of speaking in tongues in Corinth against the background of the kind of ecstatic frenzy depicted in ancient literature in regard to certain Dionysiac cults and similar groups.[3] Nor should it be viewed primarily in terms of the type of oracular revelations attributed to messengers of the divine such as the famous Pythia of Delphi. The women chosen for this task were understood to enter a trance-like state (whether induced by intoxicants or not is highly debated) in which they received and communicated a message from Apollo, which was then translated and written down in verse by the priests. The Corinthians engaged in glossolalia (tongue speaking) do not seem to have become frenzied or unconscious. They seem to have been aware of what they were doing but not in control of it. What they spoke came from within themselves (their unconscious), yet they could not comprehend their own words. Hence, they were conscious of what they were doing but not conscious of what they were saying. That is why Paul urges them also to seek the gift of interpretation (14:13). Since Paul believes that the interpretation of tongues can edify the church, then he must have seen interpreted tongues, much as prophesy, as the communication of a word from the Lord. In this respect, the Delphic oracle is relevant. For pagan believers, the Pythia's mutterings were a message from the divine. For the Corinthians, who regularly saw Mount Parnassos, where the Delphic oracle was located, to the north across the Corinthian Gulf, it would have been quite natural to associate unintelligible speech with a divine revelation. Paul agrees that the Lord may speak through glossolalia, but he sees it to be of no communal value if it cannot be interpreted.

Delphi

(Credit: Scott Nash)

Delphi was the site of the most respected oracle in the Greek and Roman world. Believed by the Greeks to sit at the center of the world, it was located on the southern side of Mount Parnassos in central Greece, which was (and is) visible from Ancient Corinth across the Corinthians Gulf to the south. At Delphi, the Pythia, a woman over 50 years of age and chosen especially for the task, going into a state of divine illumination, received Apollo's response to questions posed by visitors seeking a divine answer to their human problems. The answer came in the form of unintelligible speech, which was translated and rendered into verse by the priests.

Paul ends his preliminary discussion of manifestations of the Spirit by repeating his initial point that the same Spirit lies behind each. Different things may be given to different people, but it is the one Spirit that dispenses them all, in accordance with the Spirit's choosing of who gets what. In Paul's emphasis on the Spirit as the source of all things spiritual, we are reminded of 1 Corinthians 4:7: "If then you received it, why do you boast as if it were not a gift?"

12:12-31a. In v. 12, Paul introduces the metaphor of the church as a body. The metaphor was commonly used in Stoicism to describe the cosmos, and it appears in political writings to stress the interdependence of the various parts of the polis (city) or state. [The Body Politic] While the cosmological examples have little relevance to Paul's usage of the metaphor, the numerous examples of its use

The Body Politic

A commonwealth resembles in some measure a human body. For each of them is composite and consists of many parts; and no one of their parts either has the same function or performs the same service as the others. 2 If, now, these parts of the human body should be endowed, each for itself, with perception and a voice of its own and a sedition should then arise among them, all of them uniting against the belly alone, and the feet should say that the whole body rests on them; the hands, that they ply the crafts, secure provisions, fight with enemies, and contribute many other advantages toward the common good; the shoulders, that they bear all the burdens; the mouth, that it speaks; the head, that it sees and hears and, comprehending the other senses, possesses all those by which the thing is preserved; and then all these should say to the belly, "And you, good creature, which of these things do you do? What return do you make and of what use are you to us? Indeed, you are so far from doing anything for us or assisting us in accomplishing anything useful for the common good that you are actually a hindrance and a trouble to us and—a thing intolerable—compel us to serve you and to bring things to you from everywhere for the gratification of your desires. 3 Come now, why do we not assert our liberty and free ourselves from the many troubles we undergo for the sake of this creature?" If, I say, they should decide upon this course and none of the parts should any longer perform its office, could the body possibly exist for any considerable time, and not rather be destroyed within a few days by the worst of all deaths, starvation. No one can deny it. Now consider the same condition existing in a commonwealth.

Dionysius of Halicarnassus, *Roman Antiquities*, 6.82.1-3 (LCL; trans. Earnest Cary; Cambridge MA: Harvard University Press, 1937–1950).

in political writings to bolster harmony come closer to Paul's purpose in promoting harmony and interdependence in the church.[4] Whereas the political writers sought harmony through adherence to established hierarchies of power, Paul urges equal respect and appreciation for the parts of the body whose significance is usually discounted. Murphy-O'Connor is absolutely correct in his contention that the aims of the political writers "were precisely the antithesis of what he [Paul] was trying to achieve," but he is absolutely wrong in suggesting that the "trigger experience" for Paul's application of the body metaphor to the church was the apostle's observance of the ceramic, anatomical votives discovered in the sanctuary of Asklepios in Corinth.[5] Those artifacts belong to the time of the pre-Roman city of Corinth and would have been underground and invisible in Paul's time.[6] If Paul needed a "trigger" to prompt him to apply the metaphor to the church, he would have had to look no further than what he had written in 1 Corinthians 11:27-29. There he connected profaning the Lord's body with the discriminatory behavior of the wealthier church members against the poorer members. With that connection established, it is no giant leap to depicting the church itself as Christ's body. When Paul does so in chapter 12, he makes the same point he did in chapter 11. Those who considered themselves "higher" members of the body because of their exercise of certain spiritual gifts should not discriminate against those they viewed as lower members of the body. While the two bases of discrimination are different in chapter 11 and chapters 12–14, Paul's point is the same: all members of the body of Christ should be respected and appreciated equally.

Paul's introduction of the body metaphor in v. 12 contains a surprise. One might have expected him to apply the metaphor to the church since the practice of applying it analogically to groups of people, such as the city, was well established, as we have noted. Instead, Paul applies it to Christ.[7] As a body has many members but remains one body, so it is with Christ. This leap over the church to Christ suggests that Paul saw the image of the body as more than a metaphor. Later, in v. 27, he confirms this when he proclaims, "Now you *are* the body of Christ." He immediately connects the body of Christ with his emphasis on the one Spirit in vv. 4-11 by stressing that it is the Spirit that brings one and all into Christ's body. All are "baptized" by one Spirit into the one body, whoever and whatever they might be, and all "drink" of the same Spirit. Overtones of the sacraments may be found in these two statements, but I think Paul's real point lies elsewhere. Baptism is an external washing, while drinking is internal. Paul's point is that entrance into the body of Christ involves a complete saturation of the Spirit, inside and out. His omission of "male or female" from the triad of pairs in v. 13 probably reflects Paul's remembrance of his argument in 11:2-16 and his inclination not to reopen the issue he addressed there.

Following the pattern of the body metaphor's use by political writers, Paul envisions different parts of the body disclaiming membership in the body. Claiming to be separate from the rest of the body, however, does not make it so. Forgoing amputation, each member remains a part of the body, which is fortunate. If the body consisted of only certain members, it would be dysfunctional, which is not God's design (vv. 17-19). God arranged (*etheto*) the parts, each one in the body as God willed. Because each part of the body is essential, furthermore, no part can claim to be independent of the others. By contrast, each and every part needs each and every other part. Furthermore, those parts of the body that may on the surface appear to be unimportant are, in fact, the most indispensable. In veiled language Paul refers to the genitalia (our unpresentable parts). Except for athletes and statues of deified persons, the general practice in Greece and Rome, as in most civilized cultures, was to cover up the unpresentable parts rather than expose them. Paul asserts that this constitutes honoring those parts. As a sign of respect and dignity, those parts are given a special treatment that other parts do not require. Rather than argue that those parts are covered out of shame, Paul affirms their essential value.

Comparing Paul's Lists

The sequence in which Paul names functions and persons in the two lists is different, except for the placement of tongues and/or their interpretation at the bottom in both instances. The fluidity of the sequence and the naming of different items suggest that Paul is not trying to be exhaustive in either case.

1 Corinthians 12:8-10	1 Corinthians 12:28
the speech of wisdom	apostles
the speech of knowledge	prophets
faith	teachers
gifts of healing	miracles
the working of miracles	healings
prophecy	assistances
discerning spirits	guidances
kinds of tongues	kinds of tongues
interpretation of tongues	

This represents concord in the body, whereby all parts express mutual care for the others. The inescapable interdependence of the body's parts means that all share equally in suffering and rejoicing.

In v. 27, Paul states explicitly what has been implicit in his use of the metaphor all along: "You (collectively) are the body of Christ and (individually) members of it." In this body, as in the human body, God has arranged (*etheto*; cf. v. 18) for there to be different parts. Paul then lists a variety of functional positions within the church in a way that indicates some degree of hierarchy. [Comparing Paul's Lists] He specifically says "first" apostles, "second" prophets, and "third" teachers. The functions performed by persons in these positions are oriented toward the whole community rather than individuals alone. That may account for their having been listed as they are. The rest are introduced by "then": miracles, gifts of healing, "assistances," "guidances," and kinds of tongues. This last group specifically names functions and not the performers of those functions. We may infer that Paul had in mind persons who exercise these gifts (as most translations indicate), but it could also be the case that Paul saw these functions as more fluid. Different persons at different times might be "gifted" to perform these actions. Paul's point in listing these positions and functions is to show that God has arranged for there to be differences. He reinforces that point by a series of questions that points out that none of these positions or functions belongs to everyone. Different persons do different things within the body of Christ. Once again in his questions, as in each of his lists, tongues and/or their interpretation comes last.

Verse 31 provides a transition from Paul's prelude, in which he has laid a foundation for addressing the problem more directly in chapter 14, to his interlude, which presents the model by which their behavior in regard to "spiritual things" should be guided. As noted above, Paul elsewhere inserts exemplary models into the middle of his arguments. He paves the way for that insertion here by affirming their zeal for "spiritual things."[8] Paul deliberately refers to them, however, as "gifts" (*charismata*) to keep their focus on their divine source rather than their human possessor. The word *zēloute* may be read as an indicative ("you are zealous for"), but it used as an imperative in other places (14:1, 39) and should be taken as such here ("be zealous for"). The continuous force of the present tense should also be recognized: "Continue to be zealous for the greatest gifts!"

What are the *greatest* gifts? According to the Corinthians, they would probably be wisdom, knowledge, tongues, and the interpretation of tongues, though perhaps with the last two placed before the other two. Conceivably, Paul considers all of the gifts he has mentioned among the "highest gifts." If Paul's listing immediately above informs his reference to the "highest gifts," then Paul meant apostleship, prophecy, and teaching since he specifically places them in a prior position to the others. But how could one be zealous for the position of apostle or teacher? In the discussion that follows in chapter 14, Paul urges them to be zealous for prophecy (14:1, 39). Apostleship, teaching, and prophecy have in common that they are oriented toward the up-building of the whole community. The only one of the three that Paul discusses in the context of a *charisma* that might be given to them during corporate worship is prophecy. All three are the "highest gifts," but without a special calling from God, the one they can aspire to is prophecy.

The Corinthians have shown that they are already zealous regarding gifts of the Spirit. Paul affirms their zeal, but they need more than zeal for *charismata.* They need a model for using whatever gifts they might receive. Hence, Paul intends to *show* them yet a surpassing way. We might have expected Paul to write that he will *tell* them. By indicating that he will *show* them a way, Paul moves the idiom of senses from sound to sight. Seeing requires a visual model. Paul provides that by once again pointing to himself. He begins and ends the next chapter with repeated references to "I." These "I" passages will serve as a frame around his description of love as the surpassing way. This is *how* he will show them another way. The way *that* he will show them is the way beyond zeal for gifts. It is a way that will put gifts in their proper perspective. It is a way that will overcome the divisiveness to which their competitive spirit chronically leads them. Furthermore, it is not presented as another "gift" among others, nor is it the "highest" of the "highest gifts." It is not a "gift" at all; it is a *way.* It is not parceled out to those to whom the Spirit chooses to give it. It is a way available to, even mandated for, all believers (cf. the new commandment in John 13:34).

13:1-13. Too often 1 Corinthians 13 has been read without any regard for its context. This usually results in misreading a biblical text. One can appreciate the appeal of this chapter, though, as a distinct unit in itself. Both thematically and stylistically it rises above the trenches of Paul's battles with the Corinthians and takes on a life of its own. We have to remember, however, that Paul was still in the trenches when he composed these words. They are not unrelated to his larger campaign against the ills that beset the Corinthian congregation. As beautiful and lyrical as the words of this chapter may be, they are still, in a sense, fighting words. They serve a crucial function in Paul's attempts to dissuade the Corinthians from certain practices.

In terms of ancient rhetoric, trying to convince someone to follow a certain course of action or not to follow another course belonged to the domain of deliberation. Most of 1 Corinthians is, in fact, deliberative rhetoric. At times, however, even in a deliberative speech or writing, one could interject other kinds of rhetoric if it served the overall deliberative purpose. That is what Paul has done here. He has drawn from the well of epideictic or demonstrative rhetoric to enhance and buttress his argument for chapters 12–14.[9] In epideictic rhetoric, one celebrated certain commonly held values by praising those who exhibited them and blaming those who did not. The purpose could simply be to gain honor for some and shame for others, but it could also, by inference, intend to persuade those who are shamed to be more like those who are honored. In chapter 13, Paul praises not a person but a virtue, love. Likewise, he does not cast blame on any persons but, instead, depreciates another supposed virtue, gifts (*charismata*). The inference that the Corinthians were supposed to draw from this was that, in their excessive glorification of the lesser virtue to the neglect of the greater, they should be ashamed. To soften the blow of this stinging indictment, Paul places himself in the picture as if he were the one with the inadequate view. This tactic, along with Paul's demonstration of his poetical skills, was designed to win approval from his readers. It also sets the stage for Paul's more direct assault on the problem in chapter 14. [The Structure of 1 Corinthians 13]

The Structure of 1 Corinthians 13

A—vv. 1-3: Paul as subject; my gifts are useless without love
B—vv. 4-7: Love as subject; the qualities of love
B'—vv. 8-10: Love as subject; the endurance of love
A'—vv. 11-12: Paul as subject; my understanding is incomplete
B''—v. 13: Love as subject; the greatest is love

As one reads this chapter, he or she will undoubtedly find allusions to earlier parts of Paul's letter. This is not accidental. In a sense, everything comes to a head at this point. In chapters 12–14,

Paul is dealing with the last of a series of major behavioral problems confronting the Corinthian church. Those problems have a common root: the absence of love. In dealing with this final problem, Paul addresses not only the specific issues this problem entails but also the root cause of all the problems. His word of the cross, with which he began the debate, now takes on very human flesh in his depiction of love. The love Paul portrays is not some abstract concept but rather the concrete point where the love of God expressed in the death of Jesus becomes embodied in the lives of believers. We do his work an injustice when we de-incarnate this chapter and turn it into an ode to love.

Paul uses the first person in the first three verses as he places himself in the position of the Corinthians who have been zealous for gifts. In contrast to all of his lists of gifts thus far, he begins with the "problem child," *glossolalia*. This is the gift his audience seems to value most. The phrase "tongues of human beings and angels" shows that Paul can use the word *glōssa* ("tongue") to mean human language as well as "spiritual" speech (cf. *phōnē* in 14:10-11). The "tongues of angels" reflects the way speaking in tongues was viewed by the Corinthians, and apparently by Paul (14:2). It is the speech of the abode of heaven that is incomprehensible to human beings (unless an interpreter is present). The idea that direct communication with God may involve such angelic language is found in other ancient writings. [Angel Speech] Without love, however, such speech becomes noise. Paul uses two images to depict the useless sounds. The second, "clanging cymbals," is fairly clear in that cymbals make loud, crashing sounds, though the sound itself may not be irritating in certain contexts. The first image (*chalkos ēchōn*), however, is uncertain. *Chalkos* could refer to any number of metals (not only bronze or copper) or metal objects. The word *ēchos* could mean a sound, a voice, or even an echo. Since there is no known occurrence of *chalkos* in connection with musical instruments, other objects have been suggested, including the acoustic vases used in theaters to amplify sound or simply "clunky" metal.[10] The term was used of pots and cauldrons, so I suggest a good rendition of Paul's meaning would be "clanging pot." Whatever object Paul intended, his point is that the noise (tongues) is useless without love.

Angel Speech

The *Testament of Job* (1st century BC–AD 1st century) describes one of Job's daughters engaging in angel speech.

> Thus, when the one called Hemera arose, she wrapped around her own string just as her father said. And she took on another heart—no longer minded toward earthly things—but she spoke ecstatically in the angelic dialect, sending up a hymn to God in accord with the hymnic style of the angels. And as she spoke ecstatically, she allowed "The Spirit" to be inscribed on her garment.

T. Job 48:1-3 (trans. R. P. Spittler) in *The Old Testament Pseudepigrapha*, Vol 1: *Apocalyptic Literature and Testaments* (ed. James H. Charlesworth; Garden City NY: Doubleday & Company, 1983) 865–66.

What Paul contends about the uselessness of *glossolalia* without love applies as well to other manifestations of the Spirit, including both those that the Corinthians are zealous for and those Paul considers more edifying. In v. 2, he names prophecies, mysteries, knowledge, and faith. The first three come in one conditional clause, while faith stands in its own clause. The first three involve things one might know. Paul amplifies the examples of mysteries and knowledge by inserting "all." Of course, he does not know all of these things, but even if he did, this insight would be meaningless without love. The same applies even to faith. In the reference to "moving mountains," Paul uses what was probably a proverbial statement about being able to do the impossible (cf. Matt 17:19-20; Mark 11:23-24; Luke 17:6). Even with such knowledge and power, Paul concludes, without love, "I am nothing,"

Even performing magnanimous and selfless deeds remains without merit if not accompanied by love. In v. 3, Paul first mentions giving away all his belongings. The verb he uses to describe this act (*psōmisō*) is normally associated with feeding. (The most commonly used term for "bread" in Modern Greek is *psōmi.*) The idea expressed is that of giving away everything one has to feed the needy. One thinks naturally here of Jesus' instructions to the rich man to give all of his possessions to the poor (Mark 10:17-22 and par.). Doing so in obedience to Jesus' command or for the sake of honor would still be inadequate without love. Paul's second example in v. 3 is perplexing in several ways. First of all, the ancient manuscripts differ as to what word Paul used, with a slight majority having *kauchēsōmai* ("I might boast") but a large number having *kauthēsomai* ("I will be burned"). [The Text of 1 Corinthians 13:3] Choosing which reading was the original is difficult, but whichever choice is made only leads to a second problem, which is the meaning. If Paul wrote, "If I hand over my body so that I might boast," what did he mean both as to the "handing over" and the "boasting"? *First Clement* 55:2 mentions persons' "handing

The Text of 1 Corinthians 13:3

The manuscripts give witness to four variant readings for 1 Cor 13:3, only two of which (*kauchēsōmai* and *kauthēsomai*) are significant. "Boast" (*kauchēsōmai*) is supported by important early unicials (P46 ℵ A B), several minuscules, a few early translations, and some Church Fathers. "Burn" (*kauthēsomai*) is attested to by some uncials (C D F G L), most minuscules, more early translations, and more Church Fathers. The geographical distribution of the manuscripts for *kauthēsomai* is also broader than those for *kauchēsōmai*. One could argue that the numerous witnesses to *kauchēsōmai* stem from a single source. The committee responsible for the UBS Greek NT 3rd ed., however, decided in favor of *kauchēsōmai* mainly because it is easier to explain how it was changed by a scribe to *kauthēsomai* than to explain the opposite switch. The scribes who favored *kauthēsomai* lived at a time when death of martyrs by burning was more common. "Burning," furthermore, may have made more sense to these scribes than "boasting." How would handing over one's body enable boasting? Such a question indicates that *kauchēsōmai* is the "harder reading," which is one criterion for determining the original. Without any degree of certainty, I accept the committee's judgment that *kauchēsōmai* is more likely the term Paul used.

David E. Garland, *1 Corinthians* (BECNT; Grand Rapids: Baker Academic, 2003) 627–28.

Bruce M. Metzger, *A Textual Commentary on the Greek New Testament* (3rd ed.; Stuttgart: United Bible Societies, 1971) 563–64.

Anthony C. Thiselton, *The First Epistle to the Corinthians: A Commentary on the Greek Text* (NIGTC; Grand Rapids: Eerdmans, 2000) 1042–44.

themselves over" to slavery and using the proceeds to feed others. Such a sacrifice might constitute grounds for "boasting" for Paul. While Paul normally views boasting negatively, he does acknowledge legitimate grounds for boasting when one performs selfless and sacrificial acts (9:15-16; 2 Cor 11:16–12:13). If he wrote, "If I hand over my body so that I will be burned," he was apparently thinking in terms of surrendering to an especially painful death. While persecution of Christians by burning them at the stake still lay in the future at this point, Jewish literature described martyrs' dying by fire during the Maccabean period (2 Macc 7:1-6; 4 Macc 6:24-30). Paul could have had such stories in mind as examples of the ultimate personal sacrifice. Either reading is plausible, with a slight edge going to "boast" on the basis of the textual evidence. We should not lose sight of Paul's main point here. Without love, no sacrifice, however great, gains anything for the person who makes it.

Venus before a Mirror

Peter Paul Reubens. *Venus before a Mirror.* 1614–1615. Oil on wood. Sammlung Fùrst von Liechtenstein, Vaduz Liechtenstein. (Credit: Erich Lessing/Art Resource, NY)

Reubens's portrayal of Venus, goddess of love, captures her vainly observing her reflection in the mirror. Paul's portrayal of love stresses, by contrast, that love is not conceited or arrogant. Later, in v. 12, he also points out that we see only indirectly with a mirror and cannot yet know God as we are known by God.

In the next section (vv. 4-7), Paul switches from himself as the subject to love personified. In doing so, he uses verbs rather than adjectives. Paul does not describe what love *is* but rather what love does or does not *do.* The section may be divided into three parts. The first identifies two actions of love. The second includes a long list of actions love does not perform. The third section (v. 7) identifies what love *always* does. Thus, Paul begins and ends with the positive. Despite doing so, however, his real emphasis seems to be on the central negative part. This is where he appears to allude to the Corinthians' own behavior. In contrast to the positive frame that surrounds his description of love, the Corinthians are guilty of behaving exactly in the ways that love does not behave. Thus, what appears at first to be a praise of love serves as a device for blaming the Corinthians.

Even the first two positive actions of love may be taken as representative of what the Corinthians fail to do. They are not patient, nor are they kind. Their divisiveness, inconsiderate treatment of one another, and competitive status seeking are proof of that. As for what love does not do, they are jealous (3:3), conceited (1:29-31; 3:21; 4:7; 5:6), and "puffed up" (4:6, 18-19; 5:2; 8:1). They are shameful (5:1-2; 7:36), self-seeking (10:24), and quarrelsome (1:11). The last three items may be taken together. While many interpreters read *ou logizetai to kakon* in v. 5 as "not keeping a record of wrong" (i.e., "holding a grudge"), it could as easily mean "not calculating evil" in the sense of not considering an evil course of action. This joins with "not rejoicing over injustice" in v. 6. Both of these, then, would be contrasted with the last part of v. 6: "rejoices together in the truth." These last three items may not allude to any particular actions of the Corinthians, but they do characterize their overall behavior.

Verse 7 returns to the positive actions of love. The word *panta* often means "all things," but it can also have an adverbial sense and mean "always." The first and last verbs here (*stegei* and *hypomenei*) both mean "endure," which is the theme of Paul's next section (vv. 8-10). Translating *panta* as "always" provides a transition to the next section in which Paul stresses the enduring quality of love. The two verbs in the center (*pistei* and *elpizei*) point forward to the last verse in the chapter where Paul states that faith (*pistis*), hope (*elpis*), and love (*agapē*) remain.

The next section (vv. 8-10) contrasts the permanence of love with the transitory nature of gifts. Love never "ends" (lit., "falls"). Prophecies, tongues, and knowledge, however, will cease to be. Paul does not mean by this that such manifestations of the Spirit are only for a limited period in the early history of the church, as dispensational theology holds. Rather, Paul means that they are part of the present age in which the church lives. Paul was anticipating the end of the present age to come soon, but he did not envision a time in the church's life, however long the present age may actually be, when these manifestations of the Spirit would not be present. Still, they are of limited duration. When the kingdom of God comes in its fullness, there will no longer be a need for prophecy, tongues, or knowledge.

Even the knowledge that the Corinthians treasure so highly and prophecy, which Paul considers the most edifying gift, will come to an end. Paul explains why. They are simply incomplete. We know only in part, and we prophesy only in part. This is a remarkable confession. It acknowledges that even those who are endowed by the Spirit with knowledge do not know everything. Those who proclaim the church's message do not testify to the whole truth. They each only have a part of the total picture. This confession by Paul should inject a necessary element of humility into all theological discussions and proclamations. We neither know nor tell the whole truth because it is not ours to possess or pass on to others. When the whole truth (the "perfect") comes, the incomplete will pass away.

To drive home his point about the incompleteness of knowledge and prophecy, Paul returns to speaking of himself as the subject. As a child, Paul behaved as a child in thought and speech. But those childish ways were incomplete. When he became an adult, those ways were no longer adequate; they had to be given up. The analogy of the transition from childhood to adulthood relates to his contention that incomplete knowledge and prophecy will disappear when the kingdom of God comes in its fullness, but it also has another function. Those who place supreme value on the incomplete gifts are behaving as children, not adults. The Corinthians, whom Paul has already called "babies" (3:1-2), would not have failed to see the covert allusion to themselves in this analogy. In case they should miss the point, however, Paul will tell them in 14:20 explicitly not to be childish in their thinking.

Paul shifts his analogy slightly to reinforce his point. What we now see is incomplete, as if we were peering into a mirror rather than at the object itself. Paul adds that we see with this mirror in "puzzlement" (*ainigmati*). The image in the mirror may be clear, but it is still only an image. We have only indirect knowledge of the real thing. The metaphor of the mirror was used by Plato and others to argue that we normally base our knowledge on images rather than on reality.[11] Paul may have drawn the metaphor of the mirror from the philosophical traditions, but his use of it appears to have been shaped by the description of God's speaking to Moses in Numbers 12:6-8. [Numbers 12:6-8] The account in Numbers holds that God spoke to Moses "face to face" and not "in riddles" (*di' ainigmatōn*). Paul affirms that the time will come when he will see "face to face." Then he will know fully what he now knows only in part. What he will know fully when seeing "face to face" is the One who already knows him fully. There is a connection here to 8:2-3 where Paul argued that those who think they know something do not know what they ought to know. They only know in part. But if they love God, they will be known by God. What God knows of us and how God knows us is not available to us now, but it will be, Paul contends, when the imperfect and childish ways of knowing and speaking are replaced by the perfect.

Numbers 12:6-8

And he said,
"Hear my words:
When there are prophets among
you,
I the Lord make myself known
to them in visions;
I speak to them in dreams.
Not so with my servant Moses;
he is entrusted with all my
house.
With him I speak face to face—clearly,
not in riddles;
and he beholds the form of the
LORD. (NRSV)

In the meantime, love remains, along with faith and hope (v. 13). Verse 13 begins with a word (*nyni*) that could be read as a temporal adverb ("now") or as a logical connective ("therefore"). How one translates the word affects whether one takes the verb *menei* ("I remain") in a present or future sense. Is Paul saying that right now faith, hope, and love remain, but they too will pass away, or that these three will continue to abide even beyond the close of the age? It is difficult to see what role faith or hope could have at that time, for they are both forward-looking. Then again, if Paul sees love also remaining only until the end of this age, then his argument about the surpassing endurance of love loses some of its force. Commentators strongly advocate one view or the other. I agree that hope and faith do not seem to belong to the time when God's kingdom has fully come, but I do not think that Paul was being overly precise in his poetry at this point. Both faith and hope prove to be more enduring and empowering than any manifestation of the Spirit that excites the Corinthians. As great as they are, however, they too pale in comparison to love. Love is the surpassing way both now and forever.

The Gifts of Prophecy and Tongues, 14:1-40

Everything Paul has written to this point has been preparatory for directly confronting the problem of speaking in tongues. Thus far, he has alluded to tongues only in conjunction with other manifestations of the Spirit. Finally, he shows his hand, and we see what he has been driving toward all along. This gradual buildup to a direct confrontation of the problem reflects Paul's awareness that the issue of speaking in tongues can quickly result in the dissolution of community within the church. The issue is prone to explode the bonds of fellowship even today by the centripetal forces of those both supporting and opposing the practice. Rather than blow up the church, Paul strives to build it up by finding a way to integrate a phenomenal, personal experience into the life of the community.

Paul's approach to defusing the situation comes in two parts (vv. 1-25 and vv. 26-40). He first contrasts tongues with prophecy, which he asserts has a clear purpose in edifying the church (vv. 1-25). He points out that the edification of tongues is limited to the person doing the tongue-speaking (vv. 1-5). He then explains that is the case because, unlike prophecy, tongues are unintelligible (vv. 6-12). He follows this by pointing out the need for interpretation of tongues before they can be edifying (vv. 13-19). Finally, he urges them to consider the effects of tongues on those outside the church (vv. 20-25).

In the second part (vv. 26-40), Paul prescribes how order should be maintained during worship. He first addresses the orderly practice of tongues (vv. 27-28). He then does the same for prophecy and its discernment (vv. 29-36). Following in this section are special instructions regarding wives (vv. 33b-36). He adds an admonition regarding any who might reject his prescription (vv. 37-38) and then offers a conclusion to his whole argument (vv. 39-40). [The Structure of 1 Corinthians 14]

The Structure of 1 Corinthians 14

Prophecy Edifies More Than Tongues, vv.1-25
- Tongues edify the speaker, vv. 1-5
- Tongues are unintelligible, vv. 6-12
- Tongues must be interpreted, vv. 13-19
- Tongues confuse outsiders, vv. 20-25

Order Should Prevail in the Church, vv. 26-40
- Let everything be done for edification, v. 26
- Let tongues be regulated, vv. 27-28
- Let prophecy and its discernment be regulated, vv. 29-33a
- Let women be silent in church, vv. 33b-36
- Let everyone recognize this practice, vv. 37-38
- Let everything be done decently and in order, vv. 39-40

14:1-25. Paul begins by referring back to the surpassing way of love that he has described in chapter 13. "Pursue love," he urges. He also instructs them to be zealous for "spiritual things." This is the first time Paul has used the word *pneumatika* since v. 1. He could not discuss the quest for *pneumatika* without first setting the context for the distinctions between them and their use. The theme of vv. 1-25 becomes clear when he states, "But even more so that you might prophesy." The preferred "spiritual thing" is prophecy. Though we have not made this observation to this point, it is clear from the discussion that follows that by prophecy, Paul means "inspired preaching." Prophecy is the disclosure of a spirit-induced word from the Lord. "Are all prophets?" Paul asked in 12:29. No, but Paul does believe that everyone can prophesy (v. 31). The church may have those among its ranks who are recognized as prophets, but this does not preclude the possibility of others being inspired to speak.

Paul points out the essential difference between prophecy and tongues in vv. 2-5. Speaking in tongues is typically an individual experience. The person so speaking speaks only to God, not to other persons. No one "hears" the message because it remains mysterious. The person doing the speaking speaks "by spirit" mysteries. "By spirit" could refer to a spirit that comes into the person to inspire them, or it could mean the person's own spirit, that is their deepest inner self, the part that can communicate most directly with God.[12] In light of Paul's distinction between praying with the mind and praying with the spirit in vv. 14-15, the latter understanding is preferable. The one who prophesies, in contrast, speaks to other persons and offers edification, encouragement, and consolation. Prophecy is communal speaking. The tongue-speaker only edifies himself or herself. Granted, the phenomenon of glossolalia may cast an aura of the supernatural over a congregation that could inspire reverence toward God, but the content of the tongue-speech remains undisclosed. Prophecy, however, directly by its content (and not the charismatic displays of preacherly excellence) contributes to the edification of all.

Unlike numerous modern denominations, Paul makes it clear that he is "pro-tongues." He asserts that he wants all the Corinthians to speak in tongues (v. 5). Unlike numerous other modern denominations, however, he makes it clear that he does not consider tongues to be the highest gift. He also repeats his statement from v. 1: "but even more so that you would prophesy." The simple reason for preferring prophecy to tongue-speaking is that it edifies the church while the other does not. This makes prophecy and the one who prophesies "greater" in Paul's view than tongues or its practitioner.

In v. 6, Paul elaborates on what he has already hinted, that the basic problem with tongues is their unintelligible nature. Adopting the first-person voice again as he did in 13:1, perhaps to soften the obvious criticism of their position, he supposes what benefit he could bring to them if he only came speaking in tongues. Obviously he would need to impart to them some revelation, knowledge, prophecy, or teaching to do them any good. Tongues cannot communicate any of these constructive things. He then employs the analogies of musical instruments and the military bugle. A flute or harp must produce an intelligible pattern of notes before any recognizable music can be heard. The bugler must issue a clear call to arms before anyone will get ready for battle. An unclear signal will leave soldiers not knowing whether to attack or retreat. Likewise, the unintelligible sounds of tongue-speaking leave the hearer clueless as to the message. The noise simply floats meaningless into the air.

Paul gives another example to prove his point in v. 10. The variety of languages (*genē phōnōn*) existing in the world all have linguistic meaning, but unless one knows the meaning (lit., "power") of the specific language spoken, then it remains meaningless. The speaker and hearer remain as "barbarians" (*barbaros*) to each other. "Barbarian" was the term Greeks applied to all persons who could not speak Greek. The same applies to those speaking in tongues. They remain in a state of "foreignness" to their fellow believers. Because of this, and because of their zeal for "spirits," Paul instructs them to strive to abound for the edification of the church. [Zeal for Spirits] Since Paul has already specified that certain gifts, namely prophecy, contribute to edifying the church, their zeal for those that do not is essentially misplaced.

At this point (vv. 13-19), Paul explains the need for interpretation before the practice of speaking in tongues can serve any edifying purpose for the church. The one who speaks in a tongue should also pray that he or she might interpret the tongue. Paul does not say that the person should pray for someone else to interpret the tongue. He puts the responsibility on the shoulders of the tongue-speaker. Paul then once more puts himself in the place of his target audience. "If I should pray in a tongue, my *spirit* prays but my *mind* is fruitless." Paul seems to hold that a person has both mind and spirit and that both should be involved in prayer. If the mind is not in operation in the experience, then it receives no benefit. One can engage in prayer without engaging the mind. That is what one is doing when speaking in a tongue. Only a part of the self is engaged.

Zeal for Spirits

AΩ 1 Cor 14:12 literally reads, "Since you are zealots of spirits (*pneumatōn*), for [the purpose of] the edification of the church seek so that you might abound." The statement is worded in such a way that the object of "abound" is unclear. Most interpreters understand Paul to mean that they should strive to abound *for the edification of the church*. This certainly fits the thrust of Paul's argument throughout. The syntax of the sentence, however, also allows for understanding the assumed object to be "spirits." Thus, the sense would be, "Since you are zealots of [i.e., for] spirits, for the edification of the church, strive to abound [*in spirits*]. "Spirits" would be understood in this case as external spirits that inspire speech, both *glossolalia* and prophecy. Most interpreters also hold that the word that literally means "spirits" should be read as essentially equivalent to *pneumatika* ("spiritual things"). If so, one wonders why Paul did not use *pneumatika* instead of *pneumatōn*. Translating *pneumatōn* as "spirits" is more in keeping with its normal meaning and probably more accurately reflects the Corinthians' perspective. They were seeking to be inspired by "spirits" that would empower them to speech in tongues. That may be one reason stressed that Paul stressed in 12:4-10 that it is the *one* Spirit that lies behind all gifts. Taking "spirits" as the object of "abound," however grammatically possible, misses Paul's point, which is that their zeal should be directed toward the things that will edify the church.

Clint Tubbs, "The Spirit (World) and the (Holy) Spirit among the Earliest Christians: 1 Corinthians 12 and 14 as a Test Case," *CBQ* 70 (2008): 324–25.

Dale Martin has argued that Paul's dichotomy of mind and spirit reflects similar dichotomies found in Plato, Philo, and Iamblicus.[13] According to those philosophers, the mind normally governs the person's thinking and acting. When in communication with a higher realm, however, the mind gives way to a higher agent. Indeed, this is considered necessary lest the mind interfere with the working of the higher agent. Paul seems to have a similar view in that when one is communicating with God directly by the spirit, the mind becomes inactive. For the purpose of edifying the church, however, Paul insists that the mind be brought back into the picture. Both agents must work in tandem. Martin holds that this means Paul is arguing for a reduction in the status of the higher agent, the person's spirit. By placing the mind and spirit on the same level, Paul is rejecting the Corinthians' valuation of experiences that involves the spirit but not the mind.

Paul states that the solution to the problem of praying only in the spirit is to pray with the mind also (v. 15). The same holds for singing. Both the spirit and the mind should be engaged. The Corinthians may hold that praying or singing in the spirit constitutes a higher level of spiritual experience, but Paul disagrees. Such actions do not benefit the community, and so, according to his view of what constitutes the "higher" gifts, they should be considered lesser gifts. He gives an example of how praying only in spirit presents problems in v. 16. How can *someone* say the "Amen" to one's thanksgiving prayer if that *someone* does not understand what the prayer is saying? Paul identifies the *someone* with a phrase that literally means "one who fills the place of the outsider (*idiōtou*)." Who would that have been? Some interpret the difficult phrase to mean an unbeliever who is in attendance. The same word is used in conjunction with "unbeliever" in v. 23. But why would not knowing when to say "amen" be problematic for an outsider? Others think it means a person who is sympathetic to the church but not yet baptized, while others hold that it refers to novices in the faith. Still others hold that it refers to anyone who does not understand what is being said when a person prays in tongues. Paul's point is that the tongue-praying serves no benefit for the other person. That person is not edified in any way.

Paul's final statement in this section serves several purposes. The first is to deflate the pride some of his readers may have in regard to tongues. Paul is no novice in the matter. He thanks God that he can speak in tongues more than any of the Corinthians. Any smugness they may have had about their tongue-speaking experiences is unjustified. Paul excels any of them who would consider the gift of tongues to be a sign of their spiritual superiority. The second purpose is to show how little regard Paul has for his own tongue-speaking in comparison to more edifying speech. He asserts that he would rather speak a mere five intelligible words with his mind engaged than ten thousand unintelligible words in a "mindless" tongue. If he and the Corinthians were to get into a "tongue-speaking contest," Paul would win hands down, but he would prefer to achieve a little understanding on the part of his listeners than to take home that trophy. The final purpose is to offer himself once again as an example of one who willfully gives up rights and privileges for the sake of others. Though endowed with the gift of tongues to a degree superior to his readers, he forgoes this practice in the context of community worship. "In church" Paul is concerned with edifying his sisters and brothers in Christ rather than enjoying whatever personal benefit might be his through the experience of speaking in tongues.

The last point Paul wishes to make about the limitations of tongues and the greater benefits of prophecy for the community involves their effect on unbelievers (vv. 20-25). While tongues may serve no edifying function for the church, they may actually prove detrimental to unbelievers. Paul begins this part with an exhortation that they not become children in their thinking. He has already called them "babies" in 3:1-2, and he probably implied in 13:11 that "giving up childish ways" meant reassessing the maturity of those who were so infatuated with tongues. They should "be as babies" in regard to evil, but maturity was required of them in their thinking.

The language of children and babies reflects Paul's basic stance in relationship to them as their "father" (4:14-15). But it may also reflect the source of Paul's quotation in v. 21, Isaiah 28. [Isaiah 28:9-12] His quotation includes only a paraphrased rendition of Isaiah 28:11 and a snippet of the following verse. The two verses that precede the part paraphrased by Paul include a reference to babies recently weaned. Verses 9-10 of Isaiah 28 are generally concerned to be the response made to Isaiah's preaching by the "drunken" priests and prophets described in v. 7. These obstinate religious leaders consider Isaiah's words to be childish gibberish fit only for babies, and they mock him with childlike talk about "precept upon precept" and "line upon line." The part Paul cites gives Isaiah's response to their ridicule. God is speaking to them "with a stammering lip and with a foreigner's tongue." Paul alters this to read "by men of strange tongue and by the lips of foreigners." Because the religious leaders cannot understand the message, they do not hear or heed it. In Isaiah 28, this is followed by God's pronouncement that "strange baby talk" is all they will receive from the Lord. As a result, they shall meet their doom. The unheard message, then, becomes a word of judgment.

Isaiah 28:9-12

"Whom will he teach knowledge,
and to whom will he explain
the message?
Those who are weaned from milk,
those taken from the breast?
For it is precept upon precept,
precept upon precept,
line upon line, line upon line,
here a little, there a little.

Truly, with stammering lip
and with alien tongue
he will speak to this people,
to whom he has said,
"This is rest;
give rest to the weary;
and this is repose";
yet they would not hear. (NRSV)

This larger context from Isaiah may partly explain Paul's surprising statement in 14:22 that tongues are a sign not for believers but for unbelievers and that prophecy is not for unbelievers but for believers. Asserting that tongues are not for believers appears to contradict what Paul has already said (and will say) about the benefit of tongues, when interpreted, for believers. Likewise, claiming that prophecy is not for unbelievers seems to contradict what he says in vv. 24-25 about the positive effect prophecy can have on unbelievers. The Isaiah passage shows that a strange tongue comes as a word of judgment for those who do not believe. The seemingly childish gibberish of *glossolalia* actually prevents unbelievers from coming to belief. It stands in the way of their hearing the gospel and confirms them in their disbelief, which ultimately leads to their judgment. But in what sense would prophecy not be for unbelievers as well as believers? Paul's words to this effect cannot be completely reconciled with vv. 24-25. One either has to suppose that Paul meant prophecy was primarily, but not exclusively, for believers or that Paul's two contrasts in v. 22 do not have parallel meanings. The first contrast stresses that tongues are a *sign* for one but not the other, but the second contrast refers to the possession or use of prophecy by one but not the other, in the sense that believers may prophesy but unbelievers cannot. Neither of these attempts to resolve the apparent contradiction is satisfactory because they both read into the text more than what the words permit. Probably, Paul's habit of juxtaposing opposites simply led him a little too far in stating that prophecy was not for unbelievers.

The last three verses in this section pose a more understandable contrast between tongues and prophecy (vv. 23-25). If unbelievers come into an assembly where the whole church is present and find everyone speaking in tongues, they will conclude that the church members are crazy (*mainesthe*). Hays argues that "manic" behavior may not have necessarily led the unbelievers to assess that the church was crazy but only that is was like other cultic groups that practiced frenzied behavior and speech.[14] This assessment, however, overlooks the repulsion that most Romans felt toward such groups. They looked with suspicion, not complacency, on such groups and considered them both crazy and dangerous. [Bacchic Cults] By contrast, Paul points out, if they come into an assembly in which everyone is prophesying, they will be converted (vv. 24-25). They will be convicted and called to account by everything that is said, which they can hear clearly. The secrets of their hearts will be exposed, and they will fall on their faces worshiping God. Rather than blurting out, "You are all crazy," they will declare (in the words of Isa 45:14), "God is certainly among you." Paul's optimism about the response of unbelievers reflects his conviction that prophecy, clearly spoken, has the power to change lives.

14:26-40. The second section of Paul's argument in chapter 14 focuses on the maintenance

Bacchic Cults

The Roman historian Livy devotes 12 chapters of his *History of Rome* to describing the excesses of the Bacchic cult in Rome.

> To think nothing unlawful, was the grand maxim of their religion. The men, as if bereft of reason, uttered predictions, with frantic contortions of their bodies; the women, in the habit of Bacchantes, with their hair dishevelled, and carrying blazing torches, ran down to the Tiber; where, dipping their torches in the water, they drew them up again with the flame unextinguished, being composed of native sulphur and charcoal. They said that those men were carried off by the gods, whom the machines laid hold of and dragged from their view into secret caves. These were such as refused to take the oath of the society, or to associate in their crimes, or to submit to defilement. Their number was exceedingly great now, almost a second state in themselves, and among them were many men and women of noble families. During the last two years it had been a rule, that no person above the age of twenty should be initiated; for they sought for people of such age as made them more liable to suffer deception and personal abuse.

Livy, *History of Rome* 39.13.11-14 (trans. William A. McDevitte; London: Bungay, 1850).

of order when the church assembles together for worship. After stating a general principle that should guide everything that occurs in worship, Paul gives specific guidance regarding tongues, prophecy, and the role of women. He closes with an admonition to any who would oppose his view and then ends with a reminder that everything should be done decently and in order.

In v. 26, Paul begins to explicate the implications of what he has argued thus far. When they come together, each one may have something different to contribute, but everything that happens should be for edification. He specifically mentions hymns, teachings, revelations, tongues, and interpretations. This should be taken only as a representative list of worship activities and not an exhaustive one, especially since he does not include prophecy. Nor should his reference to "each" be taken to mean that he sees worship as "pot luck" where everyone always contributes. The variety of contributions to worship simply sets up his basic principle that whatever one contributes, it should be for edification.

The general principle of edification applies especially to tongues, as his previous argument makes clear. So Paul follows this principle with specific instruction for the regulation of tongues toward the goal of edification. If anyone does speak in tongues, there should be only two, or three at most, and someone should interpret. Paul has already argued that glossolalia is inappropriate in communal worship if not accompanied by interpretation. Presumably the "one" who should interpret is anyone to whom the *charisma* of interpretation has been give (12:10). Without the presence of someone who can interpret, the tongue-speaking should remain silent, speaking only to the self and to God.

Paul gives a similar regulation for prophecy. Two or three prophets should be allowed to speak, and then what they say should be "discerned" (*diakrinetōsan*) by "the others." The identity of "the others" is unclear. Some commentators see this referring to the whole church, while others think it designates specific persons. In 12:10, Paul listed "discernment of spirits" right after prophecy in his list of gifts of the Spirit. As 14:32 shows, Paul understood prophecy to involve spirits. It seems likely that "the others" who should discern the spirit that has inspired the prophecy are those who have received the gift of discernment. The prophets themselves should become silent and promptly surrender the floor to another prophet when that one receives a revelation. Verse 31a is often taken to mean that everyone present may potentially prophesy in turn. I read the verse somewhat differently: "For by going one at a time you enable all (the prophets) to prophesy." This

The Prophet's Spirit

If the gift is subject to the prophets, how can it not also be subject to you, so that you may keep quiet when you are meant to?

Oecumenius, *Pauline Commentary from the Greek Church*, in Gerald Bray, ed., *1–2 Corinthians* (vol. 7 of ACCS NT; ed. Thomas C. Oden; Downers Grove IL: InterVarsity Press, 1999) 145.

reading makes more sense of v. 32, which states that "spirits of prophets are submissive to prophets." A spirit may inspire the prophecy, but the prophet is not controlled by the spirit. The prophet may subject his or her inspiring spirit and become silent so that each of the prophets present may speak in turn. [The Prophet's Spirit] This way, everyone may learn and be encouraged (v. 32b). This orderly procedure for worship conforms to the nature of God, Paul holds, because God is not a God of disorder but of peace (v. 33a).

The next unit (vv. 33b-36) contains instructions regarding women that have caused much debate. Paul's statement that women should keep silent in the churches seems to be a clear contradiction of 11:2-16, where Paul specified only that women should have their heads covered when praying or prophesying in church. How can they do either if they must remain silent? The basic questions any interpretation are the following: (1) Does this passage belong in the text? (2) Does this passage reflect Paul's position or that of the Corinthians? (3) Does this passage contradict 11:2-16? (4) What exactly does the passage mean?

(1) Does this passage belong in the text? This passage appears in all known ancient copies of 1 Corinthians, but in a few manuscripts it appears in a different location in chapter 14. Without going into detail about the critical issues of the text, we can still note a few aspects of the debate.[15] Some interpreters take the appearance of this passage in different locations in different texts as a sign that it is an interpolation by a scribe, possibly using 1 Timothy 2:11-12 as a basis for the interpolation's content. Since nearly all of the manuscripts in which the passage is moved are late Western texts, however, any interpolation would have had to be done very early and would have had to be accepted as authentic over a broad geographical area. No text omits the passage. This alone gives strong grounds for its authenticity.

(2) Does this passage reflect Paul's position or that of the Corinthians? Some interpreters hold that Paul is quoting the

Corinthians once again here. Verse 36 is read as Paul's rebuttal to the attempt by Corinthian men to subject the women to silence. The attraction of this view is twofold: It removes the contradiction with 11:2-16, and it gets the monkey off Paul's back since the Corinthians, not he, are arguing for the silencing of the women. Despite the attractiveness, this view flounders on the improbability that vv. 33b-35 is a quotation and that v. 36 is a rebuttal. Verse 36 is better read as a continuation of the point made in the preceding verses. Any slogans of the Corinthians quoted by Paul elsewhere in the letter are brief, and Paul immediately and directly challenges or qualifies the quoted slogan. Whether one likes it or not, these verses appear to express Paul's view on the matter.

(3) Does this passage contradict 11:2-16? The answer to this question, of course, depends on what the passage means. If it is a blanket suppression of women's voices in all the churches at all times, then we have no recourse but to acknowledge that Paul has spoken out both sides of his mouth. Total silence bans any praying or prophesying in church, whether they have their heads covered or not. If Paul intended for women to be silent at all times, then what did he mean in 11:2-16? If we accept the two passages as contradictory, then we still have to decide which of the two really represents Paul's position in regard to women. If 14:33b-36 reflects the "real" Paul, then what are we to make of his positive references to all of his female coworkers (1 Cor 16:19; Rom 16; Phil 4:2-3; Col 4:15)?[16] Did they do their work in silence? If we accept 11:2-16 as reflecting Paul's position, then we have to find some way to interpret 14:33b-36 that does not contradict his view. Otherwise, we have to concede that Paul was either duplicitous or schizophrenic.

(4) What exactly does the passage mean? Taking the passage to be Paul's own words, original to the text, and non-contradictory of 11:2-16, I hold that in 14:33b-36 Paul is addressing a situation in which wives are speaking in a way that may be considered shameful for their husbands (v. 35). Shame was very much Paul's concern in 11:2-16, and a similar concern underlies his instruction here. He is not prescribing a ban on all speaking by all women in all instances. He is trying to resolve a particular problem that he sees occurring in the Corinthian assemblies. Wives are speaking up in a certain way that brings shame directly to their husbands and indirectly to the church.

The difficult section begins in 14:33b with Paul's appeal to custom: "As in all the churches of the saints." Some see here a specific reference to the Jerusalem saints and hold that Paul is seeking to impose on the Corinthians a custom rooted in Jewish aversion to the participation of women in the synagogue. Paul identifies the Corinthians themselves as "saints," however, and ties them with "all those who call upon the name of the Lord Jesus Christ in every place" (1:2). He is referring to what he considers a universal custom in the churches. In all the churches, the women are to be silent, are not permitted to speak, and should be subordinate (v. 34). Subordinate to whom? In all instances in the New Testament where the verb "be subordinate" (*hypotassomai*) appears in connection

with women, it refers to their being subordinate to their husbands.[17] Paul is referring here to wives' being subordinate to their husbands, not to all women being subordinate to all men. This subordination to their husbands, Paul argues, means that the wives should remain silent in church.

Paul bases the prohibition against wives' speaking in church not only on the custom of the churches, but also on the "law" (v. 35). This statement has puzzled interpreters in two ways. First, it appears to be "un-Pauline" for Paul to appeal to a teaching of the Mosaic Law since he was so adamant that Gentiles were free from the law. Second, the Old Testament contains no specific command either for the woman to be silent or to be subordinate to her husband. As for the first matter, Paul appeals to the Old Testament law in 14:21 and elsewhere in 1 Corinthians (7:19; 9:8-10). As for the second, the absence of a specific Old Testament commandment does not require us to conclude that by "law" Paul was referring to some other law. Winter has suggested that Paul had in mind the Vellian decree passed by the Roman senate during the time of Claudius that restricted the right of women to testify in court, but this seems to be too specific to apply to Paul's situation.[18] Paul's contemporary, Philo, held that the Law of Moses did teach the subordination of wives to their husbands, and he asserted that husbands should be the ones to teach the law to their wives. [Philo on the Law] Paul may have shared the view that the Law of Moses taught the subordination of wives to their husbands and the propriety of the wife's learning from her husband at home.

Philo on the Law

Two relevant passages appear in Philo's *De Hypothetica.* In a summary of the laws of Moses, he wrote:

Wives must be in servitude to their husbands, a servitude not imposed by violent ill-treatment but promoting obedience in all things. (*Hypoth*. 7.3.5a)

The husband seems competent to transmit knowledge of the laws to his wife. (*Hypoth*. 7.14)

Paul bases his position on custom, the law, and the fact that it is shameful for the wives to speak in church. In the "honor-shame" culture of the time, the "shame" would have fallen not on the wife but on the husband. Praying and prophesying without her head covered would have shamed a woman's husband because she was appearing in public as though she were not married. Speaking up in the assembly in a way forbidden by custom and the law would have shamed the husband because the wife was acting in an insubordinate way.

Apparently, however, it was not considered insubordinate for a wife to pray or prophesy in the assembly as long as she had her head covered. Why is one act of speaking a sign of insubordination and another not? Some try to answer this question by translating the verb for speaking (*laleō*) as "chattering," "gossiping," or some other kind of offensive speaking. But the word *laleō* carries none of these negative connotations in itself. I think interpreters have focused on the wrong verb. In v. 35, when Paul states that the wife should learn at home by "asking" her husband, he uses a word that he never uses elsewhere except in a quotation of Isaiah 65:1 in Romans 10:20. The verb *eperōtaō* carries a much stronger sense than merely asking. It suggests "scrutinizing," "interrogating," or "investigating."[19] It suggests a much more aggressive form of asking, one that could easily be seen as disrespectful "grilling" of the husband. If the aggressive interrogation came in the context of "discerning" what was said by the one prophesying, then the offense was amplified, even more so if the one prophesying was the husband. (I suspect many preachers can relate to the embarrassment that would come from having a spouse—who knows best the contradictions between what is preached and practiced by the preacher—"scrutinize" the sermon in public.) In the context of a male-dominated culture in which a wife's failure to behave modestly in public brought shame to the husband, Paul accepted and affirmed the custom of silence for the wives, except when they were inspired to prophesy and preach.

Paul's final word on the subject is his own interrogation of the Corinthians for allowing a practice that disrupts orderly worship (v. 36). "Did the word of God come forth from you, or has it reached you alone?" The Corinthians, of course, are neither the originators of the gospel nor its sole recipients. They are part of that larger body of persons who call upon the name of the Lord. In Paul's view, they are not free to flaunt what has become the accepted practice of the church at large. To do so is to be insubordinate.

Verses 37-40 function as a *peroratio* (concluding summary) for the argument Paul began in 12:1. Thus, the strong statement Paul makes in vv. 37-38 should not be restricted in application to the immediately preceding section. Given that Paul's argument begins softly and only reaches a harsh tone in chapter 14, however, the warning of these final verses applies especially to what Paul has just written. He began in 12:1 to address the matter of "Spiritual things" (*pneumatikōn*). He ends by stating that any persons who consider themselves to be prophets or "spiritual persons" (*pneumatikos*) should recognize that what he has written comes with the force of a command from the Lord. Anyone truly spiritual would acknowledge the truth of his argument. If they do not, then they are not "recognized." The sense of this statement is much stronger than it might at first appear. Their spirituality or status as a prophet is repudiated, and also perhaps is their presence within the community of faith.

The last word in vv. 39-40 reiterates Paul's desire that they desire the higher gift of prophecy. That is the gift most conducive to edification. Tongues still has its place, so Paul urges them not to forbid the practice of speaking in tongues. Overall, his approach to the problem, while forceful, has been diplomatic. The final statement that everything be done decently in order captures succinctly the point of his whole argument.

CONNECTIONS

The Body of Christ

Paul's metaphor of the church as the body of Christ in 1 Corinthians 12 has often been used in proclamation to stress the unity that should exist within the church. The history of Christianity is such that one can easily understand how any text that promotes unity would be welcomed. The fractured state of the body of Christ that Paul encountered in Corinth pales in comparison to the brokenness that has transpired since his day. Division, rather than unity, characterizes the church today. Incredibly, much of this division has occurred because of the quest for unity understood as uniformity. *Oneness* in Christ has been interpreted to mean *sameness.* Those who are different are perceived as threats to the health of the body; thus, they are subjected to pressure to conform or leave. [The Captive Body]

The Captive Body

In much of the much of the tradition of received interpretation, the "body of Christ" has been long held captive, while serving ecclesial interests and legitimizing the powerful in society and the church. The fossilized "body of Christ' as a metaphor for a unified organism precludes other possibilities of meaning that would open the opportunity for cross-cultural dialogue with "others."

Yung Suk Kim, *Christ's Body in Corinth: The Politics of a Metaphor* (Minneapolis: Fortress Press, 2008) 30.

Ironically, some of the basis for this understanding of the body of Christ as a unified whole comes from Paul's own language. In 1 Corinthians 12:4-11, Paul stresses that the different manifestations of the Spirit in the church all come from the same Spirit. In 12:12-13, he points out that just as the body has many members but remains a single body, so it is with the church. In 12:24-25, he argues that God has so designed the body of Christ that all of the members respect and care for each other so that there may be no discord in the body. All of this emphasizes the oneness of the body.

What is easily overlooked is Paul's emphasis on the diversity of the body. Yes, it is one and the same Spirit that stands behind the different spiritual manifestations, but the Spirit does not impart to everyone the same gift. A diversity of gifts exists in the church. Yes, the different parts of the body belong to one and the same body, but each part has its own distinctive function. Yes, the different parts of the body show respect and care for the other parts, but each part remains different. Yes, we are all baptized into one body, but we that are baptized do not lose our distinct identities.

What we so easily overlook in stressing the oneness of the body is the reason Paul was compelled to use the body metaphor. Some elements in the church were discounting the importance of other elements. In particular, those who experienced the Spirit's manifestation of certain gifts were devaluing other manifestations. They viewed the body in terms of a hierarchy in which some gifts placed those who possessed them at the top. Paul's response to this way of seeing the body was to subvert it by arguing that those parts of the body that one might consider to be lower in status or less important were actually the ones that are honored the most. The thrust of this reversal was not to place the foot (or any other lower part) above the head but to dispense with the hierarchy altogether. If there is to be any ranking at all, it is based on the degree to which particular gifts contribute to the well-being of all the other parts of the body. In Paul's view, all the gifts can serve for the edification of the whole body. The problem he faced was that certain gifts exercised by some parts of the body were being used for individual enhancement of power and prestige rather than for the good of all.

Paul's objective was not simply to bring all of the Corinthians together into a unified body in which the bonds of togetherness superceded the forces of separation. He envisioned a community in which all of the diverse parts would be welcomed and allowed to function *as diverse parts* within the body. Tongues as well as prophecy belong to this community. Healers and helpers belong in this community. Teachers and miracle workers have a place as well. His promotion of prophecy as "greater" than tongues because of its power to edify in 14:5 includes an interesting aside: "unless someone interprets." He holds out the possibility that interpreted tongues might prove to be even more edifying than prophecy. His aim was not to root out certain gifts but to redirect the thoughts of those who exercised any gift to do so for the good of everyone else. Mutuality of concern, compassion, and respect were his objectives, not uniformity or conformity.

The body of Christ is that place where persons of various backgrounds (Jew or Greek), various roles in society (slave or free), and various perspectives (perhaps Paul should have added male or female) find they are welcomed to exercise their different gifts, conscious of their interdependence and their interconnectedness in Christ. Not to do so is tantamount to trying to be the body of Christ with some of the limbs or organs missing. If Paul was right about the need for diversity within the body, then the church should be wary of self-amputation through exclusion of those who do not match our perception of unity. [Our Need for the "Other"]

Our Need for the "Other"

The existence of "others" is not something to remove or simply overcome but to live through because we may learn from them Christ-like manifestations. In an individualistic faith and life context today, what is at stake is how to reconstruct a community for "all"—in which the rich and the poor, the happy and the unhappy, gather together in acknowledging others, comforting and being comforted, challenging and being challenged.

Yung Suk Kim, *Christ's Body in Corinth: The Politics of a Metaphor* (Minneapolis: Fortress Press, 2008) 90.

Love Is a Verb

Sentimentality may abound when 1 Corinthians 13 is read at weddings, but Paul hardly intended that his Corinthians readers mistake his words as a sentimental tribute to love. The poetic beauty of his writing may easily draw the modern reader's attention away from the sharp critique embedded in his praise of love, but the Corinthians would have probably understood his point quite well. He was on the attack. The very qualities of love that he enumerated stood in clear contrast to their own behavior. The primacy of love over tongues, knowledge, and even prophecy rendered petty their competition over acclamation for having the higher spiritual gifts.

Paul described love not as a gift but as a "way." The way of love leads away from competition and self-assertion. The way of love departs from the jealousy, boasting, arrogance, and inconsiderateness that characterized their interaction with each other. The way of love transcends the pursuit of individual fulfillment and leads to true community. The way of love endures.

In describing love, Paul showed a preference for verbs rather than adjectives, though translations somewhat obscure this. By using verbs, Paul made the point that love is not simply a feeling; it is a lifestyle. Love involves action. [Luv Is a Verb] For Paul, the action required by love is defined by the cross of Christ. Through the foolishness of the cross, God has acted on behalf of the foolish, the weak, the lowly, and the despised—all the "nothings" and "nobodies" of the world—in order to transform them into children of the kingdom (1:27-28). To follow the way of love, the Corinthians

Luv Is a Verb

The rap group dc Talk seems to have understood something of Paul's point in 1 Cor 13, as indicated by the excerpt from their song "Luv Is a Verb" given below.

Pullin' out my big black book
'Cause when I need a word defined that's where I look
So I move to the ls quick, fast, in a hurry
Threw on my specs, thought my vision was blurry
I looked again but to my dismay
It was black and white with no room for grey
Ya see, a big v stood beyond my word
And yo that's when it hit me, that luv is a verb.

Words come easy but don't mean much
When the words they're sayin' we can't put trust in
We're talkin' 'bout love in a different light
And if we all learn to love it would be just right.

would have to change not only the way they viewed the "lessers" in the church but also the way they acted toward them. Whatever gifts they had received from the Spirit were to be employed in the building up of the whole body of Christ, with special attention to "inferior" parts.

For the modern church, following the way of love also means using its gifts for the edification of the whole body and giving special attention to the "least of those among us." Sadly, for many modern churches, the "least" are not among us at all. They are outside the body, or at least outside the ranks of the local group of fellow believers though they may, in fact, not be outside the full body of Christ in the world. Using the gifts of the church in the way of love today may mean spending less time and energy on "building up" the power and status of the local community of believers and expending more on the up-building of those less powerful and less esteemed outside the ranks of the church.

For Leif and Anita Kratz, following the way of love has meant caring for children discarded by the world. They do this, of all places, in Ancient Corinth. To aid the children displaced by the Balkan wars of the 1990s, they helped establish an international organization known as "Children's Ark." Their efforts resulted in the construction of an orphanage for homeless children in the small village of Ancient Corinth. They are currently involved in a new effort to aid one of the most despised and displaced groups in Europe and much of the world today, the Roma people (Gypsies). Against governmental discouragement and without local support, they began to build a center for the education and care of Roma children. Once again, they have chosen to base this venture in Ancient Corinth. About ten years ago, I asked the director of the orphanage, Phillip Larsen, why the Kratzes had chosen Ancient Corinth as the location for their orphanage. After all, the modern

The Children's Ark

School for Roma children. (Credit: Scott Nash)

Sign constructed by Mercer University students. (Credit: Scott Nash)

village is a small place without many of the resources that one needs for such a venture. He told me it was simple. They were driven by Paul's words in 1 Corinthians 13 to locate their operations in the place where Paul had first sent his message about the way of love.

What Do We Do about Tongues?

Having witnessed more than a few modern congregations torn apart by controversy over tongues, I must confess that I am leery of the practice. Tongues appear to be no less divisive now than when Paul addressed the matter in 1 Corinthians. One sure way of igniting a church fight is to bring up the subject of tongues. There seems to be little common ground between those who are opposed to speaking in tongues and those who see it as one of the greatest of gifts, if not the greatest. [The SBC and Tongues] My first instinct when it comes to the question of tongues is to leave it alone.

The SBC and Tongues

In 2005 the Southern Baptist Convention's International Mission Board's trustees voted to bar new missionary candidates who practice a "private prayer language" from serving on the mission field. The SBC's North American Mission Board had already banned missionaries from "promoting glossolalia," including having a private prayer language. It appears that the Apostle Paul would not be qualified to be a Southern Baptist missionary.

Deann Alford, "Tongues Tied: Southern Baptists Bar New Missions Candidates from Glossolalia," *Christianity Today*, January 2006, p. 21.

Paul, of course, could not and did not ignore the issue. To do so would have been to leave the Corinthian church to suffer the same fate of modern churches that have been torn asunder by the debate over tongues. Given the explosive situation Paul had on his hands, his resolution of the problem appears both diplomatic and instructive. He neither forbade speaking in tongues nor exalted it above other gifts. He subsumed the practice under the larger principle of doing all things for edification (14:26). He furthermore tried to incorporate speaking in tongues into the framework of orderly worship.

To argue that the phenomenon Paul dealt with was different from what is happening in charismatic churches today is unhelpful. Nor does it cancel the debate by holding that Paul saw tongues as something that would fade away after the apostolic age. People today engage in a practice that involves unintelligible speech, and they affirm that it is a meaningful spiritual experience, whether what they experience is the same phenomenon as the one Paul addressed or not. The growth of charismatic churches throughout the world, especially in the southern hemisphere, confronts the church with the reality that speaking in tongues has not passed away. In fact, if Philip Jenkins is even partially correct in his prognosis of future trends, the majority of Christians in the future will be from the less developed parts of the world and they will be more charismatic.[20]

Some churches and church bodies, no doubt, will continue to resist allowing members of their congregations to speak in tongues. Other churches may embrace the practice as a necessary way to keep their membership from declining. Others may find creative and effective ways to incorporate the experience into their worship services without sacrificing their convictions about reverent worship and theological depth. Some churches may acknowledge the validity of tongues for other churches but continue to find ways to experience meaningful worship without encouraging the practice among their members. I confess that I am more comfortable with this last type of church.

Even for churches that do not embrace tongue-speaking in communal worship, the reality of tongues could be edifying. Worship does not have to be purely cerebral. [Cerebral Worship] Paul stated that he would pray and sing with his spirit and with his mind (14:15). In response to those who were enthralled with the "spirit" dimension of worship, Paul stressed the importance of the "mind." Some of us have heard his call to "mindful" worship, but we have forgotten his more than token acknowledgment of the role of "spirit" in worship. Perhaps the growth of charismatic churches is a healthy reaction to this neglect. We are more than our "minds." Feeding only the mind results in malnutrition for the rest of our being. Charismatic churches appeal to people who are spiritually hungry. Non-charismatic churches must find ways to feed the spirit as well as the mind.

Cerebral Worship

Worship that is solely cerebral is an aberration. Feelings are a legitimate part of the human personality and should be employed in worship. To make such a statement doesn't mean that our worship should do violence to our rational faculties, but it does mean that our rational faculties alone are inadequate.

Richard J. Foster, *Celebration of Discipline: The Path to Spiritual Growth* (rev. and exp. ed.; San Francisco: Harper & Row, 1988) 168.

Lectionary Connections

In Year A of the Revised Common Lectionary, 1 Corinthians 12:3b-13 is read on Pentecost Sunday, along with Numbers 11:24-30 (or Acts 2:1-21) and John 20:19-23. The Gospel text gives the Johannine version of Jesus' imparting of the Spirit on his disciples. The reading from Numbers 11 tells of God's Spirit falling on Israel and leading some to prophesy, while Acts describes the descent of the Spirit and Peter's resultant Pentecost sermon.

Two readings from 1 Corinthians 12 and one from 1 Corinthians 13 are used on the second, third, and fourth Sundays after Epiphany in Year C. On the second Sunday, Isaiah 62:1-5 contains the prophet's assurance of Israel's coming vindication. The Gospel reading is about the wedding at Cana. First Corinthians 12:1-11 focuses on the diversity of gifts bestowed by the Spirit. The third Sunday joins 1 Corinthians 12:12-31a with Nehemiah 8:1-3, 5-6, 8-10 and Luke 4:14-21. The texts from Nehemiah 8 recall Ezra's reading of the Torah for the Jerusalem community after the exile. Luke 4 describes Jesus' sermon at Nazareth. The fifth Sunday readings include 1 Corinthians 13:1-13, Jeremiah 1:4-10, and Luke 4:21-40. The texts from Jeremiah and Luke describe the beginnings of the ministries of the prophet and Jesus respectively.

NOTES

1. Ambrosiaster, *Commentary on Paul's Epistles* 81.132, in Gerald Bray, ed., *1–2 Corinthians* (vol. 7 of ACCS NT; ed. Thomas C. Oden; Downers Grove IL: InterVarsity Press, 1999) 118.

2. See Anthony C. Thiselton, *The First Epistle to the Corinthians: A Commentary on the Greek Text* (NIGTC; Grand Rapids: Eerdmans, 2000) 972–88.

3. Christopher Forbes, *Prophecy and Inspired Speech in Early Christianity and Its Hellenistic Environment* (WUNT 2/75; Tübingen: Mohr, 1995) 129–39.

4. Margaret M. Mitchell, *Paul and the Rhetoric of Reconciliation: An Exegetical Investigation of the Language and Composition of 1 Corinthians* (Louisville: Westminster John Knox, 1991) 68–83.

5. Jerome Murphy-O'Connor, *St. Paul's Corinth: Texts and Archaeology* (Collegeville MN: Liturgical Press, 1983) 175.

6. As correctly observed by Richard E. Oster Jr., "Use, Misuse and Neglect of Archaeological Evidence in Some Modern Works on 1 Corinthians (1Cor 7,1-5; 8,10; 11,2-16; 12,14-26)," *ZNW* 83 (1992): 69–73.

7. I owe this observation to Richard B. Hays, *First Corinthians* (IBC; Louisville: John Knox Press, 1997) 213.

8. Contra Joop F. M. Smit, "Two Puzzles: 1 Corinthians 12.31 and 13:3: A Rhetorical Solution," *NTS* 39 (1993): 246–64, who argues that Paul is using a rhetorical *permissio* to ridicule their zeal.

9. Here I am more positively influenced by the arguments of Joop F. M. Smit, "The Genre of 1 Corinthians 13 in Light of Classical Rhetoric," *NovT* 33 (1991): 193–216.

10. Murphy-O'Connor, *St. Paul's Corinth*, 75–77; David E. Garland, *1 Corinthians* (BECNT; Grand Rapids: Baker Academic, 2003) 611–13.

11. Thiselton, *The First Epistle to the Corinthians*, 1069.

12. Clint Tubbs, "The Spirit (World) and the (Holy) Spirit among the Earliest Christians: 1 Corinthians 12 and 14 as a Test Case," *CBQ* 70 (2008): 313–30, argues that all instances of the word "spirit" without the article (and some with) refer to external spirits that enter into the person and inspire speech.

13. Dale B. Martin, *The Corinthian Body* (New Haven CT: Yale University Press, 1995) 96–102.

14. Richard B. Hays, *First Corinthians* (IBC; Louisville: John Knox Press, 1997) 238–39.

15. For a discussion of the details, one may consult Thiselton, *The First Epistle to the Corinthians*, 1147–50; Garland, *1 Corinthians*, 675–77; and Gordon D. Fee, *The First Epistle to the Corinthians* (NICNT; Grand Rapids: Eerdmans Publishing, 1987) 699–702.

16. A point made by Jouette M. Bassler, "1 Corinthians," in *The Women's Bible Commentary* (ed. Carol A Newsom and Sharon H. Ringe; Louisville: Westminster/John Knox, 1992) 327–28.

17. Robert Scott Nash, "The Role of the *Haustafeln* in Colossians and Ephesians," (Ph.D. diss. The Southern Baptist Theological Seminary, 1982).

18. Bruce W. Winter, *Roman Wives, Roman Widows: The Appearance of the New Women and the Pauline Churches* (Grand Rapids: Eerdmans, 2003) 93, 177–79.

19. Thiselton, *The First Epistle to the Corinthians*, 1159–60, suggests "sifting."

20. Philip Jenkins, *The Next Christendom: The Coming of Global Christianity* (Oxford; New York: Oxford University Press, 2002).

THE RESURRECTION OF THE DEAD

1 Corinthians 15:1-34

"Every parting gives a foretaste of death; every coming together again a foretaste of the resurrection."[1]

Up to this point in his letter to the Corinthian church, Paul has primarily confronted matters of behavior. Undoubtedly, as we have seen at times, the various practices that Paul opposed were rooted in ideas that were contrary to his own thinking. Thus, at the appropriate points, Paul has sought to correct the undesirable behaviors by undermining the perspectives undergirding them. In 1 Corinthians 15, however, Paul seems to have no particular errant behavior in his sights. Rather, his target is fundamentally theological in nature, namely, misunderstanding about the resurrection of believers.

Nonetheless, his objective of correcting erroneous theological thinking here is not disconnected from his previous behavioral concerns. [Barth on 1 Corinthians 15] In fact, one can argue (as many have done) that confusion about the nature of the resurrection has contributed to many of the practices that Paul finds so unacceptable. The connection between 1 Corinthians 15 and other problems engaged in the letter is more evident in some cases than in others. In particular, the problem of immorality addressed in 1 Corinthians 5–6, as framed by Paul, stems from the same basic disregard for the significance of the body in respect to ultimate consequences that lies at the heart of the disagreement between Paul and some of the Corinthians about the resurrection. The connection between 1 Corinthians 15 and other problems addressed in the letters, however, is more subtle. Paul grounded his opening argument in 1 Corinthians 1:10–4:21 in his word of the cross; his concluding argument here rests on his teaching about the resurrection. The two

Barth on 1 Corinthians 15

It cannot be by chance that 1 Cor. xv, the chapter which deals with the most positive subject that can be imagined, forms the very peak and crown of the essentially critical and polemically negative Epistle. What is disclosed here is Paul's key position. The Resurrection of the Dead is the point from which Paul is speaking and to which he points. From this standpoint, not only the death of those now living, but, above all, their life *this side* of the threshold of death, is in the apostolic sermon, veritably seen, understood, judged, and placed in the light of the last severity, the last hope.

Karl Barth, *The Resurrection of the Dead* (Eng. trans.; London: Hodder & Stoughton, 1933) 101.

events, crucifixion and resurrection, are parts of the single act of God performed for the sake of those whom God loves. The resurrection, pointing forward, no less than the cross that points backward, forms the basis for Christian identity and lifestyle in the present. The two stand, then, as the frame around the rest of the letter and as the twin towers of Christian faith. Thus, Paul begins his discussion of the resurrection by reminding them of the *gospel* he has preached to them.

Structurally, the chapter falls into two clearly noticeable parts. [A Thematic Outline of 1 Corinthians 15:1-34] In 1 Corinthians 15:1-34, Paul gives an argument in support of the idea of the resurrection of the dead. In 1 Corinthians 15:35-58, he gives an explanation of the resurrection of the body. Questions about the nature of the resurrected body, which Paul addresses in the second part, probably led some of the Corinthians to doubt that *dead bodies* would be *raised* at all, which is the subject in the first part. Verses 1-2 prepare for the discussion of the topic, while v. 58 provides a concluding exhortation based on the discussion. If the usual English translation of *eikē* ("unless you believed *in vain*") in v. 2 is correct (see below), then vv. 1-2 can be seen with v. 58 ("your labor is not *in vain*" [*kenos*]) as an *inclusio* around the whole chapter.[2]

A Thematic Outline of 1 Corinthians 15:1-34

- I. An Argument for the Resurrection of the Dead (15:1-34)
  - A. The Gospel of First Importance (15:1-11)
    - 1. Tradition as Witness to the Resurrection (15:1-7)
    - 2. Paul as Witness to the Resurrection (15:8-11)
  - B. The Consequences of Denying the Gospel (15:12-19)
    - 1. Preaching and Faith are in Vain (15:12-16)
    - 2. Sin Remains and the Dead Perish (15:17-19)
  - C. The Confirmation of the Resurrection of the Dead (15:20-34)
    - 1. Resurrection and God's Sovereignty (15:20-28)
    - 2. Resurrection and Faithful Living (15:29-34)
- II. An Explanation of the Resurrection of the Body (15:35-58)
  - A. The Glory of the Resurrected Body (15:35-49)
    - 1. Different Kinds of Bodies (15:35-41)
    - 2. The Body of Spirit (15:42-49)
  - B. The Mystery of Transformation (15:50-58)
    - 1. The Final Victory (15:50-57)
    - 2. The Present Work of the Lord (15:58)

Rhetorically, 1 Corinthians 15 is predominately deliberative in character. (See the section titled "1 Corinthians as Rhetoric" in the Introduction.) It is better viewed as a self-contained argument about the resurrection than as one of the "proofs" in a larger argument for unity.[3] As such, it exhibits most of the parts one expects to see in such an argument. Verses 1-2 function as an *exordium* by establishing the transmitted tradition as a common basis for Paul and the recipients. The creedal tradition itself (15:3-7), along with Paul's addition of his own witness to the resurrection (15:8-11) serves as a *narratio*.[4] The argument proper begins in 15:12 with a question that flows from the statement of facts in the *narratio* and serves as a *propositio*: "If Christ is preached that he was raised from the dead, how can some among you say that there is no resurrection of the dead?" Verses 13-19 give the first proof as a *refutatio*, followed by a *confirmatio* in vv. 20-33.[5] The exhortation in v. 34 functions as a *peroratio* for the first half of the argument. A second *propositio* comes in 15:35, also stated interrogatively: "How are the dead raised? With what kind of body will they come?" Verses 36-41 function as another *refutatio*, and vv. 42-49 and 50-57 comprise a two-part *confirmatio*. The exhortation in v. 58 closes the second half of the argument, but it also serves as the *peroratio* for the whole argument.[6] [A Rhetorical Outline of 1 Corinthians 15]

A Rhetorical Outline of 1 Corinthians 15

Exordium		15:1-2
Narratio		15:3-11
Argumentatio I		15:12-57
	Propositio	15:12
	Refutatio	15:13-19
	Confirmatio	15:20-33
	Peroratio	15:34
Argumentatio II		15:35-58
	Propositio	15:35
	Refutatio	15:36-41
	Confirmatio	15:42-49
		15:50-57
	Peroratio	15:58

COMMENTARY

An Argument for the Resurrection of the Dead, 15:1-34

To understand the logic of Paul's argument, we have to realize certain presuppositions upon which it is based. First of all, Paul's apocalyptic perspective shaped his views about the destiny of believers. For him, the resurrection was an end-time event. He shared the belief of many Jews (but not all) that God would raise the dead at the end of the age. The concept of the resurrection of the dead developed late in Israel's theology, and even in the first century AD not all Jews had accepted the idea (e.g., Sadducees). [Daniel and Resurrection] Those who did differed in their understanding of exactly who or what would be resurrected. Some saw only the righteous being raised, while others saw the unrighteous also being raised, but for final annihilation or eternal damnation. Some held that the soul would be resurrected (e.g., Josephus), while others believed that the bodies of dead persons would be raised again. In any case, those Jews who accepted the idea of resurrection understood that it would happen at the end of this age. This view is reflected in the story of Lazarus in John 11, in a Gospel that otherwise reflects little apocalyptical thinking. When Jesus told Martha that her brother would rise again, she answered, "I know that he will rise again in the resurrection on the last day" (John 11:24). For Paul, the resurrection of Jesus was a signal that

Daniel and Resurrection

The earliest clear reference to resurrection in biblical literature appears in the book of Daniel, which was probably written in the mid-2d century BC.

> Many of those who sleep in the dust of the earth shall awake, some to everlasting life, and some to shame and everlasting contempt. Those who are wise shall shine like the brightness of the sky, and those who lead many to righteousness, like the stars forever and ever. (Dan 12:2-3; NRSV)

the "last day" had begun to unfold. At the appropriate time, presumably soon, the rest of the dead would also be raised. Jesus was the "first fruits" of the harvest (to use Paul's metaphor), and the rest would be harvested when Jesus returned (15:23). The resurrection of Jesus, then, was tied to the resurrection of the others. Since resurrection in its totality was an end-time event, one could not accept the reality of the resurrection of Jesus without also affirming the completion of the event in the resurrection of believers.

Schweitzer on Paul's Mysticism

The original and central idea of the Pauline Mysticism is therefore that the Elect share with one another and with Christ a corporeity which is in a special way susceptible to the action of the powers of death and resurrection, and in consequence capable of acquiring the resurrection state of existence before the general resurrection of the dead takes place.

Albert Schweitzer, *The Mysticism of Paul the Apostle* (trans. William Montgomery; New York: The Seabury Press, 1931) 115–16.

Secondly, as Albert Schweitzer observed some time ago, Paul believed that believers have been joined in some mystic way to the person of Christ.[7] [Schweitzer on Paul's Mysticism] They have been baptized *into* Christ and are one *in* him (Gal 3:27-28). Through the death of Christ, believers have also died to sin (Rom 6:11) and the law (Rom 7:4). They live as one body *in* him (Rom 12:5) and he lives *in* them (Rom 8:10). The same Spirit of God that raised Jesus from the dead will also resurrect their mortal bodies (Rom 8:11). Paul's view that believers are joined as a corporate entity to the actual being of Christ lies behind his contrast between Christ and Adam in 1 Corinthians 15:21-22, 45-49. All human beings corporately and corporally participate in the being of the first human being, Adam. This participation is not figurative or representative; it is actual. Likewise, believers participate corporately and corporally in the being of the second Adam, Christ. As participants in Adam, all human beings die. As participants in Christ, believers shall be made alive. Because they are joined to Adam, the whole race of human beings shares in his death. Because they are joined to Christ, the whole body of believers shares in his resurrection. What happened to Christ necessarily and inevitably happens to believers.[8] Again, Christ's resurrection cannot be affirmed, according to Paul, without also affirming the resurrection of those who are joined to him.

Thirdly, Paul understood the resurrection to involve the "body" of persons. Disembodied existence appears to have been inconceivable to Paul, except, perhaps, in the case of God. For Paul, the body is who and what we are. It is our physical self, but it is also our emotional and mental self. It is all that we are except for that life force, the soul, that God has breathed into us. The soul invigorates the earthly body, being so intertwined with it that the two cannot be disentangled in this life. When the life force (soul) desists, the body dies. Conversely, when the body dies, the life force desists; it does not go marching on. This body, as we now experience it, cannot itself experience the new life ahead (15:50). That life calls for a transformation of this body into the glorious state of the resurrection body, which is invigorated by the spirit. God did not rescue Jesus' soul from its bodily prison; God raised up Jesus' body and transformed it. Likewise, the bodies of believers will be raised up and transformed. This aspect of resurrection was what proved troubling to some in Corinth. The idea that the body had any enduring worth was alien to their thinking. They could accept the idea of an afterlife but not a bodily one. For Paul, to reject the idea of raised bodies is to reject the hope for future life since that life involves a body, although it is a transformed one (15:42-44). To reject that future hope is to reject the reality of Christ's bodily resurrection since his resurrection is tied to the bodily resurrection of others.

These three presuppositions guide Paul's logic as he moves through his argument. The resurrection of Jesus and of believers is a single, though not simultaneous, end-time event. Believers are joined as a corporate whole to Christ. Existence now and in the future is embodied. We cannot assume that his audience in Corinth shared his presuppositions. In fact, doubts about his third presupposition probably gave rise to the theological problem Paul addresses here.

15:1-11. Paul begins his argument by establishing some basis of common understanding between himself and the Corinthians: "I call to your mind the gospel that I preached . . . in what terms I preached to you" (15:1-2). His opening words, fashioned in a notoriously awkward sentence, constitute more than a simple reminder of old sermons.[9] [Paul as "Speech-act"ivist] In reminding them, he proclaims again the basis of their faith, which he labels "the gospel." [Paul's Gospel] This noun is followed by four (perhaps five) relative clauses, giving this parallel construction:

Paul as "Speech-act"ivist

Alexandra Brown points to 1 Cor 15:1 as an example of Paul's use of utterances that constitute acts. She writes, "Here Paul does more than report a fact; in saying, 'I remind you,' he actually does remind, provided his utterance invokes the conventions that allow the expression 'I remind you' to function as a reminder in a given setting."

Alexandra R. Brown, *The Cross and Human Transformation: Paul's Apocalyptic Word in 1 Corinthians* (Minneapolis: Fortress, 1995) 19.

the gospel
which I proclaimed to you,
and which you received,
and on which you have taken a stand,
and through which you are [being] saved,
(with which word I proclaimed to you).

Paul's Gospel

AΩ Paul's letters mark the earliest known usage of the word "gospel" (*euangelion*) in Christian literature. In fact, 60 of the 76 occurrences of the word in the NT appear in writings attributed to him. Since the noun *euangelion* does not appear in the LXX or other Greek writings of the period, James Dunn has suggested that Paul himself coined the term to refer to his proclamation.

James D. G. Dunn, *The Theology of Paul the Apostle* (Edinburgh: T & T Clark, 1998) 168.

Alternatively, the clause in parenthesis may be taken not as a relative construction tied to *euangelion* but as a clarifying repetition of *euangelion* further defining the substance of Paul's reminder.[10] In either case, the clause points forward to the content of the gospel that Paul outlines in vv. 3-5. Significantly, Paul points out, between his two references to his proclamation of this gospel, their response. They received it, have taken their stand on it, and are being saved by it. Thus, this gospel constitutes a ground for agreement between Paul and the Corinthians, with two caveats: (1) if they hold fast to it, and (2) unless they have believed *in vain* (*eikē*). [Translating *eikē*]

Translating *eikē*

AΩ The word usually translated "in vain" (*eikē*) can be taken two ways. (1) The final clause in v. 2 can be rendered "unless you have believed *in vain*." Perhaps the testimony is unreliable. Perhaps the witnesses were wrong. Perhaps Christ was not raised. If any of these is true, then they have been deceived and their faith is pointless. (2) An alternative way to translate the last part of v. 2 is, "unless you believed *incoherently*." In other words, they have heard the message of first importance, but they do not really "get it." They have not seen the full implications of what it means to believe that Christ has been raised from the dead. Both of these ways of understanding what Paul means here can be supported by what follows. Paul considers what the implications are if Christ was not raised (15:12-19). He also gives attention to the misunderstanding some of the Corinthians have about the nature and meaning of Christ's resurrection (15:35-50).

Paul then recites for them a succinct statement of the gospel that he identifies as "of first importance" (v. 3a). What he has passed on to them was what he himself has received (cf. 11:23). Thus, both he and they have received a gospel that was passed on, not one that Paul has invented. Paul has accepted that message in the same way that they have accepted it. He, too, has taken his stand on it and is being saved by it. Thus, this basic statement of the gospel forms a bond between Paul and the Corinthians and between them and the larger body of believers (cf. 1:2). It also provides Paul with a mutually received basis for his argument.

The recitation that follows appears to be an early creedal statement.[11] It reads:

> Christ died for our sins in accordance with the Scriptures;
>   he was buried;
> he was raised on the third day in accordance with the Scriptures;
>   he appeared to Cephas, then to the twelve.

The first and third lines in the statement (death and resurrection) are the crucial elements for Paul. The second line, "he was buried," confirms the reality of his death without further elaboration regarding an empty tomb such as we find in the Gospels. The fourth line, "he appeared to Cephas, then to the twelve," serves to confirm the reality of his resurrection, but since this is the element of the traditional statement that concerns Paul the most, additional confirmation is added. The importance of Christ's death *and* resurrection for Paul is reflected in the creedal statement itself in that both are held to be "in accordance with the Scriptures." [The Scriptures] While particular Scriptures were used in the early church to buttress and illuminate its claims about Christ's death and resurrection, the creedal statement itself probably does not point to those texts but rather signifies that these two pillar events in the story of Christ were witnessed to and supported by the whole of the Scriptures.

The Scriptures

The Scriptures to which the early creedal statement cited by Paul in 15:3-5, of course, refers to what eventually became the Christian Old Testament. The early church inherited its Scriptures from Israel, but it interpreted those Scriptures in the light of Jesus Christ. Passages of the Hebrew Bible (used predominately in Greek translations) that originally spoke about other matters were reinterpreted to apply to Jesus. For example, Jesus was seen as the fulfillment of the passage in Isaiah 53 that refers to the suffering of God's servant "for our sins." Psalms that praise God for delivering the righteous from death (such as Ps 16) were viewed as references to Jesus' resurrection. For Paul, the reinterpretation of Israel's Scriptures through the lens of the story of Christ enabled the early church to incorporate its own story into the larger story of God's long history of redemptive activity.

The statement includes specific human witnesses to the resurrection: Cephas and the twelve. The use of "then" (*eita*) in reference to the twelve suggests a sequence. Unlike the accounts in the canonical Gospels (except, perhaps, Luke), the tradition asserts that the resurrected Christ appeared first to Cephas before appearing to the other members of the twelve. [Where Are the Women?] The importance of the witnesses to Christ's resurrection leads Paul to add to the creedal statement references to other persons who could confirm that it happened. He then appeared to more than five hundred "brothers" at one time, Paul asserts, stressing that most of them are still alive (in case anyone needs to check out their story). He then appeared to James, the leader of the Jerusalem church, and then to all the apostles. (Note that the statement distinguishes between "the twelve" and that larger body of church leaders referred to as "the apostles.")

To this impressive list of witnesses to the claim that Jesus was raised from the dead Paul adds his own name, which he stresses is of one who in certain respects is unimpressive. While his reference to his own experience of the resurrected Christ as "last of all" may mean that Paul saw himself as the final apostolic recipient of such a visitation, the phrase may also join other self-descriptive terms Paul uses to indicate his unworthiness to receive such a gift.[12] When Paul refers to himself here as "one untimely born" (NRSV), he uses a word (*ektrōmati*) that often referred to an aborted or miscarried fetus, a stillborn baby, or a deformed newborn. Whether the

Where Are the Women?

The creedal statement cited by Paul in 1 Cor 15:3-5 identifies Cephas as the first witness to the resurrected Christ, followed by the rest of the twelve. Paul adds to this statement other witnesses, all of whom presumably were men. It is possible that the 500 "brothers" in v. 6 and "all the apostles" in v. 7 included women since the plural masculine form of such terms could be used inclusively of men and women. What remains striking, however, is that no women are specifically referred to either by the tradition or by Paul. The Gospel of Mark (followed by Matthew) and the Gospel of John clearly indicate that women were the first witnesses to the resurrection. In fact, the Gospel of John and the longer ending of Mark (16:9-20) identify Mary Magdalene as the first person to whom Jesus appeared. While one can argue for the greater historical probability of the tradition rehearsed by Paul, given its earlier appearance in the literature, one can also entertain the possibility that even at an early stage, the tradition reflecting the primacy of women as witnesses to the resurrection could have been neglected or suppressed, only to resurface later in Gospels offering a different perspective to the one reflected in the pre-Pauline traditions, the Pauline literature, and in the Pauline-oriented work Luke-Acts. The different versions regarding who was the first witness to the resurrection reflect conflicting, even competing, traditions. In light of the male-dominated church that preserved all the traditions, one can appreciate the assessment of Elisabeth Schüssler Fiorenza: "Since the tradition of Mary Magdalene's primacy in apostolic witness challenged the Petrine tradition, it is remarkable that it has survived in two independent streams of the Gospel tradition."

Elisabeth Schüssler Fiorenza, *In Memory of Her: A Feminist Theological Reconstruction of Christian Origins* (New York: Crossroad, 1983) 332.

emphasis intended is on the "suddenness" of his "birth" or on the "undeveloped nature" of the newly born Paul is much debated.[13] We might think in terms of the Caesarean birth of a premature baby. Paul did not come to his new life in Christ in any normal way; he was taken by God from the womb of his old life and suddenly "birthed" as a new Paul when he met the resurrected Christ. This fits well, incidentally, with the accounts of his conversion found in the book of Acts. The stress is not so much on Paul's inclusion among the privileged witnesses to the resurrection so much as it is on his unworthiness to be included at all. Paul insists that he was undeserving of this new birth and unfit to be numbered among the apostles because of his earlier persecution of the church. By the grace of God, however, he was reborn from his former grotesque life of death to a new life as an apostle. The contrast between Paul the formerly death-dealing persecutor of the church and the new Paul who proclaims the life-giving gospel finds a parallel later in the juxtaposing of Adam and Christ (15:22). God's gift of new life to Paul was not wasted either, Paul insists. Though he might be the least of the apostles, he has worked harder than the rest. As if this might sound overly boastful and subversive of his main point, Paul explains that it was actually the grace of God working with him.

Paul then reinforces why he has reminded them of the message "of first importance" and why he has backed it up with his list of witnesses to the resurrection. "All of us (Paul and the other apostles) preached the same message," he writes, "and it was that very message about the resurrected Christ that you yourselves believed" (15:11). The last verse here takes us back to the first two verses. This is the message they received, the one they have taken their stand on, and the one that is saving them—unless they have erroneously believed this message "in vain" (15:2). The narration of the traditional creedal statement and the additional witnesses to the resurrection of Christ, therefore, establish the common basis for refuting challenges to belief in the resurrection of the dead.

15:12-19. Formally, the refutation begins with the identification of the point to be rebuffed: that there is no resurrection of the dead (v. 12). At issue here, however, is not simply the opposing idea but also the testimony of those who espouse the idea. Some of the Corinthians are *saying* that the dead are not raised in contrast to the testimony of the apostles and the apostolic tradition that God does, indeed, raise the dead. The primary issue is the credibility of the claim that the dead are raised. Secondarily, the credibility of the opposing voices is at stake. The evidence supporting the proponents of resurrection has already been presented (15:3-8). Their testimony was previously accepted as valid, but now dissenting voices have created doubt about the validity of their testimony. Paul does not present the arguments of the opposition. Instead, he outlines the consequences of accepting their claims rather than that of the apostolic witnesses. His presentation of the consequences comes in two parallel movements (vv. 13-15 and 16-18). In each movement, Paul connects the claim that the dead are not raised to a denial of the resurrection of Jesus. He then identifies a pair of losses resulting from that denial. He then expands on one of those losses by adding another negative consequence. The result is an A-B-C, A'-B'-C' pattern. [The Pattern of 1 Corinthians 15:13-18] Verse 19 concludes the litany of losses by pointing out the pathetic state to which the opposing claim reduces all would-be believers.

The refutation itself substantially involves pointing out the consequences of denying the gospel, which is what Paul insists questioning the reality of bodily resurrection actually entails. Note that Paul does not say that anyone in Corinth was denying the resurrection of Jesus. His opening question in v. 12, however, indicates that some of them were having problems with the idea of dead bodies being brought back to life. While it is not so obvious in English translations that render *nekros* simply as "dead," the Corinthians' misgivings are more under-

The Pattern of 1 Corinthians 15:13-18

The pattern of Paul's refutation of the view that the dead are not raised consists of two parallel movements, each beginning with the same premise (A), followed by a two-fold consequence (B1&2, B'1&2), and then followed by an expansion of one item in each pair (C, C').

First Movement

A—But if there is no resurrection of the dead, then Christ has not been raised. (15:13)

B—If Christ has not been raised,

1—then our preaching is in vain

2—and your faith is in vain. (15:14)

C—And we are also exposed as false witnesses concerning God . . . (15:15)

(C expands B1)

Second Movement

A—For if the dead are not raised, then Christ has not been raised. (15:16)

B'—If Christ has not been raised,

1—your faith is futile

2—and you are still in your sins. (15:17)

C'—Then also those who have died in Christ have perished (15:18)

(C' expands B'2)

standable if the term is given its more usual sense of "corpse." The raising of corpses appeared both unnecessary and undesirable to some of them. Several scholars have argued that the concept was problematic for the higher-status members of the church who would have ascribed to certain philosophical notions gained through education that considered the human body to be significant only for this life.[14] Such may have been the case, but one does not have to restrict the aversion to raised corpses to the upper classes or to the intellectually elite. The prospect of reinvigorated corpses was alien to most Gentiles, and even for many Jews the apocalyptic construct of resurrected bodies required reinterpretation. For Paul, the denial of the general idea of the resurrection of dead bodies also meant that one must reject the possibility that Christ himself was raised. If one rejected Christ's resurrection, the personal consequences were serious.

Paul begins by asking how anyone could deny the reality of the dead being raised if he and other apostles are preaching that Christ has been raised, a proclamation that the Corinthians have already accepted. Paul has reminded them of the teaching about Christ's resurrection and of the fact that they have accepted and believed it. What amazes him is that some people cannot see the connection between the proclamation of Christ's confirmed resurrection and the raising of other persons' dead bodies. For those who did not share the presuppositions of Paul described above, however, the disconnect is not so mysterious. Eventually, Paul will have to include some discussion of those presuppositions in his argument, but for the moment he focuses only on the personal consequences of denying the resurrection of Christ.

The Text of 1 Corinthians 15:14

One of the most common textual variants found in the NT, the switching of *hymōn* (your) and *hēmōn* (our), appears in this verse in several ancient manuscripts. The two words differ only in the second letters and were probably pronounced alike (*ee-mōn*). The original reading here was probably *hymōn*, as the oldest papyrus copy and oldest uncial codices indicate. Two very old uncials, however, read *hēmōn*, along with nine later minuscules and seven ancient lectionary texts. Since Paul clearly states in 15:17, "If Christ has not been raised, your (*hymōn*) faith is futile," he most assuredly also wrote in 15:14 that "your (*hymōn*) faith is empty" for the same reason.

What is the result of denying the resurrection of the dead? Twice he insists that it also means denying the resurrection of Jesus (15:13, 16). The first consequence of this denial is that his preaching and their acceptance of it have been in vain (15:14). [The Text of 1 Corinthians 15:14] He has proclaimed and they have believed something that is simply not true. Furthermore, Paul and the other apostolic proclaimers are exposed (*heuriskometha*) as false witnesses regarding God (15:15). Their preaching is not only "empty" (*kenon*), it is libelous. They have testified *against* (*kata*) God by claiming that God did something God did not do. If, however, it should prove to be the case that they have testified truthfully regarding God's resurrection of Christ, then those on the other side would be exposed as false witnesses against God because they have claimed that God did not do what God actually did do.

The second consequence is that their faith is meaningless and they are still "dead" in their sins (15:17). That "Christ died *for our sins* in accordance with the Scriptures" is affirmed by the creedal statement. But that statement also affirms that "Christ was raised on the third day in accordance with the Scriptures." If the latter affirmation is invalid, then so must be the former. Furthermore, all those who have died believing have simply perished, for there is no afterlife of any kind (15:18). They died *in their sins* and have suffered the fate that awaits all unredeemed persons. Believing or not believing the gospel matters nothing because believers and nonbelievers both perish.

Paul's final loss that comes from denying the resurrection adds a poignant note of *pathos.* If there is no afterlife, and Christ only has significance for this life, then believers are the most pitiable fools of all (15:19). His last point may raise some eyebrows. "Would it not be better to live now for Christ, to follow his teachings now, to practice Christian love now, and to try to improve the world in his name—even if there is no afterlife—then not to do so?" For Paul, even though such a life might be virtuous, noble, and more commendable than one of immoral self-indulgence, it would still be pitiable. It would be based on an understanding of God that is too limited. It would be rooted in resignation to the admission that the gospel's message of God's ultimate triumph over evil is a pipe dream. It would abdicate the hope for justice to the realities of an unjust world. It would sadly accept that human life has no ultimate value or meaning beyond the few fleeting moments experienced here. For some persons, such a perspective might be considered "realistic." For Paul, it is supremely pitiable. [Chrysostom on the Body]

Chrysostom on the Body

Even if the soul remains, being infinitely immortal, without the flesh it will not receive those hidden blessings. If the body does not rise again, the soul remains uncrowned with the blessings stored up in heaven. In that case, we have nothing to hope for, and our rewards are limited to this life. What could be more wretched than that?

Chrysostom, *Homilies on the Epistles of Paul* 39.4, in Gerald Bray, ed., *1–2 Corinthians* (vol. 7 of ACCS NT; ed. Thomas C. Oden; Downers Grove IL: InterVarsity Press, 1999) 156.

15:20-34. In v. 20, Paul moves from refuting the contention that dead bodies are not raised by enumerating the negative consequences of that view to affirming the counterpoint, that Christ has been raised, by explaining the positive consequences that Christ's resurrection holds for believers. This affirmation unfolds in two parts: 15:20-28 and 15:29-34. The first part focuses on the theological basis of his understanding of the resurrection of believers. The second part points to actions that support his contention. The final

First Fruits

Paul refers to Christ as the "first fruits" (*aparchē*) of those who are to be raised from the dead. The term appears in Greek literature primarily in reference to the first part of the harvest, but it almost always also depicts that first part as an offering to a deity. By extension, the term also came to refer to offerings other than the first fruits and to other obligatory payments such as taxes. Paul refers to Epaenetus (Rom 16:5) and the household of Stephanas (1 Cor 16:15) as the first fruits of converts in Asia and Achaia respectively. The metaphor in these instances points not only to the temporal priority of these converts but also to the fact that they are part of a larger "harvest." In Rom 11:16, Paul uses the holiness of the portion of dough (first fruits) offered to God during Pentecost to remind Gentiles of the holiness of the rest of the dough (Israel). In this instance, the metaphor stresses the connection between the part and the whole. In Rom 8:23, God is the giver, rather than the recipient, of the first fruits of the Holy Spirit imparted to believers. There, the stress is twofold: (1) believers have a portion of the Holy Spirit as a guarantee or promise, but (2) the bulk of the gift lies in the future. Several of the nuances found in other usages converge in 1 Cor 15:20. The cultic sense of an offering dedicated to God forms the backdrop in that Christ and resurrected believers are God's chosen ones. The temporal priority of the resurrected Christ is evident; the believers are resurrected only at his return (15:23). More important for Paul's point is the connection between the first fruits (Christ) and the rest of the harvest (believers). Christ is, thus, representative of the rest; what happened to him will happen to believers.

Gerhard Delling, "ἄρχω, ἀρχή, ἀπαρχή κτλ," *TDNT* 1:484–86.

Joost Holleman, *Resurrection and Parousia: A Traditio-Historical Study of Paul's Eschatology in 1 Cor 15* (NovTSup 84; Leiden: E. J. Brill, 1988) 49–57.

Anthony C. Thiselton, *The First Epistle to the Corinthians: A Commentary on the Greek Text* (NIGTC; Grand Rapids: Eerdmans, 2000) 1122–23.

verse (34) is an exhortation that flows from his last point regarding action and serves as a conclusion (*peroratio*) to his first major argument in chapter 15.

In 15:20-28, Paul uses two metaphors to describe what will happen at the general resurrection and interprets each metaphor with references to Scripture. The first metaphor is drawn from the realm of agriculture. The resurrected Christ is the "first fruits" (*aparchē*) of those who have died. [First Fruits] The harvest imagery here serves to join the resurrection of Christ to the assured resurrection of the rest of the harvest. As Paul points out in 15:23, however, there is also a disjuncture since Christ's resurrection has already occurred and the resurrection of believers still lies in the future. Nonetheless, the first fruits and the rest of the crop are part of the same harvest. In a harvest, some fruit ripens earlier than others, yet all are reaped or picked in the same season. Likewise, the resurrection of Christ and the resurrection of believers are part of a single harvest that will culminate in the appointed season (*kairos*; cf. 1 Cor 7:29).

That Paul places more emphasis on the connection between Christ and believers than on the difference in the time of their respective resurrections at this point in his argument seems apparent from his immediate allusion to the story of Adam in Genesis 3. Though shifting from metaphor to typology, Paul continues with his dual focus on connection and representation. In Adam all died (v. 22). Adam, as the primordial representative of the human race, experienced what all human beings experience, namely, death as the result of sin. [Romans 5:12-14] All human beings also participate in the being of Adam in experiencing both sin and death. Paul's simple, unexplained statement of this connection between all people and Adam indicates that he considered it to be a given that his readers would understand and accept, probably because it had been a part of his preaching while he was present with them. As all humans are represented by Adam and participate corporately in his being, so it is with Christ and those who belong to him. As Christ was raised, so shall believers be raised. What happened to him will happen to them. As all persons experience sin and death *in* Adam, so shall believers experience resurrection *in* Christ. The universalism seemingly implied in v. 22 is qualified by v. 23 where Paul specifies that it is only those who belong to Christ who are raised (cf. Rom 5:18-19).

Romans 5:12-14

Paul's use of Adam typology is more developed in his letter to the Romans. The basic thrust of Adam as the representative of the human race and as the one *in whom* the human race experiences sin and death is already in view in 1 Cor 15. A portion of Paul's use of Adam typology in Rom 5 appears below.

> Therefore, just as sin came into the world through one man, and death came through sin, and so death spread to all because all have sinned—sin was indeed in the world before the law, but sin is not reckoned where there is no law. Yet death exercised dominion from Adam to Moses, even over those whose sins were not like the transgression of Adam, who is a type of the one who was to come. (Rom 5:12-14; NRSV)

In v. 23, Paul begins to use a military metaphor that extends through v. 28. While vv. 21-22 stress the singleness of Jesus' resurrection and that of believers, here Paul clarifies that not everyone's resurrection happens at the same time. They are raised according to their own "rank" or "corps" (*tagma*). [*Tagma*] Numerous scholars have seen in Paul's specification that the resurrection of believers does not occur until the *parousia* ("coming") of Christ a concern that some of the Corinthians were already claiming to have experienced some type of resurrection.[15] Thus, they are thought to have subscribed to an "overly realized eschatology" that focused on present experience and had little or no regard for any future resurrection. Paul's objective here, according to this view, is to establish firmly the principle that resurrection is a future event for believers, not a present experience. If we are correct, however, in holding that the erroneous Corinthian view that Paul challenges in 1 Corinthians 15 was not a total disbelief in an afterlife of any kind but rather a rejection of the idea of resurrected bodies, then Paul's stipulation regarding the "order" of the resurrection should not be seen as a corrective to a premature claim of already being resurrected but rather as another affirmation on Paul's part as to the necessity of the raising of corpses in the future. The sequence of Christ-then-believers follows the end-of-the-age eschatological plan of God.

Tagma

AΩ The word *tagma* is often translated as "order" (NRSV), and numerous times in Greek literature it is used to denote a social grouping in accordance with a prescribed arrangement of the social order. It may also be used in the sense of one's "status." Another common usage of the term, however, is in reference to the orderly arrangement of soldiers, as in a legion, division, or cohort. In light of the prevalence of military imagery throughout the section 1 Cor 15:24-28, it seems best to give *tagma* a military connotation in v. 23. In a sense, then, Paul depicts the general (Christ) as being raised first, followed by the troops (believers). The word *tagma* is derived from the verb *tassō*, which often is used in the sense of ordering or directing soldiers. Another word derived from *tassō*, *hypotassein* ("to subject") appears six times in vv. 27-28 and refers to God's final subjecting of all things after having destroyed all enemies.

H. G. Liddell, Robert Scott, and H. Stuart Jones, *Greek-English Lexicon* (9th ed.; Oxford: Clarendon Press, 1995) 1752.

Ben Witherington has argued that Paul may be battling here not against an "overly realized eschatology" but a "Roman realized eschatology."[16] He points to significant archaeological evidence from Corinth and elsewhere that indicates that the imperial cult included celebration of the emperor's role in bringing in the "golden age" for the inhabitants of the empire. A common title appearing on inscriptions attributes supreme benefaction to the empire from the emperor as *pater patriae* ("father of the fatherland"). The focus of imperial leaders was on the present "salvation" imparted by the deified emperors. He also argues that those wealthier, higher-status Corinthians in the church would have been the ones most likely to discount a future resurrection because they already enjoyed the most significant benefits of the new order inaugurated by imperial rule. Paul labors here, then, to show that "true salvation" lies in the future and is the accomplishment of God, not the emperor. Witherington asserts, "Paul, by contrast, associates salvation not with the coming of Caesar, but with the coming and return of Christ."[17] The scenario Paul describes involves the destruction of "*every* rule and *every* authority and power" (15:24), including Caesar's. The *parousia* (coming) of Christ will culminate in all things being subjected to God. Witherington further argues that Paul's reference to *tagma* (which he understands as "proper ordering") intends to point the Corinthians who are concerned about status-ranking to the only "ordering" of significance, namely, Christ first and then the believers.[18]

Porta Maggiore Inscription

Frontal view of the Porta Maggiore from the side facing Piazzale Labicano. Porta Maggiore, Rome, Italy. (Credit: Alinari/Art Resource, NY)

The emperor Claudius was awarded the title *pater patriae* by the Roman senate in January of 42. That title appears among others on the inscription above a double monumental arch that carried parts of two aqueducts built by Claudius, the *Aqua Claudia* and the *Anio Novus*, which were completed in the year 52. The full inscription reads (in translation):

> Tiberius Claudius Caesar Augustus Germanicus, the son of Drusus, pontifex maximus (=chief priest), in his twelfth year of tribunician power, consul for the fifth time, imperator twenty-seven times, father of his country (*pater patriae*), saw to it that, at his own expense, the aqua Claudia be brought from the 45th milestone, from the springs which are called the Caeruleus and Curtius, and too the Anio Novus be brought from the 62nd milestone into the city of Rome.

Chris Scarre, *Chronicle of the Roman Emperors* (London: Thames and Hudson, 1995) 41.

Witherington's view has much to commend it in light of the pervasive influence of the Roman imperial cult, especially in a Roman colony such as Corinth. (See the section titled "The Imperial Cult" in the Introduction.) Paul's apocalyptic perspective leads him to depict the end (*telos*; v. 24) in terms of a military campaign in which God ultimately triumphs over all opposing forces. Christ delivers the "kingdom" to God, the *real* father, after destroying "every rule (*archēn*) and every authority (*exousian*) and power (*dynamin*)" (cf. 1 Cor 2:6). The terms *archē* and *exousia* probably carry here the same metaphorical force as in Ephesians 6:12 where they refer to spiritual (demonic) powers. That would be in keeping with the apocalyptic background from which the imagery is drawn in that evil is typically depicted as supernatural forces at war against God and God's chosen ones. Even in apocalyptic portrayals of evil, however, the imagery generally has some referent that is both earthly and recognizable.[19] The bizarre and picturesque symbolism of apocalyptic is designed to reveal the true, otherworldly force behind the earthly manifestation of evil powers. We should not forget that the earthly power most visibly manifested in Paul's day was the Roman Empire that dominated his world. While Paul might consider the power of Rome only to be that which God permits it to have (cf. Rom 13:1), he also holds that ultimately even that power must give way to God's total subjection of all things. The political implications of Paul's proclamation that God would ultimately subdue all powers would not have been lost on the citizens of the Roman colony of Corinth. His assertion that *every* power would be destroyed subversively challenges the Roman claim to have delivered the lasting benefits of the golden age.

Nevertheless, we should probably not restrict the referent of Paul's imagery here to Roman imperial power nor see his target solely in terms of Roman realized eschatology.[20] His view is larger than that. Imperial Rome was but one earthly manifestation of the powers that wage war in heaven as well as upon the earth. The apocalyptic vision that guides Paul's description of the end includes the destruction of *all* God's enemies, including the final foe, Death (vv. 25-26). As the ultimate destructive force in the cosmos, Death entered human experience through Adam and continues to plague the human race in that all die, including the faithful. The raising of

Death of Paul

Alessandro Algardi. *Beheading of St. Paul.* 1650. Marble. San Paolo Maggiore, Bologna, Italy.

Algardi's sculpture group depicts Paul as he is about to be beheaded by a Roman soldier. In high Baroque fashion, he portrays both the soldier and Paul as powerful figures, but both Paul and the executioner express reserve in the face of the impending death. Unlike many depictions of a frail, bald-headed Paul, Algardi's Paul appears noble and unfazed by the power of Rome.

the faithful dead at Christ's coming, however, signals the demise of Death itself. Death and the other powers may work through earthly institutions of power, such as imperial Rome, but they are not limited to such institutions.[21] They exist as forces beyond the scope and structure of earthly manifestations of their power. Furthermore, limiting Paul's target audience to those in the church who, by virtue of whatever higher status they may have had, benefited the most from imperial rule ignores the influence that imperial propaganda was designed to have (and probably did) on the inhabitants of the empire as a whole. The impact of imperial success heralded in architecture and ritual was felt by all, even those who had reason to resent it. Paul's vision of the end of imperial domination may have served as a warning to those invested in the empire's success, but it would have also pointed toward radical and traumatic change for those who were not so invested. Moreover, especially for people of lower status and power who often understood their lives to be shaped by other forces in addition to human institutions of imperial rule and social ordering, the claim that *every* rule, authority, and power would be destroyed offered hope for liberation by God from every evil power they believed to be dominating their lives.[22]

To support his assertion that Christ's victory over the powers will be complete, Paul quotes from two psalms. The reference to putting "all his enemies under his feet" in v. 25 comes from Psalm 110:1 (LXX 109:1). In its original context, Psalm 110:1 referred to God's installation of a king on the Jerusalem throne. Since the Old Testament verse begins "The LORD says to my lord," Paul takes the rest of the verse to apply to Christ ("my lord"). Since it is the LORD (God) who speaks, then the decree carries the determinism of a typical apocalyptic scenario in which "it is necessary" (*dei*) that God's decree be enacted. The quotation in v. 27, "he [God] subjected all things under his [Christ's] feet," is from Psalm 8:6 (LXX 8:7). While the psalm originally referred to humankind in general, Paul treats the singular "his" as referring solely to Christ. He also takes the past tense of the verb "subjected" (*hypetaxen*) to imply that what will happen at the end is already assured. Thus, Paul interprets the two psalms both christologically and apocalyptically. While his usage of the psalms might appear suspect from a modern, historical-critical perspective, rhetorically it adds weight to his major point that the resurrection of the dead is a part of the triumphal events of "the end." All of these events, including the general resurrection (since "all things" includes Death), have already been determined by God and announced through

Scripture. Similar to his previous clarification that the resurrection of believers follows that of Christ, Paul clarifies that "all things" does not include God (v. 27b). Ultimately, however, it does include the Son (v. 28a). [Incipient Arianism?] When Christ has subdued everything else, then Christ, the Son, will subject himself to the rule of the one who gave him the victory over his enemies. The final scene in Paul's apocalyptic scenario finds "all things" subjected to God to the point that God is "all things (*ta panta*) in all things" (v. 28b). While *ta panta* appears to echo Stoic usage of the term in reference to the totality of the cosmos, the apocalyptic background, in which God marches toward the final consummation of the cosmos, remains foremost.[23] The dynamic nature of God's interaction with the cosmos (and not absorption of it) is clearer in Romans 11:36; 1 Corinthians 15:28b simply depicts the conclusion of the process whereby the long-suffered fracture and alienation of the creation are resolved. [Romans 11:36]

The last part of Paul's argument confirming the resurrection of the dead (15:29-34) includes two examples from human conduct: baptism on behalf of the dead (v. 29) and his own struggles as an apostle (vv. 30-33).[24] Some resemblance exists here to the refutation part of his argument in 15:12-19 since Paul once again discusses the futility of certain actions if the dead are not raised.[25] In vv. 12-19, Paul points out the negative consequences of denying the resurrection, but in vv. 29-34 he is appealing to specific conduct that confirms his contention that the dead will be raised. The conduct itself supports his claim, but if his claim is false, then the conduct is futile. [*Ad hominem* Arguments?]

The first practice Paul points to is baptism on behalf of the dead. Undoubtedly, v. 29 is one of the most enigmatic verses in the New Testament. Paul's words may be literally translated: "Otherwise, what will those who are being baptized on behalf of the dead do? If the

Incipient Arianism?

A few centuries after Paul, Arians and others used his words in 1 Cor 15:28 to support a subordinationist view of Christ. Paul was not attempting to lay out a full trinitarian theology here; he was focused on showing that the resurrection of the body was a part of God's plan for the creation. Nor was Paul espousing pantheism when he wrote that Christ's victory would lead to God's being "all in all." His point was that ultimately God would prevail over all things.

Romans 11:36

Paul concludes his long discussion in Rom 9–11 about the place of Jews and Gentiles in God's eschatological plan with this benedictory prayer. The prepositions (italicized below) do not depict a static condition of an absorption of the cosmos into the being of God but rather a dynamic movement in God's relationship with the cosmos. 1 Cor 15:28 envisions the culmination of this movement when "all things" have at last reached their proper relationship with God.

"For *from* him and *through* him and *to* him are all things. To him be the glory forever. Amen." (NRSV)

***Ad hominem* Arguments?**

Several interpreters have referred to Paul's arguments in 1 Cor 15:29-34 as *ad hominem*, apparently because Paul appeals to personal examples. But *ad hominem* arguments typically attack one's character or motives or appeal to one's emotions rather than one's reasoning. Paul does question the motivations behind the conduct named in these examples, but he does not charge that they are false. He assumes that the motivations and the conduct are genuine. He simply questions the practicality of doing certain things *if* his premise, that the dead are raised, is false. He is also not appealing to emotions but rather to reason.

dead are not raised at all, why are they even baptized for them?" The future tense verb *poiēsousin* ("will they do") may be taken as a simple future active and mean essentially, "What will happen to those people if the dead are not raised?" Alternatively, the verb could be taken as a logical present in the sense of "What are those people doing [i.e., Why are they doing that?] if the dead are not raised?"[26] More problematic is the question of exactly what Paul means by "being baptized on behalf of the dead."[27] Numerous answers to this question have been offered by interpreters through the centuries, but none has attained a broad consensus. Among these interpretations, three will be discussed here. [Recent Studies of 1 Corinthians 15:29]

Recent Studies of 1 Corinthians 15:29

DeMaris, Richard E. "Corinthian Religion and Baptism for the Dead (1 Cor 15:29): Insights from Archaeology and Anthropology," *JBL* 114 (1995): 661–82.

———. *The New Testament in Its Ritual World*. New York: Routledge, 2008.

Downey, James. "1 Cor 15:29 and the Theology of Baptism." *Euntes Docete* 38 (1985): 23–35.

Hull, Michael F. *Baptism on Account of the Dead (1 Cor 15:29): An Act of Faith in the Resurrection*. SBLABi 22. Atlanta: Society of Biblical Literature, 2005.

Kennedy, Charles. "The Cult of the Dead in Corinth." In *Love and Death in the Ancient Near East: Essays in Honor of Marvin H. Pope*. Edited by J. Marks and R. Good. Pages 227–36. Guilford CT: Four Quarters, 1987.

Murphy-O'Connor, Jerome. "'Baptized for the Dead' (I Cor., XV, 29): A Corinthian Slogan?" *RB* 88 (1981): 532–43.

Patrick, James E. "Living Rewards for Dead Apostles: 'Baptised for the Dead' in 1 Corinthians 15.29." *NTS* 52 (2006): 71–85.

Reaume, J. D. "Another Look at 1 Corinthians 15:29, 'Baptized for the Dead'." *BSac* 152 (1995): 457–66.

Walker, William O. Jr. "1 Corinthians 15:29-34 as a Non-Pauline Interpolation." *CBQ* 69 (2007): 84–103.

White, Joel R. "'Baptized on account of the Dead': The Meaning of 1 Corinthians 15:29 in Its Context." *JBL* 116 (1997): 487–99.

The simplest, yet most theologically difficult, answer to this question is that some Corinthian Christians were being baptized vicariously for persons who had died without being baptized themselves. If so, then they understood baptism to be more than a symbolic rite of initiation into the church. Baptism would have been for them an effective ritual in which the person baptized was transformed in the actual process. As an act with "contagious magical" properties, the effectiveness of baptism could be imparted to a dead person by performing the ritual on someone connected to that person, presumably through a familial relationship. If such an understanding of baptism guided the practice, then the dead person would not necessarily have had to be a believer for the ritual to be effective. Through proxy baptism, the unbaptized dead would be able to reunite with their Christian loved ones in the resurrection. A variation of this view is to see the ritual of being baptized on behalf of a dead person as intended to facilitate the dead's entrance into the underworld, not as an effort to include them among those who would be resurrected.[28] Paul, of course, would not have seen baptism only as a ritual for transition to the world of the dead but as a participation in the death of Christ that enables one to share in the resurrection. His use of the practice as an example confirming his argument assumes his own understanding of the purpose of baptism, whether or not that was the understanding of the persons who engaged in the practice of being baptized on behalf of the dead.

Many Christians see this understanding of the practice to be theologically troubling. Those who do not view baptism sacramentally find it difficult to believe that some in the early church saw baptism as a "magical" ritual. The absence of criticism in Paul's brief reference to the practice confirms for them that vicarious baptism is not what the verse addresses.[29] Others who do view baptism as sacramental and efficacious may still be bothered by the idea that someone could be effectively baptized on behalf of another person without the dead person's own confession of faith. They may accept that the ritual could have been performed on behalf of a convert who died before being able to be baptized, but they insist that the rite would have been only symbolic. A purely symbolic ritual, however, would not support Paul's use of the practice as a confirming example. Still others, whether holding a sacramental or nonsacramental view of baptism, think that even though Paul did not agree with the practice of vicarious baptism, he chose not to challenge it in this instance because it served his purpose to use it as an example. Their presumption is that Paul's views on faith and baptism expressed elsewhere in his writings precludes his acceptance of such a practice as legitimate. Hays points out, however, that Paul's soteriology may, in fact, have allowed room for the church to act on behalf of those who could not act for themselves.[30]

The difficulties associated with seeing the Corinthian practice in terms of vicarious baptism have spawned other interpretations of "baptism on behalf of the dead." One that several scholars favor is that the preposition *hyper* should be rendered "for the sake of," "in regard to," or "because of" rather than "on behalf of." Thus, some special consideration of the dead leads a person to be baptized. One version of this view is that the faithfulness of the crucified Jesus or of Christian martyrs or of other apostolic witnesses has inspired someone to be baptized.[31] Another version of this view allows one to see the practice as one in which a person undergoes baptism out of consideration for deceased loved ones who are persons of faith.[32] Thus, not on the basis of one's own faith in Christ but out of a desire to be reunited with departed loved ones, a person receives baptism. Such baptism of a nonbeliever assumes the reality of the resurrection of the dead, so Paul would not have criticized the practice, even if he did not see such a baptism as genuine, since it suited the purpose of his larger argument. Thiselton accepts this last mentioned view as "the least problematic and most convincing of all."[33] Less problematic this view may be, in some respects, but in light of Paul's references to deceased believers in 15:6, 20, as "those who have fallen asleep" rather than as "the dead," it is hardly the most convincing. It also requires Paul to have condoned a practice, at least for the momentary sake of his argument, that he presumably otherwise would not have supported. Somewhat more plausible is the view of Michael Hull that baptism *because of* the dead was practiced out of a conviction that the dead would be raised.[34] Hull's position, however, restricts the practice of baptism itself to a small group within the church, whom Paul holds up as an example to those who doubt in the resurrection.

Another approach to this difficult passage that dates from the time of Chrysostom is to understand "the dead" here to refer to the "dead bodies" of the *living* persons who are being baptized.[35] [Chrysostom on the Dead] In Romans 7:24, Paul depicts the struggle with sin as bondage to a "body of death." Although the word for death there is the noun *thanatos* and not the adjective *nekros,* Paul's view that Death has reigned over humankind since Adam (Rom 5:17) means that the body is in a sense already dead. It is to these dead bodies (ourselves) that resurrection promises new, death-free life. As noted above, the word *nekros* most often referred to a "corpse" in both Greek literature and inscriptions.[36] If "the dead" in v. 29 holds the same meaning that it seems to have in much of chapter 15, then Paul would have been questioning the validity of baptism in general if the corpses being baptized are not going to be raised. Some Corinthians had doubts about corpses being raised from the dead. They saw the body as important only for this life. At death, the body would be left behind. "So," Paul asks them, "if the body is not going to be resurrected, then why are people bothering to have their bodies baptized?" This view fits with Paul's emphasis throughout 1 Corinthians on taking what one does with the body seriously. It also fits with his concern for faithful living in the rest of this section. This view is mainly problematic, however, if Paul's reference in v. 29 to baptism on behalf of the dead pertains only to *some* persons who were engaged in a special practice, as proponents of vicarious baptism generally hold. In fact, however, Paul does not specifically indicate that he is referring to some and not all of the Corinthians. His question would apply to all believers: "Why would anyone bother baptizing a corpse [this body of death]

Chrysostom on the Dead

"Sin has brought death into the world, and we are baptized in the hope that our dead bodies will be raised again in the resurrection. If there is no resurrection, our baptism is meaningless and our bodies will remain *as dead as they are now*." (Italics added)

Chrysostom, *Homilies on the Epistles of Paul to the Corinthians* 40.2, in Gerald Bray, ed., *1–2 Corinthians* (vol. 7 of ACCS NT; ed. Thomas C. Oden; Downers Grove IL: InterVarsity Press, 1999) 166.

that will not be resurrected?" Such a practice would be pointless if the dead are not raised.[37]

The second practice Paul points to in this section has to do with faithful living (15:30-34). Such living is also futile if there is no resurrection of the body. Paul first points to his own conduct (vv. 30-32) and then concludes the first section of his argument with a warning against living unfaithfully (v. 34). Verse 33 provides the bridge between Paul's faithful striving, which he considers not to be futile, and his admonition not to be hoodwinked into a lifestyle that wrongly considers affairs of the body to be insignificant and ignorantly leads to a life that is futile.

Two questions frame the argument here: (1) v. 30, "Why are we endangered every hour?" and (2) v. 32a, "If, according to a human perspective, I fought wild beasts at Ephesus, what would I profit?" The "we" of the first question is unspecified, but it probably refers to Paul and his coworkers. More broadly, it could mean the whole of the apostolic witnesses or even all believers.[38] The more restricted reference to Paul and his associates currently located in Ephesus (cf. 16:8-9) coincides with Paul's later description of their difficulties there in 2 Corinthians 1:8-10. In that letter Paul asserts that they were able to endure what seemed a "death sentence" through their reliance on "the God who raises the dead." The question also takes us back to the description of the dangerous plight of apostles that Paul gave in his sarcastic denunciation of Corinthian arrogance in 1 Corinthians 4:8-13. The point of the question is not stated here, but it is the same as that given in the *apodosis* of the second question: "What is the profit in this?" Why should Paul and the others constantly put their lives on the line if there is no resurrection of the dead? Paul then narrows this general question about the futility of apostolic struggles to a forceful statement about his own predicament in v. 31a: "I die every day!" To capture Paul's point here, this might be rendered, "I face death every day." The solemnity with which Paul makes this assertion is reinforced by an oath-like contention: "[I swear] by your confidence, brothers and sisters, which I have in Christ Jesus our Lord."[39] With deep passion, Paul calls upon that bond that still exists between himself and the Corinthians despite the strain in their relationship—a bond that stems from his sacrificial, even life-threatening, labors on their behalf. Implied in this passionate assertion is the question, "Why would I be doing all of this for you if it were futile?"

The second question regarding "fighting with wild beasts" can be taken literally or figuratively. The literal sense would indicate that Paul had actually endured a trial against wild beasts in the Ephesian arena, but both the probability of one who was apparently a Roman citizen being subjected to that punishment and the possibility of surviving such an ordeal seem remote, if not impossible. If Paul were speaking hypothetically about fighting wild beasts, then he would have used a different kind of conditional statement in Greek. Some figurative sense seems more probable. Some interpreters take the "wild beasts" to be a metaphor for the "adversaries" that Paul mentions in 1 Corinthians 16:9.[40] Abraham Malherbe, and others, however, have pointed to the common use of the metaphor of "wild beasts" in philosophical discussions about controlling the passions.[41] Paul's inclusion of the phrase *kata anthrōpon* ("according to a human perspective") may suggest that he intends the image of "wild beasts" to be taken in the well-known metaphorical sense of "human passions."[42] If Paul intended such an allusion, then his second question has turned the focus from outer threats to inward adversaries.

This seems probable in light of the direction that the rest of his argument takes. Paul's point is, Why bother engaging in this relentless struggle against human passions if the dead are not raised? Why not, instead, "Let us eat and drink, for tomorrow we die"? The words of Paul's quotation come from Isaiah 22:13, which describes the hopeless hedonism of some Jerusalemites during a time of national uncertainty in the seventh century BC. The words also reflect the widespread sentiment of anti-Epicurean moralists of Paul's own time who criticized the alleged self-indulgence of Epicureans. [Plutarch on Hedonism] One does not have to hold the view that members of the Corinthian church were actually subscribing to the tenets of a particular philosophical school to appreciate Paul's point of contact with his audience here. Nor does one have to assume that Paul's words were directed toward exorbitant hedonistic behavior by certain church members. The idea that the pleasures of the body could only be enjoyed this side of the grave was a common one. Persons who held that belief, however, did not have to accept the corollary idea that sensual pleasures should therefore be exploited to the fullest. Undoubtedly, many

Plutarch on Hedonism

Plutarch expressed a typical view against Epicurean hedonism, though his caricature misconstrues Epicurus's actual views, in this excerpt from his *Moralia*, titled "That It Is Not Possible to Live Pleasurably according to the Doctrine of Epicurus."

> For it will not perhaps seem strange if I assert, that the memory of pleasure past brings no pleasure with it if it seemed but little in the very enjoyment, or to men of such abstinence as to account it for their benefit to retire from its first approaches; when even the most amazed and sensual admirers of corporeal delights remain no longer in their gaudy and pleasant humor than their pleasure lasts them. What remains is but an empty shadow and dream of that pleasure that hath now taken wing and is fled from them, and that serves but for fuel to foment their untamed desires. Like as in those that dream they are adry [thirsty] or in love, their unaccomplished pleasures and enjoyments do but excite the inclination to a greater keenness. Nor indeed can the remembrance of past enjoyments afford them any real contentment at all, but must serve only, with the help of a quick desire, to raise up very much of outrage and stinging pain out of the remains of a feeble and befooling pleasure.

Plutarch's Morals, Translated from the Greek by Several Hands. Corrected and Revised by William W. Goodwin, with an Introduction by Ralph Waldo Emerson, 5 vols. (Boston: Little, Brown, and Co., 1878) 2:4B.

persons did follow both the logic and the practice of that corollary (perhaps even some persons within the church), but many did not, especially those who were influenced by the more prevalent Stoic perspective on controlling the passions. Paul's point is simply that if one gives up the hope for bodily resurrection, then one may as well focus entirely on the present moment.

Paul immediately points out, however, that while "living it up now" may be a logical conclusion to the dismissal of resurrection hope, it is a dangerous one. Disregarding the significance of the body for the future opens the door to discounting the importance of disciplining bodily appetites in the present. At least some of Paul's readers have been deceived in this regard, so he issues a blunt command using the negative present-tense imperative *mē planasthe* ("Stop being deceived!"). He then quotes what was probably a well-known maxim: "Bad company ruins good morals." The saying appears in several ancient writings but seems to have been attached especially to Menander, who included it in his play *Thais* in a section describing a manipulative prostitute.[43] [Menander] Winter observes that *homiliai* ("company") usually has some connotation of sexual intercourse, so he takes Paul's use of this saying as an indication that he was targeting young, elite men in the church who were exercising their rights to participate in private parties that involved eating, drinking, and having sex with prostitutes.[44] Horsley, however, argues that the plural form of *homiliai* suggests not sexual intercourse but rather "conversations." For him, Paul's target would be those who have been deceived by speculative wisdom.[45] The use of this saying in conjunction with the quotation from Isaiah 22:13, as well as the imperatives in v. 34 to "sober up" and "stop sinning," support Winter's view over Horsley's. Still, we do not have to accept the idea that Paul was concerned primarily with a relatively small group of elite men who were indulging in hedonism. His target audience was that group that denied the idea of a bodily resurrection. Whether or not they therefore indulged in hedonism, their perspective was itself dangerous because it could lead them to be cavalier in regard to all ethical behavior. Their cloudy thinking on this matter prevented them from seeing the negative consequences of their conduct, whether that conduct was especially egregious or not.

Menander

Commentators frequently note the similarity between Paul's statement regarding "bad companionship" in 1 Cor 15:33 and a line found in the surviving fragment of Menander's play *Thais* (LCL fragments 215-28). The saying itself appears in other ancient writings. In the play it appears to be directed toward a prostitute.

> "Loose-bridled? Pest! Methinks, though I have suffered this, that none the less I'd be glad to have her. Sing to me, goddess, sing of such a one as she: audacious, beautiful, and plausible withal: she does you wrongs; she locks her door; keeps asking you for gifts; she loves none, but ever makes pretense. Evil companionship corrupts good character."

As cited by Bruce W. Winter, *After Paul Left Corinth: The Influence of Secular Ethics and Social Change* (Grand Rapids MI: Eerdmans, 2001) 98–99.

Paul's concluding word in this section is a call to clear-headed thinking and appropriate behavior: "Come to your senses and think properly and stop sinning" (v. 34a). The propensity to sin is rooted in muddled thinking. It exposes the sad truth that "some have no real understanding of God" (34b). Their denial of the hope of bodily resurrection is ultimately a profound ignorance about the power and working of God. It is also ignorance about the transformative working of God in the present. Resurrection hope not only pertains to the future; it informs the shape and character of life in the present. For Paul—whose presuppositions of apocalypticism, corporate mysticism, and embodied existence framed his perspective—their denial of resurrection hope was simply the tip of an iceberg of theological and ethical confusion. His final word here, "To your shame I say this," is shock therapy designed to crack the ice. It represents the only true *ad hominem* argument in the section. (See [*Ad hominem* Arguments?].) His statement here is almost a verbatim repetition of his words in 6:5, where he criticized the church for not handling internal disputes internally. Both later statements (6:5; 15:34) contrast with his earlier assurance that his sarcastic lambasting of the arrogant among them was not intended to shame the church (4:14).

An Explanation of the Resurrection of the Body, 15:35-58

Paul finally begins to speak directly to the central objection that some of the Corinthians have apparently raised about the idea of the resurrection of the body. In doing so, he identifies the *propositio* to be argued in this second part of his larger argument: "How are the dead raised? With what kind of body do they come?" Like the *propositio* of 15:12, the thesis is framed as a question, except this time it is expressed in two related questions and the questions themselves are attributed to a fictive interlocutor, not to Paul. The refutation of the deficient questions follows in vv. 36-42, while the bulk of the rest of chapter 15 gives two distinct proofs (vv. 42-49 and vv. 50-57) correcting the erroneous viewpoint behind the questions. The final verse (58) contains an appropriate concluding exhortation.

15:35-49. Paul utilizes a device commonly referred to as a diatribe as he begins to address the central problem his views about resurrection have raised among some of the Corinthians. [Diatribe] He poses two related questions as if they are asked by an imaginary opponent representing their perspective. The first question ("How are the dead raised?") should not be read as a challenge to the idea of life after death but rather as a genuine inquiry as to the mode of resurrection existence. The second question ("With what kind of body do they come?") gets to the heart of their perplexity. Physical bodies age, die, then decompose. So how can they be resuscitated in any kind of meaningful form? Furthermore, why would anyone, once shedding the limits of earthly life imposed by bodily existence, want to carry such baggage into the next life? Dale Martin is probably correct in suggesting that the Corinthians' questioning of Paul's teaching regarding the resurrection probably reflects both certain ideas they had about the nature of the body and Paul's lack of attention to details regarding the resurrected body in his earlier preaching.[46] The anxiety of the church in Thessalonica about the fate of those believers who died before the coming of Christ (1 Thess 4:13-18) probably also stemmed from Paul's failure to give detailed information about his views on that subject while he was present with them.

Diatribe

The diatribe has often been seen as a preaching device adopted by Paul and other early Christian preachers and writers from the public speaking of Cynic and Stoic philosophers. Stanley Stowers has shown, however, that its origins lay in classroom discussions and discourses by philosophical schools following the dialogical pattern of Socrates. The diatribe often features an imaginary opponent who voices a view that the speaker or writer considers fallacious and necessarily refutable. The inconsistent and inadequately informed view of the imaginary opponent may be indicated initially by addressing the fictive person as a "fool," which is exactly what Paul does in 1 Cor 15:36.

Stanley K. Stowers, *The Diatribe and Paul's Letter to the Romans* (SBLDS 57; Chico CA: Scholars Press, 1981).

David E. Aune, *The New Testament in Its Literary Environment* (LEC; Philadelphia: Westminster Press, 1987) 200–202.

To refute the questions posed, especially the second, Paul employs an agricultural metaphor, namely, the planting of seed. But first, he ridicules the erroneous assumption behind the stated question by calling his imaginary interrogator a "fool." The nomenclature points forward to the coming argument as well as backward to the questions that express the mistaken perception that makes the argument necessary. Paul's initial point may be paraphrased, "Do you not understand how planting works? When you plant seed, the seed has to die before it grows into something." Paul's statement reflects a horticultural and theological perspective similar to that of John 12:24 in that he views the planted seed as "dying" and that such "dying" is necessary for rebirth. [John 12:24] In point of fact, the planted seed does not actually "die," but it does cease to be a seed. It becomes something far more significant than the "naked seed" (*gymnon kokkon*) that was planted (see v. 53 below). The sown seed does not have the "body that *will become*" (*genēsomenon*, a rare future participial form), but when it "dies" it becomes the "body" that God has chosen to give it. Indeed, God gives to each kind of seed its own appropriate body.

John 12:24

"Unless a grain of wheat falls into the earth and dies, it remains alone; but if it dies, it bears much fruit."

Paul does not press the issue of how the planted seed is transformed into the "body that will become" at this stage, because his point in the use of the seed metaphor here is that a difference exists between the seed that is planted and the body that emerges. Later, however, in vv. 51-53, he describes the process of transformation into the resurrected body as a "mystery." Even here, though, his assertion that it is God who gives the seed its chosen body already places the matter in the realm of God's mysterious activity. As in the parable of the seed growing secretly in Mark 4:26-29, where the sower does not know how the miracle of transformation occurs, the choosing of appropriate bodies is God's doing. [Mark 4:26-29]

Mark 4:26-29

He also said, "The kingdom of God is as if someone would scatter seed on the ground, and would sleep and rise night and day, and the seed would sprout and grow, *he does not know how*. The earth produces of itself, first the stalk, then the head, then the full grain in the head. But when the grain is ripe, at once he goes in with his sickle, because the harvest has come." (NRSV; italics added)

As it is with flora, so it is with fauna, Paul asserts. Human beings, animals, birds, and fish all exist in different forms. Here, though, Paul uses the term flesh (*sarx*) rather than body (*sōma*). By flesh here, Paul seems to mean something like "muscular corporeality."[47] He recognizes a certain commonality in the physical makeup of the various members of the animal kingdom, but he also stresses that each type of animal is different. Each kind of "animated" earthly creature has its own type of flesh. These differences in flesh conform to the different kinds of bodies that such creatures have. Paul's differentiation between bodies of plants (v. 38), the flesh of earthly bodies (v. 39), and the glory of heavenly bodies (vv. 40-41) possibly reflects the same view about a hierarchy of living things based on the composition of their bodies and the regions they inhabit found in Philo and some Stoic philosophers.[48] [Philo on Plants and Animals]

Philo on Plants and Animals

Those then that are affected by motion, inducing change of place, which we call animals, are attached to the most important portions of the universe; the terrestrial animals to the earth, the animals which swim to the water, the winged animals to the air and those which can live in flame to the fire (which last are said to be most evidently produced in Macedonia), and the stars are attached to the heaven. For those who have studied philosophy pronounce the stars also to be animals, being endowed with intellect and pervading the whole universe; some being planets, and moving by their own intrinsic nature; and others, that is the fixed stars, being borne along with the revolutions of the universe; so that they likewise appear to change their places. But those which are regulated according to a devoid of all sensation, which are peculiarly called plants, have no participation in that motion which involves a change of place.

Philo, *Concerning Noah's Work as a Planter* 12–13, as found in *The Works of Philo: New Updated Edition* (trans. C. D. Yonge; Peabody MA: Hendrickson Publishers, 1993) 192.

In v. 40, Paul begins to shift the focus from the earthly realm to the heavenly by making a contrast between the two. The inhabitants of the heavenly realm also have "bodies." These bodies, however, are very different from those of the earthly realm—so different, in fact, that Paul uses the word "glory" in reference to them instead of "flesh." In v. 40a, he affirms that bodies exist for both the earthly and heavenly regions, but in v. 40b he stipulates that the glory of the heavenly bodies (*hē tōn epouraniōn doxa*) is different (*hetera*) from that of the earthly. Though the word "glory" (*doxa*) in reference to earthly bodies is implied by the presence of the feminine article (*hē tōn epigeiōn*), the absence of the word *doxa* in the second part of the contrast may reflect Paul's hesitancy to use "glory" in connection with earthly bodies.[49] Flesh characterizes earthly, animal bodies, but glory characterizes heavenly ones, including the resurrection body (v. 43). As earthly bodies have different kinds of flesh, so heavenly bodies have different kinds of glory. The sun, moon, and stars have different glories, and even the different stars vary in glory (v. 21).

We should not lose sight of Paul's main points here. First of all, existence involves embodiment. Every living thing has a body, including plants (seeds), animals, and celestial entities, but presumably excluding God. This point is crucial to Paul's affirmation of *bodily* resurrection. Secondly, however, bodies differ. Within the earthly realm, bodies differ in their "flesh." In the heavenly realm, bodies differ in their "glory." More importantly, a fundamental difference holds between the two realms. Bodies of the earthly realm cannot exist in the heavenly realm. Paul has outlined these differences using a chiastic pattern that centers on the difference between the two realms:

A—Earthly bodies differ in *flesh* (v. 39)
B—Earthly bodies differ from heavenly bodies (v. 40)
A'—Heavenly bodies differ in *glory* (v. 41)[50]

This difference between earthly and heavenly bodies is crucial to his explanation of the *nature* of the resurrected body.

Paul began his rebuttal of his imaginary interlocutor's question about "what kind of body" the resurrected will have with the metaphor of planted seed. Having established that different kinds of bodies exist for different living things, he returns to his metaphor in v. 42. As the seed is transformed through "death" into the body chosen by God, likewise the earthly body that is "sown" is transformed through the resurrection. The difference between the preresurrection body and the transformed body is highlighted by a series of four pairs of contrasts in vv. 42-44, followed later in vv. 48-49 by two more contrasting pairs. Paul will repeat the first contrasting pair ("corruption" vs. "incorruption") in v. 53 and add another contrast ("mortal" vs. "immortal"). [Contrasts between the Body before and after Resurrection] While many modern versions prefer to translate *phthora* in v. 42 and elsewhere as "perishable," the KJV's "in corruption" actually fits Paul's own view better.[51] No doubt, his Corinthian detractors would have seen the body as "perishable," but Paul's range of vision extends beyond the deterioration that a corpse might undergo in the grave. In fact, the state of corruption

Contrasts between the Body before and after Resurrection

The body before resurrection		The body after the resurrection
sown in degeneration (*en phthora*)	v. 42	raised in generation (*en aphtharsia*)
sown in humiliation (*en atimia*)	v. 43	raised in glory (*en doxē*)
sown in weakness (*en astheneia*)	v. 43	raised in power (*en dynamei*)
a "soulful" body (*sōma psychikon*)	v. 44	a "spiritual" body (*sōma pneumatikon*)
of the dust (*ek choikos*)	v. 47	of heaven (*ex ouranou*)
bears the image of the man of dust (*ephoresamen tēn eikona choikou*)	v. 49	bears the image of the man of heaven (*phorosōmen tēn eikona tou eporaniou*)
degenerated (*to phtharton*)	v. 53	generated (*aphtharsian*)
mortal (*to thnēton*)	v. 53	immortal (*athanasian*)

in which bodies exist precedes death and is not limited to physical decline. Whatever the extent of bodily rot that might occur for those saints already buried, Paul does not see the body as something that passes out of existence, as "perishable" implies. Rather, he sees this earthly, degenerating body as being transformed in the resurrection. The second pair of contrasts, "humiliation" (*atimia*) and "glory" (*doxē*), expresses the language and sentiment found in Philippians 3:21. [Philippians 3:21] The third pair, "weakness" (*asthenia*) and "power" (*dynamei*), highlight the difference between human frailty and the transformative power of God at work in the resurrection (cf. 6:14).

Philippians 3:21

He will transform the body of our humiliation that it may be conformed to the body of his glory, by the power that also enables him to make all things subject to himself. (NRSV)

In vv. 37-41, Paul pointed out that the resurrected body is different from the earthly body. Here he elaborates on exactly how different it is. The earthly body is corrupt, humiliated, and weak. The resurrected body is incorruptible, glorious, and powerful. Paul's stress here is on the difference between the two, not on the insignificance of the earthly body. He has gone to great pains elsewhere in this letter to stress the significance of the earthly body, so we would be misconstruing the point of his contrasts here if we should see him depicting earthly existence as wretched. In comparison to the resurrection body, our present bodies are clearly inferior, but that does mean that they are to be discounted as of no importance. If Paul were to voice that sentiment, he would be playing into the hands of those who dismissed the lasting importance of the earthly body and the deeds done in it. Rather, he is trying, as Richard Hays has argued, "to make the resurrection of the dead seem *appealing* rather than *appalling* to the Corinthians."[52]

Paul's label for the earthly body in v. 44 is difficult to put into English. He calls it a *sōma psychikon*, which literally means something like "soulful body." To translate it as "physical body" obscures the distinction he wants to make since the resurrected body is also in some sense "physical," though a different kind of physicality. Paul does not pit the physical over against the spiritual. Paul also does not pose body over against soul, nor does he pose body over against spirit. He juxtaposes soul and spirit. The "soulful body" is that body invigorated by the vital force of life that the Bible often refers to as the "soul." Paul recalls the account in Genesis 2:7 where God breathed into Adam the breath of life and he became a "living soul" (15:45). Like Adam, we are living souls embodied in a frail form made from the elements of the earth. The soul and the body are one, not two separate entities that can be disentangled. When the life force desists, the body dies. Conversely, when the body dies, the life force desists; it does not go marching on. [2 Corinthians 5:1-10]

The difficulty of putting all of this into language is evident in Paul's use of "spiritual body" (*sōma pneumatikon*) to identify the resurrected body. If we think of the body as primarily material, then Paul's reference to "spiritual matter" appears to be an oxymoron. For Paul, the body is who and what one is. It is the physical self, but it is also the emotional and mental self. It is all that one is, invigorated by that life force, the soul, that God has breathed into it. This body, as now experienced, cannot experience the new life ahead. That life calls for a transformation of this body into the glorious state of the resurrection body. The gospel song that claims "I'll have a new body" is partly correct, but it gives the impression that the old body is to be left behind. Paul's conviction in 1 Corinthians is not that this old body will be replaced but rather that it (who one is) will be transformed. The resurrection body will not be invigorated by the time-bound soul but by the eternal spirit.

2 Corinthians 5:1-10

Scholars have long noted that Paul's description of the resurrected body in 1 Cor 15 seems to be in some tension with his portrayal of what happens after death in 2 Cor 5:1-10. In particular, in 2 Cor 5:6 Paul characterizes "dwelling (*endēmountes*) in the body" as "dwelling (*ekdēmoumen*) away from the Lord," and in 2 Cor 5:8 he asserts a preference for being "out of the body" and "with the Lord." At the judgment, one receives payment according to what one has done "through the body" (2 Cor 5:10). The tension lies in Paul's apparent restriction of the *body* to earthly existence in 2 Cor 5. Even so, the same metaphorical language of "clothing" that appears in 1 Cor 15:53-54 also appears in 2 Cor 5:2-4. In 1 Corinthians, the dead and the living "put on" the qualities of resurrection existence at the parousia, while in 2 Corinthians the heavenly dwelling is "put on" in place of the earthly tent. Paul's insistence on *bodily* resurrection in 1 Cor 15 reflects his concern to correct views about the body that affected the Corinthians' behavior. Other matters govern 2 Cor 5.

The quotation of Genesis 2:7 identifies the nature of human beings as "living souls." Paul's insertion of "Adam" into his quotation of this verse also enables him to return to the Adam-Christ typology that he introduced in 15:21-22. The first Adam received life and the qualities of earthly existence (for good and bad) from God; the second Adam (Christ), who has become a "life-giving" spirit, gives life and the qualities of resurrection existence. Unlike Philo, who saw the Adam of Genesis 1 as the archetypical and ideal human being, Paul sees the first Adam as partaking of a nature that is incapable of "inheriting the kingdom of God" (v. 50). [Philo on Adam] The second Adam, Christ, represents a kind of existence that has come into being *after* the first Adam. Thus, the focus is not on reclaiming some lost ideal from the primordial past; rather, it is on attaining the future mode of existence proleptically revealed in the resurrected Christ. The first Adam was from the dust of the earth and returned to that dust in death. The second Adam is from heaven and returned to that heaven through resurrection. As it is with that first "dust man" (*ho choikos*), so it is with all the "dust people" (*hoi choikoi*), for in Adam all die (v. 22a). Likewise, as it is with the "heavenly man" (*ho epouranios*), so it is with the "heavenly people" (*hoi epouranioi*), who "in Christ shall be made alive" (v. 22b). Paul reminds his

readers that "we have *worn* the likeness (*eikona*) of this dust man" (v. 49).[53] He does not appeal to Genesis 1:27 and describe human beings as being made in the "image (*eikona*) of God." Instead, human beings have worn the image of Adam. For Paul, Adam never represents a model for humanity but rather a picture of humanity's limitations.

The second half of v. 49, which refers to wearing the image of the man of heaven, is textually problematic. [The Text of 1 Corinthians 15:49] Most modern versions read, "*we will* also bear the image of the

Philo on Adam

Philo distinguished between the "heavenly man" *fashioned* in the image of God in Gen 1 and the "earthly man" *made* from the dust of the earth in Gen 2 (*Allegorical Interpretation* 1:31-32). The heavenly man, in Philo's thinking, conformed to the Platonic idea of the "Form" on which the earthly man was modeled. Thus, for Philo, the first Adam (of Gen 1) represents the ideal of humanity for which all human beings should aspire.

See Anthony C. Thiselton, *The First Epistle to the Corinthians: A Commentary on the Greek Text* (NIGTC; Grand Rapids: Eerdmans, 2000) 1283–84.

The Text of 1 Corinthians 15:49

The vast majority of ancient manuscripts have the aorist hortatory subjunctive *phoresōmen* ("let us wear") rather than the future indicative *phoresomen* ("we will wear"). Nonetheless, the UBS Committee's *Greek New Testament* (inc. the latest edition) gives the future indicative as the preferred reading. While in the 3rd ed. the committee gave the future indicative a "C" classification (indicating that the committee had difficulty deciding between the variants), the 4th ed. carries a "B" label for *phoresomen* (indicating that this reading is almost certain). In explaining the committee's choice of the less-attested future indicative, committee chair Bruce Metzger explained, "Exegetical considerations (i.e., the context is didactic, not hortatory) led the Committee to prefer the future indicative, despite its rather slender textual support" (TCGNT, 569). C. K. Barrett (369 n.2) has observed that both words were pronounced alike and that in the dictation of the original or early copies the aorist may have been mistaken for the intended future. Thiselton (1289) favors the future indicative adopted by most commentators, but Fee (794–95) supports the aorist. Clearly, the future indicative is the easier reading to take for exegetical purposes, but, as Fee observes, this would have been as true early in the history of the transmission of the text as it is today. One can understand why ancient copyists would have preferred the future form, so the wide attestation of the aorist strongly supports it as the original. Despite the challenge the aorist holds for interpretation, it is most likely the correct reading. Thus, the reading "let us wear," while more difficult for interpretive purposes, is the reading preferred here.

C. K. Barrett, *A Commentary on the First Epistle to the Corinthians* (2d ed.; London: Black, 1971) 369.

Gordon D. Fee, *The First Epistle to the Corinthians* (NICNT; Grand Rapids: Eerdmans Publishing, 1987) 794–95.

Bruce M. Metzger, *A Textual Commentary on the Greek New Testament* (Stuttgart: United Bible Societies, 1971) 569.

Anthony C. Thiselton, *The First Epistle to the Corinthians: A Commentary on the Greek Text* (NIGTC; Grand Rapids: Eerdmans, 2000) 1288–89.

man of heaven." This fits with Paul's contrast between the earthly body now and the resurrected body then. But nearly all the ancient manuscripts actually read, "*let us* bear the image of the man of heaven." This does not seem to fit with Paul's main point so well. If it is the correct reading, as is likely, then perhaps Paul was saying that though we have worn the image of Adam, we should now look to Christ and strive to conform our lives to his. Though we do not yet possess that resurrected body that shall fully reflect the image of Christ, we should live in such a way that Christ is reflected even in these earthly bodies. Both "we will wear" and "let us wear" stress that becoming like Christ is the glory of the resurrection. The exhortation "let us," however, adds to the basic message of future hope an appropriate note of responsibility in the present. The full experience of that glory must await our own resurrection, but to the degree that we can reflect the image of Christ now, we already wear the likeness of resurrection existence.

1 Corinthians 15.50

While numerous commentators and some translations (inc. RSV) understand 1 Cor 15:50 to be the concluding statement in the section begun in v. 42, the Greek text of both the Nestle-Aland *Novum Testamentum Graece* (26th ed.) and the United Bible Societies' *The Greek New Testament* (4th rev. ed.) see v. 50 as the beginning of a new paragraph. The general subject in v. 50, of course, is the same as vv. 35-49, but here Paul turns to focus on the process of transformation that occurs in the resurrection. Verse 50 aptly introduces this shift in focus.

Gordon D. Fee, *The First Epistle to the Corinthians* (NICNT; Grand Rapids: Eerdmans Publishing, 1987) 798.

Anthony C. Thiselton, *The First Epistle to the Corinthians: A Commentary on the Greek Text* (NIGTC; Grand Rapids: Eerdmans, 2000) 1290.

15:50-58. The final movement in Paul's long argument about the resurrection begins in v. 50. [1 Corinthians 15:50] Here Paul shifts attention to the transformation of the body that occurs at the resurrection. While vv. 36-49 were directed toward the second question posed in v. 35, what follows seems to pertain more to the first question: "How are the dead raised?" That is not to say, however, that the question about the nature of the resurrected body disappears from view. In the preceding section, Paul has asserted that God gives the appropriate body for each kind of living being. Here Paul describes how the resurrected body is given, within the limits of what can be said about this "mystery" (v. 51). In addition to describing this mysterious process, Paul also reveals for the first time that the scope of transformation extends beyond the resurrection of dead bodies to include the living.

While v. 50 constitutes the beginning of a new section, namely the second proof in Paul's *confirmatio* of his argument explaining the nature of the resurrected body, the section is not independent of what he has argued to this point. In fact, Paul's opening words, "What I am saying," point out the implications of his previous argument. His assertion that "flesh and blood cannot inherit the kingdom of God" in all probability also expresses the main objection that his detractors had about the idea of a bodily resurrection.

Surreptitiously, as often happens in this letter, Paul "takes captive" this idea (cf. 2 Cor 10:5) and utilizes it for his final thrust. Bodies of mere flesh and blood, indeed, cannot inherit the kingdom; furthermore, persons in a state of corruption cannot inherit what is incorruptible. The two parts of v. 50 should both be seen as referring to human beings in general and not to two different groups (i.e., the "living" and the "dead") as Jeremias has argued.[54] The two descriptions, however, are not merely synonyms. The phrase "flesh and blood" focuses attention on the frailty of human bodily existence, while "corruption" expands beyond the physical to the moral dimension.[55] The Corinthians consistently failed to see the connection between the two. Thus, Paul again tethers the physical to the moral, stating a point that they affirmed while adding a corollary that they failed to grasp.

Paul signals the full import of his statement in v. 50 by beginning his next line with the imperative *idou* (Look!). The incompatibility of earthly, bodily existence and life in the heavenly realm—the scandal of which initiated the doubts about the resurrection that Paul is attempting here to dispel—will be resolved in a mystery that Paul now divulges. The language of "mystery" is common to apocalyptic depictions of the end in that the truth about what is to happen remains hidden until it is unveiled to the chosen recipient of divine revelation. Paul claims the status of such a recipient of divine mysteries in 2 Corinthians 12:4-7. Here he discloses the secret answer to their questions about the resurrection as the climax of his argument: "We will all be changed." Everyone will not die, he confides, but everyone will be changed. The transforming power of the resurrection will affect the living as well as the dead. His assertion that the dead will be raised and that "we will be changed" in v. 52 has often been taken to indicate Paul's belief that he would be included among those still living at the parousia. Perhaps Paul did believe that, but his words here should not be pressed too far in that direction.[56] His point here is that everyone who inherits the kingdom must be transformed into a kind of being appropriate for existence in that realm. Death of the body is not required, but transformation beyond flesh, blood, and corruption is.

Paul's actual depiction of the transformative moment is much more concise than his similar description in 1 Thessalonians 4:15-17. [1 Thessalonians 4:15-17] In 1 Thessalonians, Paul addressed the concern that those who had died might in some sense be left behind, so he gave

1 Thessalonians 4:15-17

For this we declare to you by the word of the Lord, that we who are alive, who are left until the coming of the Lord, will by no means precede those who have died. For the Lord himself, with a cry of command, with the archangel's call and with the sound of God's trumpet, will descend from heaven, and the dead in Christ will rise first. Then we who are alive, who are left, will be caught up with them to meet the Lord in the air; and so we will be with the Lord forever. (NRSV) some attention to the sequence of events. That account, however, omits what was crucial to the concern of his Corinthian audience, namely that merely earthly bodies cannot exist in the heavenly realm. The brevity of his account here coincides with the suddenness of its occurrence. In an instant (*atomō*), in an eye's blink (*rhipē*), at the last trumpet (*salpiggi*), the change suddenly happens. Though trumpets were used to announce the beginning of athletic competitions, funeral processions, civic ceremonies, and the verdicts of judges, they most commonly were associated with military events. In vv. 24-28, Paul used military metaphors to depict the final victory of Christ, so the trumpet's blast here reflects a return to that imagery. [The Last Trumpet] When the trumpet sounds, the dead are raised in an incorruptible form and the living are changed into the same form. Paul's description of the altered state mimics the language of vv. 42-43 but also includes "immortality" along with the previously mentioned "incorruption." His language also describes the changes as something "put on" (*endysasthai*). Those who have worn the image of the dust man Adam (v. 49) now at last wear the incorruptible and immortal image of the heavenly Christ. Paul reiterates that it is necessary for this change to occur, recalling his major point in v. 50. By using the language of clothing here, furthermore, Paul again underscores that there is continuity between the earthly body and the resurrection body. *This* (*touto*) corruption puts on incorruption; *this* (*touto*) mortality puts on immortality. The "this" is that body previously sown in dishonor and weakness but now raised in glory and power (v. 43). Paul may define "this" in 2 Corinthians 4:16 as "our inner nature" (*ho esō hēmōn*), but in 1 Corinthians 15 he cannot give ground to any allowance for a disembodied state.

The Last Trumpet

While the trumpet appears in the OT in several contexts indicating the powerful presence of God, in the postexilic prophets the sounding of the trumpet took on a more eschatological sense when it came to be associated with the coming of the "day of the Lord" (Joel 2:1; Zeph 1:14-16). In Zech 9:14, the trumpet signals God's gathering of dispersed Israelites, a motif that reappears in an altered form in the Matthean apocalyptic discourse (Matt 24:31) wherein the Son of Man signals with a trumpet for his angels to gather his elect. In 1 Cor 14:8, Paul clearly associates the trumpet with warfare but not in an eschatological sense. In 1 Cor 15:52 and 1 Thess 4:16, the trumpet signals both the military triumph envisioned in the prophets' "day of the Lord" and the gathering of God's people. Paul identifies the trumpet in 1 Cor 15:52 as the "last" (*eschatē*) trumpet. While this *last* trumpet may not be the final blast in a series of horns, as in Rev 11:15, its sound signals the same complete victory where "The kingdom of the world has become the kingdom of our Lord and of his Christ."

Ambrosiaster was not mistaken when he took the last trumpet to signal the victory of a battle won.

Ambrosiaster, *Commentary on Paul's Epistles*, CSEL 81.183.

(Credit: Dave Jones)

When all of this happens, Paul writes, then certain Scriptures will have been fulfilled. While the particular Scriptures Paul means is certain, their form is not. His quotations differ from what came to be the established Hebrew and Greek texts. His version of Isaiah 25:7 reads: "Death has been swallowed up in victory." [Isaiah 25:7] The Hebrew text (MT 25:7) actually reads: "He will swallow up death forever." The LXX version (25:8) reads: "Death swallowed up, having prevailed."[57] Though Paul makes Death the subject of the verb, as in the LXX, he follows the meaning of the Hebrew. If Paul was responsible for changing the future tense of the Hebrew verb to a past tense Greek verb, it was possibly because he was looking at the event from the perspective of the time when it has been fulfilled. What appears in Isaiah 25:7 as a promise becomes a reality in the resurrection. Death, long the great consumer of life, will itself have been consumed. The phrase "in victory" appears in neither the MT nor the LXX, but it does appear in the second-century AD Greek versions known as Aquila and Theodotion. Paul may have drawn from a Greek version that already included the phrase and that had also made Death the subject of the verb "swallowed up," perhaps already in the passive voice.

Isaiah 25:7

And he will destroy on this mountain
The shroud that is cast over all peoples;
the sheet that is spread over all nations;
he will swallow up death forever. (NRSV)

Whether of Pauline or pre-Pauline origin, the phrase "in victory" provides a word-link with Paul's quotation of Hosea 13:14: "Where, O Death, is your victory? Where, O Death, is your sting?" [Hosea 13:14] Paul's rendering here clearly follows the LXX rather than the MT, in which the two statements about Death express God's judgment on Israel. In the LXX Greek version, though, they are part of God's promise to deliver God's people. The LXX Greek text of Hosea 13:14, however, has "penalty" (*dikē*) where Paul has "victory" (*nikos*). The differences in wording may have already been in the scriptural tradition from which Paul drew. If Paul altered the wording, he may have done so to emphasize the contrast between God's ultimate victory over death in the quotation from Isaiah and death's final failure to achieve the victory it has always previously known, which Hosea's slightly altered words express in a pair of mocking taunts. The Greek text of Hosea 13:14 has *hadē* (= Hades; Heb *sheol*) in the second taunt, while Paul has substituted "Death." "Hades" is often used in Greek literature as the name of the residence of the shadowy residues of those who once lived, which is the same role played by *sheol* in the Old

Hosea 13:14

Shall I ransom them from the power of Sheol?
Shall I redeem them from Death?
O Death, where are your plagues?
O Sheol, where is your destruction?
Compassion is hidden from my eyes. (NRSV)

Testament. In point of fact, however, Hades was the name of the god who ruled over the realm of the dead. The sorry shades of former life lingered in the "house of Hades." Paul's substitution of Death for Hades and his personification of Death, signified by the direct address of the taunts, is highly appropriate. The one who has lorded over the dead shall do so no more, as a result of the resurrection. Furthermore, God's victory over Death shall bring an end to meaningless resignation to the "shadowlands," for that victory entails the resurrection of the body to a glorious state of incorruption and immortality.

Paul adds some commentary to his quotation of Hosea as he continues the contrast between death's usual victory and God's final triumph in vv. 56-57. He defines the "sting" of death as sin. As in Romans (5:12-14; 7:7-13), Paul closely connects sin and death. What Paul developed in great detail in his letter to the Roman believers, which was probably penned in Corinth, he states succinctly here. Sin is the tool death uses to work its way into human life. Death stings human beings again and again through sin until the poison of sin causes one to succumb to death. "Death spread to all because all have sinned," Paul wrote in Romans 5:12b. The inclusion of "sin" in Paul's brief depiction of the resurrection scenario is not odd at all since his discussion of the resurrection of the body in this chapter is not isolated from his concern for how one lives in the body elsewhere in the letter. The sudden insertion of the "law" in a letter that otherwise has little to say about the subject is more surprising. Again, however, what appears here in succinct form flows in all probability from the kind of teaching that Paul had already done in Corinth, though we see it most fully developed in a letter written from Corinth. As sin is death's tool, so the law becomes the operative power for sin. For Paul, though the law is holy and good, it participates in death's destruction of human life because it identifies sin and, in doing so, makes sin more powerful (Rom 7:7-8). Thus, the

Hades

Bust of Hades. Marble. Roman copy after a Greek original from the 5th C. BC; the black mantle is a modern addition. Former Ludovisi collection. Museo Nazionale Palazzo Altemps, Rome, Italy. (Credit: http://commons.wikimedia.org/wiki/File:Hades_Altemps_Inv8584.jpg)

Though the term "Hades" is often applied to the realm of the dead, Hades was actually the god of that realm. The shades of those formerly alive lingered in the house of Hades.

law is sin's power. Despite the perpetual onslaught of suffering that this trio of terror has inflicted on the human race, however, the victory over all three destructive powers has been won by God through our Lord Jesus Christ (15:57). The captives have been set free, thanks to God. Paul's extended argument about the resurrection of the dead ends in a word of celebration.

But there is an epilogue. As the first part of Paul's long argument ended with an exhortation (v. 34), so ends the second part. Whereas that earlier exhortation was intended to shame, this one is intended to inspire those whom he now embraces with terms of endearment: "Therefore, *my beloved*, be steadfast, immovable, always excelling in the work of the Lord, because you know that in the Lord your labor is not in vain" (15:58). If *eikē* in v. 2 is correctly translated as "in vain," then the final verse of this chapter contains an *inclusio* (*kenos* = in vain, empty) that frames the entire discussion. (See [Translating *eikē*] above.) It also echoes in reverse Paul's earlier statement in v. 14 that his preaching and their faith were "in vain" (*kenon*) if Christ had not been resurrected. Believing in the resurrection of the dead is not in vain, and laboring in the work of the Lord who raises the dead is not futile. The exhortation to "be steadfast, immovable" also resonates with the beginning of Paul's argument where he referred to their "standing" and "holding fast" to the gospel he had preached to them (v. 2). His call to be "always abounding in the work of the Lord" is a reminder that "holding fast" is an ongoing enterprise. With this concluding exhortation, then, Paul's long argument about future resurrection returns the focus of his audience to the present. It further reminds us that Paul has written so much about the resurrection here not merely because eschatology was the "center" of his theology, but *because* some of the Corinthian Christians were not taking *this present life* seriously enough. I repeat here the words with which I closed the Introduction: "The hope provided by Paul's eschatological vision, therefore, could not be divorced from the ethical consequences such a vision impressed (and impresses) upon the church."

CONNECTIONS

The Message of First Importance, 15:3

The basis of Paul's argument in 1 Corinthians 15 is his conviction that Jesus was raised from the dead. He passed on the traditional affirmation of Jesus' resurrection as a "message of first importance."

According to this tradition, Jesus did not stay dead. For many people, this affirmation too closely resembles the stuff of horror movies. Like a vampire, ghost, or zombie, Jesus came back from the dead. And much as is the case with movie monsters, when Jesus came back, he was different. He was transformed into a different kind of creature. Unlike those movie monsters, however, the transformed Jesus did not come back to wreak havoc or to terrify people. Jesus came back as part of God's effort to save persons. In fact, according to Paul, his resurrection is an essential part of God's redemption of the whole creation. His resurrection gives the basis for hope in our own transformation into new creatures. His resurrection gives us hope for our own resurrection.

The gospel affirms that, unlike the fictional monsters of movies, the resurrection of Jesus was a historical event. For some persons, both inside and outside the church, accepting the historical reality of Jesus' resurrection is as difficult as believing in vampires, ghosts, and zombies. According to Acts 17:32, when Paul preached about the resurrection of the dead in Athens, some of the listeners mocked him. Some of the believers in Corinth apparently also had doubts about the resurrection. They do not appear to have doubted, however, that Jesus had been raised from the dead. What some of them seem to have found incredible was that Jesus' *body* had been raised. They could accept that Jesus' spirit (or soul) had survived death and that theirs would, too (somewhat like ghosts). The idea that bodies of flesh could be raised, though, sounded too much like tales of vampires and zombies.

Resurrection of the Dead

Paul Chenavard (1807–1895). *Resurrection of the Dead.* 1845. Eglise Parochiale, Bohal, France. (Credit: Erich Lessing/Art Resource, NY)

In response to their doubts, Paul penned his long argument in 1 Corinthians 15 that affirmed the reality and importance of bodily resurrection. He began with what he considered most important: the church's traditional testimony to the risen Jesus. For

Paul that testimony plus his own experience provided the solid basis for believing in our own resurrection. In his case, it was experience that led to belief, not vice versa. That same tradition does not hold the same irrefutable claim to legitimacy for some persons that it did for Paul. Perhaps, however, those same persons may be able to supplement the tradition with their own experience of the risen Lord. The church continues to proclaim the tradition of first importance, trusting that experience may lead to its affirmation.

Believing in the Resurrection, 15:12

Christopher Hitchens recently published a book titled *God Is Not Great.* In the book he does not really attack God, mainly because he does not believe in God. Instead, he attacks religion, which he thinks poisons all of life and is a great threat to meaningful existence and true ethical living. For him, the question of God is a pointless one. We would do well to shelve all our questions about God and all of the insane attempts to answer those questions in the archives of the oldest libraries. That, of course, is not likely to happen—for most people.

In a real sense, questions about the resurrection are questions about God, not questions about us. We may wonder about life after death: Is it real? What will it be like? When does it happen? Fundamentally, though, we are asking: What is God up to? If we believe in God and we believe that God is good, then we may despair of the insane suffering and inconsolable sorrow that fill this life. How could a good God let this happen? The despair or disillusionment it sometimes brings may even lead us to doubt that God exists. If we hold on to our belief in God and God's goodness, then the conviction that this life is not all there is allows us to trust that God will set things right. [This Life Only?]

This Life Only?

Therefore Christ is not to be hoped in for this life only, in which the bad can do more than the good, in which those who are more evil are happier, and those who lead a more criminal life live more prosperously.

Maximus of Turin, *Sermons* 96.1, in Gerald Bray, ed., *1–2 Corinthians* (vol. 7 of ACCS NT; ed. Thomas C. Oden; Downers Grove IL: InterVarsity Press, 1999) 156.

That appears to be what happened to those Jews who first began to affirm the idea of resurrection. They were not simply looking for some promise of vindication for themselves after death. They were struggling to find some way to hold on to their convictions about God. If God's righteousness does not, in fact, prevail in this life, then what does that say about God? If God is really God, then righteousness must be the final word sometime, somewhere. In a sense, the idea of resurrection arose not so much to give us another chance at life as to give us a way of expressing confidence in God and giving God another chance.

Many people, such as Hitchens, hold that people believe in God because they want to believe in life after death. I think it is the other way around. I think we believe in life after death because we believe in God and we believe that God is good.

Victory over Death?, 15:55

In Margaret Edson's play *W;t*, Vivian Bearing, a professor of seventeenth-century literature, is in the hospital dying of ovarian cancer. Her career has been one marked by careful, astute scholarship on the Holy Sonnets of John Donne. While in her last days of treatment, she fantasizes about the encounter with one of her professors (E.M.) that determined the direction of her career. The professor was critical of a paper she had written on Donne, claiming that it was flawed because she used an inferior edition of his work.

Margaret Edson

(Credit: Dave Smiley)

> E.M.: The sonnet begins with a valiant struggle with death, calling on the forces of intellect and drama to vanquish the enemy. But it is ultimately about overcoming the seemingly inseparable barriers separating life, death, and eternal life.
>
> In the edition you chose, this profoundly simple meaning is sacrificed to hysterical punctuation:
>
> And Death—*capital* D—shall be no more—*semicolon*!
> Death—*capital* D—*comma*—thou shalt die—*exclamation point*!
>
> If you go for this sort of thing, I suggest you take Shakespeare. Gardner's edition of the Holy Sonnets returns to the Westmoreland manuscript sourcc of 1610—not for sentimental reasons, I assure you, but because Helen Gardner is a *scholar*. It reads:
>
> And death shall be no more, *comma*, Death thou shalt die.
>
> (*As she recites this line, she makes a little gesture at the comma.*)
>
> Nothing but a breath—a comma—separates life from life everlasting. It is very simple really. With the original punctuation restored, death is no longer something to act out on a stage, with exclamation points. It's a comma, a pause.
>
> This way, the *uncompromising* way, one learns something from this poem, wouldn't you say? Life, death. Soul, God. Past, present. Not insuperable barriers, not semicolons, just a comma.[58]

Later, when Vivian knows that her death is imminent, she rises to give her final recitation to the audience.

> These are my last coherent lines. I'll have to leave the action to the professionals.
>
> It came so quickly, after taking so long. Not even time for a proper conclusion.
>
> (*Vivian concentrates with all her might, and she attempts a grand summation, as if trying to conjure her own ending.*)
>
> And Death—*capital* D—shall be no more—semicolon.
> Death—*capital* D—thou shalt die—*ex-cla-mation point*!
>
> (*She looks down at herself, looks out at the audience, and sees that the line doesn't work. She shakes her head and exhales with resignation.*)
>
> I'm sorry.[59]

What does not work about the line is that even though Vivian has spent her career engaging Donne's baffling poetic genius and wit as if it were a game between the two of them, in the end she wants something more than what a life of intellectual combat can give her. The senselessness of her death cannot overcome her longing for meaning. Though she has prided herself on her own wit and skepticism, she wants death to be followed by a *comma*, with something after the pause.

Clarence Jordan

Clarence Jordan putting faith to work.
(Credit: Koinonia Farm)

Clarence Jordan was a New Testament scholar and translator whose "Cotton Patch" version of the Gospels inspired a musical by the same name. He is better remembered, though, as a prophetic voice and activist servant on behalf of civil rights. His vision of racial unity led him to establish an integrated Christian community near Americus, Georgia, called Koinonia Farm. It also earned him the wrath and hostility of many in the white community in South Georgia, including most Baptist churches there. When he died, he was buried at Koinonia in a plain cedar box. Millard Fuller, a resident of the farm and the founder of Habitat for Humanity, delivered the eulogy. After Jordan was buried, Fuller's two-year-old daughter spontaneously broke into a simple song.

Happy birthday to you.
Happy birthday to you.
Happy birthday, dear Clarence.
Happy birthday to you.

To see death as an occasion for victorious rejoicing may strike some of us as inappropriate or insensitive to the grief of the survivors. The sting of death is real, and any flippant remark to the effect that the deceased has "gone to a better place" overlooks the real pain that death inflicts upon us. The question for us is this: in the midst of our very real and appropriate grief, can the hope embedded in a child's simple song give us cause to trust that death does not have the final word? Paul held that those who die "in the Lord" have a reason to look forward to that coming day of new birth. If he was right, then on that day, it would be appropriate to sing with the child. "Happy birthday."

Resurrection and Our Present Work, 15:58

Many of the hymns sung in the church where I grew up were about heaven. "There Is a Land that Is Fairer than Day," "When We All Get to Heaven," and "When the Morning Comes" were always called out on "Pick-a-Hymn" night. They are great hymns. They do, however, reflect a longing for the next life that can sometimes become so obsessive that we do not give enough attention to the here and now. Paul did not share that obsession. No one can doubt that Paul looked forward to God's final triumph and the resurrection of the dead. No one who reads his letters, though, could ever accuse him of neglecting the importance of this life. In fact, in 1 Corinthians, most of what he wrote about concerned everyday matters. Only in 1 Corinthians 15 does he focus on the life to come. If we read the whole letter and look at this chapter in context, we will see that Paul talked about the resurrection *because* some of the Corinthian Christians were not taking this present life seriously enough. They believed that what they did with their earthly bodies was of no eternal consequence. Paul confronted that erroneous perspective by showing the connection between the earthly body and the heavenly one.

We should not be surprised, then, that Paul ends his great exploration of resurrection by calling his readers back to the present. "Therefore, my beloved, be steadfast, immovable, always excelling in the work of the Lord, because you know that in the Lord your labor is not in vain" (15:58). The hope of the resurrection is not an excuse to ignore the demands of this life. Rather, it is the inspiration we need to give this life the attention it requires. It tells us that we do not labor to be the people God wants us to be in vain. What we do now matters. It matters now. It matters for eternity.

Lectionary Connections

Several readings from 1 Corinthians 15 are included in the Revised Common Lectionary. Both Years B and C include 1 Corinthians 15:1-11 among the readings for Easter Sunday morning. In Year B, a text from Isaiah 25:6-9 or Acts 10:34-43 may be used. The standard Gospel lesson for Easter is John 20:1-18, but Mark 16:1-8 may be substituted. In Year C, the same Acts text or Isaiah 65:17-25 may be read with either the Johannine Easter account or Luke 24:1-12. The readings from the Old Testament look forward to God's coming vindication of God's people. The Acts text rehearses the death and resurrection of Jesus in the context of the Gentile mission.

Year C has selections from 1 Corinthians 15 for the fifth through eighth Sundays after Epiphany. On the fifth Sunday, 1 Corinthians 15:1-11 is joined with the vision of Isaiah in Isaiah 6:1-8 and the miraculous catch of fish in Luke 5:1-11. On the sixth Sunday, 1 Corinthians 15:12-20 is read with Jeremiah 17:5-10, which focuses on trusting the Lord, and Luke 6:17-26, which includes the first part of Jesus' Sermon on the Plain. The seventh Sunday has 1 Corinthians 15:35-38, 42-50 along with the story of Joseph's disclosure of his identity to his brothers in Genesis 45:3-11, 15 and the portion of the Sermon on the Plain in Luke 6:27-38 that deals with love for enemies and judging. Finally, on the eighth Sunday (if there is one), the readings are 1 Corinthians 15:51-58, Isaiah 55:10-13, and Luke 6:39-49, the last of which concludes the Lukan Sermon on the Plain. The Isaiah passage stresses that the word of God shall not fail to accomplish its purpose.

NOTES

1. Arthur Schopenhauer, "Psychological Observations," *Studies in Pessimism* (trans. Thomas Bailey Saunders; 1851).

2. Anthony C. Thiselton, *The First Epistle to the Corinthians: A Commentary on the Greek Text* (NIGTC; Grand Rapids: Eerdmans, 2000) 1186, challenges the usual translation and prefers, instead, "without coherent consideration."

3. Margaret M. Mitchell, *Paul and the Rhetoric of Reconciliation: An Exegetical Investigation of the Language and Composition of 1 Corinthians* (Louisville: Westminster John Knox, 1991) 283–90, sees it as a "sub-argument within the larger compositional whole." Ben Witherington III, *Conflict and Community in Corinth: A Socio-Rhetorical Commentary and 1 and 2 Corinthians* (Grand Rapids: Eerdmans, 1995) 292–92, agrees with Mitchell on the function, but not on the rhetorical structure, of this chapter.

4. Burton L. Mack, *Rhetoric and the New Testament* (GBS; Minneapolis: Fortress Press, 1990) 56, extends the narratio to include vv. 12-20 and identifies v. 20 as the thesis. Witherington, *Conflict and Community in Corinth*, 292, labels vv. 12-19 as the *propositio* with v. 20 as thesis. Both fail to see how 15:13-19 already begins the argument against the questioning of the resurrection.

5. Except for my identification of the double *propositio* and *peroratio*, the rhetorical scheme I suggest follows that of Anders Eriksson, *Traditions as Rhetorical Proof: Pauline Argumentation in 1 Cor* (*ConBNT* 29; Stockholm: Almqvist & Wiksell, 1998). See also Thiselton, *The First Epistle to the Corinthians*, 1177–78.

6. Mitchell, *Paul and the Rhetoric of Reconciliation*, 290–91, argues unpersuasively that v. 58 is the *epilogos* (*peroratio*) for the entire argument that began in 1:10. Witherington, *Conflict and Community in Corinth*, 292–92, and others disagree.

7. Albert Schweitzer, *The Mysticism of Paul the Apostle* (trans. William Montgomery; New York: The Seabury Press, 1931).

8. See the discussion of "participation" by Dale B. Martin, *The Corinthian Body* (New Haven: Yale University Press, 1995) 131–32.

9. For discussions of the complexity of v. 2, see Hans Conzelmann, *1 Corinthians: A Commentary* (Hermeneia; trans. James W. Leitch; Philadelphia: Fortress Press, 1975) 248 n4; Gordon D. Fee, *The First Epistle to the Corinthians* (NICNT; Grand Rapids: Eerdmans Publishing, 1987) 719–21; and Thiselton, *The First Epistle to the Corinthians*, 1185–86.

10. See Thiselton, *The First Epistle to the Corinthians*, 1185, and Fee, *The First Epistle to the Corinthians*, 720.

11. Still informative for the structure and meaning of this creedal statement is Reginald H. Fuller, *The Formation of the Resurrection Narratives* (New York: The Macmillan Company, 1971) 9–49.

12. See Peter Rhea Jones, "1 Cor 15:8: Paul the Last Apostle," *TynBul* 36 (1985): 5–34.

13. See the discussion of options by Thiselton, *The First Epistle to the Corinthians*, 1208–10.

14. See, in particular, Richard B. Hays, *First Corinthians* (IBC; Louisville: John Knox Press, 1997) 253, 259–60; Bruce W. Winter, *After Paul Left Corinth: The Influence of Secular Ethics and Social Change* (Grand Rapids MI: Eerdmans, 2001) 76–109; and Martin, *The Corinthian Body*, 106–107.

15. C. K. Barrett, *A Commentary on the First Epistle to the Corinthians* (HNTC; New York: Harper & Row, 1968) 109; Charles Talbert, *Reading Corinthians: A Literary and Theological Commentary on 1 and 2 Corinthians* (rev. ed.; Macon: Smyth & Helwys, 2002) 123–24; and foremost, Anthony C. Thiselton, "Realized Eschatology at Corinth," *NTS* 24 (1978): 510–26. In his later commentary, Thiselton has reaffirmed his earlier view regarding an "overly realized eschatology" on the part of the Corinthians, but he

has also acknowledged that this was not the sole contributor to the host of problems in the Corinthian church (40).

16. Witherington, *Conflict and Community in Corinth*, 295–305.

17. Ibid., 297.

18. Ibid., 298.

19. Neil Elliott, "The Anti-imperial Message of the Cross," in *Paul and Empire: Religion and Power in Roman Imperial Society* (ed. Richard A. Horsley; Harrisburg PA: Trinity Press, 1997) 172–74.

20. Witherington, *Conflict and Community in Corinth*, 298, seems to suggest that Roman realized eschatology is Paul's only target here and that his objective is to lead certain higher-status Corinthian believers to "disengage from previous commitments to imperial eschatology" (305). The view that Paul's imagery can only be referring to supernatural powers *or* to earthly powers is argued by Wesley A. Carr, *Angels and Principalities: The Background, Meaning and Development of the Pauline Phrase "hai archai kai hai exousia"* (SNTSMS 42; Cambridge: Cambridge University Press, 1981).

21. Thiselton, *The First Epistle to the Corinthians*, 1232.

22. See Luke Timothy Johnson, *Religious Experience in Earliest Christianity* (Minneapolis: Fortress Press, 1998) esp. 6–10.

23. Thiselton, *The First Epistle to the Corinthians*, 1239.

24. William O. Walker Jr., "1 Corinthians 15:29-34 as a Non-Pauline Interpolation," *CBQ* 69 (2007): 84–103, argues that this entire section interrupts the flow of Paul's argument, contains vocabulary and content uncharacteristic of Paul, can be isolated as a self-contained unit, and was probably added in the early second century by a Marcionite or proto-Marcionite advocate of baptism on behalf of the dead. I disagree with his contention that the unit does not contribute to Paul's argument here.

25. Hays, *First Corinthians*, 266.

26. Thiselton, *The First Epistle to the Corinthians*, 1241.

27. Significant discussions of the numerous interpretations offered for this verse include Mathias Rissi, *Die Taufe für die Toten* (ATANT 42; Zurich: Zwingli Verlag, 1962); Michael F. Hull, *Baptism on Account of the Dead* (1 Cor 15:29) (SBLAB 22; Atlanta: Society of Biblical Literature, 2005); Thiselton, *The First Epistle to the Corinthians*, 1242–49; and Fee, *The First Epistle to the Corinthians*, 765–66.

28. Richard E. DeMaris, "Corinthian Religion and Baptism for the Dead (1 Cor 15:29): Insights from Archaeology and Anthropology," *JBL* 114 (1995): 661–82. DeMaris has recently buttressed his argument that baptism on behalf of the dead was a "boundary-crossing" ritual marking the dead's entrance into the community of the dead in an insightful study of early Christian ritual. See his *The New Testament in Its Ritual World* (London and New York: Routledge, 2008) esp. 57–71.

29. DeMaris, "Corinthian Religion and Baptism for the Dead," 680, notes the apparent Protestant bias in arguments against viewing the Corinthian practice as vicarious baptism.

30. Hays, *First Corinthians*, 267.

31. Variations of this basic approach are argued by John D. Reaume, "Another Look at 1 Corinthians 15:29, 'Baptized for the Dead'," *BSac* 152 (1995): 457–75, and Joel R. White, "'Baptized on account of the Dead': The Meaning of 1 Corinthians 15:29 in Its Context," *JBL* 116 (1997): 487–99.

32. See esp. Maria Raeder, "Vikariatstaufe in 1 Cor 15:29," *ZNW* 46 (1955): 258–60, and Joiachim Jeremias, "Flesh and Blood Cannot Inherit the Kingdom of God," *NTS* 2 (1955–1956): 151–59.

33. Thiselton, *The First Epistle to the Corinthians*, 1249.

34. Hull, *Baptism on Account of the Dead (1 Cor 15:29)*, 230–35.

35. Chrysostom, *1 Cor. Hom.* 40:2; Winter, *After Paul Left Corinth*, 103–105, accepts this view but allows that vicarious baptism is a viable option.

36. Martin, *The Corinthian Body*, 107–108. Martin's textual and inscriptional evidence for this appears on p. 271 n9.

37. If Hull had given more weight to Martin's discussion of the body and of dead bodies, he may have been more inclined toward this position. It is not incompatible with his own view, except for his restriction of the practice of baptism to a small group within the church.

38. Thiselton, *The First Epistle to the Corinthians*, 1249.

39. Many commentators, including Thiselton (The First Epistle to the Corinthians, 1250–51), and Fee (The First Epistle to the Corinthians, 761) take the construction *tēn hymeteran kauchēsin* (lit., "your boasting") to refer to Paul's pride in the Corinthians, but that ignores the simple force of the possessive adjective *hymeteran*. Rudolf Bultmann, "καυχάομαι, καύχημα, καύχησις," *TDNT* 3:650 n43, is more true to the sense of the phrase when he suggests "by the renown which I have (won) in you."

40. See the discussion of options in Thiselton, *The First Epistle to the Corinthians*, 1251–52.

41. Abraham J. Malherbe, "The Beasts at Ephesus," *JBL* 87 (1968): 72–80. See also Winter, *After Paul Left Corinth*, 101–102.

42. See Winter, *After Paul Left Corinth*, 102.

43. Thiselton, *The First Epistle to the Corinthians*, 1254, and Winter, *After Paul Left Corinth*, 98–99.

44. Winter, *After Paul Left Corinth*, 98–106.

45. Richard A. Horsley, *1 Corinthians* (ANTC; Nashville: Abingdon Press, 1998) 208.

46. Martin, *The Corinthian Body*, 120–21.

47. I borrow the term "muscular corporeality" from Eduard Schweizer, "*sarx*," *TDNT* 7:125 n215.

48. See Martin's discussion, *The Corinthian Body*, 118–19.

49. I make this suggestion despite Thiselton's nearly persuasive argument that no problem exists in ascribing "glory" to earthly bodies (*The First Epistle to the Corinthians*, 1269–71).

50. Fee, *The First Epistle to the Corinthians*, 783, also identifies a chiastic pattern here.

51. Thiselton, *The First Epistle to the Corinthians*, 1271–72, correctly argues against the contrast between *phthora* and *aphtharsia* as primarily one of "duration," which the common modern translations "perishable" and "imperishable" imply. He also points out that the terms have a moral dimension as well as a physical one. His choice of "decay" and "decay's reversal" as appropriate translations, however, do not seem to me to be as inclusive of both dimensions as does the KJV's rendering of "corruption" and "incorruption." Fee, *The First Epistle to the Corinthians*, 784–85, correctly sees that "in a

perishable state" would describe the body as Paul's Corinthian opponents saw it. Paul, however, would not have accepted their estimation of the body as merely perishable. It is subject to corruption, but by the power of God at work in the resurrection, it is also subject to transformation.

52. Hays, *First Corinthians*, 272. Italics added.

53. Thiselton, *The First Epistle to the Corinthians*, 1289, points out that the verb *phoreō*, unlike *pherō*, while also meaning "bear," is commonly used in reference to clothing. Thus, "worn" is preferred to "born."

54. Joiachim Jeremias, "Flesh and Blood Cannot Inherit the Kingdom of God," *NTS* 2 (1955–1956): 151–59.

55. Here I agree more with Thiselton, *The First Epistle to the Corinthians*, 1291, than with David E. Garland, *1 Corinthians* (BECNT; Grand Rapids: Baker Academic, 2003) 741–42.

56. Garland, *1 Corinthians*, 742–43.

57. The transposition of Death from the object of the active verb to the subject in the LXX remains unexplained, since the alteration completely reverses the sense of the original Hebrew. The replacement of "forever" (Hebrew *lanetsach*) with an aorist participle of *ischyō* (*ischysas*) may have been based on association with the cognate Aramaic verb that means "to overcome," as Thiselton, *The First Epistle to the Corinthians*, 1299, suggests. The LXX may, however, have used *ischyō* in the sense of "having become permanent" (LSJ 844, citing such a use in the Epicurean Epistles) as a substitute for the Hebrew "forever."

58. Margaret Edson, *W;t* (New York: Faber & Faber, 1999) 14–15.

59. Ibid., 72–73.

FINAL MATTERS

1 Corinthians 16:1-24

Marana tha

"Our Lord, come!"

Having addressed the major issues confronting the Corinthian congregation, Paul begins to bring his letter to a close. Some of the elements of this closing simply reflect epistolary convention in that Paul follows the typical pattern for ending a letter. Two matters that Paul addresses briefly in this final chapter, however, may tie directly to the emphasis he has placed on selfless service to others throughout the letter. These are his instructions about the collection (16:1-4) and his commendation of Stephanas and others like him (16:15-18). Sandwiched between these two matters are travel plans for Paul, Timothy, and Apollos (16:5-12). Paul typically mentions his travel plans near the close of the body of his letters, but in this case they hold special importance for the implementation of his instructions in the rest of the letter. As Paul has already indicated in 4:17-21, Timothy's anticipated arrival and reception in Corinth will determine the tone of Paul's subsequent visit. The brief mention of Apollos's delayed return to Corinth may also reflect uncertainty about his continued role among the Corinthians in light of the propensity of some of them to gravitate toward teachers of his reputed eloquence. [A Thematic Outline of 1 Corinthians 16]

A Thematic Outline of 1 Corinthians 16

I. Preparations for the Collection (16:1-4)
II. Travel Plans for Paul and Associates (16:5-12)
   A. Paul (16:5-8)
   B. Timothy (16:9-11)
   C. Apollos (16:12)
III. Final Instructions for the Corinthians (16:13-18)
   A. Exhortations (16:13-14)
   B. Commendations (16:15-18)
IV. The Closing of the Letter (16:19-24)
   A. Greetings (16:19-20)
   B. Autograph (16:21-24)

COMMENTARY

Preparations for the Collection, 16:1-4

The importance of the collection for the "saints" for Paul is apparent from the references he makes to it in his letters. In Galatians 2:6-10,

Paul stated that when he had visited the church in Jerusalem and met with the "pillars" of the church, they affirmed his ministry to the Gentiles and placed no additional stipulations on him except that he remember the poor. Paul added that he was more than glad to do so. In Romans 15:22-29, Paul informed the Roman believers that he had to deliver the collection to Jerusalem before coming to visit them. He specifically named the churches of the provinces of Macedonia and Achaia as contributors to the collection. He pointed out that it was proper for the Gentile churches to contribute material blessings to the poor Jewish believers because of the Gentiles' debt to them in spiritual blessings. He also added that the Gentile congregations were pleased to join in this effort. In 2 Corinthians 8–9, which may or may not have originally been part of the letter we call 2 Corinthians, he dealt extensively with the Corinthians' contributions to this collection. The attention Paul gave to the matter in both chapter 8 and chapter 9 indicates that some problems had apparently developed in this regard after the writing of 1 Corinthians. Paul's assessment of the importance of this collection is also apparent in the different terms he used to describe it. [Paul's Terms for the Collection]

Paul's Terms for the Collection

1 Cor 16:1, 2	"contribution" (*logeia*)
1 Cor 16:3	"gift" (*charin*)
Rom 15:25	"serving" (*diakonōn*)
Rom 15:26	"sharing" (*koinōnia*)
Rom 15:28	"fruit" (*karpos*)
Rom 15:31	"service" (*diakonia*)
2 Cor 8:4	"service" (*diakonia*)
2 Cor 8:6, 7, 19	"this gift" (*charin tautēn*)
2 Cor 8:20	"this generosity" (*adrotēs tautē*)
2 Cor 9:1, 13	"service" (*diakonia*)
2 Cor 9:11	"this offering" (*leitourgia tautē*)
2 Cor 9:13	"sharing" (*koinōnia*)

But why was this collection so important to Paul? Four possible reasons may be surmised. The first is simply that a tangible need existed and Paul felt an obligation and desire to respond to that need. The Jerusalem believers were predominately poor, as were most residents of Palestine. The perpetual poverty of a region systematically fleeced by the Roman administration, however, was aggravated by the tension between the Jewish followers of Jesus and other Jews, a tension that deprived those followers of any support available from the synagogues. Secondly, Paul wanted the Gentile believers to appreciate their inclusion within God's chosen people, Israel. As wild olive branches grafted into the tree late in God's history with Israel, they should recognize their indebtedness to the trunk. They were privileged to be a part of Israel and should express their gratitude through their giving. Thirdly, Paul's desire was that Jewish believers would accept the validity and equal standing of their Gentile sisters and brothers. To accept a "benevolence" from another party in Roman culture implied an acceptance of that party's equal or superior status. A subordinate party might render a "service," but only an equal or superior could bestow a "gift." Paul's language describing the collections flows back and forth between "gift" and "service." For the Gentiles, he stressed that their contributions were a "service" in recognition of the priority of their Jewish predecessors. For the Jews, he hoped that the contributions would be accepted as a "gift" from persons who were their equals in standing before God. A final possible reason the collection was so dear to Paul is that he may have viewed his work in taking the offerings of the Gentiles to Jerusalem as a type of fulfillment of Old Testament prophecies about the Gentiles coming to Jerusalem in the last days bearing gifts (Isa 2:2-3; 45:14; 60:5-17; 61:6, 18-21; Mic 4:1-2, 13). If so, then he may have understood the collection to be an event signaling the end.

Paul turns to the topic of the collection in v. 1 with the same phrase ("and concerning" = *peri de*) that he has used throughout the letter to indicate a new subject. He points out that his instructions are in line with those given to the churches in Galatia. His more detailed instructions in 2 Corinthians 8–9 show that Paul informed the churches in different provinces what the other churches were doing. His instructions here appear to be quite simple. On the first day of the week, the day that they assemble in remembrance of the day of Christ's resurrection, in the context of worship, they are to collect and store the contributions. Each person is to give according to individual means. The regular collection of smaller offerings will make it unnecessary to request a larger, more difficult contribution when Paul arrives. Upon his arrival, he will write letters of recommendation for the persons the Corinthians select to transport the collection. If it appears advisable, perhaps because of the size of the collection but more probably because of unanticipated circumstances, Paul will lead the transport party himself.

Travel Plans for Paul and Associates, 16:5-12

As he usually does near the end of his letters, Paul discusses his travel plans. The discussion of his travels serves to reinforce the letter. He will come to see them again. Whether he comes with open arms to embrace them for following his instructions or with a rod to discipline them (4:17-21) depends on them. One thing they can count on is that he will return to Corinth.

16:5-8. Paul's plans involve a tour through the northern province of Macedonia. After that, he hopes to spend a good amount of time in Achaia, if the Lord permits. The qualification of his plans

Macedonia, Achaia, and Asia

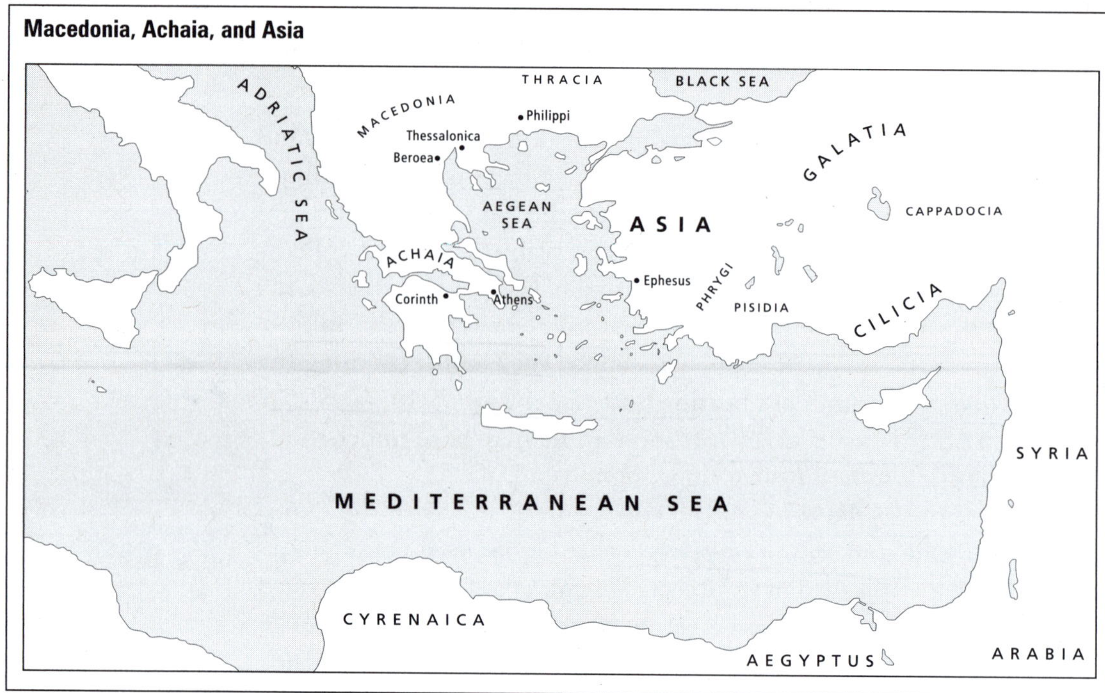

by "if the Lord permits" reflects more than the oriental custom of piously adding "if God wills it" at the end of one's expression of intentions for the future. For Paul, his itinerary is subject to the intervention of the Lord's guidance; everything is contingent upon that. He may only pass through Macedonia, but he wants to linger with the Corinthians. Expressing his intention of staying a longer period with them reveals his hope that their relationship will be such that a long stay would be desirable by both parties.

Before any traveling will occur, however, he must attend to matters in Ephesus. He states that a door has been opened for him, one that is wide and effective. His preaching there has apparently found a good hearing. The door of opportunity also opens to the challenge of opposition. Paul acknowledges that by candidly stating that there are also many adversaries. Paul's awareness of resistance to his ministry in Ephesus apparently was well founded, if the first part of 2 Corinthians is any clue to what happened to him after writing 1 Corinthians. He would write to the Corinthians about his hardships in Asia later in that letter and confess that he was almost driven to despair (2 Cor 1:8-9). His stance in the face of looming danger, however, was to focus on the opportunity. That work would keep him there, he indicated, until the time of Pentecost and the end of the spring rains, after which travel by land and sea would be much easier.

16:9-11. Paul's visit to Corinth will be preceded by Timothy's arrival, as Paul has already indicated in 4:17. Timothy's stated purpose for traveling to Corinth in that verse is "to remind you of my ways in Christ." Paul appears to be more tentative about Timothy's travel plans in 16:10 ("If Timothy comes"), but the conditional tone of his language probably reflects once more the apostle's awareness that plans are subject to being changed ("if the Lord permits").

Ephesus

Facing northwest down Curetes Street toward the Library of Celsus. (Credit: Scott Nash)

When Timothy arrives, the church is to "see to it" (*blepete*) that he is "free of fear" (*aphobōs*) toward them. Some interpreters prefer to read this: "Beware that he is *fearless* toward you."[1] The idea would thus be that they should know that Timothy comes with the same authority and determination to reprimand them that Paul would exhibit should he be the one coming. For this reading to be possible, however, we should expect Paul to have used *hoti* ("because") after *blepete* rather than *hina* ("so that"). *Hina* indicates that the purpose of *blepete* is so that Timothy will not be afraid. But why should Timothy be afraid? Most likely, it is because of the anticipated opposition to Paul's instructions in 1 Corinthians. As Paul's representative sent to guide the Corinthians in "Paul's ways," he will be subjected to the venting of their hostility toward Paul. Paul wishes to avoid this, and so he reminds them that what Timothy is about is "the Lord's work," as is Paul. For this reason, not because he is Paul's emissary but the Lord's, no one should "despise" him. To "despise" is not "to express hatred toward" but rather "to dismiss as of no importance." Some of the Corinthians have already shown that they are quite capable of heaping scorn on those they consider to be less important than they status-wise. Timothy comes as the Lord's representative, and they should see to it that by the time he leaves, he departs in peace and with their full support. Paul does not want Timothy's stay in Corinth to be prolonged by bickering and resistance. He wants Timothy to return to him in Ephesus on schedule with the other brothers and sisters who will be coming from Corinth. There is no point in speculating on the identify of the other persons who were to travel with Timothy.

16:12. The person who clearly will not be traveling to Corinth in the immediate future is Apollos. [Didymus the Blind] Because Paul uses the phrase *peri de* in turning to discuss Apollos's travel plans, many

Didymus the Blind

Apollos was the bishop of Corinth, but he had left the church on account of its divisions and gone to be with Paul. He would not go back with the letter, because he did not want to return until the divisions were healed.

Pauline Commentary from the Greek Church 15:12-13, in Gerald Bray, ed., *1–2 Corinthians* (vol. 7 of ACCS NT; ed. Thomas C. Oden; Downers Grove IL: InterVarsity Press, 1999) 188.

interpreters think that the Corinthians had requested that he return to them. It is highly conceivable that those persons in the church there who had a preference for sophist-like teaching may have considered Apollos to be a superior teacher to Paul and would have requested that he, and not Paul or his surrogates, be the one to come to Corinth and guide them through their problems. If so, then the return of Apollos would only have aggravated the situation.

Paul indicates that he has strongly encouraged "the brother" Apollos to return with other "brothers" to Corinth but that there was not a "will" that he should return now. If it was Apollos's "will" that he should not return, then that may indicate that he realized his presence in Corinth would only make matters worse. If it was the "will" of Paul, Apollos, and the "brothers" combined, then it reflects a collective decision. Some interpreters think that the "will" in question is God's will. Ker argues that for Paul to say that God had "willed" that Apollos not go, while Paul was urging him to go, would have unwisely given the impression that Paul was not in line with God on this matter.[2] He thinks it was Apollos who was not willing to go. He also suggests that part of Apollos's unwillingness to return to Corinth may have been that he did want to be identified as a member of a Pauline embassy, but he also grants that Apollos probably did not want to make the situation in Corinth worse than it was. In light of Paul's indication that his own travel plans were subject to what "the Lord permits," however, it does not seem so far-fetched that Paul meant that the Lord was not yet ready for Apollos to return. Paul's assurance that Apollos would visit Corinth "whenever he has opportunity" was probably not too reassuring to those Corinthians who were hankering for him to return.

Final Instructions to the Corinthians, 16:13-18

16:13-14. Paul moves toward the close of this letter as he often does by interjecting a string of brief exhortations. While the substance of the exhortations could fit almost any context, Paul is not throwing out these particular instructions at random. They succinctly relate to matters he has addressed before. "Be on guard!" may have an eschatological tone to it, as several commentators have suggested. That is, it may relate to being vigilant until the coming of the Lord. In this context, though, it seems more to be a warning to watch out for imminent danger. The Corinthians must be alert to the consequences of the aberrant behavior that has been taking place in the church. This understanding of the first exhortation ties it more directly to the other three. "Watching out" means standing firm in the faith. While "faith" in Paul's letters generally refers to "faithfulness" or "trusting" in the Lord, here it seems to refer more to the idea of holding fast to "the faith" in the sense of "maintaining the traditions" Paul has delivered to them (11:2). Paul has appealed to those traditions in combating several problems in this letter. He urges them to remain true to his teaching whatever resistance may arise in the church. The last two exhortations reinforce this: "Be courageous!" "Be strong!" The same aggressive resistance to Paul's instructions that Timothy might encounter upon his arrival may already be pressing upon those whose orientation is to follow Paul's guidance. They are to stand up against any pressure without fear. Finally, reminding them of the surpassing way of Christ that has served as the undertone throughout the letter, Paul urges them to let everything be done in love.

16:15-18. The probability that the exhortations of vv. 13-14 were not simply generally applicable but rather specifically targeted toward the Corinthian congregation may be strengthened by Paul's last instruction before closing the letter. He gives a commendation of the household (*oikia*) of Stephanas for doing exactly what the exhortation to do everything in love entails. Paul appeals to what the Corinthians already know about this household: "they are the first-portion of Achaia and they devoted themselves to the service of the saints." [First Fruits of Achaia] Most commentators hold that *oikos* and *oikia* are used interchangeably by Paul. The reference to the *oikia* of Stephanas should, therefore, be viewed as synonymous with the mention of the *oikos* of Aquila and Prisca in v. 19. Winter, however, presents evidence to show that when both words are used in the same writing, a distinction between the two is intended.[3] The *oikos* of Aquila and Prisca is their home, in which a church meets. The *oikia* of Stephanas, however, is his family. This family was the first converted to the faith in Corinth.

First Fruits of Achaia

Paul calls these people the "first fruits" of Achaia, either because they were the first to be converted or because their piety was greater than that of others or because they refused to be ordained on account of their great humility and instead dedicated themselves to the service of others.

Didymus the Blind, *Pauline Commentary from the Greek Church* 15:12-13, in Gerald Bray, ed., *1–2 Corinthians* (vol. 7 of ACCS NT; ed. Thomas C. Oden; Downers Grove IL: InterVarsity Press, 1999) 188.

In accordance with the patron-client network of relationships that existed in the Roman world, one might suppose that the family of Stephanas would have exercised a position of prominence among the other families of the church in Corinth. Paul affirms that they do, but that prominence is not based on the fact that they were the first to be baptized or because their extended household includes more clients than that of other patron families in the church. Their prominence is based on the fact that they have devoted themselves to the service of the saints. They have followed the way of love in putting the resources of their home at the disposal of those in need. Patrons typically expected services to be rendered to them by their many clients. The Stephanas family has done exactly the opposite and has rendered services to the many.

Paul urges the church to be subject to such people. By advocating that they "be subject" (*hypotassēsthe*) to them, he does not mean that they should transfer their allegiance from their current patrons and become clients of Stephanas. This is evident from the fact that Paul urges similar subjection to everyone "working together" (*synergounti*) and "doing hard labor" (*kopiōnti*) in the same way. The subjection Paul has in mind is following the model of such persons and working stridently with them in service to the whole church.

Apparently Stephanas has visited Paul in Ephesus, as have Fortunatus and Achaicus. The names of these latter two, being somewhat like "nicknames," may indicate that they are freedmen, perhaps descended from that first generation of freedpersons brought from Rome in the first century BC to populate the new Roman colony of Corinth. Whether they all visited Paul at the same time is not clear. Many interpreters think they may have carried the letter from the Corinthians that Paul responds to throughout much of the second half of 1 Corinthians. In any case, Paul states that he has rejoiced at their coming because they "refreshed" his spirit (v. 18). In Philemon 20, Paul uses the same term in asking for some "benefit" from Philemon in regard to the slave Onesimus: "Refresh my heart (lit., "bowels")." Refreshing in both instances means more than "reviving" one's mood. It refers to rendering a tangible service. Paul reminds the Corinthians that these three men have also "refreshed" them. Whether Fortunatus and Achaicus were of similar affluence as Stephanas cannot be determined, but they appear to have been of the same disposition. They, too, have followed the way of love in striving to be of benefit to others. Such persons should be "recognized." The contrast between these who should be recognized and those who should not be recognized because of their disregard of Paul's instructions regarding the edifying and orderly use of gifts in 14:38 is striking. Those who should be recognized are those who do not assert themselves but understand the message of the cross and implement that message in their sacrificial care for others.

The Closing of the Letter, 16:19-24

The closing of Paul's long letter includes two basic parts: an exchange of greetings and a final, brief section written by Paul himself.

16:19-20. Paul first sends greetings from all the churches of the province of Asia. Then he extends a special, hearty greeting from Aquila and Prisca and the church that meets in their home. According to Acts 18, Paul met this couple in Corinth. They had in common with Paul three main things: They were Jews, they were fellow believers, and they worked at the same trade. According to Acts, Paul stayed with them while in Corinth. Acts also describes Aquila and Prisca (Priscilla) as hailing from Pontus, a province in Asia Minor. They had come to Corinth by way of Italy when Claudius had expelled the Jews from Rome (AD 49). They had left Corinth when Paul did and had settled down, for the time being, in Ephesus. They were apparently successful in their trade since they had a home large enough in Ephesus for a church to meet there. Along with their greeting, Paul extends that of all the "brothers and sisters." Since he has already sent greetings from all the churches, this last group must refer to a circle of coworkers, which included the "brothers and sisters" Paul mentioned earlier in vv. 11-12. The importance of these greetings is reflected in Paul's exhortation that the Corinthians greet one another with a holy kiss. [Holy Kiss] The Corinthians should remind themselves through their regular embracing of one another that they are part of an important family that transcends geography and, of special importance for them, social class.

Holy Kiss

The holy kiss is the sign of peace, doing away with discord.

Ambrosiaster, *Commentary on Paul's Epistles* 1.12:265, in Gerald Bray, ed., *1–2 Corinthians* (vol. 7 of ACCS NT; ed. Thomas C. Oden; Downers Grove IL: InterVarsity Press, 1999) 190.

16:21-24. Paul then takes up the pen to add his own greeting. Some of his letters include a postscript of sorts in which Paul writes an additional note after the scribe has finished the main letter. In this instance, Paul seems to be concluding the letter proper himself. This greeting is followed by a curse, a grace wish, and a final word of assurance. In the first and last of these components, love is emphasized.

Paul's curse (v. 22) is often taken as being addressed toward non-believers. In light of everything he has written in this letter about love, it seems more appropriate to take it as a final warning to those believers in the church who are not showing love for God. In 8:3, Paul stated that anyone who loves God is known by God. This statement came in the context of an argument against those who thought their knowledge about God qualified them to engage in eating food offered to idols without repercussions. Paul argued that such behavior had potentially harmful effects on others and should, therefore, not be tolerated. The curse is on anyone who does not love God.

The Aramaic expression *marana tha* that follows this curse is typically read as distinct from the curse itself. It literally reads, "Our

Marana tha

ΑΩ The expression *marana tha* appears only in 1 Cor 16:22 in the NT and only in the *Didache* (10:6) in other early Christian writings. It is a Greek transliteration of an Aramaic expression and, thus, would appear to go back to the earliest days of the Jesus movement. Since the original early Greek texts typically had no spaces between words, it is unclear whether the expression should be divided *marana tha* or *maran atha*. The *mar* stems from the Aramaic word for "lord" or "master" and is, thus, equivalent to the Greek *kyrios*. The personal suffix *an* or *ana* means "our." If the division should be *maran atha*, then *atha* would mean either "is coming" or "has come." If, as most scholars hold, the division should be *marana tha*, then *tha* is an imperative: "Our Lord, come!" Rev 22:20 has an Greek imperative construction ("Come, Lord Jesus!") probably based on the Aramaic expression.

Max Wilcox, "Maranatha," *ABD* (ed. David Noel Freedman et al.; New York: Doubleday, 1992) 4:514.

Lord, come." Whether the tense of the verb *tha* is past, present, or future is debated. [*Marana tha*] Since this is the only occurrence of this expression in the New Testament, it is tenuous to extrapolate theories about its usage in the Pauline churches beyond its presence here following the curse. If the verb is read as future ("Our Lord will come" or "Our Lord is coming"), then it may be understood to be expressing hope. A future sense, however, may also (or rather) denote judgment, much as do Paul's other references to the Lord's coming in 1 Corinthians. If so, then the expression may, in fact, serve as the conclusion to Paul's curse. The warning that the Lord is coming to judge those who do not love may be Paul's final rebuke of those who insist on having their own way without regard for others.

Judgment is not the final word of this letter, however. Paul concludes with a wish for the grace of the Lord Jesus to be with them and an assurance that his own love will be with all those who are in Christ Jesus. At the end of this long, tortuous letter, in which Paul has confronted again and again an unloving congregation, the assurance that his love for them endures may be the final irony.

CONNECTIONS

Giving a Little

When Paul gave instructions to the Corinthians about the collection for the saints, he exhorted them to place something aside every week for this cause. That way, he explained, when he arrived they would not have to make large contributions. In one sense, Paul's advice was simply a good "fundraising" strategy. Giving a little each week would not seem like much of a sacrifice, and before they realized what had happened, a significant sum might accrue. Except for those persons who preferred to make a splash with large, one-time gifts, most of Paul's constituents would have probably found it much easier to contribute on the regular-payment plan. So his stewardship program simply made good fiscal sense.

On two other levels, however, his strategy may have something to say beyond financial stewardship. First, cultivating the habit of regular service is a good idea in matters other than money. If one practices a particular service on a regular basis, it is more likely to become a normal part of one's life than if one only performs the service sporadically. Even if the service one does on a sporadic basis is large and noticeable, it is less likely to become ingrained. One is less apt to become a good golfer by playing seventy-two holes twice a year than by playing nine every day. One is less likely to cultivate a spirit of compassion, caring, and benevolence by going on the annual church mission trip than one would by helping with the church's clothes closet or food pantry every week. Paul's strategy of regular service is a sound one if our goal is to develop people who are sensitive to need and prone to respond to need whenever it arises.

Second, there is much to be said for encouraging small acts of service over the large. Opportunities for grand and impressive service present themselves rarely. The need for smaller acts of compassion is constant. Francis de Sales likened the great virtues and small fidelities to sugar and salt.[4] Sugar has a more exquisite taste, but its use is less frequent than salt's. Like salt, the service of small things is everywhere and always present. Giving a little of ourselves constantly touches more lives than does holding back until we can make a "real contribution." It also reminds us that service in the name of Christ is not a valve that can be opened full blast only on certain occasions; it needs to "drip "all the time. [Fénelon]

Ancient Offering Box

Man carrying a box, possibly for offerings. Early Dynastic I–II; 2900–2600 BC. Mesopotamia. Arsenical copper. Harris Brisbane Dick Fund, 1955. (Credit: © The Metropolitan Museum of Art/Art Resource, NY)

The giving and collection of offerings has been a part of religious devotion since at least the 3rd millennium BC. After the invention of coinage (prob. 6th century BC), sanctuaries sometimes had boxes or other containers for the deposit of monetary offerings. The artifact located near the entrance to the temple of Asklepios is often identified as such a treasury box, but it is actually a type of millstone from a period after the temple's destruction. We can only speculate as to how the weekly contributions made by the church in Corinth were stored.

The Open Door

As he brought his letter to a close, Paul discussed his plans for travel in the future. He expressed his desire to pass through Macedonia and then spend some time with the church in Corinth. First, however, he needed to stay in Ephesus and take advantage of an "open door" (16:9) for effective work. In sharing his optimism about the opportunities that had developed in Ephesus, Paul also acknowledged that there were many adversaries. Earlier in the letter, he referred to "fighting the wild beasts at Ephesus" (15:32). In the context of that comment, he was probably not referring literally to facing wild beasts in the arena but to other kinds of struggles both internal and

Fénelon

It is not elevation of the spirit to feel contempt for small things. It is, on the contrary, because of too narrow points of view that we consider as little what has such far reaching consequences.

François Fénelon, *Christian Perfection* (Minneapolis: Bethany Fellowship, 1975) 34.

external. Little did Paul know at the time he made that metaphorical allusion to facing the wild beasts that his days in Ephesus would prove to be more turbulent than even he could imagine. From 2 Corinthians, we learn that his trials there after writing 1 Corinthians would almost send him to his grave. Paul knew some dangers existed, but he did not know the full extent of those threats when he expressed his desire to go through the open door.

We can only speculate about this, but given his track record and his determination, we can surmise that even if Paul had known the scope of what lay ahead, he would have still wanted to go through the door. Opposition, however threatening, did not deter Paul from seizing opportunity. One cannot help wondering what the church could accomplish today if that same attitude prevailed. Too often the threat of difficult days ahead causes a church to shrink from going through the open doors that present themselves. Retreat, rather than advance, seems to characterize our approach to challenge. "Circle the wagons and protect ourselves from the dangers that lie outside the fold" is often our strategy for dealing with opposition. We forget, it seems to me, that the church has never flourished with a strategy of retreat or entrenchment. It has only advanced when it was willing to go though the open door, despite the adversaries.

Wayfaring Friends

In her book *Christianity for the Rest of Us*, Diana Butler Bass has observed that Christianity is not a "map" religion. "Maps are about seeing from above, about perspective from a god's-eye view, about getting to a destination by avoiding the pain." In contrast, she points out, "Christianity is a religion of the streets, of signposts on the ground, of people walking along the way." She goes on to describe Christianity as "kind of vast spiritual and historical migration, a mobile city of pilgrims, all on their way to a country where there are no maps."[5]

Bass's description of Christianity fits what we see in 1 Corinthians 16 where Paul sends greetings to and from a people on the move. Paul himself, of course, was in many ways the epitome of a pilgrim. He appears in perpetual motion, moving from one center of mission to another. He traveled through much of his known world on the ground, often on foot, establishing communities of faith in the process. Perhaps our image of Paul as a *uniquely* mobile person is derived from the fact that we know about his travels because of the letters left behind. When the author of Acts penned an account of Paul's activities some year's after the apostle's death, the foremost feature of his portrayal was that of Paul the traveling preacher.

What we do not know is how typical such mobility was for countless other early Christians. Because they have not left behind letters and because no one chronicled their many travels, we simply are not aware of the extent of their movement in the name of Christ. Here and there in Paul's letters, though, we get a glimpse of those other pilgrims whose journeys have not been as fully reported as his. Among those early travelers that we bump into in Paul's letters from time to time are Prisca and Aquila. At the close of 1 Corinthians we find them with Paul in Asia. At the end of his letter to the Romans, we find them apparently back again in Rome. When Paul met them in Corinth for the first time, they had recently arrived there from Rome, according to Acts. Acts also informs us that they were from Pontus in Asia Minor.

Something else that we learn about this couple from Acts and Paul is that they opened their home to strangers. They took in Paul when he arrived in Corinth. When Paul sends greetings from them back to Corinth, he adds that those greetings come also from the church in their house. Aquila and Prisca were on the move as much as Paul, it seems, but they always made a place in their home for strangers. They were practitioners of that ancient Christian custom of hospitality. [Hospitality] Hospitality is one of those "signposts on the ground," as Bass puts it, that points Christians in the right direction. Prisca and Aquila were gleaming beacons of hospitality, with the "vacancy" light always on at their place. Their willingness to put their home at the disposal of fellow pilgrims played no small role in helping Christianity become transformed from a small cult into a worldwide "movement."

Hospitality

Hospitality draws from the ancient taproots of Christian faith, from the soil of the Middle East, where it is considered a primary virtue of community. Although it is a practice shared by Jews and Muslims, for Christians hospitality holds special significance: Christians welcome strangers as we ourselves have been welcomed into God through the love of Jesus Christ. Through hospitality, Christians imitate God's welcome. Therefore, hospitality is not a program, not a single hour of ministry in the life of a congregation. It stands at the heart of a Christian way of life, a living icon of wholeness in God.

Diana Butler Bass, *Christianity for the Rest of us: How the Neighborhood Church Is Transforming the Faith* (San Francisco: HarperSanFrancisco, 2006) 82.

The whole world now seems to be on the move. Transience and temporary residency have become more the order of the day than the exception. Increasingly, we are becoming strangers in a strange land. As a result, the old practice of Christian hospitality is becoming almost as important as it was in those earliest days of the faith. The turmoil of displacement is a problem for the modern world, and for the church. For the church, however, the mobility of the world presents an opportunity to recapture something that was key to Christianity in the beginning. We can once again become a people whose identity and purpose do not depend on being settled in any one place. We can become a people who are constantly moving toward that destination for which there is no map, only a guide. And on the way, we can open our temporary homes to our fellow travelers, whether they are following our guide or not. Bass reminds us once again of who we are: "Christian people, themselves wayfarers, welcome strangers into the heart of God's transformative love."[6]

NOTES

1. David E. Garland, *1 Corinthians* (BECNT; Grand Rapids: Baker Academic, 2003) 759–60.

2. Donald P. Ker, "Paul and Apollos—Colleagues or Rivals?" *JSNT* 77 (2000): 95.

3. Bruce W. Winter, *After Paul Left Corinth: The Influence of Secular Ethics and Social Change* (Grand Rapids MI: Eerdmans, 2001) 206–11.

4. Richard J. Foster, *Celebration of Discipline: The Path to Spiritual Growth* (rev. and exp. ed.; San Francisco: Harper & Row, 1988) 135.

5. Diana Butler Bass, *Christianity for the Rest of us: How the Neighborhood Church Is Transforming the Faith* (San Francisco: HarperSanFrancisco, 2006) 74.

6. Ibid., 87.

BIBLIOGRAPHY

I. Selected Commentaries

Barrett, Charles K. *A Commentary on the First Epistle to the Corinthians.* 2d ed. Harper's New Testament Commentaries. London: A. & C. Black, 1971.

Bassler, Jouette M. "1 Corinthians." Pages 411–19 in *The Women's Bible Commentary.* Exp. ed. Edited by Carol A. Newsom and Sharon H. Ringe. Louisville: Westminster/John Knox, 1998.

Conzelmann, Hans. *1 Corinthians.* Translated by James W. Leitch. Hermeneia. Philadelphia: Fortress Press, 1975.

Fee, Gordon D. *The First Epistle to the Corinthians.* New International Commentary on the New Testament. Grand Rapids: Eerdmans, 1987.

Garland, David E. *1 Corinthians.* Baker Exegetical Commentary on the New Testament. Grand Rapids: Baker Academic, 2003.

Hays, Richard B. *First Corinthians.* Interpretation: A Bible Commentary for Teaching and Preaching. Louisville: John Knox Press, 1997.

Horsley, Richard A. *1 Corinthians.* Abingdon New Testament Commentaries. Nashville: Abingdon Press, 1998.

Minor, Mitzi. *2 Corinthians.* Smyth & Helwys Bible Commentaries. Macon GA: Smyth & Helwys, 2009.

Moffatt, James. *The First Epistle of Paul to the Corinthians.* Moffatt New Testament Commentary 7. London: Hodder & Stoughton, 1938.

Orr, William F., and James Arthur Walther. *I Corinthians.* Anchor Bible 32. New York: Doubleday, 1976.

Robertson, Archibald, and Alfred Plummer, *First Epistle of St. Paul to the Corinthians.* 2d ed. International Critical Commentary. New York: Charles Scribner's Sons, 1914.

Sampley, J. Paul. "The First Letter to the Corinthians." Vol. 10 in *The New Interpreter's Bible.* Nashville: Abingdon Press, 2002.

Schrage, Wolfgang. *Die erste Brief an die Korinther* (EKKNT 7/1-4; 4 vols.; Zurich and Braunschweig: Benziger Verlag, and Neukirchen-Vluyn: Neukirchener Verlag, 1991–2001.

Soards, Marion L. *1 Corinthians.* New International Biblical Commentary: New Testament Series. Peabody MA: Hendrickson, 199.

Talbert, Charles H. *Reading Corinthians: A Literary and Theological Commentary on 1 and 2 Corinthians.* Rev. ed. Macon: Smyth & Helwys, 2002.

Thiselton, Anthony C. *The First Epistle to the Corinthians: A Commentary on the Greek Text.* New International Greek Testament Commentary. Grand Rapids: Eerdmans, 2000.

Witherington, Ben, III. *Conflict and Community in Corinth: A Socio-Rhetorical Commentary and 1 and 2 Corinthians.* Grand Rapids: Eerdmans, 1995.

II. Sources for Ancient Works

Aesop's Fables. A New Translation by Laura Gibbs. World Classics. Oxford: Oxford University Press, 2002.

Boring, M. Eugene, Klaus Berger, and Carsten Colpe, eds. *Hellenistic Commentary to the New Testament.* Nashville: Abingdon Press, 1995.

Bray, Gerald, ed. *1–2 Corinthians.* Vol. 7 of *Ancient Christian Commentary on Scripture: New Testament.* Edited by Thomas C. Oden. Downers Grove IL: InterVarsity Press, 1999.

Celsus. *De Medicina.* Vol. 3. Translated by W. G. Spencer. Loeb Classical Library. Cambridge MA: Harvard University Press, 1938.

Charlesworth, James H., ed. *The Old Testament Pseudepigrapha.* 2 vols. Garden City NY: Doubleday & Co., 1983, 1985.

Danby, Herbert. *The Mishnah.* Translated from the Hebrew with Introductory and Brief Explanatory Notes. London: Oxford University Press, 1933.

Dio Chrysostom. *Discourses.* Vol. 5. Translated by H. Lamar Crosby. Loeb Classical Library. Cambridge MA: Harvard University Press, 1951.

Dionysius of Halicarnassus. *Roman Antiquities.* Vol. 4. Translated by Earnest Cary. Loeb Classical Library. Cambridge MA: Harvard University Press, 1943.

Epictetus. *Discourses.* Vol. 2. Translated by W. A. Oldfather. Loeb Classical Library. Cambridge MA: Harvard College, 1928.

Hennecke, Edgar, and Wilhelm Schneemelcher, eds. *The New Testament Apocrypha.* English trans. by Robert McL. Wilson. 2 vols. Philadelphia: Westminster Press, 1963, 1964.

Josephus. *The Life. Against Apion.* Translated by H. St. J. Thackeray. Loeb Classical Library. Cambridge MA: Harvard University Press, 1926.

———. *Jewish War.* Vol. 3. Translated by H. St. J. Thackeray. Loeb Classical Library. Cambridge MA: Harvard University Press, 1927.

Juvenal. *Satires.* Translated by G. G. Ramsay. Loeb Classical Library. Cambridge MA: Harvard College, 1918.

Kovacs, Judith L., trans. and ed. *1 Corinthians: Interpreted by Early Christian Commentators.* In *The Church's Bible.* Edited by Robert Louis Wilken. Grand Rapids: Eerdmans, 2005.

Livy, *History of Rome.* Translated by William A. McDevitte. London: Bungay, 1850.

Menander. Vol. 3. Edited and translated by W. G. Arnott. Loeb Classical Library. Cambridge MA: Harvard College, 2000.

Neusner, Jacob. *Sifré to Numbers. An American Translation.* I. *1-58.* Atlanta: Scholars Press for Brown Judaic Studies, 1986.

Ovid. *Heroides, Amores.* Translated by Grant Showerman and revised by G. P. Goold. Loeb Classical Library. Cambridge MA: Harvard College, 1914.

———. *The Art of Love and Other Poems.* Translated by J. H. Mozley and revised by G. P. Goold. Loeb Classical Library. Cambridge MA: Harvard College, 1929.

Pausanias. *Guide to Greece. Volume 1: Central Greece.* Translated by Peter Levi. New York: Penguin Books, 1971.

Petronius. *Satyricon, Apocolocyntosis.* Revised by E. H. Warmington. Translated by Michael Heseltine and W. H. D. Rouse. Loeb Classical Library. Cambridge MA: Harvard College, 1913.

Plutarch's Morals. Translated from the Greek by Several Hands. Corrected and Revised by William W. Goodwin, with an Introduction by Ralph Waldo Emerson. 5 vols. Boston: Little, Brown, and Co., 1878.

Sallust. *The War with Catiline.* Translated by John C. Rolfe. Loeb Classical Library. Cambridge MA: Harvard University Press, 1921.

Strabo. *Geography.* Vol. 4. Translated by Horace Leonard Jones. Loeb Classical Library. Cambridge MA: Harvard College, 1927.

———. *Geography.* Vol. 8. Translated by H. L. Jones. Loeb Classical Library. Cambridge MA: Harvard University Press, 1927.

Suetonius. *Lives of the Caesars.* Vol. 2. Translated by J. C. Rolfe. Loeb Classical Library. Cambridge MA: Harvard College, 1914.

Tacitus. *The Histories and The Annals.* Translated by Clifford H. Moore and John Jackson. 5 vols. Loeb Classical Library. Cambridge MA: Harvard University Press, 1937.

The Apostolic Fathers: Revised Greek Texts with Introductions and English Translations. Edited and translated by J. B. Lightfoot and J. R. Harmer. Grand Rapids: Baker Book House, 1984.

The Ante-Nicene Fathers. Edited by Alexander Roberts and James Donaldson. 1885–1887. American Reprint of the Edinburgh Edition. Grand Rapids: Eerdmans, 1993.

The Works of Philo: New Updated Edition. Complete and Unabridged in One Volume. Translated by C. D. Yonge. Peabody MA: Hendrickson, 1993.

The Tosefta. Translated from the Hebrew. New York: Ktav Publishing House, 1977–1985.

III. Other Relevant Works

Amjad-Ali, Christine. "The Equality of Women: Form or Substance (1 Corinthians 11.2-16)." Pages 185–93 in *Voices from the Margin: Interpreting the Bible in the Third World.* New ed. Edited by R. S. Sugirtharajah. Maryknoll NY: Orbis Books, 1995.

Aune, David. *The New Testament in Its Literary Environment.* Library of Early Christianity 8. Philadelphia: Westminster Press, 1987.

Balch, David L. *Let Wives Be Submissive: The Domestic Code in 1 Peter.* Society of Biblical Literature Monograph Series 26. Chico CA: Scholars Press, 1981.

Barclay, John M. G. "Thessalonica and Corinth: Social Contrasts in Pauline Christianity." *Journal for the Study of the New Testament* 47 (1992): 49–74.

Barth, Karl. *The Resurrection of the Dead.* Eng, trans. London: Hodder & Stoughton, 1933.

Bartschy, Scott S. *MALLON CHRESAI: First Century Slavery and the Interpretation of 1 Cor. 7:21.* Society of Biblical Literature Dissertation Series 11. Missoula: Scholars Press, 1973.

Bassler, Jouette M. "Paul's Theology: Whence and Whither?" Pages 3–17 in *Pauline Theology, Vol. II: 1 & 2 Corinthians.* Edited by David M. Hay. Minneapolis: Fortress Press, 1993.

Beker, J. Christiaan. *Paul the Apostle: The Triumph of God in Life and Thought.* Philadelphia: Fortress, 1980.

Bernard, J. H. "The Connexion between the Fifth and Sixth Chapters of 1 Cor." *Expository Times* 7 (1907): 433–43.

Blue, Bradley. "The House Church at Corinth and the Lord's Supper: famine, Food Supply, and the *Present Distress*." *Criswell Theological Journal* 5 (1991): 221–39.

Bookidis, Nancy, et al. "Dining in the Sanctuary of Demeter and Kore at Corinth." *Hesperia* 68 (1999): 1–54.

———, and Ronald S. Stroud. *The Sanctuary of Demeter and Kore: Topography and Architecture.* Corinth XVIII.8. Princeton: American School of Classical Studies at Athens, 1997.

Boswell, John. *Christianity, Social Tolerance, and Homosexuality.* Chicago: University of Chicago Press, 1980.

Bowe, Barbara Ellen. *A Church in Crisis.* Harvard Dissertations in Religion 23. Minneapolis: Fortress Press, 1988.

Braxton, Brad Ronnell. *The Tyranny of Resolution: I Corinthians 7:17-24.* Society of Biblical Literature Dissertation Series 181. Atlanta: Society of Biblical Literature, 2000.

Broneer, Oscar. *The South Stoa and Its Roman Successors.* Corinth I.4. Princeton: American School of Classical Studies at Athens.

———. "The Apostle Paul and the Isthmian Games." *Biblical Archaeologist* 25 (1962): 1–31.

———. "Paul and the Pagan Cults at Isthmia." *Harvard Theological Review* 64 (1971): 169–87.

———. "The Isthmian Victory Crown." *American Journal of Archaeology* 66 (1962): 259–63.

Brown, Alexandra R. *The Cross and Human Transformation: Paul's Apocalyptic Word in 1 Corinthians.* Minneapolis: Fortress, 1995.

Bünker, Michael. *Briefformular und rhetorische Disposition im 1. Korintherbrief.* Göttinger theologische Arbeiten 28; Göttingen: Vandenhoeck & Roprecht, 1983.

Cadbury, Henry J. "Erastus of Corinth." *Journal of Biblical Literature* 50 (1931): 42–58.

Carr, Wesley A. *Angels and Principalities: The Background, Meaning and Development of the Pauline Phrase "hai archai kai hai exousia."* Society for the Study of the New Testament Monograph Series 42. Cambridge: Cambridge University Press, 1981.

Carrington, Phillip. *The Primitive Christian Calendar.* Cambridge: Cambridge University Press, 1952.

Cary, M. and H. H. Scullard. *A History of Rome: Down to the Reign of Constantine.* 3d ed. New York: St. Martin's Press, 1975.

Charlesworth, James H., ed. *The Old Testament Pseudepigrapha.* 2 vols. Garden City NY: Doubleday & Company, 1983.

Cheung, Alex T. *Idol Food in Corinth: Jewish Background and Pauline Legacy.* Journal for the Study of the New Testament: Supplement Series. Sheffield: Sheffield Academic Press, 1999.

Chow, John K. *Patronage and Power: A Study of Social Networks in Corinth.* Journal for the Study of the New Testament: Supplement Series 75. Sheffield: Sheffield Academic Press, 1992.

Clarke, Andrew D. *Secular and Christian Leadership in Corinth: A Socio-Historical and Exegetical Study of 1 Corinthians 1–6. Arbeiten zur Geschichte des antiken Judentums und des Urchristentums* 18. Leiden: E. J. Brill, 1993.

Collins, Adela Yarbro. "The Function of 'Excommunication' in Paul." *Harvard Theological Review* 73 (1980): 251–63.

Conzelmann, Hans. "Korinth und die Mädchen der Aphrodite." *Nachrichten (von) der Akademie der Wissenschaften in Göttingen* 8 (1967): 247–61.

Dahl, Nils. *Studies in Paul: Theology for the Early Christian Mission.* Minneapolis: Augsburg Press, 1977.

Dawes, Gregory W. "The Danger of Idolatry: First Corinthians 8:7-13." *Catholic Biblical Quarterly* 58 (1996): 86–91.

de Vos, Craig Steven. *Church and Community Conflicts: The Relationships of the Thessalonian, Corinthian, and Philippian Churches with Their Wider Civic Communities.* Society of Biblical Literature Dissertation Series 168. Atlanta: Scholars Press, 1999.

de Young, James B. "The Source and NT Meaning of ἀρσενοκοῖται, with Implications for Christian Ethics and Ministry." *The Master's Seminary Journal* 3 (1992): 191–215.

Delobel, Joël. "1 Cor 11:2-16: Towards a Coherent Explanation." Pages 369–89 in *L'Apôtre Paul: Personalité, style et conception du ministére.* Edited by A. Vanhoeye. Leuven: Peeters, 1986.

DeMaris, Richard E. "Corinthian Religion and Baptism for the Dead (1 Corinthians 15:29) : Insights from Archaeology and Anthropology." *Journal of Biblical Literature* 114 (1995): 661–82.

———. *The New Testament in Its Ritual World.* New York: Routledge, 2008.

———. "Demeter in Roman Corinth: Local Development in a Mediterranean Religion." *Numen* 42 (1995): 105–17.

Deming, Will. "The Unity of 1 Corinthians 5–6." *Journal of Biblical Literature* 115 (1996): 289–312.

———. *Paul on Marriage and Celibacy: The Hellenistic Background of 1 Corinthians 7.* Society for New Testament Studies Monograph Series 83. Cambridge: Cambridge University Press, 1995.

Derrett, J. Duncan M. "Judgement and 1 Cor 6." *New Testament Studies* 37 (1991): 22–36.

Doty, William G. *Letters in Primitive Christianity.* Guides to Biblical Scholarship. Philadelphia: Fortress, 1973.

Downey, James. "1 Cor 15:29 and the Theology of Baptism." *Euntes Docete* 38 (1985): 23–35.

Dunn, James D. G. *The Theology of Paul the Apostle.* Edinburgh: T & T Clark, 1998.

Elliott, Neil. "The Anti-imperial Message of the Cross." Pages 167–83 in *Paul and Empire: Religion and Power in Roman Imperial Society.* Edited by Richard A. Horsley. Harrisburg PA: Trinity Press, 1997.

Engels, David. *Roman Corinth: An Alternative Model for the Classical City.* Chicago: University of Chicago Press, 1990.

Eriksson, Anders. *Traditions as Rhetorical Proof: Pauline Argumentation in 1 Cor.* Coniectanea neotestamentica 29. Stockholm: Almqvist & Wiksell, 1998.

Fant, Clyde E., Jr., and William M. Pinson Jr., eds. *20 Centuries of Great Preaching: An Encyclopedia of Preaching*. Waco TX: Word Books, 1971.

Fee, Gordon D. "Toward a Theology of 1 Corinthians." Pages 37–58 in *Pauline Theology, Vol. II: 1 & 2 Corinthians*. Edited by David M. Hay. Minneapolis: Fortress Press, 1993.

Fiore, Benjamin. "'Covert Allusion' in 1 Cor 1–4." *Catholic Biblical Quarterly* 47 (1985): 85–102.

Fiorenza, Elisabeth Schüssler. "Rhetorical Situation and Historical Reconstruction in 1 Corinthians." *New Testament Studies* 33 (1987): 386–403.

———. *In Memory of Her: A Feminist Theological Reconstruction of Christian Origins*. New York: Crossroad, 1983.

Fisk, Bruce N. "Eating Meat Offered to Idols: Corinthian Behaviour and Pauline Response in 1 Corinthians 8–10." *Trinity Journal* 10 (1989): 49–70.

Fitzgerald, John T. *Cracks in an Earthen Vessel: An Examination of the Catalogues of Hardships in the Corinthian Correspondence*. Society of Biblical Literature Dissertation Series 99. Atlanta: Scholars Press, 1988.

Fitzmyer, Joseph A. "Another Look at Κεφαλή in 1 Corinthians 11:3." *New Testament Studies* 35 (1989): 32–59.

———. "*Kephalē* in 1 Cor. 11:3." *Interpretation* 47 (1993): 32–59.

Forbes, Christopher. *Prophecy and Inspired Speech in Early Christianity and Its Hellenistic Environment*. Wissenschafliche Untersuchungen zum Neuen Testemant 2/75. Tübingen: Mohr, 1995.

Fotopoulos, John. *Food Offered to Idols in Roman Corinth: A Socio-Rhetorical Reconsideration of 1 Corinthians 8:1–11:1*. Tübingen: Mohr Siebeck, 2003.

Friesen, Steven J. "The Wrong Erastus: Status, Wealth, and Paul's Churches." In *Corinth in Context: Comparative Perspectives on Religion and Society*. Edited by Steven J. Friesen and Daniel N. Showalter. Cambridge MA: Harvard University Press, forthcoming.

Fuller, Reginald H. *The Formation of the Resurrection Narratives*. New York: The Macmillan Company, 1971.

Funk, Robert W. "The Apostolic *Parousia*: Form and Significance." Pages 248–68 in *Christian History and Interpretation: Studies Presented to John Knox*. Edited by W. R. Farmer, C. D. F. Moule, and R. Niebuhr. Cambridge: Cambridge University Press, 1967.

Garnsey, Peter. *Social Status and Legal Privilege in the Roman Empire*. Oxford: Clarendon Press, 1970.

Gelpi, Barbara Charlesworth. *Feminist Theory: A Critique of Ideologies*. Edited by Nannerl Keohanne, et al. Chicago: University of Chicago Press, 1982.

Gill, David H. "*Trapezomata*: A Neglected Aspect of Greek Sacrifice." *Harvard Theological Review* 67 (1974): 117–37.

Gooch, Peter D. *Dangerous Food: 1 Corinthians 8–10 in Its Context*. Studies in Christianity and Judaism 5. Waterloo Ont.: Wilfred Laurier University Press, 1993.

Gooch, Paul W. "'Conscience' in 1 Corinthians 8 and 10." *New Testament Studies* 33 (1987): 244–54.

Gregory, Timothy E. *The Corinthia in the Roman Period.* Journal of Roman Archaeology Supplementary Series 8. Ann Arbor MI: Journal of Roman Archaeology, 1993.

Grudem, Wayne. "The Meaning of *kefalē* ('Head'): A Response to Recent Studies." *Trinity Journal* 11 (1990): 3–72.

Hall, David R. *The Unity of the Corinthian Correspondence.* Journal for the Study of the New Testament Supplement Series 251. London: T & T Clark Int., 2003.

———. "A Disguise for the Wise: METASCHMATISMOS in 1 Corinthians 4.6." *New Testament Studies* 40 (1994): 143–49.

Hans-Josef Klauck. *Ancient Letters and the New Testament: A Guide to Context and Exegesis.* Waco TX: Baylor University Press, 2006.

Hanson, Anthony T. *Studies in Paul's Technique and Theology.* Grand Rapids: Eerdmans, 1974.

Harland, Philip A. "Familial Dimensions of Group Identity: 'Brothers' (*Adelfoi*) in Associations of the Greek East." *Journal of Biblical Literature* 124 (2005): 491–513.

Hays, Richard B. "Relations Natural and Unnatural." *Journal of Religious Ethics* 14 (1986): 184–215.

Hock, Ronald F. *The Social Context of Paul's Ministry: Tentmaking and Apostleship.* Philadelphia: Fortress Press, 1980.

Holleman, Joost. *Resurrection and Parousia: A Traditio-Historical Study of Paul's Eschatology in 1 Cor 15.* Novum Testamentum Supplements 84. Leiden: E. J. Brill, 1988.

Holmberg, Bengt. "The Methods of Historical Reconstruction in the Scholarly 'Recovery' of Corinthian Christianity." Pages 255–71 in *Christianity at Corinth: The Quest for the Pauline Church.* Edited by Edward Adams and David G. Horrell. Louisville: Westminster John Knox, 2004.

Hooker, Morna D. "Beyond the Things That are Written? St. Paul's Use of Scripture." *New Testament Studies* 27 (1980–1981): 295–309.

Horrell, David G., and Edward Adams. "The Scholarly Quest for Paul's Church at Corinth." Pages 13–26 in *Christianity at Corinth: The Quest for the Pauline Church.* Edited by Edward Adams and David G. Horrell. Louisville: Westminster John Knox, 2004. *Christianity at Corinth,* 13–26.

Horsley, Richard A. "1 Corinthians: A Case Study of Paul's Assembly as an Alternative Society." Pages 242–52 in *Paul and Empire: Religion and Power in Roman Imperial Society.* Edited by Richard A. Horsley. Harrisburg PA: Trinity International Press, 1997.

———. "Gnosis in Corinth: I Corinthians 8.1-6." *New Testament Studies* 27 (1981): 32–52.

———, ed. *Paul and Empire: Religion and Power in Roman Imperial Society.* Harrisburg PA: Trinity Press, 1997.

Hoskins-Walbank, Mary E. "Evidence for the Imperial Cult in Julio-Claudian Corinth." Pages 201–14 in *Subject and Ruler: The Cult of the Ruling Power in Classical Antiquity.* Edited by Alastair Small. Journal of Roman Archaeology Supplementary Series 17. Ann Arbor MI: Journal of Roman Archaeology, 1996.

Hull, Michael F. *Baptism on Account of the Dead (1 Cor 15:29).* Society of Biblical Literature Archaeology and Biblical Studies 22. Atlanta: Society of Biblical Literature, 2005.

Hurd, John Coolidge, Jr. *The Origin of I Corinthians.* Macon GA: Mercer University Press, 1983.

Hurley, J. B. "Did Paul Require Veils or the Silence of Women? A Consideration of 1 Cor 11:2-16 and 1 Cor 14:33b-36." *Westminster Theological Journal* 35 (1973): 190–220.

Instone-Brewer, David. "1 Corinthians 7 in the Light of the Jewish Greek and Aramaic Marriage and Divorce Papyri." *Tyndale Bulletin* 52 (2001): 238–39.

Jeremias, Joachim. "Flesh and Blood Cannot Inherit the Kingdom of God." *New Testament Studies* 2 (1955–1956): 151–59.

Johnson, Luke Timothy. *Religious Experience in Earliest Christianity.* Minneapolis: Fortress Press, 1998.

Jones, Peter Rhea. "1 Cor 15:8: Paul the Last Apostle." *Tyndale Bulletin* 36 (1985): 5–34.

Judge, Edwin A. *The Social Pattern of Christian Groups in the First Century: Some Prolegomena to the Study of New Testament Ideas of Social Obligation.* London: Tyndale Press, 1960.

Kagan, Donald. *The Peloponnesian War.* New York: Viking Penguin, 2003.

Käsemann, Ernst. "On the Subject of Primitive Christian Apocalyptic." Pages 108–37 in *New Testament Questions for Today.* Translated by W. J. Montague. Philadelphia: Fortress Press, 1969.

Kennedy, George A. *Classical Rhetoric and Its Christian and Secular Tradition from Ancient to Modern Times.* Chapel Hill: University of North Carolina Press, 1980.

———. *New Testament Interpretation through Rhetorical Criticism.* Chapel Hill: University of North Carolina Press, 1984.

Kennedy, Charles A. "The Cult of the Dead in Corinth." Pages 227–36 in *Love and Death in the Ancient Near East: Essays in Honor of Marvin H. Pope.* Edited by John. H. Marks and Robert M. Good. Guilford CT: Four Quarters, 1987.

Kent, John Harvey. *The Inscriptions 1926–1950.* Corinth VIII.3. Princeton: American School of Classical Studies at Athens, 1966.

Ker, Donald P. "Paul and Apollos—Colleagues or Rivals?" *Journal for the Study of the New Testament* 77 (2000): 75–97.

Kim, Yung Suk. *Christ's Body in Corinth: The Politics of a Metaphor.* Minneapolis: Fortress Press, 2008.

Kittel, Gerhard, and Gerhard Friedrich, eds. *Theological Dictionary of the New Testament.* Translated by Geoffrey W. Bromiley. 10 vols. Grand Rapids: Eerdmans, 1964–1976.

Koester, Helmut. "Melikertes at Isthmia: A Roman Mystery Cult." Pages 355–66 in *Greeks, Romans, and Christians: Essays in Honor of Abraham J. Malherbe.* Edited by David L. Balch, Everett Ferguson, and Wayne A. Meeks. Minneapolis: Fortress Press, 1990.

Lampe, Peter. "The Eucharist: Identifying with Christ on the Cross." *Interpretation* 48 (1994): 36–49.

Lanci, John R. *A New Temple for Corinth: Rhetorical and Archaeological Approaches to Pauline Imagery.* Studies in Biblical Literature 1. New York and Bern: Peter Lang, 1997.

Levick, Barbara. *Claudius.* New Haven: Yale University Press, 1990.

Liddell, Henry G., Robert Scott, and H. Stuart Jones. *Greek-English Lexicon.* 9th ed. Oxford: Clarendon Press, 1968.

Lightfoot, J. B. *Notes on the Epistles of St. Paul.* London: Macmillan, 1895.

MacDonald, Margaret Y. "The Shifting Centre: Ideology and the Interpretation of 1 Corinthians." Pages 273–94 in *Christianity at Corinth: The Quest for the Pauline Church.* Edited by Edward Adams and David G. Horrell. Louisville: Westminster John Knox, 2004.

Mack, Burton L. *Rhetoric and the New Testament.* Guides to Biblical Scholarship. Minneapolis: Fortress Press, 1990.

MacLachlan, Bonnie. "Sacred Prostitution and Aphrodite." *Studies in Religion* 21 (1992): 145–62.

Malherbe, Abraham J. *Paul and the Popular Philosophers.* Minneapolis: Fortress Press, 1989.

———. *Social Aspects of Early Christianity.* 2d ed. Philadelphia: Fortress Press, 1983.

———. "The Beasts at Ephesus." *Journal of Biblical Literature* 87 (1968): 72–80.

Martin, Dale B. *The Corinthian Body.* New Haven: Yale University Press, 1995.

———. *Slavery as Salvation: The Metaphor of Slavery in Pauline Christianity.* New Haven: Yale University Press, 1990.

Martyn, J. Louis. "Epistemology at the Turn of the Ages: 2 Corinthians 5:16." In *Christian History and Interpretation: Studies Presented to John Knox.* Edited by W. R. Farmer, C. F. D. Moule, and R. R. Niebuhr. Cambridge: Cambridge University Press, 1967.

McDonald, Margaret Y. "Women Holy in Body and Spirit: The Social Setting of 1 Corinthians 7." *New Testament Studies* 36 (1990): 161–81.

Meeks, Wayne A. *The First Urban Christians: The Social World of the Apostle Paul.* New Haven: Yale University Press, 1983.

Meggitt, Justin J. "The Social Status of Erastus (Ron 16:23)." *Novum Testamentum* 38 (1996): 219–25.

———. *Paul, Poverty and Survival.* Studies of the New Testament and Its World. Edinburgh: T & T Clark, 1998.

———. "Sources: Use, Abuse, Neglect. The Importance of Ancient Popular Culture." Pages 241–53 in *Christianity at Corinth: The Quest for the Pauline Church.* Edited by Edward Adams and David G. Horrell. Louisville: Westminster John Knox, 2004.

Merklein, Helmut. *Der erste Brief an die Korinther. Kapitel 1-4.* Ökumenischer Taschenbuch-Kommentar 7/1. Gütersloh: Mohn, 1992.

Metzger, Bruce M. *A Textual Commentary on the Greek New Testament.* 3d ed. Stuttgart: United Bible Societies, 1971.

Mikalson, Jon D. *Ancient Greek Religion.* Oxford: Blackwell, 2005.

Mitchell, Alan C. "Rich and Poor in the Courts of Corinth: Litigiousness and Status in 1 Cor 6:1-11." *New Testament Studies* 39 (1993): 562–86.

Mitchell, Margaret M. "Concerning peri de in 1 Corinthians." *Novum Testamentum* 31 (1989): 229–56.

———. *Paul and the Rhetoric of Reconciliation: An Exegetical Investigation of the Language and Composition of 1 Corinthians.* Louisville: Westminster John Knox, 1991.

Moulton, James H., and George Milligan. *The Vocabulary of the Greek Testament.* Grand Rapids: Eerdmans, 1960.

Munck, Johannes. "The Church without Factions: Studies in I Corinthians 1–4." Pages 137–67 in *Paul and the Salvation of Mankind.* London: SCM, 1959.

Murphy-O'Connor, Jerome. "'Baptized for the Dead' (I Cor., XV, 29): A Corinthian Slogan?" *Revue biblique* 88 (1981): 532–43.

———. *Paul the Letter-Writer: His World, His Options, His Skills.* Collegeville MN: Liturgical Press, 1995.

———. "The Divorced Woman in 1 Cor, 7:10-11." *Journal of Biblical Literature* 100 (1981): 601–606.

———. "Freedom or the Ghetto (I Cor. viii, 1-13; x,23-xi,1)." *Revue biblique* 85 (1978): 543–74.

———. "Interpolations in the 1 Corinthians." *Catholic Biblical Quarterly* 48 (1986): 81–94.

———. "Sex and Logic." *Catholic Biblical Quarterly* 42 (1980): 482–99.

———. *St. Paul's Corinth: Texts and Archaeology.* Collegeville MN: Liturgical Press, 1983.

Nash, Scott. "Heart." *Mercer Dictionary of the Bible.* Edited by Watson E. Mills. Macon GA: Mercer University Press, 1990.

———. "The Role of the *Haustafeln* in Colossians and Ephesians." Ph.D. diss. The Southern Baptist Theological Seminary, 1982.

Newton, Derek. *Deity and Diet: The Dilemma of Sacrificial Food at Corinth.* Journal for the Study of the New Testament: Supplement Series 169. Sheffield: Sheffield Academic Press, 1998.

O'Brien, Peter T. *Introductory Thanksgivings in the Letters of Paul.* Novum Testamentum Supplements 49. Leiden: Brill, 1977.

Osiek, Carolyn, and David L. Balch. *Families in the New Testament World: Households and House Churches.* Louisville: Westminster John Knox Press, 1997.

Oster, Richard E., Jr. "Use, Misuse and Neglect of Archaeological Evidence in Some Modern Works on 1 Corinthians (1Cor 7,1-5; 8,10; 11,2-16; 12,14-26)." *Zeitschrift für die Neutestamentliche Wissenschaft und die Kunde der Älteren Kirche* 83 (1992): 52–73.

Patrick, James E. "Living Rewards for Dead Apostles: 'Baptised for the Dead' in 1 Corinthians 15.29." *New Testament Studies* 52 (2006): 71–85.

Patterson, Orlando. *Slavery and Social Death: A Comparative Study.* Cambridge MA: Harvard University Press, 1982.

Perriman, A. C. "The Head of a Woman: The Meaning of κεφαλή in 1 Cor 11:3." *Journal of Theological Studies* 45 (1994): 602–22.

Pesch, Rudolf. *Paulus ringt um die Lebensform der Kirche. Viere Briefe an die gemeinde Gottes in Korinth.* Freiburg: Herder, 1986.

Petersen, William L. "Can *arsenokoitai* Be Translated by 'Homosexuals'?" *Vigiliae christianae* 40 (1986): 187–91.

Pfitzner, Victor C. *Paul and the Agon Motif: Traditional Athletic Imagery in the Pauline Literature.* Leiden: Brill, 1967.

Plank, Karl A. *Paul and the Irony of Affliction.* Society of Biblical Literature Semeia Studies. Atlanta: Scholars Press, 1987.

Pogoloff, Stephen M. *Logos and Sophia: The Rhetorical Situation of 1 Corinthians.* Society of Biblical Literature Dissertation Series 134. Atlanta: Scholars Press, 1992.

Porter, Stanley E., and T. H. Olbricht, eds. *Rhetoric and the New Testament: Essays from the 1992 Heidelberg Conference.* Sheffield: Sheffield Academic Press, 1993.

Powell, Benjamin. "Greek Inscriptions from Corinth." *American Journal of Archaeology* 7 (1903): 60–61.

Price, Simon R. F. *Rituals and Power: The Roman Imperial Cult in Asia Minor.* Cambridge: Cambridge University Press, 1984.

Probst, Hermann. *Paulus und der Brief: Die Rhetorik des antiken Briefes als Form der paulinischen Korintherkorrespondenz.* Wissenschaftliche Untersuchungen zum Neuen Testament 2/45. Tübingen: J. C. B. Mohr, 1991.

Raeder, Maria. "Vikariatstaufe in 1 Cor 15:29." *Zeitschrift für die neutestamentliche Wissenschaft und die Kunde der älteren Kirche* 46 (1955): 258–60.

Ramsara, Rollin A. "More Than an Opinion: Paul's Rhetorical Maxim in First Corinthians 7:25-26." *Catholic Biblical Quarterly* 57 (1995): 531–41.

Reaume, John D. "Another Look at 1 Corinthians 15:29, 'Baptized for the Dead'." *Bibliotheca sacra* 152 (1995): 457–75.

Reese, David George. "Demons: New Testament." Pages 140–42 in vol. 2 of *The Anchor Bible Dictionary.* Edited by David Noel Freedman. New York: Doubleday, 1992.

Richardson, Peter. "Judgement in Sexual Matters in 1 Corinthians 6:1-11." *Novum Testamentum* 25 (1983): 35–58.

Rissi, Mathias. *Die Taufe für die Toten.* Abhandlungen zur Theologie des Alten und Neuen Testaments 42. Zurich: Zwingli Verlag, 1962.

Roetzel, Calvin J. *The Letters of Paul: Conversations in Context.* 3d ed. Louisville: Westminster/John Knox, 1991.

Rosner, Brian S. "'Stronger than He?' The Strength of 1 Corinthians 10:22b." *Tyndale Bulletin* 43 (1992): 171–79.

———. "Moses Appointing Judges: An Antecedent to 1 Cor 1–6?" *Zeitschrift für die neutestamentliche Wissenschaft und die Kunde der älteren Kirche* 82 (1990): 275–78.

———. *Paul, Scripture and Ethics: A Study of 1 Corinthians 5–7.* Leiden: E. J. Brill, 1994.

Rothaus, Richard M. *Corinth, the First City of Greece: An Urban History of Late Antique Cult and Religion.* Leiden: Brill, 2000.

Saffrey, H. D. "Aphrodite à Corinthe: réflexions sur une idée reçue." *Revue biblique* 92 (1985): 359–74.

Salmon, J. B. *Wealthy Corinth: A History of the City to 338 B.C.* Oxford: Oxford University Press, 1984.

Scarre, Chris. *Chronicle of the Roman Emperors.* London: Thames and Hudson, 1995.

Schottroff, Luise. "Holiness and Justice: Exegetical Comments in 1 Corinthians 11:17-34." *Journal for the Study of the New Testament* 79 (2000): 56–57.

Schrage, Wolfgang. "Leid, Kreuz und Eschaton. Die Peristasenkatologe als Merkmale paulinischer theologia crucis und Eschatologie." *Evangelische Theologie* 34 (1974): 141–75.

Schubert, Paul. *Form and Function of the Pauline Thanksgiving.* Beihefte zur Zeitschrift für die neutestamentlische Wissenschaft 20. Berlin: Alfred Töpelmann, 1939.

Schweitzer, Albert. *The Mysticism of Paul the Apostle.* Translated by William Montgomery. New York: The Seabury Press, 1931.

Scranton, Robert. *Medieval Architecture in the Central Area of Corinth.* Corinth XVI. Princeton: American School of Classical Studies at Athens, 1957.

Scroggs, Robin. *The New Testament and Homosexuality.* Philadelphia: Fortress Press, 1983.

———. "Paul and the Eschatological Woman." Pages 69–95 in *The Text and the Times: New Testament Essays for Today.* Minneapolis: Fortress Press, 1993.

Shanor, Jay. "Paul as Master Builder: Construction Terms in First Corinthians." *New Testament Studies* 34 (1988): 461–71.

Showalter, Daniel N., and Steven J. Friesen, eds. *Urban Religion in Roman Corinth: Interdisciplinary Approaches.* Harvard Theological Studies 53. Cambridge MA: Harvard University Press, 2005.

Smit, Joop F. M. *"About the Idol Offerings": Rhetoric, Social Context and Theology of Paul's Discourse in First Corinthians 8:1–11:1.* Beitrag zur evangelischen Theologie 27. Leuven, Belgium: Peeters, 2000.

———. "Epideictic Rhetoric in Paul's First Letter to the Corinthians 1–4." *Biblica* 84 (2003): 184–201.

———. "1 Corinthians 8,1-6, a Rhetorical Partitio: A Contribution to the Coherence of 1 Cor 8,1-11,1." Pages 577–91 in *The Corinthian Correspondence.* Bibliotheca ephemeridum theologicarum lovaniensium 125. Edited by Reimund Bieringer. Leuven, Belgium: Peeters Press, 1996.

———. "The Genre of 1 Corinthians 13 in Light of Classical Rhetoric." *Novum Testamentum* 33 (1991): 193–216.

———. "The Rhetorical Disposition of First Corinthians 8:7–9:27." *Catholic Biblical Quarterly* 59 (1997): 480–81.

———. "Two Puzzles: 1 Corinthians 12.31 and 13:3: A Rhetorical Solution." *New Testament Studies* 39 (1993): 246–64.

Smith, Dennis Edwin. "The Egyptian Cults at Corinth." *Harvard Theological Review* 70 (1977): 201–31.

Smyth, Herbert Weir. *Greek Grammar.* Cambridge MA: Harvard University Press, 1920, 1984.

Spawforth, Anthony J. S. "Corinth, Argos, and the Imperial Cult: *Pseudo-Julian, Letters* 198." *Hesperia* 63 (1994): 211–32.

Spawforth, Anthony J. S. "Markets and Fairs." Page 926 in *The Oxford Classical Dictionary.* 3d ed. Edited by Simon Hornblower and Anthony Spawforth. Oxford: Oxford University Press, 1996.

Stegemann, Ekkehard W., and Wolfgang Stegemann. *The Jesus Movement: A Social History of Its First Century.* Minneapolis, Fortress Press, 1999.

Still, E. Coye, III. "Paul's aims regarding *EIDWQUTA*: A New Proposal for Interpreting 1 Corinthians 8:1–11:1." *Novum Testamentum* 44 (2002): 333–43.

Stowers, Stanley K. *Letter Writing in Greco-Roman Antiquity.* Library of Early Christianity 5. Philadelphia: Westminster, 1986.

———. "Social Status, Public Speaking and Private Teaching: The Circumstances of Paul's Preaching Activity." *Novum Testamentum* 26 (1984): 59–82.

———. *The Diatribe and Paul's Letter to the Romans.* Society of Biblical Literature Dissertation Series 57. Chico CA: Scholars Press, 1981.

Strugnell, John. "A Plea for Conjectural Emendation in the New Testament, with a Coda on 1 Cor 4:6." *Catholic Biblical Quarterly* 36 (1974): 543–58.

Theissen, Gerd. *The Social Setting of Pauline Christianity: Essays on Corinth.* Philadelphia: Fortress Press, 1982.

Thiselton, Anthony C. "Realized Eschatology at Corinth." *New Testament Studies* 24 (1978): 510–26.

Thompson, Cynthia L. "Hairstyles, Head-coverings, and St. Paul: Portraits from Roman Corinth." *Biblical Archaeologist* (1988): 99–115.

Thomson, Peter J. *Paul and the Jewish Law: Halakha in the Letters of the Apostle to the Gentiles.* Vol. 1 in Jewish Traditions in Early Christian Literature. Section 3 in *Compendia Rerum Iudaicarum ad Novum Testamentum.* Minneapolis: Fortress Press, 1990.

Tonier, Henrik. "The Corinthian Correspondence between Philosophical Idealism and Apocalypticism." Pages 186–82 in *Paul beyond the Judaism/Hellenism Divide.* Edited by Troels Engberg-Pederson. Louisville: Westminster John Knox Press, 2001.

Tubbs, Clint. "The Spirit (World) and the (Holy) Spirit among the Earliest Christians: 1 Corinthians 12 and 14 as a Test Case." *Catholic Biblical Quarterly* 70 (2008): 313–30.

Tyler, Ronald L. "First Corinthians 4:6 and Hellenistic Pedagogy." *Catholic Biblical Quarterly* 60 (1998): 97–103.

Veyne, Paul. "The Roman Empire." Pages 5–234 in *From Pagan Rome to Byzantium.* Edited by Paul Veyne. Translated by Arthur Goldhammer. Vol. 1 of *A History of Private Life.* Edited by Philippe Ariès and George Duby. Cambridge: Harvard University Press, 1987.

Vos, Johan S. "Der μετασχηματισμος in 1 Kor. 4.6." *Zeitschrift für die neutestamentliche Wissenschaft und die Kunde der älteren Kirche* 86 (1995): 154–72.

Wagner, J. Ross. "'Not beyond the Things Which Are Written': A Call to Boast Only in the Lord (1 Cor 4.6)." *New Testament Studies* 44 (1998): 279–87.

Walker, William O., Jr. "1 Corinthians 15:29-34 as a Non-Pauline Interpolation." *Catholic Biblical Quarterly* 69 (2007): 84–103.

Wallace, Daniel B. *Greek Grammar beyond the Basics: An Exegetical Syntax of the Greek New Testament.* Grand Rapids: Zondervan, 1996.

Wallace-Hadrill, Andrew. *Houses and Society in Pompeii and Herculaneum.* Princeton: Princeton University Press, 1994.

Weiss, Johannes Weiss. *Der erste Korintherbrief.* 9th ed. Kritisch-exegetischer Kommentar über das Neue Testament. Göttingen: Vandenhoeck & Ruprecht, 1910.

Welborn, Laurence L. "Discord in Corinth: First Corinthians 1–4 and Ancient Politics." *Journal of Biblical Literature* 106 (1987): 85–111. Rev. and repr. pages 1–42 in *Politics and Rhetoric in the Corinthian Epistles.* Macon: Mercer University Press, 1997.

———. "A Conciliatory Principle in 1 Corinthians 4:6." *Novum Testamentum* 29 (1987): 320–46. Rev. and repr. pages 43–75 in *Politics and Rhetoric in the Corinthian Epistles.* Macon: Mercer University Press, 1997.

White, Joel R. "'Baptized on account of the Dead': The Meaning of 1 Corinthians 15:29 in Its Context." *Journal of Biblical Literature* 116 (1997): 487–99.

White, John L. *Light from Ancient Letters.* Foundations and Facets: New Testament. Philadelphia: Fortress, 1986.

Wilcox, Max. "Maranatha." Page 514 in vol. 4 of *The Anchor Bible Dictionary.* Edited by David Noel Freedman. New York: Doubleday, 1992.

Williams, Charles K., II. "A Re-evaluation of Temple E and the West End of the Forum in Corinth." Pages 156–62 in *The Greek Renaissance in the Roman Empire: Papers from the Tenth British Museum Classical Colloquium.* Edited by Susan Walker and Averil Cameron. *Bulletin of the Institute of Classical Studies Supplement* 55; London: University of London, 1989.

———, and Orestes H. Zervos. "Corinth, 1985: East of the Theater." *Hesperia* 55 (1986): 147–48.

Willis, Wendell Lee. *Idol Meat in Corinth: The Pauline Argument in 1 Corinthians 8 and 10.* Society of Biblical Literature Dissertation Series 68. Chico CA: Scholars Press, 1985.

Wimbush, Vincent L. *Paul the Worldly Ascetic: Response to the World and Self-understanding according to 1 Corinthians 7.* Macon GA: Mercer University Press, 1987.

Wink, Walter. *Naming the Powers: The Language of Power in the New Testament.* Philadelphia: Fortress Press, 1984.

———. *Unmasking the Powers: The Invisible Forces That Determine Human Existence.* Philadelphia: Fortress Press, 1986.

Winter, Bruce W. *After Paul Left Corinth: The Influence of Secular Ethics and Social Change.* Grand Rapids MI: Eerdmans, 2001.

———. "Civil Litigation in Secular Corinth and the Church: The Forensic Background to 1 Cor 6:1-8." *New Testament Studies* 37 (1991): 559–72.

———. *Philo and Paul among the Sophists: Alexandrian and Corinthian Responses to a Julio-Claudian Movement.* 2d ed. Grand Rapids MI: Eerdmans Publishing, 2002.

———. "Puberty or Passion? The Referent of Ὑπέρακμος in 1 Corinthians 7:36." *Tyndale Bulletin* 20 (1998): 71–89.

———. *Roman Wives, Roman Widows: The Appearance of New Women and the Pauline Communities.* Grand Rapids MI: Eerdmans, 2003.

———. *Seek the Welfare of the City: Christians as Benefactors and Citizens.* First-Century Christians in the Greco-Roman World. Grand Rapids: Eerdmans, 1994.

———. "Theological and Ethical Responses to Religious Pluralism—1 Corinthians 8–10." *Tyndale Bulletin* 41 (1990): 218.

Wire, Antoinette Clark. *The Corinthian Women Prophets: A Reconstruction through Paul's Rhetoric.* Minneapolis: Fortress Press, 1990.

Wiseman, James. "Corinth and Rome I: 228 B.C.–A.D. 267." *Aufstieg und Nieedergang der römischen Welt: Geschichte und Kultur Roms im Spiegel der neuren Forschung.* 7.1:461–62. Part 2. *Principat,* 7.1. Edited by H. Temporini and W. Haase. New York: de Gruyter, 1979.

———. *The Land of the Ancient Corinthians.* Studies in Mediterranean Archaeology 50. Göteborg: Paul Aström Förlag, 1978.

Witherington, Ben, III. "Not So Idle Thoughts about *Eidolothuton.*" *Tyndale Bulletin* 44 (1993): 237–54.

———. *Paul's Narrative Thought World: The Tapestry and Tragedy of Triumph.* Louisville: Westminster/John Knox, 1994.

Wright, David F. "Homosexuals or Prostitutes? The Meaning of *arsenokoitai* (1 Cor 6:9; 1 Tim 1:10)." *Vigiliae christianae* 38 (1984): 125–53.

———. "Translating ARSENOKOITAI: 1 Cor 6:9; 1 Tim 1:10." *Vigiliae christianae* 41 (1987): 396–98.

Wuellner, Wilhelm. "Greek Rhetoric and Pauline Argumentation." Pages 177–88 in *Early Christian Literature and the Classical Intellectual Tradition*: in honorem *Robert M. Grant.* Edited by W. R. Schoedel and R. L. Wilken. Théologie Historique 54. Paris: Etudes Beauchesne, 1979.

Yeo, Khiok-Khng. *Rhetorical Interaction in 1 Corinthians 8–10: A Formal Analysis with Preliminary Suggestions for a Chinese, Cross-Cultural Hermeneutic.* Biblical Interpretation Series 9. Leiden: Brill, 1995.

Zaas, Peter S. "Catalogues and Context: I Corinthians 5 and 6." *New Testament Studies* 34 (1988): 622–29.

INDEX OF MODERN AUTHORS

INDEX OF SIDEBARS AND ILLUSTRATIONS

Text Sidebars

Illustration Sidebars

INDEX OF SCRIPTURES

Old Testament

INDEX OF TOPICS

C

I

J

K

L

M

N

O

P

Q

R

S

Z